The State of State Reform in Latin America

The State of State Reform in Latin America

Edited by

Eduardo Lora

INTER-AMERICAN DEVELOPMENT BANK

A COPUBLICATION OF STANFORD ECONOMICS AND FINANCE,
AN IMPRINT OF STANFORD UNIVERSITY PRESS, AND THE WORLD BANK

A copublication of Stanford Economics and Finance, an imprint of Stanford University Press, the World Bank, and the Inter-American Development Bank.

Stanford University Press	The World Bank •	The Inter-American
1450 Page Mill Road	1818 H Street, NW	Development Bank
Palo Alto, CA 94304	Washington, DC 20433	1300 New York Ave, NW
		Washington, DC 20577

The views and opinions expressed in this publication are those of the authors and do not necessarily reflect the official position of the Inter-American Development Bank.

ISBN-10 0-8213-6575-4	(World Rights except North America)
ISBN-13 978-0-8213-6575-5	(World Rights except North America)
ISBN-13 (soft cover) 978-0-8047-5529-0	(North America)
ISBN-13 (hard cover) 978-0-8047-5528-3	(North America)

Library of Congress Cataloging-in-Publication Data has been applied for.

Latin American Development Forum Series

This series was created in 2003 to promote debate, disseminate information and analysis, and convey the excitement and complexity of the most topical issues in economic and social development in Latin America and the Caribbean. It is sponsored by the Inter-American Development Bank, the United Nations Economic Commission for Latin America and the Caribbean, and the World Bank. The manuscripts chosen for publication represent the highest quality in each institution's research and activity output and have been selected for their relevance to the academic community, policy makers, researchers, and interested readers.

Advisory Committee Members

About the Contributors

Juan Benavides is a senior infrastructure specialist in the Sustainable Development Department at the Inter-American Development Bank, Washington, DC.

Alberto Chong is principal research economist in the Research Department at the Inter-American Development Bank, Washington, DC.

Juan Carlos Cortázar is a modernization of state specialist in Regional Operations Department 1 of the Inter-American Development Bank, Washington, DC.

Robert Daughters is a principal urban development specialist in the Sustainable Development Department at the Inter-American Development Bank, Washington, DC.

Koldo Echebarría is the country office representative in Chile of the Inter-American Development Bank, Santiago, Chile.

Gabriel Filc is a project coordinator and researcher at CIPPEC (Centro de Implementación de Políticas Públicas para la Equidad y el Crecimiento), Buenos Aires, Argentina.

Arturo Galindo is a professor in the Department of Economics at Universidad de los Andes, Bogotá, Colombia.

Leslie Harper is a modernization of state specialist in the Sustainable Development Department at the Inter-American Development Bank, Washington, DC.

Eduardo Lora is the principal adviser in the Research Department at the Inter-American Development Bank, Washington, DC.

Gustavo Márquez is the principal labor adviser in the Research Department at the Inter-American Development Bank, Washington, DC.

Alberto Melo is a senior country economist in Regional Operations Department 3 at the Inter-American Development Bank, Washington, DC.

Carmelo Mesa-Lago is distinguished professor emeritus, University of Pittsburgh, Pittsburgh, Pennsylvania.

Alejandro Micco is the director of Capital Markets at the Ministry of Finance of Chile, Santiago, Chile.

Juan Carlos Navarro is chief of the Education Unit of the Sustainable Development Department at the Inter-American Development Bank, Washington, DC.

Ugo Panizza is a senior research economist in the Research Department at the Inter-American Development Bank, Washington, DC.

J. Mark Payne is a civil society specialist in the Sustainable Development Department at the Inter-American Development Bank, Washington, DC.

Juan Cruz Perusia is an assistant program specialist in the Education Survey Operations Section of UNESCO Institute for Statistics, Montreal, Canada.

Andrés Rodríguez-Clare is a professor of economics at Pennsylvania State University, University Park, Pennsylvania.

Carlos Scartascini is an evaluation economist in the Office of Evaluation and Oversight at the Inter-American Development Bank, Washington, DC.

Mariana Sousa is a graduate student at the University of Notre Dame, South Bend, Indiana.

Contents

Foreword   xv
Francis Fukuyama

Acknowledgments   xix

Abbreviations   xxi

1 STATE REFORM IN LATIN AMERICA: A SILENT REVOLUTION   1
Eduardo Lora

2 REFORMING THE RULES OF THE GAME: POLITICAL REFORM   57
J. Mark Payne and Juan Cruz Perusia

3 A BRIEF OVERVIEW OF JUDICIAL REFORM IN
LATIN AMERICA: OBJECTIVES, CHALLENGES,
AND ACCOMPLISHMENTS   87
Mariana Sousa

4 PUBLIC ADMINISTRATION AND PUBLIC
EMPLOYMENT REFORM IN LATIN AMERICA   123
Koldo Echebarría and Juan Carlos Cortázar

5 BUDGETARY INSTITUTIONS   157
Gabriel Filc and Carlos Scartascini

6 TRENDS AND OUTCOMES OF TAX REFORM   185
Eduardo Lora

7 FISCAL AND POLITICAL DECENTRALIZATION REFORMS   213
Robert Daughters and Leslie Harper

8 PRIVATIZATION AND REGULATION IN LATIN AMERICA   263
Alberto Chong and Juan Benavides

9   Two Decades of Financial Reforms   291
    Arturo Galindo, Alejandro Micco, and Ugo Panizza

10 Productive Development Policies and Supporting
    Institutions in Latin America and the Caribbean   317
    Alberto Melo and Andrés Rodríguez-Clare

11 Reform of Pension and Social Assistance Systems   355
    Carmelo Mesa-Lago and Gustavo Márquez

12 Education Reform as Reform of the State:
    Latin America Since 1980   387
    Juan Carlos Navarro

Index   423

Boxes
4.1   Uruguay: A Turning Point in the Size
      of the Bureaucracy   135
4.2   Peru: The Ineffective Reduction of the Size
      of the Public Administration   137
4.3   The Progress of Meritocracy in Chile   140
4.4   Merit and Flexibility in the Costa Rican Central
      Government   143
4.5   Brazil: Reform and Adaptation of a Classic
      Administrative Bureaucracy   145
4.6   Clientelistic Bureaucracies in the Central
      American Countries   150
4.7   Creation of Meritocratic Bureaucracies in
      Tax Administrations   152
5.1   Restrictions on Subnational Governments:
      The Brazilian Fiscal Responsibility Law   167
12.1 A Catalog of Education Reforms: Broad and Sustained
      Education Reform in Chile   389

Figures
1.1a Voice and Accountability and Political Stability, 2004   8
1.1b Rule of Law and Control of Corruption, 2004   9
1.2   Quality of Public Administration   17
1.3   Decentralization Maturity Index   29
1.4   Regulatory Quality, 2004   30
1.5   Social Public Expenditure per Capita   38

1.6	Distribution of Social Public Expenditure	39
2.1	Presidential Election Systems (number of countries)	63
3.1	Remuneration of Judges and the Compression Rate, 2000	105
3.2	Subjective Indicators of Judicial Independence in Selected LACs	106
3.3	De Jure and De Facto Judicial Independence Indicators in Selected Latin American Countries	107
4.1	Strategies for Public Administration Reform	127
4.2	Total Public Sector Employment, 1995 and 1999	134
4.3	Public Sector Payroll, 1995 and 1999	136
4.4	Strategic Consistency Index of Public Administrations	138
4.5	Merit Index	139
4.6	Functional Capacity Index	141
4.7	Functional Capacity Subindexes (average indexes by group of countries)	142
4.8	Size and Quality of the Public Administration	147
4.9	Bureaucratic Configurations	148
5.1	The Path of Reform	164
5.2	Budgetary Institutions in 2000 and Fiscal Results, 2000–02	173
6.1	Tax Revenues in Latin America	196
6.2	Tax Revenues by Tax Type (as GDP percentage)	198
6.3	Combined Neutrality Index	201
7.1	Fiscal Decentralization Trends (regional averages 1985–2004, percentage)	214
7.2	Priority Decentralization Policy Reform Areas, 1996 and 2004	217
7.3	Decentralization of Expenditure	224
7.4	Shifts in Sectoral Decentralization, 1985–2004	236
7.5	Principal Obstacles to Decentralization, 1996 and 2004	238
8.1	Economic Activity of State-Owned Enterprises	266
8.2	Developing Countries' Proceeds from Privatization, 1990–99	268
8.3	Privatization in Latin America, 1990–2000	271
8.4	Worldwide Privatization Revenues by Sector, 1990–2000	271
8.5	Worldwide Privatization Proceeds by Sector, 1990–2000	272
8.6	Profitability Changes after Privatization	277
8.7	Operating Efficiency after Privatization	278
8.8	Telecommunications Regulation Index	281

8.9   Electricity Regulation Index   282
9.1   Share of State-Owned Banks in Total Bank Assets,
       by Region   295
9.2   Share of State-Owned Banks in Total Bank Assets,
       Latin America   296
9.3   Relative Performance Indicators of State-Owned
       Banks vs. Private Banks   298
9.4   Financial Liberalization   300
9.5   Financial Liberalization in Latin America   301
9.6   Average Compliance with Basel Principles
       for Effective Banking Supervision   304
9.7   Capital Market Reforms   306
9.8   Domestic Bonds as a Share of GDP (weighted average)   307
9.9   Pension Fund Assets   308
9.10   Effective Creditor Rights   310
9.11   Duration of Bankruptcy Procedures   311

TABLES
1.1   Changes in Presidential Election Rules, 1978
       (or year of transition to democracy) to 2004   10
1.2   Quality Indicators of Judicial Reform in Selected
       Countries   15
1.3   Budget Institution Reform   20
1.4   Tax Revenues in 1985–89 and 2000–03
       (percentages of GDP)   24
1.5   Models and Characteristics of Pension Reforms
       in Latin America, 2005   41
1.6   Institutional Reforms in Education: Decentralization
       and Academic Tests   46
2.1   Changes in Presidential Election Rules, 1978
       (or year of transition to democracy) to 2005   61
2.2   Reforms to Presidential Election Systems   64
2.3   Reforms to Presidential Reelection Rules   68
2.4   Duration of Presidential Terms   70
2.5   Lower House Electoral Reforms   73
2.6   Electoral System Reforms for the Senate   74
2.7   Theoretically Expected Effects of Reforms:
       Lower House (or National Assembly)   75
2.8   Theoretically Expected Effects of Reforms:
       Upper House   75
2.9   Primary Elections   78
2.10   Current Laws in Selected Areas of Regulation of
       Electoral and Party Financing   79
2.11   Limits on Electoral Campaign Spending and Duration   81

2.12	Significant Reforms Affecting the Regulation of the Financing of Politics	82
3.1	Reform Goals, Means, Indicators of Success, and Major Promoters	89
3.2	Types of Reform by Types of Reformer, 1985 to 2004	92
3.3	Main Obstacles to Judicial Independence by Country	96
3.4	The Role and Composition of Judicial Councils in Selected Latin American Countries	101
3.5	Judicial Reform Index in 10 Selected Latin American Countries	109
4.1	Reform Processes in Peru, Brazil, and Chile	130
5.1	Summary of Fiscal Reforms	162
5.2	Numerical Restrictions	165
5.3	Interbranch Relations: Powers of the Legislative Branch to Make Changes in the Executive Proposal	169
5.4	Restrictions on Line Ministries in Negotiations with Finance Ministry, 2005	170
5.5	Cash Management, 2005	171
5.6	Average Fiscal Balance (percent)	173
5.7	Regression Analysis Dependent Variable: Fiscal Balance of General Government	175
6.1	Tax Rates, 1985, 1995, and 2003 (percentage)	189
6.2	Tax Incentives to Production and Investment, around 2000	190
6.3	Personal Income Tax Exemption Level and Upper Income Bracket (multiples of GDP per capita)	193
6.4	Tax Revenue as Percentage of GDP, by Country (simple averages)	197
6.5	Selected Latin American Countries: Cost of Tax Collection, 1998	199
6.6	Tax Neutrality Index, Selected Countries	202
6.7	Financial Transactions Taxes	202
6.8	Summary of Income and Value-Added Tax Incidence Studies	204
6.9	Tax Expenses in Selected Countries	206
6.10	Tax Revenue Loss from a Free Trade Agreement with United States (percentage of GDP)	207
7.1	First Year of Democratic Elections for Municipal and Intermediate Government Chief Executives	218
7.2	Some Reforms Affecting Political Autonomy and Citizen Participation at the Subnational Level	221
7.3	Fiscal Reform Sequence in Countries with Advanced Levels of Decentralization	226

7.4	Fiscal Reform Sequence in Countries with Intermediate Levels of Decentralization	228
7.5	Reform Processes in Countries with Limited or Incipient Decentralization	232
8.1	Characteristics Affecting Scope and Sequence of Privatization	275
8A	Regulation Index Questionnaire	285
9.1	Share of Public Bank Assets (percent)	297
9.2	Capital Requirements in Latin America	303
9.3	Implementation of Private Pension Funds	307
9.4	Measures of Equity Market Development for Selected Countries, 2003	309
10.1	Import Protection in the Developing World in 1985 and in the 2000s (percentages)	320
10.2	State-Owned Enterprises' Activity as a Percentage of GDP (percentage points of GDP)	322
10.3	Technological Sector Funds in Brazil	332
10.4	Funds to Support Science and Technology Activities in Chile	335
10.5	Programs to Promote Horizontal, Vertical, and Territorial Production Networks	339
10.6	Financial and Fiscal Incentives for Specific Sectors in Latin America and the Caribbean, 2001	340
10.7	Summary of Fiscal Incentives for Exports	344
10.8	Financial Support for Exports from Government Financial Agencies	345
10.9	Credit Granted by Public Development Banks	348
11.1	Characteristics of Pension Systems in Latin America, 2005	358
11.2	Private and Public Systems: Performance Indicators, 2000–04	362
11.3	Characteristics of Conditional Cash Transfer Programs	377
12.1	Level of Government with Responsibility for Education	391
12.2	Evaluation Systems in Latin America	399
12.3	Enrollment Rates, 1990 and 2000 (percent)	409
12.4	Years of Enrollment, 1990 and 2000	410
12.5	Comparison of Enrollment Rates in Income Distribution Quintiles 1 and 5	412

Foreword

Francis Fukuyama

Over the past decade, a broad consensus has emerged that "institutions matter" and that the capacity of states to deliver critical public goods is a key determinant of economic growth. The emphasis on economic policies that characterized much of the 1980s and early 1990s has given way to a greater appreciation of the fact that policies must be executed within the proper institutional framework: if the framework does not exist or does not function properly, an otherwise good policy, such as privatization or capital market liberalization, might have perversely negative consequences. The quality of institutions, in turn, and the ability to reform them, depend on a host of political factors, because institutions affect and reflect the interests of important actors in each society.

Consensus on the importance of institutions has masked a number of areas of uncertainty, however. One such area concerns exactly which institutions are the most important for economic growth. Economists have tended to emphasize property rights and the legal institutions necessary to protect them. A property-rights regime exists within another set of institutions, that is, the larger political system whose functions are to facilitate collective action, resolve disputes, and legitimize decisions made by the political community. A given political system may not be sufficient to generate the political "will" to, for example, reform a corrupt judicial system, or may be destabilized by an inability to resolve social conflicts over distribution or political access. Furthermore, the term "institutions" as it is currently used by economists encompasses not just formal rules such as constitutions and legal systems, but informal norms and habits as well. These interact with formal laws and rules in complex ways and are even harder to observe and manipulate than their formal counterparts.

So while the empirical relationship between institutions and growth has been well established, we know a great deal less about the mechanisms that shape institutions, and what practical, workable strategies can bring about institutional reform. It is therefore especially important to be able to

Francis Fukuyama is Bernard L. Schwartz Professor of International Political Economy at the Johns Hopkins School of Advanced International Studies.

study the actual experience of countries that have undertaken institutional reform, to see what progress has been made, what obstacles exist, and what the effects of successful reform have been. It is in this regard that this volume on state reform in Latin America is of particular value.

Perhaps the most remarkable finding of this book is that a quiet institutional revolution, which has escaped the notice of many observers, has taken place across the region. Latin America has seen its share of setbacks. Argentina underwent a severe crisis in 2001 that led to the demise of its currency board and a massive default on sovereign debt. Venezuela has seen a steady dismantling of its democratic institutions under the presidency of Hugo Chávez as well as a politicization of its economic institutions. Like-minded populists have appeared on the scene in Bolivia, Ecuador, and elsewhere, and in Haiti, the region boasts a genuine failed state.

These very visible cases of instability deflect attention, however, from the broad progress in building institutional capacity made in other parts of the region. *The State of State Reform in Latin America* documents a number of areas in which this has occurred. Most important are the economic policy-making institutions responsible for monetary and fiscal policy—central banks, finance ministries, and budgeting authorities. The Latin American debt crisis of the early 1980s emerged, after all, precisely because of weak policy making in these areas. The sharp rise of oil prices due to the oil shocks of the 1970s put pressure on current accounts; unlike the East Asian fast developers, many Latin American countries responded not by cutting government expenditures to keep fiscal balances in line, but by borrowing recycled petrodollars. Central banks covered fiscal deficits through monetary emissions, which led to inflationary spirals, declining currencies, devaluations, and recessions. The consequences of this mismanagement of macroeconomic policy were devastating: growth rates and per capita incomes stagnated or fell, and poverty rates increased as countries such as Argentina, Brazil, Mexico, and Peru struggled with debt burdens for the next decade.

The situation today is very different. Central bank independence has increased, and the technical capacity of governments to manage budgets is vastly superior. The ability to control deficits often requires major political reform. In large federal countries such as Argentina, Brazil, and Mexico, individual states were able to abuse their constitutional powers and run up deficits even if the central government maintained budget discipline; national budgets could not be brought into line without a reallocation of power between central and state governments.

Today, Latin America faces challenges not entirely different from those of the late 1970s, with rapidly rising energy prices and an abundant supply of external finance that could translate into fiscal and current account deficits. Yet overall, few governments in the region seem inclined to repeat the macroeconomic mistakes of the past. This has been true in countries such as Argentina and Brazil led by presidents of the left, who have been cautious in challenging the new consensus on prudent macroeconomic management.

A second important area of reform has been the attempt to decentralize political power, not just to the state level (long the case in the region's large federal countries), but to municipalities and localities. Argentina, Bolivia, Brazil, Colombia, Peru, and Venezuela have all undertaken major initiatives in this direction. In Brazil, the city of Pôrto Alegre engaged in a widely noted experiment in participatory budgeting during the early 1990s, which has had the positive effect of undermining traditional patronage networks and forcing local governments to be more transparent about their use of funds. Participatory budgeting has now spread to more than 140 cities in Brazil and has been copied elsewhere in the region. In Colombia, direct election of mayors has allowed municipalities to engage in experiments in dealing with drug gangs and educational reform.

Decentralization is not, of course, a panacea; its impact depends heavily on the way responsibilities and budgets are shared between the central and local authorities. Bolivia's 1994 decentralization law created a large number of small administrative units, but did not provide them with real power in critical areas such as education. The ability of subnational states to run budget deficits has long hindered the ability of federal countries such as Argentina and Brazil to maintain overall fiscal discipline, although Brazil's 2000 Law of Fiscal Responsibility has gone some way to fixing this problem in Brazil.

As the current volume indicates, the design of decentralized systems is critical to their success or failure. It is not enough simply to move responsibility to a lower level of government; if the lower-level unit remains dependent on higher-level ones for resources, or does not face hard budget constraints, the intent of the reform can be vitiated. It is important to keep lines of authority distinct; if they are up for constant renegotiation, effort will flow into that activity rather than to implementing public policy.

Finally, numerous efforts to reform political systems have been undertaken, either to make them more representative, or to increase the efficiency of decision making. Two decades ago, the political scientist Juan Linz criticized presidentialism as an institution in Latin America.[1] The inherently winner-take-all nature of presidential elections often produced leaders elected by only a minority of the electorate; such leaders thus lacked legitimacy. In the debate that Linz provoked, attention shifted from the form of the executive to electoral systems. In Latin America, legislatures often could not generate strong and stable majorities in support of initiatives coming from the executive. In this, the precise rules (such as the inability of political parties in Colombia to control who ran under their own lists) mattered a lot.

The great deal of activity in this area has often had mixed results. Argentina, Colombia, and Peru all extended term limits for presidents, a reform that may or may not be desirable in itself, but that coincided with the ambitions of particular presidents to remain in office. The introduction of second-round voting solves the problem of minority presidents, but also tends to fragment party systems. The design of political systems involves trade-offs between competing social goods (for example, decisiveness versus resoluteness), with the result that there is no clearly optimal institutional design.

As the current volume makes abundantly clear, enormous weaknesses remain in Latin American institutions that will continue to constrain the region's prospects for economic development and stable democracy. Most serious are corruption and weak rule of law in virtually all countries except Chile, making property rights insecure and driving much economic activity into the informal sector. General public administration remains poor, and governments that fail to deliver necessary public services to their constituents undermine their own legitimacy and provoke cynicism about democracy itself. Hugo Chávez's Venezuela has seen substantial institutional regression because the president has politicized or put under his control virtually all institutions of horizontal accountability—the congress, the trade unions, the central electoral commission, the state oil company, and the court system.

It is understandable that progress has been so much slower in an area such as legal reform than in the reform of institutions dealing with macroeconomic policy. The latter involves public agencies with low transaction volume and high specificity. That is, an institution such as a central bank makes relatively few decisions, and the decisions it makes are readily monitorable. It is therefore relatively easy for principals to hold agents accountable for their behavior. The same is much less true of legal systems, because high transaction volume and low specificity make it much more difficult to hold agents accountable.

An earlier publication of the Inter-American Development Bank, *The Politics of Policies,*[2] argued that the agenda facing researchers in the area of institutions had changed. The general importance of institutions is well understood, as are the theoretical ways in which different types of institutional design affect policy making. What is less well understood are the specific features of particular institutions—many of which are the product of informal rather than formal rules—that often spell the difference between effectiveness and dysfunctionality. Local context, history, and tradition are extremely important in shaping the way in which specific institutions work; without an empirical understanding of these factors, it is impossible to move forward with a workable program of institutional reform. It is in this context that *The State of State Reform in Latin America* makes a very valuable contribution to the growing literature on institutions and suggests specific ways forward in the next stage of Latin America's institutional development.

Notes

1. See Juan J. Linz, "Democracy: Presidential or Parliamentary—Does It Make a Difference?" (Paper prepared for the Workshop on Political Parties in the Southern Cone, Woodrow Wilson International Center for Scholars, Washington, DC, 1984); and Juan J. Linz, "The Perils of Presidentialism." *Journal of Democracy* 1 (Winter 1990): 51–69.

2. Ernesto Stein, Mariano Tommasi, Koldo Echebarría, Eduardo Lora, and Mark Payne. 2005. *The Politics of Policies: Economic and Social Progress in Latin America, 2006 Report.* Washington, DC: Inter-American Development Bank.

Acknowledgments

This book is part of a large, ambitious project on political institutions and government in Latin America being carried out by the Inter-American Development Bank (IDB). The seeds for this project were sown over four years ago with a Latin American Research Network study led by Ernesto Stein and Mariano Tommasi, which became the basis for the IDB's 2006 Economic and Social Progress Report entitled *The Politics of Policies*. The preparation of that groundbreaking report involved virtually all the contributors to this volume, who were originally asked to prepare succinct notes on the status of different types of public institutions in Latin America. Realizing that there were major lacunae to produce even a basic description of Latin American governments, the contributors generously agreed to embark on a more ambitious undertaking, which is now reflected in this book. *The State of State Reform in Latin America* has benefited from many synergies with the other components of that larger project.

A veritable army of researchers, writers, editors, and administrative personnel contributed to making this book a reality. Apart from the authors of the chapters, many others deserve special recognition for their economic research and substantive comments on numerous drafts, including Martín Bes, Cecilia Calderón, Mauricio Cárdenas, Regina Cárdenas, Cindy Clement, Eduardo Fernández-Arias, Florencio López-de-Silanes, Claudio Storm, Vito Tanzi, Luiz Villela, and an anonymous referee. Everyone who participated in the Workshop on State Reform held at the IDB's headquarters in August 2005, and other related seminars deserve special thanks as well.

Much of the information for the chapters in this book came from sources within the countries of the region. To all the ministries, statistical institutes, government authorities, and other data sources in countries throughout Latin America, I would like to offer my thanks. In particular, authorities from numerous countries responded to a series of surveys on budget institutions that were key to the preparation of chapter 5.

Ideas become successful books thanks to capable editorial and administrative support. For their exceptional support in this area, I would like to acknowledge Heather Berkman, Juan Camilo Chaparro, Rita Funaro, Elton Mancilla, María Helena Melasecca, and Mariela Semidey. For pulling everything together I am most grateful to the editorial team at the World Bank led by Dina Towbin under the direction of Santiago Pombo. Finally, this book would not have been possible without the multiple contributions of Carlos Andrés Gómez-Peña, who provided meticulous research assistance and carefully followed the production process from start to finish.

Eduardo Lora

Abbreviations

ABA/CEELI	American Bar Association's Central and East European Law Initiative
ADI	Activity Decentralization Index
AIOS	International Association of Latin American Pension Fund Supervisors
AVEC	Venezuelan Catholic Schools Association
CARCE	Colombia Competes Network and the Regional Advisory Committees for External Trade
DMI	Decentralization Maturity Index
FDI	foreign direct investment
FEIREP	Fund for Stabilization, Social and Productive Investment and Public Borrowing Reduction (Ecuador)
FEP	oil stabilization fund, Ecuador
FUNDEF	Fund for Maintenance and Development of the Fundamental Education and Valorization of Teaching (Brazil)
GATT	General Agreement on Tariffs and Trade
GDP	gross domestic product
GRADE	Group for the Analysis of Development
IDB	Inter-American Development Bank
JRI	Judicial Reform Index
LLECE	Latin American Laboratory of Education Quality
OECD	Organisation for Economic Co-operation and Development
PIRLS	Program in International Reading Literacy Study
PISA	Program for International Student Assessment
PREAL	Partnership for Educational Revitalization in the Americas
R&D	research and development
SOE	state-owned enterprise
TIMSS	Third International Math and Science Study
VAT	value added tax

1

State Reform in Latin America: A Silent Revolution

Eduardo Lora

WITH THE 1980s, crisis began in the interventionist, paternalist, and centralist state that for half a century Latin American countries, following the example of Europe, had attempted to establish, with varying degrees of success.[1] The crisis of the state in Latin America fully manifested itself beginning with the foreign debt crisis that erupted when Mexico declared a moratorium on its obligations in 1982. The crisis emerged first as a fiscal problem because the sources that had financed the expansion of the bureaucratic apparatus for decades finally dried up. These included the gradual monetization of economies in expansion,[2] income from the provision of public services under monopolistic conditions to the upper and middle classes, workers' contributions to the social security systems that still had very few pensioners, and tax revenue that was easy to collect but that stifled international trade and distorted investment and production decisions. The signs of exhaustion of these sources of fiscal revenue were evident in several countries in the 1970s but the solutions were delayed because high oil prices, apart from creating new revenue in crude-exporting countries such as Mexico and Venezuela, recycled the financial surpluses of Middle Eastern oil-producing countries through bank loans for Latin American governments. When the rise in international interest rates and the consequent debt crisis put an end to this source of loans, some countries turned increasingly to unbridled issuance of currency, setting into motion or exacerbating the inflationary processes already under way in several countries. In a few years, this method[3] would also lose effectiveness as the public fled from national currencies.

The crisis of the Latin American state was not only fiscal, it was also a crisis of the functioning of the administrative apparatus and, as a consequence, a crisis of political legitimacy. The expansion of the state since the

1930s had been founded on a firm base in Argentina, Chile, and Uruguay, which already had administrative capacity and skilled human resources, and was also consolidated to a large extent in Brazil, Colombia, Costa Rica, and Mexico, each of which had established a dense network of relatively efficient public bodies. By the 1980s, the complexity of the administrative apparatus in most countries led to "bureaucratization," that is, an excess of public employment,[4] and to decreasing returns to the resources used, as revealed in the stagnation of coverage and the deterioration of the quality of education, health, water, electricity, and telecommunications services. In the countries with more modest bureaucratic capacities and weaker public institutions, it was not only the deficiencies of coverage and quality that were evident but also the more critical problems of corruption and waste of resources, and in some countries the capture of economic policies by powerful interest groups and sectors.[5]

The crisis of state legitimacy took on a variety of expressions depending on the political context. The developmentalist military regimes in power in much of South America—promoters of industrial development and massive infrastructure investment directly supported by the state, without much consideration given to their financial and economic viability—lost the limited popular support on which they had relied, along with the economic capacity to co-opt the business and financial elites. Although the Pinochet dictatorship did implant a state model more in tune with the new free-market trends—neoliberalism—and succeeded in rapidly reactivating the economy after the deep crisis of 1982, as living conditions improved the deeply rooted democratic institutional tradition of Chileans achieved a completely peaceful return in 1990. The one- or two-party democracies of Colombia, Mexico, and Venezuela were forced to make room for the participation of marginalized political and social groups, which ultimately caused deep changes in the political systems of these countries in the 1990s. Some of the poorest Central American countries, still ruled by patrimonialist governments, experienced civil wars and political instability as the forerunner to democracy.

This multidimensional crisis of the state contributed decisively to producing three phenomena common to all Latin American countries that changed the economic and political features of the region. These phenomena were democratization, macroeconomic stabilization (that is, the reduction of inflation and the control of the great fiscal disorder associated with it), and the opening up of countries to international commerce by reducing tariffs and other barriers to trade. Of the 18 Latin American countries in 1980, only 6 were governed by popularly elected presidents. Twenty years later, all countries had regular elections and, although 11 presidents were deposed between 1992 and 2005 (Stein and others 2005), in all cases they were replaced in a few days or weeks by constitutional mechanisms. Stabilization was equally generalized. At the end of the 1980s, in the same group of 18 countries, 11 had inflation rates over 20 percent and 4 suffered price increases of over 1,000 percent annually. By contrast, in the 2001–05 period no country had an average inflation rate over 20 percent, and only 5 countries recorded inflation in one of these years above this mark (with a maximum of 41 percent in Argentina in 2002). Trade liberalization was also a common phenomenon. The average tariff on imports in South American countries dropped from 55 percent in 1985 to approximately 10 percent in 2000, and in the group of Central American countries and Mexico the fall was even steeper—from 66 percent to 6 percent. The international opening of trade also applied to trade in services, foreign direct investment, and international finance.

Obviously the crisis of the state was not the only cause of democratization, stabilization, and trade liberalization. Globalization also contributed, because the reduction in transport costs and the spread of new information and communication technologies raised the potential gains from trade and from technological change, at the same time as the exposure of the countries to the new ideological tendencies of the state and economic management intensified. The collapse of the communist systems of Eastern Europe in 1989 and the return of international capital to Latin American countries—due to the Brady Plan[6] and growing international liquidity—helped consolidate the democratization process and created incentives to initiate economic reforms. The frustration left by the lost decade of the 1980s and the promise offered by replicating the policies adopted by Chile contributed to strengthening interest in economic stabilization and trade opening. The success of countries in Southeast Asia with growth models based on fiscal discipline and exports provided more impetus to follow a new policy direction.[7] The most common elements of the first wave of reform in this context resulted in the well-known Washington Consensus (Williamson 1990).

Democratization, stabilization, and trade liberalization are the starting points for this book.[8] These trends that, as we have seen, were in part brought about by the crisis of the state, helped propel state reform since the mid-1980s (a process that began in many cases before these phenomena).[9] By its very nature, democratization led to reform of the political systems, especially electoral systems and the functioning of parties, not only to make suffrage possible but also to broaden the representativeness and relevance of the legislative bodies. Democratization also produced various reforms to the judicial systems to prevent the abuse of presidential power that had occurred under the authoritarian regimes and to expand access to justice beyond the elites. In most countries, democratization was expanded in the 1980s and 1990s to provincial and municipal governments, increasing popular demand to widen and improve residential and social services provided by these subnational governments, thus influencing reform in these sectors.

From the start, price stabilization was a tenuous victory because in practically all countries it was initially based on sudden cuts in public spending or on manipulation of the exchange rate, both of which were impossible to sustain indefinitely. The political dividends of controlling inflation were so great,[10] however, that the parties in power rapidly closed ranks to shore up the achievements through other reforms, such as granting independence to the central bank, strengthening tax systems, or privatization, and when these supports turned out to be insufficient, reforming budgetary institutions. The consensus on the importance of price stability, and on the need for it to be based on a strong fiscal situation, also contributed to reform of the financial and pension systems. The threat of a crisis in these sectors was—and in many countries still is—a factor of fiscal weakness because the state is the ultimate guarantor of these systems.

The decision to integrate the economies more closely into trade, investment, financing, and technology flows influenced the reform of various state functions since the mid-1980s. Trade liberalization was in itself recognition that the state was losing the independence it needed to protect the economy and maintain competitiveness, to manage macroeconomic policy in opposite directions to international financial trends, or to finance itself from taxes on international trade.[11] Consequently, tax policies and institutions were reformed partly to compensate for lower tariff receipts, but also to improve the competitiveness of national products and attract investment. The regulatory practices of the financial systems and infrastructure were adapted as far as possible to applicable international standards. In countries most exposed to international competition, liberalization also contributed to the initiation of reforms in the education and justice sectors and to strengthening intellectual property rights. Moreover, increased international integration probably also contributed to the spread of ideas, facilitating, for example, propagation of the pension system reform inspired by the Chilean model, the multiplication of independent regulatory agencies,[12] and the diffusion of some successful social protection systems, such as the Mexican *Oportunidades* program.

When the crisis of the state became evident in the 1980s with sudden cuts in public spending, liquidation of state companies, and the virtual collapse of some state functions in the hardest hit countries, opponents of reform created the myth that the old model of the paternalist, interventionist state that generated unnecessary public employment would be replaced by a minimalist state concentrated on protecting property rights, ensuring macroeconomic stability, and guaranteeing access to only the most basic services of justice, health, and education. This feared neoliberal state never became a reality. As this book extensively documents, the new state that is taking shape after 20 years of reform is more "socially liberal," to use the term coined by Luiz Carlos Bresser Pereira (1998), architect of Brazilian state reform during the presidency of Fernando Henrique Cardoso. In comparison with the previous state model, this is a state that is more limited in size and objectives; more representative and legitimate; less centralized; more managerial and less bureaucratic; a promoter rather than protector of the private sector and employment; and a guarantor of access to the basic services of education, health, and social security, although not necessarily the producer of these services in their entirety. However, just as the neoliberal state never completely materialized, neither does this socially liberal ideal correspond exactly with any Latin American state.

This book does not attempt to analyze all the aspects of state reform since the mid-1980s. Its more limited objective is to concentrate on the most important areas of institutional reform, which have been much less systematically studied than the economic reforms resulting from stabilization and deregulation—the backbone of the Washington Consensus. As pointed out by Naím (1994), and verified by numerous subsequent studies, institutional or "second-generation" reform is a necessary complement for the Washington Consensus reforms to effectively accelerate growth and contribute to achieving other development objectives.[13]

Although valuable studies review different areas of state reform, no work offers a panoramic view of overall reform. This book attempts to fill part of this gap, using a series of monographs commissioned by the Research Department of the Inter-American Development Bank (IDB) to describe the scope of the main aspects of the reform of state institutions that has taken place silently and gradually in Latin America. This effort is part of a larger project on public policy that includes studies on the political aspects of the reform process and the role of actors and political institutions in decision making. These issues are touched upon only tangentially in this book (see Stein and others [2005]).

This book is structured around four major areas of institutional reform: (a) political institutions and organization of the state; (b) fiscal institutions, tax policy, and institutional decentralization institutions; (c) institutions of sectoral economic policies; and (d) social policy institutions. It is an imprecise grouping because, as will be seen later, these reform areas intersect at various points. Likewise, the separation from first-generation economic reform is not totally clear—not surprising given that liberalization and institutional reform measures act in common spaces.

In each of these areas, this book summarizes the objectives of the reforms, describes and measures their scope, and identifies the main obstacles to their implementation and effectiveness, especially institutional obstacles. The methodological approach is essentially comparatively static between the situation before and after the reform. This approach does not do justice to the complexity of the process, or to the diversity of national experiences, because it ignores the political process of reform and the roles of the various economic and social actors in these processes.[14] However, it does identify the most common features of the reforms and their results based on quantitative indicators and common criteria.

The central conclusion of this review of state reform is that Latin America has experienced a silent revolution in which many dimensions of the state have been gradually transformed. The degree and depth of state reform contrast with current opinion that the region has put too much emphasis on macroeconomic and free-market reform and ignored the institutional dimensions of development.

Political Institutions and State Organization

Paradoxically, the crisis of the centralist and bloated state in the 1980s created the opportunity to recover or establish democratic institutions in several Latin American countries,[15] instead of producing abrupt or improvised changes in government structures or in the organization of the state, as had happened in various countries in past crises. Since the restoration of democracy, Latin American societies have broadly supported those democracies, although they persistently express discontent with the results as the opinion indicators of *Latinobarometer* survey, available since 1996, clearly reveal.[16] When the surveys began, a majority in 16 of the 17 countries surveyed considered that "democracy is preferable to any other form of government" (the only exception was Honduras), and a minority (not exceeding 26 percent of those surveyed in any country) considered that "in certain circumstances an authoritarian government could be preferable to a democratic government." Ten years later, support for democracy has fallen in almost all countries except Chile, El Salvador, Mexico, and Venezuela. Apart from these four, a majority supports democracy in another six countries (Argentina, Costa Rica, the Dominican Republic,[17] Nicaragua, Panama, and Uruguay); however, the percentage that might favor authoritarianism is less or has changed very little (except in Paraguay and to a lesser extent Peru). Consequently, democracy is far from being consolidated, but Latin Americans continue to consider it, as Winston Churchill said, "the worst system of government, except all the others."

In this light, it is not surprising that reform of the democratic institutions of government has been a continuous and inconclusive process. The main reforms have strengthened the legitimacy of the presidential system, but have limited the power of the executive in relation to the legislative branch, which is more representative of the diversity of political interests, and in relation to a judicial branch that has acquired a level of independence previously unknown in Latin America. Although the executive is now subject to greater political control than at any other time in the past, its capacity has been strengthened by public administration reform, which has had varying degrees of success depending on the country.

In this global context, political institutions in Latin America have made great progress when compared with other developing regions, albeit incomplete compared with the patterns in developed countries; and the progress varies from country to country. The indicators "voice and accountability" and "political stability" constructed by Kaufmann, Kraay, and Mastruzzi (2005) point to this progress and are presented in figure 1.1a. Other international indicators confirm that Latin America leads the developing world in democratic and civil freedoms based on the advances of recent decades (see IDB [2000], 14–16). However, Latin American countries are positioned less favorably in other aspects of government, especially "rule of law" and "corruption control." These deficiencies suggest the region still has a long way to go in terms of judicial reform and modernization of the state apparatus.

Political Reform

The basic structure of Latin American political regimes has changed little since the transition to democracy. All countries continue to have presidential systems; all have remained either federal structures (Argentina, Brazil, Mexico, and Venezuela), or unitary countries; and the structure of the legislative chambers is essentially unchanged, except for Peru and Venezuela, which moved from bicameral to unicameral systems.

However, as Payne and Perusia warn in chapter 2 of this book, it would be a mistake to conclude that the political regimes are unaltered. Without changing the basic structure, the multitude of reforms has altered many important aspects of the rules of the political game. Reform policies have not had a single orientation, which is not surprising given the complex and even unpredictable relationship between the political rules and their resulting effectiveness, legitimacy, representativeness, and level of citizen participation; and given that some of these objectives, although desirable in principle, can be partially exclusive. For example, an electoral reform that improves the representativeness of all political parties in congress could very possibly reduce the effectiveness of congressional decision making. The lack of a uniform direction in political reform is also the result of the frequent opportunistic motives of the leaders of the reform measures.

Presidential election systems have been subject to important changes, summarized in table 1.1. Only El Salvador, Honduras, Mexico, and Panama have maintained their presidential election rules essentially unchanged. In general terms, the number of countries that use a simple majority system has declined and the use of two-round runoff systems has increased, either with an absolute majority (as in half the countries of the region) or with a lower threshold (as occurs in four cases). No country has transformed a two-round system into a simple majority. That is, no country has moved contrary to the general trend of increasing the legitimacy of the president.

The possibility of presidential reelection has been another central aspect of reform of electoral rules. The general trend has been to introduce changes to permit immediate reelection, as have Argentina (1994), Brazil (1997), Colombia (2005), the Dominican Republic (2002), and Venezuela (1998). In Costa Rica and Ecuador nonimmediate reelection

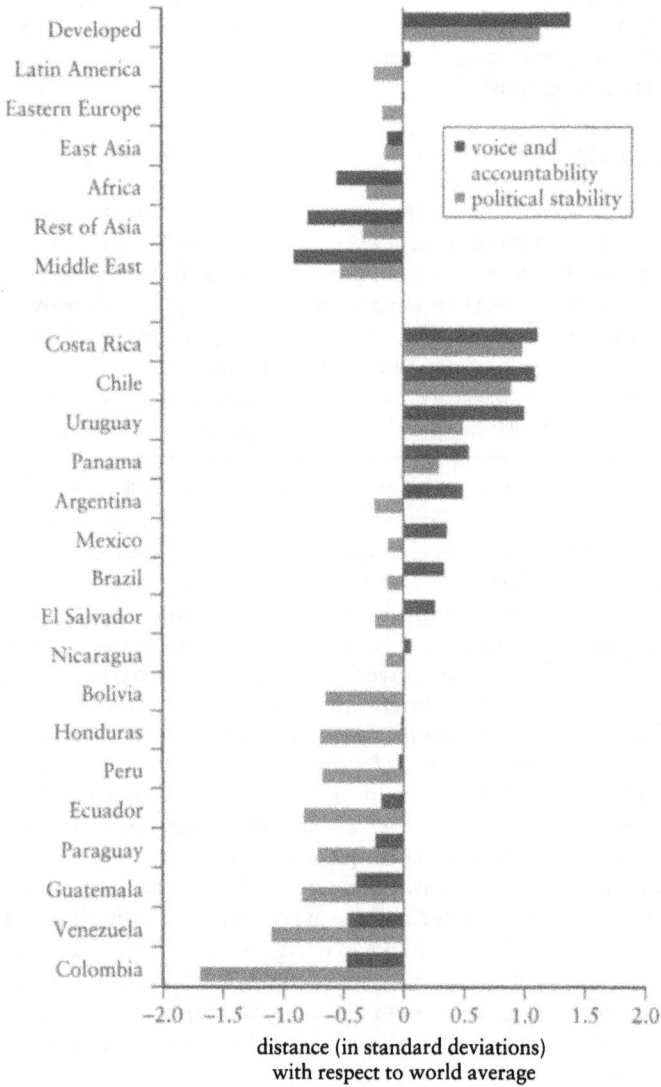

Figure 1.1a Voice and Accountability and Political Stability, 2004

distance (in standard deviations)
with respect to world average

Source: Kaufmann, Kraay, and Mastruzzi 2005.

Figure 1.1b Rule of Law and Control of Corruption, 2004

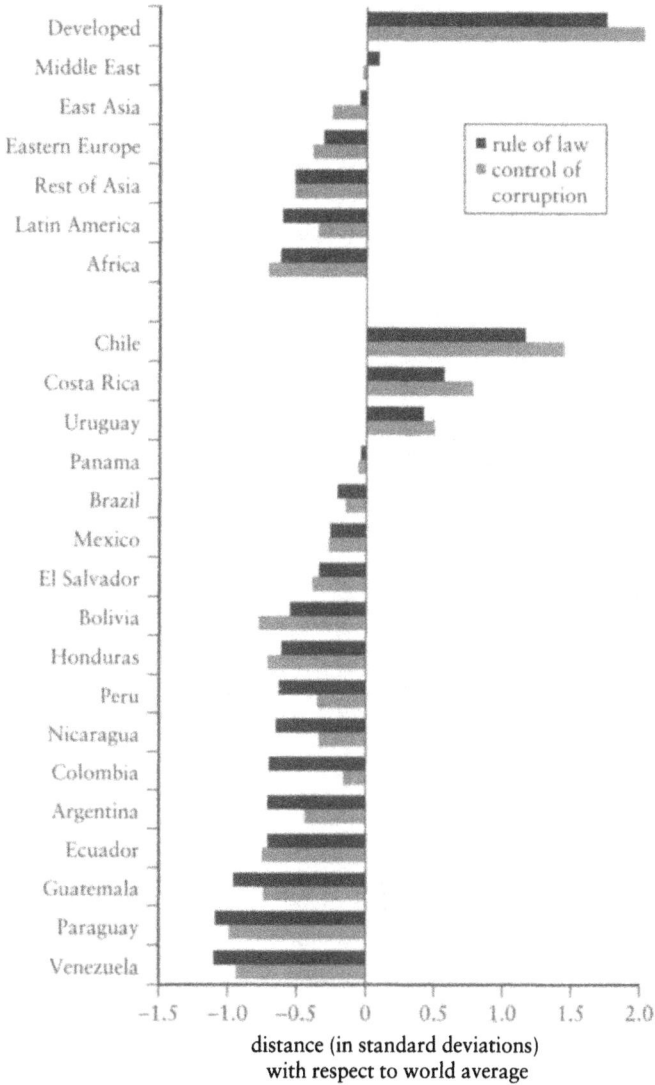

distance (in standard deviations)
with respect to world average

Source: Kaufmann, Kraay, and Mastruzzi 2005.

Table 1.1 Changes in Presidential Election Rules, 1978 (or year of transition to democracy) to 2004

	Election system	Simultaneity of elections	Duration of term	Reelection[a]	Countries with some changes
Argentina	From plurality to runoff	More concurrent	Reduced	Enabled	X
Bolivia	Congress runoff		Increased		X
Brazil	From congress vote to direct vote	More concurrent	Reduced	Enabled	X
Chile		Less concurrent	Reduced		X
Colombia	From plurality to runoff			Enabled[b]	X
Costa Rica				Nonimmediate, enabled	X
Dominican Republic	From plurality to runoff	Less concurrent		Enabled	X
Ecuador	From majority runoff to runoff with threshold	More concurrent		Nonimmediate, enabled	X
El Salvador					
Guatemala			Reduced		X

(*continued*)

Table 1.1 Changes in Presidential Election Rules, 1978 (or year of transition to democracy) to 2004 *(continued)*

	Election system	Simultaneity of elections	Duration of term	Reelection[a]	Countries with some changes
Honduras					
Mexico					
Nicaragua	From plurality to runoff		Reduced	Nonimmediate, enabled	X
Panama					
Paraguay				Not permitted	X
Peru				Nonimmediate, enabled	X
Uruguay	From plurality to runoff				X
Venezuela		Less concurrent	Increased	Enabled	X
Total of countries with changes	8	6	7	10	14

Source: Chapter 2.
Note:
a. Refers to last change until 2004. For further details see chapter 2, table 2.3.
b. Reelection enabled in 2005.

was permitted. Reform in Nicaragua and Peru moved in the opposite direction (where immediate reelection was prohibited) and in Paraguay (where reelection in general was prohibited). Another clear trend has been the shortening of the presidential term, which on average was reduced from 5.0 to 4.7 years (although in Bolivia and Venezuela, the presidential term was extended). Partly as a result of these changes in the length of terms, in most countries presidential and legislative elections are no longer simultaneous. It is also important to note that in most countries it is common practice for political parties to hold primary elections.

The electoral rules for the lower chamber have also been transformed. Only three countries (Brazil, Costa Rica, and Chile) have not adopted reforms in this area, while Argentina and El Salvador introduced relatively marginal reforms. The general trend has been to redesign electoral districts to improve representativeness, as well as to change closed lists to open lists where voters may choose between different candidates of a single party. In the Senate, two countries merged their congresses into a single chamber (Peru and Venezuela), while Argentina, Colombia, and Mexico significantly reformed election rules for senators.

In chapter 2, Payne and Perusia evaluate the possible effects of these reforms on the capacity of election systems to be participative, representative, and effective. The authors conclude that reform of the election systems for lower chambers has produced a clear gain in participation, understood as the facility offered by the electoral system for a direct relation between voters and their representatives. In the areas of representativeness and effectiveness the results are less clear, partly because of the tension that tends to occur in practice between these two characteristics. Representativeness measures the degree to which each party is represented in proportion to its vote, while effectiveness relates to the capacity of the system to make majority decisions. In general terms, in Central America there has been a trend in favor of representativeness (with some cost in effectiveness), while in countries such as Colombia and Peru the opposite has occurred. In the case of the Senate, the trend shows a gain in representativeness in the countries that have introduced reform (Argentina, Colombia, and Mexico).

In conclusion, the political institutions of Latin America have been in the process of change since the return of the democracies. The frequency of the changes reflects the fact that the rules of political competition are not yet firmly established, and that the region's democracies are still exploring ways of reconciling objectives that are not totally compatible. Citizen pressure and the dynamic of electoral competition have produced reform measures that have tended to increase the legitimacy of the executive and to bring voters closer to their representatives in the legislature. However, in other respects the effects have been more diverse and occasionally the reform has strengthened the political interests of certain groups to the detriment of others and at the cost of the system's capacity to pursue the collective benefit.

Judicial Reform

As part of second-generation reform, many countries of the region have made important changes in their judicial systems since the mid-1980s. The central purpose of such reform has been to strengthen the judicial branch in relation to the executive and legislative branches, at the same time as improving the administration of justice in areas that range from the selection and management of personnel to dispute settlement by alternative mechanisms. Given that judicial reform can vary significantly, Mariana Sousa in chapter 3 of this book uses a classification that identifies three types of reform: Type I reform relates to changes in the law itself; Type II reform relates to the effective implementation of the laws in the judicial sector and its supporting institutions; and Type III reform affects the role of the judicial branch in the public policy-making process, as control and counterweight to the decisions and actions of the other branches.

Argentina and Ecuador stand out as the most active reformers. Brazil, Colombia, Costa Rica, and the Dominican Republic fall into the intermediate category of substantial reform; followed by Bolivia, Chile, Guatemala, Mexico, Paraguay, Peru, and Venezuela, which have put through some reforms; and finally El Salvador, Honduras, Nicaragua, Panama, and Uruguay have seen very little reform activity. However, the scope of reform does not indicate the degree of success in achieving the desired objectives, as will be seen later.

Legal or Type I reform has been most frequent. In the great majority of countries, procedural codes, especially criminal codes, have been simplified with the aim of facilitating access to justice by broader sectors of the population, and laws have been passed to permit the use of alternative dispute settlement mechanisms. The scope of Type II reform has been much narrower. Such reform is more institutional, involving the operation of the courts, police, and other agencies of the judicial branch. Type II reform measures include managerial and administrative strengthening of the courts, the creation of specialized bodies such as councils of the judicature, training of judges, and the use of information systems to improve efficiency.

The scope of Type III reform has also been limited. Type III reform relates to the independence of the judicial branch in areas such as the appointment and selection mechanisms of judges, budgetary independence, the creation of constitutional courts, and judicial review mechanisms by the higher courts. These reforms have aimed at reducing political interference in the selection of magistrates and judges, improving pay and lengthening terms, increasing the budget, and creating specialized bodies responsible for budget management and the selection and promotion of judges. In a separate area of reform, the Supreme Courts, and in some cases new constitutional courts, have been granted greater review powers. These reforms are designed to affect the incentive structure that influences the conduct of judges and their capacity to make independent decisions; as such, their effectiveness depends not only on the rules and how they are implemented, but also on the perceptions and attitudes of politicians and the public in general toward the judicial system. (In Latin America, levels of confidence in justice are precarious and perceptions of the independence of the system vary greatly from one country to another, with Chile and Uruguay at the head, and Paraguay and Venezuela in the rear).

The results of judicial reform, especially Types I and II, have varied. For example, in the field of the appointment of judges with technical criteria, some countries have had success with judicial councils (Costa Rica), while others have abandoned them as ineffective (Ecuador). Similarly, in the area of pay systems, while some countries have managed to establish relatively high salaries (Brazil), others have not raised pay levels sufficiently (Ecuador), or the higher pay has favored only the higher courts (Nicaragua). With respect to budgetary independence, although the situation has improved on paper in most countries, for various reasons true independence has made much less progress.

In summary, there is great diversity both in the judicial reform initiatives and in the achievement of the desired objectives. In a valuable attempt to synthesize the progress of reform, Sousa has constructed an index based on 26 qualifying factors of the judicial systems in 10 countries; the results are summarized in table 1.2. The highest scores relate to factors that measure the formal powers and operating guarantees that have been granted to the judicial systems. Scores are less favorable for budget resources and pay levels. In most cases the results in the area of the qualification and selection of judges, transparency, responsibility, and efficiency leave much to be desired. Considering the set of judicial reforms, Chile and Costa Rica have made the most progress, while El Salvador, Guatemala, and Honduras have a long road ahead.

Public Administration

The reform of public administration is one component of the changes in state organization that has received little attention, partly because it has usually taken place in the shadow of political and economic reform, and has only occasionally been undertaken as a separate reform. The central purpose of explicit public administration reform measures has been to introduce models of organization and management practices to improve responsibility, independence, and technical capacity in state bureaucracies. As a by-product of other reforms, however, many changes have taken place in public administration, resulting in a great variety of organiza-

Table 1.2 Quality Indicators of Judicial Reform in Selected Countries

Indicators	Costa Rica	Chile	Argentina	Panama	Paraguay	Bolivia	Dominican Republic	El Salvador	Guatemala	Honduras
Total	18	15	8	3	-1	-2	-3	-3	-10	-16
Judicial powers	5	5	4	5	3	3	2	3	1	1
Operating guarantees	4	3	5	2	2	0	0	-1	-3	-4
Financing resources	2	1	1	-1	-2	-1	0	2	2	-1
Judges rating and selection	1	3	-1	-3	-1	0	0	-2	-2	-3
Transparency and responsibility	5	2	-1	1	1	-3	-2	-3	-3	-4
Efficiency	1	1	0	-1	-4	-1	-3	-2	-5	-5

Source: Chapter 3.
Note: Larger numbers indicate better quality reforms.

tional forms and bureaucratic structures, even within the same country. The evaluation of the progress of these reforms is a complex task not only because of this diversity, but also because of the limited basic information on the size and functioning of the civil service.

With some important exceptions, the reforms have reduced the size of public employment, which for the region as a whole dropped from 5.4 percent of the population in 1995 to slightly over 4 percent in 1999. However, the regional averages conceal large differences between countries. The bureaucracies in Chile and Colombia are the smallest (1 percent of the population), while in Panama, Uruguay, and Venezuela, to mention only some cases, over 5 percent of the population are public employees. State payrolls represent between 6 percent and 10 percent of gross domestic product (GDP) in most countries, with the exception of Chile and Guatemala where this cost is below 4 percent of GDP. In most countries, although reform has reduced public employment, it has also increased its cost.

The information on the size and cost of the state payroll tells little about the quality of public administration. For this reason, the Public Policy Management and Transparency Dialogue of the Inter-American Development Bank has constructed a series of qualitative indicators that measure the efficiency of the bureaucracy; the degree of connection between the civil service systems and the strategic priorities of governments; and the degree of independence, professionalism, and technical capacity of the civil service. In their analysis of these variables, Koldo Echebarría and Juan Carlos Cortázar in chapter 4 conclude that only two countries, Brazil and Chile, have functional, efficient, and independent bureaucracies that are, above all, in tune with their governments' priorities (figure 1.2). A second group of countries, which includes Argentina, Colombia, Costa Rica, Mexico, Uruguay, and Venezuela, is in the intermediate category where modest progress has been made, suggesting the need for additional reform. Finally, a broad group comprising Bolivia, Ecuador, Peru, and all the Central American countries with the exception of Costa Rica, has unsatisfactory bureaucratic quality indexes.

Public administration reform has varied across countries in depth and effectiveness. Three key features of reform have been the size of the bureaucracy, the introduction of merit criteria for selection of officials, and more flexible management of human resources. All three reveal a marked contrast from one country to another. Consider, for example, Uruguay and Peru in relation to the size of the bureaucracy. Between 1997 and 2000 in Uruguay, the state payroll was cut as part of a program that included restructuring functions, voluntary retirement with incentives for numerous officials, and redesign of pay systems. The program successfully supported the relocation of about 3,500 workers outside the public sector, cut the operating costs of the public system, and facilitated functional reorganization. In Peru, in 1991 the government started a program to "buy" the resignations of public officials, which reduced the payroll

Figure 1.2 Quality of Public Administration

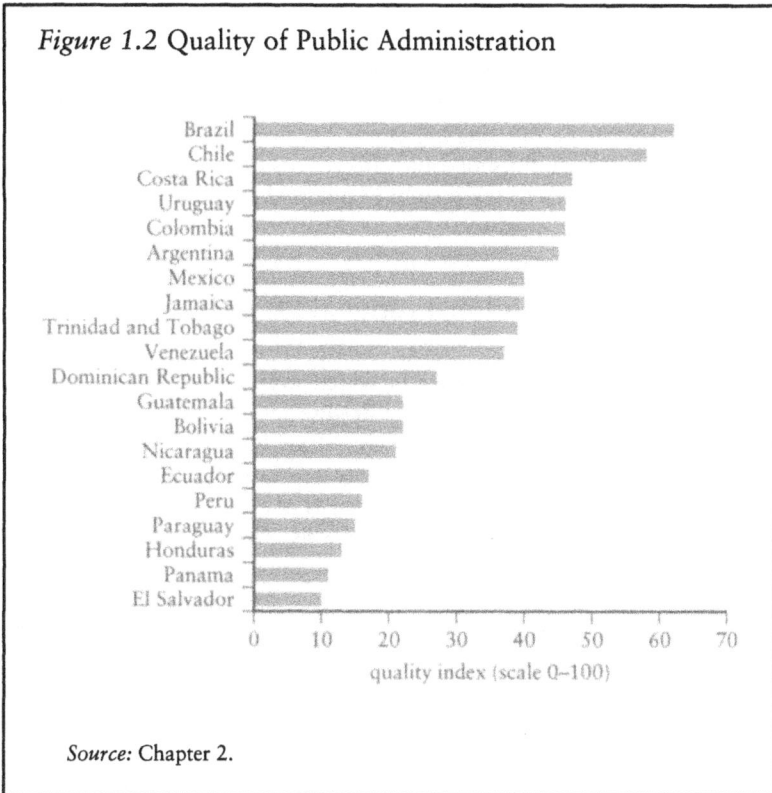

Source: Chapter 2.

by about 300,000 workers. However, the following year hiring resumed using "contracts for nonpersonal services" to evade restrictions, resulting in practice in the informalization of public employment, with no significant reduction in the number of public sector workers.

The introduction of merit and performance criteria has also had a range of outcomes. In Chile, performance criteria are a central component of the management-by-results strategy that has gradually but effectively deepened in recent years. In Brazil, the strengthening of the meritocracy in the federal government has raised the proportion of officials with university degrees from 39 percent in 1995 to 63 percent in 2001. In Costa Rica, about half the jobs in central government are covered by merit-based selection—a result of the relative independence enjoyed by the agency that controls these processes. In contrast, in the other Central American countries, entry into public administration and promotion are both strongly influenced by political criteria or patronage, and efforts to introduce technical selection mechanisms have been swiftly abandoned. The increasing

flexibility of resource management has gone hand in hand with professionalization in most countries. In Brazil, however, despite the success
of the public administration reform initiated in 1995, its end result was
to strengthen the traditional meritocracies of the central administration
rather than reforming the state apparatus under managerial criteria. More
than in any other area, the scope and effectiveness of public administration
reform are determined by the weight of political practices and the culture
of each country.

Fiscal, Tax, and Institutional Decentralization

The fiscal and inflationary crises in which most of Latin America was
immersed in the late 1980s were the driving forces behind the first-generation reform, which was primarily concerned with macroeconomic stabilization and liberalization of the more repressed markets. The crises
convinced political leaders of the advantages of granting independence to
central banks, which was one of first reforms of macroeconomic institutions. Between 1988 and 1996, the central banks of 12 Latin American
countries were reformed by law or by the constitution, granting them
greater independence in the design and conduct of monetary policy with
the objective of guaranteeing price stability. A key element of this new
independence consisted of limiting government access to central bank
financing. These reforms effectively reduced inflation but, in a very revealing way, the degree of success had more to do with the operational independence of the central banks in the management of monetary policy
instruments and the definition of policy targets than with the level of formal or de jure independence granted by legal provisions (Jácome 2001).

In this situation, limiting government's access to central bank credit
turned out in many countries to be insufficient to guarantee the monetary
independence of the central banks and to prevent excessive government
borrowing, especially in a context of renewed government access to external financing, the growing need for fiscal revenue following the loss of
tax receipts caused by trade opening, the increased international mobility of tax bases, and last, increased expenditure pressure resulting from
democratization and decentralization tendencies in some countries. These
parameters explain the importance of institutional reform in the fiscal
arena in the 1990s.

Reform of Budgetary Institutions

Fiscal results are not the outcome of the decisions of a social planner anx-
ious to safeguard the collective welfare, but the result of political processes
used by a diverse group of actors to pursue their own interests or those
of the people they represent. Budgetary institutions must discipline the

behavior of these actors to prevent the "problem of the commons," that is, excessive and inefficient expenditure of public resources. A pioneering study on this subject, prepared by the IDB in the mid-1990s (Alesina and others 1996), identified three groups of rules that contribute to preventing the problem of the commons in the fiscal area: (a) numerical restrictions that establish limits on the amount or path of the deficit, public expenditure, or borrowing; (b) procedural rules that establish a clear separation of responsibilities between the executive and congress on budgetary decisions to prevent the latter from increasing the fiscal deficit or total expenditure, and that centralize in the finance ministry the decisions on final control of expenditure to impose discipline on the line ministries; and (c) transparency rules that facilitate public oversight and centralized control of the budget.

In chapter 5, Gabriel Filc and Carlos Scartascini use this analytical approach to study the reform trends in budgetary institutions between the early 1990s and 2004.[18] As summarized in table 1.3, practically all reform has been in the direction of improving control of fiscal results. Twelve of the 18 countries considered made progress with numerical restrictions. A number of countries opted to pass integrated "fiscal responsibility" laws that imposed limits on spending, the deficit, or the public debt.[19] In Chile, although there is no law, the rule of a 1 percent surplus of GDP was established for normal years, and higher when copper prices rise or the economy is buoyant (and vice versa). Apart from these limits, various countries have multiyear frameworks to give predictability and flexibility to annual targets. The fiscal responsibility laws of Argentina and Peru also set up funds to stabilize tax revenue, and the Ecuadorian law created an oil revenue stabilization fund. Oil stabilization funds were created in Colombia, Mexico, and Venezuela (in addition to the Chilean copper fund in operation since 1987 and the coffee fund in Colombia since 1940).[20] Several countries have also established numerical fiscal restrictions on subnational governments, as will be mentioned later in the section on decentralization.

In the area of hierarchical or procedural rules, reform has been far less extensive. Except for Guatemala, legislatures in Latin America are restricted from modifying total spending or the deficit proposed by the executive (although in Bolivia and Paraguay these restrains are circumvented). Similarly, except for six countries (Bolivia, Guatemala, Honduras, Panama, Peru, and Venezuela) the finance minister has the last word in budgetary decisions, which facilitates fiscal control. Ecuador is one of the few countries where the distribution of powers changed significantly as it sought to limit the power of congress over the executive.

With the idea of strengthening the authority of the ministry of finance in relation to the other spending authorities, the principal changes had to do with how to administer resources, especially cash and debt. A key element of such reform was the introduction of the single treasury account, which

Table 1.3 Budget Institution Reform

Country	Fiscal rules			Hierarchical rules			Transparency norms	
	Numeric rules	Countercyclical fund	Multiyear programming framework	Power of the executive	Power of the minister of finance	Single account	Transparency law	Disclosure regulations
Argentina	+®	+®		+	+	+	+®	
Bolivia	+					+		
Brazil	+®		+			+	+®	
Colombia	+®	+	+®		+	+	+®	
Chile	+®[a]	+®[a]		–			+	
Costa Rica						+		+
Dominican Republic					+		+	
Ecuador	+®	+®	+®	+		+	+®, +	
El Salvador						+		+
Guatemala	+		+			+		

(continued)

Table 1.3 Budget Institution Reform *(continued)*

Country	Fiscal rules			Hierarchical rules			Transparency norms	
	Numeric rules	Countercyclical fund	Multiyear programming framework	Power of the executive	Power of the minister of finance	Single account	Transparency law	Disclosure regulations
Honduras			+			+		
Mexico	+	+	+				+	
Nicaragua	+		+		+			+
Panama	+®		+			+	+	
Paraguay			–	–		+		
Peru	+®	+®	+®			+	+®, +	
Uruguay	+			+		+		
Venezuela	+	+	+			+		

Source: Chapter 5.
Note: + = improvement; – = worsening; ® = indicated reform is part of the Fiscal Responsibility Law (FRL).
a. In Chile the FRL does not have the force of law.

14 countries adopted. This measure improves cash control (although not necessarily control of accruals) over fiscal resources.

The transparency rules have acquired importance since the mid-1990s with the passage of laws that establish free access to information and dissemination of fiscal results. Twelve countries have issued regulations to improve transparency, and in five of them, these rules are an integral part of the legal principles of fiscal responsibility.

As in the 1996 study (Alesina and others 1996), the recent research by Filc and Scartascini finds that the fiscal results clearly tend to be better in countries with good fiscal institutions. The primary fiscal deficit in the countries with the worst institutions is 2.5 percentage points of GDP higher than in the countries with the best institutions. The authors note that the numerical restrictions and procedural rules are more clearly related to the fiscal results than the transparency rules, possibly because transparency rules play a supplementary role. However, as the Alesina and others study warns, a good index is no guarantee of success because even the best fiscal rules may not work when the political incentives are not well aligned or when extraordinary circumstances occur that cannot be politically accommodated. A similar conclusion was reached by a detailed evaluation of case studies on the effectiveness of the numerical rules included in the fiscal responsibility laws (Kopits 2004). More than the technical design or the legal hierarchy of the rules, what is important for compliance is transparency of the fiscal accounts, quality of the budget processes, and support of the electorate. Consequently, the efficiency of formal institutions (which are most susceptible to definition and measurement) depends strongly on informal institutions, especially political culture and practices.

Tax Reform

Tax policy and administration have been active reform areas since the economic crises of the 1980s, especially in the first half of the 1990s. Trade opening measures, globalization, and the substantial drop in inflation—which limited the possibilities of financing the fiscal deficit by issuing currency—were the factors that drove this pressure for reform.

In this context the primary (but not only) objective of tax reform since 1985 has been to increase collections without generating excessive administrative costs. Following international trends, reform measures proposed by governments since the late 1980s have also aimed at improving neutrality and horizontal equity, reducing differences in treatment between sectors, and eliminating incentives and exemptions.

The pursuit of neutrality usually facilitates tax administration, but the opposite is not always the case. Taxes on financial transactions, the spread of tax-withholding mechanisms, large taxpayer units, and the introduction of simplified collection systems for small businesses have been effective administrative measures for increasing collections, but they conflict not only with horizontal equity but also with the effectiveness of the legal rules, making Richard Bird's comment that in developing countries, administration is tax policy more true than ever (Bird and Casanegra 1992, in Shome 1999).

The pursuit of progressivity (vertical equity) has been relegated to a modest role in reforms proposed by governments, which have given priority to value added tax (VAT) as a collection instrument. It has been the congresses that have frequently opposed proposals to expand the VAT base and unify its rates on the grounds of the regressive nature of this tax.

Chapter 6 shows how the pursuit of higher receipts, greater neutrality, and a more effective tax administration produced profound changes in Latin American tax regimes. For corporate taxes, the most important change was the cut in the rate from an average of 42.0 percent in 1986 to 31.7 percent in 1990 and 30.0 percent since the late 1990s. The rates for personal income taxes fell more steeply: the highest marginal rate dropped on average from 50.0 percent in 1985 to 33.7 percent in 1990 and to 25.0 percent in 2001. This apparent loss of progressivity was offset by the increase in exempt basic income (from an average of 60 percent of income per capita in the mid-1980s to 230 percent in 2001), and by the reduction in the level of income at which the highest marginal tax rate applies (from 121 times income per capita in the mid-1980s to 20 times at the beginning of the present decade). The most important transformation in the tax structure came from the expansion of VAT and the increase in its rate from an average of 10 percent in the late 1980s to around 15 percent since the early 1990s. The other indirect taxes lost ground, with the notable exception of the financial transactions tax, whose use has spread since the late 1990s. Many other taxes were eliminated or simplified.

To judge by total tax receipts, the effect of the reform measures seems modest. In 2004, average tax collections in Latin America were 15.7 percent of GDP, not a very different level from the 15.4 percent in 1985 and only 1.9 percentage points above the lowest point of tax collections in 1989. Although Argentina, Bolivia, Brazil, Colombia, and the Dominican Republic strongly increased collection since the late 1980s, in Chile, Mexico, Panama, Trinidad and Tobago, and Venezuela the trends were in the opposite direction (table 1.4). However, reform took place in an adverse context for taxation, and higher receipts were not the only objective.

The reforms had a much more significant effect on tax productivity (measured by the ratio between receipts as a proportion of GDP and the tax rate).[21] For income taxes, productivity increased on average 70 percent, and productivity increased 54 percent for VAT. The combined effect of the changes in rates and higher tax productivity was to improve the neutrality of the entire tax system, which was especially clear until the mid-1990s, because of the simultaneous loss of importance of the more distorting taxes, such as taxes on trade, excise taxes (on specific consumer items), and numerous small taxes. In recent years, however, reform has been less effective and has introduced taxing methods and collection mechanisms more damaging to the neutrality of the system. Improvements

Table 1.4 Tax Revenues in 1985–89 and 2000–03 (percentages of GDP)

Country	Total tax revenues		Trade taxes		Direct taxes		VAT		Other	
	1985–89	2000–03	1985–89	2000–03	1985–89	2000–03	1985–89	2000–03	1985–89	2000–03
Argentina	12.9	18.4	2.0	1.6	1.2	3.8	2.2	5.7	7.5	7.2
Bolivia	14.2	17.4	n.a	1.1	0.4	2.4	1.5	6.0	10.9	7.9
Brazil	16.0	21.0	0.6	0.7	4.4	5.8	5.6	8.3	5.5	6.3
Chile	19.2	16.5	2.6	1.0	3.0	4.4	8.3	8.0	5.4	3.1
Colombia	9.3	13.0	2.2	1.0	3.4	5.1	2.6	5.3	1.2	1.5
Costa Rica	—	12.8	—	1.0	—	3.0	—	4.9	—	3.9
Dominican Republic	11.6	15.2	4.6	4.1	2.5	3.9	1.3	3.7	3.5	3.5
Ecuador	16.8	18.3	2.7	1.6	1.6	2.7	2.5	6.5	10.0	7.6
El Salvador	12.3	11.0	3.2	1.1	2.6	3.2	n.a.	6.0	3.5	0.7
Guatemala	7.9	10.0	2.0	1.3	1.5	2.5	2.2	4.5	2.2	1.7
Honduras	13.6	16.2	5.1	2.3	3.5	3.5	1.6	5.5	3.4	4.9

(continued)

Table 1.4 Tax Revenues in 1985–89 and 2000–03 (continued) (percentages of GDP)

Country	Total tax revenues		Trade taxes		Direct taxes		VAT		Other	
	1985–89	2000–03	1985–89	2000–03	1985–89	2000–03	1985–89	2000–03	1985–89	2000–03
Jamaica	23.8	25.3	5.4	7.4	10.1	10.0	n.a.	3.9	8.4	4.0
Mexico	15.6	13.1	0.7	0.5	4.5	5.0	3.3	3.6	7.2	4.1
Panama	12.1	9.1	2.2	1.6	5.2	3.7	1.3	1.4	3.5	2.4
Paraguay	8.5	9.8	1.4	1.7	1.3	1.7	n.a.	4.2	5.9	2.1
Peru	10.8	12.4	2.3	1.4	2.0	3.1	2.1	4.9	4.4	3.0
Trinidad and Tobago	24.0	21.0	2.5	1.5	9.7	7.5	n.a.	3.8	11.8	8.2
Venezuela	16.2	11.5	1.9	1.1	11.5	4.2	n.a.	4.3	2.9	1.9
Average	14.4	15.3	2.6	1.8	4.0	4.3	2.9	5.0	5.7	4.1

Source: Author's calculations based on government finance statistics, IMF Article IV consultations, and IMF "Recent Economic Developments" reports.

Note: Total tax revenues do not include social security. Averages do not include Costa Rica. — = not available. n.a. = not applicable.

in the productivity and neutrality of the system were common until the mid-1990s in all countries. Later changes have been more heterogeneous.

The increased importance of VAT as a source of collection has generated concern in certain circles because of possible effects on income distribution. Although it is true that VAT affects low-income groups much more than an income tax, its final effect on income distribution is insignificant. What is really important for income distribution is the amount of the collection, which has much more influence on the redistributive potential of taxes. Without higher VAT collections, it would not have been possible to raise public social expenditure, as in fact has occurred in almost all the countries of the region since 1990 (see below). A different issue is that public spending is not sufficiently concentrated in the low-income groups, thus missing opportunities for redistribution.

The challenges that stimulated tax reform since 1985 have not disappeared. Globalization will continue creating "fiscal termites" that will find new ways of eroding tax receipts.[22] The growing importance of hemispheric and world economic integration agreements will involve additional sacrifice of tariff revenues. Political regimes will continue to exert pressure to make the tax regimes more responsive to the diverse interests of their constituencies, to the detriment of total revenue.[23] In the face of these pressures, some governments will certainly resort to new taxes, effective for collection although damaging to investment and efficiency, especially in countries where the possibilities of continuing to raise VAT are limited for political or practical reasons. With luck, others will attempt to more thoroughly exploit the potential of income taxes and personal assets taxes, and help subnational governments develop their own tax capacities.

Fiscal and Political Decentralization

With the exception of Argentina and Brazil, which are organized on a federal basis, the other countries of Latin America were politically, administratively, and fiscally very centralized until the 1980s. The return of democracy in the more prosperous, urbanized, and economically and politically complex societies started a decentralization process that is still far from over. In 2004, 19.3 percent of public spending was executed by subnational governments, an important increase compared with the decentralization coefficients of 13.1 percent in 1985 and 17.3 percent in 1996. Currently Argentina, Brazil, and Colombia have expenditure decentralization ratios of around 15 percent, and Bolivia, Mexico, and Venezuela around 30 percent (although Bolivia is one of the few countries with a tendency to recentralization). In several of the small countries, however, there has been no clear trend toward decentralization.

Following the approach of recognized IDB work in this area (IDB 1997), in chapter 7 Robert Daughters and Leslie Harper assess the progress of the institutional aspects of decentralization since the mid-1990s. In the area of political decentralization, they find that the election of mayors, which was already widespread a decade ago, has been followed by election of chief executives at intermediate levels of government—states, provinces, departments, or regions. This is an incipient trend because, apart from the four federal countries (Argentina, Brazil, Mexico, and Venezuela), only Colombia, Paraguay, and Peru conduct elections at this intermediate level. Some countries have changed the method of mayoral election from indirect to direct (Chile, Costa Rica, the Dominican Republic, and Venezuela) and have separated the timing of subnational elections from the national elections (Brazil, Costa Rica, the Dominican Republic, Ecuador, and Nicaragua).

The election of mayors has stimulated political demand for other aspects of institutional reform that are part of the decentralization process. Until the mid-1990s, decentralization of responsibility for provision of services to local communities had concentrated on basic infrastructure services (trash collection, road maintenance, and urban works). Since 1996, this has spread to such services as nutrition, hospital management, potable water, and interurban roads, all of which have more complex requirements for organization and skills. There has also been a certain trend toward greater decentralization in education and other social services, as discussed later, although limited by the resistance of labor unions. Other factors that have limited decentralization according to Daughters and Harper include the lack of clarity in the separation of responsibilities between the different levels of government (Brazil, Colombia, Ecuador) or, on occasion, the assignment of responsibility without supporting resources or tax powers (Mexico). Because effective decentralization of responsibility is a gradual and laborious process, lack of continuity in the priorities of decentralization in national governments has held up progress (Ecuador and Peru).

Because very few taxes can be managed more efficiently by local governments than by a central government, decentralization of tax powers is always insufficient in relation to expenditure decentralization. However, Latin America holds unexploited potential for local taxes (for example, taxes on real estate and gas consumption), but accompanied by little political interest at all levels of government in developing it. The subnational governments do not have any incentive to assume the political costs and accountability that local taxation implies. National governments have not promoted greater tax decentralization because they fear the erosion of national revenue and do not wish to spark competition or widen inequalities between jurisdictions. Argentina, Brazil, and Colombia have granted the most tax powers to subnational governments. Brazil is the only country that has a subnational VAT, whose receipts represent about one-quarter of the country's tax burden.

The growing disequilibrium between expenditure responsibilities and tax collection efforts at the local level has been covered by increased transfers of funds from the central government, regulated in most countries by systems of coparticipation in national tax revenue. The literature on decentralization has found that transfers generate fewer problems of inefficiency and corruption in expenditure when they are made automatically based on a transparent formula. Four of five countries with comparable information between 1996 and 2004 demonstrated an improvement according to this criterion (Chile, Ecuador, El Salvador, and Peru), while in Argentina discretion increased slightly in some programs.

Beginning in the mid-1990s, Brazil and Colombia faced serious problems of overborrowing by subnational governments, as later did Bolivia, Ecuador, and Peru, which led to a series of reforms to limit borrowing powers and improve the fiscal institutions of subnational governments. In Brazil, Colombia, Ecuador, and Mexico, limits were placed on borrowing (in the first three cases as part of fiscal responsibility laws). Colombia established a system of oversight of fiscal accounts, whose results determine the financing limits for each subnational government. In Mexico, the amount of credit that subnational development banks could lend to their governments was limited and national government bailouts were prohibited. Despite these measures, in most of the other countries the possibility of borrowing by subnational governments depends on discretionary approval by the national government, which does not guarantee discipline.

Daughters and Harper present an indicator that attempts to measure the quality and consistency of the various institutional aspects of decentralization. Their indicator takes into account (a) whether mayors and governors are elected, (b) the responsibilities of subnational governments for expenditure execution, (c) the extent of taxing powers, (d) the extent to which transfers of fiscal revenue are automatic or freely allocated, and (e) the level of control over the borrowing of subnational governments.[24] This index of the "maturity of the decentralization process," as they call it, demonstrates progress in the decentralization of institutions in all countries during the last decade, with pronounced changes in Bolivia, Ecuador, and Peru (figure 1.3). Argentina, Brazil, and Colombia made the most progress in the set of institutional aspects of decentralization, followed by Bolivia, Chile, and Ecuador. The institutional maturity of the decentralization process is closely correlated with the ratio of subnational expenditure to national expenditure[25] (as are the changes in both variables),[26] which suggests that there is a process of learning and institutional adaptation as decentralization deepens.

Sectoral Policy Institutions

The criteria for state intervention in the various economic sectors have changed radically since the late 1980s. With fiscal, administrative, and legitimacy crises of the state in the 1980s, the old forms of intervention

Figure 1.3 Decentralization Maturity Index

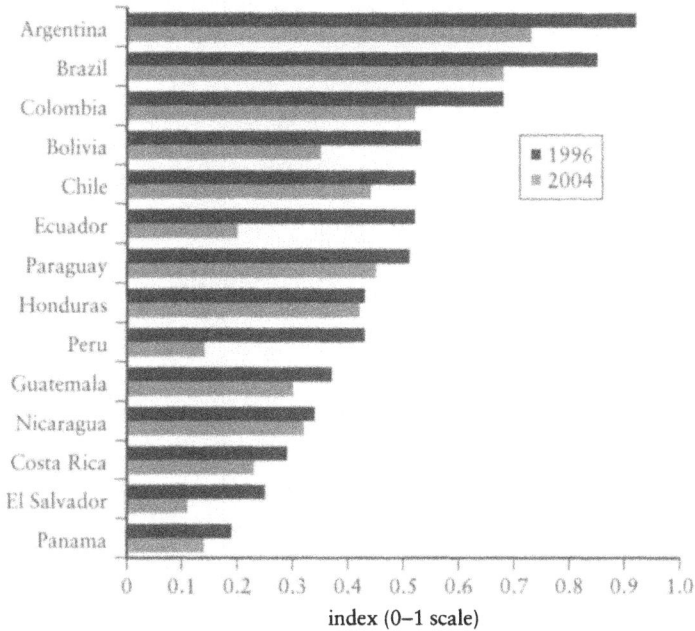

Argentina
Brazil
Colombia
Bolivia
Chile
Ecuador
Paraguay
Honduras
Peru
Guatemala
Nicaragua
Costa Rica
El Salvador
Panama

■ 1996
■ 2004

0   0.1   0.2   0.3   0.4   0.5   0.6   0.7   0.8   0.9   1.0
index (0–1 scale)

Source: Chapter 7.

lost support. Until the mid-1990s, reform was largely aimed at reducing direct state participation in productive and financial activities and removing obstacles to private initiative in a number of areas of the economy. As privatization and liberalization processes lost momentum, practically coming to a halt in the late 1990s, the importance—and limitations—of regulatory institutions were recognized. Thus, a new paradigm of state intervention is taking shape in which the central role is taken by institutions specializing in the regulation and supervision of the economic sector, but in which other forms of state action have space to promote the development of private initiative in certain sectors, activities, regions, or market segments in which the presence of externalities or failures of coordination limit investment or innovation. This section discusses reform of state institutions related to the public service sector, the financial sector, and the industrial sector in general.

The few indicators that compare Latin America with other regions of the world according to the quality of regulation of economic sectors suggest that institutional reform in this area has produced important benefits. According to the indicator devised by Kaufmann, Kraay, and Mastruzzi (2005), which is presented in figure 1.4, the typical Latin American

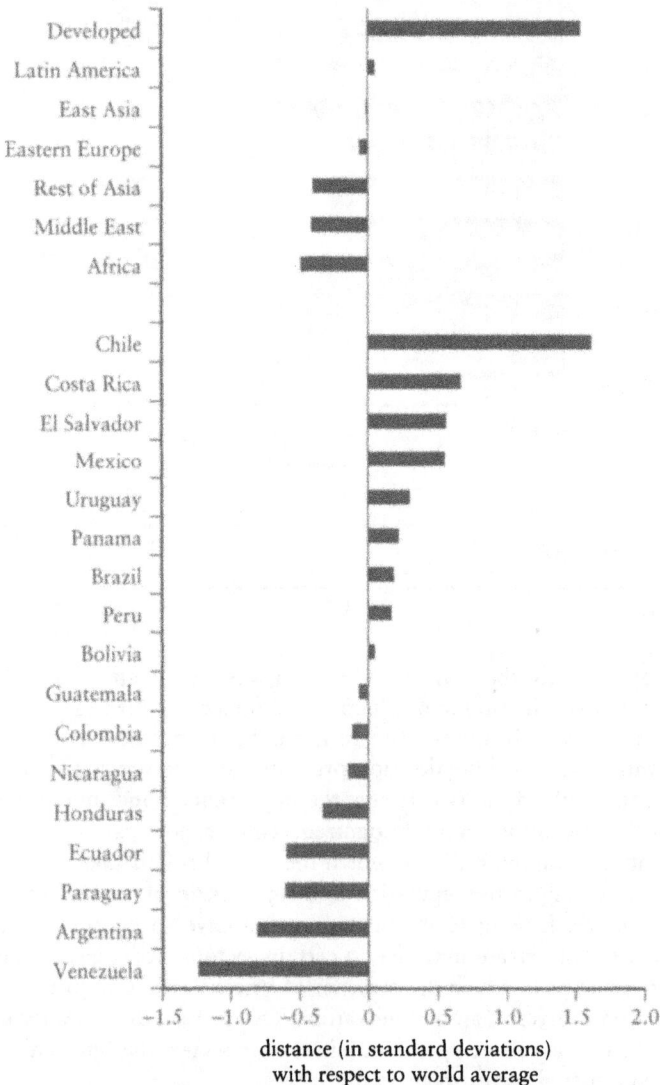

Figure 1.4 Regulatory Quality, 2004

distance (in standard deviations)
with respect to world average

Source: Kaufmann, Kraay, and Mastruzzi 2005.

country has a regulatory framework similar in quality to the countries of Southeast Asia and in some cases not significantly different from that of typical developed countries. As in other areas, there are wide differences among countries in the region and from one regulatory area to another. Moreover, as emphasized in this book, no universal regulatory methods are applicable to all situations in countries with distinct economic and political structures. Consequently, these general comparisons must be viewed with caution.

Ownership and Regulation of the Public Service Sectors

Privatization has played a leading role in the reformist agenda in Latin America. Measured by the number of companies sold off, contribution to GDP, market value, and, naturally, the amount of fiscal revenue obtained, the privatization process has no parallel. As a result of privatization, public companies' share of GDP fell from 10 percent in 1987 to half this a decade later. Governments received revenue from the sale of companies totaling over US$170 billion in the 1990–99 period, over three times the figure for Central Europe and Asia, the region with the second highest sales of state assets. Most countries privatized totally or partially their telecommunications, electricity, gas, water, and sanitation services. In fact, 75 percent of the revenue from privatization came from the sale of utilities and infrastructure companies, while 11 percent originated in the financial services sector and 14 percent in other sectors. However, privatization did not make equal headway in all Latin American countries. Argentina, Bolivia, Chile, and Peru were the most ambitious privatizers, while Costa Rica, Ecuador, Nicaragua, and Uruguay decided to maintain a strong state presence in various economic activities, especially in the public service and infrastructure sectors.

An interesting aspect of the privatization process that Alberto Chong and Juan Benavides analyze in chapter 8 was the exclusion of certain sectors, considered "strategic"—such as electricity in Brazil; telecommunications in Colombia, Costa Rica, and Uruguay; transport and sanitation services in Peru; and copper, ports, and oil in Chile. Almost all countries maintained an important state presence in the banking sector. The great heterogeneity of the strategic sectors suggests that political, cultural, and historical considerations were dominant in the selection of the sectors susceptible to privatization. In recent years, the process of selling state assets seems to have halted, partly because of the difficulty of reforming state ownership in the most politically sensitive sectors, which, again, vary from country to country.

The political difficulty contrasts with recent evidence on the results of privatization, especially in the public service and infrastructure sectors. From an economic viewpoint, the studies offer convincing estimates of the gains in efficiency associated with the process of selling off public assets. On average, the operating-income-to-sales ratio increased 14 percentage points in companies privatized in the region. Based on studies for five countries summarized in the chapter, the main reason for the increased profitability was clearly the improvement in efficiency, in large part due to technological modernization and the elimination of redundant employment, and not the exploitation of monopolistic advantage. Unit costs fell on average 16 percent after privatization, the sales-to-assets ratio increased 26 percent and the sales-to-employment ratio grew an impressive 70 percent, all in a context of expansion of services and higher quality. Obviously, in some cases the results were not so favorable. Based on available information, it can be concluded that the failures in the privatization process were associated with deficiencies in the regulatory framework that allowed private investors to exercise market power, preventing consumers from participating in the benefits of privatization. The public reaction against privatization results not only from the economic success that these privatized companies represent for new investors but from the resistance and visibility of the workers who were laid off and the aura of corruption that surrounded many of these operations.

Given that the bulk of privatization was concentrated in public services and infrastructure, the greatest challenge facing governments was to develop adequate regulatory frameworks, especially in the sectors with natural monopolistic conditions or oligopolistic market structures. In some sectors regulation worked very well. For example, in the telephony sector, evidence shows that when privatization took place in contexts with an independent regulator, the results were favorable in terms of labor efficiency and line density. Also, because sale prices of privatized assets were higher in the countries that already had regulatory agencies, it was desirable to have efficient regulation before the privatization processes began. Consequently, it seems paradoxical that this has been more the exception than the rule, because most privatizations have taken place without an adequate regulatory framework. The transport infrastructure sector is a good example of the philosophy "privatize now, regulate later." The cost of this strategy has not been insignificant in this sector, where the opportunistic renegotiation of contracts has been the norm. Chong and Benavides explore the practical difficulties of establishing a regulatory framework before privatization and set out the main challenges currently faced by regulation.

Public Institutions in the Financial Sector

Reflecting a radical change of view toward the role of the state in financial activities, in recent decades the participation of public banks in the banking sector has appreciably declined, and all aspects of financial intermediation have been liberalized. The share of public banking fell in the sector from 64 percent in 1970 to 40 percent in 1995,[27] and Latin America moved up from being the region with the lowest level of financial liberalization in the early 1990s to levels similar to developed countries by the end of the decade.[28] Practically all the region's economies eliminated regulations on interest rates, terms, and sectoral allocation of credit. Legal reserves were also reduced and restrictions on foreign-owned banks were lifted. Restrictions on external borrowing by the private sector were also removed, as were controls on capital and the multiple exchange rate systems.

However, as Arturo Galindo, Alejandro Micco, and Ugo Panizza warn in chapter 9, these reforms did not result in a more dynamic expansion of the financial sector, as had been expected. Financial depth in Latin America only reaches one-third the level of East Asia and half the average of the developed economies. In practice, the low level of financial depth reflects the fact that the financing requirements of many companies are not met, or they are met outside the formal lending mechanisms. Apart from its scarcity, credit in Latin America is costly and extremely volatile, as documented in a recent IDB study (IDB 2004).

In part as a result of this limited progress, liberalization has retreated in some countries of the region since the late 1990s. Brazil, Colombia, Ecuador, and Mexico, among other countries, have maintained or reintroduced forced investments, credit directed at certain sectors, and ceilings on interest rates. Argentina, Bolivia, Brazil, Colombia, Peru, and Venezuela have taxes on financial transactions—an expedient measure for tax collection but with potentially harmful effects on financial intermediation. The limited advances made in expanding and stabilizing credit have also rekindled interest in public banking, although with an approach influenced by the lessons of the past.

The "new" public intervention has been guided by the use of private criteria in the approach to state banking, both in compliance with prudential regulation and in hiring and management. Although the new approach does not rule out the possibility that public banks might grant subsidies, it is accepted that the mechanisms for granting them must be transparent and explicit. This is the case, for example, for partial guarantees and the creation of specialized institutions for supporting certain segments of the credit market, such as mortgages.

Galindo and colleagues argue that the lack of better results after financial liberalization can be partly attributed to the absence of supplementary reforms that interact with financial deregulation. Liberalization has a poor effect on growth when the institutions that back credit contracts and protect creditors are weak. If the judicial system is not prepared and the regulations inhibit the use of instruments to mitigate risk—such as guarantees—the benefits of liberalization will not materialize.

Worse still, liberalization can become a double-edged sword, increasing the tendency toward financial crisis when the quality of the regulatory and supervisory agencies is bad. With respect to financial regulation standards, capital requirements in Latin America are apparently relatively strict and in accord with international standards. However, the more institutional aspects of regulation exhibit many deficiencies. Of a total of 30 principles required for effective banking supervision according to the Basel Capital Accord,[29] Latin American countries comply with only half. For example, in most countries, banks do not adequately evaluate loans or make the recommended provisions; there is no consolidated supervision of financial groups; and regulatory agencies lack independence.

Two important areas of institutional reform that were virtually ignored until a few years ago relate to creditors' rights and the use of credit information. These areas are fundamental in the credit relation because they can help solve problems associated with moral hazard and information asymmetries. Protection of property rights in financial contracts is weak in Latin America, but countries such as Brazil and Mexico have recently reformed their legal provisions to improve this situation. A few countries have also taken measures in recent years to facilitate the use and recovery of collateral, which is difficult in most Latin American countries because of the lack of adequate property registers, and the slow pace and high costs of judicial processes. The institutions involved in processing and exchanging credit information (known as credit bureaus or credit reporting centers) are relatively well developed in Latin America, but in some countries they are now threatened by attempts to limit the use of this information through the introduction of legislation that mistakenly advocates the privacy of the information.

Industrial Policy Reform

One of the main components of first-generation reform was the dismantling of industrial policies associated with protectionism, selected subsidies, and direct state intervention in certain productive activities. The closing of the formerly influential economic development ministries exemplified the end of productive development policies in the framework of the import-substitution model, and led not a few analysts to suggest the end of industrial policy. Under the new model, the market would take over the allocation of resources, and industrial policies would be unnecessary and even inconvenient.

However, around the mid-1990s—partly as a result of the poor outcome of reform—authorities began to show interest in a new type of industrial policy. In most countries this change took place between 1994 and 1996, when medium- and long-term plans or strategies were adopted for development of the industrial sector. The new industrial policies became the escape valve for much of the criticism of the effects of structural reforms, especially those related to industrial restructuring of the sectors most affected by trade liberalization.

The new policies were accompanied by a renewed language in which the search for greater competitiveness became the unifying and integrating factor. Rather than proposing a return to the import-substitution model, the new industrial policy proposed directing the state into activities and services critical for improving the competitiveness of local production, such as transport and communications infrastructure, availability of skilled labor, and scientific and technological research, among others. The new industrial policy does not ignore the importance of macroeconomic stability or try to obscure or counteract price signals through the use of massive subsidies, which used to be common in some countries.

As Alberto Melo and Andrés Rodríguez-Clare note in chapter 10, the new industrial policies have essentially been adopted under two alternative models. The first, the strategy-driven model, is characterized by a scheme in which all interested sectors (government, unions, employers) discuss the vehicles or instruments required to improve competitiveness. Commitments are acquired in this process, normally structured around the concept of production chains, in which the private and public sectors set specific targets aimed at raising productivity and competitiveness. The striking aspect of this model is that the strategies and commitments are designed to improve the existing production chains, rather than introducing new sectors or creating new industries in a medium- and long-term development strategy. Colombian industrial policy is a good example of this model.

In contrast, the second approach, which the authors term demand driven, deliberately sets out to change the vector of goods and services produced, rather than supporting and promoting the existing sectors. Brazilian industrial policy is embedded in the framework of this model, which aims to stimulate the development of sectors considered strategic for long-term development, such as semiconductors, software, pharmaceutical and biotechnology products, and nanotechnology. Although the private sector also participates in this model, the public sector clearly plays a more active role in prioritizing the productive sectors.

The new industrial policies in Latin America combine diverse elements: trade, science and technology, promotion of small and medium enterprises, training, regional development, and many others. Melo and Rodríguez-Clare do not attempt to evaluate them all. The chapter concentrates on the policies and institutions of technological innovation and development, on the incentives for production and investment, and on the fiscal and financial mechanisms for export promotion. These areas are of interest because they are in the midst of change and allow the identification of contrasts between new and old.

The policies for promoting technological innovation have changed dramatically in recent years. The model has shifted from one based on the supply of research and development by state agencies to an incentives system for demand for technological innovation. The main components of the new model are (a) increased formalization of the science and technology systems; (b) creation of funds (which may or may not be sectoral) to support technological modernization; (c) active participation of the private sector in the process; and (d) a separate government entity for the policy design function, and another for the programming, promotion, execution, and evaluation functions. Brazil provides to date the most complete example of support for technological innovation through specific sectoral funds, in line with a demand-driven approach. In contrast, Chile is the best example of the more horizontal system of support for science and technology through funds that grant subsidies for demand without distinction between sectors, the strategy-driven approach.

Incentives for production and investment survive in a few countries in the form of programs for the provision of long-term credit for specific sectors, along with a number of fiscal incentives to support specific sectors of the economy, especially tourism (in the Andean, Central American, and Caribbean countries), as well as mining, reforestation, and other activities based on natural resources. Together with these traditional incentives, countries such as Argentina and Brazil have begun to develop public-private association programs to invest in specific production chains, with incentives ranging from a mutual commitment to make supplementary investments, to financing of seed capital.

Export promotion policies have a long history in the region. Although in the past, tax incentives were common, under the new World Trade Organization criteria they were reduced to reimbursement of taxes and tariffs on imports in export processes, especially in the major economies of South America. However, unlike these countries, tax exemptions (for both direct and indirect taxes) on export activities are still prevalent in Mexico, Central America, and the Caribbean. Special export processing zones are a separate case. They exist in practically all the region's economies, and are a favorite instrument for channeling tax incentives to foreign investors and export activities located in specific areas. In addition, financial incentives for exports are frequent in South American economies (except Bolivia) and in Mexico, which maintain public banks specializing in export finance through lines of credit, normally on more favorable terms and rates. In contrast, the Central American and Caribbean countries have left export finance to the private commercial banks. Nonfinancial export promotion agencies are a constant in the region, with the exception of the Bahamas, Haiti, Paraguay, and Suriname. There is a wide range of possible institutional configurations, depending on the degree of private sector participation and on the activities of the agency, which, in addition to supplying market information, is sometimes responsible for promoting foreign direct investment in the country.

No empirical evaluations of the effectiveness of the new industrial and innovation policies have been undertaken. According to Melo and Rodríguez-Clare, the results are difficult to observe because these policies are nascent, and have been applied timidly and inconsistently. For example, credit granted by development banks is very low in comparison with the experience in the Republic of Korea, and the fiscal revenue earmarked for innovation promotion is scarce and unstable. Although the high level of experimentation is desirable, some recognized principles are often disregarded; for example, that subsidies should be temporary. It is reasonable to conclude that industrial innovation policies are still being reinvented.

Social Policy Reform

The organization of the social portion of the public sector reflects the centralized, paternalistic, and bureaucratic state model adopted in Latin America in the 1930s, following the European pattern. This model was found, until the 1980s, to be effective for extending services and improving health and education conditions.[30] For example, in the health area, life expectancy rose from 40 years in 1942 to over 60 in 1980, and progress was even more significant in the infant mortality indicators. Notable progress was also made in primary education. Men born about 1960 (who would have been in the education system between 1966 and the mid-1980s) received an average of 7.7 years of education, while men born about 1930 received only 4.7 years of education. Women made even faster progress: from 3.7 years for those born about 1930 to 7.2 years 30 years later.

Although these advances have continued since the mid-1980s, the rate of progress slowed and the traditional state organization generated significant deficiencies in quality and equity. This was especially evident in education, although it is also true of social security. Latin Americans born about 1978 received 8 years of education, with an improvement over one decade of only 0.4 years for men and 0.9 years for women. The education gap with the United States, which had narrowed appreciably until the generation born in 1960, changed very little later (and widened in relation to the countries of Southeast Asia, where educational achievements continued to improve) because the region was incapable of expanding the coverage achieved in primary education to secondary education. Even more serious, the quality of education in Latin America was far inferior to levels in Asia and Eastern Europe, let alone developed countries.

With the fiscal crisis of the late 1980s, fear spread that the social sectors would be subject to budgetary asphyxia, which would destroy the achievements of the previous decades. Paradoxically, the slowing of progress in health and education took place amid a degree of fiscal abundance for these sectors. Social public expenditure per capita (in constant prices) rose almost 50 percent in the 1990s,[31] with increases in every country except Ecuador. In Bolivia, Colombia, the Dominican Republic, Guatemala, Paraguay, and Peru, this expenditure has doubled, although starting from very modest levels (figure 1.5). But the fiscal effort to support the social sectors has not been effective: the increase in expenditure on education in the 1990s has had no discernable impact on the coverage of primary or secondary education.[32] (It is illustrative to note that in developed countries there is no correlation between public expenditure and human development indicators, and that social conditions in some countries that substantially reduced the size of their public sectors did not deteriorate as had been feared [see Tanzi 2005].) The inefficiency of social spending can also be due to the fact that, in Latin America in general, spending is

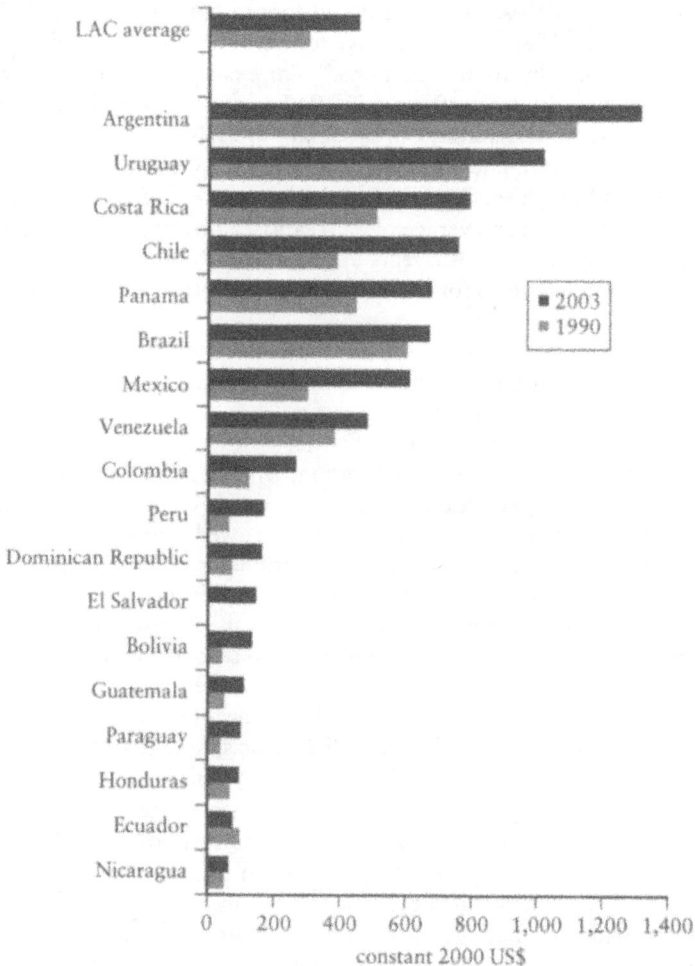

Figure 1.5 Social Public Expenditure per Capita

Source: ECLAC 2005.

not very concentrated on low-income groups, with the notable exception of Chile (see figure 1.6). This problem will tend to worsen in the coming decades with the increase in spending on pensions, which is the most inequitable component of social spending (and is not included in the statistics of the figure).

In solving the problems of stalled coverage, low quality, and inequality that affect the social sectors in Latin America, the institutional reforms designed to change the incentives of the providers and users were more important than the fiscal efforts to strengthen the old systems. This section outlines the main conclusions of the chapters of the book on pensions and education.[33]

Reforms of the Pension and Social Protection Systems

The traditional pension systems, guaranteed by the state through a simple collective distribution mechanism, underwent sweeping reform in 11 countries. Between 1993 and 2004, fully funded systems (in which the pension is based on the amount saved by the individual) were introduced,

Figure 1.6 Distribution of Social Public Expenditure

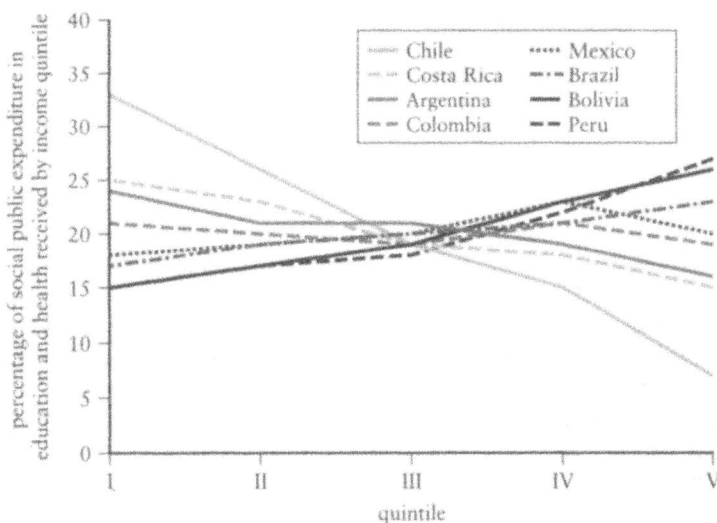

Source: ECLAC 2005.

inspired by the Chilean model created in 1981. The aim was to improve social security coverage, reduce administrative and financial inefficiency, stimulate the development of capital markets, and prevent future fiscal disequilibrium in the system. In Bolivia, the Dominican Republic, El Salvador, Mexico, and Nicaragua, the reforms envisaged the total replacement of the old public pay-as-you-go system with the new fully funded system, as in Chile (table 1.5). In contrast, Colombia and Peru opted for parallel systems (where workers join the system of their choice). Argentina, Costa Rica, Ecuador, and Uruguay decided on models that mix the public system (or partial collective capitalization) with fully funded systems for all workers. The other countries have not established fully funded systems, although some have made important changes to the conditions of membership and benefits of the public systems. Brazil established national accounts for private workers who are members of the system (maintaining public management) and began to unify the regimes for public servants. Venezuela passed a mixed-type reform in 1998 that was not implemented because of the change of government. In 2002, the new government ordered the integration of the entire provisional system with public management and partial collective funding.

The objectives of pension reform have only been partially achieved, according to the evaluation by Carmelo Mesa-Lago and Gustavo Márquez in chapter 11. With respect to coverage the results are not favorable. On average in the countries that put through reforms by 2004, the pension systems' coverage rate, measured by the number of contributors, was only 26 percent of the labor force,[34] whereas before the reforms the average was 38 percent, and 46 percent in the countries where there were no reforms. The possible causes of this low coverage include the trend toward informalization of employment, the high rates of contribution by workers and companies after reform, the high administrative costs of the pension funds (see following), and the minimum pension guarantee, which can prompt low-income workers to stop contributing once they have acquired this right.

The results for administrative and financial efficiency have been mixed. On the one hand, administrative costs in the private system are very high, averaging one-fifth of contributions because of the high costs of marketing, advertising, and seller commissions (whereas in the public system they average less than 4 percent of contributions). However, the real returns on the balances saved in the private funds are respectable: since the start of each operation until 2004, they were above 10 percent in three countries and between 6 percent and 10 percent in the other countries, with the exception of the Dominican Republic. But this is not because the pension funds have significantly diversified their investment portfolios. In seven of nine countries with information, over half the balance is invested in public paper and very little in stock market shares or other instruments. Capital market diversification in Chile is an isolated case attributable only partly

Table 1.5 Models and Characteristics of Pension Reforms in Latin America, 2005

Models of pension systems[a]	Coverage (contributors as % of labor force)		Administrative cost (% of revenues)	Cumulative Fund (% GDP)	Annual average of real yield, until 2004 (%)	Fiscal reform cost, 2001 (% GDP)
	Before the reform	After the reform				
Structural reforms						
Substitutive model (private, based on individual capitalization)						
Chile: May 1981	64.0 (1980)	57.3	19.8	59.1	10.2	−7.2
Bolivia: May 1997	12.0 (1996)	10.5	9.0	20.5	10.4	−3.5
Mexico: Sept. 1997	37.0 (1997)	28.0	40.3	5.8	7.7	−0.5
El Salvador: May 1998	26.0 (1996)	20.1	18.7	13.7	9.9	−1.4
Dominican Rep.: 2003–06	30.0 (2000)	14.5	7.0	1.9	−8.8	—
Parallel model (Public distribution or partial collective capitalization; and private, based on individual capitalization)						
Peru: June 1993	31.0 (1993)	12.0	21.9	11.0	7.6	−0.7
Colombia: April 1994	32.0 (1993)	22.0	40.3	10.3	6.9	−1.6

(continued)

Table 1.5 Models and Characteristics of Pension Reforms in Latin America, 2005 (continued)

Models of pension systems[a]	Coverage (contributors as % of labor force)		Administrative cost (% of revenues)	Cumulative Fund (% GDP)	Annual average of real yield, until 2004 (%)	Fiscal reform cost, 2001 (% GDP)
	Before the reform	After the reform				
Mixed model (like the parallel model but with no choice)						
Argentina: July 1994	50.0 (1994)	20.7	17.4	12.0	9.9	−2.5
Uruguay: April 1996	73.0 (1997)	58.8	11.9	16.1	12.9	−4.0
Costa Rica: May 2001	53.0 (2000)	46.6	—	2.7	6.7	—
Average	38.0[b]	29.1	20.7	15.3	7.3	−2.7
Parametric reforms or no reform						
Brazil	45.9; 51.0[c]	45.9	1.6	18.0	n.a.	n.a.
Guatemala	21.8; 27.9[c]	21.8	8.7	2.4	10.4	n.a.
Honduras	15.7; 19.2[c]	15.7	0.5	—	6.2	n.a.

(continued)

Table 1.5 Models and Characteristics of Pension Reforms in Latin America, 2005 *(continued)*

Models of pension systems[a]	Coverage (contributors as % of labor force)		Administrative cost (% of revenues)	Cumulative Fund (% GDP)	Annual average of real yield, until 2004 (%)	Fiscal reform cost, 2001 (% GDP)
	Before the reform	After the reform				
Parametric reforms or no reform (continued)						
Panama	58.9	58.9	4.8	13.0	5.6	n.a.
Paraguay	7.3; 12.9[c]	7.3	—	—	—	n.a.
Venezuela	26.3; 32.7[c]	26.3	—	—	n.a.	n.a.
Average	46.6[b]	41.4	3.9	11.1	4.4	n.a.

Sources: Chapter 11 and Mesa-Lago (2004) for data of coverage before the reforms.

Note:

— = Not available. n.a. = Not applicable.

a. Excludes Ecuador and Nicaragua, where the private systems created by law in 2004 have not been implemented, and Haiti, with no reform.

b. Weighted by population covered.

c. The lower number is for the general program and the higher number includes almost all programs.

to pension reform, and much more to other institutional factors. However, the gradual accumulation of funds can be favorable to the development of capital markets in other countries with adequate financial regulation and political isolation (see later).

The effect of pension reform on fiscal sustainability is the subject of intense debate. In principle, the individually funded accounts limit the emergence of future fiscal obligations to pay pensions. However, the creation of privately managed accounts generates "transition costs" because the public system no longer receives contributions from the fund members. There are also transition costs stemming from the issuance of recognition bonds for workers who transfer from the public to the private system. Finally, there are fiscal costs for payment of the minimum pension guarantees in the new system (which are not transition costs). The discussion centers on the fact that transition costs can last a long time and require considerable fiscal effort, which can raise the amount and cost of public debt, and even threaten macroeconomic stability. For example, in Chile, after almost two decades of reform, the fiscal cost of the reform in 2001 was 7.2 percent of GDP, and in Argentina before the crisis, 4.6 percent of GDP. On average, in eight countries the fiscal costs in 2001 were 2.7 percent of GDP. Consequently, the creation of a fully funded system can be inconvenient in countries that start off with high levels of public debt or institutions that are inadequate for making deep fiscal adjustments. These problems are greater where the public pay-as-you-go systems are older and the age structure of the population is more mature.

The replacement of public systems by privately managed fully funded systems promised in principle to reduce the state role in social security and, by extension, the possible intrusion of politics into the protection of workers. But this did not happen. The state continues to be essential for promoting membership, regulating and supervising the system, financing transition costs, and providing minimum and social assistance pensions. In practice, the roles played by the state have multiplied: the state continues to manage the public regimes, which have hardly begun the unification process in most countries (with the continuation of separate regimes for the armed forces and, in many cases, the justice system and other sectors). Also, the reforms have rarely been implemented in a single stroke, as in Chile. The more common reform process requires considerable state interference and opens spaces for political negotiation. Inevitably, worker protection continues under political influence, especially in countries that lack fiscal soundness and solid budgetary institutions to absorb the transition costs without mishap.

During the 1990s, pension systems were not the only components of the social protection system to be reformed. The new conditional cash transfer programs to relieve poverty are especially important. About the mid-1990s, Brazil and Mexico led the introduction of this subsidy, which has been extended to Argentina, Brazil, Chile, Colombia, Ecuador, Honduras, Jamaica, and Nicaragua. Conditional cash transfer programs are exclusively targeted (at least in principle) at low-income beneficiaries, and aim to break the cycle of poverty through incentives for the education, nutrition, and medical care of children. Evaluations of programs in Colombia, Mexico, and Nicaragua show that they have considerably increased school enrollment.[35] The effect on school attendance is less impressive but also positive; in contrast, there is no indication that these programs contribute to better test results. Favorable effects have also been found for prevention and incidence of various diseases and for family dietary patterns.

The rapid introduction of the transfer programs is promising because it shows that innovative and effective reform is possible in countries with diverse institutional conditions. In fact, these programs are a new form of social policy outside the regular organizational and policy channels. However, as happened with the social investment funds (parallel entities were created to circumvent institutional obstacles to the execution of social programs supported by the international organizations), they could reduce the possibility of reforming the ministries and other public bodies traditionally responsible for social policy. There is also a discussion on whether these national programs are eroding the political power and space for local government action. Finally, how they should be integrated with other social security programs is also subject to debate.

Education Sector Reform

Traditionally, education systems in Latin America have been organized around a central ministry that provides financing, resource allocation, hiring, and administrative control. This monopolistic organization produces weak users because families and students are unable to influence decisions; generates strong teachers' unions by creating incentives for centralization; and creates inefficient command structures because governments operate with shorter horizons than users or teachers (and therefore tend to underestimate the long-term costs and benefits of their actions), because the nature of education services generates serious contractual (or agency) problems, because the actions of teachers and schools are difficult to monitor and evaluate, and because the size and complexity of the sector hinders efforts at coordination.

In this context, reforms aimed at expanding the system are more feasible than is the introduction of structural changes into the system or into the incentives that schools and teachers receive (see Stein and others [2005], chapter 10). However, since the mid-1980s, important progress has been made with three types of structural reform designed to solve problems of efficiency, lack of innovation and adaptation of the system, and the low quality of educational results. The three reforms are decentralization, development of evaluation systems, and public–private alliances for provision of education services. These are analyzed by Juan Carlos Navarro in chapter 12 and summarized in table 1.6. In addition to these supply

Table 1.6 Institutional Reforms in Education: Decentralization and Academic Tests

Country	Principal responsibility for administration, 2005	Starting year	Degree of institutionalization	International academic tests				
				LLECE	PISA	TIMSS	PIRLS	Others
Argentina	Provincial (1976, 1991)	1993	Intermediate	X	X			X
Bolivia	Municipal (1994)	1996	Intermediate	X				
Brazil	State/municipal (1988, 1995)	1988	Advanced	X	X			X
Chile	Municipal (1981)	1988	Advanced	X	X	X	X	X
Colombia	Departmental/municipal (1991, 2000)	1991	Intermediate	X		X		X
Costa Rica	National	1988	Intermediate	X				
Dominican Rep.	National	1991	Intermediate	X				
Ecuador	National	1996	Initial					
El Salvador	National/school	1993	Advanced					X

(continued)

Table 1.6 Institutional Reforms in Education: Decentralization and Academic Tests *(continued)*

Country	Principal responsibility for administration, 2005	Starting year	Degree of institutionalization	International academic tests				
				LLECE	PISA	TIMSS	PIRLS	Others
Guatemala	National/school	1997	Intermediate					
Honduras	National[a]	1990	Intermediate	X				
Mexico	State	1992	Advanced	X	X			
Nicaragua	National/school	1997	Initial					
Panama	National[a]	1997	Intermediate	X				
Paraguay	National[a]	1995	Intermediate	X				X
Peru	National	1997	Intermediate	X	X			X
Uruguay	National	1996	Advanced		X			X
Venezuela	National[a]	1995	Initial	X		X		X

Source: Chapter 13.
Note:
a. Decentralization process is either not consolidated or has been completely reversed.

reforms, on the demand side a new generation of subsidy systems has emerged creating incentives for families to keep their children in school, as mentioned in relation to conditional cash transfers.

The decentralization of the administration and, to a lesser extent, the financing of public school systems to subnational governments (or directly to the schools) have been the most common reforms in the region since the 1990s. Decentralization is a response to the organizational problems of the sector, bringing decision making closer to users, thus creating some democratic control over education decisions, with the expectation that this will improve efficiency, innovation, and adaptation to local conditions. In six countries (Argentina, Bolivia, Brazil, Chile, Colombia, and Mexico), administrative decisions are handed down to subnational governments, and in three Central American countries (El Salvador, Guatemala, and Nicaragua) directly to the schools. In Honduras, Paraguay, Panama, and Venezuela, decentralization attempts have not been consolidated and have even been reversed. Although the main fear with decentralization has been inadequate capacity of local governments and communities, the evidence clearly shows that institutional improvement has been, in fact, the main effect of decentralization, resulting in better management capacity and the appearance of effective coordination mechanisms between levels of government. Evidence also indicates that decentralization has contributed to educational innovations, such as the school independence program in Minas Gerais state in Brazil, the introduction of all-day schools in Mérida state in Venezuela, and various innovations in the Bogotá School District in Colombia.

The most serious weakness of education decentralization has been the difficulty of adapting the system of fiscal transfers or creating tax powers in subnational governments to support the process. In Brazil, however, decentralization has been combined with reforms to financing and incentive mechanisms, with very promising results in coverage and efficiency throughout the system (Kaufmann and Nelson 2004). In contrast, in Argentina, the lack of fiscal backing delayed the start of the program, which was part of a fiscal adjustment policy, and led paradoxically to the federal government eventually taking over the financing of education through the "teaching incentive." In Venezuela, transferring management of schools to subnational governments was completely halted after those governments refused to assume the costs of teacher severance pay and pensions because of lack of funds. In Mexico, transfers to the states for school financing are subject to continuous renegotiations, which limit the effectiveness of decentralization.

The second important reform was the introduction of evaluation systems in 14 countries. This apparently simple reform has involved considerable institutional development associated with the formation of groups of specialists in ministerial departments or semi-independent evaluation institutes, the establishment of international networks that create viable conditions for comparative international tests, and the political and social legitimation of the tests. However, evaluations are still underused for changing the functioning and incentives of the sector, because incomplete and inadequate results become available too late for use in decision making by families and the administrators of the sector. This deficiency is less evident in university evaluation and accreditation programs in various Central America countries and in the practice examinations for certain professions that have recently been established in Brazil and Colombia.

The third reform area involves public-private alliances that exploit the apparent advantages of private education in the areas of costs, management, and incentive schemes to expand the coverage and improve the quality of publicly financed education. Three basic ways to create these alliances have emerged. The oldest is the voucher model adopted by Chile in the 1980s, which currently covers about 40 percent of primary and secondary enrollment in that country. In this model, private providers compete for students who are the owners of public subsidies. Second is the "competitive bidding" model, exemplified by Bogotá, where private providers compete to manage schools built by local governments; and third, the "negotiated agreement" model, typified by the *Fe y Alegría* network in Venezuela and other countries, in which the government partially finances privately administered schools in exchange for those schools accepting children from low-income sectors. All these modalities share the advantage of cost-effectiveness, but an intense technical discussion revolves around their quality benefits. Although the academic results of the beneficiaries of the voucher programs are better than the public schools, it is not clear if this is because the private schools produce better results or simply because they select the students with the best academic potential. Similarly, the negotiated agreement schools show a clear superiority over public schools in intermediate indicators such as repetition or dropout rates, but not in learning results. Although very recently introduced, the "bidding" model suggests that it is possible to design contracts with adequate incentives for improving the performance of administrators and teachers.

These organizational reforms seek to affect education results through supply-side intervention. Only the voucher system takes direct action on the demand side, by conferring power on students (evaluation systems also strengthen users although this potential has not been sufficiently exploited). On the demand side, the most important reform has been the creation of cash transfer systems conditional on, among other things, school attendance, as mentioned in the section on social protection systems.

Conclusion

State reform has silently revolutionized many aspects of the institutional landscape in Latin America. Given the widespread preconception that the region has neglected the institutional reforms essential for development, the most surprising feature of this revolution is its extent and scope. Improvement predominates in practically all the areas analyzed in this book, or at least institutional innovation, even in areas of relative technical and political complexity, such as fiscal and tax institutions or pension systems. Going backward (to inadequate organizations or practices in the light of existing experience) tends to be the exception or relatively marginal.

The reform process summarized in this book is not a chance occurrence, but neither is it a response to any preconceived plan. The reforms have tended to come in waves partly because the debt crisis, which began in 1982 and ended in 1989 with the Brady Plan, had similar effects on many countries. For example, the most sweeping tax reforms were concentrated in a few years in the early 1990s; the majority of the most ambitious pension reforms occurred between 1993 and 1998; and the fiscal responsibility laws were passed around 2000. Privatization, which flourished in the early 1990s, was virtually suspended after 1998. The creation of independent agencies responsible for regulating the privatized sectors also came in waves,[36] although the process of adapting such regulation was more continuous. The reforms less concentrated in time were those closely related to the organization of the state administrative apparatus and the functioning of the education and justice services. It is remarkable that after the first wave in each area of institutional reform, later attempts in the newly reforming countries tended to be more cautious, and were followed everywhere by adjustments to strengthen and consolidate the initial reforms, rather than reverse them. This suggests not only that some external causes common to the region were important in triggering reform processes, but also that countries learned from and emulated one another.

Institutional reforms have tended not to be bundled, as they apparently were in some countries with first-generation economic reforms (Lora and Olivera 2004). On the contrary, the institutional reforms are characterized by their fragmentation—at the cost very often of timing consistency or the integrity of the sectoral reform process. For example, all aspects of decentralization of government to the provinces and municipalities should ideally be synchronized (assignment of responsibilities for provision of services, tax collection powers, transfers from the central government to local governments, and borrowing powers and limits), but in practice, progress is made first in the assignment of responsibilities, then in the area of fiscal transfers, then in disciplining borrowing, and so forth. For pension reform, the ideal would be to simultaneously introduce fiscal reforms to finance the transition costs from a public to a private or mixed system, because in the new systems the public sector stops receiving contributions from members who join the private systems. With the sole exception of Chile, the fiscal adjustment measures needed to accommodate the transition were not adopted simultaneously. The same observation applies to privatizations of public services where the most common pattern was to privatize first and regulate later, or education reform where progress in decentralization of responsibilities was not backed by adequate transfers of fiscal revenue to finance these responsibilities, or where the emergence of student performance evaluation systems was not accompanied by changes in the incentive system for schools and teachers to improve the quality of teaching.

This unbundling of reforms seems to have been the result of governments trying to exploit political spaces, however small, to push change in the desired direction, with the hope perhaps of later generating interest to continue the process. The early privatization waves in Argentina and Peru, or the Colombian pension reform, are outstanding examples of this opportunist reform strategy, but are by no means the only ones. These strategies do not always work: occasionally promising institutional reforms have been reversed (decentralization in Venezuela) and frequently the opportunist reforms have taken their own, difficult to alter, course (for example, emergency taxes, such as the financial transactions taxes in various countries, which become permanent despite their defects), or they have produced powerful antibodies against making more progress (for example, the charter schools in Bogotá).

Although quite a few institutional reforms have attempted to reduce the space for discretionary decisions by politicians (fiscal rules, automatic transfers to the regions, flat taxes with no exceptions, single pension systems, and so on), these spaces reappear, revealing that, as in nature, politics abhors a vacuum. A paradigmatic example is pension reform. This conclusion does not apply to many of the first-generation economic reforms, which effectively closed the spaces to the political game, at least so far: central banks continue to be independent, the opening of imports has not been reversed, and interest rates remain unregulated in most countries.[37] This has also been the case, at least until now, with the new generation of subsidies for low-income families (such as *Oportunidades* in Mexico), even though they were established outside the traditional administration and policy channels.

All this reinforces the central conclusion of this book: it is surprising that such profound changes have been achieved in the most diverse political, economic, and social institutions, and that these changes have taken place and are continuing to take place so silently. However, state reforms have not always been successful as has been shown in some cases in this chapter and as is discussed in more detail in the rest of the book. The unbundling or incomplete adoption of certain reforms can explain some of these failures. Nevertheless, because there is rarely an articulated plan for implementing reforms, what seems after the fact as a case of unbundling may simply be ignorance of the requirements of reform. This might have been the case with the early decentralization initiatives in Brazil and Colombia.

This example also reveals that, unlike most of the first-generation economic reforms, which eliminated or simplified state intervention, institutional reforms are by their nature more complex, more uncertain, and more difficult to implement. Moreover, unlike first-generation economic reform, they generally involve a diversity of actors during the design, approval, and start-up phases, which makes them more dependent on the political process. Consequently, their possibilities of success depend not only on the consistency and refinement of their technical details, but on whether the political process for approving and implementing them is achieving solutions that, although not technically optimal, are stable, adaptable, coherent, and oriented to the public interest, and can be implemented with the existing formal and informal institutions.[38]

Finally, the success of state reform can depend on the unplanned or unforeseeable effects of these or other reforms. We have seen, for example, that reform of the parliamentary election regimes has improved representativeness at the cost of reducing the effectiveness of congressional decision making. This may also have had an impact on the effectiveness of fiscal institutions because more representative but more fragmented congresses are more likely to increase public expenditure and the fiscal deficit. This tendency toward excessive spending can in principle be counteracted by more hierarchical budgetary institutions, which confer more power on the executive to make spending cuts, but this discretionary power can harm the efficiency of the spending programs affected, and result in a deterioration of the composition of all public expenditure, especially when there are restrictions on cuts in some types of expenditures and not others (wages and salaries of public officials or payment of retirement pensions are less likely to be cut than investment spending).

Clearly, therefore, there are no magic formulas for state reform. Throughout this book we will see that some general principles can be useful as initial hypotheses to guide certain reforms. However, the success of any institutional reform depends on respecting certain basic technical criteria, and on adapting its specific details to the institutional and political context.

Notes

1. Whitehead (1994) provides an excellent historical review of the transformation of the state in Latin America since 1930. Pereira (1998) analyzes the causes and implications of the crisis of the state.

2. The increase in the circulation of fiduciary money (that is, money whose only backing is the promise of the sovereign government) is a source of inexpensive financing for the Treasury, known as "seigniorage."

3. This method is known as the "inflationary tax" because it is a fiscal resource derived from the loss of purchasing power of money in the hands of the public.

4. According to Whitehead (1994), while public employment on average in Latin America absorbed only 0.8 percent of the population in 1925, it had risen to

1.2 percent in 1960, and by 1980 had reached 4.8 percent of the total population (although the latter figure includes state companies). In developed countries the tendency was similar: as a percentage of total employment, public employment went from 3.7 percent in 1913 to 12.3 percent in 1960 and 17.5 percent in 1980, according to Tanzi and Schuknecht (2000, 26).

5. Corrales (2003) concisely describes the deficiencies of the state and its capture.

6. Initiative led by the U.S. government under the leadership of Nicholas Brady to convert the nonperforming bank debts of the developing countries into long-term bonds to restore access by those countries to international finance.

7. Today, however, it is recognized that the version of this model that was so successfully disseminated by the World Bank (1993) exaggerated the role of markets and minimized the actual importance of the state in promoting new sectors and coordinating investment and innovation.

8. Among the many studies on Latin American democratization, Huntington (1991) is worth special mention. On macrostabilization and trade opening, see Edwards (1994) and Kuczinsky and Williamson (2004).

9. There are many precedents for reform of state institutions in various countries before democratization, stabilization, or trade liberalization as they responded to signs of crisis in the traditional social service systems or to intervention in economic sectors. A notable case is Chile, where important reforms took place during the dictatorship (1973–90). However, in the majority of countries it is only since the middle or end of the 1980s that attempts at state reform have implied a rupture with the previous forms of state organization and management.

10. See the review of studies and econometric estimates by Lora and Olivera (2005). The principal beneficiaries of the reduction in inflation were wage earners and the urban middle classes, both of which are decisive electoral groups in many countries.

11. Corrales (2003) shows that, even though it is often affirmed that trade liberalization resulted from external pressure, state deficiencies were a powerful cause.

12. On the international diffusion of regulatory capitalism, see Levi-Faur and Jordana (2005).

13. See, for example, Burki and Perry (1998) and Lora and Panizza (2002).

14. On the political process of reform, consult the work of Stein and others (2005). On social sectors, an excellent study is Kaufmann and Nelson (2004). Navia and Velasco (2004) offer a general overview of the policy of reform and a copious bibliography.

15. However, the connection between crisis of the state and democratization is less narrow and mechanical than this assertion suggests. It is important to consider, for example, that in Peru the crisis of the state was confronted in the early 1990s with measures that implied a reversal in democratic institutions.

16. See *The Economist*, October 29, 2005, 39–40.

17. Not included in 1996.

18. The original IDB study obtained information for 1990–03, which is the basis for the comparison with the current situation. However Filc and Scartascini take into account other aspects of the budgetary institutions that were not studied or are not comparable with the previous study.

19. Argentina (1999), Brazil (2000), Peru (2000 and 2003), Panama (2002), Ecuador (2002), Colombia (2003), and Venezuela (2003). In Guatemala, a fiscal pact was signed in 2000 that established numerical targets, but it was not legally binding.

20. The coffee fund is private, not fiscal in nature.

21. For VAT, productivity is calculated more exactly as the ratio between collections as a proportion of domestic demand (GDP less exports plus imports) and the basic VAT rate. However, these measures are still rough approximations that mix together the effects on collections of the exclusion of certain income or goods from the tax bases, the special treatment and exemptions given to diverse sectors, and the problems of evasion.

22. The expression "fiscal termites" is from Tanzi (2001).

23. An analysis of the role of political systems in the definition of tax policy can be found in Stein and others (2005).

24. An index on a scale of 0 to 1 is constructed for each of these aspects, where 1 represents the institutions most ripe for decentralization. The "maturity of the decentralization process" index is calculated as the average of these five indexes less one-half of the standard deviation of the five indexes. This correction is intended to capture the degree of inconsistency between the various aspects of decentralization.

25. 0.92, calculated for 2004, based on figure 7.8.

26. 0.71, calculated for the changes between about 1995 and 2004, based on figure 7.8.

27. However, there are large differences between countries. In the mid-1990s, state banks represented over 50 percent of the total banking sector in Argentina, Colombia, Costa Rica, Nicaragua, Paraguay, Uruguay, and Venezuela.

28. According to the indicators of Kaminsky and Schmukler (2003).

29. The Basel Capital Accord is a set of basic principles accepted by developed countries to regulate and supervise their banking systems; the principles are increasingly used as the benchmark to assess the quality of banking regulation in the developing countries.

30. The historical patterns summarized in these paragraphs are analyzed in more detail in chapter 1 of IDB 2000.

31. Increasing from US$303 in 1990 to US$458 in 1998 (1990 prices), with no great changes in the next five years (US$455 in 2003). The data are taken from ECLAC (2005).

32. The correlations are –0.088 and –0.06, respectively, for the data from 12 countries that measure the changes between 1990 and 2000 in expenditure per capita on education and coverage of enrollment for the 12–15 and 16–19 age groups, respectively (according to the figures given by Navarro in chapter 12).

33. For an assessment of the few and mostly incipient reforms in health, see Baeza and Packard (2006).

34. The figures for some countries are not strictly comparable before and after reform because they do not use the same number of months to establish the number of contributors. Based on household surveys, the World Bank calculates higher coverage after reform in Argentina, Chile, El Salvador, and Mexico than those given in the table.

35. In Mexico, the increase in enrollment at the secondary level due to the program is calculated at between 7.2 and 9.3 percentage points for girls and 3.5 and 5.8 percentage points for boys; in Colombia between 4 and 6 percentage points in rural areas and 12 and 14 percentage points in urban areas; and in Nicaragua 22 percentage points in the areas covered by the program (Rawlings and Rubio 2004).

36. See Levi-Faur and Jordana (2005) for a quantitative analysis of the diffusion process of the independent regulatory agencies.

37. However, recent developments in Argentina under Néstor Kirchner and in Venezuela under Hugo Chávez, and the policy announcements of Evo Morales during his election in December 2005, suggest that the resistance of the first-generation reforms to political interference is limited.

38. The study by Stein and others (2005) is an extended development of this analytical approach.

References

Alesina, Alberto, Ricardo Hausmann, Rudolph Hommes, and Ernesto Stein. 1996. "Budget Institutions and Fiscal Performance in Latin America." NBER Working Paper No. 5586, National Bureau of Economic Research, Cambridge, MA.

Baeza, Cristian, and Truman Packard. 2006. *Protecting Households from Health Shocks in Latin America.* Washington, DC: World Bank.

Bird, Richard, and Milka Casanegra, eds. 1992. "Improving Tax Administration in Developing Countries." International Monetary Fund, Washington, DC.

Burki, Shahid Javed, and Guillermo Perry. 1998. *Beyond the Washington Consensus: Institutions Matter.* Washington, DC: World Bank.

Corrales, Javier. 2003. "Market Reforms." In *Constructing Democratic Governance in Latin America.* 2nd ed., ed. Jorge I. Dominguez and Michael Shifter. Baltimore and London: Johns Hopkins University Press.

ECLAC (Economic Commission for Latin America and the Caribbean). 2005. "Informe de Desarrollo Social." Santiago, Chile.

Edwards, Sebastián. 1994. *Crisis and Reform in Latin America: From Despair to Hope.* Oxford: Oxford University Press and the World Bank.

Huntington, Samuel P. 1991. *The Third Wave: Democratization in the Late Twentieth Century.* Norman, OK: University of Oklahoma Press.

IDB (Inter-American Development Bank). 1997. *Latin America after a Decade of Reforms. Economic and Social Progress Report.* Washington, DC: IDB.

———. 2000. *Development Beyond Economics. Economic and Social Progress Report.* Washington, DC: IDB.

———. 2004. *Unlocking Credit. Economic and Social Progress Report.* Washington, DC: IDB.

Jácome, Luis I. 2001. "Legal Central Bank Independence and Inflation in Latin America during the 1990s." IMF Working Paper WP/01/212, International Monetary Fund, Washington, DC.

Kaminsky, Graciela, and Sergio Schmukler. 2003. "Short-Run Pain, Long-Run Gain: The Effects of Financial Liberalization." NBER Working Paper No. 9787, National Bureau of Economic Research, Cambridge, MA.

Kaufmann, Daniel, Aart Kraay, and Massimo Mastruzzi. 2005. "Governance Matters IV: Governance Indicators for 1996–2004." Policy Research Working Paper No. 3630, World Bank, Washington, DC.

Kaufmann, Robert R., and Joan M. Nelson. 2004. *Crucial Needs, Weak Incentives: Social Sector Reform, Democratization, and Globalization in Latin America.* Washington, DC, and Baltimore: Woodrow Wilson Center Press and Johns Hopkins University Press.

Kopits, George. 2004. "Overview of Fiscal Policy Rules in Emerging Markets." In *Rules-Based Fiscal Policy in Emerging Markets: Background, Analysis, and Prospects,* ed. George Kopits. New York: Palgrave Macmillan.

Kuczinsky, Pedro Pablo, and John Williamson. 2004. *After the Washington Consensus: Restarting Growth and Reform in Latin America.* Washington, DC: Institute for International Economics.

Levi-Faur, David, and Jacint Jordana, eds. 2005. "The Rise of Regulatory Capitalism: The Global Diffusion of a New Order." *The Annals of the American
Academy of Political and Social Science* 598 (1).

Lora, Eduardo, and Mauricio Olivera. 2004. "What Makes Reforms Likely: Political Economy Determinants of Reforms in Latin America." *Journal of Applied
Economics* VII (1): 99–135.

———. 2005. "The Electoral Consequences of the Washington Consensus." *Economia* 5 (2): 7–61.

Lora, Eduardo, and Ugo Panizza. 2002. "Structural Reforms in Latin America
Under Scrutiny," Research Department Working Paper No. 470, Inter-American
Development Bank, Washington, DC.

Mesa-Lago, Carmelo. 2004. "Las reformas de pensiones de América Latina y su
impacto en los principios de seguridad social." Series on Development Finance,
No. 144, ECLAC, United Nations, Santiago, Chile.

Naim, Moisés. 1994. "Latin America: The Second Stage of Reform." *Journal of
Democracy* 5 (4): 32–48.

Navia, Patricio, and Andrés Velasco. 2004. "The Politics of Second Generation
Reforms in Latin America." In *After the Washington Consensus: Restoring
Growth and Reform in Latin America,* ed. Pedro Pablo Kuczinsky and John
Williamson. Washington, DC: Institute for International Economics.

Pereira, Luiz Carlos Bresser. 1998. "La Reforma del Estado de los Años Noventa.
Lógica y Mecanismos de Control." *Desarrollo Económico* 38 (150): 517–50.

Rawlings, Laura, and G. Rubio. 2004. "Evaluating the Impact of Conditional Cash
Transfer Programs: Lessons from Latin America." Policy Research Working
Paper No. 3119, World Bank, Washington, DC.

Shome, Parthasarathi. 1999. "Taxation in Latin America: Structural Trends and
Impact of Administration." IMF Working Paper 99/19, International Monetary
Fund, Washington, DC.

Stein, Ernesto, Mariano Tommasi, Koldo Echebarría, Eduardo Lora, and Mark
Payne. 2005. *The Politics of Policies: Economic and Social Progress in Latin
America. 2006 Report.* Washington, DC: Inter-American Development Bank
and David Rockefeller Center for Latin American Studies, Harvard University.

Tanzi, Vito. 2001. "Globalization, Technological Developments, and the Work of
Fiscal Termites." *Brooklyn Journal of Political Economy* 49 (1): 116–27.

———. 2005. "The Economic Role of the State in the 21st Century." *Cato Journal*
25 (3): 617–38.

Tanzi, Vito, and Ludger Schuknecht. 2000. Public Spending in the 20th Century: A
Global Perspective. Cambridge, UK: Cambridge University Press.

Whitehead, Laurence. 1994. "State Organization in Latin America Since 1930."
In *The Cambridge History of Latin America.* Vol. 6, ed. Leslie Bethell, 3–95.
Cambridge, UK: Cambridge University Press.

Williamson, John, ed. 1990. *Latin American Adjustment: How Much Has Happened?* Washington, DC: Institute for International Economics.

World Bank. 1993. *The East Asian Miracle: Economic Growth and Public Policy (A
World Bank Policy Research Report).* Oxford, UK: Oxford University Press.

2

Reforming the Rules of the Game: Political Reform

J. Mark Payne and Juan Cruz Perusia

THE WAVE OF STATE REFORMS THAT swept across the Latin American region arose in most countries during transitions from relatively closed political systems to more open, democratic ones. The demise of authoritarian and semi-authoritarian political regimes resulted, in part, from the crisis of legitimacy associated with the broader fiscal and administrative crises of the developmentalist state discussed in chapter 1. In some countries, mainly those of the Southern Cone (Argentina, Chile, and Uruguay), political liberalization consisted of the restoration of preexisting democratic constitutions or fairly long-standing democratic traditions and practices (or both). In a second group of countries, such as those in Central America and Bolivia and Ecuador, regime transition was initiated with a process of democratization in states with scarce previous experience with democracy. For a third group (such as Mexico and Paraguay, and to a lesser extent, Colombia and Venezuela), political liberalization brought about the opening of one-party or two-party systems to previously marginalized political and social groups. The relative underdevelopment of most of the newly implanted democracies, and the need to wrestle with the various difficulties confronting the state, including that of building social and political legitimacy, contributed to an environment ripe for frequent, and sometimes profound, reform of the configuration of political rules inherited at the moment of the democratic transition. From this unsettled environment came repeated calls for more inclusive, accountable, and efficient decision making as well as continual interest by political groups in restructuring rules to their advantage. Thus, along with the profound reforms of fiscal, economic, and social institutions that took place since 1985, political institutions also underwent frequent and far-reaching change.

Political institutional reforms have pursued different purposes. If reforms are to be adopted into law, they must be compatible with the interests of the leading political and social groups. Thus, political reform inevitably is shaped in part by the narrow motives of power and privilege. In some instances, such motives have been dominant, even though proponents of reform might still portray it as a means to strengthen democratic governance. For instance, Peru's 1993 constitutional reforms eliminated the upper house of congress, created a single national district for electing legislators (replacing the former multidistrict system), and allowed presidential reelection, all of which served the purposes of weakening the potential political opposition and centralizing power in the Fujimori administration. However, reforms of political institutions are also prompted by demands of citizens and civil society organizations for more effective and representative democratic governance. Such demands can change elected politicians' calculus of the costs and benefits of reform, at least for brief periods, and lead to reforms that meaningfully enhance some dimension of democratic performance.

Political institutional reforms are intrinsically important given democratic institutions' impact on the ability of citizens to exercise their political and civil rights. They are also, however, instrumentally valuable given their effects on the capacity of citizens to conceptualize and articulate the needs of society (Sen 1999). The construction of efficient social and economic institutions appears to be based in part on the presence of effective democratic institutions that permit fair and efficient rules to be designed; that ensure the evenhanded and consistent enforcement and adjudication of those rules; and that guarantee their adaptation to the particular social, economic, historical, and cultural conditions and needs of a country (Payne and others 2006; Rodrik 2000). Thus, advances in the areas of state reform covered in this book depend to some extent on the development of a set of political institutions that foster cooperation among social and political actors and responsiveness to broad social interests (Stein and others 2005).

However, several factors complicate the analysis of "progress" in political reform. First, unlike most other areas of institutional reform, actors agree less on which ultimate objectives of reform should be prioritized. Considering them separately, most persons would concede the merits of a number of objectives of political reform, including political stability, decision-making efficiency, inclusive political participation, equitable representation, political legitimacy, transparency, and accountability. It is much more difficult to obtain agreement on which one of these objectives should be prioritized in a particular country at a particular moment, let alone for the region as a whole. Therein lies the problem, because typically the pursuit of one of these objectives, such as more inclusive representation, may come at the expense of another objective, such as decision-making efficiency. Second, the theory relating political institutional reform and these ultimate objectives is less well developed than is typically the case in other areas of state reform. In part this is because the ultimate qualities of democratic governance and of the policy-making process result from an interaction among multiple political institutional dimensions. To understand the effects of a given political reform on democratic system performance dimensions, one must take into account the broader institutional context in which the reform takes place, as well as political culture and history (Stein and others 2005). In addition, discerning the effects of reform is difficult because other factors, such as economic crisis or the broad erosion of the legitimacy of the political system, may overwhelm the effects of a particular reform. Thus, ascertaining the effects of political reforms in the region on particular qualities of democratic governance would require detailed country-by-country analysis and would be colored by the normative biases of the analyst toward the ultimate objectives of reform.

Given the broad regional perspective of the book and space constraints, this chapter will take a modest approach to analyzing the state of progress in political reform. For each of the reform areas, it first discusses the theoretically expected effects of reform, holding other institutional rules constant. In some cases reform choices involve trade-offs among competing theoretical objectives while for other types of reforms, the benefits appear to be more clear-cut. Then the chapter describes the reforms that have taken place and some of the different motivations behind them. Finally, some preliminary and partial conclusions are given about the effects of the reforms, if any.

Overview of Political Reform in Latin America

During the 1970s and 1980s, an important part of the academic discussion about the reasons for the breakdown of democratic systems in previous decades centered on the presidential nature of the political regimes found across the Latin American region. Some argued that presidentialism, with its popularly elected heads of government and fixed terms of office, contributed to problems of governability that could have been avoided, or at least managed better, in a parliamentary system in which built-in incentives for cooperation between the executive and legislature are greater (Di Palma 1990; Linz 1990; Linz and Stepan 1978; Linz and Valenzuela 1994). Whatever the merits of the arguments of these critics of presidentialism, none of the Latin American countries opted to shift to a fully parliamentary system.

Not only did countries not change the basic structure of the political regime, but also they did not formally change the territorial structure of their political systems. The region continues to have four formally federalist countries—Argentina, Brazil, Mexico, and Venezuela—while the rest are unitary. With regard to another key characteristic, the structure of the legislative branches, Peru and Venezuela changed from bicameral to unicameral systems.

The stability in such broader structural characteristics of the political systems could lead to the conclusion that the last two decades of democracy in the region have brought little change to the organization of the political systems. This is not the case. Although in general the core structure of the political systems in the region has changed relatively little, reforms of institutions and rules have been implemented that would be expected to directly affect the dynamics of electoral competition and representation, and more broadly, the functioning of the democratic regime. Reforms have taken place in numerous areas, including the systems used for electing the president and legislators, the rules regarding the reelection of presidents, the constitutional powers of presidents and legislatures, the process by which parties select candidates for elected office, and the financing of political parties and electoral campaigns. In addition, decentralization has resulted in greater political, financial, and administrative autonomy for subnational levels of government, driven primarily by changes in the methods used for selecting subnational officials (see chapter 7).

In countries with presidential regimes, in which the executive and legislative branches are elected separately, the interaction between the systems used for electing the president and legislators is important in shaping the nature of executive-legislative relations and the nature of the electoral accountability links that develop between elected representatives. The first two sections examine the reforms that have occurred in the election of officials to these two branches. A final section examines reforms to the way in which political parties nominate candidates and to the regulation of political party and electoral campaign financing.

Reforms of Systems for Electing the President

The reforms that have been adopted for the election of presidents have included changes to the vote share required for winning, the rules regarding reelection, the duration of presidents' terms of office, and the timing of presidential elections relative to legislative elections. From 1978 (or the year of the democratic transition in each country)[1] to 2005, 14 countries reformed at least one of these aspects of the system for electing the president (table 2.1). Only El Salvador, Honduras,[2] Mexico, and Panama did not introduce changes in the electoral rules related to the presidency.

Presidential Election Systems—Threshold for Election

The presidential election systems used in the region include plurality systems, majority runoff systems, and runoff systems with reduced thresholds. In the first system, the candidate with the most votes wins. In the second,

Table 2.1 Changes in Presidential Election Rules, 1978 (or year of transition to democracy) to 2005

Country	Election system	Simultaneity of elections	Duration of term	Reelection	Countries with some change
Argentina	X	X	X	X	X
Bolivia	X		X		X
Brazil	X	X	X	X	X
Colombia	X			X	X
Costa Rica				X	X
Chile		X	X		X
Dominican Republic	X	X		X	X
Ecuador	X	X		X	X
El Salvador					
Guatemala			X		X
Honduras					
Mexico					
Nicaragua	X		X	X	X
Panama					
Paraguay				X	X
Peru				X	X
Uruguay	X				X
Venezuela		X	X	X	X
Total	8	6	7	10	14

Source: Payne and others 2006.

a candidate must win a majority (or 50 percent plus one) of the votes to be declared the winner in the first round. If no candidate obtains a majority, a second round is held between the two candidates who received the most votes in the first round. In the third system, a threshold lower than a majority is required for a candidate to be declared a winner in the first round and to avoid a runoff between the two candidates with the most votes. For example, in Costa Rica, the first country to adopt a reduced threshold system, the threshold is 40 percent; in Argentina the threshold is 45 percent, or 40 percent and a 10 percentage point advantage over the candidate finishing in second place.

The system used to elect the president has both direct and indirect effects. Arguably it has direct effects on the legitimacy of the mandate of the elected president. An objective of some of the advocates of changing to a majoritarian two-round system was to ensure that even in a multiparty system, the winning presidential candidate would obtain, through the second round, a broadened popular mandate and, it was supposed, would be able to govern more effectively. In the second round competition it was thought that the two remaining candidates would have to reach out to other parties and interests, thus resulting in a stronger basis for governing than would result from a victory by a minority of the votes in a plurality system.

However, the indirect effects of such a majority runoff system on the party system may mean that such a system ends up negatively affecting the manageability of executive-legislative relations over the longer term because of the tendency of such a system to increase the number of parties obtaining representation in the legislature. This may happen because it is less likely that a candidate will win the presidency in the first round. As a consequence, the incentives for parties to merge or form coalitions before the elections are reduced and smaller parties are more likely to present independent presidential candidates and separate lists of legislative candidates. The majority runoff system also frees citizens to vote according to their true party preferences in the first round, which is also likely to increase the fragmentation of representation in the congress and reduce the chances that the president's party will obtain a majority (Jones 1995; Payne and others 2006; Shugart and Carey 1992). Cross-national empirical studies support the hypothesis that the number of presidential candidates and the effective number of legislative parties tend to be larger in majority runoff systems than in plurality systems (Cox 1997; Jones 1995, 1999).

The adoption of a runoff system with a reduced threshold requires a compromise between the objectives of broadening the mandate of the elected president and promoting more workable relations between the executive and legislative branches. The runoff with reduced threshold systems increases the chances that a candidate will win the presidency in the first round. As a consequence, parties have greater incentives to form preelectoral coalitions, which then also tends to reduce the number of parties presenting separate lists of legislative candidates, thus concentrating the legislative vote.

Reforms of systems for electing the president have not been driven purely by objectives of strengthening governmental mandates, and little thought may have been given to the potential consequences for party system fragmentation. As with other types of political reform, the self-interest of key political actors was sometimes a guiding motive. A majority runoff system was favored in some cases when two or more parties wanted to lower the chances that a particular party, representing a sizable minority, could win the presidency. A reduced threshold system was favored in some cases by parties with a strong hold on a near majority of the electorate, because this was thought to favor the chances of their candidates winning in the first round. Of the 18 countries considered, only five use the plurality system for electing the president: Honduras, Mexico, Panama, Paraguay, and Venezuela. By contrast, Argentina, Costa Rica, Ecuador, and Nicaragua use runoff systems with different types of thresholds. The other nine countries use the majority runoff system.

The system used for electing the president has been the object of reform in many countries in the region since 1978. At the beginning of the period studied a majority of the countries elected their presidents through a plurality system; now a preponderant majority use some form of runoff system (figure 2.1). Changes to a majority runoff system occurred in Colombia, the Dominican Republic, and Uruguay. In Argentina and Nicaragua the plurality system was replaced by a runoff with reduced threshold system (table 2.2). There have been no changes from a runoff system to a plurality system. Only Ecuador, with the shift from a majority runoff to a runoff with a reduced threshold system, changed in the contrary direction between the start of the democratic period and 2005 (Payne and others 2006).

Evidence of the tendency for the majority runoff system to result in party system fragmentation and governance complications can be found in a comparison of the effective number of resulting legislative parties in the two types of systems. Whereas an average of 4.6 effective parties resulted from elections in which the president was elected through majority runoff, only 2.7 effective parties resulted from plurality elections and 3.4 from runoff with reduced threshold elections (Payne and others 2006).

Simultaneity of Presidential and Legislative Elections

The relative timing of presidential and legislative elections also affects the fragmentation of representation in congress and the likelihood that the

---

Figure 2.1 Presidential Election Systems
(number of countries)

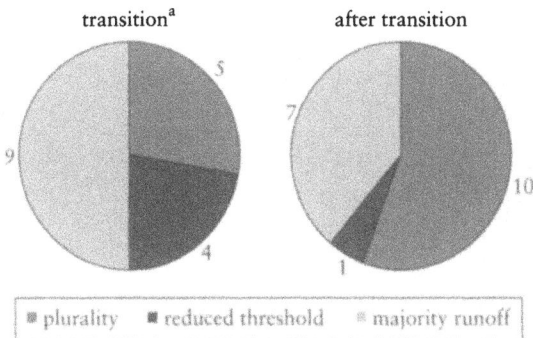

transition[a]

after transition

plurality   reduced threshold   majority runoff

Source: Payne and others 2006.
Note: a. For each country, this is the year of transition to democracy or 1978 if the countries were democratic before 1978.

Table 2.2 Reforms to Presidential Election Systems

Country	Majority runoff	Runoff with reduced threshold	Plurality	Year of change	Description of change
Argentina		X		1994	From plurality to runoff with reduced threshold (45 percent or 40 percent and advantage of 10 percent over second place finisher). Also change from election through electoral college to direct popular election.
Bolivia	X[a]			1990	Instead of choosing among the top three finishers, the congress chooses between the top two finishers from the first round if no candidate obtains a majority.
Brazil	X			1988	From indirect voting of congress to direct popular vote.
Chile	X			—	No change.
Colombia	X			1991	From plurality to majority runoff.
Costa Rica		X[b]		—	No change.
Dominican Republic	X			1994	From plurality to majority runoff.
Ecuador		X		1998	From majority runoff to runoff with reduced threshold (50 percent + 1 or 40 percent and an advantage of 10 percent or more over nearest competitor).
El Salvador	X			—	No change.
Guatemala	X			—	No change.
Honduras			X	—	No change.

(continued)

Table 2.2 Reforms to Presidential Election Systems *(continued)*

Country	Majority runoff	Runoff with reduced threshold	Plurality	Year of change	Description of change
Mexico			X	—	No change.
Nicaragua		X		1995	From plurality to runoff with a reduced threshold (45 percent). Later in
				1999	1999 the threshold was reduced further to 40 percent or 35 percent and an advantage of 5 percent over the nearest competitor.
Panama			X	—	No change.
Paraguay			X	—	No change.
Peru	X[c]			—	No change.
Uruguay	X			1997	From plurality to majority runoff.
Venezuela			X	—	No change.
Total	9	4	5		

Source: Payne and others 2006.

Note:

a. If no candidate obtains a majority of the vote, the legislature chooses the president from between the first two finishers in the first round.

b. The threshold is 40 percent of the votes.

c. In the 1979 constitution a majority system was adopted but this system was not to be applied in the first election in 1980. In this election a runoff system was applied with a low threshold of 33 percent for winning in the first round. Otherwise the congress was to decide the winner between the two candidates with the most votes. As it turned out, Fernando Beláunde Terry reached the presidency with 45 percent of the votes.

president's party will control a majority of the seats. When elections for the two branches are held at different times, voters' choices among competing legislative party lists are not constrained (or channeled) by their choice for president, as is the case when elections for the two branches are held simultaneously. Given the weaker constraints on voter choices, more parties are likely to compete for and obtain votes, which will tend to increase the number of parties gaining representation in congress. In addition, with nonconcurrent or midterm congressional elections, candidates from the president's party will not benefit from the coattails of the presidential election and are likely to be left with fewer legislative seats than if presidential elections were always held simultaneously with congressional elections. However, nonconcurrent elections, including the separation of presidential elections from legislative and subnational elections, could be viewed as beneficial from the standpoint of permitting closer accountability links between voters and elected officials and of allowing a midterm opportunity for voters to express their approval or disapproval of the government's or legislative parties' performance.

By the end of 2005, 12 countries had systems in which presidential and legislative elections were always held simultaneously: Bolivia, Brazil, Chile, Costa Rica, Ecuador, Guatemala, Honduras, Nicaragua, Panama, Paraguay, Peru, and Venezuela. The remainder had systems in which elections for the two branches were not concurrent or were only partially simultaneous.

As shown in table 2.1, six countries altered in some manner the simultaneity of presidential and legislative elections during the period. Brazil and Ecuador, two of the countries with the greatest degree of party system fragmentation, changed their systems from nonconcurrent or partially simultaneous to concurrent. In Brazil, the move to fully concurrent elections resulted from the reduction in 1994 of the length of the presidential term from five to four years, the same as that of legislators.[3] In Ecuador, the midterm legislative elections were eliminated so that now all legislators are elected at the same time as the president.[4] In Argentina, given that the presidential term was reduced from six to four years, in theory the simultaneity of elections was increased with the elimination of one of the midterm legislative elections.[5] Chile experienced two reforms that affected the simultaneity of elections. In the first, the presidential term was reduced from eight to six years, which changed the system from partially simultaneous to one in which presidential and legislative elections are held concurrently only every 12 years. However, in 2005 the presidential term length was reduced further to four years, resulting in fully concurrent presidential and legislative elections.[6]

In the two remaining countries, however, the system was changed in the opposite direction. In the Dominican Republic the system was changed from fully concurrent to completely nonsimultaneous as a consequence of the one-time reduction of the term of a president (Joaquin Balaguer, 1994–96) to two years while the four-year term of legislators was not interrupted. Finally, in Venezuela, the increase of the presidential term from five to six years, while leaving legislators' terms at five years, resulted in elections for the two branches generally being held in different years—to coincide only every 30 years.

Clearly in the Dominican Republic the shift to nonconcurrent elections resulted in complications for democratic governance. In 1996, Leonel Fernández Reyna won the presidential election, but as a result of the 1994 congressional elections his party controlled only about 11 percent of the seats in the lower house and 3 percent of the seats in the upper house. Similarly, when Fernández was reelected to the presidency in 2004 his party controlled only 27 percent of the lower house seats and 7 percent of the upper house seats, resulting from the 2002 legislative elections. By contrast, the change to fully concurrent elections in Brazil in 1994 appears to have facilitated the formation and duration of governing coalitions and enhanced the bargaining power of presidents.

Presidential Reelection and Term

Whether to permit presidents to be reelected has been a highly contentious issue in the region. While theoretical considerations, such as whether permitting immediate reelection facilitates electoral accountability or increases the risk of accumulating and abusing power, have been given some attention, the most important force behind reform to reelection typically has been the political self-interest of popular governing presidents and their parties. Prohibitions on reelection have usually been led by political forces opposed to presidents who had been reelected and were viewed to have abused power.

Liberal democratic theory would tend to support the notion of allowing at least one immediate presidential reelection. Reelection provides for a greater range of choice for voters. Prohibiting reelection of popular and successful presidents interrupts the progress being achieved, shortens time horizons, and creates legitimacy problems for successors. Reelection also provides for greater accountability, because presidents concerned about reelection are theoretically more likely to be responsive to citizen interests. Furthermore, one would expect presidential reelection to promote more efficient governance because presidents are more likely to retain power and influence over the course of their terms of office. However, if the rule of law and effective checks on the executive's abuse of authority and state largesse are not secure, presidential reelection can provide an opening to the accumulation of power and the progressive erosion of democracy.

Among rules related to presidential election systems, reelection rules have been the ones most frequently changed. Ten countries changed their stance on reelection and three countries did so twice in contrary directions (see table 2.3). Immediate reelection was enabled through reforms enacted in Argentina (1994), Brazil (1997), Colombia (2005), the Dominican Republic (2002), and Venezuela (1998). In addition, in Ecuador and Costa Rica[7] limitations on reelection became somewhat less restrictive because reelection became possible after the passage of one or more presidential terms instead of being banned completely. Reelection rules were made more restrictive in Paraguay and Nicaragua. While in Paraguay

Table 2.3 Reforms to Presidential Reelection Rules

Immediate reelection permitted	*Nonimmediate reelection permitted*	*Reelection not permitted*
Argentina (1994–present)	Argentina (1983–94)	
	Bolivia	
Brazil (1997–present)	Brazil (1985–97)	
	Chile	
Colombia (2005–present)	Colombia (1978–91)	Colombia (1991–2005)
	Costa Rica (2003–present)	Costa Rica (1978–2003)
Dominican Republic (1978–94 and 2002–present)	Dominican Republic (1994–2002)	
	Ecuador (1996–2004)	Ecuador (1979–96)
	El Salvador	
		Guatemala
		Honduras
		Mexico
Nicaragua (1990–95)	Nicaragua (1995–present)	
	Panama	
Paraguay (1989–92)		Paraguay (1992–present)
Peru (1993–2000)	Peru (1980–93 and 2000–present)	
	Uruguay	
Venezuela (1998–present)	Venezuela (1978–98)	

Source: Payne and others 2006.

reelection was banned completely, in Nicaragua immediate reelection was prohibited but reelection after the passage of a presidential term was still permitted.

Finally, in three countries rules on reelection were changed twice in opposite directions. In 1991 Colombia's new constitution changed the rules such that reelection was banned altogether instead of permitting nonimmediate reelection of presidents. Then in 2005 a reform made it possible for presidents to be immediately reelected. In the Dominican Republic immediate reelection was prohibited in 1994 but then permitted again eight years later. In Peru the 1993 constitutional reform permitted the immediate reelection of the president, but a reform enacted in 2000 made reelection possible only after the passage of one presidential term. In the Dominican Republic immediate reelection was prohibited in 1994 but then permitted again eight years later.

It is difficult to assess the impact of reforms in this area. The restrictions on reelection imposed in the Dominican Republic, Nicaragua, and Paraguay appear to be aimed at blocking the possibility that a strong leader could once again dominate politics over a long period, as was the case in those countries with Joaquín Balaguer, Anastasio Somoza (or Daniel Ortega), and Alfredo Stroessner, respectively. In such circumstances, the reforms mark a positive departure from the past style of politics and may be needed to ensure ongoing plurality in the division of national political power. However, the pressures to allow popular presidents the opportunity to continue is evident in Argentina, Brazil, Colombia, the Dominican Republic, Peru, and Venezuela. Depending upon the effectiveness of checks and balances and the qualities of the president, reelection can be either beneficial or harmful to democratic institutionalization and effectiveness.

With respect to the duration of the presidential term, there were changes in seven countries (table 2.4). Five countries—Argentina, Brazil, Chile, Guatemala, and Nicaragua—reduced the length of presidents' terms. Chile did so twice, first from eight years to six years and then from six years to four years. Two countries—Bolivia and Venezuela—increased it. As a consequence of these changes, the average length of the presidential term decreased from 5.0 to 4.6 years.

Reforms to Legislative Election Systems

The design of an optimal system for electing members of the legislative branch is difficult, not only because the way in which a given system functions depends upon the broad social, political, and historical context of the country, but also because the desirable qualities of an electoral system are difficult to obtain, in their optimal levels, at the same time. Among

Table 2.4 Duration of Presidential Terms

4 Years	5 Years	6 Years
Argentina (6)	Bolivia (4)	Chile (8)
Brazil (5)	El Salvador	Mexico
Chile (6)	Nicaragua (6)	Venezuela (5)
Colombia	Panama	
Costa Rica	Paraguay	
Dominican Republic	Peru	
Ecuador	Uruguay	
Guatemala (5)		
Honduras		

Source: Payne and others 2006.
Note: Number in parentheses denotes the term length before the reform.

these are the qualities of representativeness, effectiveness, and participation (Nohlen 1998, 1999).

Representativeness is the extent to which each party is represented in
the legislature in a similar proportion to the votes it obtains in the elections
and the extent to which minority parties are able to obtain representation.
Effectiveness is the extent to which the partisan composition of congress
facilitates the formation of consensus and sufficient capacity of the government to adopt needed policy changes in response to social problems.
Finally, participation is the extent to which the electoral system favors a
strong connection between constituents and their representatives.

Reforms aimed at optimizing an electoral system's fulfillment of one
of these functions usually results in inferior performance for one or both
of the other functions. For example, a reform that aims to make it easier
for minority parties to obtain representation is likely to result in increased
fragmentation of the party system, making it more difficult to reach agreements in the congress, while also limiting the ability of electors to assign
responsibility for governmental performance or policy actions. Reforms
aimed at improving participation in the system, such as by changing from
proportional multimember districts to single-member districts, can result
in unequal political representation and an underrepresentation of minority parties. Efforts to enhance participation by unblocking party lists and
permitting voters to cast a preference vote may also reduce effectiveness
by fostering intraparty divisions and competition and by making it more
difficult to build majorities to pass legislation.

As is the case with other types of reform, election system reform is typically motivated as much by the self-interests of the major political parties
as by considerations of trade-offs among abstract democratic values and
objectives. However, while the interests of elected politicians and the dominant parties are usually best served by the electoral system through which

they gained their current positions and political status, there are occasions (such as when parties are losing popular support or when there are strong demands from citizens for reform) when incumbent political parties will support reform. Nonetheless, enacted reforms typically reflect a combination of the asserted public interest objectives of reform advocates and the interests of politicians.

Numerous legislative electoral system reforms were carried out since 1980, but a relatively small proportion of these changes fundamentally altered the nature of the electoral system. The most profound changes to the lower house (or the national assembly in unicameral systems) occurred in Bolivia (1994), Colombia (2003), Ecuador (1998 and 2002), Mexico (several), Paraguay (1990), Peru (1993 and 2000), and Venezuela (1990). In Bolivia and Venezuela, reforms were adopted that changed the electoral system from proportional representation with closed party lists to personalized proportional representation systems in which a proportion of the representatives are elected individually in single-member districts. A reform adopted in 2003 in Colombia required that each party present a single electoral list in each electoral district (instead of multiple lists as was typical before the reform) such that votes are now awarded to parties in proportion to their votes instead of to faction lists. In addition, this reform reduced incentives for party system fragmentation by changing the formula for allocating seats from the Hare and greatest remainder system to D'Hondt.[8] In Ecuador, a 1998 reform shifted the system from closed list proportional representation to majoritarian in multimember districts; a subsequent reform in 2002 reestablished the proportional nature of the system but with open lists in which voters can choose multiple candidates from different party lists. While Mexico maintained its mixed-member electoral system, in which legislators are elected both through majority vote in single-member districts and through proportional representation in large multimember districts, it adopted a series of reforms that have significantly changed the weight of the two components in the system. In 1990, Paraguay changed from a pure proportional system (with a single national district) to a proportional system using multimember districts. Peru changed its electoral system in 1993 from proportional representation in multimember districts to a purer form of proportional representation (using a single national district), and in 2000 reverted to the previous system, but with a smaller congress and fewer deputies elected per district.

Aside from these more comprehensive reforms, many countries of the region have adopted reforms that could be expected to subtly affect the three main electoral system functions. The reforms included changing the formula used to translate parties' vote shares into shares of legislative seats in each district; changing the number of seats per district resulting from changes in the overall size of congress or from the creation or elimination of districts, including in some cases the addition of a national-level district;

moving from closed and blocked lists to open lists in which voters have the option of choosing a particular candidate in addition to a party list; splitting or separating the ballot so that voters have the option of voting for different parties for president, the legislative chambers, and subnational offices; and altering the timing of legislative elections relative to presidential elections. Table 2.5 summarizes the reforms carried out in the region between 1980 and 2005 according to these reform categories.

Table 2.5 clearly shows the variability in the stability of electoral rules. As mentioned above, six countries adopted fairly significant electoral reforms for the lower house and three of these (Ecuador, Mexico, and Peru) did so at least twice. Three countries did not change their electoral systems (Brazil, Chile,[9] and Costa Rica) and two countries introduced only a relatively minor reform in one year (Argentina and El Salvador). The remaining eight countries adopted reforms that affected multiple features of the electoral system or adopted two or more reforms in different years (Payne and others 2006).

Reforms have also been adopted in the election systems for the Senates of those countries that began the period with bicameral legislatures (table 2.6). Two countries consolidated their formerly bicameral legislatures into a single chamber (Peru and Venezuela) while three (Argentina, Colombia, and Mexico) adopted significant reforms to the systems used for electing senators. Argentina's reform replaced the indirect method of electing two senators per state by the provincial legislative assemblies to election by direct popular vote through a plurality system in which the majority party obtains two seats and the first minority obtains one. Colombia changed from electing senators by proportional representation in multimember constituencies to proportional representation in a single national constituency. Mexico changed its system from a plurality system to a segmented system combining plurality with representation of the minority and proportional representation in a national district. Other electoral reforms for the Senate mainly aimed at separating the vote for Senate candidates or lists from the vote for president or for the lower house.

What effects would these reforms be expected to have on the functioning of the electoral systems in the region? Tables 2.7 and 2.8 indicate the direction of the change to the three theoretical electoral system functions between the start and end of the period. The direction of the reforms clearly says nothing about the extent to which the systems actually fulfill the specified functions. Directional indicators are assigned only when the theoretically expected change implied by the reform is relatively unambiguous. The significance of the change resulting from the reforms varies greatly, but the directional signs do not encompass degrees of significance.

The electoral reform efforts for the lower house (or national assembly) maintained proportionality as the basic principle of representation in the region. The only current exceptions are Chile with its binominal system and Mexico with its segmented system. These systems were both

Table 2.5 Lower House Electoral Reforms

Country	Systemic reform	Electoral formula	District size	Structure of vote choice	Ballot structure in conjunction with other offices	Simultaneity
Argentina						1994
Bolivia	1994	1986, 1991				
Brazil						
Chile						
Colombia	2003	2003	1991	2003		
Costa Rica						
Dominican Rep.	1998, 2002		1997	2002	1985, 1990, 1994	1994
Ecuador			1994, 1998, 2002			1998
El Salvador			1988			
Guatemala			1990, 1994, 1998, 2003	1994		
Honduras			1985, 1988		1992, 1993	—
Mexico		1986, 1989, 1990, 1993, 1996	1996	1986, 1989		
Nicaragua						
Panama	1990	1988, 1992	1996		1993	
Paraguay		1993			1990	
Peru	1993, 2000		1993, 2000			
Uruguay		1996[a]			1996	
Venezuela	1990		1997, 1999		1990	1998, 1999

Source: Payne and others 2006.

Note: Table applies to national assembly for countries with unicameral system.

a. The electoral reform in Uruguay allowed parties to continue to present multiple lists in each district provided that seats would be allocated according to vote shares of the faction lists rather than to the cumulated votes of the party in the district as was the case before the reform.

73

Table 2.6 Electoral System Reforms for the Senate

Country[a]	Systemic reform	Electoral formula	District size	Structure of vote choice	Ballot structure in conjunction with other offices	Simultaneity
Argentina	1994[b]					1994
Bolivia						
Brazil						
Chile						
Colombia	1991[c]	2003	1991	2003		
Dominican Republic					1985, 1990, 1994	
Mexico	1996[d]	1993	1993		1990	
Paraguay	1993[e]					
Peru						
Uruguay						
Venezuela	1999[e]				1990	

Source: Payne and others 2006.
Note:
a. Countries excluded have no Senate.
b. Changed from the election of two senators per province by the provincial assemblies to direct popular election in a plurality system with representation of the first minority party.
c. Changed from multimember regional constituencies to a single national district and created special circumscriptions for indigenous representation.
d. Segmented the system for electing senators such that three-quarters are elected in three-member state districts by plurality with representation of the first minority party and one-quarter is elected by proportional representation in a national district.
e. Changed from a bicameral to a unicameral system.

Table 2.7 Theoretically Expected Effects of Reforms:
Lower House (or National Assembly)

Country	Representation	Effectiveness	Participation
Argentina		+	
Bolivia			+
Brazil			
Chile			
Colombia	−	+	
Costa Rica			
Dominican Republic	−		+
Ecuador		+	+
El Salvador	+	−	
Guatemala	+	−	+
Honduras	+	−	+
Mexico	+		
Nicaragua			
Panama	+		+
Paraguay			+
Peru	−	+	
Uruguay		+	
Venezuela			+

Source: Payne and others 2006.

Table 2.8 Theoretically Expected Effects of Reforms:
Upper House

Country[a]	Representation	Effectiveness	Participation
Argentina	+		+
Bolivia			
Brazil			
Chile			
Colombia	+	−	−
Dominican Republic		−	+
Mexico	+	−	
Paraguay			+
Peru		+	
Uruguay			
Venezuela		+	

Source: Payne and others 2006.
Note: a. Countries excluded have no Senate.

adopted prior to the countries' democratization and thus are not included among the reforms in tables 2.5 and 2.6. Ecuador's 1997 reform is the one case involving a short-term departure from the principle of proportional representation, but by 2002 this principle was restored. Thus, the main changes that have taken place to the trade-off between representation and effectiveness result more from subtle changes in the degree of proportional representation caused by modifications to such features as the size of electoral districts and the type of electoral formula used. Overall, the reforms across the region have tended to favor greater representation but to a limited extent.

A fairly uniform tendency throughout the region has been the adoption of changes that give citizens greater latitude in the selection of representatives. In a few cases, such as the adoption of personalized proportional representation systems in Bolivia and Venezuela and the opening of party electoral lists in the Dominican Republic and Ecuador, the reforms have been significant. In others, a potentially closer link between representatives and constituents has been fostered more subtly by separation of the vote for the two houses of congress or between the congress and the presidency (Guatemala, Honduras, Panama, and Paraguay), by the separation of the timing of presidential and legislative elections (the Dominican Republic), or by the creation of new, smaller electoral districts (the Dominican Republic and Paraguay).

For the upper house, the most significant change was to the function of representativeness for three countries—Argentina, Colombia, and Mexico. In Argentina, the 1994 constitutional reform changed the election system so that senators are now elected directly, rather than by the provincial legislatures; their mandates were reduced from nine to six years; and the number of senators elected per province was increased from two to three, with the third seat being allocated to the party with the second most votes. Colombia eliminated its regional electoral districts in favor of a single national district, while also creating special circumscriptions for indigenous persons and persons of African descent. Finally, Mexico in 1993 increased the number of senators elected per state from two to four, with the last seat being allocated to the party with the second most votes. Then in 1996 a reform reduced the number of seats elected per state to three (two seats allocated to the party obtaining a plurality of the vote and one to the party finishing in second place), while creating a 32-member national district so that one-fourth of the senators are elected by proportional representation. Aside from the change to unicameralism in Peru and Venezuela, the only other reforms were those in the Dominican Republic and Paraguay that favored the function of participation by separating the elections for president and congress in the former and separating the vote choice for the Senate and the lower chamber in the latter.

Political Party and Political Financing Reform

The regulation of political parties has always been difficult because of their dual public and private nature. While the strict internal organization of political parties could be considered a private matter, the nomination of candidates for public office is a public matter. This latter area stimulates greater demands for transparency and participation. A reform trend can be traced since the beginning of the 1990s oriented toward giving the state greater involvement in regulating the processes of selecting candidates for public office and the sources of financing for parties and for electoral campaigns.

Internal Democratization of Political Parties

The internal democratization of political parties initiated during the 1990s responded to increasing societal demands for greater transparency and participation and to the declining legitimacy of political parties. Given their resistance to giving up control and the fear of eroding party cohesion, party leaders have generally been reluctant to support the adoption of regulations that would require them to use more democratic and open procedures for selecting leaders and candidates for political office. In some cases, however, the threat of losing public support and of competition from new political forces has sparked an interest in reform.

At the same time, the use of primary elections for the selection of candidates not only resulted from a demand for more accountable and democratic political parties, but also aided the selection of candidates where there were interparty coalitions. This was the case of the *Concertación* in Chile in 1993 and 1999, and of the *Alianza* in Argentina in 1999, for which open primary elections permitted the designation of the presidential candidate of the parties that comprised the political coalition. Similarly, in some countries individual political parties have resorted to primaries to resolve internal disputes over leadership even when not required by law. Although in the short term internal elections may threaten the unity of parties, over the longer term they should help strengthen and diversify leadership structures and make parties more accountable to their members and to the broader citizenry

Table 2.9 shows the countries in which an obligation to hold primaries is regulated by law or the constitution. With the adoption of primaries in Argentina, Bolivia, Honduras, Panama, Paraguay, Peru, Uruguay, and Venezuela in the past decade, nine countries now stipulate primaries in the law. In addition, primaries have been held by individual parties on some occasions in Argentina,[10] Chile, the Dominican Republic, Ecuador, El Salvador, Mexico, and Nicaragua.

Table 2.9 Primary Elections

Country	Year of incorporation of the obligation to hold primaries	Have primaries been used?
Argentina	Law (2002). Established open and simultaneous primaries. Eliminated temporarily in 2003.	Sometimes (open and closed)
Bolivia	Law (1999). This law has not been applied yet.	Sometimes
Colombia	No obligation to hold primaries but if the parties choose to do so they are regulated by law.	Sometimes
Costa Rica	Law (1952)	Yes
Honduras	Law (2000)	Yes
Panama	Law (1997)	Yes
Paraguay	Law (1996)	Yes
Peru	Law (2003). Still with option of nomination by internally elected party leaders.	No
Uruguay	Constitution (1996)	Yes
Venezuela	Constitution (1999)	Sometimes

Sources: Friedenberg 2005; Payne and others 2006.

Electoral and Political Party Financing

The intervention of the state in the financing of electoral campaigns and the activities of political parties was also not considered a priority during the first years of the transitions to democracy. Recently, however, this topic has become one of the principal political reforms under discussion. The objectives for reforming political financing include promoting greater equality in electoral competition; lowering financial barriers for individuals to run for political office; reducing the extent to which politicians' policy decisions are oriented toward appeasing their financial backers rather than the interests of their constituents; and lowering the risk that dirty or illicit money will corrupt the system and undermine the rule of law (USAID 2003).

Whatever their primary objectives, Latin American countries have implemented measures to reform political financing with different degrees of success. Reforms were adopted across the region beginning in the early 1980s; now in all countries but one (Venezuela) the state provides direct financial support to political parties (or candidates) for electoral campaigns or for other organizational needs (table 2.10). In addition, seven countries mandate that private television networks provide time to political parties for electoral advertising. However, in Bolivia, the Dominican Republic, El Salvador,[11] Guatemala, Panama, and Uruguay access is provided only to

Table 2.10 Current Laws in Selected Areas of Regulation of Electoral and Party Financing

Country	Direct public financing for electoral campaigns	Direct public financing for party operations	Free access to private media	Limits to individual and/or total private contributions	Publication of financial statements of parties required by law	Prohibitions on origin of private contributions (from foreign or corporate sources)
Argentina	X	X	X	X	X	X
Bolivia	X			X		X
Brazil	X	X	X	X	X	X
Chile	X		X	X		X
Colombia	X	X	X		X	
Costa Rica	X	X		X	X	X[a]
Dominican Republic	X	X			X	X
Ecuador	X	X		X	X	X
El Salvador	X					
Guatemala	X	X				
Honduras	X					X
Mexico	X	X	X	X	X	X
Nicaragua	X	X				X[a]
Panama		X			X[b]	
Paraguay	X	X	X	X		X
Peru	X	X	X	X		X
Uruguay	X					
Venezuela						X

Source: Griner and Zovatto 2004.

Note:

a. Foreign private contributions are allowed only for training and technical assistance.

b. For public financing only.

the state-run media, which tend to have a considerably smaller audience than private media outlets (Griner and Zovatto 2004).

Ten countries have placed limits on the size of individual contributions to political parties, to campaigns of individual candidates, or on the total amount of private contributions that parties or candidates can receive. Reforms have also prohibited donations from various entities, such as foreign companies, governments, or individuals; state contractors; corporations; or social and political groups. Regulations have also become more strict in requiring parties and candidates to report and account for the origins of contributions, the amounts of their earnings, and the nature of their expenditures, especially for funds received from the state (Griner and Zovatto 2004; Payne and others 2006). In eight of the countries, campaign spending is limited, either through a literal limit on total spending or through some manner of restrictions on the amount of media advertising. At the same time, 12 countries limit the length of the electoral campaign or the period in which candidates and parties can advertise in the media (table 2.11). Nevertheless, the real effectiveness of such restrictions varies greatly.

Political finance reform since 1985 has trended toward the direct provision of public funds to cover some proportion of campaign costs or political party operating budgets (table 2.12). However, a mixed system of public and private financing has been preserved, with parties and candidates defending their freedom to devote large sums of private money to their campaigns. In some cases, regulations have stipulated that all or a portion of public financing be directed toward investment in political parties rather than purely electoral spending, and in a small number of cases steps have been taken to attempt to limit total campaign spending. The imposition of regulations to ensure more equitable access to media for advertising has been an incipient trend (Payne and others 2006).

The reforms intended to enhance transparency and accountability have generally fallen short of their ultimate objectives. Account statements of parties are generally not widely publicized, audits are not performed in a timely manner, and in many cases revenue and expenditure reporting is only applied to the portion of party budgets related to public monies or is otherwise inaccurate or incomplete. In addition, transparency and accountability standards are usually applied to party organizations but not to individual candidates. Political finance reform has accomplished the least toward strengthening supervisory mechanisms and institutions, as well as toward the creation and effective application of sanctions for noncompliance with transparency and other political finance regulations. Nevertheless, increasing attention is being paid to the issue and civil society organizations are growingly involved in helping to monitor party finances.

Table 2.11 Limits on Electoral Campaign Spending and Duration

Country	Total campaign spending limits	Limits on duration of campaign or duration of media advertising
Argentina	X	X
Bolivia	X[a]	
Brazil		X
Chile	X[b]	X
Colombia	X	X
Costa Rica		
Dominican Republic		
Ecuador	X	X
El Salvador		X
Guatemala		
Honduras		X[c]
Mexico	X	X
Nicaragua		X
Panama		
Paraguay		X
Peru	X[a]	X
Uruguay		X
Venezuela	X[a]	

Source: Griner and Zovatto 2004.
Note:
a. The limit is not on total spending but on amount of advertising time that can be purchased per TV or radio channel or in total.
b. Only in relation to expenses reimbursable by the state.
c. In practice this limit is not enforced.

Conclusions

The relative stability of democratic regimes over the past two decades in Latin America has not fostered stability in the rules of the democratic system. Rather, the majority of countries have significantly revised or overhauled their constitutions or adopted changes in political party and electoral laws. In part, the ferment of political reform is associated with the democratic transition and consolidation in contexts in which there was limited prior experience with democracy before the 1980s. However, the frequency of political reform also results from the unsettled nature of democratic political competition and the struggle to build the legitimacy and functioning of democracy in the face of wavering citizen support.

Table 2.12 Significant Reforms Affecting the Regulation of the Financing of Politics

Country	Public financing	Subsidized access to state or private media for advertising	Prohibition against foreign or other sources of contributions	Limits to individual and/or total private contributions	Limits to total campaign spending	Registering or reporting sources of financing and use of state and private funds
Argentina	1961, 1985, 2002	2002	1985, 2002	2002	2002	2002
Bolivia	1997, 1999		1999	1999		1999
Brazil	1995	1997	1997	1997[a]		1995
Chile	1988 (indirect) 2003 (direct)	1988	1988, 2003	2003	2003	1987, 2003
Colombia	1985, 1994	1994				1994
Costa Rica	1949					1996
Dominican Republic	1997	1997	1997			
Ecuador	1978		2000	2000	2000	2000
El Salvador	1983	1992, 1993, 1996 (removed private)	1983			
Guatemala	1985	1985				1989 (only public funds)

(continued)

Table 2.12 Significant Reforms Affecting the Regulation of the Financing of Politics *(continued)*

Country	Public financing	Subsidized access to state or private media for advertising	Prohibition against foreign or other sources of contributions	Limits to individual and/or total private contributions	Limits to total campaign spending	Registering or reporting sources of financing and use of state and private funds
Honduras	1981		1981			
Mexico	1977, 1987, 1990, 1993, 1996	1996	1996	1996	1996	1996
Nicaragua	1974, 2000					
Panama	1997	1983, 1988, 1993, 1998				2002
Paraguay	1990	1990	1990	1996		
Peru	2003	2003	2003	2003		2003
Uruguay	1928, 1999	1998				
Venezuela	1999 (eliminated)					

Source: Griner and Zovatto 2004.
Note:
a. The limit is with respect to the donor's income rather than an absolute amount or relative to the total budget of the party.

In some cases reform has been inspired by democratic activists seeking to improve democratic accountability and enhance citizens' involvement and influence. In others, reform has mainly or partly sought to bring advantage to one or more political groups over others, though it may have been represented as having been directed at promoting the broader public interest.

What is clear is that the rules of the policy-making process themselves are objects of reform and are to some extent endogenous to the broader processes of state reform examined in other chapters of this book. At the same time, the existing rules of the political game help shape the political reforms that are possible and the effects that such reforms ultimately have on the functioning of democracy. The experience of Latin American countries since 1985 vividly demonstrates that where democracy continues to function, citizen pressures and the dynamics of electoral competition can at times induce political reforms that, at least in a limited way, go against the narrow interests of the status quo political interests and have the potential to improve the way democracy works and to strengthen the legitimacy of democratic institutions. Advances in enhancing the responsiveness of politicians to broader public interests, improving the possibilities for intertemporal cooperation among political actors, and strengthening institutional checks and balances would seem to be necessary for progress in reform in other state-related institutions.

Notes

1. The starting years for the examination of reforms for this chapter are 1978 or the year that is considered to be the year of the transition to democracy. (Because Mexico experienced a prolonged process of political liberalization and democratization during the period, a particular year of transition is not specified. The year chosen as the start year for analysis of Mexico is 1982, because this is the year in which the first president of the 1978–2005 period was elected.) The starting years for each country are the following: Argentina (1983), Bolivia (1982), Brazil (1985), Chile (1990), Colombia (1978), Costa Rica (1978), the Dominican Republic (1978), Ecuador (1979), El Salvador (1984), Guatemala (1985), Honduras (1982), Mexico (1982), Nicaragua (1990), Panama (1989), Paraguay (1989), Peru (1980), and Venezuela (1979).

2. Though the reform is not captured within the dimensions considered here, in 1985 Honduras experimented with a double simultaneous vote system for electing the president in which parties could field multiple candidates and the candidate with the most votes from the party with the most votes was the winner.

3. Elections for both the Chamber of Deputies and the Senate are held simultaneously with the presidential elections, but only one-third or two-thirds of the members of the Senate are elected every four years.

4. Before 1998, deputies elected out of provincial districts were elected every two years while those elected out of the national district were elected every four years.

5. Given that in Argentina the Chamber of Deputies and the Senate have elections every two years, with the four-year term for the president there is now

only one midterm legislative election instead of two. There is no law that obliges the provinces to hold national legislative elections the same day as the presidential elections. For this reason, in 2003 in many provinces deputies and senators were elected on a date that was different from the date of the presidential election.

6. The only exception is that only half of the Senate is elected every four years because senators serve eight-year terms.

7. In Costa Rica presidential reelection was banned by constitutional reform in 1969. However, the *Sala Constitucional* struck down this reform in 2003, and the country went back to the original rule from the 1949 constitution in which former presidents can stand for reelection after eight years (two terms) of being out of office.

8. In the Hare and greatest remainder system, the total number of valid votes in a given electoral district is divided by the number of seats to be awarded. In the first distribution parties are awarded seats according to the number of quotients they obtain. If there are still seats to be awarded, these are allocated to the parties with the greatest number of remaining votes after the full quotients are subtracted from their vote totals. In the D'Hondt system the total votes obtained by each party are divided by a series of divisors (1, 2, 3, and so on) and seats are awarded to each party in the order of the size of these quotients.

9. In 2005 a constitutional reform in Chile eliminated the appointed and lifetime senators. As a result, all senators are now directly elected out of two-member districts.

10. The law obligating open and simultaneous primaries in Argentina has yet to be applied. The primaries that have been held so far have been at the discretion of individual parties.

11. In practical terms, the time provided is not used in El Salvador, while in Guatemala state television ceased operating by the beginning of 2004.

References

Cox, Gary W. 1997. *Making Votes Count: Strategic Coordination in the World's Electoral Systems.* New York: Cambridge University Press.

Di Palma, Giuseppe. 1990. *To Craft Democracies: An Essay on Democratic Transitions.* Berkeley, CA: University of California Press.

Friedenberg, Flavia. 2005. "Democracia interna en los partidos politicos." In *Tratado de Derecho Electoral Comparado de América Latina,* ed. Dieter Nohlen, Sonia Picado, and Daniel Zovatto. Mexico City: Fondo de Cultura Económica.

Griner, Steven, and Daniel Zovatto, eds. 2004. *De las normas y buenas practices: El desafío del financiamiento politico en América Latina.* San José, Costa Rica: Organización de los Estados Americanos (OEA) and el Instituto Internacional para la Democracia y la Asistencia Electoral (IDEA).

Jones, Mark P. 1995. *Electoral Laws and the Survival of Presidencial Democracies.* Notre Dame, IN: University of Notre Dame Press.

———. 1999. "Electoral Laws and the Effective Number of Candidates in Presidential Elections." *The Journal of Politics* 61 (1): 171–84.

Linz, Juan J. 1990. "The Perils of Presidentialism." *Journal of Democracy* 1 (1): 51–69.

Linz, Juan J., and Alfred Stepan, eds. 1978. *The Breakdown of Democratic Regimes.* Baltimore: Johns Hopkins University Press.

Linz, Juan J., and Arturo Valenzuela, eds. 1994. *The Failure of Presidential Democracy*. Baltimore: Johns Hopkins University Press.

Nohlen, Dieter. 1998. *Sistemas electorales y partidos politicos*. Mexico City: Fondo de Cultura Económica.

———. 1999. "El distrito electoral." Paper presented at the International Seminar on Electoral Legislation and Organization, Lima, Peru, February 9–11.

Payne, J. Mark, Daniel Zovatto, Mercedes Mateo Díaz, Edmundo Jarquín, and Fernando Carrillo. 2006. *La política importa. Democracia y desarrollo en América Latina*. Washington, DC: Inter-American Development Bank and International IDEA.

Rodrik, Dani. 2000. "Institutions for High-Quality Growth: What They Are and How to Acquire Them." *Studies in Comparative Development* 35 (3): 3–29.

Sen, Amartya Kumar. 1999. *Development as Freedom*. New York: Knopf.

Shugart, Matthew Soberg, and John M. Carey. 1992. *Presidents and Assemblies: Constitutional Design and Electoral Dynamics*. Cambridge, UK: Cambridge University Press.

Stein, Ernesto, Mariano Tommasi, Koldo Echebarría, Eduardo Lora, and Mark Payne (coordinators). 2005. *The Politics of Policies: Economic and Social Progress in Latin America, Report 2006*. Washington, DC: Inter-American Development Bank and David Rockefeller Center for Latin American Studies, Harvard University.

United States Agency for International Development (USAID). 2003. *Money in Politics Handbook: A Guide to Increasing Transparency in Emerging Democracies*. Washington, DC: USAID.

3

A Brief Overview of Judicial Reform in Latin America: Objectives, Challenges, and Accomplishments

Mariana Sousa

AS PART OF SO-CALLED SECOND-GENERATION REFORM, many Latin American countries have taken important steps toward transforming the judicial system since the mid-1980s.[1] The content and the speed of these reforms have varied across countries. Although not all of the intended objectives have been achieved and some consequences of policy adjustment were not foreseen, the consensus is that the process of judicial reform has not only strengthened the judicial branch in relation to the executive and the legislative branches, but has also improved the mechanisms of case management, judicial training, administration, and dispute resolution (Hammergren 2002b; Popkin 2001; Santiso 2003). This chapter reviews the general trends of the judicial reform process in Latin America, highlighting its main objectives, results, and challenges. It presents a judicial reform index for selected countries in the region and it concludes with a brief overview of the main implications of judicial reform for the policy-making process.

In the period immediately preceding the 1980s, the judiciary in Latin America played a subservient role in the policy-making process when compared with the other two branches of government. In a context of military dictatorships and recurring economic crises, judicial independence was rare. Judges were appointed according to their political preferences and the Supreme Court was generally seen as a mere "rubber stamp" to the will of the governing administrations. At the time, political scientists, policy makers, and public opinion in general considered Latin American judiciary systems to be irrelevant, weak, and largely dominated by the executive.[2]

Recently, however, as many countries in the region underwent a process of authoritarian-rule decay, newly established democratic governments stated as important policy objectives the implementation of the rule of law, an independent judiciary, and a well-functioning court system (Dakolias 1996). Some underscored the importance of an independent judicial sector on the basis of human rights concerns (Keith 2002; Skaar 2001). Others recognized that the rule of law was a necessary (even if not sufficient) condition for democracy (Méndez, O'Donnell, and Pinheiro 1999; O'Donnell 1999; Prillaman 2000) and economic development (Feld and Voigt 2003; Posner 1999). Throughout the region, the amount of foreign aid and loans geared toward the improvement of the court system received a considerable boost (Biebesheimer and Payne 2001; Buscaglia and Dakolias 1996). Not surprisingly, interest in the literature on the judiciary has increased; this work has provided significant evidence of the active political role of Latin American courts and their rising impact in public policy and governance (Gargarella 2003; Schedler, Diamond, and Plattner 1999).

The Objectives, Means, Promoters, and Strategies of Judicial Reform

Within the context of democratization and economic liberalization, more specific means for achieving more efficient, independent, and accountable judiciaries were delineated, such as the incorporation of new technologies and information systems, the implementation of training methods for the professionalization of the bench and the bar, the modernization of procedural codes, and the creation of new courts (Messick 1999). In some cases, the intended objectives and means were readily achieved. In other circumstances, powerful political forces have been able to capture the reform process and either reverse it or tilt it to favor certain political or economic interests (or both) that were not originally intended (Blair and Hansen 1994; Eyzaguirre 1996). Even if couched in socially desirable goals, some changes in the judicial system have been the product of self-interested pressure from narrow political groups. Table 3.1 summarizes the various goals of judicial reforms, the common means of achieving these goals, indicators to measure the success of reforms, and their major promoters.

Although these goals are not independent of each other, they are analytically distinguishable. This becomes especially important when considering the process of implementation of these reforms, which in many circumstances revealed important trade-offs among the stated objectives (Biebesheimer and Cordovez 2000; Jarquín and Carrillo 1998). Higher levels of judicial independence, for instance, were aimed at curtailing the possible abuses of power by the executive. In reality, judicial independence

Table 3.1 Reform Goals, Means, Indicators of Success, and Major Promoters

Objectives	Common means	Indicators of success	Major promoters
Building a strong, independent judiciary as a key democratic political actor	Depoliticized appointment systems, budgetary autonomy, enhanced judicial review powers	Ability to review and oppose government programs; judgments against political elites	Judges, civic interest groups, external actors
Judicial modernization as a goal in itself or to meet rising demand	New technologies, organization, administrative techniques	More efficient service, more cases resolved, backlog reduced	Government, donors, the judiciary (but more for the inputs than the results)
Elimination of traditional vices (corruption, bias, incompetence, delays)	Training, equipment, monitoring and evaluation systems, citizen complaints bureaus, judicial inspection offices, ethics codes and laws	Better public image; decreased delays; over longer run, fewer complaints; over shorter run, more judges disciplined, dismissed for cause	Civic action groups, sometimes elements of local bar or judiciary
Increased accessibility to wider range of social groups for rights protection, equitable treatment, and effective conflict resolution	More courts and judges, simplified and alternative procedures, rights-oriented training, subsidized legal services, popular legal education	Change in socioeconomic identity of users, decisions upholding constitutional rights	Political parties, civic groups, external actors
Enhancing crime control functions for increased citizen security, decreased social violence	New procedures, strengthening of other sector institutions (police, prosecution), judicial training and protection	Higher clearance rate for criminal cases, decline in crime rate	Government, public
Enhancing judiciary's ability to deal with economically relevant disputes	Law modernization, training, specialized commercial courts, delay reduction	More economic cases to courts, faster resolution, economic growth	Economic groups, government, donors

Source: Reprinted with permission from Hammergren (2002c), chart 1.

has often created incentives for judicial personnel to misuse resources or make politically motivated decisions, as they take advantage of an excessive amount of discretion and lack of accountability (Gloppen, Gargarella, and Skaar 2004; Vargas Viancos 1999).[3] Similarly, even though changes in laws and procedural codes have generally been interpreted as a sign of modernization, they have also decreased efficiency (at least in the short run) to the extent that it became necessary to train judges to use the new legislation.[4] The evolution of judicial reform has thus revealed the difficulty of pursuing all objectives simultaneously.

Moreover, the various objectives of reform entail the use of different means, measures of success, and major promoters, which can create debates about the best strategies for a successful judicial reform program. The divide is clear between those who argue that reform cannot be achieved without a prior societywide consensus (such as Blair and Hansen [1994]; Dakolias [1995]) and those who contend that a reform project itself can help create this consensus (for example, Hammergren (2001)). The former group believes that when such support is lacking, judicial reform should be forgone; instead, they suggest concentrating efforts on building consensus (that is, forging workable partnerships) for reform by opening the dialogue between the government, bar associations, business groups, and other nongovernmental organizations. The latter group contends that even without an initial large consensus within society, external donors and other reform supporters can create enough political will to at least start the process of change.[5] According to this group, the process of reform should not wait for an optimum level of support because it gives more chances for antireform forces to effectively derail any attempts to change the status quo.

Such divided opinions highlight the broad factors influencing the rate and the seriousness of reform, including historical experiences, the political skill of the nations' leaders, the organization and discipline of the nations' political parties, institutional capacity, and finally, the level of consensus in civil society and how well that can be harnessed by political leaders. Most important, it draws attention to the fact that judicial reform takes place in at least two stages: *initiation* (promulgation of constitutional revisions and new laws) and *implementation* (translation of abstract concepts into concrete structures). In some circumstances, reform is initiated but not implemented because of the high cost of change and a lack of consensus within society on the need as well as the benefits of reform (Finkel 2003). As a result, institutional judicial advances have sometimes remained purely paper changes.

Types of Judicial Reforms and Reformers

Indeed, the efforts for reforming the judicial sector amount to an ongoing process of cumulative changes in the law itself (Type I reforms), in law-related institutions (Type II reforms), and in the role of the judiciary as an independent actor in the policy-making process (Type III reforms) (Carothers 1998). In each of these three types of reform, varying objectives and means are fostered, and the extent of success can be measured only on a country-by-country basis. While an exhaustive list of successful reforms cannot be provided here, table 3.2 highlights the main categories of judicial reform experienced by 18 Latin American countries during the 1985–2004 period.[6] These countries are divided into three groups according to the extent of reform.[7] Argentina, Chile, Costa Rica, the Dominican Republic, and Ecuador are classified as *broad* reformers for having enacted changes in at least nine (out of the possible 11) reform categories during the period under analysis. Bolivia, Brazil, Colombia, Paraguay, and Peru fall under the *medium* reformers group because they enacted judicial reforms in seven or eight categories during the same period. Finally, El Salvador, Guatemala, Honduras, Mexico, Nicaragua, Panama, Uruguay, and Venezuela showed a *narrow* inclination to reform with visible efforts to change the judicial sector in six or fewer categories. Albeit at different paces and levels of success, all 18 countries have taken steps to change the judicial system in at least 4 of the 11 identified categories.

Type I reform includes important modifications to pieces of legislation or entire substantive and procedural codes.[8] Often the intent is to modernize the judicial system, to improve efficiency, and to increase the accessibility of the judicial system to larger sectors of the population by simplifying procedural codes and changing the laws regarding the use of alternative dispute resolution mechanisms. In general, the redrafting of laws has focused on the criminal justice domain;[9] some countries doing so include Argentina (1992), Bolivia (2000), Chile (2000), Colombia (1991), Costa Rica (1997), Ecuador (2001), El Salvador (1998), Guatemala (1994), Honduras (2000), Paraguay (2000), and Venezuela (1999). These changes have introduced a more adversarial system, replacing written documents with oral arguments and public trial before a jury or a judge (Payne and others 2002). The main promoters of such reforms have been external donors and members of government. Some visible common results include an increase in case backlogs (at least in the short run) for lack of experience and interpretative jurisprudence with regard to the new legislation, improved interest of the general public in courtroom proceedings (because of its more dynamic nature), and changes in the management of cases (Vargas Viancos 1996). Although important improvements have been made in writing and passing new codes, in some countries there is still progress to be made in drafting enabling legislation, which is supposed to produce the institutional capacity for the implementation of legal changes (Hammergren 1998a).

Type II reform involves efforts to strengthen the functioning of the courts, the police, or other judicial institutions through information systems, changes in organizational management, enhanced human resources

Table 3.2 Types of Reform by Types of Reformer, 1985 to 2004

Types of Reform	Types of Reformer		
	Broad	*Medium*	*Narrow*
All types of reform	Argentina, Chile, Costa Rica, Dominican Republic, Ecuador	Bolivia, Brazil, Colombia, Paraguay, Peru	El Salvador, Guatemala, Honduras, Mexico, Nicaragua, Panama, Uruguay, Venezuela
Type I			
Changes in laws and codes	Argentina, Chile, Costa Rica, Dominican Republic, Ecuador	Bolivia, Brazil, Colombia, Paraguay, Peru	El Salvador, Guatemala, Honduras, Nicaragua, Panama, Uruguay, Venezuela
Access to justice (creation of institutions or alternative methods of dispute resolution to facilitate access to judicial system)	Argentina, Chile, Costa Rica, Dominican Republic, Ecuador	Bolivia, Brazil, Colombia, Paraguay, Peru	El Salvador, Guatemala, Mexico, Nicaragua, Uruguay, Venezuela
Training and human resources management	Argentina, Chile, Costa Rica, Dominican Republic, Ecuador	Bolivia, Peru	Honduras, Nicaragua, Uruguay
Type II			
Information systems	Argentina, Chile, Dominican Republic, Ecuador	Colombia	Guatemala, Honduras
Strengthening or creation of institutions such as public ministry and judicial councils	Argentina, Chile, Costa Rica, Dominican Republic, Ecuador	Bolivia, Brazil, Colombia, Paraguay, Peru	El Salvador, Guatemala, Honduras, Mexico, Nicaragua, Panama, Venezuela
Case management and other management	Argentina, Chile, Costa Rica, Dominican Republic, Ecuador	Bolivia, Brazil, Peru	Guatemala, Mexico, Venezuela

(continued)

Table 3.2 Types of Reform by Types of Reformer, 1985 to 2004 *(continued)*

Types of Reform	Types of Reformer		
	Broad	*Medium*	*Narrow*
Budget autonomy (autonomy over management; autonomy in determination of budget amount)	Argentina, Dominican Republic, Ecuador	Brazil, Paraguay	
Remuneration and term of judges	Chile, Costa Rica, Dominican Republic, Ecuador	Bolivia, Brazil, Colombia, Paraguay	El Salvador, Panama, Venezuela
Type III Career system: nomination, evaluation, promotion of judges	Argentina, Chile, Costa Rica, Dominican Republic, Ecuador	Bolivia, Brazil, Colombia, Paraguay, Peru	El Salvador, Guatemala, Honduras, Mexico, Panama, Uruguay
Size and structure of highest court	Argentina, Chile, Costa Rica, Ecuador	Paraguay, Peru	Honduras, Mexico, Nicaragua, Uruguay, Venezuela
Constitutional review powers of highest court	Argentina, Costa Rica, Dominican Republic, Ecuador	Bolivia, Brazil, Colombia, Peru	Mexico

Sources: The main sources consulted include—among others—the various issues of the country reports of *The Economist* (1996–2004), the USAID's (2001) various reports of the *Informes Nacionales sobre Independencia Judicial*, and the CEJA's various "Reports on Judicial Systems in the Americas 2004–2005."

Note: To construct table 3.2, the author counted the number of significant reforms within each category (i.e., reforms cited in expert reviews, in the press, or in both as important changes to the status quo) undertaken by each country during the period analyzed. Although many judicial reform projects take various years to be implemented, the author has recorded only the year of the project's enactment.

training programs, and the creation of (or reformulation of existing) organisms such as the judicial council and the public defender's office. Even though some of these institutional revisions are relevant to judicial independence, their stated objectives lie elsewhere: increased accessibility to the justice system, elimination of traditional vices such as corruption, and an overall improvement in courts' performance. The main promoters of this type of reform have been civic groups (both domestic and international) and they have hoped to improve the judiciary's image in public opinion. Given the intrinsic difficulty in making cross-country comparisons of institutional strengthening, progress in this type of reform should be assessed by evaluating country-based reports (Hammergren 1998b).[10]

Type III reform includes any change to the process of nomination, promotion, and evaluation of judges; modifications affecting the tenure and remuneration of judges; granting the judiciary more autonomy with respect to the stipulation and management of its budget; reforms in the size and structure of the highest court; the creation of a constitutional court; or the revision of the judicial review powers of the highest court. Together these reforms are aimed at achieving greater levels of judicial independence.[11] Although the sources of judicial independence vary, a successful Type III reform requires a profound modification in the incentive structure for policy makers. That is, beyond legal and institutional changes, politicians need to start perceiving an independent judiciary as an essential and valued feature of the policy-making process. Not surprisingly, civic groups, external donors, and judges themselves have joined forces to push for sweeping change in the attitude of government officials so as to accept the judiciary as an independent decision-making entity in various Latin American countries. The satisfactory achievement of these reforms depends on the extent to which these attitudinal changes can be developed.

In reviewing the types of reforms carried out by Latin American countries, shown in table 3.2, it is possible to identify some general trends in the region. Whereas Type I reform has been frequently undertaken by all three groups of reformers, the narrow set of reformers has found it particularly difficult to carry out Type III reform. Within Type II reform, the creation and strengthening of judicial institutions and modifications to provide better access to justice have been common; the same cannot be said about changes that improve information systems and the training of judges and judicial personnel. Within Type III reform, restructuring of the career system has often been observed in all three groups of reformers; changes favoring greater budget autonomy were mostly enacted by broad reformers.

These general patterns suggest that there is no uniform formula for restructuring the judicial system. Approaches to reform varied from "shock treatment" to "piecemeal." While some reforms were far-reaching (usually undertaken by the broad reformers), others focused on altering specific aspects of the judicial system. In neither case does the initiation of reforms guarantee their success.

Overall, changes since the mid-1980s have been largely in the direction of less politically motivated mechanisms of selection for Supreme Court magistrates and lower judges, pay increases, life or longer terms, increases in budget allocation to the judicial sector, creation of judicial councils (responsible for budget administration and promotion and appointment of judges), more education programs to enhance professionalism of judges, greater constitutional review powers to Supreme Courts, and in some cases, creation of separate constitutional courts. At least some visible partial improvements can be seen in human rights protection: more cases are being heard, judges are better prepared and take their jobs more seriously, decisions are made in a more unbiased manner, and corrupt judges are being punished (USAID 2001). Even critics agree that the achievement of more independent judiciaries, efficient case management, increased judicial resources, and enhanced human rights protection should not be underappreciated (Correa Sutil 1999; Hammergren 2002b; Prillaman 2000; Ungar 2002).

The Challenges to Judicial Reform

The objectives of reform have not been easily achieved. The process of change is necessarily full of conflict and direct resistance to reform has come from opposition parties, the political class that benefited from a controlled judiciary, and sometimes, the judiciary itself (Popkin 2001). For instance, in 1990, Chile's new democratic government attempted to pass reforms that would have created a National Justice Council and changed the structure of the Supreme Court. Such suggestions were never approved because of severe opposition by both the judiciary (which interpreted the reforms as a threat to its independence) and the opposition parties (which were afraid of the consequences for human rights violators of the Pinochet regime). The executive itself has, in some instances, tried to regain control over the judiciary. In Argentina, President Menem's interest in regaining control of the court was behind the increase in the size of the Supreme Court from five to nine members. Similar efforts on the part of the executive have been observed in Guatemala, Honduras, Panama, and Peru. Table 3.3 is revealing in its summary of the main obstacles to judicial independence identified in a survey (among other sources) conducted by the Due Process of Law Foundation in collaboration with the *Fundación Internacional para Sistemas Electorales* in selected Latin American countries in 2000 (USAID 2001).

Two other barriers to the successful fulfillment of reform objectives can be added to these forces of resistance. Despite the reform efforts, the

Table 3.3 Main Obstacles to Judicial Independence by Country

Country	Obstacles
Argentina	Executive branch appointment of judges with similar preferences; powerful lawyers lobbying for the nomination of judges; certain politically appointed judges
Bolivia	Low salaries for judges, which leads to corruption and low qualifications; no periodic evaluation of judges and no incentives for promotion; inadequate disciplinary regime; external pressures, especially over those judges nominated before the reforms of 1998; sensitive areas (such as drug trafficking) that are especially subject to international pressures; pressure by the media and public opinion; the process of reform itself, which requires judges to be constantly updated
Brazil	Judicial system still extremely slow (duration of cases is high and costly); in some areas, such as labor, decisions always favor the employee
Chile	Social legitimacy of the sector, especially given its omissions in dealing with human rights issues during the military dictatorship; excessive hierarchical structure (Supreme Court judges exert pressure on lower court judges); procedural rules allowing lawyers to lobby in the nomination of judges
Colombia	Sensitive areas (such as drug trafficking); no de facto budget autonomy; still high levels of corruption; external pressure coming from the United States
Costa Rica	Political class believes the judicial sector does not need any major changes in its organization; vision is shared by the members of the judicial elite (especially within the Supreme Court); vertical, hierarchical, and concentrated structure of the judicial system; lack of internal independence; media concentration on access to justice and improvements in the speed of the adjudication process
Dominican Republic	Slow hearings; lack of public access and confidence in the justice system; hierarchical and centralized system; political forces impinge on judicial independence via the control of its budget

(continued)

Table 3.3 Main Obstacles to Judicial Independence by Country (continued)

Country	Obstacles
Ecuador	"Selective activism" by constitutional court; poor working conditions and lack of career stability; no review or evaluation of performance; lack of predictability; poorly trained judges; overburdened legal system; susceptible to corruption
El Salvador	Absence of a de facto judicial career; political instability and poor institutionalization; overburdened with administrative tasks; corruption of judicial sector employees
Guatemala	Lack of consciousness of their political importance on the part of lower court judges; job instability; possibility of promotion of judges for political reasons; tradition of making declarations to the media without any factual evidence; threats against judges and their families, especially when they are involved in human rights cases; no institutional policy for protection of people who denounce crimes; overwhelming caseload resulting in delegation of decisions to aides; constant threat of the *Ministerio Público* when judges make unfavorable decisions
Honduras	Deficient academic preparation of judges; low salaries; hierarchical influence of superiors; nominations still follow the results of presidential elections; influence of powerful economic groups over judges' decisions; release of news about parties in a hearing, which may not be true, but end up influencing public opinion and judges' decisions
Mexico	Bribes used for any government action; judges rarely overturn the decisions of presidents who have appointed them; judiciary has given great discretion to the president by incorporating the "nonjusticiability" doctrine whereby the courts refuse to hear a case because the justices believe they will be deciding an issue that is political in nature and should be made by the president; lack of public's confidence in the judiciary

(continued)

Table 3.3 Main Obstacles to Judicial Independence by Country *(continued)*

Country	Obstacles
Nicaragua	Lack of professional training; corruption; slow and inefficient case management procedures; lack of legal aid and public defense (despite law providing for public defense free of charge since 1998); legal illiteracy; lack of resources to enforce rulings; general lack of resources (low salaries of judges, insufficient geographical coverage, infrastructure, and dissemination of jurisprudence)
Panama	Lack of professional training; low salaries except for Supreme Court justices; low public opinion
Paraguay	Widespread corruption; lack of de facto budget autonomy; lack of public's credibility; lack of job security; influence of political parties and powerful lawyers; the media
Peru	Lack of uniform jurisprudence criteria; corruption; inadequate substantive and procedural codes; lack of job stability
Uruguay	Financial restrictions; inadequate judicial offices; not enough information processing equipment; lack of specialization in economic and financial problems and crime; lack of financial independence; limited judicial review powers
Venezuela	Power struggle between the judicial council and the Supreme Court; executive control of nomination of Supreme Court judges

Sources: Alston and others 2005; Aninat and others 2004; Araujo and others 2004; Hammergren 2002a; Lehoucq and others 2005; Popkin 2001; USAID 2001.

general public's perception of the sector has not improved. The Latinobarometer survey (2004) shows that only 32 percent of the respondents in 18
surveyed Latin American countries hold "high" or "some" degree of trust
in the judicial system.[12] In Argentina, for instance, the levels of "low"
trust reached 90.3 percent in 2003, followed by Paraguay (88.0 percent),
Ecuador (84.6 percent), and Mexico (81.1 percent) (Popkin 2004). Only
in Costa Rica did more than half of respondents hold "high" confidence
in the judicial system. Without widespread public support, citizens' control mechanisms over traditional vices of the judicial sector are impaired,
and the demand for increased transparency and judicial independence
decreases. In addition, the media have not always played a positive role in
legitimating reforms and the work of the courts. Often they only under-
score the failures of the sector, blaming it for the high levels of crime and
impunity in certain Latin American countries. Taken together, these two
factors make it more difficult to create a consensus in favor of change in
the justice system (Domingo and Sieder 2001).

The Determinants of Successful Judicial Reform

Despite numerous challenges, the search for the main factors shaping the
success stories of judicial reform in Latin America is extremely valuable.[13]
Although it is difficult to transfer the content of successful judicial reform
from one country to another, many lessons can be drawn from the analysis of shared experiences across borders. This is particularly relevant if
Latin American countries want to avoid replicating mistakes and instead
promote further improvements in both the performance of their judicial
systems and the quality of their democratic governance. Some of these lessons are identified below.

Based on the observation that the adequate implementation of reforms
depends on committed political and judicial will and a broad base of
societal support, a successful process of judicial reform must be transparent and subject to systematic monitoring. Transparency ensures access to
quality information about the state of reform and its effect on the activities of the judiciary. Systematic monitoring motivates continuous compliance with standards and reform strategies. Taken together, these features
allow for higher levels of public awareness and consensus regarding the
problems of the judiciary and the importance of reform. Higher levels of
awareness and consensus, in turn, invite the involvement and participation
of not only key stakeholders but also different groups in civil society. Ultimately, greater involvement and participation reinforces public demand
and the commitment by elites to reform.[14]

A well-defined reform strategy, coupled with efficient coordination
and capable leadership, also contributes to the success of judicial reform.
These factors facilitate the identification of weaknesses and the elabora-

tion of best practices, thus avoiding duplication of effort and the waste of resources. In addition, they serve as extra mechanisms to detect and punish corruption in both the judicial system and the reform process. The maintenance of the integrity and the legitimacy of reform programs are fundamental for progress to be achieved.

Moreover, the success of judicial reform depends on the inclusion of reform efforts into broader institutional and economic restructuring agendas (Henderson and Autheman 2003). Because the judiciary does not exist in a vacuum, complementary political and socioeconomic reform can improve the sustainability of judicial reform. A free press, for instance, can disseminate information vital for the implementation of judicial reform.

Finally, having an accurate understanding of each country's needs and vulnerabilities is essential for the appropriate design of successful reform. Magic formulas and "one size fits all" reform recipes from abroad have limited applicability (Hammergren 2003). If reformers do not know the peculiarities of the national socioeconomic and political environment, the definition of problems, causes, and solutions is impaired.

The Differentiated Results of Judicial Reforms

Beyond the determinants of successful judicial reforms, it must be highlighted that the same type of reform has often produced different results across (and within) countries. The issue of judicial councils is a case in point. To improve the procedures for selecting and promoting judges as well as to increase the independence of the judiciary by administering its budget, many Latin American countries decided to follow the European model of establishing judicial councils. Often, however, these new bureaucracies have become subject to the same kind of politicization that they were supposed to help reduce (Hammergren 2002a). Supporters of the creation of judicial councils claim that despite all the problems, the establishment of judicial councils is a significant advance over the previous criteria for appointment of judges, as in Costa Rica. Skeptics do not agree and propose to disband judicial councils, as happened in Ecuador due to lack of effectiveness. Regardless of the merits of the arguments of both groups, what is evident is that the composition and responsibilities assigned to judicial councils are not the same in all Latin American countries, suggesting that the effects of reforms to these entities have varied significantly (see table 3.4).

Two other examples of the differentiated impact of judicial reforms in various Latin American countries follow. First, although judicial salaries have generally improved, they remain low in many countries when compared to salaries in the private sector, and are therefore not attracting enough qualified professionals (an important exception is Brazil). In some cases, salary improvement occurred only at the top of the judicial

Table 3.4 The Role and Composition of Judicial Councils in Selected Latin American Countries

Country	Judicial council composition	Council selected by	Council's role in Supreme Court selection	Council's role in selection of other judges	Additional council responsibilities
Argentina	Composed of: Supreme Court president; 8 legislators (4 from each chamber; 2 from the majority party and 2 from the leading minority parties); 4 lawyers in federal practice, chosen by election; 1 member of the academic community; 1 executive delegate	Judicial representatives are elected by federal judges; legislators are selected by the presidents of the two chambers, based on proposals from the different chambers	None	Selection of candidates for judgeships through merit-based public competition; preparation of lists of three candidates for executive selection	Administers judiciary's budget and discipline of judges; initiates proceedings to remove judges; issues regulations related to judicial organization and independence
Bolivia	Supreme Court president and 4 other members	Congress	Nominates candidates	Nominates candidates for lower courts	Administrative and disciplinary responsibility for the judiciary; runs training program

(continued)

Table 3.4 The Role and Composition of Judicial Councils in Selected Latin American Countries *(continued)*

Country	Judicial council composition	Council selected by	Council's role in Supreme Court selection	Council's role in selection of other judges	Additional council responsibilities
Costa Rica	Composed of 5 members: 4 from the judiciary and 1 outside lawyer; Supreme Court president presides	Supreme Court	None	Merit-based selection	An administrative council has delegated responsibility for various administrative and disciplinary matters
Dominican Republic	President; president of Senate and opposition party senator; president of chamber and opposition deputy; president of Supreme Court and another justice	Not applicable	Recruits and screens candidates; appoints justices; can hold public hearings	None	Not applicable
El Salvador	3 lawyers; 1 professor from the law faculty of the University of El Salvador and 1 from the private universities; 1 lawyer from the Public Ministry	Legislature chooses from lists of 3 nominated by each sector represented	Proposes candidates to the legislature, half of whom must come from an election organized by the country's lawyers' associations	Proposes candidates on a merit basis; provides the Supreme Court lists of 3 candidates for its selection	Periodic evaluations of judges; runs the Judicial Training School

Table 3.4 The Role and Composition of Judicial Councils in Selected Latin American Countries *(continued)*

Country	Judicial council composition	Council selected by	Council's role in Supreme Court selection	Council's role in selection of other judges	Additional council responsibilities
Guatemala	President of Supreme Court; head of judiciary's human resources unit; head of training unit; 1 representative of judges; 1 representative of appellate magistrates	Judge and magistrate to be elected in their respective assemblies	To advise congress of need to convoke Postulation Commission for selection of Supreme Court and appellate magistrates	In charge of merit-based entry system; training unit evaluates candidates; successful completion of 6-month course makes candidates eligible to be named by Supreme Court	Names and removes head of institutional training unit; evaluates performances of judges and magistrates; defines policies and training unit
Paraguay	1 member of the Supreme Court; 1 representative of executive; 1 member of each legislative chamber; 2 lawyers; 1 professor from the National University's Law Faculty; 1 professor from the private universities	Not applicable	Proposes list of 3 for Senate selection and appointment	Proposes list of 3 for appointment as judges or prosecutors by Supreme Court	Not applicable

Source: Reprinted with permission from M. Popkin, "Efforts to Enhance Judicial Independence in Latin America: A Comparative Perspective," in *Guidance for Promoting Judicial Independence and Impartiality*, (Washington, DC: Due Process of Law Foundation and U.S. Agency for International Development. http://www.dplf.org and www.usaid.gov/our_work/democracy_and_governance/publications/pdfs/pnacm007.pdf, 2001), table 3.1.

hierarchy, which has not necessarily solved the problem of poorly qualified judges and attorneys. Figure 3.1 portrays this situation. It shows the
annual salaries of Supreme Court and lower court judges in purchasing
power parity U.S. dollars (PPP/US$) in 2000. Although in Ecuador, judges'
salaries increased 100 percent in 1992 and 40 percent in 2002, the compensation of first instance judges is still considered low and uncompetitive
(World Bank 2002). In Nicaragua, while Supreme Court judges receive
high salaries, lower court judges struggle to maintain a reasonable income
(thus, the highest compression rate in Latin America). Finally, Brazil is an
example of competitive remuneration at all judicial hierarchical levels and
a low compression rate.

The judicial budget provides a second example of the differentiated
impact of judicial reforms. Even though changes in the law have made
the judiciary responsible for *drafting* its own budget in many countries,
such as Argentina, Chile, Colombia, Paraguay, and Uruguay, in practice,
only in some democracies is its *execution* independent of the approval
of the executive or legislature. In most countries, financial resources for
the judiciary are controlled either because the executive disburses these
resources in quotas or because the judicial budget requires some special
authorization by the other branches of government. Not surprisingly, the
degree of de facto budget autonomy has varied significantly across the
region (USAID 2001).

When looking at quantitative indicators of the success of reforms there
is still considerable variation at the individual country level of analysis.
Subjective indicators of judicial independence show Brazil, Chile, Costa
Rica, and Uruguay as examples of countries with high levels of judicial independence. Conversely, the majority of the other Latin American
countries score lower than the world average in judicial independence (see
figure 3.2). As an illustration of how the initiation of reforms does not
necessarily lead to their complete implementation, figure 3.3 presents de
jure and de facto indicators of judicial independence. Their correlation
coefficient is only 0.334.

The Judicial Reform Index

Once again, the initiation of reforms does not necessarily mean they were
successfully implemented or the intended goals were achieved. The sections on the challenges to reform and the differentiated results of judicial
reform provide evidence for such an assertion. In an effort to provide an
overall assessment of how well a country's judicial sector matches with
the expectations of a particular reform objective, this section presents a
judicial reform index (JRI) for 10 selected Latin American countries. This
index is based on the index developed by the American Bar Association's

Figure 3.1 Remuneration of Judges and the Compression Rate, 2000

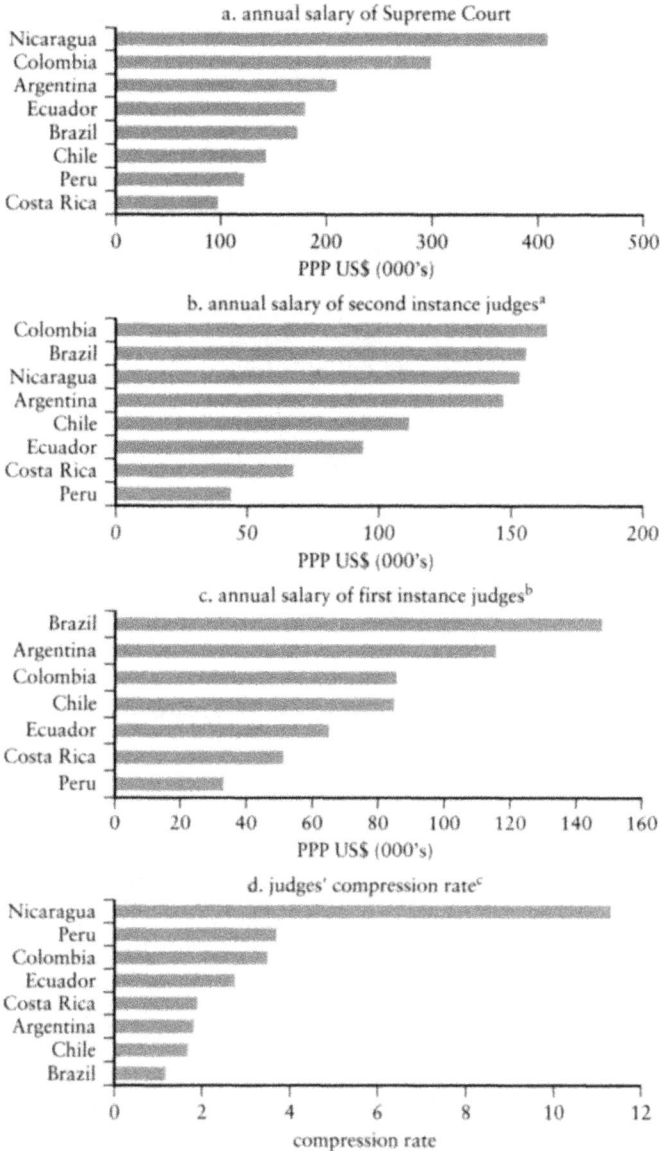

a. annual salary of Supreme Court

Nicaragua	
Colombia	
Argentina	
Ecuador	
Brazil	
Chile	
Peru	
Costa Rica	

0   100   200   300   400   500
PPP US$ (000's)

b. annual salary of second instance judges[a]

Colombia	
Brazil	
Nicaragua	
Argentina	
Chile	
Ecuador	
Costa Rica	
Peru	

0   50   100   150   200
PPP US$ (000's)

c. annual salary of first instance judges[b]

Brazil	
Argentina	
Colombia	
Chile	
Ecuador	
Costa Rica	
Peru	

0   20   40   60   80   100   120   140   160
PPP US$ (000's)

d. judges' compression rate[c]

Nicaragua	
Peru	
Colombia	
Ecuador	
Costa Rica	
Argentina	
Chile	
Brazil	

0   2   4   6   8   10   12
compression rate

Source: The World Bank, Legal and Judicial Reform Practice Group, http://www4.worldbank.org/legal/leglr/.

Note: PPP US$ = purchasing power parity U.S. dollars.

a. Second instance judges are responsible for hearing cases initially adjudicated in the lower courts and correcting possible legal errors made by first instance judges.

b. First instance judges are responsible for trying and ascertaining the facts on cases of a civil, commercial, or criminal nature, when they first arrive at the (lower) judicial courts.

c. Compression rate is the ratio between the highest and lowest salary.

Figure 3.2 Subjective Indicators of Judicial Independence in Selected LACs

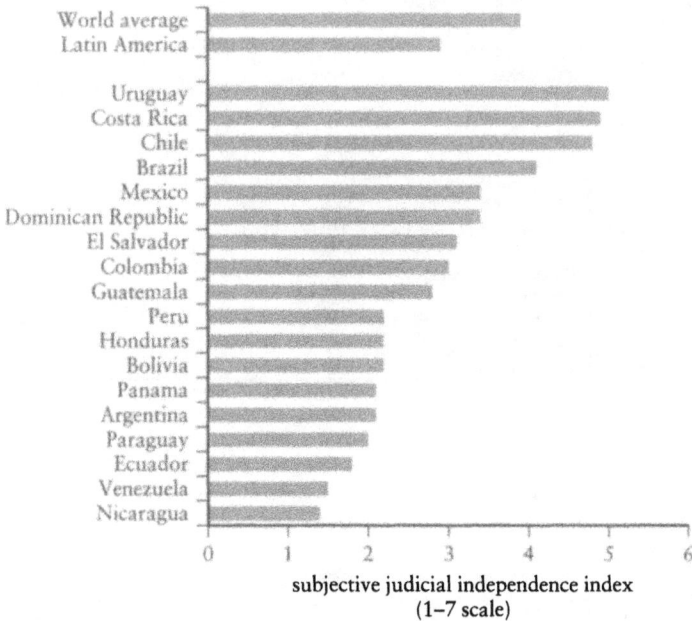

subjective judicial independence index
(1–7 scale)

Source: World Economic Forum 2005.

Central and East European Law Initiative (ABA/CEELI 2002) and it serves as an analytic device to evaluate the accomplishments of reform efforts.

The JRI is *not* a quantitative indicator, in which countries score points as more reforms are achieved. Because of the methodological difficulties of developing a quantitative measure of countries' reform progress, each of the selected countries is simply recorded here as having a negative, neutral, or positive correlation with each of the "factors" analyzed.[15] Each reform factor corresponds to a statement of what would be expected after completion of a country's judicial reform process.[16] If the reality of a given country's judicial system fully corresponds to the statement, a positive correlation is marked. On the contrary, if what is stated does not match up with the facts of each country's judicial sector, a negative correlation is recorded. Finally, if there are signs of mixed correlation with the statement—in which some positive factual evidence is tempered by some negative—a country receives a neutral evaluation. The 26 statements used as the factors of reform are shown in appendix 3A.

Figure 3.3 De Jure and De Facto Judicial Independence Indicators in Selected Latin American Countries

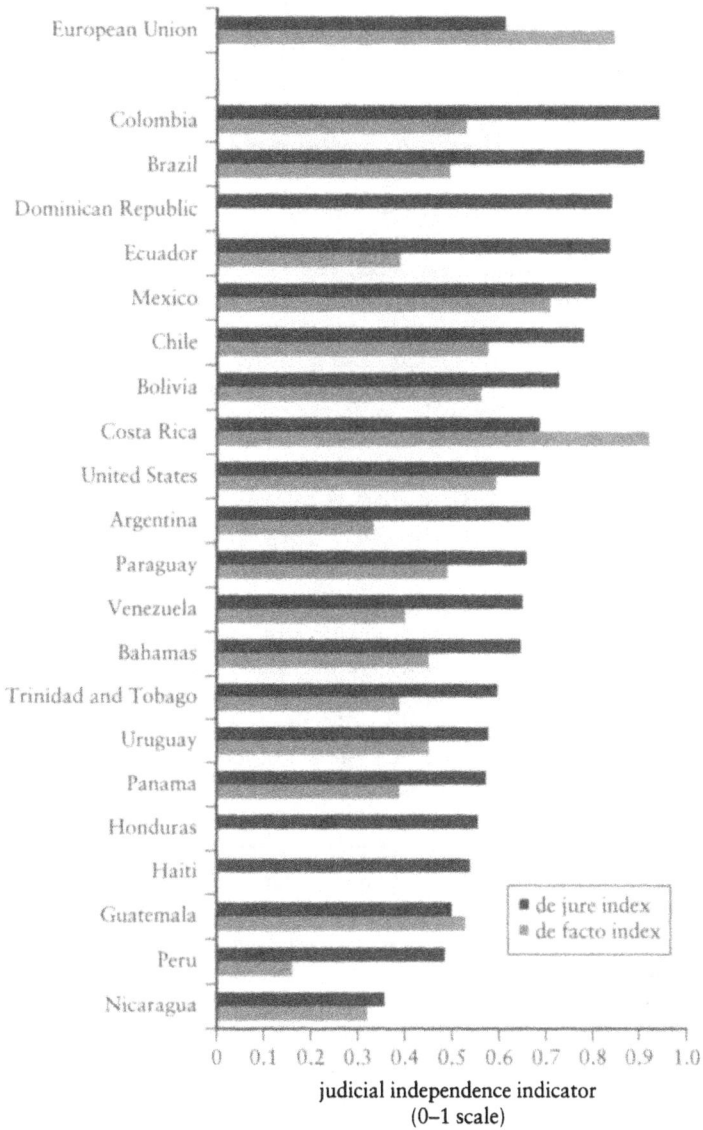

Source: Feld and Voigt 2003.

In addition, it is important to note that the *Informes Nacionales sobre Independencia Judicial* produced by the *Fundación para el Debido Proceso Legal* in collaboration with the *Fundación Internacional para Sistemas Electorales* was used as the basis for the evaluation of each country's judicial system. These reports were prepared in 2000 and produced as USAID's technical publication *Pautas para promover la independencia y la imparcialidad judicial* (or Guidance for Promoting Judicial Independence and Impartiality) published in 2001. Further progress may have occurred in the time that has elapsed since these reports were published. As a result, all of the information presented in table 3.5 should be interpreted cautiously.

Among the 10 Latin American countries reviewed, Chile and Costa Rica have achieved the most positive concrete results in the process of judicial reform. El Salvador, Guatemala, and Honduras are lagging behind: despite the efforts to reform, they have yet to accomplish their intended outcomes. Furthermore, the evidence suggests that, in all countries, the goals of efficiency, accountability, and transparency have been the most difficult to achieve. Judicial review powers of the highest court demonstrate important expansion.

Conclusion and Implications of Judicial Reforms for the Policy-Making Process

Since 1985, Latin American countries have gone through an important process of judicial reform, albeit at different speeds. Within the context of political and economic liberalization, these reforms were aimed at increased levels of judicial independence, efficiency, access to justice, and the elimination of corrupt practices. The implementation of these reforms revealed important trade-offs and the simultaneous achievement of all goals has proved difficult (if not impossible). The challenges to change come from various sources ranging from entrenched political interests to lack of support by the media and public opinion. The effects of reform have varied across (and within) countries, but some considerable advances have been observed. Countries that made sure the process of reform was transparent, open to broad participation, and adequate to their own socio-economic and political contexts were able, for the most part, to capitalize on the benefits of successful judicial reform. What this brief examination of the Latin American experience shows is that reforms in the judicial sector have produced some differentiated but significant changes in the structure and the functioning of courts, which, in turn, may have an impact on how courts veto laws, shape their content, enforce other policy reforms, and act as an alternative representative of society. At the very least, judicial reforms have started the debate over what role the judicial branch could and should assume in the policy-making process.

Table 3.5 Judicial Reform Index in 10 Selected Latin American Countries

		Argentina	Bolivia	Chile	Costa Rica	Dominican Republic
I. Quality and education						
Factor 1	Judicial qualification and preparation	Neutral	Negative	Positive	Positive	Neutral
Factor 2	Selection and appointment process	Neutral	Neutral	Positive	Neutral	Neutral
Factor 3	Continuing legal education	Negative	Neutral	Positive	Neutral	Neutral
II. Judicial powers						
Factor 4	Judicial review of legislation	Positive	Positive	Positive	Positive	Neutral
Factor 5	Judicial oversight of administrative practice	Neutral	Neutral	Positive	Positive	Neutral
Factor 6	Judicial jurisdiction over civil liberties	Positive	Neutral	Positive	Positive	Positive
Factor 7	System of appellate review	Positive	Positive	Positive	Positive	Positive
Factor 8	Contempt, subpoena, and enforcement powers	Positive	Positive	Positive	Positive	Neutral
III. Financial resources						
Factor 9	Budgetary input	Positive	Neutral	Neutral	Positive	Negative
Factor 10	Adequacy of judicial salaries	Neutral	Negative	Positive	Positive	Positive
IV. Structural safeguards						
Factor 11	Guaranteed tenure	Positive	Neutral	Positive	Positive	Positive
Factor 12	Objective judicial advancement criteria	Positive	Neutral	Neutral	Positive	Positive
Factor 13	Removal and discipline of judges	Positive	Neutral	Positive	Neutral	Neutral
Factor 14	Case assignment	Positive	Negative	Neutral	Positive	Negative
Factor 15	Judicial associations	Positive	Positive	Positive	Positive	Negative

(continued)

Table 3.5 Judicial Reform Index in 10 Selected Latin American Countries (continued)

		Argentina	Bolivia	Chile	Costa Rica	Dominican Republic
V. Accountability and transparency						
Factor 16	Judicial decisions and improper influence	Neutral	Neutral	Neutral	Neutral	Neutral
Factor 17	Code of ethics	Negative	Negative	Negative	Positive	Neutral
Factor 18	Judicial conduct complaint process	Positive	Negative	Neutral	Positive	Neutral
Factor 19	Public and media access to proceedings	Negative	Neutral	Positive	Positive	Neutral
Factor 20	Publication of judicial decision(s)	Neutral	Negative	Positive	Positive	Negative
Factor 21	Maintenance of trial records	Neutral	Neutral	Positive	Positive	Negative
VI. Efficiency						
Factor 22	Court support staff	Neutral	Neutral	Neutral	Positive	Negative
Factor 23	Judicial positions	Neutral	Neutral	Positive	Neutral	Neutral
Factor 24	Case filing and tracking systems	Neutral	Neutral	Neutral	Neutral	Neutral
Factor 25	Computers and office equipment	Neutral	Neutral	Neutral	Neutral	Negative
Factor 26	Distribution and indexing of current law	Neutral	Negative	Neutral	Neutral	Negative

(continued)

Table 3.5 Judicial Reform Index in 10 Selected Latin American Countries *(continued)*

		El Salvador	Guatemala	Honduras	Panama	Paraguay
I. Quality and education						
Factor 1	Judicial qualification and preparation	Negative	Negative	Negative	Negative	Negative
Factor 2	Selection and appointment process	Neutral	Neutral	Negative	Negative	Neutral
Factor 3	Continuing legal education	Negative	Negative	Negative	Negative	Neutral
II. Judicial powers						
Factor 4	Judicial review of legislation	Positive	Neutral	Positive	Positive	Positive
Factor 5	Judicial oversight of administrative practice	Neutral	Negative	Negative	Positive	Neutral
Factor 6	Judicial jurisdiction over civil liberties	Positive	Positive	Positive	Positive	Positive
Factor 7	System of appellate review	Positive	Positive	Positive	Positive	Positive
Factor 8	Contempt, subpoena, and enforcement powers	Neutral	Neutral	Negative	Positive	Neutral
III. Financial resources						
Factor 9	Budgetary input	Positive	Positive	Neutral	Neutral	Negative
Factor 10	Adequacy of judicial salaries	Positive	Positive	Negative	Negative	Negative
IV. Structural safeguards						
Factor 11	Guaranteed tenure	Positive	Negative	Negative	Positive	Neutral
Factor 12	Objective judicial advancement criteria	Neutral	Negative	Negative	Negative	Neutral
Factor 13	Removal and discipline of judges	Negative	Negative	Negative	Positive	Positive
Factor 14	Case assignment	Negative	Neutral	Negative	Positive	Neutral
Factor 15	Judicial associations	Neutral	Neutral	Neutral	Neutral	Positive

(continued)

Table 3.5 Judicial Reform Index in 10 Selected Latin American Countries *(continued)*

	El Salvador	Guatemala	Honduras	Panama	Paraguay
V. Accountability and transparency					
Factor 16 Judicial decisions and improper influence	Negative	Negative	Negative	Neutral	Neutral
Factor 17 Code of ethics	Negative	Negative	Negative	Neutral	Negative
Factor 18 Judicial conduct complaint process	Neutral	Positive	Neutral	Negative	Positive
Factor 19 Public and media access to proceedings	Neutral	Neutral	Neutral	Positive	Neutral
Factor 20 Publication of judicial decisions	Neutral	Negative	Negative	Positive	Positive
Factor 21 Maintenance of trial records	Negative	Negative	Negative	Neutral	Neutral
VI. Efficiency					
Factor 22 Court support staff	Neutral	Negative	Negative	Positive	Negative
Factor 23 Judicial positions	Neutral	Negative	Negative	Negative	Negative
Factor 24 Case filing and tracking systems	Neutral	Negative	Negative	Neutral	Negative
Factor 25 Computers and office equipment	Negative	Negative	Negative	Neutral	Neutral
Factor 26 Distribution and indexing of current law	Negative	Negative	Negative	Negative	Negative

Source: Author's compilation.

More specifically, it appears the division of powers and the role of the judiciary in the policy-making process are not as neatly and narrowly defined as traditionally supposed.[17] First, with the establishment of institutional structures conducive to higher levels of judicial independence, courts have become less subservient and the judiciary has repositioned itself in relation to other branches of government. The number of judicial rulings against the executive's preferences has generally increased in many countries, and overall, the greater importance of court decisions in both public policy and politics is apparent (Shapiro and Stone Sweet 2002; Tate 1992). Moreover, the broadening of judicial review powers has forced legislators to consider constitutional adequacy when elaborating legislation (Stone Sweet 2000). The policy debate now includes efforts to anticipate the reaction of judicial institutions (Ferejohn 2002). Finally, the appointment of higher court judges remains largely political. If courts were irrelevant for the policy-making process, the strategic interest in the control of appointments to the courts would not be so prevalent

A greater understanding of why and how courts affect both the policy-making process and policy outcomes is still lacking. Although discussions about the "judicialization of politics" emphasize the role of courts in affecting public policy and their influence in politics (Tate and Vallinder 1995), the literature has yet to explore the link between reform, the role of the judiciary in the policy-making process, and the features of public policy. A comprehensive study on this issue would be of great value.

Here, it suffices to speculate about what judiciaries in Latin America are *capable* of doing in the policy-making process. First, courts can act as "veto players." Following Tsebelis's (2002) work—which argues that policy change becomes more difficult as the number of veto players increases—courts assume this role when their "agreement is required to enact policy change" (Andrews and Montinola 2004, 56). Second, courts can shape the content of policies according to their own preferences, fulfilling their role as a "policy player." Rather than being a simple seal of approval, when judiciaries review laws to determine their legislative intent or when they give new interpretations to a piece of legislation, they are engaging in the process of law crafting because they are impressing their own policy preferences onto policy outcomes. The third possible role that judiciaries can undertake is similar to that of a "quality inspector." Courts can be called upon to ensure the effective application of other state policy reforms (such as privatization, or fiscal and pension reform), and in this case, would act as external enforcers of agreements and mediators between contracting parties. When acting as a quality inspector, courts are not primarily concerned with judging the constitutionality of laws passed by governments, but rather with the supervision of activities and day-to-day disputes involving the government that cannot be solved by the two contracting parties alone or the regulatory agency. Finally, a fourth possible role for the judicial branch is that of "society representative." In general, it is difficult for certain, usually lower, classes within society to have a direct impact on the policy-making process. Because judiciaries make certain issues or conflicts more salient than others, they can provide a voice for the marginalized groups and an alternative channel for societal representation.

Given this variety of possible roles for the judiciary in the policy-making process, it is important to be cautious about the road ahead. Fearing the increase of judicial power in the policy-making process, some Latin American governments have either stopped or reversed the advances made by judicial reforms. Countries providing examples of reform backlashes include Ecuador and Venezuela. In these countries, the executive encroached on the workings of the judicial system and interfered with the normal proceedings of separation of powers. The process of judicial reform is far from complete. Its results remain uncertain and its effects on the dynamics of the policy-making process are not yet clear. Although the time of weak, dependent, and irrelevant judiciaries has passed, the ultimate accomplishments of judicial reform will depend on the degree to which Latin American countries can overcome the barriers to change.

Appendix 3A. The Factors of Judicial Reform

(Adapted from ABA/CEELI's Judicial Reform Index country reports):

I. Quality and Education

Factor 1: Judicial Training. Judges are required to have a Bachelor's degree in legal studies and some practical experience, or have specific academic training on pertinent substantive and procedural law and the role of judges in society before they are appointed.

Factor 2: Selection/Appointment Process. Judges are selected and appointed according to impartial and apolitical criteria through the use of standardized exams, professional experience requirements, and performance thresholds.

Factor 3: Continuing Legal Education. Judges are required to continuously take courses (free of charge) in various areas of law to keep them updated with the most recent legislation changes.

II. Judicial Powers

Factor 4: Judicial Review of Legislation. There is a judicial entity that can establish the constitutional adequacy of all other legislation and the decisions are enforced.

Factor 5: Judicial Oversight of Administrative Practice. The judicial branch has the power to supervise administrative acts, forcing the government to accomplish its legal duties.

Factor 6: Judicial Jurisdiction over Civil Liberties. The judicial branch is the sole authority entitled to evaluate cases regarding civil rights and liberties.

Factor 7: System of Appellate Review. There is a system of appellate review which allows judicial decisions to be reconsidered and, whenever appropriate, reversed.

Factor 8: Contempt/Subpoena/Enforcement. The judiciary may exercise its contempt, subpoena, and/or enforcement powers without fear of encroachment and disrespect by other branches of government.

III. Financial Resources

Factor 9: Budgetary Input. The judicial branch collaborates with the legislature and/or the executive to determine its budgetary allocations, and it solely manages how its resources are spent.

Factor 10: Adequacy of Judicial Salaries. Judicial salaries are considered competitive and adequate to attract and retain well-trained judges.

IV. Structural Safeguards

Factor 11: Guaranteed Tenure. A judge's appointment is either for a fixed-term or guaranteed life-long tenure.

Factor 12: Objective Judicial Advancement Criteria. Judges are promoted based on objective criteria and impartial standards.

Factor 13: Removal and Discipline of Judges. Judges can only be removed from the bench via a transparent and impartial trial process for misconduct.

Factor 14: Case Assignment. The process of case assignment is guided by an objective method, such as by lottery.

Factor 15: Judicial Associations. A judicial association exists and it is active in promoting the interests of the members of the judiciary.

V. Accountability & Transparency

Factor 16: Judicial Decisions and Improper Influence. Judges make their decisions according to their examination of the evidence and their understandings of the law and justice, without inappropriate interference from other governmental authorities, private interests, and superior judges.

Factor 17: Code of Ethics. A judicial code of ethics exists and judges are expected to abide by it during their tenure.

Factor 18: Judicial Conduct Complaint Process. An important process exists to record public complaints against judges' conduct.

Factor 19: Public and Media Access to Proceedings. The general public and the media have open access to courtroom proceedings.

Factor 20: Publication of Judicial Decisions. Judicial decisions are published and/or generally available for public examination.

Factor 21: Maintenance of Trial Records. Courtroom proceedings are recorded/transcribed and maintained for open access by the public.

VI. Efficiency

Factor 22: Court Support Staff. Judges have a well-equipped staff to help them perform their job in an efficient manner.

Factor 23: Judicial Positions. The creation of new judicial positions follows objective procedures.

Factor 24: Case Filing and Tracking Systems. Efficient case filing and tracking systems ensure that cases are heard without long delays.

Factor 25: Computers and Office Equipment. A sufficient number of computers and office equipment is available for a more efficient management of caseloads.

Factor 26: Distribution and Indexing of Current Law. Judges constantly receive jurisprudence and updates in legislation.

Notes

1. In this chapter, "judicial system" includes not only the workings of the judicial courts, but also the broader legal and institutional framework related to the administration of justice (that is, lawyers, the police, prosecutors, public defenders, and all civil, penal, and constitutional legislation).

2. See Verner (1984) for possible explanations for the judiciary's historical role of dependence.

3. It is worth noting that the abuse of resources and lack of accountability has raised questions about the very desirability of providing the judiciary with greater levels of independence. Critics claim that the judicial branch cannot be a "black box" without any external oversight.

4. The extremely slow pace of the adjudication process is a perennial complaint in many Latin American countries.

5. That does not mean that the sustainability of reforms would be guaranteed.

6. The 18 countries included are Argentina, Bolivia, Brazil, Chile, Colombia, Costa Rica, the Dominican Republic, Ecuador, El Salvador, Guatemala, Honduras, Mexico, Nicaragua, Panama, Paraguay, Peru, Uruguay, and Venezuela.

7. Table 3.2 does not tell the reader the degree of *success* of the enacted judicial reforms. It only shows whether a country has taken significant steps to change the status quo within each of the possible types of judicial reform.

8. Type I reforms can also be called legal reforms. Because of the predominance of the civil law tradition in Latin America, judicial reforms have often been equated to legal reforms. Here, legal reforms constitute one type of judicial reform.

9. Although it has not been restricted to it. Other areas include commercial and family law.

10. The difficulty has to do with the fact that the concept of institutional strengthening is very particular to each country's history as well as its social, political, and economic context.

11. Although judicial independence has many meanings and dimensions, this chapter follows Keith S. Rosenn's definition of the concept: "the degree to which judges actually decide cases in accordance with their own determinations of the evidence, the law and justice, free from coercion, blandishments, interference or threats of governmental authorities or private citizens" (Rosenn 1987).

12. Although the reasons for these low levels of confidence in the judiciary are beyond the scope of this chapter, some plausible explanations can be identified: lack of accountability, limited access to the judicial system, high levels of corruption, and significant delays in the judicial process.

13. "Success" means the degree to which the objectives of a certain judicial reform program are actually achieved.

14. Building broadly based coalitions in favor of reform is especially important when judges themselves tend to be conservative and opposed to change (Buscaglia and Dakolias 1996).

15. For a good overview of the methodological difficulties of composing a quantitative index, see any of the country reports of ABA/CEELI's Judicial Reform Index available at http://www.abanet.org/ceeli/publications/jri/home.html.

16. Although these statements were elaborated by the ABA/CEELI for Eastern European countries, they can be applied to the Latin American context as well.

17. Traditionally, the role of courts in the policy-making process has been reactive in nature: interpreting laws and establishing their legality given an already existing body of rules and norms only when requested.

References

ABA/CEELI (American Bar Association's Central and East European Law Initiative). 2002. Various Reports on Judicial Reform Index. http://www.abanet.org/ceeli/publications/jri/home.html.

Alston, Lee, Marcus Melo, Bernardo Mueller, and Carlos Pereira. 2005. *Political Institutions, Policymaking Processes and Policy Outcomes in Brazil.* Latin American Research Network Working Paper No. R-509. Washington, DC: Inter-American Development Bank.

Andrews, Josephine T., and Gabriella R. Montinola. 2004. "Veto Players and the Rule of Law in Emerging Democracies." *Comparative Political Studies* 37: 55–87.

Aninat, Cristóbal, John Londregan, Patricio Navia, and Joaquín Vial. 2004. "Political Institutions, Policymaking Processes, and Policy Outcomes in Chile." Latin American Research Network, Research Department, Inter-American Development Bank, Washington, DC.

Araujo, María Caridad, Andrés Mejía Acosta, Aníbal Pérez-Liñán, Sebastián M. Saiegh, and Simón Pachano. 2004. "Political Institutions, Policymaking Processes, and Policy Outcomes in Ecuador." Photocopy. Latin American Research Network, Research Department, Inter-American Development Bank, Washington, DC.

Biebesheimer, Christina, and Carlos Cordovez. 2000. *Justice Beyond our Borders.* Washington, DC: Inter-American Development Bank.

Biebesheimer, Christina, and J. Mark Payne. 2001. "IDB Experience in Justice Reform: Lessons Learned and Elements for Policy Formulation." Sustainable Development Department Technical Papers Series SGC-101, Inter-American Development Bank, Washington, DC.

Blair, Harry, and Gary Hansen. 1994. "Weighing in on the Scales of Justice: Strategic Approaches for Donor-Supported Rule of Law Programs." Assessment Report No. 7, U.S. Agency for International Development, Washington, DC.

Buscaglia, Edgardo, and Maria Dakolias. 1996. "Judicial Reform in Latin American Courts: The Experience in Argentina and Ecuador." Technical Paper No. 350, World Bank, Washington, DC.

Carothers, Thomas. 1998. "The Rule of Law Revival." *Foreign Affairs* 77 (2): 95–106.

CEJA (Centro de Estudios de la Justicia de las Americas). 2004–05. "Report on Judicial Systems in the Americas 2004–2005." http://www.cejamericas .org/reporte/.

Correa Sutil, Jorge. 1999. "Latin America: Good News for the Underprivileged?" In *The Rule of Law and the Underprivileged in Latin America*, ed. Juan Mendez, Guillermo O'Donnell, and Paulo Sérgio Pinheiro. Notre Dame, IN: University of Notre Dame Press.

Dakolias, Maria. 1995. "A Strategy for Judicial Reform: The Experience in Latin America." *Virginia Journal of International Law* 36 (1): 167–231.

———. 1996. "The Judicial Sector in Latin America and the Caribbean: Elements of Reform." World Bank Technical Paper 319, World Bank, Washington, DC.

Domingo, Pilar, and Rachel Sieder, eds. 2001. *Rule of Law in Latin America: The International Promotion of Judicial Reform.* London: Institute of Latin American Studies.

The Economist. 1996–2004. The Economist Intelligence Unit, various countries' reports.

Eyzaguirre, Hugo. 1996. "Institutions and Economic Development: Judicial Reform in Latin America." DPP Strategy and Working Paper No. 103, Inter-American Development Bank (IDB), Washington, DC.

Feld, Lars, and Stefan Voigt. 2003. "Economic Growth and Judicial Independence: Cross Country Evidence Using a New Set of Indicators." *European Journal of Political Economy* 19 (3): 497–527.

Ferejohn, John. 2002. "Judicializing Politics, Politicizing Law." *Law and Contemporary Problems* 65 (3): 41–68. http://www.law.duke.edu/journals/lcp/articles/ lcp65dSummer2002p41.htm.

Finkel, Jodi. 2003. "Initiation versus Implementation: Judicial Reform in Argentina in the 1990s." Paper presented at the American Political Science Association Conference, Philadelphia, PA, September 1.

Gargarella, Roberto. 2003. *La Justicia Frente al Gobierno: Sobre el Caracter Contramayoritario del Poder Judicial.* Barcelona: Ariel.

Gloppen, Siri, Roberto Gargarella, and Elin Skaar, eds. 2004. *Democratization and the Judiciary: The Accountability Functions of Courts in New Democracies.* London: Routledge.

Hammergren, Linn. 1998a. "Code Reform and Law Revision." PN-ACD-022, USAID, Washington, DC. http://www1.worldbank.org/publicsector/legal/Code%20Reform.pdf#search='hammergren%20&%20code%20reform'.

———. 1998b. "Institutional Strengthening and Justice Reform." PN-ACD-020, USAID, Washington, DC. http://www1.worldbank.org/publicsector/legal/Institutional%20Strengthening.pdf#search='Institutional%20Strengthening%20and%20Justice%20Reform'.

———. 2001. "Enhancing Cooperation in Judicial Reforms: Lessons from Latin America." Paper presented at the World Bank Conference "Empowerment, Security, and Opportunity Through Law and Justice," St. Petersburg, Russia, July 8–12.

———. 2002a. "Do Judicial Councils Further Judicial Reform? Lessons from Latin America." Working Paper No. 28, Carnegie Endowment for International Peace, Washington, DC.

———. 2002b. "Fifteen Years of Judicial Reform in Latin America: Where We Are and Why We Haven't Made More Progress." USAID Global Center for Democracy and Governance, Washington, DC. http://www.undp-pogar.org/publications/judiciary/linn2/index.html#intro.

———. 2002c. "¿Hemos Llegado? El Desarrollo de Estrategias Empíricas para la Reforma Judicial." *Revista del CLAD Reforma y Democracia* 23: 41–80.

———. 2003. "Use of Empirical Research in Refocusing Judicial Reforms: Lessons from Five Countries." World Bank, Washington, DC. http://www1.worldbank.org/publicsector/legal/UsesOfER.pdf.

Henderson, Keith, and Violaine Autheman. 2003. "A Model Framework for a State of the Judiciary Report for the Americas: Lessons Learned and Monitoring and Reporting Strategies to Promote the Implementation of the Next Generation Reforms." Paper prepared for the "Third Conference on Justice and Development in Latin America and the Caribbean: Principal Trends of the Last Decade and a View to the Future," Quito, Ecuador, July 24–26. http://www.iadb.org/sds/doc/SGC-Panel_I_EN2.pdf.

Jarquín, Edmundo, and Fernando Carrillo, eds. 1998. *Justice Delayed: Judicial Reform in Latin America.* Washington, DC: Inter-American Development Bank.

Keith, Linda Camp. 2002. "Judicial Independence and Human Rights Protection Around the World." *Judicature* 85(4): 195–200.

Latinobarometer. Various years. "Latinobarometer: Latin American Public Opinion." http://www.latinobarometro.org.

Lehoucq, Fabrice, Francisco Aparicio, Allyson Benton, Benito Nacif, and Gabriel Negretto. 2005. "Political Institutions, Policymaking Processes, and Policy Outcomes in Mexico." Latin American Research Network Working Paper No. R-512, Inter-American Development Bank, Washington, DC.

Méndez, Juan E., Guillermo O'Donnell, Paulo Sérgio Pinheiro, eds. 1999. *The (Un)Rule of Law and the Unprivileged in Latin America.* Notre Dame, IN: University of Notre Dame Press.

Messick, Richard. 1999. "Judicial Reform and Economic Development: A Survey of the Issues." *The World Bank Research Observer* 14 (1): 117–36.

O'Donnell, Guillermo. 1999. "Horizontal Accountability in New Democracies." In *The Self Restraining State: Power and Accountability in New Democracies*, ed. Andreas Schedler, Larry Diamond, and Marc Plattner. Boulder, CO: Lynne Rienner Publishers.

Payne, J. Mark, Daniel Zovatto, Fernando Carrillo Florez, and Andres Allamand Zaval. 2002. *Democracies in Development: Politics and Reform in Latin America*. Washington, DC: Inter-American Development Bank.

Popkin, Margaret. 2001. "Efforts to Enhance Judicial Independence in Latin America: A Comparative Perspective." In *Guidance for Promoting Judicial Independence and Impartiality*, 100–32. Washington, DC: Due Process of Law Foundation and U.S. Agency for International Development, Office for Democracy and Governance. http://www.dplf.org and www.usaid.gov/our_work/democracy_and_governance/publications/pdfs/pnacm007.pdf.

———. 2004. "Fortalecer la Independencia Judicial." In *En busca de una justicia distinta: Experiencias de reforma en América Latina*, ed. Luis Pásara. Lima, Peru: Consorcio Justicia Viva. http://www.bibliojuridica.org/libros/4/1509/12.pdf.

Posner, Richard. 1998. "Creating a Legal Framework for Economic Development." *The World Bank Research Observer* 13 (1): 1–11.

Prillaman, William C. 2000. *The Judiciary and Democratic Decay in Latin America: Declining Confidence in the Rule of Law*. Westport, CT: Praeger.

Rosenn, Keith S. 1987. "The Protection of Judicial Independence in Latin America." *University of Miami Inter-American Law Review* 19 (1): 1–35.

Santiso, Carlos. 2003. "Insulated Economic Policymaking and Democratic Governance: The Paradox of Second Generation Reforms in Argentina and Brazil." SAIS Working Paper Series WP/02/03, Paul H. Nitze School of Advanced International Studies, Johns Hopkins University, Baltimore, MD.

Schedler, Andreas, Larry Diamond, and Marc F. Plattner, eds. 1999. *The Self Restraining State: Power and Accountability in New Democracies*. Boulder, CO: Lynne Rienner Publishers.

Skaar, Elin. 2001. "Judicial Independence and Human Rights Policies in Argentina and Chile." CMI Working Paper 15, Chr. Michelsen Institute, Bergen, Norway.

Shapiro, Martin, and Alec Stone Sweet. 2002. *On Law, Politics, and Judicialization*. New York: Oxford University Press.

Stone Sweet, Alec. 2000. *Governing with Judges: Constitutional Politics in Europe*. New York: Oxford University Press.

Tate, C. Neal. 1992. "Comparative Judicial Review and Public Policy: Concepts and Overview." In *Comparative Judicial Review and Public Policy*, ed. Donald W. Jackson and C. Neal Tate. Westport, CT: Greenwood Press.

Tate, C. Neal, and Torjorn Vallinder, eds. 1995. *The Global Expansion of Judicial Power*. New York: New York University Press.

Tsebelis, George. 2002. *Veto Players: How Political Institutions Work*. Princeton: Princeton University Press.

Ungar, Mark. 2002. *Elusive Reform: Democracy and the Rule of Law in Latin America*. Boulder, CO: Lynne Reinner Publishers.

USAID. 2001. *Informes Nacionales sobre Independencia Judicial.* Reports on judicial independence in 10 Latin America countries prepared as part of the judicial independence study that resulted in the USAID technical publication *Pautas para promover la independencia y la imparcialidad judicial.* Available at http://www.dplf.org/JIT/span/la_jit01_indice.htm.

Vargas Viancos, Juan Enrique. 1996. "Lessons Learned: Introduction of Oral Process in Latin America." In *Lessons Learned,* ed. Madeleine Crohn and William E. Davis. Williamsburg, VA: National Center for State Courts.

———. 1999. "Poder Judicial, Políticas Judiciales y Corrupción." Paper presented at *la Novena Conferencia Mundial Anti-Corrupción,* Durban, South Africa, October 10–15. http://www.cejamericas.org/doc/documentos/cl_poder_jud.pdf.

Verner, Joel. 1984. "The Independence of Supreme Courts in Latin America: A Review of the Literature." *Journal of Latin American Studies* 16: 463–506.

World Bank, Legal and Judicial Reform Practice Group, http://www4.worldbank.org/legal/leglr/.

World Bank. 2002. "Ecuador: Legal and Judicial Sector Assessment." Legal Vice Presidency Unit, Washington, DC. http://www4.worldbank.org/legal/leglr/LJR—Ecuador.pdf#search='ecuador%20legal%20and%20judicial%20sector%20assessment'.

World Economic Forum. 2005. *The Global Competitiveness Report 2004–2005.* New York: Oxford University Press.

4

Public Administration and Public Employment Reform in Latin America

Koldo Echebarría and Juan Carlos Cortázar

THE YEARS SINCE 1990 BROUGHT ABOUT important transformations in the politics, societies, and economies of Latin American countries and, by extension, their state apparatuses. Public sector reform has affected a large number of institutions and policies, producing significant changes in the role of the state and the way it performs its functions. Two major political and economic trends stimulated these changes: the democratization process and the deepening of the market economy. As a result, although the state has narrowed its functions, it has acquired greater political responsibility for the welfare of citizens.

This chapter analyzes how these major trends have affected the public administration, an institution to which the great political and economic theories pay scant attention, but which forms the black box of state operations. Public administration is the aggregate of organizations, people, formal and informal rules, capacities, and practices. Its statutory mission is to convert policies, laws, and the budget into useful services for citizens. In this intermediation process, the public administration is not neutral, and its form and the incentives that it creates have transcendent effects on citizens. The public administration transforms expectations and desires about the role and mode of operation of the state into the reality that citizens experience.

This chapter analyzes the evolution of the public administration amid the transformations in the region. The analysis focuses on empirical variables that describe the circumstances of public employment, which is one of the most important aspects of public administration. The degree to which employment is merit based and stable, its professional capacity, and its consistency with government policies are basic institutional factors for a competent and neutral public administration.

Surprisingly, the transformation of public administration in the region can be explained more as a reflection of other political or fiscal reforms than as the fruit of an independent reform effort. This means that the important pending challenge—the construction of a merit-based administration—is not very different from that proposed in the 1960s. Even so, these reforms have resulted in a less centralized and more complex administration in which a variety of bureaucratic considerations can emerge within a single country. For the future, this creates the need for the public administration reform strategy to be more tolerant of the diversity of structures and organizations that have developed.

The next section describes public administration as the object of reform. The region's record in the last few years is analyzed, taking into account that public administrations can be transformed either by economic and political reforms of which they are not the main target, or by reforms specifically aimed at their transformation. The second section discusses the strategies followed by different governments to reform their public administrations. The third describes the changes in public employment, which are important for understanding the transformations of public administration. Next, a system of indicators is presented that evaluates the most important qualitative aspects of public administration. Based on this information, the main models of public administration that have developed in the region after the reforms are described, and some of their most relevant examples, are identified. The final section presents an overview of the transformations achieved and future challenges.

Public Administration as an Object of Reform Policies

Public administration has been described as the submerged part of the iceberg that forms the core of the state apparatus. This metaphor expresses two attributes of public administration relevant for analyzing its transformation. The first is that the administration is the most voluminous part of the state apparatus, grouping the immense majority of the material and human resources at the service of the state; the second is that, despite its size, public administration has a subordinated and instrumental position within the state, operating under the direction of the government and under the control of the other two branches of the state. This subordination often gives it a secondary role in state reform, being more a subject of transaction in the major political and economic reforms rather than an object of reform itself.

This does not mean that the administration is a pure organizational implement of the government and, therefore, easy to transform. Because of the size of the resources that compose it, the public administration acquires its own institutional substance, which gives it a dynamic that goes beyond the political and economic sphere. Political and economic reforms tend to ignore this dynamic and operate under simple hypotheses that tend to produce undesirable effects in the operation of the administration. For example, applying a political logic that considers public administration subordinate to democratically elected governments, in many countries a large number of public positions are left to government discretion. Given the relative independence of the administrative apparatus, this discretion can simply result in filling posts rather than moving the administration toward the political objectives of the government currently in office. Likewise, based on the logic of fiscal policy, drastic plans to contain wages can be formulated that, if they fail to recognize the negotiating capacity of the unions, can end in conflicts that lead to more costly wage settlements than would be obtained from a view of wage policy as part of employment policy.

The traditional view of administrative reform, which considered the organization and operation of the administration in isolation and projected its transformation without considering its political and economic importance, could also be considered unrealistic. In developing countries, the administration has tended to evolve more as a public resource than as an independent institution that, based on the neutrality and capacity of its officials, serves the rule of law. The political component of the administration means that any transformation has to be based on a transformation of the underlying political model. The same can be said of its fiscal importance, which means that the public administration must be considered a part of budgetary policy, especially in relation to resources and wages. Any reform of the administration that ignores fiscal parameters is condemned to be unviable or unsustainable.

Since 1990, considering the state as a whole, public administrations in Latin America have rarely been the direct object of the most important reforms, which have been dominated by political and economic considerations. The region has undergone a strong democratizing process that has introduced, for the first time in some countries, the basic rules of a plural competitive political system, where opinions are freely expressed and access to power is possible. In this context, it is normal for institutional attention to tend to shift from the executive to the legislative branch and other components indispensable for a functioning democracy. Subnational governments gain political space through democratization and decentralization processes, which also have an impact on the administrative apparatus. Moreover, in this period the region also experienced a radical change in the dominant development paradigm. The Washington Consensus proposed a set of measures aimed at creating a more limited and fiscally disciplined state, which transferred development impetus to market forces. Thus, public administration was displaced from the center of attention, except for its relevance to fiscal policy.

Although administrative reform since 1990 has tended to take a back seat to political and economic reform, public administration has been subject to transformation because the latter reforms have altered its organization and operation. Although many countries have proposed specific administrative reform agendas, the effect has been marginal, with exceptions such as Brazil and Chile, and sometimes has not even counteracted the pernicious effects of other reforms on the effectiveness and capacity of the public administration.

Despite this, the region has not been isolated from the wider theoretical and practical movement toward reform of public administration, which took place in this period in the developed countries. As an initial outcome of restrictive fiscal policies, but gaining independence from them, administrative reform policies under the sign of "new public management" opened the way with their impact on the organization and operation of the state in many Western countries. The central issue has been the introduction of organizational models and management practices that move public administration toward economic as well as administrative rationality. Although the new public management is not transferable to existing models or techniques, the routines of the public administration have been altered in many countries by the effort to improve performance and the satisfaction of the users of public services.

The region has echoed this movement and, with the support of multilateral financial organizations, many countries have introduced models and techniques inspired by the new public management. Although little data are available to evaluate these initiatives, one finding is the diversity of effectiveness in transforming the routines of countries and in achieving higher levels of effectiveness and efficiency. As the data presented below reveal, most of the administrations in the region continue the patrimonial model with low levels of independence and effectiveness, leaving only a few countries or enclaves of rationality and effectiveness. Moreover, it can be argued that the application of management techniques in a context of high politicization and low administrative neutrality is contradictory to the basic requirements of stability and independence, which require the strengthening of the public administration in developing countries.

Strategies of Public Administration Reform in the Region

As already mentioned, public administration is the aggregate of organizations, people, formal and informal roles, capacities, and practices, the statutory mission of which is to convert policies into laws and the budget into useful services for citizens. The rules and routines that cross the entire public administration—such as those related to budgetary and financial management, civil service, procurement, organizational development, and control—generate incentives that guide, constrict, and motivate the action of the organizations and public officials (Barzelay 2001). So public administration reform consists of a set of coherent interventions that attempt to redirect these institutional incentives to increase the efficiency and effectiveness of organizations and officials and their responsibility for the generation of services that are useful to citizens.

This chapter describes two aspects of administrative reform efforts . The first is breadth, or the degree to which the reform processes have attempted to affect, or have achieved an impact on, the various cross-sectional components of the public administration (budget, control, civil service, procurement, organizational development, and so forth). The second aspect is the depth attempted or achieved in modifying these cross-sectional components. The typology shown in figure 4.1 is based on these two aspects.

The typology identifies reform processes that combine varying degrees of comprehensiveness and depth of the proposed or achieved changes. For example, reform processes that are usually identified as exemplary models of new public management—as in Australia, New Zealand, and the United Kingdom—could be classified in or near quadrant IV because they achieved reforms that affected most of the cross-sectional components of the public administration with significant depth.

Three recent reform processes in Latin America allow us to appreciate the internal logic of those processes in relation to the comprehensiveness and depth proposed and effectively achieved. The first was the reform of the public apparatus in Brazil from 1995 to 1998 during the first Cardoso administration, which led to a constitutional amendment supported by a

Figure 4.1 Strategies for Public Administration Reform

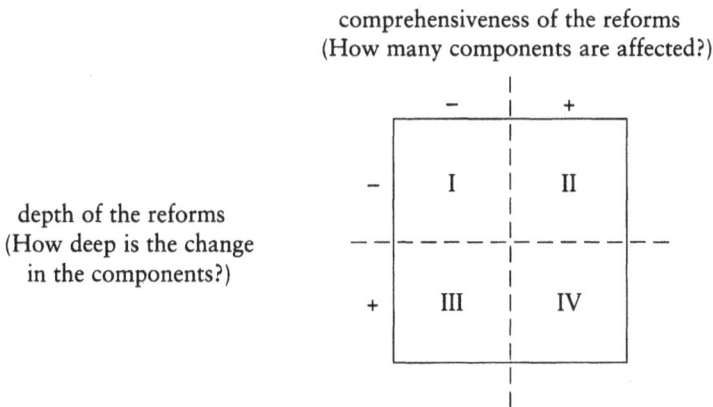

Source: Authors' compilation.

majority in congress. The reforms consisted of the authorization of new forms of organization (such as agencies and quasi-autonomous nongovernmental organizations), new forms of public employment, and increased flexibility in the job security of public officials (Gaetani 2003). These reforms substantially strengthened the merit-based character of the central administration, promoting its professionalization and reducing the weight of the public payroll in the federal budget. After passage of the reforms, the ministry created to implement them—the Ministry of Administration and State Reform—was deactivated, so the process lost some of its impetus, but it was not discontinued or reversed in any way.

In contrast, since 1990 Chile has been implementing an ongoing reform that has gained impetus and scope over time. Initially (1990–94), administrative reform was not an explicit priority on the government agenda, but specific initiatives were developed for unifying conditions in the administration and modernizing the management of some agencies. From 1994 to 1996 the issue moved up the government agenda, generating a set of initiatives aimed at changing the focus of the public administration toward efficiency, effectiveness, and quality of service. An interministerial committee was set up to oversee the reform process, in which the Ministry of Finance took a leading role. Beginning in 1997, a structured reform program was implemented in various elements of the administration, with more comprehensive strategic definition and initiatives in areas of information technology, government purchasing, management redesign, and management by results (Armijo 2002). Among other things, the program established a system of management agreements and a system of evaluation by results, both linked to the budgetary appropriations of every agency. Last, in 2003 a significant reform to public employment was implemented with establishment of the Public Senior Management System for the merit-based selection of senior civil servants, and a new policy on access to jobs and the professional career path.

The reform initiative in Peru between 1995 and 1997 took a different course. Starting from concerns about the fiscal weight of the public sector payroll during the first Fujimori administration (1990–95), the reform effort entered the government agenda in 1995. With shared but conflicting leadership between the Presidency of the Council of Ministers (which emphasized the organizational and management aspects of the reform) and the Ministry of Economy and Finance (which emphasized reduction of the fiscal weight of the payroll), an attempt was made to exploit the opportunity opened in the 1995 Budget Law that delegated legislative powers to the executive for approval of a vast set of reforms. These ranged from organizational restructuring of the ministries to the modernization of personnel management, government purchases, and control systems. In a race against time in 1996, a team of consultants prepared a vast package of legal reform proposals, which finally collided with the insurmountable obstacle of presidential disapproval. This veto was caused by fear of the high political cost of an initiative that would significantly reduce the workforce, and that faced resistance from important sectoral interests in the cabinet itself because several ministers would have lost power in the organizational restructuring. In view of this, the consulting team was disbanded and the reform proposals were sent to congress after the powers delegated to the president had expired, never to be passed (Cortázar Velarde 2002).

Returning to the typology proposed in figure 4.1, the Chilean experience seems to have begun in quadrant I and moved gradually toward quadrant IV, gaining on the way a better position on the government agenda and the necessary political support; thus, this case is an example of an *incremental* reform strategy. In contrast, the opposite path was followed in Peru. After proposing comprehensive, deep reform of the public administration (quadrant IV) only some minor organizational restructuring was achieved (quadrant I). The Brazilian case is situated around the center of figure 4.1. The reforms proposed and executed had a moderately comprehensive scope and intermediate depth (for example, no substantive reform of public employment was proposed or achieved, unlike the success in Chile, and fewer aspects of public administration were attempted than in Peru). Unlike the Chilean outcome, the Brazilian and Peruvian processes provide examples of a *comprehensive* reform strategy because both initiatives were explicitly aimed at achieving global and sweeping changes, although with very different results.

It is not possible or appropriate to recommend which reform strategy—incremental or comprehensive—is more useful or successful. The strategy adopted has to correspond to the government's analysis of the problems, the resources needed, and the desired outcome. It is possible, however, to delve briefly into the internal logic of each of the three reform processes to make some suggestions (which need to be examined in more detail in the future) about which factors can lead to relatively successful reform or total failure.[1]

Table 4.1 describes three dimensions of the reform initiatives in Brazil, Chile, and Peru:

- Predecision processes—How did the reform ideas get onto the agenda and remain there? How were the specific reform proposals generated and selected?
- Decision-making process—Who made the reform decisions and how were they made?
- Implementation of the changes—How were the changes put into practice and the impetus maintained?

Table 4.1 Reform Processes in Peru, Brazil, and Chile

	Predecision process	Decision-making process	Implementation
Brazil (1995–98)	• Reform ideas unexpectedly entered the agenda	• Weak direct commitment of the president: the reforms depended on congress and to a lesser extent on the executive	• Start-up of new organizational models and of management by provisional measures (before legislative passage)
	• High visibility	• Opposition from some cabinet members	• Resistance to change from organizations
	• Promoting entity: new ministry competing with other entities	• Great need for legislative changes (need for constitutional change)	• A new ministry given charge of execution but disappears shortly afterward
	• Team with training and certain experience		
	• Weak linkage with economic policy		
	• Proposals developed rapidly		

(continued)

Table 4.1 Reform Processes in Peru, Brazil and Chile *(continued)*

	Predecision process	Decision-making process	Implementation
Chile (1990–2003)	• Reform ideas gradually entered the agenda • Low visibility • Promoting entity: Interministerial Committee with decisive role played by Finance Ministry • Link with economic policy was solid and stable • Proposals were developed very gradually	• Decisions depended heavily on the executive • Growing need for legal changes: these became necessary toward the end of the process	• Gradual implementation: specific experiences prior to the expansion of the changes
Peru (1995–97)	• Reform ideas unexpectedly entered the agenda • High visibility • Promoting entity: committee of consultants with little experience • Linkage with economic policy was conflictive • Proposals prepared extremely rapidly • Proposals with a marked legal character	• Process depended entirely on the president's decision • Resistance to the reforms in the cabinet • Great need for legislative decision (using the powers delegated to the executive in the Budget Law to amend the Executive Branch Law)	• Implementation of minor and insignificant changes

Sources: Cortázar Velarde 2002; Gaetani 2003; Armijo 2002.

A comparison of the three cases allows some general reflections on the development of public administration reform:

- The priority of reforms on the government agenda is no guarantee of success. Although high priority can attract important political support, it overexposes the reform to debate and general political conflict, as happened in Peru. A less visible position protects reform from political fatigue and helps gradually gather political support, as in Chile. The gradual rise of reform on the Chilean government agenda seems to be a factor behind why it remained there for over a decade (while in the other cases it rapidly disappeared or gradually faded).
- The degree of experience and institutional participation of the technical-political team responsible for reform is key. The serious conflicts of competence in Peru and Brazil interfered with the coherence of the reform process and its permanence on the agenda. Clearly, the process of selecting and designing reform proposals should fall on the executive, although decision making falls fundamentally on the executive or the legislative branch.
- The rate of development of the reform proposals should allow time for lessons to be learned from the initial experiences. One of the virtues of the Chilean process was that, with the incremental progression of the reforms, the team and the government were able to gain experience before wider application and legislative passage. The opposite path, which opts for major legal reform that is later implemented on a relatively wide basis can be successful (Brazil), but can also be exposed to blockage in the decision-making process that virtually extinguishes the effort (Peru).
- The linking of the reform initiative with other important areas on the government agenda can help its success, provided the reform maintains its own identity. The link of public administration reform to economic policy concerns in Chile and Brazil—which did not reduce it to a simple derivation of the fiscal problems—provided the necessary impetus. In contrast, the ambivalent relationship of the reform initiative to fiscal problems in Peru contributed to severe political attrition, imposing on public opinion a view of the reform as basically an effort to cut the workforce in a context of widespread underemployment and unemployment.
- The concentration of reform decision making in the executive is not necessarily an effective option; it failed in the Peruvian case, whereas the Brazilian experience shows that reform in which the decisions mainly devolve to the legislature can be successful. However, postponing the legislative decisions until the process was more mature worked adequately in Chile. Appropriate sharing of the weight of the decisions that the various actors have to make and their sequence is a key element in the design of reform strategies.

These points confirm that the vulnerability and success of the reform process does not depend exclusively on whether the strategy adopted tends to be more comprehensive or more incremental. Success seems to depend greatly on the design and implementation of actions to include reform on the government agenda, the technical preparation of the policy proposals, the engineering of decision making, and implementation. Both incremental and comprehensive change can be successful if these aspects are taken into account and are deployed with relative coherence.

Reform and Its Impact on the Size of Public Administrations

The region has been involved in ongoing fiscal adjustment and discipline since the mid-1980s. What has been the resulting effect on the size of the public administration, especially on public employment? This is difficult to answer because the data on public employment are not sufficiently up to date and fiscal statistics are not always accurate, or coherent between countries. For example, to escape inclusion in employment statistics, part of employment, especially contracted or temporary labor, does not appear or part of the wage bill is not shown. Public administration has also been affected in some countries by decentralization and external hiring, which have not always led to a net reduction in public service employment. The absence of data prevents an analysis of this impact, although decentralization likely has produced a net increase in the number of employees (by reducing economies of scale and increasing exposure to clientelistic practices), and external hiring may have reduced the cost rather than the number of employees, with a downward impact on the pay of such workers.

The data available generally show that these processes reduced public employment, except in Argentina, Bolivia, and Brazil (figure 4.2). According to data compiled by the Inter-American Development Bank in surveys of the countries, public civil employment as a proportion of the total population fell from an average of 5.3 percent in 1995 to 4.1 percent in 1999 with broad dispersion between countries (6.3 percent in Uruguay and 1.8 percent in Nicaragua in 1999).[2] The reduction is real although less dramatic than might be expected given the warnings about decentralization and contracting of services. While some employment reduction processes have been successful and lasting, although limited in scope, such as in Uruguay (see box 4.1), others have been reversed, as in Peru (box 4.2).

The public payroll in the region grew from 7.3 percent of GDP in 1995 to 7.8 percent at the end of the decade,[3] with the only exceptions to the general increase being Brazil, Guatemala, and Nicaragua (figure 4.3). So, the decline in public employment has not been reflected in lower costs, implying that average employee remuneration has increased (although possibly not for external contractors, as already mentioned). Moreover,

Figure 4.2 Total Public Sector Employment, 1995 and 1999

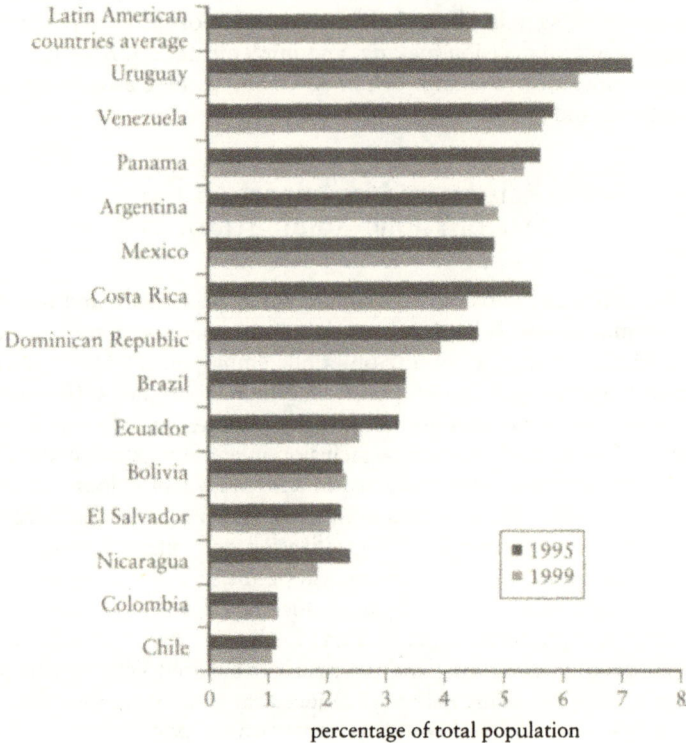

percentage of total population

Source: Authors' compilation based on information from comparative studies of civil service systems in 18 Latin American countries conducted as a part of the IDB's Network on Public Policy Management and Transparency.

Note: Data for Chile, Colombia, and Ecuador are for the level of general government. The average for Latin America and the Caribbean includes data from only those countries with data for level of total public sector.

according to studies based on information from individuals employed in the public sector and outside, public officials receive significantly higher wages than workers with similar characteristics of age, gender, education, and experience in the formal manufacturing sector.[4] Naturally, this information says little about the capacity of the bureaucracy to perform its functions, a point dealt with in the next section.

Box 4.1 Uruguay: A Turning Point in the Size of
the Bureaucracy

Between 1997 and 2000, a selective process of bureaucracy reduction
took place in Uruguay, marking a turning point in the growth dynamic
of the public administration. Annual savings estimated at US$86 million
were generated, of which US$53 million annually were reallocated to the
ministries to improve internal management and working conditions. The
State Reform Program had a significant effect on human resources management (which remained in the central administration) with very important results: (a) the functions of the executing units were restructured,
leading to the elimination of 9,000 jobs and voluntary resignation with
incentives of over 7,000 public servants; (b) approximately 100 highly
specialized new full-time jobs were created with competitive salaries; (c)
in the context of a new training strategy, 1,940 middle and higher managers were requalified; (d) a system for supervision of objective working
conditions was designed and implemented to inspect conditions and offer basic information to all units of the central administration; and (e) a
remuneration information system was designed to improve transparency
and to include all items received by public officials.

The program provided training and technical assistance services to
affected officials; approximately 2,400 workers were retrained and relo-
cated. At the end of the program, targets had been exceeded with assistance for over 3,500 job profiles and business plans. External evaluations
of the program reveal that it was successful in its acceptance by affected
workers and in its effectiveness for rehiring in the labor market: 90 percent of workers who left public service were rehired in the private sector,
almost all in microenterprises.

Source: Authors' compilation based on IDB's previous operations on the issue in
Uruguay.

Evaluation of the Quality
Attributes of Public Administrations

A qualitative approach to evaluating public administrations requires an
examination of the extent to which they are equipped with the institutional attributes necessary for performance of the normative roles assigned
to them in a representative democracy. Ideally, the public administration
should be *responsible* to the democratically elected authorities for the
preparation, management, and introduction of policies that respond to
the political mandate that these authorities represent. At the same time,

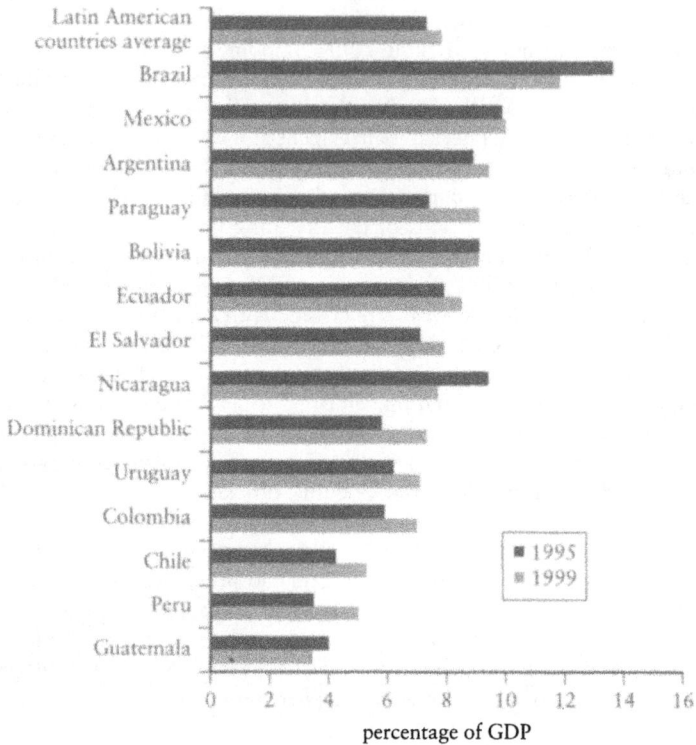

Figure 4.3 Public Sector Payroll, 1995 and 1999

Source: Carlson and Payne 2003.
Note: Data for Chile, Colombia, and Peru are for the level of general
government.

however, administrations have to protect the values and interests of citizens, which are above the political interests of the leaders in power, and defend the neutrality of state action against possible abuses by leaders. To do this, administrations have to have *independence* from the demands of politicians and power groups that go against the interests of citizens or the neutrality of public action. Obviously, these two requirements mean that the public administration should have the necessary *technical capacity* to effectively exercise its role in policy making and policy adoption and in the neutral exercise of public authority.

Box 4.2 Peru: The Ineffective Reduction of the Size of the Public Administration

The new government in Peru in 1990 found the fiscal accounts in a critical situation. Tax collections had fallen from 13 percent to 9.9 percent of GDP in five years, generating a growing public deficit. Because the public payroll represented 26 percent of total current expenditure, its reduction became an important objective. The government's fiscal problems led to the identification of the overstaffing of the public apparatus as a priority issue on the economic agenda.

On the initiative of the economic authorities, in 1991 the government began a process of purchasing the resignations of public employees, followed by a reorganization of public agencies to eliminate jobs. As a result, the volume of public jobs was drastically cut in 1992. An undesired consequence was the transfer to the private sector of a large part of the most qualified professional staff in the public sector.

Employment in the Peruvian Public Sector

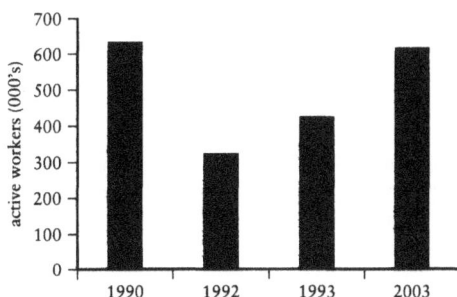

Sources: IDB 2005c; Webb and Fernández Baca 1994.

However, in 1993 the workforce of public agencies began to grow again, through hiring of new personnel under "nonpersonal service contracts." This type of contract was unprecedented in Peruvian labor legislation, and unrelated to any specific legal category (generically based on the Civil Code and the State Contracting Law). Lacking adequate regulation, it escaped the strict limitations on the hiring of public officials. The possibilities that it offered for evading these severe restrictions on contracting and remuneration of public workers facilitated the renewal of the labor force in some of the existing agencies, and the setting up of new decentralized agencies that were created alongside the ministries and line entities. As a result, in the next decade the Peruvian public administration returned to near its 1990 size (see figure).

Source: Authors' compilation.

Figure 4.4 Strategic Consistency Index of Public
Administration

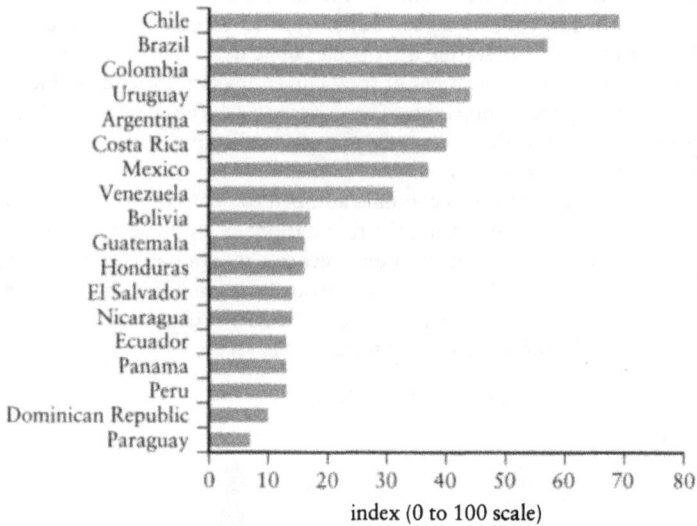

index (0 to 100 scale)

Source: Authors' compilation based on information from comparative
studies of civil service systems in 18 Latin American countries conducted as a
part of the IDB's Network on Public Policy Management and Transparency.

To assess the quality of public administration, this chapter uses the results of a work prepared for the Regional Policy Dialogue on Transparency and Public Management of the Inter-American Development Bank. The study, carried out between 2002 and 2005, evaluated the quality of public employment in 18 Latin American countries under a common framework designed to reflect to what extent countries meet a series of institutional requirements on the quality of employment.[5]

The degree to which public administrations respond to government mandates and priorities is measured by the strategic consistency index (figure 4.4). This index reveals the link between the management processes and practices of the civil service systems, and the strategic priorities of government. On a scale of 100 points, only the administrations of Brazil and Chile achieved indexes over 50, while Argentina, Colombia, Costa Rica, and Uruguay had indexes of about 40 points, and Mexico and Venezuela had just over 30 points. In the other countries—all with indexes lower than 20—there is a persistent disconnect between the civil service systems and the strategic priorities of governments. Under these conditions, leaders have

Figure 4.5 Merit Index

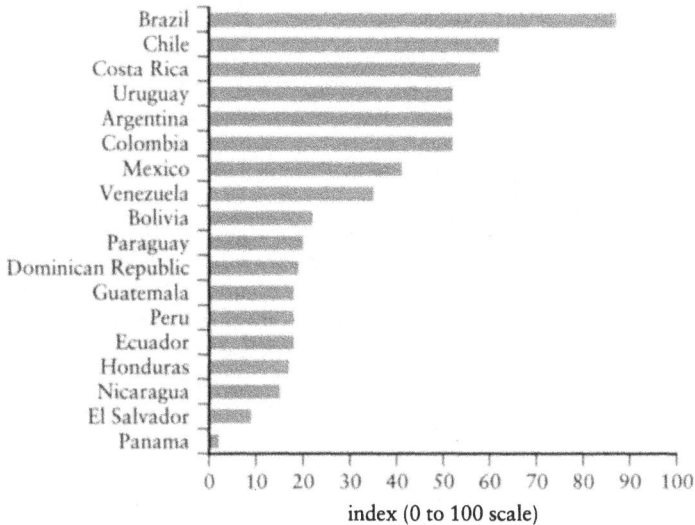

Source: Authors' compilation based on information from comparative studies of civil service systems in 18 Latin American countries conducted as a part of the IDB's Network on Public Policy Management and Transparency.

difficulty designing and adopting policies that respond to their political mandates and citizens' expectations.

The degree of independence of the bureaucracy is measured by the merit index (figure 4.5), which evaluates to what extent effective guarantees of professionalism exist in the civil service, and the degree of effective protection from officials in the face of abuses, politicization, and rent seeking. Three groups of countries can be discerned according to the values of the merit index. Brazil, Chile, and Costa Rica lead the group, with indexes between 55 and 90 (out of 100), reflecting the widespread use of the merit principle in selection, promotion, and discharge decisions, of which Chile and Costa Rica are good examples (boxes 4.3 and 4.4). They are followed by a group of countries with indexes between 30 and 55, including Argentina, Colombia, Mexico, Uruguay, and Venezuela, where merit-based methods coexist with clientelistic or crony traditions. Last, a broad group that comprises Bolivia, Ecuador, Peru, Paraguay, and all the Central American countries, except Costa Rica, has indexes below 25, reflecting strong politicization of entry, discharge, and promotion decisions.

Box 4.3 The Progress of Meritocracy in Chile

The Chilean administration has been one of the pioneers in the region in introducing the techniques of new public management. Under the stimulus of the Ministry of Finance, a management control system was implemented that introduced performance indicators, program and institutional evaluations (including expenditure), a set of management improvement programs linked to performance-based pay, a competitive fund for financing new programs or reformulating or expanding existing programs, and the development of public account reports (*balances de gestión integral*). This initiative is part of the government strategy to grant more managerial independence to public services in exchange for fiscal control over the execution of the programs, which will be supported by the operational start-up of the state financial management information system.

In this context, the modernization of public employment and particularly the creation of a new framework for management of public officials were considered a basic institutional requirement for deepening the strategy of management by results of the Chilean administration. The reforms began with the passage and enactment of the Law on the New Deal on Employment and the Senior Public Management System (Law 19.882 of June 2003). This initiative originated in an agreement signed in December 2001 between the government and the National Association of Fiscal Employees, which was included in January 2003 in the National Agenda for State Reform agreed to by all the democratic forces with parliamentary representation.

The reform focused on four major objectives:

- Setting up the Senior Public Management System, with public preselection and merit-based processes for senior officials (first and second level), retaining appointment by the corresponding political authorities, and establishing a system of performance-based pay incentives. The system is supervised by a Senior Public Management Council appointed by a two-thirds majority of the legislature, which results in multiparty composition.
- Promotion of a new policy for access and development of public administration staff, extending the systems of competitive professionalized access to the third level of the services and creating transparent competitive systems for internal promotion.
- An 8 percent increase in variable remunerations over three years to meet targets based on the management improvement program.
- Creation of the National Civil Service Department in the Ministry of Finance as the new institution for implementing the changes introduced in the law.

Source: Authors' compilation.

Figure 4.6 Functional Capacity Index

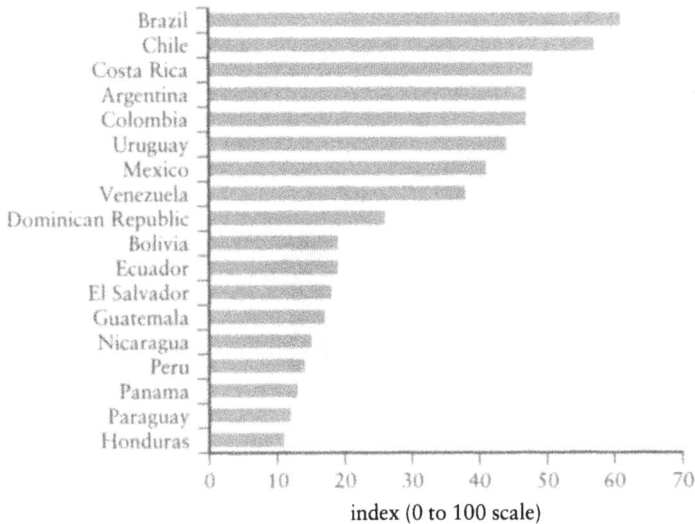

Source: Authors' compilation based on information from comparative studies of civil service systems in 18 Latin American countries conducted as a part of the IDB's Network on Public Policy Management and Transparency.

To be able to perform substantive roles in the design and introduction of public policies, in addition to independence, the public administration requires adequate technical capacity and incentives for effective performance. The functional capacity index (figure 4.6) is a good approximation of this capacity. This index considers variables related to the professional qualifications of civil servants, compensation management, performance management, and the flexibility or adaptability of the work systems, which are described next. Using these indexes, three groups of countries can be distinguished in the region, led by Brazil and Chile with indexes close to 60, showing considerable technical capacity.

They are followed by a group of countries with indexes between 35 and 50, formed by Argentina, Colombia, Costa Rica, Mexico, Uruguay, and Venezuela. The group with indexes between 10 and 25 has the worst results, and consists of Bolivia, the Dominican Republic, Ecuador, El Salvador, Guatemala, Honduras, Nicaragua, Panama, Paraguay, and Peru.

The functional capacity index combines three attributes. The first, the competence index, assesses the effectiveness of guarantees of adequate

Figure 4.7 Functional Capacity Subindexes
(average indexes by group of countries)

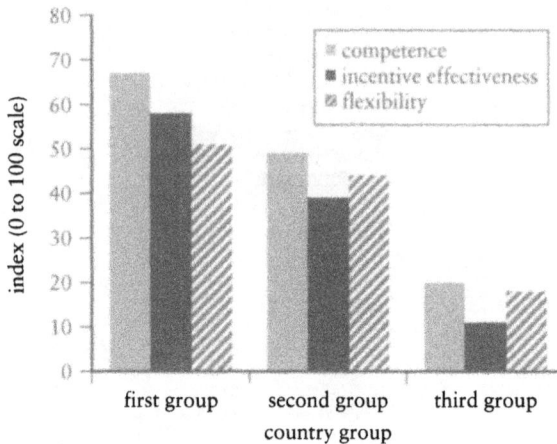

Source: Authors' compilation based on information from comparative
studies of civil service systems in 18 Latin American countries conducted as a
part of the IDB's Network on Public Policy Management and Transparency.
   Note: First group comprises Brazil and Chile; second group comprises
Argentina, Colombia, Costa Rica, Mexico, Uruguay, and Venezuela; third
group comprises Bolivia, the Dominican Republic, Ecuador, El Salvador,
Guatemala, Honduras, Nicaragua, Panama, Paraguay, and Peru.

professional qualifications for public servants. The second, the incentive
effectiveness index, measures the extent to which management policies
and human resources practices stimulate productivity, learning, and quality of service. The management practices considered especially important include compensation management and performance management.
Finally, a third aspect, reflected in the flexibility index, describes the
degree to which civil service policies and practices facilitate adaptation to
change and adoption of innovation. Figure 4.7 shows the trend in these
subindexes for each of the three groups of countries described in the
preceding paragraph.
   The scores of the countries in the first group (Brazil and Chile) reflect
civil service systems capable of positively influencing and creating incentives for the performance of public employees. In these countries, public
servants have high degrees of professional improvement as well as training

---

Box 4.4 Merit and Flexibility in the Costa Rican
Central Government

The human resources management practices in the Costa Rican central
government have incorporated merit and flexibility criteria with more
success than have most other countries of the region.

Merit and Flexibility Indexes: Costa Rica and Regional Average

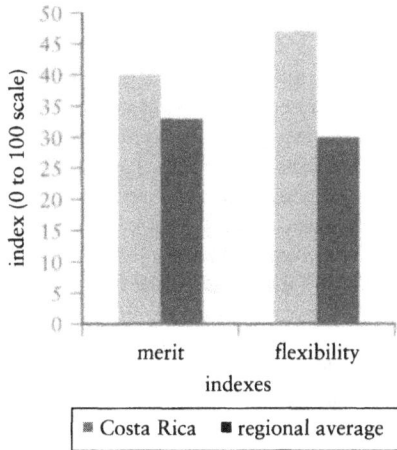

Source: IDB 2005a.

(continued)

---

systems with some degree of strategic content. The score of the incentive
effectiveness index is based on ordered systems of wage management with
relative internal equity and processes to improve wage competitiveness, as
well as evaluation processes that begin to relate individual performance to
group and institutional performance. Work systems are flexible, especially
in Brazil, where horizontal promotion is now possible (as an alternative to
hierarchical careers) and where work relations were made more flexible by
a constitutional amendment (see box 4.5).

The weakest aspect of the functional capacity of countries of the second
group (Argentina, Colombia, Costa Rica, Mexico, Uruguay, and Venezuela)
is the extent to which their civil service systems can create incentives for
public employees through the wage system and performance management.
Although these countries have undergone wage system reorganization, they
still suffer from problems of internal inequity and wage competitiveness
at management levels. In these countries, attempts to apply generalized

---

Box 4.4 Merit and Flexibility in the Costa Rican
Central Government *(continued)*

The Civil Service Statute (enacted in 1953) establishes public competitive selection processes, equality of access to public posts, appointment
based on proven suitability and merit, and administrative career and job
security. In practice there are also elements of flexibility, such as modifi-
able selection criteria, internal or external competitive selection, the possibility of eliminating jobs through restructuring, and the establishment
of differentiated regimes in each organization.

Approximately half the jobs in the central government are covered by
processes that reasonably guarantee the application of merit and professionalism criteria as the bases for income, to avoid arbitrary and politicized
practices. Most positions are open to internal or external competition with
a reasonable number of jobs reserved for personnel of confidence or appointed by political decision. Recruiting is generally open, professional,
and relatively independent at the regulatory level and in practice. One of
the main factors guaranteeing that hiring decisions are merit based is the
relatively broad margin of independence of the General Civil Service Department, the central agency that controls selection processes.

Human resources management is also broadly flexible, as revealed
in the liberal way in which work organization tools can be applied, the
existence of "escape" mechanisms from the rigidity of the wage subsys-
tem by means of wage additions, the possibility of dismissal for manifest
incapacity, the possibility of eliminating jobs for organizational reasons,
and the opportunities that training offers for transitting career paths.

Source: IDB 2005a.

---

performance evaluation systems have run into implementation difficulties.
With respect to promoting the professional competence of public servants,
although these countries require university degrees, there are situations of
overqualification of public servants (Costa Rica) and situations in which
a "degree culture" prevails over competence (Uruguay). Job manuals exist
but they are based on formal criteria (Colombia, Venezuela). Work systems are somewhat less flexible than in the previous group of countries,
with rigid job structures (Uruguay, Venezuela) and excessive rigidity of job
descriptions (Colombia).

Countries in the third group (Bolivia, the Dominican Republic, Ecuador, El Salvador, Guatemala, Honduras, Nicaragua, Panama, Paraguay,
and Peru) have very low scores in all three indexes and reveal serious
weaknesses in the technical capacity of their public administrations. As in
the second group, but with very low scores, their greatest weakness lies

---

Box 4.5 Brazil: Reform and Adaptation of a Classic
Administrative Bureaucracy

Public administration reform in Brazil is exceptional for a number of
reasons:

- No country has embarked on the introduction of management
  models with the same ambition as Brazil during the first administration of President Fernando Henrique Cardoso.
- These reforms strengthened the traditional merit-based nature of
  the central administration, rather than reforming the state apparatus under management schemes.
- Important progress was made in reforming human resources management, despite the enormous political difficulties this created in
  the context of the Brazilian political system.

Two factors were influential in giving reform priority in the first Cardoso
administration: first, the visibility of the enormous cost of the public-
sector wage bill as a result of the constitution of 1988; and second, the
appointment as Minister for State Reform of Luiz Carlos Bresser Pereira,
the intellectual and political architect of the reform, who used his friend-
ship with the president to give the process impetus and political prominence. In the second Cardoso administration, the departure of Bresser
Pereira and the disappearance of the Ministry of State Reform did not
mean the end of the reforming dynamic. On the contrary, the process
benefited from consolidating into a single ministry the areas of management, human resources, budgets, and planning. The deteriorating fiscal
situation forced the reform to concentrate on controlling the wage bill
and strengthening meritocracy in key areas of the executive branch.

As a result, the profile of human resources in the federal administration changed significantly in a few years. The public wage bill declined
from over 50 percent of current expenditure in the federal budget in 1995
to 35 percent in 2001; despite the cut in expenditure, the average wage of
public officials grew 21 percent in this period. Whereas in 1995 only 39
percent of federal officials had a university degree, by 2001 the proportion had risen to 63 percent. The reform initiated in 1995 did not succeed
in creating a totally professional and merit-based bureaucracy in the federal administration but it made important progress in that direction.

Source: Authors' compilation.

---

in their systems of remuneration and performance management. These
countries all show a diversity of pay criteria, lack of information on remuneration, high levels of inequity, and absence of performance evaluation

(despite regulations) or attempts at partial application with a strong bias toward benevolence. Wage competitiveness varies within this group, but even where public sector wages are on average reasonably competitive with private sector wages, some segments with low competitiveness persist due to the dispersion of the wage systems. As measured by the competence and flexibility indexes, these countries have workforces with very low professional skills, profiles and jobs defined without technical studies or simply not defined at all (Peru), training systems without strategic content, and very rigid "occupational systems." However, because of poorly developed employment management systems in some countries, rigidity is not a problem because there are no rules to prevent discretionary decisions (Bolivia, the Dominican Republic).

It is illustrative to compare these qualitative results with the size of the bureaucracy (figure 4.8). To do this, the chapter uses the synthetic civil service index, which incorporates efficiency of investment in the civil service, merit and functional capacity, along with other qualitative indexes. The result reveals that quantity and quality are not necessarily correlated, with countries characterized by both large and small dysfunctional bureaucracies appearing in the index. Only Brazil and Chile have public administrations of a relatively moderate size that are also acceptably functional.

Heterogeneity Inside the Public Administration: Bureaucratic Forms and Prevailing Roles

Despite the preceding general description, bureaucracies in Latin America countries are not similar homogeneous actors. Given the extraordinary heterogeneity of the components of state bureaucracies, public administration is more like a set of complex and independent organizations that do not necessarily respond similarly to the same configurations of independence and capacity. This heterogeneity can provide some keys to understanding the internal dynamic of the state apparatus and the degree to which the various parts of the bureaucracy can play different and even contradictory roles in the same country.

Taking this statement as a starting point, the forms that the bureaucracy can take in each country are now described (figure 4.9). These forms or "types" are far from being exact and are proposed for exclusively descriptive purposes. These types can coexist in the state apparatus, although their degree of presence differs from country to country with specific formations depending on historical context and predominating political practices. Also, each type of bureaucracy tends toward specific roles in the policy-making process, although exceptions can exist that are outside the framework of this analysis.

Administrative or Classic Bureaucracies

Administrative bureaucracies are characterized by low capacity and relatively high independence. They are formed by the apparatus that exercises administrative functions in all the ministries and sectors of the state, and are normally covered by formal rules of merit, which are not applied in practice and which represent frustrated or halfway attempts to develop a classic Weberian bureaucracy. In this configuration, officials have gained their posts on political criteria rather than merit, but they can have stability. They suffer from poor technical competence and it is difficult to use incentives to improve performance. These are the areas most affected by budget cuts (in some countries, such as Peru or Uruguay, entry into these bodies is frozen). Here are situated, with varying degrees of independence

Figure 4.8 Size and Quality of the Public Administration

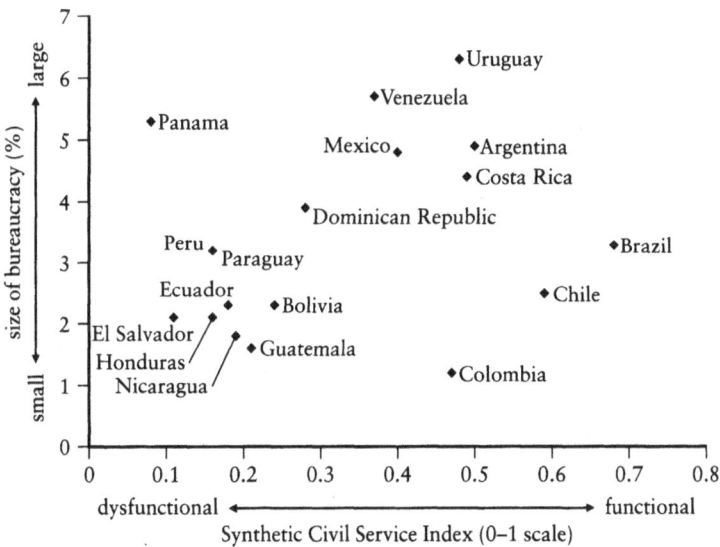

Sources: Carlson and Payne 2003; Longo 2005.

Note: The size of the bureaucracy is defined as the percentage of public employment in the total population. The Synthetic Civil Service Index is a combination of a set of indexes that combine efficiency, merit, structural consistency, functional capacity, and integrative capacity of the civil service.

Figure 4.9 Bureaucratic Configurations

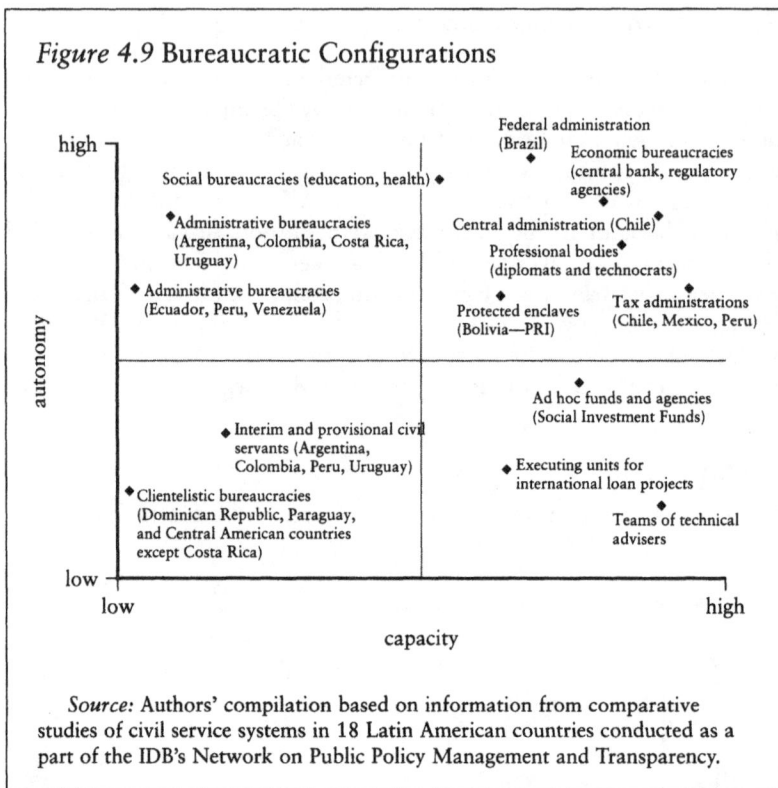

Source: Authors' compilation based on information from comparative studies of civil service systems in 18 Latin American countries conducted as a part of the IDB's Network on Public Policy Management and Transparency.

and capacity, the administrative bureaucracies of Ecuador, Peru, or Venezuela at the lowest level, and Colombia, Costa Rica, and Uruguay at the highest level.

This type of bureaucracy has little capacity to exercise an active role in the decision-making and implementation cycles of public policy. Its limited capacity prevents effective influence in the decision-making phase, which takes place mostly in the political superstructure of the ministries from which it is disconnected. It can play some role in implementation, although with a bias toward formalism and control of bureaucratic procedures rather than management of services. Its potential as a resource for political exchange is limited because of the stability of its members and the gradual decline of its quantitative importance.

Clientelistic Bureaucracies

Clientelistic bureaucracies are characterized by low levels of independence and capacity. This group is formed of officials who temporarily enter government under criteria of confidence or party affiliation. Its composition is influenced by ministerial reshuffling or changes of government, which can result in mass changes of officials. A subset of these bureaucracies occurs when access and permanence are not controlled by the party system but by labor unions or professional associations. The most extreme cases are in the Central American countries (with the exception of Costa Rica [see box 4.6]), Bolivia (except for some meritocratic enclaves), the Dominican Republic, and Paraguay. In Mexico, control of the government apparatus is traditionally divided between the governing party for the cadres (before the recently passed Career Law) and the unions for the remainder of the jobs. It is also possible to find knots of these characteristics in other countries, as in Argentina (transitory appointments), Colombia (provisional appointments), Uruguay (contracted employees), and Peru (nonpersonal services), under transitory or special employment regimes that give the government more flexibility in appointments and discharges.

The role of this configuration is linked to its character as a political resource of the governing party, which exchanges jobs for votes or political support. This bureaucracy is another extension of the political party actor, with some capacity of veto over the professional or merit-based segments of the bureaucracy, with which it can enter into conflict. Its role in policy making or implementation is almost irrelevant, except on the most operative level of simple and routine tasks.

Parallel Bureaucracies

Parallel bureaucracies are formed by "technical" or "project" teams. The unique feature of this type of bureaucracy is its low level of independence and high capacity. It is formed by cadres hired under flexible contractual forms and has expanded to most Latin American countries since the early 1990s, showing trends toward consolidation. Its labor regime is usually governed by regulations on service contracts or other legal forms. It is not part of the permanent structure, although in some countries the cadres are successively renewed. These groups of officials offer expert knowledge in some policy area and do not answer strictly to a political party. In most cases, they have entered the administration to meet specific technical needs and in some cases have developed technical-political skills. They usually form parallel institutions or so-called parallel ministries inside or outside the regular departments. These structures can be more or less successful and can meet with some resistance from the other internal bureaucratic actors.

Their participation in the public policy cycle differs according to the position they occupy. One version consists of teams of technical advisers who play a key role in the design of policy alternatives in proximity to the head of the executive branch. Another version is more focused on guaranteeing execution of policies, projects, or the effective delivery of certain public services. Here can be placed, in various combinations of

---

Box 4.6 Clientelistic Bureaucracies in the Central American Countries

The bureaucracies of the Central American countries, with the exception of Costa Rica, are characterized by the limited independence and low technical capacity typical of clientelistic systems. The merit, strategic consistency, and functional capacity indexes of El Salvador, Guatemala, Honduras, Nicaragua, and Panama are clearly lower than the regional average.

Civil Service Indexes: Central American Countries (without Costa Rica) and Regional Average

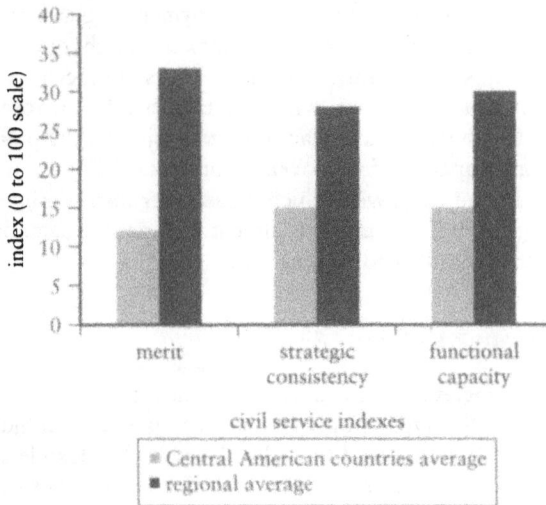

Source: IDB 2005b.   (continued)

---

independence and capacity, the organizations that manage projects with international financing or social funds.

Merit-Based Bureaucracies

Meritocratic bureaucracies are characterized by different combinations of high independence and capacity. They are formed by officials with job stability recruited on merit and assimilated into professional careers with a series of incentives for the professional performance of their work. This group comprises administrative bureaucracies in which merit and capac-

---

Box 4.6 Clientelistic Bureaucracies in the Central American Countries *(continued)*

Entry into public administration and career progress are strongly influenced by political or clientelistic criteria, either because no regulatory framework governs these processes (Nicaragua), or because such regulation is not practiced (Guatemala and Honduras). Open invitations to competitive selection processes are almost unknown and the few efforts to introduce them have been rapidly abandoned (Guatemala). However, some actions and progress toward preventing discrimination in hiring in relation to gender and ethnic origin have been made (El Salvador, Honduras, and Nicaragua). The dismissal of a significant number of public employees in state agencies following changes in political leadership is a common practice, and the widespread absence of wage policies leads to compensation practices that are easy prey to corporate and crony pressures.

The poor development of planning, performance management, and training functions disconnect human resources management from the strategic priorities of the government and public organizations.

The absence or weakness of management performance systems (marked by lack of effective performance evaluation systems) the inefficiency of wage systems, and the weakness of training supply reveal the low technical capacity of public administrations for designing, implementing, and evaluating public policies. Although there have been some efforts to improve job organization or permit dismissals for technical or organizational reasons (Guatemala and Nicaragua), in general the employment systems are still very rigid, which impedes mobility and horizontal transfer.

Source: IDB 2005b.

---

ity have been preserved as in Chile or Brazil (careers and government posts), independent agencies linked to the fiscal or economic bureaucracy (such as central banks, regulatory agencies, or tax administrations such as SUNAT and the Internal Tax Services in Peru and Chile; see box 4.7), and professional careers that have their own established personnel statutes based on merit and capacity (diplomatic careers in various countries, such as Mexico or Brazil; government administrators in Argentina; and some technicians, such as economists, lawyers, and engineers in other countries). The social sector bureaucracies (the workforce of the education and health sectors) fall halfway between the administrative and meritocratic bureaucracies, depending on the country and the sector.

Box 4.7 Creation of Meritocratic Bureaucracies in Tax
Administrations

To tackle the fiscal crisis of the late 1980s, governments began to make
important efforts to increase tax receipts (see chapter 6). At the same time,
they introduced changes into their tax policies, embarking on significant
reform of internal tax collection agencies. Until the 1980s, most of the
collection agencies were line organizations of the ministries of finance,
governed by the general rules of public employment management. In the
late 1990s, as a result of reform efforts, 10 countries (Argentina, Bolivia,
Chile, Colombia, Ecuador, Guatemala, Honduras, Mexico, Peru, and Venezuela) had tax administrations with some type of budgetary, financial, or
administrative independence.

A common component of tax administration reform was to provide
the administrations with regulatory frameworks that allowed them to
manage their human resources and give them some degree of independence from the regular public employment systems. One of the most
radical reforms was implemented in the Peruvian National Tax Administration Superintendency (SUNAT), where officials could even be hired
under the private labor regime. In most cases, changes or special regimes
were included in the general framework of human resources management, which allowed the tax-collecting agencies to hire new personnel
through competitive public processes, institute internal administrative
careers, and significantly improve wage levels. It is important to note
that these changes were not adopted provisionally or temporarily but
were part of a package of substantive reform measures in permanent and
line agencies—such as tax administrations. These measures introduced
administrative frameworks that, although they are different from most
public administrations, have so far enjoyed stability.

The reformed tax administrations succeeded in creating a highly professional workforce, recruited on merit, linked to the strategic objectives
of the organization, with the capacity to participate in the tax policy-
making process and substantially improve the processes of auditing, collection, and service to the taxpayer. The diagnosis of the Peruvian civil
service shows that SUNAT gained higher scores than the rest of the public
administration in the merit and functional capacity indexes, providing a
good example of a merit-based bureaucracy in operation.

Source: Authors' compilation.

These are bureaucracies that give opinions and act. Most of them have
specific responsibilities, such as areas of public policy that require a degree
of training or differential knowledge, that gives them influence over the
area in which they act and converts them into important factors for

maintaining the stability and public-interest orientation of policies. They may form close, specific cultures, with a strong esprit de corps, which produces corporate bias (known as "bureaucratic isolation" in Brazil). This can make them more prone to participate in policy design rather than implementation and to claim independent decision-making spaces, which generates conflict with the political power. They normally form alliances with other state powers and even with external interests, giving them capacity for external negotiation but opening them to capture.

Conclusions

In recent years, public administrations in Latin America have been the subject of numerous transformations. Most of these transformations have been the result of economic and fiscal reform but occasionally they have been the outcome of reform strategies directly focused on public management. As a result, direct public employment has declined, although the cost of the public payroll has not fallen. The success and sustainability of strategies to cut public employment have varied. A normal phenomenon has been the appearance of parallel bureaucracies and jobs with various types of contractual arrangements. Employer activity has also been transferred to subnational governments. All of these circumstances can erode the validity of the available statistics.

Although the reformers seem to have been aware of the need to improve the quality of the performance of public administration, no notable progress has been made, except in some countries (Brazil and Chile) and sectors (fiscal and regulatory bureaucracies). The administrations of the region are still strongly characterized by lack of independence and technical capacity, by their limited ability to create incentives for public workers, and by the mismatch between the available human resources and the need to meet the policy challenges in each country. Ideally, public administration reform aims at reducing the size of the bureaucracy and improving its quality, a combination that has been achieved only by Brazil and Chile. Other countries, such as Mexico and Uruguay, have raised performance but at greater cost. In general, public administration reform in other countries has had a fiscalist bias that has neither produced the expected cuts in expenditure nor improved performance.

The transformations of public administrations in the last two decades have resulted in more diverse bureaucratic forms. Even in a single country, in some policy areas, human resources management has substantially improved while in others it is immersed in the traditional problems of limited independence and low technical capacity. Although this implies partial improvement, it also creates a more complex reform scenario because it leads to different intervention routes for different sectors of the administration. An important implication of this situation is that uniform approaches to reform should be viewed with caution because of the risk of jeopardizing the progress made in some sectors (such as the tax administrations) by an homogenizing zeal. A more selective and contingent approach to reform efforts should be balanced with processes that gradually give coherence to the set by strengthening the cross-sectional functions of human resources management, based on highly professionalized central units with broad technical independence and equipped with management instruments that go far beyond pure personnel administration.

After all these years, the progress of meritocracy is still the great challenge for public administration reform in Latin America. However, in today's open societies, merit-based systems should not be confused with the creation of a cast of officials that, after demonstrating their technical competence, can evade performance and accountability requirements. Likewise, it should not be confused with the creation of parallel bureaucracies under loan from international organizations; these must be regarded as transitory situations subject to institutionalization strategies in the medium term. Countries need competent but flexible administrations capable of responding and adapting to the demands of society. The experience of some countries, like Chile, shows that progress can be made simultaneously in instituting merit-based systems and in the capacity to create incentives, maintaining an efficient and flexible public sector.

Notes

1. The proposed analysis is inspired by Barzelay (2003) and based on various cases of reform.

2. Although not strictly comparable, the calculations of Whitehead (1994) for 1980 indicated that public employment was equivalent to 4.8 percent of the total population of the region.

3. For Chile, Colombia, and Peru data correspond to general government.

4. See Panizza (1999, 2000).

5. To see all the documents related to the Dialogue on Transparency and Public Management, go to http://www.iadb.org/int/drp/esp/Red5/transparenciamain.htm.

References

Armijo, Marianela. 2002. "Modernización Administrativa y de la Gestión Pública en Chile." In *Reforma y Modernización del Estado. Experiencias y desafío*, ed. L. Tomassini and M. Armijo. Santiago, Chile: LOM, Instituto Asuntos Públicos Universidad de Chile.

Barzelay, Michael. 2001. *The New Public Management. Improving Research and Policy Dialogue*. Berkeley, CA: University of California Press/Russell Sage Foundation.

———. 2003. "The Process Dynamics of Public Management Policy-Making." *International Public Management Journal* 6 (3): 251–81.

Carlson, Ingrid, and J. Mark Payne. 2003. "Estudio comparativo de estadísticas de empleo público en 26 países de América Latina y el Caribe." In *Red de gestión y transparencia de la política pública. Servicio civil: temas para diálogo,* ed. Koldo Echebarría. Washington, DC: Regional Policy Dialogue, Inter-American Development Bank.

Cortázar Velarde, Juan Carlos. 2002. "La Reforma de la Administración Pública Peruana (1990–97). Conflicto y estrategias divergentes en la elaboración de políticas de gestión pública." Inter-American Development Bank, Washington, DC.

Gaetani, Francisco. 2003. "Public Management Policy Change in Brazil: 1995–1998." *International Public Management Journal* 6 (3): 327–41.

IDB (Inter-American Development Bank). 2005a. "Regional Policy Dialogue. Institutional Dialogue on Civil Service Systems (Abbreviated Format). Case: Costa Rica." IDB, Washington, DC.

———. 2005b. "Regional Policy Dialogue. Institutional Dialogue on Civil Service Systems (Abbreviated Format). Cases: El Salvador, Guatemala, Honduras, Nicaragua, and Panama." IDB, Washington, DC.

———. 2005c. "Regional Policy Dialogue. Institutional Dialogue on Civil Service Systems (Abbreviated Format) Case: Peru." IDB, Washington, DC.

Longo, Francisco. 2005. "Diagnóstico institucional comparado de sistemas de servicio civil: informe final de síntesis." Paper prepared for the Fifth Meeting of the Public Policy Management and Transparency Dialogue: Civil Service Reform 17–18, Inter-American Development Bank, Washington, DC.

Panizza, Ugo. 1999. "Why Do Lazy People Make More Money? The Strange Case of the Public Sector Wage Premium." Working Paper WP-403, Inter-American Development Bank, Washington, DC.

———. 2000. "The Public Sector Premium and the Gender Gap in Latin America: Evidence from the 1980s and 1990s." Working Paper WP-431, Inter-American Development Bank, Washington, DC.

Webb, R., and Graciela Fernández Baca. 1994. *Statistical Yearbook: Perú in Numbers 1994.* Lima, Peru: Cuánto.

Whitehead, Laurence. 1994. "State Organization in Latin America Since 1930." In *The Cambridge History of Latin America*, Vol. 6, ed. Leslie Bethell, 3–95. Cambridge, UK: Cambridge University Press.

5

Budgetary Institutions

Gabriel Filc and Carlos Scartascini

IN THE MID-1980S, FISCAL CRISIS HIT most Latin American economies. In some countries, external borrowing had multiplied 10 times since the preceding decade and the fiscal deficit in various cases exceeded 10 percent of GDP. The restrictions generated by the debt crisis were combated at first by an inflationary tax,[1] a solution that led to the hyperinflationary crises at the end of the decade. Under these circumstances, the budget was not operating as it should, as a planning tool for public policies. With declining inflation and the founding of the new democracies, budgets took on renewed validity because of the interest of the executive in controlling finances, of the political parties in congress in responding to demands for public expenditure and social services, and of civil society in controlling their representatives. The reopening of international capital markets to Latin American countries by the Brady Plan in 1989 generated additional incentives for good macroeconomic management and thus for improving the budgetary process.[2]

The objectives of budgetary institution reform were closely linked to the underlying impetus for reform. The democratization process in many countries fostered reforms that opened the way for new political actors to participate in the process of appropriation of public resources. These new actors were encouraged by the availability of more information following the increase in the transparency of public accounts. The debt crisis contributed to the promotion of reforms by the executive branch, particularly the finance ministries, in cooperation with international financial organizations, aimed at controlling the public deficit to guarantee the sustainability of public accounts. The process of democratization and control of public finances also generated demands from society for more effective expenditure. The executive branch, mainly through the line ministries, recognized the need to improve the provision of public goods to allay growing discontent. The multilateral organizations joined this process by encouraging expenditure appropriation mechanisms that guaranteed that expenditures were progressive and directed toward lower-income groups.

Since 1985, legal limits have been put on fiscal results, the power relationships in the budget negotiating process have been changed, and the transparency of fiscal information has been improved. This chapter concentrates on analyzing these reforms to budgetary institutions—reforms to the rules and procedures used to prepare, approve, execute, and control budgets. The specific set of budgetary institutions this chapter reviews are those Latin American institutions in the influential works of Alesina and others (1998) and Stein, Talvi, and Grisanti (1999), expanded by other institutions that have recently received government attention.

Budgets and fiscal results also depend on political institutions—institutions that affect negotiating processes and thus the incentives of the actors that participate in the budgetary process. So reforms to electoral systems, party systems, and the operations of congress, or the decentralization process itself, can affect the fiscal results as much or more than actual reform of budgetary institutions.

The following lessons are derived from this chapter:

- The reform processes and the types of reforms undertaken have been determined by policy objectives and the political context in which they took place.
- Budgetary institutions have a great deal of influence on fiscal results.
- The success of reform (and of fiscal restrictions) depends to a large extent on the situation existing when reform is introduced.
- The success of reform depends on the incentives scheme prevailing in the sector, and on the political game in general.
- Budgetary institution reform can have feedback effects on the broader political game. In some cases, this game can strengthen the new institutions and make the results more sustainable; in others it can work against the viability of the reforms.

The Importance of Budgetary Institutions

Budgetary institutions are the set of rules, procedures, and practices used to prepare, approve, and implement budgets. Budgetary institutions thus determine (a) the size of total public expenditure, the fiscal deficit, and public borrowing (and implicitly the sustainability of public sector accounts); and (b) the appropriation of resources by type of expenditure and by groups of beneficiaries.

If budgetary decisions were determined by a social planner capable of internalizing all interests, objectives, and social restrictions, a formal budgetary process would not be necessary. In reality, numerous parties interact during the budgetary process, each with its own incentives and motivations. These interactions affect the size and distribution of state resources, subject to the institutional framework that governs the interactions. This negotiation process generates results that can differ considerably from those a social planner would produce. For example, budgetary decisions can generate inefficient expenditure decisions, unsustainable deficits, or expenditures that follow the political cycle. Budgetary institutions can contribute to reducing these divergences. In particular, they can mitigate the "common pool problem" which results from the fact that each individual wants to extract the maximum he or she can from a common fund, ignoring the effect of this behavior on the total size of the fund, and so on the collective welfare. In the fiscal area, this problem appears as excessive levels of public expenditure, fiscal deficit, and borrowing.[3] Thus, budgetary institutions are important because they affect the rules of the game, either by imposing restrictions on the entire budgetary process, or by distributing the power, responsibilities, and information among the various actors, thus affecting the fiscal results. For example, the problem of common resources can be mitigated if numerical limits are imposed on total expenditure, or if the decision-making power over expenditure is concentrated in actors that have more incentives to defend fiscal discipline. This is behind the idea of granting more power to the finance ministry within the executive, and more power to the executive in relation to the legislative branch, in deciding, total expenditure.[4] Obviously, these arrangements are not sufficient for achieving other reasonable objectives, such as improving the representativeness of the budget. Thus, increasing the participation of lawmakers in the process may be desirable, giving them more freedom to make changes among the expenditure items proposed by the executive.

Reform of Budgetary Institutions in Latin America

Fiscal results do not depend solely on budgetary institutions but also on political institutions, and on the legal and institutional framework in which the state acts. This chapter, however, describes only the reforms to the aspects of budgetary institutions that have been emphasized in the literature (Alesina and others 1998; Stein, Talvi, and Grisanti 1999; Von Hagen 1992; Von Hagen and Harden 1995) because of their impact on the fiscal results; these aspects encompass fiscal rules, procedural rules, and transparency rules.

Among other things, *fiscal rules* introduce ceilings (numerical restrictions) on certain fiscal indicators and limitations on contracting debt, which can help reduce divergences produced by the problem of common resources, and can guide the strategic use of public resources.[5] These restrictions can differ according to the fiscal performance indicator to which they relate, to the legal hierarchy of the rule that establishes them, to their coverage, and so on. For example, to reduce the deficit, laws or rules favoring a balanced budget can be included at the constitutional level.

Procedural rules determine the roles and prerogatives of the actors that participate in the negotiations. For example, more hierarchical rules can concentrate budgetary power in the finance ministry inside the cabinet, and in the executive relative to the legislature.[6]

Transparency rules make information more available and thus enhance the viability of the other rules. For example, if numerical or procedural rules (or both) are introduced to reduce the deficit, increased transparency can prevent practices that distort their effectiveness, such as creative accounting.

Given the vast universe of legal changes that can affect budgetary institutions, this chapter concentrates on that subset that has been most important for fiscal results, according to academic analyses and the experience of economic authorities. For fiscal rules, this chapter considers the existence and hierarchy of numerical rules that restrict total expenditure, the deficit or borrowing, the use of medium-term fiscal frameworks, restrictions on borrowing by subnational governments, and the existence of stabilization funds. The introduction of fiscal responsibility laws takes on particular relevance in these reforms. For procedural rules, the chapter considers the power of the finance ministry over the line ministries in the preparation stage, the power of the executive over the legislature in the approval stage, and the power of the finance ministry through cash management during the execution stage. For transparency rules, the chapter considers to what extent the budget covers the totality of state outlays and the availability of this information, emphasizing the enactment of transparency laws.

The information is based on a set of surveys on budgetary practices and procedures conducted jointly by the Organisation for Economic Co-operation and Development (OECD), the World Bank, and the Inter-American Development Bank (IDB), supplemented by specific questions on the content and timing of reforms implemented since 1990. The responses to the surveys (which reflect the rules but not necessarily the practice in some cases) identify the budgetary restrictions that affect all stages of budget preparation. This information has been compared and supplemented with analysis of the legal frameworks and related documents produced by the World Bank, the IDB, and the International Monetary Fund.

Path of Reform

Since 1990, the budgetary institutions of Latin America have undergone continuing reform. Many countries introduced numerical restrictions, stabilization funds, multiyear frameworks, and restrictions on borrowing by subnational governments. Various countries introduced numerical restrictions in their fiscal responsibility laws.

With respect to procedures, the introduction of integrated financial systems involved an increase in the hierarchy of the power of the executive, mainly through the introduction of the single treasury account. In terms of transparency, the fiscal responsibility laws in some countries included special chapters on the area, while other countries enacted specific laws.

In most countries, the changes have consistently strengthened budgetary institutions and fiscal discipline, but in some cases reforms were reversed, particularly limits on the deficit. In crisis situations, some governments opted to relax the legal guidelines and reduce fiscal requirements required by the existing laws; others directly ignored or evaded compliance with the new rules and procedures.

The fiscal reform process had two clearly distinct moments. In the mid-1990s, a reform boom took place, raising finance ministries in the hierarchy of fiscal decision making, probably as part of the broader process of stabilization and structural reform. The second moment of intense budgetary reform activity occurred in the late 1990s, when most of the fiscal restrictions and transparency rules were introduced. Table 5.1 and figure 5.1 present the composition and trends in fiscal institution reform since 1990. Reforms of procedural rules are concentrated between 1994 and 2000, and reforms of fiscal and transparency rules largely from 1998. Each of the 18 countries in the sample introduced at least one budgetary institution reform in the period. The reforms reveal a high level of dispersion. For example, Argentina adopted twice as many reforms as the next country on the list. With respect to the types of reform, seven countries introduced fiscal responsibility laws, which imposed, among other components, limits on expenditure or borrowing. Four of these countries relaxed these limits in the following years.

Fiscal Rules

As table 5.1 and figure 5.1 show, most of the reforms that introduced fiscal rules took place toward the end of the 1990s and early in the 2000s. In some cases, these reforms were specific, but they were mostly included in fiscal responsibility laws. These laws have been the most innovative component of budgetary institution reform in recent years. They are designed to reduce fiscal deficits and introduce numerical limits, sometimes with medium-term horizons, with adjustable limits based on the economic cycle (to avoid fiscal adjustments that would intensify rather than moderate cycles). These laws approach fiscal problems from a more integrated point of view, including issues of transparency, responsibility, and relations with subnational governments, especially important in the most geographically decentralized countries. Argentina (1999), Brazil (2000), Peru (2000), Ecuador (2002), Panama (2002), Colombia (2003), and Venezuela (2003) all enacted fiscal responsibility laws, with features appropriate to each case.

Table 5.1 Summary of Fiscal Reforms

	1990	1991	1992	1993	1994	1995	1996	1997	1998	1999	2000	2001	2002	2003	2004	2005
Argentina	N, F				U,E[a]					R(N,C,T),S	P,r(c),S,E,F[b]	r(n),S			R(N,S,C)	
Bolivia				S							U					
Brazil									N		R(N,S,T),P					
Chile											R[e](N,C)			e[f],T		
Colombia		f			F[d]	C					N	S		R(N,P,T)		
Costa Rica												U,A				
Ecuador						U				C			R(N,P,C,T)		T	r(n)
El Salvador				U			A									
Guatemala								E[g]			P,N,U					
Honduras														P,U		
Mexico									C				C[h],P,T			
Nicaragua													S,F[i],A			P
Panama									U				R(N),S,T		r(n)	P,U
Paraguay			e[j]											P		p[k]
Peru											R(N,P,C,T)		r(n),C,T			
Dominican Republic					U				F[l]							
Uruguay							U,E[m]								T	
Venezuela									C,U		P			R(N)[n]		

(continued)

Table 5.1 Summary of Fiscal Reforms (*continued*)

Source: Authors' compilation.

Note:

N = numerical rules; C = contracyclical fund; P = multiyear framework; R = fiscal responsibility law; S = subnational govts; U = single account; E = increase in executive power; F = increase in power of finance ministry; T = transparency, and A = principles of transparency. Italic lowercase letters mean that the previously established reforms were reversed or the restrictions weakened. R(X,Y) means that the Fiscal Responsibility Law included restrictions to X and Y.

a. Decrees of need and urgency.

b. Powers of head of cabinet.

c. Constitutional mandates that make public expenditure less flexible.

d. There was a substantial reform of the way the National General Budget was executed. In 1994 Law 179 of 1979 was changed to introduce an Annual Cash Program, replacing the Expenditure Agreements.

e. R here means the establishment of a structural balance rule. A bill was sent to congress in 2005.

f. Law 19.875 (of 2003) makes the Joint Budget Committee of the National Congress permanent and establishes the Budget Advisory Unit to give technical support to parliament for budget analysis.

g. The constitution prohibits congress from increasing the estimated amount of revenue and expenditure established in the budget proposal.

h. Automatic stabilizers were introduced.

i. Some provisions to improve cash management are included in the financial administration law.

j. Congressional powers were increased.

k. Beginning in 2006 a multiyear budget is being used pursuant to a transitory decree. It was used previously but was not a legal rquirement.

l. The Integrated Financial Administration Program has made important changes in the management of the information on revenue, payments, and administration of bank accounts. These changes took place on the basis of an integrated information system that retrieves the previous information and integrates it into the full budget economic cycle.

m. Change in the review of the multiyears.

n. Includes components of the contracyclical fund and of the previously existing multiyear framework.

Figure 5.1 The Path of Reform

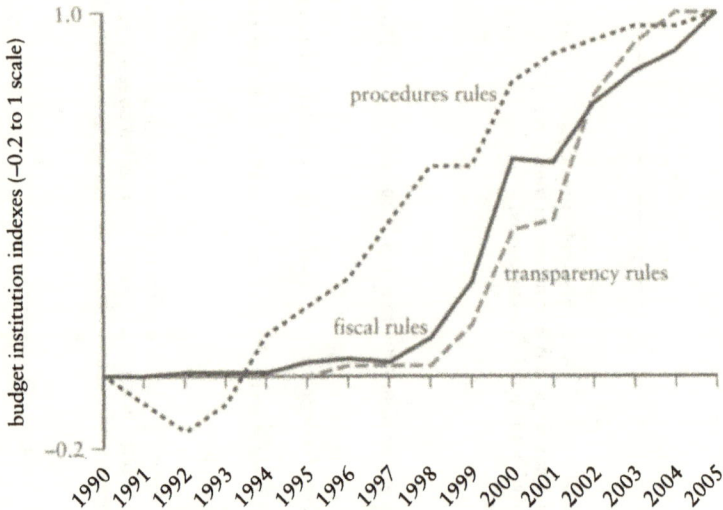

Source: Authors' calculations.
Note: To construct the figure, the reforms were weighted in accordance
with their relevance and direction and were normalized between 0 and 1.
Thus, each curve shows the transition of the institutions from their initial
situation in 1990 to their situation in 2005. The slope measures the number of
reforms and their relative importance.

Numerical restrictions. Mainly as a result of recent reform, most countries now have some numerical restriction on expenditure, deficit, or debt.
Costa Rica, Guatemala, and Nicaragua are the only exceptions. Some of
these restrictions are constitutional, while others are at the level of laws,
as shown in table 5.2. Except in Argentina, the executive has legal powers
to modify or disregard restrictions under certain conditions. The introduction of numerical restrictions has not always had immediate results, and
in many cases the restrictions have been weakened by later reforms as in
Argentina, Ecuador, Panama, and Peru.[7] Chile deserves a separate mention because of its structural balance rule, which is observed although it
does not have the status of law. This rule establishes the commitment to
maintain a 1 percent structural surplus.[8] Chile shows that the political
institutional context in which restrictions are inserted can be more important than the design.

Table 5.2 Numerical Restrictions

Country	Expenditure limit	Deficit limit	Debt limit
Argentina	Law	Law	Law
Bolivia			
Brazil	Law		Law
Chile	Law	Rule	Law
Colombia		Law	Law
Costa Rica			
Dominican Republic	Law		
Ecuador	Law	Law	Law
El Salvador	Law		
Guatemala			
Honduras			Constitution
Mexico	Law	Law	Law
Nicaragua			
Panama		Law	Law
Paraguay		Law	Law
Peru	Law	Law	
Uruguay	Law		Law
Venezuela	Law		Constitution

Source: Authors' compilation.

Note: Seven countries have included additional restrictions at the constitutional level, such as the "golden rule," which establishes that the government can only borrow for investment expenditure and not for financing current expenditure during the economic cycle.

For example, the Brazilian Fiscal Responsiblity Law puts limits on expenditure by object, by government level, and by branch of government. The law also stipulates that Congress must approve global limits for the consolidated federal, state, and municipal debt, proposed by the executive. The law also prohibits the contracting of credit operations in advance of budget revenue in the last year of mandate and prohibits increasing expenditure on employees in the 180 days before the end of the mandate. The Ecuadorian law subjects the budget bill to two fiscal rules: primary expenditure cannot increase by over 3.5 percent considering the implicit deflator of GDP; the deficit resulting from total revenue, less revenue from oil exports and less total expenditure, will be reduced annually by 0.2 percent of GDP until reaching zero. It also applies a policy of permanent reduction of the public debt, moving toward a ratio of the balance of total public debt to GDP of 40 percent.

Multiyear frameworks. Multiyear frameworks offer certain benefits of numerical rules without the costs related to excessive rigidity. These frameworks can add discipline and credibility to the budgetary process because they stipulate medium-term targets and economic expectations on which future budgets are based. However, a multiyear framework's influence on results can be modest or nil if during the passage of the annual budget, lawmakers have a large margin for deviation. The countries for which the approval of a multiyear framework is a legal requirement include Argentina, Brazil, Colombia, Honduras, Paraguay, Peru, Uruguay, and Venezuela.[9] In addition, Chile, Ecuador, Guatemala, Mexico, and Nicaragua have multiyear frameworks but without fixed limits for each of the years. Currently, multiyear frameworks do not effectively restrict the budgetary process. In most countries, the frameworks are changed year after year and annual budgets bear little relation to them.

Stabilization funds. Stabilization funds have only recently been applied in Latin American countries, with the exception of the Chilean copper fund (1985–87) and the coffee fund in Colombia (1940). The region has two types of funds: stabilization funds, and budgetary reserve or tax revenue stabilization funds. The former are funded by export revenue from non-renewable resources with the function of leveling out fluctuations in state revenue and expenditure and establishing a cushion against the eventual exhaustion of the resource. The latter are composed of revenue accumulated during years of budgetary surplus, along with nonrecurring state resources, such as privatizations. The objective of these funds is to have resources to stimulate demand and implement social expenditure policies during recessions.

In addition to the Chilean copper fund and the Colombian coffee fund, other important funds include tax revenue stabilization funds introduced in Argentina in 1999 and in Peru in 2000 (increased in 2003), as stipulated in their fiscal responsibility rules. Colombia added an oil fund in 1995, while oil stabilization funds were set up by Ecuador in 2002, and Mexico and Venezuela in 1998.

Many of the funds have been changed and have not always been used as planned.[10] As mentioned, Ecuador introduced two oil revenue stabilization funds: the Oil Stabilization Fund (FEP) and the Fund for Stabilization, Social and Productive Investment and Public Borrowing Reduction (FEIREP).[11] The FEP was designed to compensate for fluctuations in oil prices by saving when prices were above the budgeted value and permitting withdrawals when prices were lower. However, the savings that should have been accumulated for stabilization were already allocated: (a) 45 percent designated for FEIREP, (b) 35 percent to finance the repair and paving of the Amazon trunk route, (c) 10 percent to finance integrated development projects in four provinces, and (d) 10 percent for equipping and strengthening the national police. In the FEIREP, although 70 percent was set aside to repurchase foreign and domestic public debt, as of August 2005 most had been used to repurchase domestic debt, specifically bonds placed with the Ecuadorian Social Insurance Institute (which did not result in a reduction of the total stock of debt) and for social plans.[12]

Restrictions on subnational governments. With decentralization, subnational finances became important because of their potential impact on macroeconomic stability. Borrowing limits on these governments became more common.[13] The most important include Brazil, Colombia, and Ecuador. In Colombia, restrictions were placed on national government support for subnational governments. Ecuador has limits on borrowing by sectional governments in its fiscal responsibility law. Brazil now has lower borrowing limits, and restrictions on employee pay. Most countries (Costa Rica, the Dominican Republic, Honduras, Nicaragua, Panama, Uruguay, and Venezuela) require that every loan assumed by subnational governments be approved by the national government. In Brazil, these restrictions seem to have effectively controlled subnational government finances, changing the negotiation dynamic of fiscal policy in the country (see box 5.1).

Procedural Rules

Procedural rules regulate relations among the various actors in the budgetary process. In some cases these actors belong to the same branch of government (for example, during preparation), while in others, interactions are between different branches (for example, during approval). Central

---

Box 5.1 Restrictions on Subnational Governments: The Brazilian Fiscal Responsibility Law

The numerical restrictions established in Brazil's fiscal responsibility law include prudential limits on all levels of government.

Limits on employee expenditure are established as a percentage of the liquid current revenue for all levels of government:

- For the federal government, the limit is 50 percent (40.9 percent for the executive branch, 2.5 percent for the legislative branch, 6.0 percent for the judicial branch, 0.6 percent for the public prosecutor).
- For the states, the limit is 60 percent (49 percent for the executive branch, 3 percent for the legislative branch, 6 percent for the judicial branch and 2 percent for the public prosecutor).
- For municipalities, the limit is 60 percent (54 percent for the executive branch and 6 percent for the legislative branch).

Limits on public borrowing approved in the Senate in 2001 require that by 2016 debt may not exceed twice the current revenue of the federal and state governments, and 1.2 times current revenue of municipal governments. To reach these ceilings, governments must reduce at least one-fifteenth of the difference each year.

Source: Authors' compilation based on the Brazilian Fiscal Responsibility Law.

government power over cash management affects both inter- and intra-branch relations.

Fewer changes were made to procedural rules between 1990 and 2005 than to fiscal rules. Reforms were made in interbranch relations mainly after financial management laws were passed, giving the finance ministries tools to exercise this power.[14] Financial administration reforms concentrated on cash management (Treasury management) and debt management, thus leading to change within the executive branch.[15]

Brazil in 1986 was the first Latin American country to establish a single treasury account. In 1995, Argentina established a model in which the Treasury operated as a bank for all government entities, which had to deposit their funds in a single government account. Only in Guatemala and Peru are ministers able to maintain cash accounts other than the Treasury without daily transfer of balances. El Salvador and Nicaragua have single treasury account systems, but with preestablished exceptions. Paraguay introduced a single account system in 2000 after gradually reducing the number of government bank accounts. Bolivia, Ecuador, Honduras, and Uruguay also have single treasury account systems. Mexico does not have such a system, although it does have a consolidated collection account that optimizes use of funds. Table 5.1 presented the main changes in procedural rules, including the introduction of single accounts, together with increased powers of the executive and the finance ministries to impose fiscal discipline.

Interbranch relations. The rules regulating interaction between the legislative and executive branches during the approval stage of the budget are practically unchanged since the return of democracy and are relatively uniform throughout Latin America.

The existing restrictions can be divided into two major groups (see table 5.3): restrictions that prevent the legislative branch from increasing the total amount of expenditure (as in Chile, Colombia, Ecuador, El Salvador, Peru, Uruguay, and Venezuela), and those that prevent changes in the deficit level (Argentina, Costa Rica, Honduras, Mexico, Nicaragua, Panama, and Paraguay).[16] Except in Argentina, where restrictions are based on law, all countries have constitutional limits. In the Dominican Republic, any change must be passed by a two-thirds majority of lawmakers, making change difficult. These procedural regulations do not always prevent lawmakers from creatively changing budgets. In some cases, legislatures identify spurious sources of revenue to justify expenditure increases.[17] In others, spending is reallocated leading to covert increases in expenditure.[18]

Intrabranch relations. In countries with a presidential regime, the president or finance minister generally has the most influence on the budget. In the countries studied, the finance minister most commonly has the last word in budgetary discussions (Colombia, Costa Rica, Ecuador, El Salvador,

Table 5.3 Interbranch Relations: Powers of the Legislative Branch to Make Changes in the Executive Proposal

	Restriction		Form			
	No	Yes	Cannot increase or propose new expenditure	Can reallocate or increase, only if new sources of financing are identified	Can reallocate, increase, and create new expenditure only if new sources of financing are identified	Other
Argentina		X		X		
Bolivia	X					
Brazil		X		X		
Chile		X	X			
Colombia		X	X			
Costa Rica		X		X		
Dominican Republic		X				X
Ecuador		X	X			
El Salvador		X	X			
Guatemala	X					
Honduras		X		X		
Mexico		X			X	
Nicaragua		X			X	
Panama		X		X		
Paraguay		X			X	
Peru		X	X			
Uruguay		X	X			
Venezuela		X	X			

Source: Authors' compilation.

Mexico, Paraguay, and Uruguay; see table 5.4). The president decides in six countries (Argentina, Brazil, Chile, the Dominican Republic, and Nicaragua) while in the rest the final decision lies with the cabinet.

Cash management. The power of the executive branch, specifically the finance ministry, to execute the budget is another mechanism increasing its position in the hierarchy of the budgetary process. The finance ministry can reduce expenditure in downturns to control the deficit; the minister may also execute preferred items, while delaying or underexecuting expenditures introduced into the process by other actors during the preparation and approval stages. Underexecution of the budget is common in many Latin American countries.[19]

Finance ministries have broad powers in Latin America. In Argentina, Brazil, Chile, Costa Rica, the Dominican Republic, El Salvador, Guatemala, Honduras, Nicaragua, Paraguay, Peru, and Venezuela, the budgetary authority approves or determines the expenditure plans of the ministries and executing agencies. Also, as table 5.5 shows, in 11 countries the budgetary authority has powers to hold back funds already allocated to the expenditure units.

Table 5.4 Restrictions on Line Ministries in Negotiations with Finance Ministry, 2005

	Limits on expenditure for line ministries	Finance minister or president has last word in negotiations with cabinet
Argentina	X	X
Bolivia	X	
Brazil	X	X
Chile	X	X
Colombia	X	X
Costa Rica	X	X
Dominican Republic	X	X
Ecuador	X	X
El Salvador	X	X
Guatemala		
Honduras	X	
Mexico	X	X
Nicaragua	X	X
Panama	X	
Paraguay	X	X
Peru		
Uruguay	X	X
Venezuela	X	

Source: Authors' compilation.

Table 5.5 Cash Management, 2005

Country	Central budget authority can withhold allocated funds	Central budget authority can withhold allocated funds where the legal obligations have already been assumed on behalf of the state
Argentina	No	No
Bolivia	No	No
Brazil	Yes	No
Chile	Yes	No
Colombia	Yes[a]	No
Costa Rica	Yes	No
Dominican Republic	Yes	No
Ecuador	No	No
El Salvador	Yes	Yes
Guatemala	No	No
Honduras	Yes	Yes
Mexico	Yes	No
Nicaragua	Yes	No
Panama	Yes[a]	No
Paraguay	No	Yes[a]
Peru	No	No
Uruguay	Yes[a]	Yes[a]
Venezuela	No	Yes[a]

Source: Authors' compilation.
Note: a. with approval of the legislature.

Transparency Rules

The most relevant aspects of the transparency laws relate to publishing fiscal data, including

- data homogenization,
- specification of contingent liabilities,
- publication of the assumptions and statistical methods used to construct the projections,
- publication of the public debt stock (including floating) at all levels of government,
- analysis of the fiscal impact of the rules promoted by the branches of government, and
- regular disclosure of fiscal information by physical and electronic means.

Various Latin American countries have passed laws to make fiscal data more accessible to the public, including Argentina, Brazil, Chile, Colombia, the Dominican Republic, Ecuador, Mexico, Nicaragua, Panama, Peru, and Venezuela. Costa Rica and Nicaragua included publishing principles in their financial administration laws, requiring that the budget be accessible to the public in the interest of transparency. Argentina, Brazil, Colombia, Ecuador, and Peru have included transparency clauses in their fiscal responsibility laws. The formalization of transparency is a recent but rapidly expanding phenomenon, as shown in table 5.1.

Budgetary Institutions and Fiscal Results

As mentioned throughout this chapter, the purpose of reforming budgetary institutions is to affect the fiscal results. For example, the introduction of limits on expenditure or borrowing, or increased powers for certain agents, are intended to control fiscal results by restricting the problem of common resources. Alesina and others (1998) and Stein, Talvi, and Grisanti (1999) found that these rules and restrictions can affect budgetary results in Latin America. The first of these works constructed a budgetary institution index based on surveys of budget directors in 20 countries in Latin America for the 1990–93 period.[20] They found that tighter restrictions—whether based on stricter, more hierarchical, or more transparent rules—result in lower deficit and debt levels.

For this chapter, a budgetary institutions index has been constructed similar to that of Alesina and others (1998), but with new features.[21] The new index combines various elements that affect restrictions, hierarchy, and transparency in the budget into three subindexes. The first subindex, *restrictions,* takes into account fiscal rules, restrictions on borrowing by subnational governments, any requirement for reserve funds, and the presence of a medium-term fiscal framework. The second, *hierarchies,* takes into account the degree of discretion of budget authorities in cash management, restrictions on the line ministries, and restrictions on the changes that the legislative branch can make to the executive's budget proposal. The third, *transparency,* considers how comprehensive the budget document is and whether there are extrabudgetary funds and expenditures. The general index, *index,* is constructed on a weighted average of the subindexes in line with the quantity of subjects they cover. Figure 5.2 presents the relation between this index computed for 2000 and the general government primary balances for 2000–02. As can be seen, there is a positive relationship: where the index has a higher value—which is equivalent to more numerical restrictions, more hierarchical rules, and greater transparency—the fiscal results tend to be more positive.[22]

The same relation can be seen in table 5.6, where each cell shows the average fiscal balance for countries that are above and below the median for each index. For example, considering the values of *index,* the countries with better values have an average surplus of 0.8 percent of GDP, while

Figure 5.2 Budgetary Institutions in 2000 and Fiscal Results, 2000–02

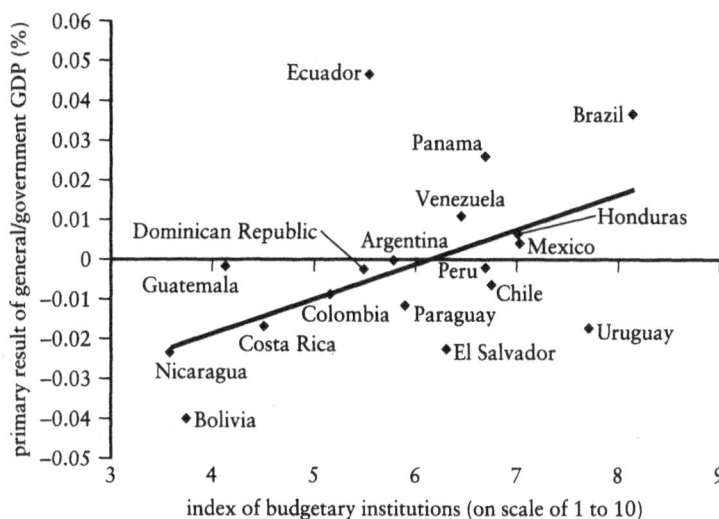

Source: Authors' calculations.

Table 5.6 Average Fiscal Balance
(percent)

Country position on index	Index	Restrictions	Hierarchies	Transparency
Above median	0.8	1.1	0.3	−0.2
Below median	−1.5	−1.8	−0.9	−0.3
Difference	2.3	2.9	1.2	0.1

Source: Authors' calculations.
Note: Each cell indicates average of general government fiscal balance as percentage of GDP in 2000–02.

countries with low values have a 1.5 percent average deficit. This means that, again on average, moving from the group of bad budgetary institutions to the group of good institutions can have a fiscal impact of over 2 percentage points of GDP.

To make the results of the regression analysis comparable to those of Alesina and others (1998), the same variables are used. The dependent variable is the general government primary fiscal balance from 2000 to 2002.[23] The independent control variables are the stock of public debt as a percentage of GDP in 1999 (*debt*), a variable constructed as the product of the change in the terms of trade multiplied by the degree of trade depth of the economy (defined as total exports and imports as a percentage of GDP) (*trade*), and a measure of the economically dependent population, defined as the percentage of the population under 15 and over 65 years old (*dependence*).[24]

The regression analysis gave the expected results, as shown in table 5.7. The results are significant for the compound index (*index*) and for the subindexes of hierarchical rules (*hierarchies*) and restrictions (*restrictions*). The evidence suggests that the countries with more hierarchical budgetary processes accompanied by restrictions on incurring significant deficits or accumulating debt have fiscal results that tend toward surplus. In economic terms, the difference between a country in the first and fourth quartiles is approximately 2.3 percent of GDP, similar to table 5.6.

The regression results of the subindexes are similar, mainly with regard to numerical restrictions and hierarchy rules. In contrast, the transparency subindex is not significant, which suggests that this measure tends to strengthen the value of the others instead of being valid in itself. It could also be the index most affected by differences between the letter of the law and actual practice. Transparency takes the most time to have a real impact on results. While limits on the deficit can have an immediate effect, the impact of transparency is felt over years, when, for example, civil society organizations are able to obtain information, analyze it, and begin to advocate change, which eventually becomes reality.

Reforms in Action

During the period under study, many budgetary institution reforms took place in Latin America. In almost all cases, the reforms included increases in restrictions based on the introduction of numerical rules, increased prominence of finance ministries in the hierarchy of budget discussions, and increased transparency. After over a decade of reform, budgetary institutions continue to be important determinants of fiscal results—the more restrictive budgetary institutions are in terms of numerical limits, and the greater prominence in the procedural hierarchy of actors with more incentives to maintain finances under control, the lower deficits tend to be.

Table 5.7 Regression Analysis
Dependent Variable: Primary Balance of General Government

	(1)	(2)	(3)	(4)	(5)	(6)	(7)
Index	0.010 (0.003)**					0.010 (0.004)**	
Numerical restrictions		0.004 (0.002)*			0.004 (0.002)*		0.004 (0.002)
Hierarchies			0.005 (0.002)**		0.005 (0.002)*		0.006 (0.002)**
Transparency				0.0001 (0.003)	-0.0001 (0.002)		0.001 (0.002)
Trade						-0.200 (0.110)*	-0.190 (0.100)
Debt						-0.000 (0.010)	-0.005 (0.010)
Dependence						-0.000 (0.001)	0.001 (0.001)
R2	0.31	0.18	0.20	0.00	0.41	0.47	0.52
Obs.	19	19	19	19	19	19	19

Source: Authors' calculations.
Note: Regressions with robust variance estimators.
Standard errors in brackets. **indicates significance to 5 percent; *to 10 percent.

However, despite this general evidence, budgetary institutions are part of a wider game that sometimes transcends the budgetary process itself.

The budgetary process has functions additional to deciding the size of public expenditure or its composition. In general, the process consists of many political transactions that permit other policies and reforms to go forward.[25] For example, the executive branch can obtain a vote in favor of a certain public policy by a fraction of lawmakers by promising (or providing) financing for works that they want, which they can then use in their political campaigns. Because these exchanges are usually necessary and common in democracies, where the interests of lawmakers (or ministers, judges, or interest groups) are different from the interests of the executive branch, the impact of budgetary process reform depends greatly on changes to the number of actors and changes to their incentives to participate in the budgetary process and political exchanges. Therefore, an analysis of the impact of budgetary process reform should study the adaptation of the actors to the new rules.

The examples below show how the impact of the rules depends on the broader political game. In general, the rules that work make political transactions more efficient. In contrast, the rules that are intended to improve certain fiscal results but that do not take into account the underlying incentives have a higher probability of being evaded.

A relatively common example in Latin America of regulations that are not observed (at least in spirit) is the rule prohibiting lawmakers from increasing spending established in the executive branch budget proposal unless alternative sources of financing are identified. The spirit of this rule is that lawmakers can increase spending to obtain political credit only if they internalize the political cost of having to increase taxes. However, this rule is violated by lawmakers who increase revenue estimates without including any practical measures, or who reallocate items. For example, as mentioned earlier, in Ecuador, to increase expenditure on certain items, lawmakers reallocated money earmarked to pay debt, thus creating additional financing needs. In Bolivia, congress increased expenditure by identifying increases in the debt or raising the collection estimates of the government as additional sources of revenue. In 1998, congress in Bolivia increased the estimates of gains in efficiency of the tax collection agency and customs by 50 percent to create a cushion to put through additional spending.[26] In fact, there were no gains in efficiency, and the deficit for that year exceeded 4 percent even though the executive branch underexecuted the budget by more than 3 percent. Naturally, this strategy is not followed only by the legislative branch. Again, in Bolivia, the executive's revenue estimate has generally been excessive, far above simple error or uncertainty in the performance of economic variables.[27] Establishing limits on the legislative branch—or alternatively on the executive branch—may have no effect if there is no political and social control over revenue estimates, and if the political exchange is such that budgetary approval can be achieved only by increasing or promising to increase state expenditure.

As a result, reforms to certain budgetary institutions can be ineffective because they are not implemented, or can be evaded. "Parliamentary assistance" (auxilios parlamentarios) in Colombia during the 1990s provides another example of a legitimate mechanism for decentralizing finances that was manipulated by lawmakers for political gain.[28] The budgetary rules in place before the 1991 constitution was passed allowed transfers to be made to lawmakers through parliamentary assistance which lawmakers could appropriate discretionally. Lawmakers could use these funds for projects with high political returns. The constitutional elimination of these predetermined and transparent "systems" gave rise to higher value and less transparent transfers instead of reducing discretion and increasing the efficiency of state expenditure. Thus, rather than being general, the transfers were even more personalized, because they were the result of negotiation between the executive and legislative branches for support of specific laws. As a consequence, the average "assistance" per lawmaker tripled in 1998 compared with the 1968–90 period. Such assistance became an important object of political transaction between the executive and the legislature, given the characteristics of the Colombian political process—a much different result than anticipated.[29] The importance assistance acquired in the political debate prompted President Uribe to include its elimination as an explicit point of his campaign and in the 100 points of his democratic manifesto.[30]

Observance of the fiscal responsibility laws also presents an interesting case study. In theory, fiscal responsibility laws should provide tools for improving a country's fiscal results, but this has not always occurred in practice, at least in the short term. The main objectives of the Fiscal Solvency Law implemented in Argentina in 1999 were to contain public spending, reduce fiscal deficits, and increase fiscal transparency. The main components of the law were an anticyclical fund, fixed numerical rules on the deficit and expenditure, rules on budgetary procedures, and measures to increase transparency.[31] The targets fixed in the law were not met: the 1999 and 2000 deficits exceeded the established limits and the law was amended to permit a new deficit reduction scheme. However, in 2001, the deficit was almost 15 percent higher than the new limit and over six times the limit established for that year in the original law.[32]

The reason for this failure was the attempt to use permanent fiscal rules, which were designed to improve medium- and long-term fiscal performance, for a short-term adjustment in response to the crisis, combined with doubts about the sustainability of the convertibility regime[33] and Argentine fiscal solvency. For example, the use of the anticyclical fund established in the law, which allowed fiscal policy to operate as a stabilizer, changed after the Russian crisis in mid-1998. The escape clauses established in the early versions of the law were eliminated and the fund became a device for accumulating resources diverted from tax receipts with the intention of keeping the country's access to financial markets open.[34]

Consequently, changes in the rules are not a sufficient condition for modifying the results when they come into conflict with the rules of political interaction of the agents involved. However, in some cases, changes in rules can have an impact because they substantially change the political game. In Brazil, the introduction of the Fiscal Responsibility Law improved fiscal results, not so much because of the direct effect of the deficit limits, but because they also changed the power relationships in the political process, especially between the federal and subnational governments.

With the constitutional reform of 1988, the states acquired extensive fiscal autonomy (and borrowing power) and state governors gained great influence in decision-making processes at local and national levels.[35] First, because they had significant control over local resources, they could use them to promote the political possibilities of local candidates to congress, and affect the decisions of federal deputies and senators. Second, because the governors had financial autonomy and no limits on borrowing, they could affect the policies of the federal government by threatening the president's macroeconomic stability targets. The new regime introduced by the Fiscal Responsibility Law changed this situation by authorizing the federal government to fix collection and expenditure targets, to limit expenditure on wages, and to withhold legal transfers if the states defaulted on their debt obligations. The measures limited the power of the state governors in the federal decision-making process because they lost the possibility of using the threat of defaulting on their debt obligations as a negotiating weapon, along with control of certain expenditure items (and over total expenditure), which they had used to influence national lawmakers.[36] In general, the numerical restrictions strengthened the authority of the federal government and the centralization of fiscal decisions.

The budgetary process and fiscal results can be affected not only by reform of budgetary institutions, but also by changes in the rules of the political game. For example, divided legislatures or restricted presidential powers can handicap fiscal management. The political reforms in Paraguay, which increased the transparency of the political process based on open and more transparent rules, intensified fragmentation of the political parties and the legislature, which created difficulties for controlling finances.[37] So, when changes are made to political institutions, the potential effects on fiscal results must be taken into account, and if necessary, compensating reforms to budgetary institutions should be made.

Conclusions

Beginning with the period of democratization, and in the wake of the economic crises, budgetary process reform has been common in Latin America. Changes were made to numerical, procedural, and transparency rules. Enactment of numerical restrictions saw limits placed on expenditure, deficit, and debt; introduction of the notion of multiyear budgetary frameworks; and limits placed on subnational borrowing (and in some cases, on the composition of expenditure). In the area of procedural rules, no substantial changes were made to the relationship between the branches of government. In contrast, a de facto advance was made toward centralizing budgetary decisions with the finance minister. Much work was done on transparency of public accounts during the period, and most countries adopted reforms. Although some enacted specific reforms, in most cases they were included in the fiscal responsibility and financial administration laws.

The persistence of fiscal weaknesses reveals that the viability and success of fiscal rules is not simply a problem of knowing good practices, and that passage of laws is not sufficient for overcoming fiscal problems. First, fiscal restrictions have been incapable of operating under the severe macroeconomic volatility that characterizes the region—regardless of the rules, deficits have overshot their legally established targets. Second, the budgetary institutions are an intrinsic part of the public decision-making process, and as such are a fundamental part of political system transactions. The approval, implementation, and enforcement of reforms depend on the incentives of the actors that interact in the budgetary process. For this reason, restrictions on practices such as "parliamentary assistance" can be ineffective if they do not produce the necessary changes in the political process and the incentives of the actors. Last, it is important to understand that reforms intended to affect only the budgetary dynamic can have an impact on negotiations in other policy areas. For example, an increase in the finance minister's power in budget negotiations or execution can have an immediate effect not only on fiscal results, but also on reform negotiations in other areas. Consequently, when fiscal problems are analyzed, a comprehensive, general equilibrium approach is critical.

In short, budgetary institutions, as part of the framework in which expenditure decisions are made, are important determinants of fiscal results, and reform can help to obtain certain effects, such as deficit reduction. But these institutions are also part of a more complex decision-making process. Therefore, policy recommendations must take into account that

- while these reforms may be necessary, they are not always sufficient to achieve the desired result;
- in some cases, reform can generate conflict between different policy objectives (for example, sustainability versus representativeness);
- while some reforms can produce the desired results, others can be evaded or not have the desired effects if they do not change the prevailing incentive schemes; and
- reforms of the budgetary process can alter the political decision-making process. Their effects can be considerable because the budget is the terrain upon which many public policy decisions are played out.

Notes

1. The inflationary tax is the potential effect when the government finances expenditure through increasing the amount of money available in the economy by printing notes and bills. When the increase in the supply is not met by an increase in money demand, a generalized increase in prices takes place. Hence, holders of cash and cash equivalents suffer a real loss in the purchasing power of their assets.

2. International conditions were also critical for stimulating budgetary reforms because of the changes that took place in various developed countries (for example, the Gramm-Rudman-Hollings Act in the United States, the Treaty of Maastricht in the European Union, and the Fiscal Responsibility Act in New Zealand) and because of new interest in the literature in explaining the events of the 1980s and the differences between countries. The so-called Washington Consensus gave additional momentum to this type of reform, two of its essential components being the search for fiscal discipline and changes in expenditure priorities.

3. The problem of common resources arises from two important characteristics of public budgets: (a) while the benefits of public programs tend to be concentrated, the costs tend to be financed from a fund of common resources; (b) the budget is the result of a collective decision-making process, which involves a variety of agents—lawmakers, expenditure ministers, the finance minister, and so on. Because most of the agents involved in the budgetary process represent geographical or sectoral interests, the combination of these two characteristics of public budgets, under certain institutional arrangements, can generate an overuse of the common resources, resulting in excessive expenditure and deficits.

4. The executive branch, particularly the president and finance minister, has an interest in the sustainability of the public accounts (at least in the short term), given that citizens tend to view them as responsible for macroeconomic management. This interest in sustainability can be seen in excerpts from the speeches of various Latin American presidents, for example, Vicente Fox (Mexico): ". . . And the third point, maintain strict fiscal discipline, applying austerity measures and programs to cutback expenditure in the public sector," in the message to the LVIII Legislature of the Congress of the Union (September 1, 2001). Abel Pacheco (Costa Rica): "We need fiscal reform to clean up public finances once and for all; to create a healthy macroeconomic environment and generate even more confidence among investors and producers" (San José de Costa Rica, May 8, 2002).

5. If they are respected, these results can eliminate some of the weaknesses of the budgetary process. However, they can also generate incentives for "creative accounting," limit the flexibility of policies, and open up the possibility that expenditure and taxes act as stabilizers (at least in the case of balanced-budget rules). Also, the budget rules can be inoperative if there are no mechanisms to enforce them.

6. Collegiate rules tend to spread power in a more equal way. The more hierarchical procedural rules, which concentrate power in actors with more interest in controlling finances, can help maintain the stability of public accounts. Obviously, increasing hierarchy does not necessarily lead to greater representativeness of expenditure, or prevent the executive from using its new powers strategically to obtain immediate political benefits, thus generating electoral cycles in the budget.

7. The Fiscal Responsibility Law in Argentina is analyzed in more detail later in the chapter.

8. This surplus is calculated according to changes in the price of copper and the economic cycle, preventing the restriction from acting pro-cyclically.

9. Uruguay is the only country with a multiyear budget.

10. In Venezuela, see, for example, "La reforma del fondo de estabilización: un aumento de la discrecionalidad del gasto," Venezuela Analítica team. Available at http://www.analitica.com/vam/1999.08/reportajes/02.htm.

11. A detailed analysis can be found in Almeida, Gallardo, and Tomaselli (2005).

12. The funds have not always been used as expected. "Ecuadorian Economy Minister Rafael Correa resigned yesterday after the World Bank did not disburse a $100-million loan as part of its fiscal support package for the country. . . . The World Bank had objected to the fact that the funds from the oil stabilization fund, which should have been destined for debt reduction, were used to finance social programs" (Oxford Analytica 2005).

13. There are previous examples, such as restrictions in Mexico introduced in the 1917 constitution.

14. The financial administration reforms adopted by most Latin American countries are designed to link the budget, treasury, and public credit and accounting subsystems with respect to normative rules, operating capacity, and information processed so that responsibility is centralized in the finance ministries. These rules are intended to develop information systems that facilitate decisions and transparency in the use of resources. Traditionally, extrabudgetary accounts and surplus government treasury accounts were the norm.

15. This reform was conceived as an integral part of the modernization of the state (Asselin 2000). The single account as institutional instrument affects intraexecutive relations insofar as it permits, by strengthening cash controls and budget management, the monitoring and timely control of transactions and expenditure, and extends to all entities a sense of fiscal discipline that previously existed only in the finance ministry.

16. Bolivia is a special case. First, the constitution states that "any bill that involves expenditure for the State shall state, at the proper time, the method of covering them and the form of investment." However, this restriction can be interpreted strictly (there must be genuine funds) or weakly (expenditures can be covered with issue of debt). This divergence of opinion exists in the country itself. Among the most important actors, the executive branch considers this a weak restriction, while the deputies consider it to be strict.

17. For example, in Bolivia in some years lawmakers increased estimates of gains in the efficiency of the regulatory agencies, which were never achieved. For more detail, see Scartascini and Stein (2003).

18. For example, in Ecuador, congress increased expenditure on certain items by reducing provisions for payment of foreign debt. Given that these payments will

have to be made in the future, the reallocation is equivalent to a covert increase in expenditure. In the 2006 budget, 18 sectors benefited from reallocation of US$396.9 million, which was offset by a reduction in the funds destined for payment of public debt from 33.4 percent to 28.8 percent.

19. For example, in Argentina, between 2002 and 2003, underexecution was between 5 percent and 11 percent; in Bolivia (1998–2002) 8 percent on average; in Paraguay (1996–2001) 20 percent on average. The most dramatic example is Brazil where in some years over 30 percent of the budget was underexecuted (see Alston and others 2005).

20. Their work is based partly on the work of Von Hagen (1992), and Von Hagen and Harden (1995), who studied the role of budgetary institutions to explain fiscal performance in the European Union.

21. Various subindexes and compound indexes were constructed based on information garnered from 22 questions on the OECD/World Bank/Inter-American Development Bank survey on budgetary practices and procedures, which valued each question according to the degree of importance of the rules, on a scale of 1 to 10. The compound index was constructed from a weighted average of the three indexes according to the number of subindexes that composed them. The fiscal rules index was constructed from the average of the subindexes of numerical rules, medium-term fiscal frameworks, borrowing restrictions, and reserve funds. The procedural rules index was constructed from the average of the subindexes of restrictions on the legislature, restrictions on the ministries, and on cash management. For a detailed analysis of the construction of the index, see Filc and Scartascini (2005).

22. Filc and Scartascini (2005) find similar results for a sample of developing countries. In contrast, according to the authors, the results are not significant for the sample of OECD countries.

23. The *index* variable is lagged (measured to 2000) with respect to the dependent variable (2000–02). The same results were obtained when the results of the balance of the central government were used (*defcen*) Source: World Development Indicators Database, World Bank.

24. Alternatively, interest payments on the public debt as a percentage of GDP (*debtserv*) were also used. Sources for these data are World Economic Outlook Database (IMF 2004) and World Development Indicators Database (World Bank).

25. For this reason, a broad set of changes can affect the budgetary process. For example, political reform such as election reform, reforms to the party system, reforms to the workings of congress, decentralization processes, and so on, can affect the fiscal results just as much or more than specific budgetary reform, such as the passage of a comprehensive financial administration law.

26. See Scartascini and Stein (2003). Araujo (1998) makes similar observations for Ecuador where, after the 1994 constitutional reform eliminated congressional power to change budgetary appropriations, the lawmakers found other ways to make special discretionary transfers outside the budgetary appropriations.

27. Naturally, overestimates are not the sole responsibility of the legislative branch. The executive branch also makes overestimates of collections, which creates a wider ambit of negotiation for it than public finances. In Bolivia, executive overestimates have been even larger than those made by congress. For example, in certain years, gains in efficiency were estimated at nearly 20 percent (while the real gains have been traditionally around 3 percent).

28. The analysis of these cases is based on the work of Hommes (1996), Vargas (1999), and Echeverri, Fergusson, and Querubin (2004). For a complete analysis of the decision-making process in Colombia, which explains the negotiations between the executive and legislative branches, see Cárdenas, Junguito, and Pachón (2004).

29. "This episode of Colombian budgetary history is illustrative because the abolition of a budgetary institution, considered undesirable at a given moment, multiplied

its value by eight, made it illegal and forced it under the table, without accountability or assignment of responsibilities" Echeverri, Fergusson, and Querubin (2004, 23).

30. President Uribe in his *Manifiesto Democrático* (2002, 7): "That there are public hearings for regional claims but not *"parliamentary assistance"* that corrupts politics. If we eliminate them, with every $10 million saved, we can finance a small enterprise and create two jobs."

31. See Gadano (2003). The law was supported not only by the executive and the legislators from the governing party in congress (*Partido Justicialista*) but also by private organizations because of the provisions to increase transparency of public accounts. Also, because it was in the conceptual scheme of the second-generation reforms promoted by the Washington Consensus, it was welcomed by the international financial institutions and the investment funds.

32. Likewise, the other provisions of the law were not observed. Debts for expenditures not recorded continued to be paid below the line. Initiatives related to reform of the state (program agreements and the Program to Evaluate the Quality of Expenditure) lacked concrete results. Last, the provisions to increase transparency, although they promoted greater dissemination of fiscal information, have not been fully implemented. The financial and employment data of the human resources system, the list of retirement and pension beneficiaries, and the state of compliance with the pension obligations of companies and persons have not been made public in due form and time. See Gadano (2003).

33. This exchange rate regime set Arg$1 equal to US$1. It required having enough reserves to match the monetary base.

34. The rules enacted in most Latin American countries are tougher than those enacted in developed countries. This severity is intended to produce macroeconomic credibility by legislation.

35. The state governors played a decisive role in the transition to democracy and in the reform of the constitution, which granted them fiscal and taxation powers and provision of certain services. This independence led to an increase in borrowing by the states, which eventually put the federal government on the spot when some governors declared a moratorium on their debt payments in 1998.

36. Other measures that worked in the same direction were the privatization of public companies and of banks operated by the states.

37. From a history of balanced budgets until the 1990s, the country moved to a growing deficit in the early part of the decade, exceeding 4 percent of GDP in 2000. For a detailed analysis of the Paraguayan case, see Molinas and Perez Liñan (2005).

References

Alesina, Alberto, Ricardo Hausmann, Rudolf Hommes, and Ernesto Stein. 1998. "Budget Institutions and Fiscal Performance in Latin America." Research Department Working Paper WP-394, Inter-American Development Bank, Washington, DC.

Almeida, M. Dolores, Verónica Gallardo, and Andrés Tomaselli. 2005. "Gobernabilidad Fiscal en Ecuador." GTZ (German Agency for Technical Cooperation) and ECLAC (UN Economic Commission for Latin America and the Caribbean), Quito, Ecuador.

Alston, Lee, Marcus Melo, Bernardo Mueller, and Carlos Pereira. 2005. "Who Decides on Public Expenditures? A Political Economy Analysis of the Budget Process: The Case of Brazil." Economic and Social Studies Series Working Paper RE1-05-006, Inter-American Development Bank, Washington, DC.

Araujo, María Caridad. 1998. "Gobernabilidad durante la crisis y políticas de ajuste." CORDES-Gobernance Project, Quito, Ecuador.

Asselin, Lynnette M. 2000. "De la política a la práctica: reformas a los sistemas de administración financiera del sector público." CEPAL – SERIE Seminarios y conferencias No. 3. 191, La política fiscal en América Latina. Santiago, Chile.

Cardenas, Mauricio, Roberto Junguito, and Mónica Pachon. 2004. "Political Institutions and Policy Outcomes in Colombia: The Effects of the 1991 Constitution." Latin American Research Network Working Paper R-508, Inter-American Development Bank, Washington, DC.

Echeverri, Juan C., Leopoldo Fergusson, and Pablo Querubin. 2004. "La Batalla Política por el Presupuesto de la Nación: Inflexibilidades o Supervivencia Fiscal." Documento CEDE 2004-01, Universidad de los Andes, Bogotá, Colombia.

Filc, Gabriel, and Carlos Scartascini. 2005. "Budget Institutions and Fiscal Outcomes: Ten Years of Inquiry on Fiscal Matters at the Research Department of the Inter-American Development Bank." *International Journal of Public Budget* 59 (November–December): 81–138.

Gadano, Nicolas. 2003. "Rompiendo las reglas: Argentina y la Ley de Responsabilidad Fiscal." *Desarrollo Económico* 43 (179): 231–63.

Hommes, R. 1996. "Evolution and Rationality of Budget Institutions in Colombia." Research Department Working Paper No. 317, Inter-American Development Bank, Washington, DC.

IMF (International Monetary Fund. 2004). World Economic Outlook Database. Available at http://www.imf.org/external/pubs/ft/weo/2006/01/data/index.htm.

Molinas, José, and Aníbal Perez Liñan. 2005. "Who Decides on Public Expenditures? A Political Economy Analysis of the Budget Process in Paraguay." Economic and Social Studies Series Working Paper RE1-05-008, Inter-American Development Bank, Washington, DC.

Oxford Analytica. 2005. "Latin America Daily Brief Executive Summaries," August 5, 2005.

Scartascini, Carlos, and Ernesto Stein. 2003. "The Bolivian Budget: A Year Long Bargaining Process." Inter-American Development Bank, Washington, DC.

Stein, Ernesto, Ernesto Talvi, and Alejandro Grisanti. 1999. "Institutional Arrangements and Fiscal Performance: The Latin American Experience." In *Fiscal Institutions and Fiscal Performance,* ed. James Poterba and Jurgen von Hagen. Chicago: University of Chicago Press.

Uribe, Álvaro. 2002. "Hacia un Estado Comunitario. Manifiesto Democrático. Los 100 puntos de Uribe." Presidencia de la República, Bogotá, Colombia.

Vargas, J. E. 1999. "Las Relaciones entre el Ejecutivo y el Legislativo." In *Hacia el Rediseño del Estado,* ed. M. Gandourand L. B. Mejía. Bogotá, Colombia: Tercer Mundo/DNP.

Von Hagen, Jürgen. 1992. "Budgeting Procedures and Fiscal Performance in the European Communities." Economic Paper No. 96, Commission of the European Communities, Brussels, Belgium.

Von Hagen, Jürgen, and Ian Harden. 1995. "Budget Processes and Commitment to Fiscal Discipline." *European Economic Review* 39: 771–79.

World Bank. Various years. World Development Indicators Database. http://web.worldbank.org/WBSITE/EXTERNAL/DATASTATISTICS/0,,contentMDK:20398986~pagePK:64133150~piPK:64133175~theSitePK:239419,00.html.

6

Trends and Outcomes of Tax Reform

Eduardo Lora

TAXATION POLICY HAS BEEN AN ACTIVE AREA OF REFORM since the late 1980s. After several years of declining tax revenues caused by low growth, high inflation, and ineffective collection efforts, many countries began overhauling their tax systems, modernizing and streamlining tax codes, and giving their tax administration offices latitude and resources to perform their tasks. A quick glance at the results of these reforms, however, is hardly encouraging: after all of these efforts, tax revenues (without social security) barely reached an average of 15.3 percent of GDP in Latin America as a whole in the early years of the 2000s, whereas in the second half of the 1980s the figure was 14.4 percent, and the average in developed countries is about 30.0 percent.

Of all the countries in the region, only Argentina, Bolivia, Brazil, Colombia, and the Dominican Republic have succeeded in raising tax collections by more than three percentage points of GDP. Most countries have managed only modest increases and six countries have had decreases. Such a superficial evaluation turns out to be a mistake, however: this apparent stagnation in taxes hides profound changes countries have had to make in their tax regimes in response to globalization.

Globalization has reduced taxation capacity through several channels: it has prompted countries to cut import tariffs and other trade taxes; led to more moderate tax rates on businesses; and eroded the taxation potential of personal capital income. This all results from the growing international mobility of goods, investments, and financial capital. Greater participation of the private sector in sectors previously reserved for state-owned enterprises, such as oil, mining, and public utilities, has reduced the monopolistic rents partly accruing as tax revenues to the governments in some countries.

Under the pressures of globalization and privatization, governments have had to introduce reforms aimed at recovering or raising tax collections to maintain fiscal and macroeconomic equilibrium. The value added tax (VAT) has been the number one tax on reform agendas. As of 2003, this tax generated revenues that on average represented 5.2 percent of GDP, which is over a third of total tax revenues. In spite of the greater mobility of tax bases, taxes on the incomes of businesses and individuals have risen slightly (from 3.7 percent of GDP in 1990 to 4.2 percent in 2003), although they are still very low compared with the average of the developed countries where they are 12 percent of GDP.

The quality of the overall tax system improved substantially, especially until the mid-1990s. However, progress has stalled, and a new crop of highly distortionary taxes, especially the financial transactions tax now in place in seven countries, has been introduced to meet the need for higher tax revenues.

This chapter offers an overview of the main trends in tax reform in Latin America since the late 1980s, starting with a discussion of their main objectives, followed by a brief synthesis of the major changes to the tax codes and tax administration systems, and an assessment of the main results in areas such as collection, neutrality, progressivity, and redistributive capacity. The chapter concludes with a tentative list of the challenges for the coming years. Social security taxes and contributions are not discussed here; that is the topic of chapter 11.[1]

The Objectives of Tax Reform

The major thrust of tax reform since the late 1980s has been to increase tax revenues without incurring high costs to the government.[2] Tax reform in earlier decades was also geared toward boosting tax revenues, but lower priority was accorded the constraints on tax administration, while other goals, such as progressivity, received more attention (Goode 1993). The imperative to increase revenues since the late 1980s was a function of two major conditions: First, periodic bouts of high inflation in several countries made it advisable to restore fiscal balance and avoid monetary funding of fiscal deficits (for this purpose, several countries granted their central banks more independence). Second, import tariffs (and, in some cases, export taxes) ceased to be an important source of fiscal revenue as all countries adopted policies to liberalize international trade. More generally, the strategy of international integration limited opportunities to tax cross-border movement of physical assets, financial resources, and proceeds from all mobile forms of capital, including human capital. Given that tax policy was largely driven by price stabilization and international trade liberalization, it is hardly surprising that the objectives of tax policy have become more modest.

Clearly, raising more revenue (on a tax base limited by globalization) has not been the only goal driving tax reform. Consistent with international trends in the tax arena (Goode 1993; Harberger 1990), reforms proposed by governments in Latin America since the late 1980s have been geared toward improving tax neutrality and horizontal equity by reducing the different treatment of sectors or revenue sources, and by limiting tax incentives and exemptions. Measures aimed at opening economies to international trade and trends in globalization have reinforced the need for tax structures that will not distort investment and production decisions. However, in practice, this objective has proven to be elusive as more independent, fragmented, and representative legislative bodies (see chapter 2) have become increasingly susceptible to pressure from interest groups, and more responsive to the diversity of their constituencies, which has led to exemptions and special treatments that run counter to the objective of neutrality.[3]

In general, neutrality is consistent with the objective of facilitating tax administration (and therefore reducing the unit costs of collection). Nevertheless, the opposite is seldom the case. In fact, various reforms promoted by tax managers to facilitate collections have frequently come into conflict with the goal of neutrality. The most significant recent instance is the taxing of banking transactions (which results in a cascading tax that disproportionately affects activities that are the least vertically integrated and have low value added per transaction). The same holds for more traditional selective excise taxes on certain consumer goods, such as tobacco, alcoholic beverages, and fuel (taxes that may be justifiable because they help offset adverse externalities). Over the past two decades, some administrative practices frequently adopted in the interest of streamlining tax administration have actually undermined neutrality and horizontal equity. Examples include tax withholdings, simplified tax systems for microenterprises, taxes on assets, and other taxes based on imputed income. In fact, it has been suggested that these mechanisms have been abused to such an extent that they have impaired the main objective of increasing collections (Shome 1999).

A number of authors have remarked on what seems to be an abandonment of redistributive goals as demonstrated by tax policies in Latin America (Agosín and others 2004; Lledo, Schneider, and Moore 2004). This trend is widespread in the developing world and among the "best practices" prescribed by international tax consultants (Goode 1993). In the past, optimism about the capacity of tax systems to achieve income redistribution seemed justified by the postwar experience of European countries. This view faded, however, as recognition grew that tax administrations in developing countries had limited capacity for handling steeply progressive tax schemes in politically adverse environments, where, in practice, elites can undermine the application of the redistributive mechanism. It is noteworthy that the worst income distributions tend to be those of the developing countries where effective tax burdens are the lightest (Agosín and Machado 2004). In the past, this correlation would have been used to promote more progressive tax systems; now, however, it is more likely to be interpreted as evidence of the administrative and political problems that tax policies face in societies where incomes and wealth are highly skewed. Even so, as argued below, the progressivity of a tax structure (that is, tax incidence by income level) should not be confused with its redistributive capacity, because the latter depends not only on incidence but above all on the size of public spending financed by tax revenues.

Key Characteristics of Tax Reforms

A brief summary of the reforms introduced to the main taxes and tax administration systems is in order before assessing their effects on revenues and other dimensions of the tax system.

Tariffs

Unlike the other tax reforms discussed in this chapter, which are enacted by the legislatures, import tariff reforms in most countries are the responsibility of the executive branch. Between the mid-1980s and mid-1990s, all governments in Latin America launched programs to open their economies to foreign trade, usually as part of a more comprehensive strategy aimed at reducing inflation, increasing competition in domestic markets, and attracting new investment, with the ultimate aim of raising productivity, employment, and income levels.[4] Tariff rates fell from an average 49 percent before the reforms to nearly 13 percent by the mid-1990s, and dispersion was significantly reduced. By 1995, all countries had average tariff rates below 20 percent (table 6.1).[5] These tariff cuts were higher for industrial than for agricultural products, which many countries still protect with high or varying tariffs depending on price conditions. Nevertheless, high agricultural tariffs are not a significant source of tax revenue because they are essentially protectionist. Although tariff reductions were substantial, tariff revenues declined on average by only 0.8 percent of GDP from the late 1980s to 2000–03 (from 2.6 percent of GDP to 1.8 percent of GDP) because import ratios increased substantially during the period and standard tariff rates were applied more effectively, as exemptions, loopholes, and evasion were curtailed. (However, the proliferation of trade agreements in the 1990s also affected effective tariff rates.) For some of the smaller, more open countries, such as Honduras and El Salvador, tariff reductions represented much larger revenue losses (2.7 percent and 2.2 percent of GDP, respectively).

Table 6.1 Tax Rates, 1985, 1995, and 2003
(percentage)

Country	Tariffs (simple average)			Corporate income tax rate (max.)			Individual income tax rate (max.)			VAT		
	1985	1995	2003	1985	1995	2003	1985	1995	2003	1985	1995	2003
Argentina	28	11	12	33	30	35	45	30	35	18	21	21
Bolivia	20	10	8	30	25	25	30	13	13	10	13	13
Brazil	80	12	12	45	25	25	60	35	28	30	31	25
Chile	36	11	6	10	15	17	50	45	40	20	18	19
Colombia	83	13	12	40	35	35	49	35	35	10	14	16
Costa Rica	53	11	6	50	30	30	50	25	25	10	10	13
Dominican Republic	—	—	—	49	25	25	73	25	25	6	8	16
Ecuador	41	12	12	40	25	25	40	25	25	10	10	12
El Salvador	23	10	7	35	25	25	60	30	30	n.a.	13	13
Guatemala	50	12	6	42	25	31	48	30	25	7	7	10
Honduras	—	—	—	46	40	25	46	46	30	5	7	12
Jamaica	43	19	9	45	33	33	57	25	25	n.a.	13	15
Mexico	34	13	17	42	34	34	55	35	40	15	15	15
Panama	—	—	—	50	45	30	56	56	30	5	5	5
Peru	64	16	11	55	30	30	50	30	27	11	18	18
Paraguay	71	9	11	30	30	30	30	0	0	n.a.	10	10
Trinidad and Tobago	83	19	10	50	38	34	70	38	35	n.a.	15	15
Venezuela	30	13	12	50	34	34	45	34	34	n.a.	13	17
Average	**49**	**13**	**10**	**41**	**30**	**29**	**51**	**31**	**28**	**12**	**13**	**15**
Median	**43**	**12**	**11**	**44**	**30**	**30**	**50**	**30**	**29**	**10**	**13**	**15**

Sources: Corporate and individual tax rates and VAT: PriceWaterhouseCoopers (various years); tariffs: Lora 2001, World Bank 2005, IDB Integration Department calculations based on the World Integrated Trade Solution.

Note: n.a. = not applicable; — = not available.

Taxes on Business Profits and Capital Gains

Corporate taxes have been an important target of reform since the mid-1980s. The most widespread and dramatic changes were the lower tax rates on business profits, which typically fell from 43 percent in 1985 to 34 percent in 1990, to finally settle at 30 percent.[6] So as not to discourage foreign investment, these rates tended to be set below the maximum rate in the United States (39.6 percent since the 1986 reform and currently 35.0 percent). As a result, rates tended to even out among the countries and stabilize over time. Between 1988 and 1995, tax rates for businesses changed 1.6 times on average per country; however, in the next seven years the average change per country was 0.4 times, and much smaller. Thus, during the 1990s the margin of action for adjusting business tax rates narrowed considerably. As might be expected, changes proliferated in other areas.

Table 6.2 Tax Incentives to Production and Investment, around 2000

Country	Horizontal tax incentives	Tax incentives to specific sectors	Tax incentives to particular regions
Argentina		Mining, forestry	
Bahamas	X[a]	Hotels, financial services, spirits and beer	
Barbados	X[b]	Financial services, insurance, information technology	
Belize	X	Mining	
Bolivia		Mining	
Brazil			X[c]
Chile	X[d]	Forestry, oil, nuclear materials	X
Colombia			X[e]
Costa Rica		Forestry, tourism	
Dominican Republic		Tourism, agribusiness	
Ecuador		Mining, tourism	
El Salvador			
Guatemala			
Guyana		Agribusiness	
Haiti	X[f]		
Honduras			
Jamaica		Motion picture industry, tourism, bauxite, aluminum, factory construction	

(continued)

Table 6.2 Tax Incentives to Production and Investment, around
2000 (*continued*)

Country	Horizontal tax incentives	Tax incentives to specific sectors	Tax incentives to particular regions
Mexico	X[g]	Forestry, motion picture industry, air and maritime transportation, publishing industry	
Nicaragua		Tourism	
Panama		Tourism, forestry	
Paraguay	X[h]		X[i]
Peru		Tourism, mining, oil	X[j]
Trinidad and Tobago	X[k]	Hotels, construction	
Uruguay	X[l]	Hydrocarbons, printing, shipping, forestry, military industry, airlines, newspapers, broadcasters, theaters, motion picture industry	
Venezuela	X[m]	Hydrocarbons and other primary sectors[n]	

Source: IDB 2001.
Note:
a. Income is tax-free and imports to be used in investment projects are duty-free.
b. The tax incentive is for foreign investors. Offshore companies are taxed at a rate significantly below the rate for local companies.
c. There are federal tax investment incentives for the Northeast and Amazon regions.
d. There are two main horizontal forms of tax incentive to investment (including reinvestment of profits): (1) Accelerated depreciation is granted for new fixed assets acquired domestically and for imported fixed assets; (2) personal income tax and additional tax apply only when profits are distributed.
e. There are two special tax regimes that favor particular regions recently affected by natural disasters. They are the Páez Law and the Quimbaya Law. The first is applicable to the zones affected by the flooding of the Páez River in 1995 and the second to the coffee-producing zone affected by the earthquake of January 1999.
f. Haiti has a comprehensive tax holiday scheme.
g. Through the Sector Promotion Program (PROSEC), firms in 22 industries in the manufacturing sector can import goods at a preferential rate to be used in the respective manufacturing sector to produce final goods either for the external or domestic market.
h. Paraguay has a five-year duration tax holiday for new investments.
i. The duration of the tax holiday mentioned in note h is longer (10 years) if the company making the investment locates in the Departments of Guairá, Caazapá, Ñeembecú, or Concepción, or in the Eastern Region.
j. Manufacturing enterprises operating in the border provinces and in the Amazon region are exempt from the income tax, the VAT, and the excise taxes.
k. Trinidad and Tobago grants comprehensive tax holidays of up to 10 years.
l. A tax exemption is available on profits reinvested in manufacturing firms, farming, and hotel facilities. In addition, there is a partial relief from capital tax through computing the fiscal value of industrial equipment at 50 percent.
m. New investments in manufacturing industry, agriculture, fishing, fish farming, livestock, and tourism receive a tax rebate of 20 percent. Furthermore, the capital gains tax is 1 percent.
n. New investments in hydrocarbons production enjoy a tax rebate of 8 percent. The purchase of capital equipment and services for new investment in oil, mining, agriculture, and fisheries is exempt from the wholesale tax.

The emphasis on sector neutrality, which had been the hallmark of the first wave of business tax reforms until the early 1990s, tended to decline from then on. For example, in Central America it was common to waive duties on foreign capital in free trade zones where *maquila* assembly plants were established, and in sectors such as tourism, mining, and fishing. (Often, this constitutes in practice a transfer of receipts to the countries of origin, because tax payments in other countries are deducted from those due in the country of origin, as is the case in the United States [Agosín and others 2004].) Exemptions from income tax in primary sector industries are quite common in Latin America (see table 6.2).

Corporate profits are usually taxed in most Latin American countries like any other income. However, in Bolivia, Paraguay, Peru, and the Central American countries with the exception of Honduras, corporate profits are taxed at lower rates, if at all. In several cases (Bolivia, Costa Rica, El Salvador, Guatemala, and Peru), the reforms that began in the mid-1980s initiated or reinforced favorable treatment of corporate profits; only in Nicaragua did the reform move in the opposite direction (Stotsky and WoldeMariam 2002).

To facilitate the administration of business taxes, several countries have long had systems of "imputed income," calculating minimum income tax payments as a percentage of asset holdings. Another common tool used to expedite collection is the withholding of a fraction of some business income in lieu of future tax obligations. The effectiveness of these mechanisms tended to decline in the 1990s because asset taxes were often modified or abolished in some countries, and withholding rates were generally reduced on payments of corporate profits and foreign remittances of dividends, interest, and royalties (Agosín and others 2004; Shome 1999; Stotsky and WoldeMariam 2002).

Individual Income Tax

The most significant reform of individual income taxes was the reduction of the maximum rates. This trend was similar to, albeit more pronounced than, the trend in business taxes. The ceiling on individual income tax fell from a median rate of 50 percent in 1985 to 34 percent in 1990, and 29 percent in 2001 (rising in 2004 to 30 percent). Even though lower rates have meant less dispersion of tax rates among countries, disparities in individual income tax rates are greater than in business tax rates. Changes in the maximum rates have become less frequent, declining from an average of 1.8 changes per country between 1988 and 1995 to 0.7 changes per country between 1995 and 2002.

Despite the appreciable drop in the maximum tax rate on individual income, the tax structures maintain significant progressive aspects: there are exemptions for minimum levels of individual income, and rates differ according to the amount of taxable income. The individual income tax exemption rose from an average of 60 percent of per capita GDP in the mid-1980s to 230 percent in 2001 (table 6.3); moreover, the income levels taxed at maximum rates were lowered. On average, in the mid-1980s, the maximum rate was only charged when taxpayers declared income 121 times higher than per capita GDP. These thresholds declined to around 20 times per capita GDP by 2001. In theory, these changes tended to make personal income taxes more progressive overall. (However, progressivity within the lower and the higher income groups, when considered separately, was reduced.) The increase in the personal exemption tended to shrink the universe of taxpayers, which streamlined collection while sacrificing little or no revenue.

Some of the attempts at reform were aimed, with scant success, at reducing exemptions, rebates, and special treatment granted to specific types of individual income, which together severely restrict the effectiveness of individual income taxes. Personal income tax continues to be poorly integrated in many countries because of reliance on withholding mechanisms that differentiate between sources of income, and that grant exemptions to different types of income, especially financial returns and corporate profits (Agosín and others 2004).

Table 6.3 Personal Income Tax Exemption Level and Upper Income Bracket (multiples of GDP per capita)

Latin America	Personal exemption level			Upper income bracket		
	1985	*1997*	*2001*	*1985*	*1997*	*2001*
Argentina	0.8	1.2	1.7	21.4	14.5	16.5
Bolivia	1.0	—	—	10.1	—	—
Brazil	0.3	2.1	1.5	10.1	4.2	3.1
Chile	0.2	0.1	0.1	2.8	1.3	1.2
Colombia	0.0	2.7	4.1	20.5	12.0	16.6
Costa Rica	1.2	1.1	0.8	1.4	5.6	3.7
Dominican Republic	1.1	0.1	2.3	413.5	34.3	5.8
Ecuador	0.4	1.8	2.4	29.2	22.7	8.3
El Salvador	—	1.4	1.2	171.7	12.7	11.0
Guatemala	0.9	6.3	5.0	356.0	17.5	22.5
Honduras	0.0	5.2	3.6	600.4	103.4	36.0
Mexico	0.7	0.1	0.1	21.3	5.0	44.0
Nicaragua	1.7	6.6	7.7	56.9	47.4	61.2
Panama	0.3	0.9	0.9	89.0	63.1	57.8
Paraguay	0.5	—	—	10.4	—	—
Peru	—	2.6	2.9	—	20.1	22.3
Uruguay	—	—	—	—	—	—
Venezuela	—	0.0	0.0	—	0.0	0.0
Average	0.6	2.1	2.3	121.0	24.2	20.7

Source: Stotsky and WoldeMariam 2005.
Note: — = not available.

Consumption Taxes: VAT and Excise Taxes

The replacement of cascading sales taxes by VAT was the most significant tax reform in Latin America in the 1980s and early 1990s. In 1995, VAT systems were in place in 21 of the 26 countries in the region. In theory, VAT is charged at each stage of production and distribution, but taxes paid on investment or export goods are discounted or reimbursed;[7] consequently, VAT functions as a tax on final consumption. In practice, however, the effectiveness of VAT is undercut by informality and the difficulty of bringing small businesses and individuals supplying specialized services into the system. Exemptions and differential tax rates on a range of products further reduce the effectiveness of the tax.

Until the late 1980s, VAT-related reforms consisted of either setting up or strengthening the system, and they were less concerned with rate changes. The typical basic VAT rate was 10 percent until the late 1980s; various reforms during the 1990s raised the basic rate to 15 percent. Rate changes became less frequent, dropping from 1.5 times per country between 1988 and 1995, to 0.6 in the next seven-year period. Since the mid-1990s, the most frequent changes were at the margins, as legislatures resisted executive attempts to improve the efficiency of the tax by broadening its base or raising the rates of what is generally considered to be a regressive tax.

Unlike VAT, excise and other minor taxes have lost importance as sources of revenue. During the early 1990s, interest in simplifying the system led to the elimination of hundreds of small taxes in many countries. In general, the only excise taxes remaining were those that raised the most revenue and were most easily justified by the nature of the goods targeted (for example, tobacco, alcoholic beverages, fuel). In contrast to other types of taxes, the difference in excise tax rates among countries has not narrowed, not even in countries whose economies are relatively well integrated, such as the Central American countries (Agosín and others 2004). Although excise taxes present an opportunity for low-cost collection, they raise opposition from producers, which are often small groups of well-organized and very vocal firms.

Administrative Reform

The goal of streamlining tax systems to facilitate tax collection was supplemented over the past 20 years by a thorough modernization of tax administrations. This was a break from the past when attempts were made to transplant tax systems wholesale from industrial countries without bothering to adjust administrative practices or capacities. By 1990, most of the tax administrations in the region had been reorganized into function-based structures (customer service, records, collections, auditing, and legal procedures), instead of the previous organization by tax type. In the 1990s, administrative reforms mainly involved functional rationalization, the

creation of special taxpayer or customer service units, tracking of large
taxpayers, the general implementation of standardized tax withholding
systems, and the introduction of simplified systems for small producers
and firms (where a single combined payment is made for income tax, VAT,
and excise taxes) (IDB 1996; Shome 1999). From an organizational point
of view, the most important change in many countries was the increased
independence granted to tax administration offices. As discussed in chapter 4, by the end of the 1990s, 10 countries had granted some type of budgetary, financial, or administrative independence to these offices. While
these organizational reforms introduced greater flexibility and accountability into tax administrations with visible results in some countries, like
Peru, their impact was less impressive in countries where the political
system retained its ability to interfere with administrative decisions. Not
all the administrative reforms in the mid-1980s required legislative action,
despite their importance to the effectiveness of the tax system. This is why
some say that in developing countries, "tax administration *is* tax policy"
(Bird and Casanegra 1992, as cited in Shome 1999).

Main Outcomes of Tax Reform

The priority of tax reform in the late 1980s and 1990s was to boost tax
revenue, and a certain measure of success was achieved in reversing the
trend in tax revenues, which had been declining since the mid-1980s.
The reforms also succeeded in improving the efficiency of the tax systems. Although the progressivity of the system was clearly reduced by
the increased importance of VAT, the redistributive capacity of taxes was
improved by the higher revenues.

Tax Collection

Between 1985 and 1989, tax revenues tended to decline in response to
sluggish economic growth, the increasing difficulty of taxing trade and
capital, and high inflation in some countries. Average tax revenues (not
including social security taxes and contributions) declined from 15.4 percent of GDP in 1985 to 13.6 percent in 1989. An upward trend starting in
most countries around 1990 raised average tax revenues to over 14 percent of GDP during the 1990s, and over 15 percent since 2000 (see figure
6.1). Although the objective of recovering and increasing tax revenues was
accomplished, the results were not impressive and tax burdens are still low
by international standards. However, these averages mask important differences among countries. Argentina and Brazil saw tax burden increases
of more than 5 percent of GDP between the late 1980s and the early
years of the 2000s, and Bolivia, Colombia, and the Dominican Republic
of over 3 percent of GDP. However, tax revenues declined significantly in

Figure 6.1 Tax Revenues in Latin America

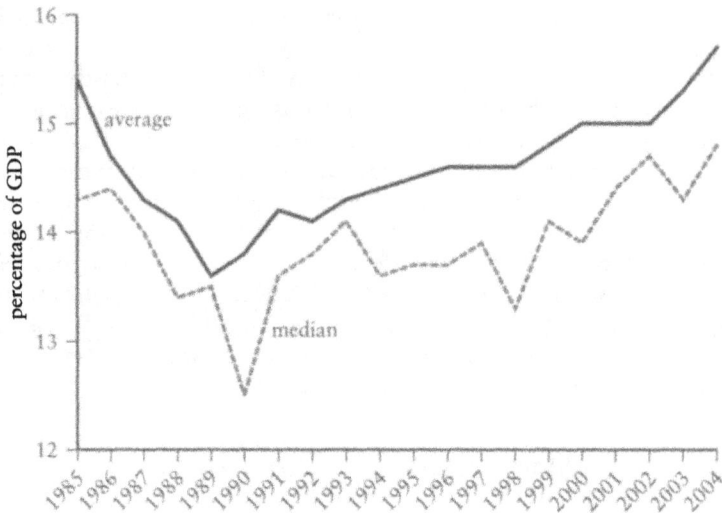

Sources: Author's calculations based on Government Finance Statistics
(GFS) and IMF Article IV consultations for 1985–89. For 1990–2004, country
statistical agencies except for Jamaica and Trinidad and Tobago, whose
data are from IMF Article IV consultations and IMF "Recent Economic
Developments" reports.

Chile, Mexico, Panama, Trinidad and Tobago, and Venezuela (table 6.4).
Furthermore, while a few countries have achieved tax collection levels
comparable to international standards (in the period 2000–03 only Brazil,
Jamaica, and Trinidad and Tobago had tax burdens—without social security contributions—over 20 percent), in several countries the tax burden is
still around 10 percent. A salient case is Guatemala at 10 percent, in spite
of a declared public consensus to reach a target of 12 percent,[8] but also
Panama, Paraguay (until 2003),[9] and Venezuela, countries that have other
important sources of fiscal revenue that discourage taxation.[10]

In light of the many factors influencing tax revenues, assessing the
impact of reform on the tax burden is no easy matter. As mentioned,
the steps taken to open economies to international trade reduced tariff
receipts, and the greater mobility of capital and other taxable bases narrowed the capacity to tax capital income of firms and individuals. However, the increased price stability achieved by many countries reduced the

Table 6.4 Tax Revenue as Percentage of GDP, by Country (simple averages)

Country	1985–89 Without social security	1985–89 With social security	1990–94 Without social security	1990–94 With social security	1995–99 Without social security	1995–99 With social security	2000–03 Without social security	2000–03 With social security	2000–03 minus 1985–89 Without social security
Argentina	12.9	16.5	14.1	18.9	16.6	20.6	18.4	21.4	5.4
without taxes on hydrocarbons	11.2	14.8	13.0	17.8	15.5	19.5	17.1	17.1	5.9
Bolivia	14.2	—	15.3	16.5	16.8	18.7	17.4	19.2	3.2
without taxes on hydrocarbons	8.0	—	8.5	10.4	11.7	14.1	12.5	14.5	4.5
Brazil	16.0	—	18.4	27.3	19.4	29.9	21.0	34.4	5.0
Chile	19.2	—	15.9	17.3	16.1	17.5	16.5	18.0	-2.7
Colombia	9.3	—	9.2	11.0	10.4	14.7	13.0	17.1	3.7
Costa Rica	—	—	11.5	17.1	12.1	18.0	12.8	19.1	1.3
Dominican Republic	11.6	—	13.0	13.6	14.4	15.1	15.2	15.9	3.6
Ecuador	16.8	19.3	16.0	18.6	13.6	15.6	18.3	20.9	1.5
without taxes on hydrocarbons	7.8	10.3	7.1	9.7	7.7	9.6	11.5	14.0	3.6
El Salvador	12.3	—	9.4	11.0	11.3	13.2	11.0	12.9	-1.3
Guatemala	7.9	—	7.7	—	8.7	8.9	10.0	10.3	2.1
Honduras	13.6	—	15.2	15.9	15.7	16.1	16.2	16.4	2.6
Jamaica	23.8	—	25.1	—	24.3	—	25.3	—	1.4
Mexico	15.6	18.0	14.4	17.0	13.1	14.9	13.1	14.7	-2.5
without taxes on hydrocarbons	11.2	13.6	11.2	13.7	9.9	11.7	11.0	12.6	-0.2
Panama	12.1	—	11.0	15.8	10.7	14.5	9.1	13.8	-3.0
Peru	10.8	—	11.7	13.4	13.7	15.4	12.4	14.1	1.7
Paraguay	8.5	—	9.0	9.5	10.6	11.6	9.8	10.8	1.3
Trinidad and Tobago	24.0	24.1	22.7	22.7	21.6	21.7	21.0	21.0	-3.0
without taxes on hydrocarbons	16.5	16.5	17.5	17.6	18.5	18.6	15.4	15.4	-1.1
Venezuela	16.2	—	15.2	16.1	13.6	14.2	11.5	12.2	-4.6
without taxes on hydrocarbons	7.5	—	5.8	6.7	9.5	10.0	9.3	9.9	1.7
Average	14.4	—	14.3	16.3	14.7	16.4	15.3	17.1	0.8
without taxes on hydrocarbons	12.6	—	12.6	14.4	13.6	15.2	14.2	15.8	1.6

Sources: Author's calculations based on the IMF's Government Finance Statistics and IMF Article IV consultations for 1985–89. For 1990–2003, country statistical agencies except for Jamaica and Trinidad and Tobago, whose data are from IMF Article IV consultations and IMF "Recent Economic Developments" reports.

Note: Averages do not include Costa Rica.

— = Not available.

"Tanzi effect"—the debilitating effect of inflation on tax receipts in real terms.[11] Given the mix of factors, it makes sense to analyze the trend not only of the total tax burden but also of the main taxes affected by reform. Revenue from income taxes, which averaged 4.0 percent of GDP from 1985 to 1989, showed only minor changes and eventually reach 4.3 percent of GDP between 2000 and 2003.[12] Even though some countries have made important progress, income taxation throughout Latin America is very low compared to international standards,[13] due largely to the inability to collect taxes on personal incomes. This contrasts with the evolution of VAT collections, which rose from an average of 2 percent of GDP in the late 1980s[14] to a remarkable 5 percent of GDP in 2000–03. In this area, the tax yield is higher than global standards.[15] Higher receipts from direct taxes and VAT managed to turn around the decline in revenues from trade, excises, and other taxes, which went from a combined average of 8.4 percent of GDP in the second half of the 1980s to 5.9 percent of GDP between 2000 and 2003. However, as figure 6.2 shows, the "other taxes"

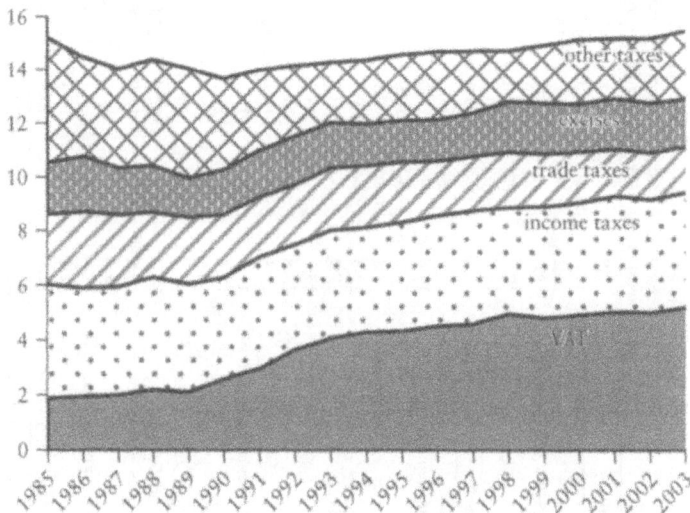

Figure 6.2 Tax Revenues by Tax Type (as GDP percentage)

Sources: Author's calculations based on GFS and IMF Article IV consultations for 1985–89. For 1990–2003, country statistical agencies except for Jamaica and Trinidad and Tobago, whose data are from IMF Article IV consultations and IMF "Recent Economic Developments" reports.

Table 6.5 Selected Latin American Countries: Cost of Tax Collection, 1998

	Percentage of Total Tax Revenue
Argentina	2.2
Bolivia[a]	1.3
Brazil	1.6
Chile[b]	0.7
Ecuador[a]	2.0
Mexico	1.5
Peru[a]	2.0
Canada	1.1
Spain	0.9
United States[c]	0.4

Source: Singh and others 2005.

Note: Primary sources are annual reports and statistical tabulations of the national tax authorities. Tax authorities generally do not reveal the approach used to derive their cost computations; and, in turn, their reported ratios may not be fully comparable.

a. National tax authorities in these countries receive a fixed proportion of revenue collected.

b. Does not include customs administration.

c. U.S. authorities compute their ratio using "gross" revenue; use of net revenue would increase the reported ratio about 10 percent.

category has shown some increase since the mid-1990s because several countries have resorted to new taxes, such as the financial transactions taxes now in place in Argentina, Bolivia, Brazil, Colombia, Ecuador, Peru, and Venezuela, to increase tax revenues.

No information is available on the administrative costs incurred in achieving these higher tax receipts. However, the cost of tax collection in most Latin American countries is high by international standards: while collection costs represent between 0.4 percent and 1.1 percent of total tax revenue in developed countries, only Chile falls within this range in the region. In Argentina, Ecuador, and Peru collection costs are 2 percent or more of tax revenue (see table 6.5). The factors that make tax collection more costly in Latin America are the complexity of the tax codes, the excessive number of exemptions and special treatments, weak administrative capabilities, lack of judicial support to enforce the tax codes, widespread labor and business informality, and a culture of tax evasion.

Neutrality

The second goal underlying tax reform since 1985 was to simplify tax structures and create tax systems that did not distort production and investment decisions. By definition, any tax exhibits greater neutrality when it charges lower proportional rates and is applied uniformly to all economic activities or agents. As has been seen, although VAT rates tended to increase, maximum rates on corporate profits and personal income taxes declined, as did import tariffs.[16]

An approximate measure of the uniformity with which taxes are levied is tax "productivity"—the ratio between real and potential tax collection, given the basic or maximum rate. Thus, the productivity of VAT is usually calculated as the ratio between the revenue raised as a proportion of GDP and the basic rate. If the entire final output of the economy was effectively taxed at the basic rate, productivity would be 1. (However, the calculations presented below are not based on the entire GDP but on internal demand because, as noted above, VAT in the region is designed as a tax on consumption.)[17] On average, the productivity of VAT rose from 0.23 in 1985 to levels of about 0.32 in 1995 and 0.35 in 2003. In general, the most significant increases in productivity took place through the early 1990s, when the tax was being consolidated. Later, however, several countries including Brazil, Colombia, and Venezuela made significant improvements while major slippages took place in Costa Rica, the Dominican Republic, Honduras, and Jamaica.

The average productivity of corporate and individual income taxes followed a similar trend. Beginning with productivity levels averaging 0.072 in the mid-1980s, substantial improvements were seen by the mid-1990s (when the average was 0.110), with more modest increases thereafter. Except for Venezuela, the productivity of income taxes is currently higher than in the mid-1980s.

To summarize the neutrality of the tax system in a single measure, this chapter applies the method used by Lora (2001), which consists of an index combining the rates of the main taxes with their respective figures for productivity. Lower tax rates and higher productivity rates are reflected in higher values for this "neutrality index." The index takes into account the tax rates of VAT, income taxes, and import tariffs, but because of data limitations on tariff revenues considers the productivity of VAT and income taxes only.[18] The results of this combined index show that the neutrality of the tax systems improved considerably between the mid-1980s and early 1990s, with few significant changes thereafter (figure 6.3). Table 6.6 shows the values of the index by country for the periods 1985–89, 1990–94, 1995–99, and 2000–03. These calculations suggest an important degree of convergence in the tax systems across the region, as differences in neutrality have become less pronounced than in the past.

This indicator of neutrality refers only to VAT, income tax, and import tariffs, and not to the entire tax system. Until the mid-1990s, the trend toward greater neutrality was probably valid for the entire tax system, as other taxes, such as export taxes, excises, and many minor taxes affecting specific economic activities or transactions, were slashed and simplified.

Figure 6.3 Neutrality Index

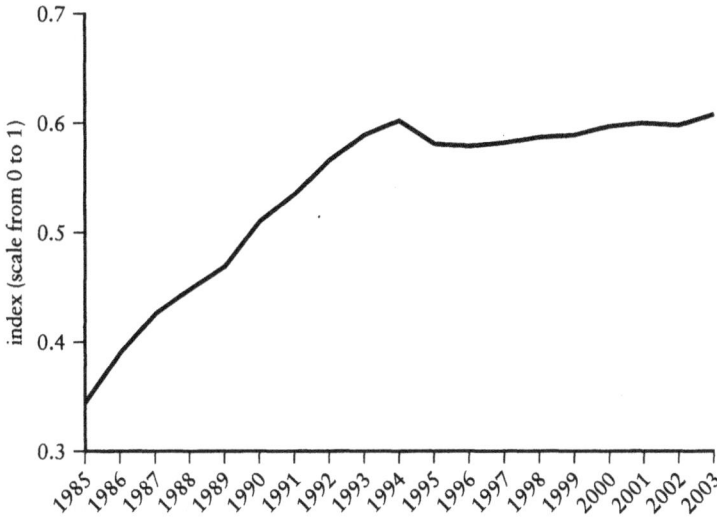

Sources: Author's calculations based on GFS and IMF Article IV
consultations for 1985–89. For 1990–2003, country statistical agencies except
for Jamaica and Trinidad and Tobago, whose data are from IMF Article IV
consultations and IMF "Recent Economic Developments" reports. For corporate
and individual tax rates and VAT, PricewaterhouseCoopers, "Corporate and
Individual Taxes, Worldwide Summaries," various years. For tariffs, Lora
(2001); World Bank (2005); and IDB Integration Department calculations based
on the World Integrated Trade Solution.

However, as mentioned, the trend has reversed recently in several countries with the introduction of financial transactions taxes and other highly
distortionary taxes. Financial transactions taxes are currently in place in
several countries, with rates (in 2000–02) between 0.3 percent and 0.8
percent and revenues as high as 2.3 percent of GDP (see table 6.7). The
cascading nature of financial transactions taxes can distort the production
chain and stimulate interenterprise netting arrangements, increased use of
cash, and recourse to offshore transactions. In the wake of the macroeconomic crisis of 2001 and the sharp devaluation of the peso, Argentina also
reintroduced export taxes (*retenciones*), which are highly distortionary.

Table 6.6 Tax Neutrality Index, Selected Countries

Country	1985–89	1990–94	1995–99	2000–03	1985–89 minus 2000–03
Argentina	0.344	0.517	0.514	0.490	0.146
Bolivia	0.572	0.704	0.644	0.678	0.106
Brazil	0.218	0.413	0.467	0.515	0.297
Chile	0.561	0.573	0.588	0.621	0.060
Colombia	0.466	0.557	0.534	0.568	0.101
Costa Rica	0.466	0.610	0.604	0.622	0.157
Ecuador	0.429	0.567	0.599	0.673	0.244
El Salvador	0.358	0.519	0.628	0.632	0.274
Guatemala	0.490	0.595	0.614	0.634	0.144
Jamaica	0.525	0.706	0.671	0.672	0.147
Mexico	0.458	0.566	0.513	0.513	0.056
Peru	0.353	0.436	0.528	0.560	0.207
Paraguay	0.353	0.543	0.700	0.677	0.324
Trinidad and Tobago	0.249	0.558	0.605	0.601	0.351
Venezuela	0.392	0.537	0.546	0.559	0.167
Average	**0.416**	**0.560**	**0.584**	**0.601**	**0.185**

Sources: Author's calculations based on GFS and IMF Article IV consultations for 1985–89. For 1990–2003, country statistical agencies except for Jamaica and Trinidad and Tobago, whose data are from IMF Article IV consultations and IMF "Recent Economic Developments" reports.

Table 6.7 Financial Transactions Taxes

Country and year	Rate (%)	Collection (% GDP)	Productivity (% GDP over avg. rate)
Argentina, 2001	0.60[a]	1.46[b]	2.43
Brazil, 2001	0.36[c]	1.45[d]	3.97
Colombia, 2001	0.30	0.76	2.53
Ecuador, 2000	0.80	2.33[e]	2.91
Venezuela, 2002	0.75[f]	1.07[d]	1.43

Source: Adapted from Gómez-Sabaini 2005.
Note:
a. In each side of the transaction; the joint rate is 1.2 percent.
b. Adjusted for the period when the tax was in force.
c. Average rates, adjusted for the period when the tax was in force.
d. Estimation based on data from partial collection and forecast GDP.
e. The tax assessed debits and credits.
f. The schedule of the rate will raise it to 1 percent between August 2002 and March 2003.

Progressivity and Redistributive Capacity

The tax reforms since 1985 have been subject to frequent criticism because of their regressive nature; specifically, the higher share of overall tax revenues contributed by VAT receipts and the reduction in the rate ceilings of taxes on corporate profits and individual income are often mentioned as regressive features of the new tax systems. A tax is considered progressive (or regressive) when lower income groups pay a smaller (or larger) proportion of their income or expenditures than higher income groups. A simple measure of the degree of pure progressivity of a tax is the difference between the concentration of the tax by income level (as measured by a quasi–Gini coefficient) and the concentration of income (as measured by the Gini coefficient). This indicator is known as the Kakwani measure of progressivity or regressivity. As table 6.8 suggests, on this basis income taxes in the region are strongly progressive: the median Kakwani measure for the seven studies considered is 0.15. The effect of the reforms since 1985 on the progressivity of this tax is not clear. The reduction in rates could have reduced progressivity, but this effect may have been offset by the combined effects of having fewer middle- and low-income taxpayers (resulting from the higher threshold of exempted income) but more high-income taxpayers subject to the top tax rates (resulting from the lower threshold at which the top rate is applied).

The Kakwani measure of progressivity for VAT suggests that, on average, this tax is highly regressive (–0.089), although it is slightly progressive in Colombia and Guatemala, according to the case studies summarized in the table. However, as the authors of the studies frequently note, the calculations tend to overestimate the degree of regressivity, especially because the concentration coefficients are calculated in terms of income and not spending,[19] and because adjustments are rarely made to account for tax evasion. The Kakwani measure is also not a satisfactory measure of progressivity because it does not take into account how much revenue is collected. Alternatively, the Reynolds-Smolensky measure, which is based on revenue collected, can be used; it simply compares the Gini coefficients before and after taxes. (Obviously, both measures yield the same sign for a given tax.) By this measure, none of the 14 income or value-added taxes considered produce any significant change in income concentration, implying that the income redistribution caused *directly* by the taxes alone is insignificant.

However, the Kakwani and Reynolds-Smolensky measures of progressivity do not account for the redistributive potential of the taxes through the use of revenues. This is a drawback because it fails to recognize that a neutral tax (neither regressive nor progressive) that yields considerable revenue may offer greater redistributive opportunities than an extremely progressive tax (such as income tax) that produces little revenue. To appreciate this redistributive potential, a third measure, inspired by Engel, Galetovic, and Raddatz (1997) is included in the table. This measure compares

Table 6.8 Summary of Income and Value-Added Tax Incidence Studies

Country and study	Year of calculations	Pure progressivity (does not take into account revenue or redistribution) Kakwani measure	Progressivity taking into account revenue (but not redistribution) Reynolds Smolensky measure	Progressivity and redistributive potential (assuming flat redistribution of the revenue) Engel, Galetovic, Raddatz measure
Income taxes				
Argentina: CEB (1997)	1996	0.156	0.00008	0.031
Chile: Engel, Galetovic, and Raddatz (1997)	1994	0.338	0.00006	0.016
Dominican Republic: Santana and Rathe (1992)	1989	0.253	0.00010	0.028
El Salvador: Acevedo and Orellana (2003)	2000	0.143	0.00002	0.007
Guatemala: Bahl, Martinez-Vásquez, and Wallace (1996)	1993	0.086	0.00001	0.009
Honduras: Gómez-Sabaini (2003)	2000	0.011	0.00001	0.024
Peru: Haughton (2005)	2000	0.157	0.00197	0.008
Median		0.156	0.00006	0.016
Value-added taxes				
Argentina: CEB (1997)	1996	-0.141	-0.00009	0.021
Chile: Engel, Galetovic, and Raddatz (1997)	1994	-0.089	-0.00008	0.040
Colombia: Steiner and Soto (1998)	1994	0.050	0.00002	0.023
El Salvador: Acevedo and Orellana (2003)	2000	-0.237	-0.00013	0.014
Guatemala: Bahl, Martinez-Vásquez, and Wallace (1996)	1993	0.076	0.00003	0.026
Honduras: Gómez-Sabaini (2003)	2000	-0.119	-0.00009	0.033
Peru: Haughton (2005)	2000	-0.015	-0.00088	0.025
Median		-0.089	-0.00009	0.025

Source: Author's compilation.

the Gini coefficient before the tax with a posttax Gini coefficient that assumes that the proceeds of the tax are distributed to all income groups in equal amounts.[20] The results indicate that the redistributive potential of VAT is significantly greater than that of income taxes, which is clearly due entirely to the fact that VAT raises higher revenues.

This analysis is not as hypothetical as it may appear. Contrary to widespread belief, social spending has grown substantially since the early 1990s on average (and in all countries of the region, except for Ecuador) from 9.3 percent of GDP in 1990 to 12.2 percent of GDP in 2003 (or 50 percent per capita in real terms). Considering the constraints imposed on tax collection by globalization and the growing informalization of economies, the increase in social spending would not have been possible without the increased tax revenues produced by VAT.

The previous analysis assumes that tax revenues are distributed equally to all income groups, which is not too distant from reality if one judges on the basis of social expenditures. As mentioned in chapter 1, Chile is the only country where social expenditures play a clearly progressive role, an example that should be followed by other countries instead of tampering with tax systems with the alleged purpose of making them more redistributive. The evidence for developed countries supports the validity of this assertion: with much higher tax burdens, they achieve much redistribution largely through transfers rather than directly through taxes.[21] The redistributive impact of the fiscal system also depends on important consumption and production fiscal subsidies. In the past, considerable fiscal resources were channeled to cover the operating losses of what used to be considered public goods, such as electricity, water, sewage, telecommunications, and all types of transportation infrastructure. Despite popular wisdom, the main beneficiaries of these subsidies were the rich and the middle classes. In all these sectors cost recovery has increased significantly, in many cases associated with the privatization process (see chapter 8), and as a result the progressivity of the whole fiscal system has probably improved.

Challenges and Pending Issues

Latin American tax systems have undergone intense reform since the late 1980s. A simple count of the significant reforms passed by national congresses suggests that reforming activity has been continuous and more frequent than in previous decades.[22] From 1977 to 1989, each country had an average of 2.5 reforms, but from 1990 to 2002 the average number per country increased to 4.2. VAT reforms were the most frequent, followed by changes to corporate and personal income taxes. Although the need to recover and raise tax revenues provided important impetus to this increase in reforming activity, no evidence indicates that the most active countries in the tax area have obtained higher tax revenue,[23] or that they have improved the neutrality of their tax systems,[24] which were the two most important objectives pursued by governments. This suggests that the results of the tax reforms depend much more on the political processes that affect their passage into law than on their technical design. Consequently, a major future challenge is to understand and improve these political processes, rather than to propose technically perfect reforms with little possibility of being passed and that, in fact, may introduce more distortions and administrative difficulties.[25]

One way to make the political processes of tax reform more transparent is to require that the cost of granting exemptions, tax incentives, and special treatment to certain sectors or groups of taxpayers be made explicit. Loss of tax revenue for these reasons is calculated as equivalent to 9.2 percent of GDP in Colombia, 7.3 percent in Guatemala, and 6.3 percent in Mexico, to mention the three most critical cases (see table 6.9). Although some countries have begun to include an estimate of these "tax costs" in their annual budgets, a separate precise quantification of each exemption or incentive that congresses pass should be required to generate political incentives to contain these costs.

Globalization trends will continue to create new challenges for tax systems. The most obvious is the deepening of free trade agreements. It is calculated, for example, that the Central American free trade agreement with the United States will mean lower tax receipts equivalent to 0.17 percent of GDP on average for the five countries in the first year, and 0.42 percent of GDP in the long term, after applying all the tariff reductions

Table 6.9 Tax Expenses in Selected Countries

	Total as percentage of GDP
Argentina	2.4
Brazil[a,b]	1.4
Chile	4.2
Colombia	9.2
Ecuador	4.9
Guatemala	7.3
Mexico[a]	6.3
Peru	2.5
Uruguay	5.3

Source: Based on Gomez-Sabaini (2005).
Note:
a. Corresponds to federal or central government.
b. Among the direct taxes income, contribution from profits (contribução sobre lucro liquido, CSLL) and contribution for financing of social security (CPSS) are included.

Table 6.10 Tax Revenue Loss from a Free Trade Agreement with USA (percentage of GDP)

	First-year effect	Total static effects
Bolivia		0.40
Colombia		0.50
Ecuador		0.60
Peru		0.40
Venezuela		0.50
Average Andean countries		**0.45**
Costa Rica	0.32	0.33
El Salvador	0.09	0.32
Guatemala	0.16	0.50
Honduras	0.22	0.61
Nicaragua	0.05	0.35
Average Central America	**0.17**	**0.42**

Sources: For Andean countries, IDB (2004b); for Central America, IMF (2005).

(not taking into account trade deviations, which can appreciably expand these effects). For the Andean countries, the estimates suggest total effects between 0.4 percent and 0.6 percent of GDP (table 6.10).

The growing trade and financial integration among the countries of the region will also intensify the trend to harmonize other aspects of tax regimes. To reduce smuggling, countries with high levels of trade integration will be forced to deepen the convergence process of VAT rates and specific taxes on certain highly mobile goods. To maintain or raise tax receipts from companies and internationally mobile capital, the process of modernizing income tax is sure to continue through mechanisms such as the broadening of the jurisdictional principle, oversight and imposition based on transfer prices between multinational parent companies and their subsidiaries, along with international agreements to limit tax competition and exchange information. However, it is naive to expect significant results from international efforts on harmonization and cooperation. There are very few instruments to impose discipline on the participant countries and very great incentives for governments, political systems, and companies to shift the ground of tax competition into new dimensions of the tax system (for example, manipulation of capitalization or depreciation rules, the appearance of new tax havens, and so forth).

An issue of growing debate in the region is the best way to increase personal taxation, which, as has been shown, is extremely low. One much underused possibility is the introduction of net worth and property taxes. The successful experiences of some provincial jurisdictions in Argentina, certain departments in Uruguay, and some municipalities in Colombia suggest that this type of tax can be an important source of subnational tax revenues (see Gomez-Sabaini 2005). The growing decentralization of taxation powers (see chapter 7) could possibly strengthen this trend. But aside from these taxes (which will be hard put to generate revenue of more than two or three percentage points of GDP in the most mature economies), the debate will continue on the options for taxing current income, either directly by taxes on personal income or sources of revenue through withholdings, or indirectly by value-added or consumption taxes. The fact that direct personal income taxes generate very low revenues and minimal redistribution is not so much the result of an ideological tendency, as is sometimes argued, but the result of globalization (which makes taxing interest and dividends more difficult), and the political processes and capacities of tax administrations in societies in which the state has little legitimacy and the culture is averse to taxation. However, it is increasingly recognized that heavy taxation of wage earners, either through a range of taxes for social security and other purposes or alternatively by continuing to raise VAT receipts, is reaching its limit for political and administrative reasons.

Also under discussion is the advisability of maintaining the new taxes on financial transactions (and export taxes in Argentina), which, despite possible distortions, are effective sources of revenue and have generated new sources of information that are beginning to be used in some countries to improve collection of other taxes. Likewise, the debate on the administrative organization of tax offices is still open. There are no definitive conclusions on the desirability of merging national tax administrations with customs administrations. The possible advantages include facilitating the integrated collection of VAT on national and imported products, speeding up the refund of VAT paid on inputs for exports under the zero rate regime (in place in most of the countries), and using information from customs to improve collection of other taxes. However, these mergers generate adaptation costs and bureaucratic and political resistance and can be counterproductive where there are very marked differences of transparency and efficiency between the two entities. Other issues of organization and administration open to debate include the concentration of collection efforts in the large taxpayer units and adoption of simplified tax systems for small taxpayers. Last, many doubts surround the practical possibility of granting budgetary and operational independence to tax administrations when effective political independence cannot be guaranteed.

Notes

1. However, see table 6.4 for country-level data on tax revenues with and without social security.

2. Useful surveys of recent tax reform trends and outcomes in Latin America are Shome (1999), Stotsky and WoldeMariam (2002) and Tanzi (2003).

3. For a discussion of the taxation policy-making process, with case studies for Brazil, Colombia, Paraguay, and Peru see Stein and others (2005), chapter 8.

4. The extent to which these objectives were achieved has been a matter of intense debate. For overviews of the discussion see Edwards (1995, chapter 5), IDB (2004a, chapter 5), Lora and Panizza (2002), and Stallings and Peres (2000).

5. See chapter 10 of this book for a discussion of the institutional implications of trade restrictions and liberalization.

6. To avoid skewing due to extreme observations, these figures refer to the medians of the 18 countries under consideration.

7. The obligation comes from the difference between the taxes charged for sales (tax debit) and those previously paid on the inputs (tax credit). This structure encourages firms to ensure that their suppliers of intermediate goods have paid their taxes correctly.

8. For a discussion of the political underpinnings of low taxation in Guatemala see Stein and others (2005), chapter 8.

9. However, tax receipts received an important boost in 2004 as the new Nicanor Duarte Frutos government strengthened the tax administration office and the legislature passed a tax reform eliminating many tax exemptions and broadening the bases of various taxes (see Stein and others [2005], chapter 8).

10. Partly due to rents from the Panama Canal and other sources, total nontax revenues of the Central Government of Panama in 2003 reached 6.5 percent of GDP. Oil tax revenues in Venezuela make up an important share of total tax revenues but vary widely (see table 6.4), depending not only on oil prices and production levels, but also on erratic government policies for the sector. Other countries that receive relatively important oil revenue are Colombia, Ecuador, Mexico, and Trinidad and Tobago.

11. This refers to loss in the real value of tax revenues between the time when the obligation is assumed and the time it is paid off.

12. See table 1.4 in chapter 1 for this information by country.

13. According to IDB (1998, chapter 8), the direct tax burden should be 8 percent of GDP, in line with global standards, for the income levels in Latin American countries. The two Caribbean countries included in this survey—Jamaica and Trinidad and Tobago—have direct tax burdens of 10.0 percent and 7.5 percent of GDP in 2000–03, which are more in line with worldwide patterns.

14. Or 2.9 percent excluding those countries that did not have VAT.

15. The tax burden from sales taxes, in line with global standards, is 4 percent of GDP (IDB 1998, chapter 8).

16. The maximum income tax rate is used, instead of the average rates, because the maximum rate has a greater influence on production, investment, and work decisions.

17. Thus, strictly speaking, productivity should be calculated in terms of private consumption. Nevertheless, we have opted to use internal demand because of the data limitations.

18. The index is a simple average of five subindexes computed on a scale of 0 to 1, as follows: (a) the average import tariff rate on a scale of 0 to 1, where 0 is the highest tax rate and 1 the lowest for the set of observations per year and country; (b) the income tax rate (which is in turn the average of the personal and the maximum corporate income tax rates) on a similar scale; (c) the productivity of income tax (computed as the ratio between the revenue-to-GDP coefficient and the average income tax rate) on a scale from 0 to 1 (in this case, 0 is the lowest level of productivity, 1 the highest); (d) the basic VAT tax rate on a similar scale (0 being the highest tax rate); and (e) the productivity of VAT (computed as the ratio between the revenue-to-domestic-demand coefficient and the basic VAT tax rate) on a similar scale (0 being the lowest productivity).

19. For example, the measure is skewed when the lowest income deciles include persons who have a temporary drop in income, but who maintain their spending in line with their permanent income level.

20. Clearly, to the extent that public spending is allocated in a more redistributive fashion, the effect on the final Gini coefficient will be greater, but it makes more sense to attribute this redistributive effect to spending decisions instead of to the tax structure. Incidentally, a "neutral" tax on 100 percent of income, which redistributes "flatly" throughout the entire population, would entirely eliminate any concentration of income.

21. For a survey of the evidence, see Perry and others (2006), chapter 5.

22. Taking the index that Mahon (2004) developed for 1977 to 1995, we have assigned quantitative values for each major congressional action beginning in 1990: (a) the reorganization of the entire tax system (assigned a value of 0.2); (b) introduction of a VAT (also 0.2); (c) significant expansion of the VAT tax base (0.1); (d) the increase in the basic VAT rate (0.1); (e) elimination of minor taxes (0.1); (f) significant expansion of the tax base for taxes on corporate profits (0.1); (g) increases in the rate ceiling for this tax (0.1); (h) significant expansion of the base for individual income taxes (0.1); (i) increases in the rate ceiling for this tax; (j) modernization of the tax administration; and (k) introduction of a tax on banking operations, tax on gross assets, or a simplified tax structure for small taxpayers (0.1). The assigned values (in parentheses) are intended to reflect the relative weight of each reform. Although Mahon does not provide this level of detail for his original indexes, a comparison of overlapping years yields similar results for both scales.

23. The correlation between the index for reform activity and the increase in tax revenues between 1990 and 2002 is virtually null (–0.04), while the correlation between the frequency of tax reforms (the number of years with tax reforms) and the increase in tax receipts is actually negative (–0.20).

24. In fact, we find a negative correlation between the intensity of the reforms and the index of tax neutrality (–0.11), and a negative correlation between the frequency of reforms and the index of tax neutrality (–0.40).

25. The case of Colombia, which is analyzed in Stein and others (2005), chapter 8, is an interesting illustration of why more intense tax reforms may be associated with worse outcomes.

References

Acevedo, Carlos, and Mauricio Orellana. 2003. "El Salvador: Diagnostico del Sistema Tributario y Recomendaciones de Política para Incrementar la Recaudación." Inter-American Develoment Bank, Washington, DC.

Agosín, M., A. Barreix, R. Machado, and J. Gómez-Sabaini. 2004. "Panorama Tributario de los Países Centroamericanos y Opciones de Reforma." Economic and Social Studies Series Working Paper RE2-04-010, Inter-American Development Bank, Washington, DC.

Agosín, M., and R. Machado. 2004. "Reforma Tributaria y Desarrollo Humano en Centroamérica." Economic and Social Studies Series Working Paper RE2-04-009, Inter-American Development Bank, Washington, DC.

Bahl, Roy, Jorge Martinez-Vásquez, and Sally Wallace. 1996. *The Guatemalan Tax Reform.* Boulder, CO: Westview Press.

Bird, Richard, and Milka Casanegra, eds. 1992. "Improving Tax Administration in Developing Countries." International Monetary Fund, Washington, DC.

CEB (Centro de Estudios Bonaerense). 1997. *Informe de Coyuntura* 7 (65–66) May. La Plata, Argentina: CEB.

Edwards, Sebastian. 1995. *Crisis and Reform in Latin America. From Despair to Hope.* Oxford: Oxford University Press.

Engel, Eduardo, Alexander Galetovic, and Claudio Raddatz. 1997. "Taxes and Income Distribution in Chile: Some Unpleasant Redistributive Arithmetic." Working Paper 41, Department of Applied Economics, University of Chile, Santiago.

Gómez-Sabaini, Juan C. 2003. "Nicaragua: desafíos para la modernización del sistema tributario." Inter-American Development Bank, Washington, DC.

———. 2005. "Evolución y Situación Tributaria Actual en América Latina: Una Serie de Temas para la Discusión," Presentation to CEPAL, Santiago de Chile, Chile, September.

Goode, Richard. 1993. "Tax Advice to Developing Countries: An Historical Survey." *World Development* 21 (1): 37–53.

Harberger, Arnold. 1990. "Principles of Taxation Applied to Developing Countries: What Have We Learned?" In *World Tax Reform: Case Studies of Developed and Developing Countries*, ed. Michael J. Boskin and Charles E. McLure, Jr. San Francisco: International Center for Economic Growth, ICS Press.

Haughton, Jonathan. 2005. "An Assessment of Tax and Expenditure Incidence in Peru." Inter-American Development Bank, Washington, DC.

IDB (Inter-American Development Bank). 1996. *Making Social Service Work.* Washington, DC: IDB.

———. 1998. *Facing Up to Inequality in Latin America.* Washington, DC: IDB.

———. 2001. *Competitiveness: The Business of Growth. Economic and Social Progress in Latin America.* Washington, DC: IDB.

———. 2004a. "The Effects of Structural Reforms on Employment and Wages." In *Good Jobs Wanted.* Washington, DC: IDB.

———. 2004b. "Integration and Trade in the Americas: Fiscal Impact of Trade Liberalization in the Americas." Periodic Note, IDB, Washington, DC.

IMF (International Monetary Fund). 2005. "Central America: Global Integration and Regional Cooperation." Occasional Paper No. 243, IMF, Washington, DC.

Lledo, Victor, Aaron Schneider, and Mick Moore. 2004. "Governance, Taxes, and Tax Reform in Latin America." IDS Working Paper 221, Institute of Development Studies, Brighton, UK.

Lora, Eduardo. 2001. "Structural Reforms in Latin America: What Has Been Reformed and How to Measure It." Research Department Working Paper No. 466, Inter-American Development Bank, Washington, DC.

Lora, Eduardo, and Ugo Panizza. 2002. "Structural Reforms in Latin America Under Scrutiny." Research Department Working Paper No. 1012, Inter-American Development Bank, Washington, DC.

Mahon, James E. 2004. "Causes of Tax Reform in Latin America, 1977–95." *Latin American Research Review* 39 (1): 3–30.

Perry, Guillermo E., Omar S. Arias, J. Humberto López, William F. Maloney, and Luis Servén. 2006. *Poverty Reduction and Growth: Virtuous and Vicious Circles.* Washington, DC: World Bank.

PricewaterhouseCoopers. Various years. "Corporate and Individual Taxes: Worldwide Summaries." Hoboken, NJ: John Wiley & Sons.

Santana, Isidoro, and Magdalena Rathe. 1992. *El Impacto Distributivo de la Gestión Fiscal en la República Dominicana.* Santo Domingo: Ediciones de la Fundación Siglo 21.

Shome, Parthasarathi. 1999. "Taxation in Latin America: Structural Trends and Impact of Administration." IMF Working Paper 99/19, International Monetary Fund, Washington, DC.

Singh, Anoop, Agnes Belaisch, Charles Collyns, Paula de Masi, Reva Krieger, Guy Meredith, and Robert Rennhack. 2005. "Stabilization and Reform in Latin America: A Macroeconomic Perspective on the Experience Since the Early 1990s." Occasional Paper 238, International Monetary Fund, Washington, DC.

Stallings, Barbara, and Wilson Peres. 2000. *Growth, Employment, and Equity: The Impact of the Economic Reforms in Latin America and the Caribbean.* Washington, DC: Brookings Institution Press.

Stein, Ernesto, Tommasi Mariano, Koldo Echebarría, Eduardo Lora, and Mark Payne. 2005. *The Politics of Policies. Economic and Social Progress in Latin America 2006 Report.* Washington, DC: Inter-American Development Bank and Cambridge, MA: David Rockefeller Center for Latin American Studies, Harvard University.

Steiner, Roberto, and Carolina Soto. 1998. *Cinco ensayos sobre tributación en Colombia.* Bogotá, Colombia: Fedesarrollo.

Stotsky, Janet, and Asegedech WoldeMariam. 2002. "Central American Tax Reform: Trends and Possibilities." IMF Working Paper 02/227, International Monetary Fund, Washington, DC.

Tanzi, V. 2003. "Taxation Reform in Latin America in the Last Decade." In *Latin American Macroeconomic Reforms: The Second Stage,* ed. J. González, V. Corbo, A. Krueger, and A. Tornell. Chicago: University of Chicago Press.

World Bank. 2005. *World Development Indicators.* Washington, DC: World Bank.

7

Fiscal and Political Decentralization Reforms

Robert Daughters and Leslie Harper

PREVIOUS CHAPTERS FOCUSED ON REFORM of the state from the perspective of the central government. Since 1985, however, the region has undergone significant decentralization, devolving important government functions and resources from the central government to the regional and local levels of government. In a few countries, especially those with federal regimes—Argentina and Brazil, in particular—decentralization reforms played a prominent role as early as the 19th century. However, most countries of the region, weighed down by a centralist colonial heritage, find decentralization a new phenomenon—one that introduces many new stakeholders and creates a contentious new arena for national policy making.

The wave of decentralization in the region has moved rapidly, producing important reforms in political and fiscal policy making. Triggered in most cases by the national democratic transitions that took place in the region during the 1980s, the decentralization reforms initially centered on the political arena, specifically the creation of representative democracies at the local level. During the 1980s and 1990s, electoral reforms were approved in most countries, thus establishing local elections for mayors and, to a lesser degree, regional elections for governors, breaking a long tradition in Latin America and the Caribbean of centrally appointed chief executives at the local and regional levels. This trend, and its close link to the broader democratic transition in the region, can be observed in table 7.1. In 1980, in all but seven countries the municipal chief executives (mayors) were appointed by the central government. By 1994, the situation had reversed; in the large majority of countries, mayors were being elected—either directly or indirectly—by their local constituencies. In countries with active regional or intermediate levels of government (about half the countries in Latin America), although it is occurring more slowly and is less widespread than at the municipal level, regional government chief executives are now popularly elected. As a result of these reforms, and for the first time in most countries, local and regional chief executives have an incentive to be more responsive and accountable to the interests of their local constituencies than to the central government bureaucracy.

In the fiscal arena, in turn, local and regional jurisdictions led by their own chief executives began to press for expanded resources and functional authority to address the preferences of their electorates, generating new grassroots demands for fiscal empowerment. The result has been a gradual but clear trend toward increasing decentralization of public expenditures in the region, as indicated in figure 7.1. This figure measures the average of the degrees of expenditure decentralization in 17 countries for which comparable data were available in 1985, 1990, 1996, and 2004. Expenditure decentralization is defined as the ratio of subnational to national expenditure.[1] As noted in the figure, on average, the share of subnational expenditure in the region increased from 13.1 percent in 1985 to 19.3 percent in 2004, moving ever closer to the level of expenditure decentralization that currently exists in Organisation for Economic Co-operation and Development (OECD) countries (29.1 percent).

Figure 7.1 Fiscal Decentralization Trends (regional averages 1985–2004, percentage)

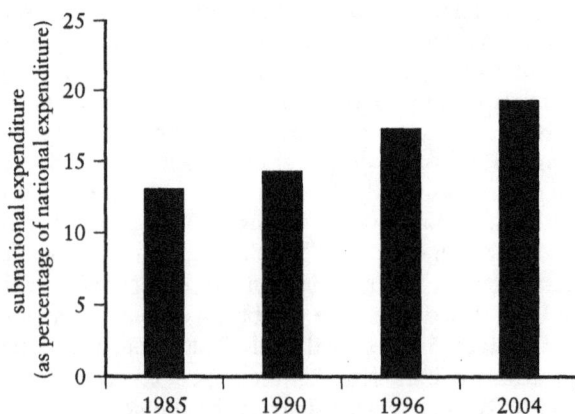

Sources: IDB (1997) and author's calculations based on a 2004 IDB survey on decentralization.

Fiscal empowerment of subnational governments in the region has not been free of controversy. During the initial phase of decentralization in the late 1980s and early 1990s, when subnational electoral reforms were in full swing, many fiscal and economic policy makers at the national level joined forces with political reformers in supporting decentralization initiatives. A broad consensus was thus created around two major benefits of decentralized regimes: (a) that decentralization helps to improve the channels of citizen participation and political accountability, and (b) that decentralization allows for a more responsive, and thus effective, government allocation of public goods to a regionally diverse citizenry. At the central macroeconomic level, moreover, the thought was that decentralization could also make a positive contribution to the structural adjustment goals that many countries were committing themselves to at the time. By devolving expenditure responsibilities, it was hoped that central governments could reduce their spending obligations and improve their fiscal balance sheets. As decentralization progressed, however, it became increasingly clear that fiscal downsizing gains to the central government had been greatly exaggerated; the devolution of expenditure responsibilities to subnational governments proved to be far more costly and complex, both politically and technically, than anticipated. In addition, the ensuing growth in central government fiscal obligations to subnational governments—whether through expanded intergovernmental transfer schemes, or periodic bailouts of overindebted subnational entities—rapidly overshadowed whatever downsizing gains had taken place. This led to a significant realignment of positions on the part of national fiscal policy makers. By the end of the 1990s, many ministries of finance in the region had taken a much more cautious, if not antagonistic, attitude toward decentralization reforms, advocating at a minimum strong regulatory frameworks for intergovernmental finances.

The cautionary attitude of central government economists has done little to slow the momentum of decentralization in the region, as this chapter shows. What has occurred as a result of the more conservative attitude of central fiscal policy makers is a sharpening of the policy debate surrounding new decentralization reform initiatives, more explicitly taking into account the risks and critical paths involved in the process, as well as the incentives needed to minimize these risks. The focus of the policy debate is on four critical risk areas:

- With excessive *dependence of local governments on central government transfers,* local governments depend more on transfers to finance their expenditure requirements than on their own revenues, distorting local fiscal discipline and accountability. Decision makers are tempted to transfer the costs of their programs to other jurisdictions and inflate costs to receive larger transfers. This results in overspending and less attention to cost-effectiveness—a classic problem of the commons. In addition, as transfers obscure the link between the cost of services and those who pay for them, the ability of voters to punish waste and rent seeking is undermined.

- Similar distortions occur when *subnational governments are allowed to borrow in a soft credit market,* where bailouts by the central government are expected to occur. In this situation, the incentive to subnational governments is to overborrow, and for lending institutions to overlend, both assuming that the final repayment burden will eventually be borne by the central government. The resulting fiscal burden on the central government can easily get out of control, as occurred in Argentina, Brazil, and Colombia in the 1990s, seriously affecting macroeconomic stability.

- A problem of common resources also occurs when *functions and responsibilities are poorly divided* between central and subnational governments because some jurisdictions will transfer costs and burdens to other jurisdictions. Inadequately defined functions and responsibilities between different levels also tend to undermine accountability and lead to duplication of efforts.

- A widespread problem throughout the region is the *weak institutional capacity that exists in most subnational governments,* making it difficult, sometimes impossible, for many local governments to effectively deliver the public goods under their responsibility. Even if in theory subnational entities should be able to respond better to local preferences, in practice, they may not be able to respond at all. This is compounded by the risk of local elites capturing power and corrupting the local decision-making process to maximize their personal rents.

This chapter provides a comparative sketch of the decentralization reform processes that have been taking place in Latin American and Caribbean countries in recent years. Using as its baseline a comprehensive comparative survey and analysis on decentralization trends undertaken in 1996 (IDB 1997), the chapter updates this analysis with a new survey covering the period 1996–2004, evaluating changes produced in key political and fiscal indicators of decentralization and linking them to the principal reform initiatives attempted during this period. In the political arena, the focus is primarily on the status of democratic elections at the local and regional levels of government. In the fiscal arena, the analysis focuses on four broad fiscal policy areas: expenditure (or administrative) decentralization, subnational tax policy, intergovernmental transfer systems, and subnational debt policy. According to the survey results, in 1996 the policy area prioritized by the greatest number of countries was that of political decentralization (that is, electoral reform), followed closely by expenditure decentralization, and, less often, intergovernmental transfers, subnational tax policy, and, least of all, subnational debt policy (see figure 7.2). In the

2004 survey, on the other hand, political decentralization shifted to the lowest priority among these five policy areas, reflecting that local democratic election reforms had already been completed in most countries by the mid-1990s. Instead, in 2004 expenditure decentralization moved into first place, followed by intergovernmental transfers as the second most active policy reform area. Subnational debt and tax policy had a lower amount of activity. The remainder of this chapter explores these trends, looking first at the policy reform trends in the area of political decentralization, followed by those that have occurred in the four fiscal policy areas. The final section of the chapter provides a consolidated review of the decentralization process in each country, based on a Decentralization Maturity Index (DMI), which permits comprehensive comparison of the progress made by each country between 1996 and 2004 in a number of strategically important political and fiscal decentralization policy areas.

Political Decentralization

One of the most compelling arguments for decentralization is the natural advantage that local and regional governments have relative to central

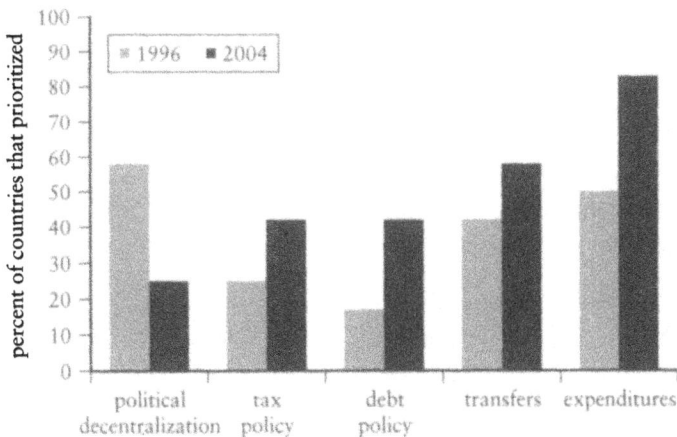

Figure 7.2 Priority Decentralization Policy Reform Areas, 1996 and 2004

Sources: IDB (1997) and authors' calculations based on a 2004 IDB survey on decentralization.

governments in achieving a good match between the public goods supplied by local governments and the preferences of the population. This fit, however, can only be obtained if local governments have mechanisms in place that permit their inhabitants to (a) hold public decision makers accountable, through *democratic elections*, and (b) properly communicate their preferences to public decision makers, through *community participation*.

As noted above, by the mid-1990s at the local level of government the first of these conditions had been largely met in the region: democratic elections for municipal mayors had been instituted in all countries in the region except Suriname (see table 7.1). At the intermediate level of government—states, provinces, departments, or regions—the democratic transition has also been progressing, but significantly more cautiously; as of 2004, only half the countries with official regional levels of govern-

Table 7.1 First Year of Democratic Elections for Municipal and Intermediate Government Chief Executives

Country	Municipal mayors[a]	State, provincial, or departmental government CEOs[a]	Year of democractic transition (DT)[b]
Argentina	1983	1983	1983
Bahamas	1997	n.a.[c]	1973
Barbados	n.a.[c]	n.a.[c]	1966
Belize	1981	n.a.[c]	1981
Bolivia	1985	2005	1982
Brazil	prior to DT[c]	1982	1985
Chile	1992	n.a.[d]	1990
Colombia	1988	1991	1958
Costa Rica	1949	n.a.[d]	1949
Dominican Republic	1966	n.a.[d]	1966
Ecuador	1983	1983	1979
El Salvador	1985	n.a.[d]	1984
Guatemala	1985	n.a.[d]	1985
Guyana	1995	n.a.[d]	1966
Honduras	1982	n.a.[d]	1982
Jamaica	1962	n.a.[c]	1962
Mexico	1917	1917	1917

(continued)

Table 7.1 First Year of Democratic Elections for Municipal
and Intermediate Government Chief Executives *(continued)*

Country	Municipal mayors[a]	State, provincial, or departmental government CEOs[a]	Year of democractic transition (DT)[b]
Nicaragua	1992	n.a.[f]	1990
Panama	1995	n.a.[d]	1989
Paraguay	1991	1993	1989
Peru	1980	2002	1980
Suriname	n.a.[g]	n.a.[c]	1987
Trinidad and Tobago	1962	n.a.[c]	1962
Uruguay	1984	n.a.[c]	1985
Venezuela	1989	1989	1958

Sources: IDB (1997) and authors' compilation based on official information. ·
Note:
n.a. = not applicable.
a. Directly or indirectly elected.
b. Year of independence, in the case of the Caribbean countries.
c. Level does not exist.
d. Level exists, but the CEO is appointed.
e. There were exceptions. During military rule, mayors of state capitals as well as around 170 cities were appointed in Brazil.
f. Nicaragua does not have an elected intermediate level of government. However, the country has two special regions (North Atlantic Autonomous Region and South Atlantic Autonomous Region), which as of 1990 have elected Regional Councils that select a regional coordinator responsible for executive functions.
g. In the case of Suriname, district councils are elected.

ment had instituted elections for their chief executives. This reflects a strong municipalist orientation in the decentralization reform processes of the region, at least among countries with unitary regimes. Many of these are reluctant to transfer the same degree of political autonomy to their departmental, provincial, or regional governments as they have to their municipalities.

The current picture among subnational governments in the region of widespread electoral democracy is a recent phenomenon, closely linked to the overall transition toward democratic regimes. Referring again to table 7.1, this link can be followed country by country. In the majority of countries, subnational elections were instituted at very nearly the same time as their respective democratic transitions at the national level (Argentina, Belize, Costa Rica, the Dominican Republic, El Salvador, Guatemala, Honduras,

Jamaica, Mexico, Peru, Trinidad and Tobago, and Uruguay), or shortly afterward (Bolivia, Chile, Nicaragua, and Paraguay). In countries such as Colombia and Venezuela, however, subnational elections did not take place until a number of years after their respective democratic transitions.

In addition to the introduction of elections as the basic method for choosing executive and legislative officials at the subnational level, political autonomy has been advanced by other important reforms (see table 7.2), such as changing the method of election of mayors from indirect to direct (Chile, 2001; Costa Rica, 2002; Nicaragua, 1995; Venezuela, 1989), and separating the timing of subnational elections from national ones (Brazil, 1997; Costa Rica, 2002; Dominican Republic, 1994; Ecuador, 1991; Nicaragua, 2000). Similarly, separate electoral ballots were established for subnational positions (Honduras, 1997), as were independent candidacies (Chile, 2001; Nicaragua 1995, then reversed in 2000), allowing voters to split their votes across executive and legislative candidates or to choose individual candidates instead of just party lists (Venezuela, 1989).

In addition to electoral reforms, important mechanisms or institutions for channeling and encouraging citizen participation were mandated or regulated by national statutes, starting with the community participation and organization mechanisms created in Brazil in 1988, which eventually spun off into the fiscal arena in the mid-1990s with pioneering participatory budgeting initiatives by a number of Brazilian municipalities. Particularly noteworthy are the strong community participation and social audit mechanisms put in place at the local level during the 1990s by Bolivia, Colombia, and Costa Rica.

Fiscal Decentralization Policy Reforms

As previously noted, the Latin American and Caribbean region achieved significant expenditure decentralization over the last two decades, climbing to a current regional average of 19.3 percent of total public expenditures controlled by subnational governments. This average, however, masks significant differences between countries, in both the degree of fiscal decentralization and the accompanying policy reform processes. As seen in figure 7.3, which maps out changes in the expenditure decentralization indexes in individual countries for the period 1996 through 2004, the region has three countries—Argentina, Brazil, and Colombia—with very high expenditure decentralization indexes (close to 50 percent), putting them in the company of some the world's most highly decentralized regimes, including Canada, the United States, and the Nordic countries in Europe. In Argentina and Brazil, this is consistent with their federal regimes and strong historical commitments to regional empowerment. It is particularly explicit in Argentina, where the power of the state is defined by its constitution as deriving from its provinces, not the central

Table 7.2 Reforms Affecting Political Autonomy
and Citizen Participation at the Subnational Level

Year	Changes
Argentina	
1983	• Elections first held. Provinces: governor; municipality: *Intendente*
1994	• Legal autonomy given to the city of Buenos Aires (its citizens now directly elect the *Intendente* and representatives to the legislative assembly). Senators directly elected instead of being appointed by provincial assemblies. New territorial entities created. Popular consultation mechanisms created.
Bolivia	
1985	• Election of mayors and municipal councils in urban areas.
1994	• Extension of election of municipal councils and mayors from departmental and provincial capitals to 311 new municipalities. Municipal council given power to revoke term of mayor after one year. Recognition given to grassroots nongovernmental organizations, which encouraged them to form oversight committees with real veto power.
Brazil	
1982	• Direct election of governors, state legislators, and all municipal mayors except for those in larger "strategic" cities.
1985	• Direct election of mayors of "strategic" cities.
1988	• Municipalities were made officially autonomous and their powers of administration were augmented relative to the other two levels of government. Introduction of popular consultation mechanisms.
1997	• Mayors elected at different dates than national and state authorities.
Chile	
1991	• Regional level of government created.
1992	• Mayors elected through municipal councils.
2001	• Direct election of mayors starting in 2004. Independent candidates allowed.
Colombia	
1986	• Direct popular election of mayors (1988).
1991	• Establishment of popular election of governors. Legal autonomy of municipalities established. Term of mayors extended from two to three years. Popular consultation mechanism established.

(continued)

Table 7.2 Reforms Affecting Political Autonomy
and Citizen Participation at the Subnational Level *(continued)*

Year	Changes
Costa Rica	
1998	• A municipal executive elected by elected municipal council members replaced by a mayor. Plebiscites and referenda introduced as well as *cabildos*. Recall provision. Election of district councils.
2002	• Direct election of the mayor. Separation of election of mayor and district councils from national elections.
Dominican Republic	
1994	• Local elections (as well as national legislative elections) separated from presidential elections.
Ecuador	
1983	• Canton: mayor.
1991	• System established that allows provincial deputies and municipal councils to be elected on different dates from national elections.
El Salvador	
1984	• Mayors elected.
Guatemala	
1985	• Mayors elected.
1995	• Terms of office for municipalities uniformly set at four years so that elections now fully concurrent with national elections.
Honduras	
1982	• Mayors elected.
1990	• Autonomy granted to municipalities; mayors directly elected; mechanisms established to promote citizen participation.
1993	• Separation of election for president, national legislature, and subnational offices. In 1997, separate ballots introduced for each office.
Mexico	
1996	• Establishment of the mayor of Mexico City being elected instead of appointed (first election in 1997). Direct elections.
Nicaragua	
1990	• Election of mayors.

(continued)

Table 7.2 Reforms Affecting Political Autonomy
and Citizen Participation at the Subnational Level *(continued)*

Year	Changes
1995	• Change from indirect election by municipal councils to direct election; reduction of mayoral term from six to four years; independent candidacies allowed; municipal governments made legally autonomous.
2000	• Independent candidacies disallowed; elections separate from national.
Panama	
1994	• Mayors elected.
Paraguay	
1991	• Mayors elected.
1992	• Established that governors are elected (1994).
Peru	
1990	• Creation of elected regional governments.
1992	• Elected regional governments replaced by temporary Regional Administration Councils.
2002	• Elected regional governments reinstated; mayors' terms extended from four to five years.
Uruguay	
1984	• Departments: *Intendente*–1984.
Venezuela	
1989	• Election of governors; system of electing mayors changed from election through municipal councils to direct election.

Sources: IDB 1997; 2004 IDB survey on decentralization; Montero and Samuels 2004; Tulchin and Selee 2004; USAID and ICMA 2004.

government.[2] Both countries, therefore, have had long periods—nearly two centuries—over which to develop, debate, and attempt to consolidate their decentralized fiscal frameworks. This process has not always moved in a predictable direction, however. Decentralization in both countries has oscillated substantially between decentralizing and recentralizing trends throughout their histories.[3] Only in recent years have they been able to achieve the high levels of expenditure decentralization found today, resulting from resurgent support for decentralization during the democratic transitions that took place in both countries in the 1980s, under the expectation that a decentralized framework of government would reduce the risk of a return to authoritarian regimes.[4]

Figure 7.3 Decentralization of Expenditure

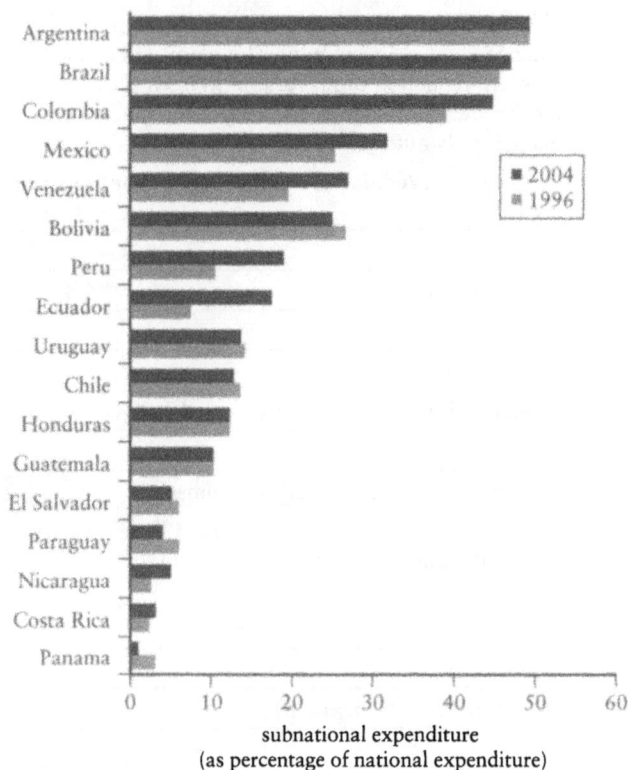

subnational expenditure
(as percentage of national expenditure)

Sources: IDB 1997; authors' calculations based on a 2004 IDB survey on decentralization.

The third strongly decentralized country, Colombia, despite its unitary regime, shares with Argentina and Brazil a deep regionalist tradition, leading to its long history of fiscal support to subnational governments, with accompanying cycles of decentralizing and recentralizing fiscal policies.[5] In terms of political decentralization, however, Colombia's history has differed significantly from that of Argentina and Brazil, because it has only chosen to relinquish central control of the selection of governors and mayors in the last two decades. Before that, the country functioned territorially under more of a deconcentrated regime,[6] assigning departments and municipalities a moderate degree of subnational fiscal power, but always maintaining central control in the naming of local and regional chief executives. Slowly, however, Colombian policy makers began to shift their interest toward greater decentralization, starting with the 1968 constitutional reform that put in place the country's first large-scale intergovernmental transfer system (the *Situado Fiscal*). Then in the mid-1980s and early 1990s, as noted in table 7.3, decentralization moved into high gear with a series of important reforms aimed principally at the municipal (rather than departmental) level of government, beginning with the creation of a new revenue-sharing mechanism for municipalities and the direct election of mayors. A new constitution followed in 1991, which enshrined the principle of decentralization; transferred responsibility for education, health, and housing services to departments and municipalities; and substantially increased the share of central revenues transferred to subnational governments. The share of subnational expenditures has since climbed steadily, increasing from 27 percent in the mid-1970s to 33 percent in 1985 and 45 percent in 2003.

The high levels of expenditure decentralization achieved by these three countries have not been without controversy in the area of national fiscal policy. To fund the expenditure responsibilities of their subnational governments, each of these countries created massive revenue-sharing systems funded by the central government budget. These transfers represent such a large proportion of central government budgets, and are so tightly earmarked, that they have significantly narrowed the freedom available to national policy makers when trying to make fiscal adjustments and achieve macroeconomic stability.

A second group of countries can be identified in figure 7.3—Mexico, Venezuela, Bolivia, Peru, and Ecuador—with more moderate, but still significant, expenditure decentralization, ranging from 17.5 percent to 31.8 percent in 2004. With the exception of Bolivia, these countries have in common a significant increase in their expenditure decentralization indexes since 1996, reflecting dynamic decentralization reform agendas instituted within the last 10 to 15 years. That is, all five countries are in the throes of consolidating their reform objectives (see table 7.4).

The nine remaining countries in the survey—Uruguay, Chile, Honduras, Guatemala, El Salvador, Paraguay, Nicaragua, Costa Rica, and Panama—are characterized by low or incipient levels of decentralization, with expenditure decentralization ratios that range from around 13 percent for Uruguay and Chile down to as little as 1–3 percent for Panama and Costa Rica. In all nine countries, decentralization of expenditures has changed little since 1996, reflecting for the most part a cautious attitude of national policy makers toward decentralization reform. Table 7.5 maps out the specific reform initiatives undertaken in five of these countries—Chile, Costa Rica, El Salvador, Guatemala, and Uruguay.

The sections that follow review more systematically and in greater detail the fiscal decentralization reform processes in the region, by comparing the changes that have occurred between 1996 and 2004 in the four principal fiscal policy areas—expenditure assignment, subnational tax policy, intergovernmental transfers, and subnational borrowing.

Table 7.3 Fiscal Reform Sequence in Countries with Advanced Levels of Decentralization

Year	Changes
Argentina	
1983	• Direct election of governors and mayors reestablished upon transition to democracy.
1988	• New Coparticipation Law gives provinces larger share of automatic fiscal transfers.
1991	• Exclusive responsibility for hospitals and secondary schools transferred to provinces (eliminating shared responsibility between provinces and federal government).
1992–93	• Fiscal pacts restrict the level of automatic transfers and encourage provinces to reform taxation systems.
1994	• New constitution enshrines Coparticipation Law. Federal District of Buenos Aires granted status of a province, with elected governor and legislature.
Brazil	
1975	• Partially reversing recentralization measures adopted since 1964 (which reduced subnational revenue shares and made gubernatorial elections indirect); military government doubles revenue share of states and municipalities.
1982	• Direct election of governors reestablished. Subnational revenue share increased again.
1985	• Direct election of mayors in state capitals reestablished.
1988	• New federal constitution enshrines autonomy of municipalities, as independent tier of government, including policy responsibility over primary education, health care, and social welfare. Also increases taxation powers of states and municipalities and doubles federal tax revenue share of municipalities. (No provision made, however, for clear assignment of shared expenditure responsibilities. Left to case-by-case negotiation.)
1992–94	• Impeachment of President Collor and Anti-inflation Plan (*Plano Real*) set stage for national consensus on need for fiscal responsibility and transparency.
1995	• National Information System on Government Debt in Arrears (CADIN) obliges all subnational governments with debt obligations in arrears to federal agencies, such as *Caixa Econômica,* to submit to careful monitoring through a system of indebtedness indicators.

(continued)

Table 7.3 (continued)

Year	Changes
1997	• Incentive Plan for Reduction of State Banks implemented (led to closing or privatization of most state banks); and Program for Financial Support and Debt Renegotiation of State Governments redefines and strengthens borrowing rules and mechanisms for states (including fiscal performance benchmarks).
2000	• Fiscal Responsibility Law passed, creating far-reaching new fiscal regime for all levels of government. In case of subnationals, consolidates and completes borrowing rules (including prohibition of intergovernmental lending) and fiscal efficiency standards (especially the latter), building on 1997 Financial Support Program. Standardizes accounting standards across all levels of government.

Colombia

Year	Changes
1986	• Direct election of mayors authorized (elections held in 1988); significant increase in automatic revenue transfers approved for municipalities.
1991	• National constitution entrenches decentralization as an organizing principal; establishes direct elections of departmental governors; establishes goal of decentralization for health, education, and housing services; substantially increases and simplifies automatic revenue transfers to departments and municipalities.
1993	• Law on Assignment of Responsibilities and Resources for education, health care, and housing (implementation of 1991 constitution), calling for phased decentralization of these three sectors and system of earmarked sectoral transfers.
1997	• Territorial Borrowing Law establishes "traffic light system" to control excesses and abuses in subnational indebtedness, followed by subnational debt restructuring law in 1999.
2000	• Indicators and benchmarks created for regulating public expenditures by subnational governments, aimed at generating budget surpluses.
2001	• Consolidation of separate intergovernmental revenue transfer systems (including *Situado Fiscal* and *Participaciones Municipales*) into a single General Share System (*Sistema General de Participaciones*) more strongly aimed at reducing horizontal regional imbalances.
2003	• Fiscal Responsibility Law, consolidating and further detailing provisions of 1997 and 2000 laws on borrowing and public expenditure regulation.

Sources: IDB 1997; 2004 IDB survey on decentralization; Montero and Samuels 2004; Tulchin and Selee 2004; USAID and ICMA 2004.

Table 7.4 Fiscal Reform Sequence in Countries with
Intermediate Levels of Decentralization

Year	Changes
Bolivia	
1987	• Sustainable process of direct municipal elections initiated (previously authorized in 1942, but interrupted after five years).
1994–96	• Laws of Popular Participation and Administrative Decentralization approved redefining territorial concept of municipality (to include rural as well as urban areas), doubling scale of subnational revenue sharing (to 20 percent of sharable taxes), giving municipalities exclusive responsibility over vehicle and property taxes, and establishing shared responsibility between municipalities and departments for primary and secondary education, and second- and third-level hospitals. Also, placed emphasis on participation of civil society organizations in allocation decisions and control and monitoring of local government activities.
1999	• Law of Municipalities further clarifies municipal responsibilities.
2000–04	• Financial Readjustment Program for municipalities put in place, establishing fiscal adjustment goals and benchmarks aimed at making local governments creditworthy, reducing ambiguities in assignment of responsibilities between departments and municipalities, and strengthening transfer system to municipalities.
Ecuador	
1991–96	• Implementation of large-scale Municipal Development Program, creating new culture of service delivery in local governments using large-scale investment lending and institutional capacity building.
1997	• Decentralization and Citizen Participation Law passed, defining services eligible for decentralization to provinces and municipalities; Revenue Sharing Law sets subnational shares of central revenues at 15 percent (to be attained gradually).
1998	• New political constitution approved, building on 1997 Decentralization Law, establishes that all public services— with exception of defense, national security, foreign policy, and economic policy—are in principal eligible for devolution to subnational governments.

(continued)

Table 7.4 Fiscal Reform Sequence in Countries with
Intermediate Levels of Decentralization *(continued)*

Year	Changes
1999	• National Decentralization Commission created, accompanied by active process of decentralization debates, with strong regionalist focus.
2000–01	• Regulations for Decentralization Law approved, defining transaction rules and institutional structure to guide transfer of responsibilities to subnationals; first Annual National Decentralization Plan approved; implementation of transfer of responsibilities proceeds very slowly, on case-by-case basis.
2002	• Subnational transfers augmented with 25 percent share of national income tax, defined on voluntary basis by each taxpayer; Fiscal Responsibility, Stabilization, and Transparency Law approved—includes restrictions on subnational borrowing; National Commission on Competencies created to arbitrate process of transfer of responsibilities.
2003–04	• Organic Law of Municipalities reformed, amending tax and revenue mechanisms for municipalities; National Decentralization Plan for 2004 approved.
Mexico	
1980	• National System of Fiscal Coordination (*pacto fiscal*) created: state governments give up old revenue-sharing system linked to federal sales tax, in exchange for new system tied to federal VAT, personal income tax, and oil royalties.
1984	• Constitutional amendment strengthening fiscal autonomy of municipalities: making revenue sharing to municipalities official; transferring responsibility for property taxes; assigning public service responsibility for water supply, street paving, and public security.
1984–85	• Breakdown of Partido Revolucionario Institucional (PRI) political monopoly gradually led to establishment of open, competitive elections at municipal level.
1992	• Transfer of functions and responsibilities from federal government to states: primary and secondary education; public health care and hospitals; nutrition programs; road infrastructure; water and sanitation. New intergovernmental transfer systems created to cover costs, including earmarked sectoral grant programs.

(continued)

Table 7.4 Fiscal Reform Sequence in Countries with
Intermediate Levels of Decentralization *(continued)*

Year	Changes
1997	• Direct election of the mayor of the Federal District.
1999	• Constitution reformed enabling municipalities to be officially recognized as the third level of government.
2000	• New regulatory framework put in place to control subnational borrowing.

Peru

Year	Changes
1965	• Direct election of mayors established (based on 1933 constitution that empowered municipalities with property tax authority as well as borrowing authority).
1979	• New constitution defines—in principle—a third autonomous, regional, level of government.
1981	• Direct municipal elections instituted (following return to democracy).
1990	• Implementation of autonomous regional level of government (creation of 12 regions agglomerating 25 existing departments); provided for gradual transfer to regional governments of taxing authority for personal income and inherited property, as well as system of transfers (including automatic revenue sharing plus earmarked sectoral transfers). Overly ambitious assignment of responsibilities with insufficient capacity-building measures, plus inadequate fiscal mechanisms and operational rules, resulted in increasingly chaotic management of regional governments.
1992	• Constitutional reform dissolves autonomous regions (only recognizes two levels of government—central and municipal).
2001	• New constitutional reform reestablishes, in principle, regional level of government.
2002–03	• Series of follow-up decentralization reforms put in place resulting in: effective creation of new regional governments with elected officials; clarification of responsibilities between three levels of government (to be gradually phased in); creation of automatic transfer mechanisms for regions (FONCOR) and municipalities (FONCOMUN), to be eventually complemented by a fund to support project investment funding (FIDE); approval of (limited) fiscal responsibility measures for subnational governments (within the National Law of Transparency and Fiscal Prudence).

(continued)

Table 7.4 Fiscal Reform Sequence in Countries with
Intermediate Levels of Decentralization *(continued)*

Year	Changes
2004	• Accreditation System Law establishing conditions for transfer of expenditure functions and resources to regions and municipalities.

Venezuela

Year	Changes
1989	• Series of legislation (sped on by *Caracazo*) authorizing direct election of mayors and governors, establishing process for gradual decentralization of federal government responsibilities to the states, on case-by-case basis, at the initiative of individual governors. In practice, decentralization has moved very slowly, due to ineffectiveness of decentralization process: mechanisms for financing new responsibilities are poorly defined and overly controlled by Central Government; cumbersome review process by Senate. Continued to depend on old top-down transfer system (*Situado Fiscal*), created in 1961, that removed most taxation authority from subnationals.
1993	• Ministry of State for Decentralization created (subsequently, in 1995, reduced to office in Ministry of Interior); Intergovernmental Decentralization Fund (FIDES) created, to finance subnational investment projects; subnational share of Situado Fiscal increased from 15–20 percent; Association of Venezuelan Governors created.
1996	• Law approved gradually increasing share of VAT transferred to subnationals through FIDES, climbing from 18 percent to 30 percent between 1996 and 2000.

Sources: IDB 1997; 2004 IDB survey on decentralization; Montero and Samuels 2004; Tulchin and Selee 2004; USAID and ICMA 2004.

Expenditure Assignments

Of the five main decentralization reform policy areas, the one showing the most reform activity and generating the most policy debate over the last 10 years has been expenditure assignments. While the measure of subnational over total government expenditures (figure 7.3) provides a sense of the relative aggregate fiscal strength of the different levels of government, it does not shed light on how much or what type of functional responsibility subnational governments are actually being assigned. Because it only measures overall spending, the rise could reflect increases in subnational expenditures without an actual increase in responsibility for service provision. To help complete the picture, the IDB constructed an Activity Decentraliza-

Table 7.5 Reform Processes in Countries with Limited or
Incipient Decentralization

Year	Changes
Chile	
1935	• Indirect election of mayors of small and intermediate-sized municipalities (appointed in four largest cities); weak functional responsibilities for municipalities; municipal taxes collected by Central Government (and frequently not returned).
1973–89	• Municipal elections dissolved under military regime. Municipalities subordinated to new regional level of government administration. Despite sharp restrictions in political autonomy of subnational jurisdictions, functional responsibilities and fiscal resources of municipalities and regions substantially strengthened: in 1979, Municipal Revenues Law created Municipal Common Fund; municipalities also given important responsibilities in administration of primary education and health programs, as well and antipoverty income support programs (funded by cost-reimbursement transfers). Result: professionalization of local governments.
1991–92	• Decentralization proposed as cornerstone of new democratic government's platform of state reform, leading to prolonged, conflictive debate on advantages and disadvantages of more explicit decentralized governments. Resulted in compromise package of constitutional reforms calling for full, formal administrative autonomy of municipalities and indirect election of mayors, establishment of regions as formal intermediate level of government, with indirectly elected regional councils, and appointed *Intendente*. Functional decentralization features created under military regime maintained and strengthened. However, definition of new subnational fiscal instruments has stalled.
1994	• Exclusive responsibility for administration of primary education and health services established for municipalities.
2000–02	• Revenue Laws (*Ley de Rentas*) I and II approved; include important provisions aimed at strengthening municipal tax performance.
2001	• Electoral reform enacted providing for direct election of mayors beginning in 2004.

(continued)

Table 7.5 Reform Processes in Countries with Limited or Incipient Decentralization *(continued)*

Year	Changes
Costa Rica	
1986–90	• Important reforms proposed but not approved under Arias administration, including constitutional amendment for automatic transfer of 10 percent of national budget to municipalities and the creation of Consultative Commission on State Reform that proposed direct election of mayors; creation of municipal public enterprises; establishment of municipal tax code.
1994–98	• Under Figueres administration, different tack followed: more responsibility transferred to Legislative Assembly; in 1995, administration of Real Estate Tax (ISBI) transferred to municipalities—however, in 1998 law was modified, lowering tax rate from 0.6 percent to 0.25 percent, as a result of which it has lost importance as source of revenue.
1998–2004	• Revenue share of fuel tax transferred to municipalities; 10 percent automatic transfer to municipalities approved in the constitution. 1998 Municipal Code approved. Bill to transfer new responsibilities to municipalities has been submitted to Congress in 2002, but has stalled there.
El Salvador	
1984–89	• Under Duarte administration, first steps to decentralization: direct election of mayors in 85 percent; automatic transfer of 1 percent of national revenues.
1988	• FODES created to fund municipal investment projects (1 percent of national revenues).
1991	• Tax code approved in 1991, authorizing municipalities to establish fees for services.
1998	• FODES law reformed, increasing transfers to municipalities to 6 percent of national revenues (split among FISDL, ISDEM, and COMURES).
1999–2000	• National Local Development Strategy proposed, coordinated by FISDL, including drafting of sectoral decentralization plans (especially water, sewers, education, health, and roads), resulting in transfer of small water systems to 21 municipalities; deconcentration in education and health; transfer (unfunded mandate) of tertiary roads by MOP.

(continued)

Table 7.5 Reform Processes in Countries with Limited or
Incipient Decentralization *(continued)*

Year	Changes
2003	• Proposal approved by Legislative Assembly to increase transfers to municipalities in FODES, from 6 percent to 8 percent; vetoed by executive (arguing that this would generate macroeconomic instability, because not linked to increase in municipal responsibilities, and that it would discourage mobilization of own-source revenues); furthermore, was declared unconstitutional by Supreme Court.

Guatemala	
1956	• Constitution allows for, direct election of mayors.
1982	• Direct mayoral elections eliminated by military government.
1985	• New constitution reestablishes direct election of mayors. Defines a transfer of 8 percent of national current revenues to municipalities (government only begins to comply in late 1980s).
Early 1990s	• Revenue-sharing formula increased to 10 percent.
1993–94	• Creation of Social Investment Fund and Solidarity Fund, to finance local regional development councils; real estate tax decentralized; programs put in place to deconcentrate health and education services.
1996	• Peace Accords lead to promotion of local social participation mechanisms, creation of Municipal Association, and creation of new additional transfer mechanism (1 percentage point surcharge on VAT).
1997	• Executive Organization Law authorizes sectoral ministries to develop deconcentration plans.
2000–04	• Portillo administration reforms Municipal Code (2002); creates COPRE (Presidential Commission for State Reform, Decentralization and Citizen Participation); passes Decentralization Law as well as its regulation (2002); IVAPAZ shared tax (percentage of VAT, car tax, oil derivatives tax) created in late 1990s as supplement to constitutional transfer; Social Funds, after growing rapidly in late 1990s, consolidated and reorganized in 2001.

(continued)

Table 7.5 Reform Processes in Countries with Limited or Incipient Decentralization *(continued)*

Year	Changes
Uruguay	
1918–34	• Period of significant political and fiscal decentralization for departments (*intendencias*), including direct elections and important authority for taxation. However, country's severe fiscal crisis in 1929 was blamed on "decentralization excesses" undercutting continued support of these policies.
1934–35	• Departments denied authority to collect taxes and issue debt. However, local officials continued to be elected. A number of agricultural services recentralized.
1966	• Constitutional reform assigns departmental planning responsibility to central planning agency (OPP).
1973–84	• Military government disbands democratically elected departmental assemblies and dismisses elected *Intendentes*.
1990–2004	• A series of Municipal Development Programs implemented, with international funding, gradually strengthening institutional and financial framework in support of decentralization, linking investment funding to attainment of institutional development benchmarks by departmental governments.
1996	• Constitutional amendment defines institutional framework for formulating and implementing decentralization policies, including designation of OPP as lead central agency in charge of promoting and guiding decentralization process, creation of a Sectoral Commission on Decentralization (includes Association of Mayors). Association of Mayors established as official representative of departmental governments.
1999	• National Budget Act increases automatic revenue sharing; creates new investment fund for interior departments (Interior Development Fund).

Sources: IDB 1997; 2004 IDB survey on decentralization; Montero and Samuels 2004; Tulchin and Selee 2004; USAID and ICMA 2004.

Note: COMURES = Corporación de Municipalidades de La República de El Salvador, FISDL = Fondo de Inversión Social para el Desarrollo Local, El Salvador, FODES = Fondo de Desarrollo Económico y Social, El Salvador, ISDEM = Instituto Salvadoreño de Desarrollo Municipal, El Salvador, IVAPAZ = Municipalities' share of VAT, Guatemala, MOP = Ministerio de Olaras Públicas, El Salvador.

tion Index (ADI), which measures the degree of autonomy of local and intermediate governments in the management of major public services.[7] Figure 7.4
maps out the regional average of ADIs for each of the major public service or
activity areas in the survey, comparing changes between 1996 and 2004 to
similar changes in the previous 10-year period (1985–96).

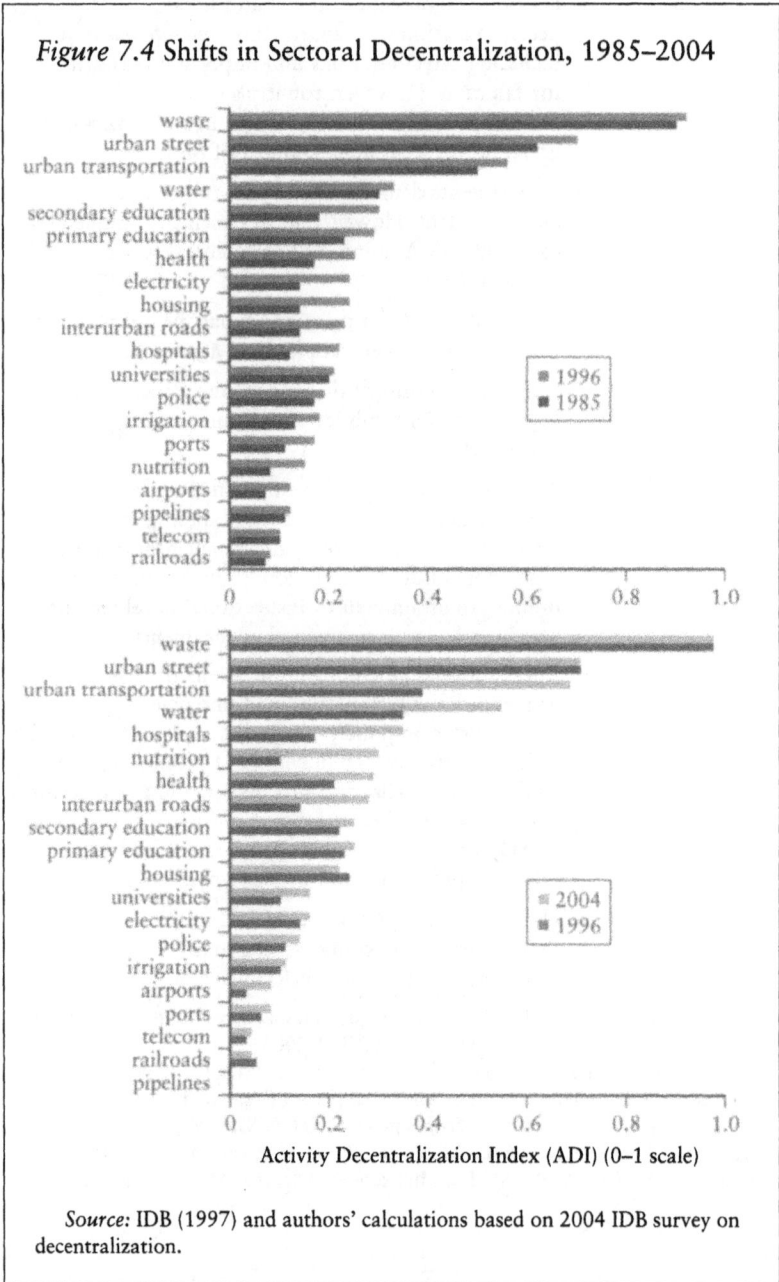

Figure 7.4 Shifts in Sectoral Decentralization, 1985–2004

Activity Decentralization Index (ADI) (0–1 scale)

Source: IDB (1997) and authors' calculations based on 2004 IDB survey on
decentralization.

The picture that emerges corresponds with what is generally known about decentralization in the region. There have been two main waves of sectoral decentralization activity. The first wave consisted of a group of basic services and infrastructure (solid waste management, urban streets, urban transportation, and water and sewerage services) that, as classic local public goods, are relatively easy to decentralize. In most countries, these sectors have been devolved to local governments for several decades. In the case of solid waste management and urban streets, in particular, as can be seen from figure 7.4, the decentralization process is now highly consolidated, having experienced no change since 1996. Urban transportation and water and sewerage services, though already relatively decentralized in 1996, took significant leaps in greater decentralization over the last eight years.

Comparing the ADIs of different countries in the region, the analysis indicates that of the countries that were actively engaged in devolving expenditure assignments to lower levels of government since 1996, the majority, including Argentina, Brazil, and Colombia, were already fairly decentralized to begin with. In that group, Argentina showed the greatest change. There has been some progress in the decentralization of water services in Mexico. For example, 118 of 135 cities with a population exceeding 50,000 now have autonomous water authorities (Diaz-Cayeros, González, and Rojas 2002). Other countries had results that indicated lower levels of activity in this area.

The second wave of decentralization is made up of a group of sectors (education, public health, interurban roads, housing, police services, electricity) that have proved considerably more difficult to decentralize. Many of these sectors require elaborate coordination—between levels of government, with private sector providers, or with national labor unions—to be effectively delivered, making it more politically controversial and technically complicated to transfer major responsibility to local or regional governments. This has been particularly true of education and public health services. Countries with federal regimes have made more progress because they have greater capacity to support decentralized social services through complementary arrangements between the local and regional levels. For the rest of Latin America the process has been more difficult, especially where support from the national level is limited. As can be seen in figure 7.4, after a period of significant decentralization reform in these sectors between 1985 and 1996, additional progress slowed considerably over the next eight years. This is the case in education, for example, because countries such as Argentina, Brazil, Colombia, and Mexico have already reached a significant level of decentralization in this sector, having carried out important reforms by the early 1990s.[8] In these countries, the main focus in recent years has been less on further decentralization and more on consolidating the reforms or improving the quality of education (for example, curriculum reform,

238

DAUGHTERS AND HARPER

teacher training and professionalization, and national testing). Brazil in particular was able to consolidate the decentralization reforms that gave significant autonomy to municipalities; especially in primary education. This, in turn, allowed the country to focus its attention on much needed improvements in the quality of the municipal education systems. In the other countries mentioned above, the consolidation of decentralization reforms has continued to absorb the attention of national policy makers throughout this period, having undergone a difficult institutional adjustment sorting new roles and functions between levels of government and other stakeholders, such as teachers' unions. The widespread absence of change between 1996 and 2004 in education can also be explained by the fact that many countries, such as Costa Rica, Guatemala, and Honduras, have been reluctant to make any significant moves toward decentralization. An important exception is Nicaragua, which has given greater decision-making autonomy to municipalities in determining how resources are spent and adjusting the curriculum according to local realities.

Many of the conflicts in the decentralization of social sectors have involved stakeholder resistance. Indeed, the second biggest obstacle to decentralization indicated by survey respondents was opposition by unions (figure 7.5). About a third of those surveyed answered that it was the most important obstacle to decentralization, preceded only by the lack of resources. This has often occurred in countries that began the decentralization process later,

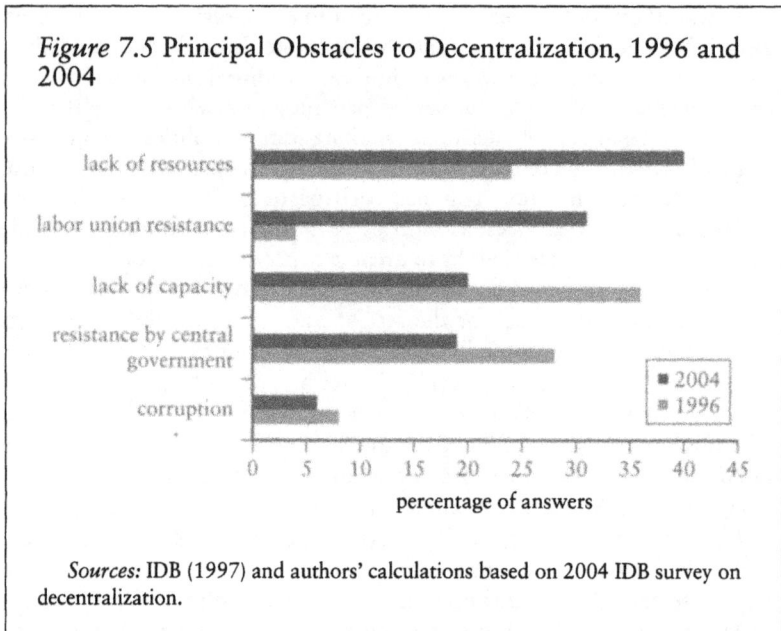

Figure 7.5 Principal Obstacles to Decentralization, 1996 and 2004

Sources: IDB (1997) and authors' calculations based on 2004 IDB survey on decentralization.

as in Ecuador and in many Central American countries. Federal regimes have not been exempt from such conflicts either. For example, opposition by unions was listed as the number one obstacle by Argentina.

Another difficulty many countries experienced was that reforms were passed that defined broad categories of responsibilities between local and national levels, but specified the details poorly. This has often led to confusion when the responsibilities local governments needed to assume were not clear. To make things worse, resource requirements for the new intergovernmental assignments of responsibilities were also often poorly worked out. On the one hand, as noted in the following sections, automatic transfers to subnational governments are frequently increased without clearly specifying the new responsibilities these governments must assume in exchange, resulting in freeloading by some subnational governments that choose not to assume their new responsibilities. This issue has been strongly debated in Brazil, Colombia, and Ecuador over the last 10 years. On the other hand, the opposite problem of unfunded mandates can also occur. Particularly in services such as education and health that have heavy operating costs and contingent liabilities, the central government might transfer these services to subnational governments without also transferring sufficient resources to cover true costs. This specific issue, for example, is being debated in Mexico now, in 2006. Both issues, too much and too little funding, point to the need for careful planning and synchronization between laws dealing with resource allocation and responsibility assignment.

Central government ministries have also not always sufficiently supported the elaborate work of fine-tuning each sector. Technocrats at the national level often do not have decentralization among their priorities, making it difficult to get effective commitment from the sectoral ministries unless a strong mandate is issued at the highest level and clearly transmitted to the relevant minister. This mandate, moreover, must be sustained for a number of years until operational and financial details are worked out between the levels of government. This has been particularly challenging for many of the countries with moderate levels of decentralization. In Ecuador and Peru, for example, sustaining a firm mandate long enough to operationalize the new division of labor between the sectoral ministries and subnational governments has proved difficult, resulting in prolonged decentralization reform processes that have tended to languish at the central government level.

Nevertheless, the level of reform activity currently under way in expenditure assignments continues to be significant. In Ecuador, through a comprehensive process centrally orchestrated by the national Modernization of the State Council, the sectoral ministries have begun to develop individual decentralization and deconcentration action plans as a basis for negotiating the transfer of responsibilities with municipal and provincial authorities; unfortunately, as noted above, implementation of these sectoral decentralization initiatives has proven difficult.[9] Between 2001 and 2002, Guatemala approved similar broad-scale decentralization reforms by way of a national Decentralization Law and a new Municipal Code that for the first time transfers responsibility for primary education to municipalities. In Chile a law is under discussion that will for the first time enable municipalities to create (or eliminate) staff positions and set salary levels—important requirements for the efficient management of public services under their responsibility. In Nicaragua, pilot programs are being developed by the central government (Ministry of Education and the Emergency Social Investment Fund) to decentralize responsibilities in primary education and in the management of social investment projects. In Panama, where municipalities still have limited responsibilities, proposed legislation would award municipalities responsibility for maintenance of schools, streets, and health centers. In Peru a law was passed in 2003 that established the principles and requirements for accreditation that local and regional governments must comply with to be transferred expenditure responsibilities that were previously carried out by the national government.

In conclusion, while many Latin American countries remain heavily centralized, sectoral expenditure decentralization has progressed significantly since 1985. Many of the countries that initiated this process in the late 1980s and early 1990s continue to refine the division of labor between levels of government. In some sectors, especially education and health, increasing attention has been given to working out the complementary relationship between intermediate and local levels of government. Other countries, Ecuador and Guatemala, for example, that began to move in this direction more recently are in the middle of the learning curve, trying to effectively implement their proposed reform objectives.

Subnational Tax Policy

Although the assignment of expenditure responsibilities to the subnational level is important, how the provision of those services is then financed by subnational governments is also a key concern. Financing is accomplished three ways: own-source revenue generation (taxation), intergovernmental transfers, or borrowing (or a combination of the three). This and the next two sections review the profile of the region in these three policy areas, starting with subnational taxation.

Public finance literature generally recognizes that robust generation of own-source revenues at the subnational level is a critical ingredient for successful decentralized governance. The more local services depend on revenues generated by the local citizenry, the more effectively will these services reflect the true preferences and willingness to pay of the local citizenry. By the same token, the more local services depend on outside funding—intergovernmental transfers, for example—the more likely that supply and demand of these services will be mismatched. Ideally, local services should be fully funded by own-source revenues to ensure internal fiscal and political accountability. In practice, however, this has not proved possible in any country. There are not enough taxes that can be efficiently administered at the local or subnational level of government to finance the expenditure obligations that these governments typically end up being assigned in a decentralized regime.

At one end of the spectrum is the assignment of taxation responsibilities to each level so that subnational governments can fully finance their expenditures. The other end would be to centralize taxation responsibilities and finance lower-level expenditures wholly through transfers. Most countries fall somewhere between these two extremes. Transfers are used to some degree in most countries because the more important tax bases can be more efficiently managed by the central government. An overreliance on transfers, however, reduces fiscal autonomy and breaks the link between the benefits of programs and those who pay for them. This undermines one of the principal goals of decentralization, which is to increase the accountability of subnational governments to their constituents. In addition, it can lead to overspending by subnational governments because it removes incentives for budgetary restraint.

In Latin America, subnational tax policy is notable by its relative absence. With the exception of Brazil, most countries in the region have not prioritized the strengthening of own-source revenues at the subnational level, preferring instead to rely on central government transfers as the principal source of revenues for their local and intermediate governments. Interestingly, the region does have an early history of allowing tax authority at lower levels of government. In the late 19th century and early 20th century, many Latin American countries permitted significant tax responsibilities at the subnational level. For example, the Argentine constitution of 1853 gave provinces the sole right to direct taxes, and in Chile the 1891 Municipal Law gave municipalities control over property taxes, personal taxes, and taxes on tobacco and alcoholic beverages and industries and professions (Montero and Samuels [2004], citing Valenzuela [1977]). Beginning in the 1930s, however, this trend reversed. Partly as a result of the Great Depression, governments began reining in subnational tax authorities in response to concerns that broad tax powers might be contributing to macroeconomic instability.[10] This trend was reinforced after the Depression by a noticeable shift in the region toward statism, which advocated a much stronger role for central government in the management of the public and private sectors. Finally, technological innovations in data processing meant that central governments could more easily collect data that in the past could only be done at the local level. As a result, it became much more efficient for central governments to manage centralized tax collection and then share the proceeds with subnational governments. These factors led to the adoption of transfer systems in most countries of the region (Argentina and Colombia being classic examples). Since then, policy concerns with expenditure decentralization have overshadowed those dealing with subnational own-source revenue generation. In recent years, as expenditure authority has expanded among subnational governments, interest in strengthening the regional and local tax systems has increased; however, this interest has not yet resulted in any important reform initiatives, neither by way of improving the effective exploitation of the current tax bases in subnational governments, nor in creatively expanding the tax base of subnational governments to expand their sources of own-source revenues.

As confirmed by the 2004 IDB survey, the broad trend in the region for tax assignment over the last 10 years has been toward relatively minor changes.[11] The majority of reforms that have been carried out have focused only on a narrow range of taxes, the most common being property taxes or vehicle licenses—for a variety of reasons. To begin with, the scope for reform is restricted by the fact that only a limited number of taxes are actually suitable for the subnational level. Although the matter generates some debate, the taxes usually considered appropriate for local and regional governments are those that are relatively simple to administer, do not foster competition among subnational governments, and whose payments are closely associated with benefits received. Common taxes include local property tax, vehicle tax, real estate transfer tax, water fees, and taxes on industry and commerce. Unfortunately, the revenue generation potential of these taxes is limited compared with the revenue potential of central government taxes, such as value added taxes (VAT) or personal income taxes. As a result, subnational governments in many countries are unable to raise, through their own sources of revenue, more than a fraction of the resources needed to cover their expenditures, forcing national governments to fill the gap with transfers.[12] Taxes levied by the central government, usually include, among others, those based on mobile tax bases (to avoid tax competition), those that involve redistribution (to avoid horizontal imbalances), those that are subject to economies of scale, and those taxes that involve persons from other jurisdictions.

This dichotomy has been reinforced by an ongoing reluctance by central government authorities in many countries to grant significant tax authority to subnationals. In addition to losing important sources of revenue to lower levels of government, they fear the creation of tax competition between different states or municipalities or exacerbating problems of regional inequalities between regions with strong and weak local tax bases. This is further complicated by the concern central authorities have about the weak institutional capacity of most local governments in tax administration.

Figures 7.6 and 7.7 show the taxes that were most frequently assigned to subnational levels of government in 1996 and 2004, in a sample of 11 countries with comparable data for both years. The first figure indicates whether, in both of these years, the tax was assigned to the intermediate

Figure 7.6 Taxes Most Frequently Assigned to Subnational Governments

1996

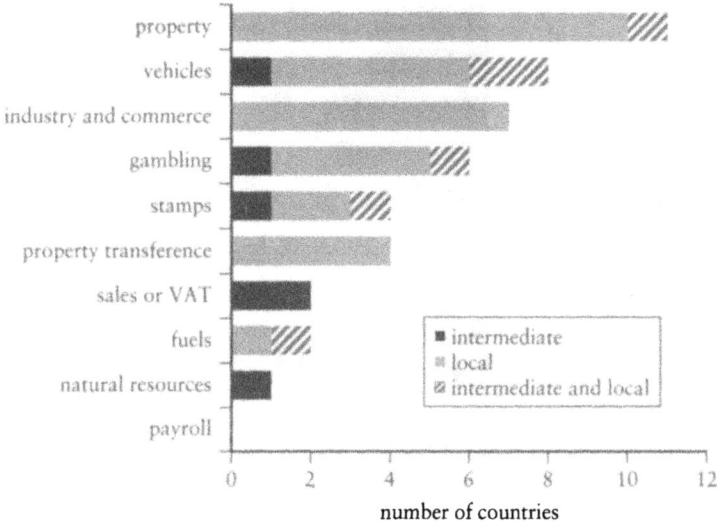

number of countries

2004

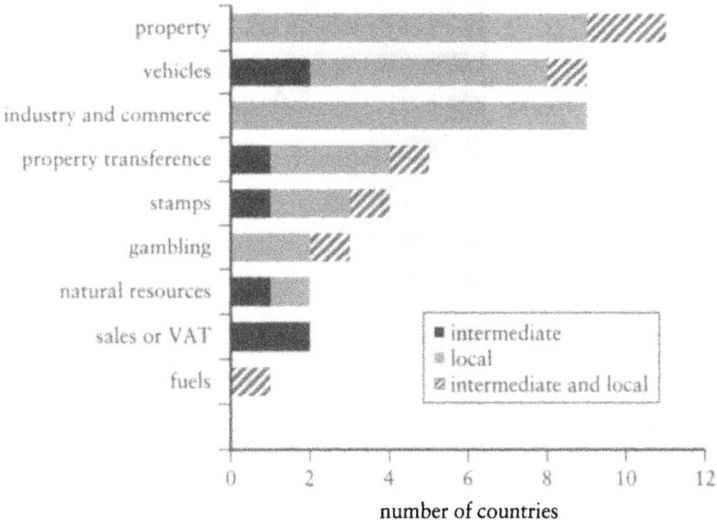

number of countries

Sources: IDB 1997; 2004 IDB survey on decentralization.

Figure 7.7 Subnational Taxes: Tax Administration and Tax Policy Responsibilities

1996

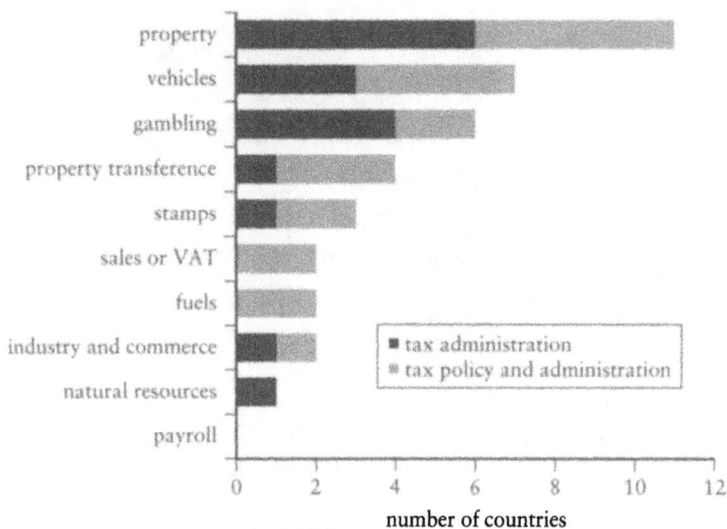

2004

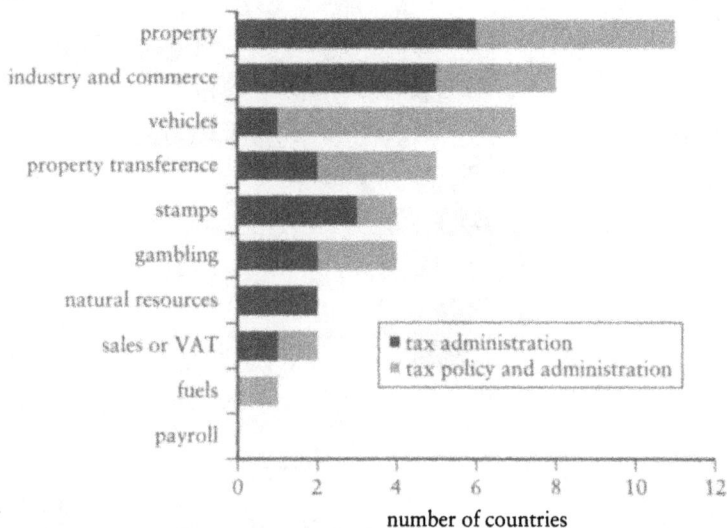

Sources: IDB (1997) and authors' calculations based on 2004 IDB survey on decentralization.

or local levels (or both). Figure 7.7 makes a distinction between taxes that are merely administered at the subnational level and those for which subnational governments also have some control over tax policy, such as fixing the tax rate or defining the tax base.

As in 1996, the tax in 2004 most often assigned to subnational levels continued to be the property tax. All 11 countries in the sample assigned this tax to either local or intermediate levels of government, almost in all cases to municipal authorities; in a little over half of these countries, local or regional governments are responsible for both tax administration and tax policy decisions. The lack of mobility of its tax base, combined with its high visibility to the local citizenry, make the property tax one of the more appropriate ones for local governments, allowing for a strong accountability link between taxpayers and government. At the same time, however, the high visibility of this tax means that it is more likely to provoke political resistance; moreover, property tax is difficult to administer, making it susceptible to weaknesses in institutional capacity. Not surprisingly, in most countries in the region, property tax systems operate with inefficient collection mechanisms and seriously outdated cadastres and property assessments, resulting in effective revenue well below potential.

As in 1996, the second and third most frequently assigned subnational taxes in 2004 were those levied on motor vehicles and on industry and commerce. The number of countries that assigned both these taxes to subnational governments has increased, with vehicle taxes now being applied in over 90 percent of the countries. As with property taxes, motor vehicle taxes function well at the local level; their high visibility makes it easy to establish clear accountability between taxpayers (drivers that use the roads) and the delivery of government services (road infrastructure). However, the increased use of industry and commerce taxes at the subnational level, though predictable, is not necessarily a positive trend. Local and regional authorities like to rely on this tax because of its ease of collection and relatively low political visibility. However, they frequently fail to take into account the negative impact these taxes have on local economies, acting as a disincentive to businesses that might otherwise be interested in locating in the region. Two other noteworthy changes during this period are the increased use of property transference taxes—a positive trend, given the natural association with regular property taxes—and, interestingly, the significant decrease in the use of gambling taxes at the subnational level. Two taxes that continue to be underutilized at the subnational level include fuel taxes and local income tax.

Not surprisingly, the countries that have given greatest tax authority to lower levels include Argentina, Brazil, and Colombia. Indeed, Brazil has been one of the most proactive countries in this area. Although the 1988 Brazilian constitution increased transfers, it also significantly strengthened subnational taxation authority. In fact, Brazil is the only country in Latin America that has a subnational VAT, making it one of the more decentralized countries in the world. While this tax has not been without controversy,[13] it successfully enabled states to have a major source of their own revenue, of which 25 percent is shared with municipalities. Currently, subnational governments collect 32 percent of taxes in the country (Souza 2004). Chile has been undergoing a process of municipalization by assigning greater tax and expenditure shares to the local level; subnational tax shares have increased from 7.2 percent of total tax revenue in 1990 to 8.6 percent in 2000. In addition, the country has two new revenue laws (*Ley de Rentas I* in 2000 and *Ley de Rentas II* in 2002) that aim to support municipal tax performance.

Other countries have also made progress, but with more conventional sources of tax revenue. In Colombia, significant progress has been made in increasing municipal tax revenues, climbing from 0.8 percent of GDP in 1990 to 1.9 percent in 2000 (Wiesner 2003). Among Central American countries, large disparities continue to exist between the expenditure obligations and tax authority of municipal governments, although significant progress has been made in recent years. El Salvador instituted payroll taxes at the local level and discussions were under way in 2005 regarding a possible reform of municipal taxes, especially property taxes. In Guatemala, a tax code bill was under discussion that would streamline municipal taxes on economic activities. Guatemala is also considering the transfer of royalties to the subnational level. In Nicaragua, the fiscal gap between tax authority and own-source revenue generation has been particularly acute, forcing municipalities to ration resources. However, the picture had begun to improve, with an important Municipal Solvency Law passed in 2003 that authorizes municipal governments to impose taxes on fixed assets and sales; two draft laws are also under consideration that aim to improve tax collection at the local level and standardize taxing procedures. Finally, in Panama the transfer to the municipalities of property tax collection is under discussion.

Intergovernmental Transfers

With few exceptions, revenue policies in the region tend to rely more on intergovernmental transfers than local taxation to address the resource needs of subnational governments. As noted earlier, in two of the three countries with the highest expenditure decentralization indexes, Argentina and Brazil, massive revenue-sharing systems (*Régimen Federal de Coparticipación, Fundos de Participacao Estadual e Municipal,* and the Situado Fiscal) were created as early as the 1930s and 1940s to fund the growing expenditure requirements of subnational governments. In the other countries of the region, similar revenue-sharing systems started to be put in place in the 1960s (Situado Fiscal in both Colombia and Venezuela) or, more frequently, in the late 1980s or 1990s (Bolivia, Ecuador, Guatemala, and Mexico).

Intergovernmental transfer systems are usually created with two over-riding objectives: (a) to reduce vertical fiscal imbalances faced by sub-national governments, or (b) to reduce regional inequalities (horizontal imbalances) between rich and poor jurisdictions (or both). Because these two types of fiscal imbalances exist in all countries to one degree or another, transfers are an indispensable fiscal policy instrument in a decentralized regime. The challenge facing policy makers is how to design transfer systems that effectively meet these objectives while minimizing distortions that may be created by the transfers.

Although there are many types of transfers, including those determined by a specific share of national revenues, a fixed amount, or on an ad hoc basis year by year, increasingly the most common in the region are trans-fers determined as a share of tax revenue. These can be formula based or ad hoc and are particularly important in Argentina, Brazil, Colombia, and Venezuela. A number of complications are frequently associated with these systems, however: (a) the problem of common resources, where subnational governments have no incentives to collaborate in the collec-tion of shared taxes; (b) distortions in local service provision from sectoral spending quotas sometimes imposed by central government transfer rules; (c) reduction in the ability of the central government to make fiscal adjust-ments during economic crises;[14] and, conversely, (d) the revenue volatility that transfers impose on subnational governments when their expendi-tures remain relatively fixed.

Another important potential distortion resulting from transfers is the risk that subnational governments will fall prey to fiscal laziness, and neglect their own local sources of revenue generation, preferring to pres-sure the central government for additional transfers rather than tackle the politically risky job of raising or improving local tax collections. This is made worse by the bailout problem—the fact that central governments will often rescue jurisdictions facing financial shortfalls with special trans-fer appropriations—which encourages undisciplined, excessive spending at the subnational level. Even in countries such as Mexico where transfer systems are relatively modest in comparison with total central govern-ment budgets,[15] the fiscal laziness impact can still be strong: 90 percent of local revenues in Mexico currently come from federal transfers. More-over, in the majority of countries in the region, the collection efficiency rates for most local taxes are generally poor. Though much of the blame for this can be attributed to weak institutional capacity, undoubtedly the collection rate problem is itself influenced by the same incentive to fiscal laziness. A second important concern associated with intergovernmental transfers is the discretion central governments have in the management of the transfer systems. The basic consensus in the public finance literature is that subnational governments will perform more efficiently if transfers are distributed to them in a nondiscretionary fashion (that is, automatically, on the basis of transparent, formula-driven criteria), and if the amount

and source of funding assigned to a given transfer are also nondiscretionary (that is, predetermined, either by formula or a fixed amount. Based
on these criteria, discretion in the transfer systems of different countries
can be measured through an index that ranks the discretion of transfers in
two dimensions: (a) how the total amount of the transfer is determined,
and (b) how these funds are distributed among the different regional and
local governments.[16]

Applying the Transfer Discretionality Index measures in 13 countries with comparable data between 1996 and 2004, a trend emerges
toward reduced discretion in the intergovernmental transfer policies of
these countries. Since 1996, four countries—Bolivia, Ecuador, El Salvador, and Peru—have shifted perceptibly toward more automatic, formula-
driven transfer policies, both for determining the transfer amount, and
for distributing the funds to subnational governments. In Peru, this shift
comes as a result of formula-driven criteria that were applied after 1996 to
two important transfer programs, the Vaso de leche (Glass of milk) poverty alleviation fund, managed by local governments, and the Common
Municipal Fund. However, because Peru's principal subnational transfer
mechanism, the Ordinary Funds for Regional Governments, continues to
be funded and distributed on a discretionary basis, the overall discretionality index for the country remains relatively high. Other countries where
discretion has been reduced are Colombia and Costa Rica.

Subnational Borrowing Autonomy and Fiscal Responsibility

As noted earlier, the regional survey showed that subnational borrowing policies have attracted increasing attention since the mid-1990s. The
increased attention has been in direct response to the fiscal crises experienced throughout the region during the 1990s and the perception by
many macroeconomic policy makers that an overly liberal subnational
borrowing policy in many countries was contributing to national macroeconomic instability. Beginning in the second half of the 1990s with Brazil
and Colombia (the first two countries in the region to face serious problems of excessive subnational indebtedness, soon thereafter chorused by
other countries in the region with intermediate levels of decentralization—
Bolivia, Ecuador, and Peru), a number of reforms have been put in place
in the region aimed at curbing the borrowing autonomy and increasing
the fiscal responsibility of subnational governments.[17] Table 7.6 presents
the changes in subnational borrowing policy that have occurred in several
countries of the region between 1996 and 2004, using four types of borrowing restrictions commonly applied to subnationals: (a) complete prohibition of borrowing, (b) borrowing conditioned on central government
acquiescence, (c) limitations on the use of borrowed funds (for example,
only for investments), and (d) quantitative limits on the amount any given
subnational government is permitted to borrow. As can be seen from table

Table 7.6 Borrowing Restriction Policies by Country, 1996 and 2004

Country	Subnational borrowing prohibited		Central government authorization required		Restrictions on use of borrowed funds		Restrictions on amount borrowed	
	1996	2004	1996	2004	1996	2004	1996	2004
Argentina				Yes	Yes	Yes	Yes	Yes
Bahamas	Yes	Yes						
Bolivia			Yes	Yes	Yes	Yes		Yes
Brazil			Yes	Yes		Yes		Yes
Chile	Yes	Yes						
Colombia				Yes	Yes	Yes	Yes	Yes
Costa Rica				Yes	Yes	Yes	Yes	
Ecuador				Yes	Yes	Yes		Yes
El Salvador				Yes		Yes		
Guatemala			Yes	Yes		Yes		Yes
Guyana			Yes	Yes	Yes	Yes	Yes	Yes
Honduras			Yes	Yes	Yes	Yes	Yes	Yes
Jamaica			Yes	Yes				
Mexico			Yes	Yes	Yes	Yes		Yes
Panama				Yes	Yes	Yes		
Paraguay			Yes	Yes	Yes	Yes	Yes	Yes
Peru				Yes	Yes	Yes		Yes
Suriname	Yes	Yes	Yes	Yes	Yes	Yes	Yes	Yes
Trinidad and Tobago				Yes	Yes	Yes	Yes	Yes

Sources: IDB 1997; 2004 IDB survey on decentralization.

7.6, both the number of countries imposing restrictions and the number of restrictions in most countries have increased.

The leaders of this reform trend have been Brazil and Colombia. Responding to the increasingly out-of-control indebtedness of their subnational governments, in the mid-1990s both countries began to gradually apply the brakes to the borrowing practices of their local and regional governments with a series of partial reforms. Brazil started with the creation of the CADIN (*Cadastro Informativo de Créditos Não-Quitados Com o Setor Público Federal* or List of Overdue Accounts with the Federal Public Sector) system in 1995, which obliged subnational governments to present detailed financial information to the federal government when their debt was in arrears; this was followed in 1997 by PROES (Incentive Plan for the Reduction of State Banking Activity), meant to address the financial liabilities faced by state governments as a result of their often insolvent state banks, and the Program for Financial Support and Debt Renegotiation of State Governments, which redefined and strengthened the borrowing rules and mechanisms for states, and greatly strengthened the use of standardized fiscal performance benchmarks. These initial reforms were brought together under the umbrella of a comprehensive Fiscal Responsibility Law, approved in 2000. Unprecedented in the region, this law created a far-reaching new fiscal regime for all levels of government. For the subnational governments, in particular, it consolidated and refined borrowing rules, including the prohibition of intergovernmental borrowing, and fiscal efficiency standards building on the 1997 Financial Support Program.

Similarly in Colombia, in 1997 a seminal reform was passed, the Territorial Borrowing Law—commonly referred to as the *Ley de Semáforos* (Traffic Light Law)—which established a fiscal and financial monitoring system to evaluate the indebtedness of its subnational governments, subjecting the borrowings of those with a "red light status" to prior approval by the Ministry of Finance. This was followed in 1999 and 2000 by a subnational debt-restructuring law that began to confront the serious liabilities being accrued by subnational governments through employee pension obligations, and Law 617, which defined a system of indicators and benchmarks to regulate subnational public expenditures with a view to generating a fiscal surplus. Finally, in 2003 the process was consolidated with the passage of Colombia's Fiscal Responsibility Law, further detailing provisions of the 1997 and 2000 laws.

Shortly after the Brazilian and Colombian reforms, several other countries followed suit with important fiscal reforms aimed at curbing subnational debt. Ecuador and Peru approved national fiscal responsibility laws in 2002 that included important first-step regulations for subnational borrowing. Although Ecuador and Peru have made progress in addressing broad categories of reform, they have not followed up with more detailed regulatory programs for disciplined accounting systems underwriting criteria for subnational loans. Of particular interest, however, is Mexico, where in 2000 a novel approach to subnational debt management was introduced by the federal government, aimed at harnessing market forces to control subnational debt, rather than direct central government supervision. As in many other countries in the region, in the 1990s the central government frequently bailed out overindebted state governments. This soft credit culture was reinforced by the use of revenue intercepts to secure subnational loans, and weaker banking regulation for subnational lending than for commercial lending. Recognizing the serious distortions this situation generated—specifically overlending to subnational entities—and the growing moral hazard enabled by the federal government, a new subnational lending framework was put in place. This new framework included (a) a commitment to not bail out municipal and state governments; (b) a sharp tightening of lending regulations by private banks to states (equivalent to commercial lending); and (c) rules for public disclosure of debt and fiscal deficits of states as a condition for borrowing from federal development banks or for federal authorization of private sector loans.

In conclusion, substantial progress was made since the mid-1990s in the area of subnational debt management. Reforms have been put in place in many countries that have improved the regulatory framework, thus hardening the subnational credit culture and, in the process, strengthening fiscal discipline in state and municipal governments.

Measuring the Effectiveness of Decentralization in the Region

If the trends reviewed in the previous sections are brought together, where does the region stand? Is it possible to get a sense of how effectively decentralization is progressing in each country? The standard, bottom-line indicator of expenditure decentralization (ratio of subnational to national expenditures) says little about the quality of the decentralization process, that is, the appropriateness of policy reforms in each country. Appropriateness is key, because increased expenditure decentralization by itself, if not correctly sequenced and orchestrated with reforms and actions in complementary policy areas such as taxation and subnational borrowing, can distort the incentives of subnational governments to act in a fiscally responsible manner and can undermine the link between the preferences of local inhabitants and the fiscal bundle of public goods and taxes provided.

This chapter uses a composite index, the Decentralization Maturity Index (DMI), that ranks countries not by how much they have decentralized their expenditures, but on how appropriate or effective their reforms have been in the five key policy reform areas reviewed in this chapter—political decentralization, expenditure assignment, subnational taxation, intergovernmental transfers, and subnational debt management. Specifically, countries are ranked by five policy reform achievements, using proxy indicators based on the data analysis in the previous sections:

- *Local democratic representation,* measured as a composite of four dummy variables, indicating whether democratic elections (direct or indirect) currently take place at the local or intermediate levels of government.[18]
- *Effective assignment of roles and responsibilities at various levels of government,* a composite indicator based on the ADI, measuring the extent to which each country has advanced in delegating responsibility over specific sectors to subnational governments, especially the key sectors of education and health.[19]
- *Strengthening of subnational taxation system* by expanding subnational authority over basic local taxes (property and vehicle) and creatively expanding the subnational tax base. The proxy indicator is a composite measure of degree of subnational authority over property and vehicle taxes, and assignment of sales or personal income tax (or both) at the subnational level (using data from figures 7.6 and 7.7).[20]
- *Reduced discretion in the intergovernmental transfer systems,* the proxy indicator for which is the level of discretion in the administration of transfers by central government, as measured by a discretionality index.[21]
- *Creation of a hard credit culture for subnational borrowing,* the proxy indicator being a composite measure of several types of borrowing restrictions set up for subnational governments (based on the inventory of reforms in table 7.6).[22]

Each of the indicators were scored between 0 and 1; the higher the score, the more effective or advanced is the policy in a given country. The overall score for a country, its DMI, is calculated as an average of the individual scores for each of these indicators adjusted by the degree of dispersion of the indicators to give better scores to countries that have more consistent levels of achievement in all five areas (see figure 7.8).[23]

When compared with the ranking of countries by levels of expenditure decentralization, the results from the index yield some interesting results. Not surprisingly, perhaps, the countries that according to the index show the greatest level of maturity in their decentralization reform processes are Argentina, Brazil, and Colombia (all with scores higher than 0.6), which are also the most decentralized from the point of view of expenditure (nearly 50 percent of total government expenditure in the three countries). Their high scores indicate that they have put in place many of the policies that make for more effective governance within a decentralized framework. In particular, all three countries have approved comprehensive

Figure 7.8 Level of Maturity in the Decentralization Reform Processes in the Region vs. Decentralization of Expediture

Decentralization Maturity Index (scale 0–1)

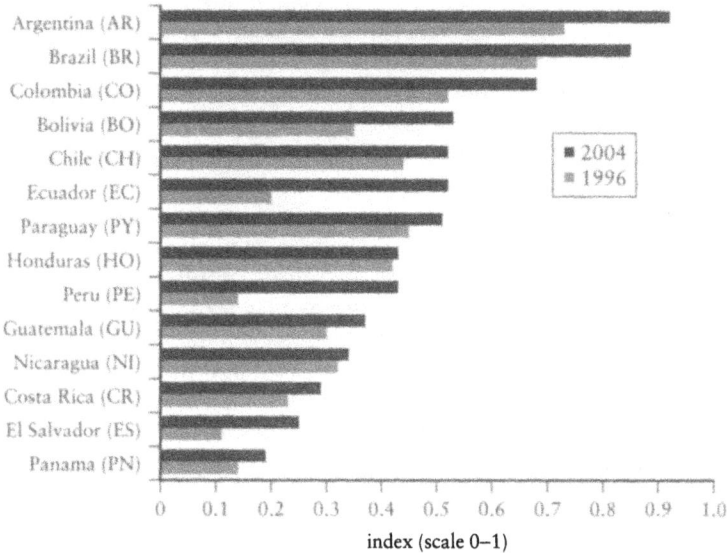

index (scale 0–1)

Decentralization of Expenditure and Decentralization Maturity Index

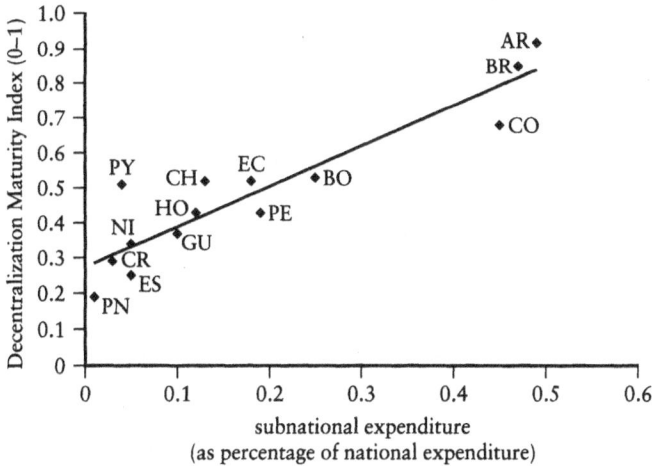

subnational expenditure
(as percentage of national expenditure)

Sources: IDB 1997; 2004 IDB survey on decentralization.

fiscal responsibility laws aimed at regulating subnational borrowing, although in Argentina, effective implementation of this regulatory framework has been slow. Argentina maintains an advantage over Brazil largely as a result of a significantly higher effective level of decentralization of its public services (as measured by the ADI), especially in the health sector and, to a lesser degree, education. Colombia, in turn, trails the other two countries for two reasons: a relatively limited level of sectoral decentralization (as measured by the ADI), especially in health and education; and a more restrictive subnational tax policy. A high overall score with this index does not automatically mean that a country has overcome all its intergovernmental fiscal woes, as witnessed by the serious fiscal problems currently faced by Argentina, resulting in large part from delays in the effective implementation of its new fiscal responsibility laws and the significant burden subnational governments continue to impose on the national fiscal system.[24] The policy indicators captured by the DMI are only meant to provide a rough measure of advances made in a country's intergovernmental policy framework. Especially in the critical policy area of subnational fiscal responsibility, the index is not fine-tuned enough to capture problems that may arise from delayed implementation or possible shortcomings in the operational design of the reforms.

In the remaining countries, the DMI rankings vary quite noticeably when compared with their respective expenditure decentralization rankings. Among the middle group of countries in the index ranking (Bolivia, Chile, Ecuador, Honduras, Paraguay, and Peru), the scores of Chile, Ecuador, and Paraguay are noteworthy because they rank considerably high in the DMI for their level of expenditure decentralization, indicating relatively well-structured policy frameworks. In Chile, key elements of this framework include its well-decentralized delivery system for public health and a fiscally conservative policy prohibiting subnational borrowing. In Paraguay, though still in a very early stage of expenditure decentralization, a system of democratic representation has already been established for municipal and departmental officials, intergovernmental transfers are funded and allocated on a formula-driven basis, and subnational borrowing is closely regulated.

Also noteworthy in this middle group of countries are the unusually large increases posted in the DMI by Ecuador and Peru, and, to a lesser degree, Bolivia, between 1996 and 2004, reflecting the large-scale policy reform agendas implemented by all three countries during this period. Ecuador experienced the greatest transformations, registering sharp increases in three of the key policy reform indicators. Subnational borrowing, previously unregulated, was subjected to a complete package of basic regulations under a new Fiscal Responsibility Law. In addition, discretion that previously existed in the system of intergovernmental transfers was eliminated, and subnational expenditures grew significantly as a percentage of total government expenditures—from 8 percent to 18 percent—as a result of the implementation of a large new revenue-sharing mechanism. In addition, small gains were also made in the devolution of basic public services to subnational governments. Peru and Bolivia also experienced important changes during this period. In Peru, the reform agenda has been particularly ambitious. Democratic elections were reestablished at the regional level, and as in Ecuador, a Fiscal Responsibility Law was approved with a complete set of subnational borrowing regulations, in contrast to 1996 when no regulations existed. Furthermore, discretion in the intergovernmental transfer system was partially curtailed, even though it continues to remain relatively high. Bolivia posted the fourth highest index value in the sample of countries in 2004, in part because of its relatively high ratio of subnational to national expenditures, but also because it made important policy gains in three key areas: establishment of direct elections for regional governors; sharp curtailment of discretion in its intergovernmental transfer rules; and approval of a regulatory framework for subnational borrowing.

At the lower end of the index are grouped a number of smaller countries (Costa Rica, El Salvador, Guatemala, Nicaragua, and Panama), most of whom also figure in the lower end of the expenditure decentralization ranking. The relatively low DMI scores of these countries reflect the limited progress they have made in their subnational and intergovernmental policy frameworks. For example, whereas all except Panama[25] have made important progress in restricting discretion in their intergovernmental transfer systems, they also have uniformly avoided setting up politically representative systems for their intermediate units of government. And although municipal borrowing is authorized by all five countries, little progress has been made other than by Guatemala in defining adequate regulatory frameworks for subnational borrowing. Likewise, all five countries continue to show unusually low levels of sectoral decentralization, particularly in public health and education services, compared with the rest of the Latin American region, as well as very restrictive policies for subnational taxation and revenue generation, with the partial exception of Nicaragua.

Conclusions

The region has committed itself broadly and deeply to a model of decentralized governance. Given the relatively weak institutional resources in the region, however, and the limited experience of most countries with this model of governance, consolidated, stable intergovernmental frameworks cannot be expected in any of the countries of the region in the short or medium term. Even in countries with long histories of federal regimes—Argentina, Brazil, Mexico, and Venezuela—only recently have effective decentralized governance frameworks with proper checks and balances begun to be put in place. In the other countries, with unitary regimes, and given Latin America's heavy-handed centralist tradition, the creation of this new framework will take that much longer.

As demonstrated by this comparative review, much progress has been made in the region. However, a great deal more work still lies in store. What are some of the signposts that policy makers need to consider on the road ahead, to build on the experience gained from the reform initiatives that have been attempted since the mid-1980s?

- *Ensure proper sequencing of decentralization reforms, particularly when considering increased revenue shares to subnational governments.* Experience shows that a gradual, customized approach is usually best, taking care not to rush reform, particularly in the relation between revenue and expenditure assignments. Special care needs to be taken to avoid advancing subnational transfers before corresponding subnational expenditure assignments have been adequately worked out, and own-revenue sources have been properly exploited. This, in turn, points to two high-priority policy areas for the future:

  - *Careful review of intergovernmental assignment of functions and responsibilities within sectors.* The countries that have advanced the most in decentralization, creating stable and effective public service delivery systems, are also those that have taken the time to carefully work out operational divisions of labor between the different levels of government. A great deal of hard, detailed work still lies ahead for most countries in the region, particularly those that are in the early phases of decentralization.
  - *Strengthen own-source revenue generation by subnational governments.* Many countries in the region are currently wrestling with intergovernmental fiscal stress as a result of an overdependence of their subnational governments on central government transfers. At the national level, this can produce rigidities in fiscal planning and budgeting. At the subnational level, it weakens the accountability of subnational governments to their constituencies. To reduce these problems, stronger efforts will need to be placed on strengthening subnational tax legislation; designing incentives for own-source revenue generation into current or new intergovernmental transfer systems; and investing heavily in strengthening revenue collection systems at the subnational level.

- *Ensure adequate political support for decentralization.* Make sure that any proposed decentralization reform initiative is a priority at all levels and among as many stakeholders as possible. Because decentralization is a lengthy and multifaceted process, it needs solid ongoing commitment from above and below, particularly as operational and financial details are worked out among the different levels of government. This requires a concerted, continuous effort at marketing and consensus building among all vital stakeholders, especially legislators and civil society representatives, as well as the subnational governments themselves and key players in the relevant sectoral ministries. Without that support, reforms can languish in central ministries for years or be blocked by powerful interest groups.

- *Invest in high-quality legislative reforms with a commitment to clear operational details.* The quality of laws, regulations, and institutions responsible for implementation (and conflict resolution) associated with decentralization reforms need to be strengthened. Too often, laws affecting intergovernmental policy are formulated without concern for inconsistencies or contradictions with existing laws. The countries with more effective intergovernmental policy frameworks have learned how important it is to fine-tune the operational details in formulating effective reforms. Because of limited government budgets and low technical expertise, this is often neglected, resulting in a policy framework that cannot be implemented.
- *Invest in the creation of uniform standards (accounting, performance measures) and information systems (platforms and data organization).* Efficient horizontal and vertical coordination mechanisms between levels of governments cannot be created without investing a great deal more in uniform information systems.
- *Support long-term institutional capacity building.* Make sure that the subnational level has the technical, managerial, and institutional capacity to handle the more complex tasks associated with fiscal decentralization. For example, subnational governments must have the necessary skills, organizational arrangements, resources, and management systems (budgeting, tax administration, and the like) to fulfill their mandates. Strong institutions are also vitally important because decentralization can exacerbate state capture and clientelism, to which subnational governments are particularly prone.

Notes

1. Where subnational expenditures include total expenditures (including investments) by both local (municipal) and intermediate (state, provincial, or departmental) levels of government.
2. Similar to the federal regime of the United States.

3. See Eaton (2004) in Montero and Samuels (2004), which maps out cycles of decentralization and recentralization in Argentina, Brazil, Chile, and Uruguay in the 19th and 20th centuries.

4. See Eaton (2004) in Montero and Samuels (2004). In Argentina, with the restoration of a democratic regime in 1983, the provincial governments gradually renegotiated upward their share of national revenues to the current level, starting from a low point of 29 percent set by the authoritarian regime in 1976 when it decided to recentralize, cutting the previous revenue-sharing level of 46 percent established for the provinces in the early 1960s. In Brazil, unlike Argentina, the military regime in the 1970s chose to support greater expenditure decentralization for subnationals by increasing their revenue transfer shares, thus setting the stage for the 1988 democratic constitution, which enshrined decentralization as a core organizing principle of Brazilian society, and assigned new sectoral responsibilities and taxation powers to subnationals, especially municipalities.

5. Fabio Sánchez and Catalina Gutiérrez (in López Murphy 1995) document the fiscal recentralization process that occurred in Colombia between 1930 and 1967, when the share of total taxes collected by subnational governments (mostly departments) decreased from 46 percent to 26 percent, setting the stage for the country's current high dependence on transfer systems as a means of funding resource needs of subnational governments. This mirrors a similar process occurring around the same time in Argentina, as noted in Eaton (Montero and Samuels 2004).

6. Where "deconcentrated," as opposed to "decentralized," refers to central government entities that have set up local or regional offices and facilities but continue to be governed or administered by central government representatives.

7. The index is a composite of four dimensions of activity decentralization, that is, which level of government is responsible for (a) deciding on the amount to be spent on the activity; (b) deciding the use of the resources (for example, recurrent versus investment spending); (c) execution of the activity (contracting, hiring of staff, disbursements); and (d) supervision (standards, regulations). The index varies from 0 to 1, depending on the degree of responsibility of the subnational governments. The index used in figure 7.4 is an average of the sectoral ADIs of all the countries in the region. Accordingly, a higher value can mean either that the activity is decentralized in more countries, or that subnational governments are more autonomous in carrying out their responsibilities.

8. See chapter 12 for a detailed analysis of these reforms.

9. As noted, implementation of Ecuador's comprehensive expenditure assignment process has been slow and cumbersome, in large part because of the complexity of the mechanism and the exacting organizational demands it places on a central government apparatus with limited human and financial resources.

10. Interestingly, this same issue regarding tax authority at the local level and concerns about macroeconomic stability was revisited during the 1980s with the debt crisis.

11. It should be noted that the countries that responded to the tax policy section of our 2004 survey were, in many cases, not the same as in the 1996 survey. Moreover, whereas the region's largest countries were strongly represented in the 1996 sample, small and medium countries were better represented in the 2004 survey. Because the subnational tax policies of large countries with federal regimes naturally tend to be more elaborate and important than those of smaller countries, with unitary regimes, the comparative analysis between both surveys reveals only broad trends rather than exact comparisons.

12. The gap, or ratio, between own-source revenues and total expenditure needs, known as the vertical imbalance, was measured in IDB (1997). On average, the region's vertical imbalance (total intergovernmental transfers to total subnational revenues) was equivalent to 52 percent, 10 percentage points greater than

the same average for OECD countries. It should be noted, however, that variations among countries in the region were substantial, ranging from more than 80 percent in El Salvador, Trinidad and Tobago, and Venezuela, to less than 25 percent in Paraguay, Peru, and Uruguay.

13. Because it has caused problems such as distortions in the tax burden and has been difficult to administer.

14. Because taxes are shared, any tax increase will have only a marginal impact at the same time it gives subnational governments more resources when fiscal restraint is needed.

15. Transfers to subnational governments represent only 7.9 percent of central government current expenditures in Mexico, compared with 39.6 percent in Argentina and 31.6 percent in Colombia (Finot 2004).

16. The Transfer Discretionality Index is a composite weighted average of the degree of discretionality of each of the transfers from the central level to subnational level governments of a given country. The index ranges from 0 to 2, where 0 represents the minimum level of discretion and 2 the maximum. To compute the index, two types of decision-making criteria were crossed in the graph: criteria used to determine the amount of a given transfer and criteria used to determine the distribution of the transfer among jurisdictions. Each of these is represented by a separate axis of the graph. The first was calculated in the following manner: if the transfer amount is (a) a predefined percentage of national revenues or of a specific national tax: 0 points; (b) a fixed amount defined by law: 0 points; (c) a reimbursement of approved subnational expenditures: 1 point; (d) an ad hoc amount: 2 points. The second criterion, in turn, was calculated as follows: if transfer funds are distributed as (a) a direct function of revenues collected in the originating jurisdiction: 0 points; (b) less explicit, objective criteria: 1 point; (c) without explicit criteria, at the discretion of the central government: 2 points. The results were then inverted and divided by 2 to be compatible with the Decentralization Maturity Index (DMI) so that the final range varied from 0 to 1, with 0 being mostly discretional and 1 being mostly automatic in amount and distribution. Borrowing autonomy was calculated in the following manner: (a) 0.75 was given if the country had no borrowing autonomy at the subnational level (if the country had borrowing at one level of subnational government but not the other, then 0.75 was given to the level that had no borrowing, which was then averaged with the score for the level that did have borrowing); (b) 1 point was given if the country had subnational borrowing and the country had limits on the quantity of debt that the subnational level was allowed to take; and finally (c) 1 point was given if subnational borrowing required central government or legislative branch authorization. Political participation was calculated by giving (a) 1 point if the country had local elections; (b) 1 point for direct local elections; (c) 1 point for regional elections; and (d) 1 point for direct regional elections.

17. Chile has had no need for reforms in support of borrowing restrictions because it prohibited subnational borrowing in the 1970s under the military regime.

18. Political participation was calculated by giving 1 point if the country had local elections; 1 point for direct local elections; 1 point for regional elections; and 1 point for direct regional elections.

19. Sectoral expenditure assignment was derived by (a) measuring whether sectoral decentralization has increased: 1 point; (b) determining whether the country was highly decentralized to begin with, having a score of 0.35 or higher on the ADI: 1 point; and (c) including the country's ADI score for health and primary and secondary education.

20. Tax authority was calculated by measuring whether (a) the local level has tax authority: 1 point; (b) the intermediate level has tax authority: 1 point; (c) the

subnational level has responsibility for tax authority for property, industry and commerce, and income and sales: 0.5 point for each; and (d) the subnational level has responsibility for administering those taxes: 0.5 for each.

21. See description of Transfer Discretionality Index in note 16. To be compatible with the scale of the DMI, the results of the discretionality index were inverted and divided by 2. As a result the final range of this indicator in the DMI varies from 0 to 1, with 0 being mostly discretional and 1 being mostly automatic in amount and distribution.

22. Borrowing autonomy was calculated in the following manner: (a) 0.75 was given if the country had no borrowing autonomy at the subnational level; (b) 1 point was given if the country had subnational borrowing and the country had limits on the quantity of debt that the subnational level was allowed to take; and finally (c) 1 point was given if subnational borrowing required central government or legislative branch authorization.

23. The index is thus calculated as the average of the five indicators minus one-half of the standard deviation of the five indicators. By construction, the index can take values only between 0 and 1.

24. Argentina's subnational governments in 2005 were responsible for approximately 21 percent of the total consolidated public debt of the country. The full extent of the burden imposed by subnational governments on the country's fiscal stability, however, goes beyond this debt indicator; it would need to include, for example, the significant amount of central government debt accrued as a result of previous debt bailouts of provincial governments. It should also register the special budget transfers periodically made in favor of provinces by the central government to address fiscal shortfalls of the provinces.

25. Panama's municipal transfer system continues to be largely ad hoc.

References

Diaz-Cayeros, A., J. González, and F. Rojas. 2002. "Mexico's Decentralization at a Cross- Roads." Working. Paper No. 153. Center for Research on Economic Development and Policy Reform, Stanford University, Stanford, CA. Available at http://scid.stanford.edu/pdf/credpr153.pdf.

Eaton, K. 2004. "The Link between Political and Fiscal Decentralization in South America." In *Decentralization and Democracy in Latin America*, ed. P. Montero and D. J. Samuels. Notre Dame, IN: University of Notre Dame Press.

Finot, I. 2004. *Descentralización Fiscal y Transferencias Intergubernamentales en América Latina*. Instituto Latinoamericano y del Caribe de Planificación Económica y Fiscal (ILPES) y la Comisión Económica para América Latina y el Caribe de las NN.UU. (CEPAL). Santiago de Chile, Chile.

IDB (Inter-American Development Bank). 1997. *Latin American after a Decade of Reform:. What Comes Next?* Economic and Social Progress in Latin America (IPES) Report, Inter-American Development Bank, Washington, DC.

López Murphy, R., ed. 1995. *Fiscal Decentralization in Latin America*. Washington, DC: Inter-American Development Bank and Johns Hopkins University Press.

Montero, A., and D. Samuels, eds. 2004. *Decentralization and Democracy in Latin America*. Notre Dame, IN: University of Notre Dame Press.

Sánchez, T. F., and Catalina Gutiérrez. 1995. "Colombia." In *Fiscal Decentralization in Latin America*, ed. R. López Murphy. Washington, DC: Inter-American Development Bank and Johns Hopkins University Press.

Souza, C. 2004. "Electoral Coalitions and Hard Budget Constraints in Brazilian States." Federal University of Bahia, Bahia, Brazil.

Tulchin, J., and A. Selee, eds. 2004. *Decentralization and Democratic Governance in Latin America*. Washington, DC: Woodrow Wilson International Center for Scholars.

USAID (United States Agency for International Development) and ICMA (International City and County Management Association). 2004. *Trends in Decentralization, Municipal Strengthening and Citizen Participation in Central America, 1995–2003. Country Reports Costa Rica, El Salvador, Guatemala, Honduras, Nicaragua, and Panama.*

Valenzuela, A. 1977. *Political Brokers in Chile: Local Government in a Centralized Polity.* Durham, NC: Duke University Press.

Wiesner, E. 2003. "Bank Lending for Subnational Development: The Policy and Institutional Challenges." Inter-American Development Bank, Office of Evaluation and Oversight, Washington, DC.

8

Privatization and Regulation in Latin America

Alberto Chong and Juan Benavides

DURING MOST OF THE 20TH CENTURY, Latin American policy makers favored state ownership and management of firms in "strategic" industries and those industries seemingly pervaded by market failures. In general, state-owned enterprises performed, and continue to perform, poorly. With a few exceptions, they have proved wasteful and inefficient, tending to produce low-quality, high-cost goods and services. They became overstaffed as governments used them to generate and maintain employment. Sheltered from competition, state-owned enterprises often were instructed to keep their prices below the cost recovery level, resulting in mounting financial losses that in some cases amounted to as much as 5–6 percent of GDP.

These distortions led to bailouts and fiscal strains, first on government budgets and finally on the banking system. Covering state-owned enterprise losses with fiscal transfers required governments to finance larger fiscal deficits and increase tax revenues, or, more commonly, reduce public expenditures in other areas, or both. Financing state-owned enterprise losses through the state banking system increased intermediation costs, reduced the private sector's access to credit, and threatened overall financial sector viability. Increasingly constrained governments also became incapable of providing capital to their state-owned enterprises, even the profitable ones, for maintenance and repair, much less badly needed network expansion and retooling. By the end of the 1980s, the purely *étatist* (statist) model had collapsed in most of the region's countries.

Coinciding with the collapse of the public ownership model, the theory of economic incentives reached a pinnacle. It is no surprise that in the early 1990s, private participation looked appealing and somehow inevitable. Broadly speaking, privatization and incentive regulation were mostly presented as tools to promote efficiency gains and improve the fiscal balance.

Privatization and regulation would introduce hard budget constraints leading to improved firm performance; in turn, reduced costs, higher quality, and capacity expansion would allow consumers to enjoy higher levels of well-being and businesses to compete under more favorable terms. In practice, however, the efficiency rationale of privatization could be pursued only in part because of the combination of two factors:

- First, the institutional endowment (rule of law, cultural traditions, and beliefs) and the corresponding risks have not been conducive to private investment in some sectors and countries. This is clearly observed in sectors such as water and sanitation, where only 11 percent of connections were private by 2003. The expropriation risk for private parties is high because this service is perceived as an entitlement and is an easy card to play in local politics. Commercial and political risks are high because of general public discontent with liberalization and privatization, as recent opinion polls (*Latinobarometro* various years) indicate. Though many hypotheses have been proposed to explain this discontent, two potential explanations are advanced here: (a) high levels of inequality and unequally shared property rights can destroy trust in both public institutions *and* private investors; (b) general discontent seems to signal a recurrent dissatisfaction with public authorities rather than being specifically targeted at privatization.
- Second, fiscal pressures frequently prevailed over efficiency considerations. A commonly used strategy was for the state to grant private concessions for legal monopolies or oligopolies (either regional or long-term exclusivity, or both) in contests organized to maximize government revenue. This practice was common in mobile telecommunications, for example. Economic rents were purposely created, then shared between private operators and the state. This led to both static and dynamic inefficiencies (short-run direct and indirect welfare loses, and reduced future entry and slow penetration of new technologies).

An examination of infrastructure is instructive in reviewing the efficacy of privatization and regulation. On the positive side, the Latin American region pioneered the attraction of private participation in infrastructure, accounting for about half the total US$786 billion investment in developing countries between 1990 and 2003.[1] Moreover, Chong and López-de-Silanes (2005) show that, on balance, privatization and other forms of private participation have contributed positively to welfare. On the negative side, the private alternative has been applied even in circumstances where (with hindsight) competition or independent regulation had little chance to flourish and deliver. Overoptimism and conceptual simplification resulted in a large number of inefficient disputes and contract breaches, which were exacerbated by technical inexperience in contest design in weak legal, fiscal, and institutional environments (see Guasch 2004).

Private participation in infrastructure, one of the key privatization areas, declined steadily after 1998 (from US$70.8 billion in 1998 to US$15.7 billion in 2003), failing to make up for generalized public cutbacks in infrastructure that affected the region.[2] Consequently, total investment in infrastructure has declined as well, yet the requirements remain huge: infrastructure outlays of about US$117 billion per year (about 6 percent of GDP) would be needed to reach the *current* per-worker infrastructure assets of the Republic of Korea.[3] The causes for private investment decline remain to be tested, although three possible explanatory factors could be driving this phenomenon: (a) a decline in economic activity; (b) reduced profitability of the remaining existing public assets after the "cream" was privatized during the 1990s; and, more fundamentally, (c) the small number of firms eligible to be privatized because the judicial system cannot be relied upon to enforce the property rights of private investors.

The first three sections of this chapter provide the basic logic for pursuing privatization, including a basic description of the privatization record in Latin America and elsewhere, and highlighting some key differences between countries in the region. The subsequent section provides empirical evidence of the impact of privatization on Latin American economies, followed by a section discussing the most relevant regulatory issues for the region. The last section summarizes and concludes.

Basic Reasons for Reform

The conceptual advantages of competition and regulation over public command and control are now well established (Kikeri and Nellis 2004). The literature emphasizes two reasons for the poor record of state ownership. First, imperfect monitoring and poor incentives for managers of state-owned enterprises translate into inferior performance. The average state-owned enterprise is not traded on the stock market and the threat of a takeover does not exist because control rests in the hands of the state. Discipline from creditors plays no role because most state-owned enterprise loans are public debt and losses are typically covered by subsidies from the treasury. In addition, the boards of directors rarely implement good corporate governance practices and management turnover obeys political rather than market forces (Vickers and Yarrow 1988).

The second strand of the literature emphasizes the political economy aspects of state production. The political view points to the inherent conflict of interest in running state-owned enterprises, as managers seek to maximize their political capital and pursue inefficient decisions. Political interference in the firm's production results in excessive employment, poor choices of products and location, and inefficient investment (La Porta and López-de-Silanes 1999). State-owned enterprises face soft budget constraints that allow them to implement such practices, because governments may not

want to risk the political cost of firms going bankrupt (Sheshinski and
López-Calva 2003). The basic claims of the two strands of the literature
have been validated by empirical research on state-owned enterprises and
firm performance after privatization around the world.

The Extent of Privatization Worldwide

Motivated by the evidence of state-owned enterprise failures, governments
in more than 100 countries have undertaken privatization programs since
1980 (Megginson and Netter 2001). Throughout the world, annual revenues from privatization soared during the late 1990s, peaking in 1998
at over US$100 billion (OECD 2001). Not surprisingly, industrial coun-
tries have pursued privatization less vigorously than developing nations.
Between 1984 and 1996, the participation of state-owned enterprises in
industrial countries declined from a peak of 8.5 to about 5.0 percent of
GDP, while in developing countries production from state-owned companies declined more steeply, in particular in Latin America (see figure 8.1).

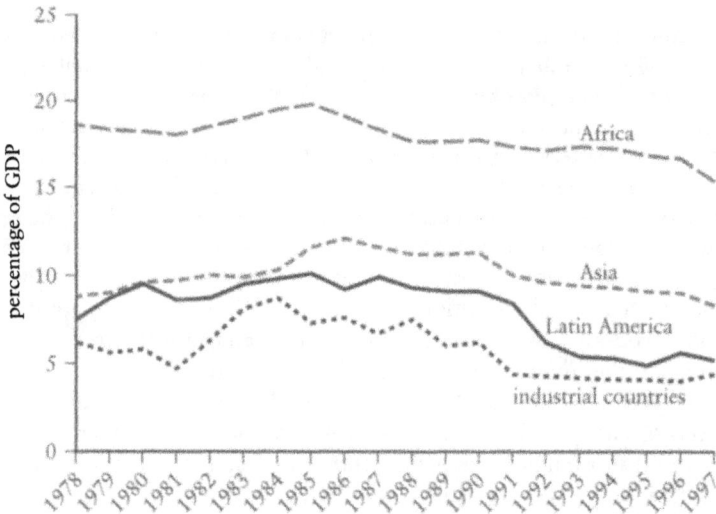

Figure 8.1 Economic Activity of State-Owned Enterprises

Source: Chong and López-de-Silanes 2005.

According to Sheshinski and López-Calva (2003), between 1980 and 1997, state-owned enterprises' activities as a percentage of GDP decreased from about 11 percent to 5 percent in middle-income countries and from 15 percent to 3 percent in low-income countries. Developing countries have also seen large reductions in state-owned enterprise employment. In middle-income countries, employment in state-owned enterprises has come down from a peak of 13 percent to about 2 percent of total employment, while in low-income countries it has dropped from over 20 percent to about 9 percent.

Privatization started slowly with only a few divestiture transactions a year through most of the 1980s. The number of transactions peaked in the mid-1990s, then declined after 1997. Between 1990 and 1999, global proceeds totaled about US$850 billion, growing from US$30 billion in 1990 to US$145 billion in 1999.

The extent of privatization has varied across and within world regions. In Sub-Saharan Africa, only a few governments openly adopted an explicit state-owned enterprise divestment strategy. The African privatization effort has been significant in only a handful of countries and state production still accounts for over 15 percent of GDP in the region.[4] Asia is another region with large variations; several Asian countries have not consistently pursued privatization strategies. China, for example, has followed an ad hoc privatization process for over two decades and only recently has the country committed to privatizing all but the largest state enterprises. In India, where privatization has thus far not figured prominently, it is reported that 43 percent of the country's capital stock is still owned by the state. Even after the Asian crisis of 1997, when private equity funds and multinationals were expecting large state-owned fire sales, many governments in the region still hung on to their assets in sectors such as energy, telecommunications, transportation, and banking (*The Economist* 2001).

In contrast, transition economies and Latin American countries have been very active in privatization. During the 1990s, transition economies in Europe and Central Asia accounted for 21 percent of total privatization revenues in developing countries, second only to Latin America. To facilitate their shift to a market economy, most transition countries launched mass privatization programs that resulted in dramatic reductions of state ownership. These programs, however, have sometimes proven unpopular, generating accusations of corruption and deliberate delays in implementing corporate governance reforms and affording poor protection to new minority investors. Even against the backdrop of massive economic transformations in transition economies, the privatization record of Latin America seems remarkable. In the 1990s, Latin America accounted for 55 percent of total privatization revenues in the developing world (see figure 8.2). The decline in economic activity of state-owned enterprises has been more substantial in Latin America than in Asia and Africa, bringing levels

Figure 8.2 Developing Countries' Proceeds from
Privatization, 1990–99

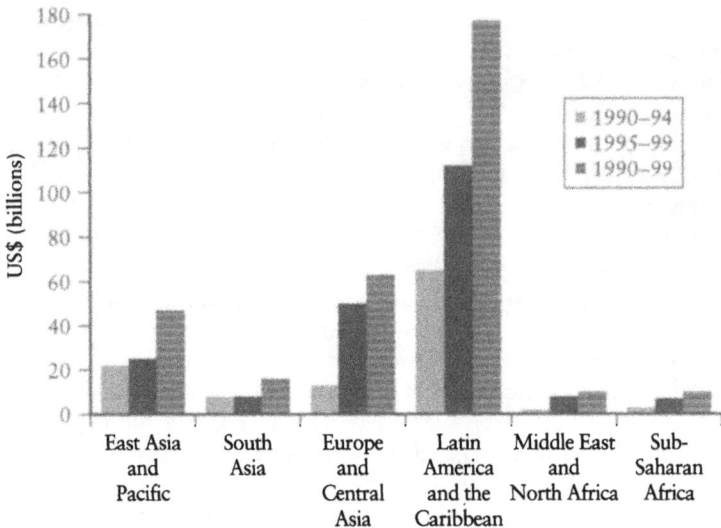

Source: Chong and López-de-Silanes 2005.

close to those of industrial countries. However, from being the most active
region in the 1990s, Latin America has virtually halted its privatization
process in recent years.

The privatization impetus has also faded in other regions, leaving
governments very much in business. In fact, state-owned enterprises still
account for more than 20 percent of investment, and about 5 percent of
formal employment worldwide (Kikeri 1999). When appropriately measured, governments may own or control much more than is apparent at
first sight. Government ownership of banks provides a clear example.
Data for the late 1990s indicate that after bank privatization programs
had been completed in many countries, the world mean of government
ownership of the top 10 banks was still 42 percent, and a somewhat lower
39 percent if former or current socialist countries are excluded (La Porta,
López-de-Silanes, and Shleifer 2002).

These data suggest that, although privatization has decreased government ownership, it has not reduced it to negligible levels. It may not even
be feasible to privatize totally: the purely private or purely public alterna-

tives are the extremes of a continuum of choices that have to be contemplated in real life, especially when projects are highly profitable but the rule of law is ineffectual. Privatization is then self-defeating because the private investor's assets will likely be expropriated. Expropriation risks are particularly acute where public funds are extremely scarce: the higher the profitability of a privatized asset, the greater will be the temptation for a government to take its profits.

Second- or third-best ownership and management tools (varieties of the public-private partnership approach) may be needed in recognition of the institutional constraints that cannot be removed in the near future. Benavides and Vives (2005) provide a taxonomy of financial structure choices based on project profitability and local conditions (summarized in two factors, fiscal space credibility and rule of law). They propose (a) profit-sharing arrangements between governments and private investors if a third party cannot enforce property rights (for example, toll road concessions); (b) use of classic public-private partnerships when the "value for money" fiscal trade-off can materialize; and (c) mobilization of noncash resources (exclusive land rights or community participation) when fiscal space is insufficient, yet the project is economically sound, just unprofitable.

A Closer Look at the Extent of Privatization in Latin America

While no accurate account is available, tens of thousands of public enterprises have been sold around the world. In fact, the resulting revenues are largely accounted for by infrastructure privatization, mainly telecommunications and power, followed by the primary sector, including petroleum, mining, agriculture, and forestry. Telecommunications accounts for about 36 percent of all privatization proceeds between 1990 and 2000, with power (16 percent), financial institutions (15 percent), and oil and gas (10 percent) claiming the next largest shares. Taken together, utilities (telecommunications, power, and oil and gas) account for 62 percent of all proceeds, while regulated industries such as telecommunications, power, and financial institutions account for about 67 percent of the total proceeds. Furthermore, a broader definition of infrastructure sales that includes national oil and gas companies accounts for 68 percent of total proceeds. Clearly, governments have sold mostly basic industrial and financial infrastructure assets in their privatization programs (Megginson 2005).

Overall, Latin America truly embraced privatization. Chile's program is particularly noteworthy, both because it was Latin America's first and because the 1990 *Teléfonos de Chile* privatization, which used a large American depository receipt share tranche targeted toward U.S. investors, opened the first significant path for developing countries to directly tap Western capital markets. Mexico's program was both vast in scope and remarkably successful at reducing the state's role in what had been an interventionist economy. La Porta and López-de-Silanes (1999) report that in 1982, Mexican state-owned enterprises produced 14 percent of GDP, received net transfers and subsidies equal to 12.7 percent of GDP, and accounted for 38 percent of fixed capital investment. By June 1992, the government had privatized 361 of its roughly 1,200 state-owned enterprises and the need for subsidies had been virtually eliminated (Megginson 2005). Several other countries in Latin America also executed large divestment programs. However, the most important program in the region is Brazil's, given the size of Brazil's economy and its privatization program, and the fact that the Cardoso government was able to sell several very large state-owned enterprises, such as *Telebras* in 1998. Thus, despite significant political opposition, Brazil's program is likely to remain influential (Megginson 2005).

For all the activity in the region, dramatic differences in the extent of privatization are also evident. For example, countries with previously large state-owned enterprise sectors, such as Ecuador, Nicaragua, and Uruguay, barely privatized in the 1990s, while others such as Argentina, Bolivia, Guyana, Panama, and Peru have raised revenues from comprehensive privatization programs that amount to over 10 percent of GDP (see figure 8.3). The difference in the extent of privatization across countries and the large amount of assets in the hands of the state highlight the importance of understanding the privatization record so far and of developing lessons for future privatization programs. In fact, the above points to a common misconception about privatization in the region because a relatively large number of countries have been reluctant to privatize.

In Latin America, 75 percent of privatization revenue came from utilities and infrastructure; 11 percent from the financial sector; and oil, gas, and manufacturing represented the rest. Relatively recent large sales have occurred in the oil and gas sectors in Argentina and Brazil. Manufacturing privatizations raised about 16 percent of total developing-country proceeds between 1990 and 1999 of which, in regional terms, Latin America accounted for a large share of non–OECD privatization activity, particularly in terms of revenues. Argentina, Brazil, Bolivia, Chile, and Mexico sold small and medium firms at first, but rapidly expanded their programs to include large infrastructure and energy firms; the largest contributions in recent years came from the sale of infrastructure and energy firms in Argentina, Brazil, and Mexico. Interestingly, manufacturing privatization in Latin America was not important except for some old strategic heavy industries such as steel, aluminum, and others (Florio, Carrera, and Checchi 2004). Figure 8.4 shows worldwide privatization proceeds by sector and figure 8.5 shows revenue shares.

The privatization process in Latin America differs markedly from that in other regions, such as Eastern Europe or Africa, and this underlines the fact that the determinants of privatization in the various regions are

Figure 8.3 Privatization in Latin America, 1990–2000

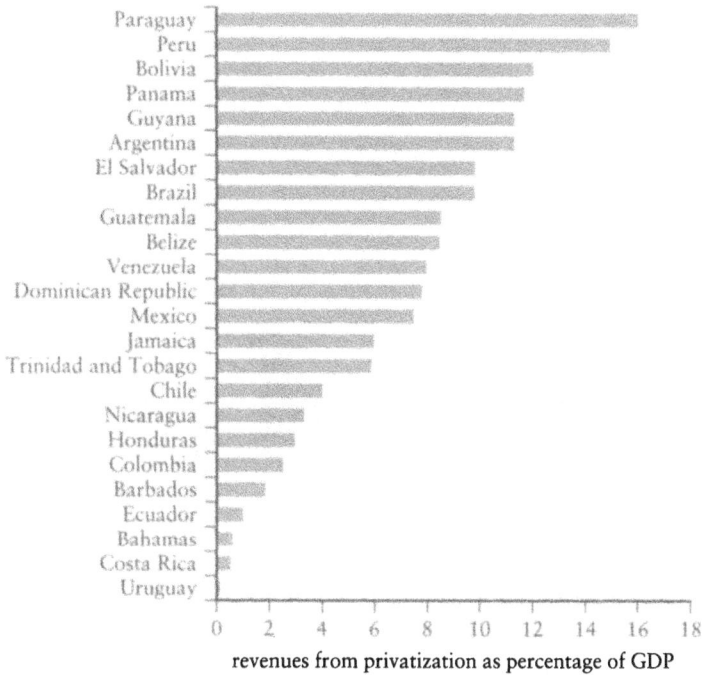

Paraguay
Peru
Bolivia
Panama
Guyana
Argentina
El Salvador
Brazil
Guatemala
Belize
Venezuela
Dominican Republic
Mexico
Jamaica
Trinidad and Tobago
Chile
Nicaragua
Honduras
Colombia
Barbados
Ecuador
Bahamas
Costa Rica
Uruguay

0   2   4   6   8   10   12   14   16   18

revenues from privatization as percentage of GDP

Source: Chong and López-de-Silanes 2005a.
Note: Calculations were made using constant 1999 dollars.

Figure 8.4 Worldwide Privatization Revenues by Sector, 1990–2000

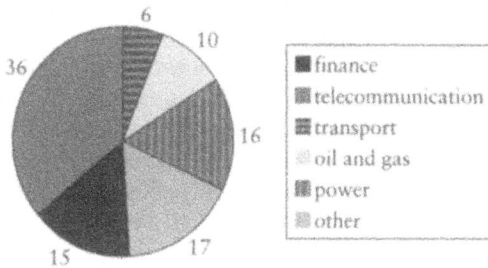

6
10
36
16
17
15

- finance
- telecommunication
- transport
- oil and gas
- power
- other

Source: Megginson 2005.

271

Figure 8.5 Worldwide Privatization Proceeds by Sector, 1990–2000

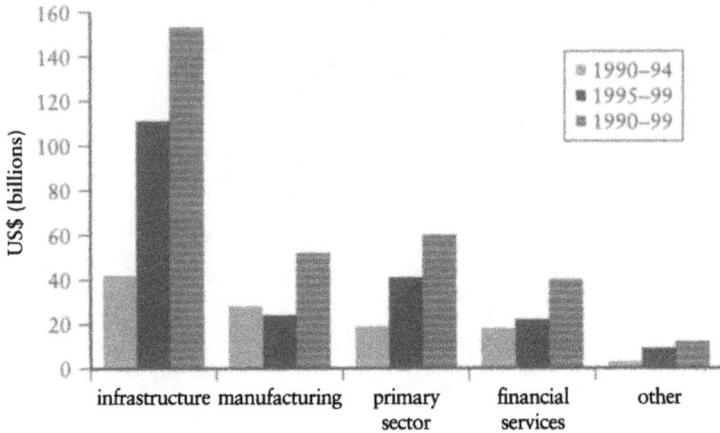

Source: Birdsall and Nellis 2002.

different. Privatization within the Latin American region also differed dramatically between countries, further reinforcing the fact that economic factors were not the only ones, and perhaps not even the crucial ones, that determined privatization policy choices. In fact, as Florio, Carrera, and Checchi (2004) point out, most countries in Latin America privatized telecommunications, electricity, gas, and, to a lesser extent, water and sanitation services, but privatization of railways, airlines, airports, and highways was less extensive. Privatization of financial and productive sectors was not so important because private participation was always present in those sectors. However, all countries except Argentina required the existence of at least one public bank, and most also retained public control of companies connected with natural resources such as oil, gas, and copper. For example, although Brazil pursued a relatively large privatization program, it still retained state participation in electricity, the financial sector, and oil (Chong and López-de-Silanes 2005). Similarly, while most countries in the region privatized their telecommunications companies, Colombia, Costa Rica, and Uruguay did not (Chong and López-de-Silanes 2005; Lora 2001; Pombo and Ramírez 2005). In Peru there was no involvement in transport, sanitation services, and a large share of agriculture and oil (Torero 2005). Even Chile retained public enterprises in key sectors, namely, copper, oil, banks, postal services, railways, and ports (Fischer and Serra 2002). Argentina stands out for retaining no important companies for the state except some national and provincial banks and some provincial sanitation companies (Galiani and others 2005). In contrast, Uruguay, a country typically regarded as similar to Argentina, privatized the least in the region. In fact, it was the only country that did not privatize electricity, oil, or telecommunications and in which privatizations were explicitly taken to a democratic vote. No other country has shown this popular participation in the privatization debate (Florio 2004).

The sequence of privatization was different among countries in the region. Bolivia, Chile, Mexico, and Nicaragua first privatized the state-owned enterprises in the competitive sectors, such as manufacturing and finance, and later, the monopolies and utilities (Florio 2004). Argentina, Brazil, Colombia, and Peru sold both types of companies simultaneously. In Argentina and Bolivia, the monopolistic structure of some sectors was maintained to maximize revenues, even in sectors like telecommunications where technology allowed more competition (Florio 2004). Governments used different methods to sell state-owned enterprises to the private sector, such as total sale through open international options, public offering of shares, concession contracts, direct transfers, and others. The intensity of use of each strategy differed across countries; for example, Argentina, Chile, Mexico, and Peru employed outright sales, but in Bolivia, capitalization schemes were used more often. Concession contracts were mainly used in sanitation services, transport infrastructure, and oil exploration and production (Florio 2004).

As Megginson (2005) argues, the differences above simply highlight the fact that deciding which sectors and public enterprises should be privatized is a contentious affair, especially if privatization is adopted by a highly divided government (Boycko, Shleifer, and Vishny 1996). A privatizing government facing sharp opposition typically feels that it must act quickly and maneuver around opposition from the party out of power, from bureaucrats within the government ministries, and from workers and managers in the state enterprises themselves. Such a government faces the real prospect of both losing power and seeing the entire privatization and economic reform halted if a major fiasco results from even one unsuccessful privatization. In theory, the choice of which sectors to privatize should be straightforward. Some sectors, such as retail or light industry operating in competitive markets will be relatively easy to sell off, while other sectors, particularly heavy industry and infrastructure assets, will be far more difficult and require more preparation (Megginson 2005).

The difficulty of privatization can be assessed based on observable characteristics of sectors, as shown in table 8.1. Based on this table, Bornstein (1999) argues that the retail trade, consumer services, and housing industries, at the start of the privatization process in most countries, operate in sectors that are already partly private, and relatively little supplemental capital investment is required to make the state assets competitive. Privatization of these sectors should be attractive and relatively noncontroversial. As one moves down in table 8.1, the sectors become increasingly difficult for a government to sell off quickly and easily. Light industry may require substantial investment and, perhaps, foreign direct investment to become economically viable. Heavy industry also requires investment, and may be qualified as "strategic" and placed off limits (Megginson 2005). Examples include copper in Chile, power in Brazil, oil in Peru, and others. The banking, telecommunications, and electricity sectors face the same challenges as heavy industry with the additional requirement of putting regulatory institutions into place. The sequence of privatization in electricity differs according to the existing level of public ownership (municipal, state, or national), the dominant type of public power generation technology, and the way subsidies are defined and transferred. In Guatemala and Nicaragua, public hydroelectric plants for which costs have already been recovered (sunk costs with almost no operating costs) are used to subsidize the power consumption of most of the population. This makes power generation an unlikely candidate for privatization because the fiscal systems of these countries are unable to support direct transfers to customers. However, in these two countries, power distribution firms were quickly privatized because they were formerly part of a single state-owned distribution firm with national coverage. In Colombia, however, large hydroelectric plants owned by the central government were among the first assets to be privatized (due to fiscal pressures) while privatization has been slow in the distribution business because many of the firms are controlled by subnational governments with little interest in losing control.

Privatization Record

Overall, the empirical record shows that privatization leads not only to higher profitability, but also to increased growth in output and productivity, fiscal benefits, and even quality improvements and better access for the poor. In telecommunications and electricity, private participation revamped the nature of service provision. At the start of 1990, only 3 percent of telephone and electricity customers were served by private firms. In 2003, 86 percent and 60 percent of telecommunications and electricity customers, respectively, were privately managed in the region. Private telecommunications became a success story in its accelerated coverage extension, lower prices, and introduction of new services. In other infrastructure sectors, the following facts were observed:

- Welfare gains in electricity materialized but are unevenly shared. Customers enjoy a more secure supply but firms enjoy an even larger share of total benefits. This happens because large electricity distribution

Table 8.1 Characteristics Affecting Scope and Sequence of Privatization

Industry	Characteristic					
	Already partly private	Small capital investment required	Substantial restructuring needed	Foreign direct investment crucial	Possibly deemed strategic	Special regulatory framework essential
Retail trade	X	X				
Consumer services	X	X				
Housing	X	X				
Agriculture	X	X	X			
Light industry			X	X		
Heavy industry			X	X	X	
Banking			X	X	X	X
Electricity			X	X	X	X
Telecommunications			X	X	X	X

Source: Bornstein 1999.

Note: An "X" in a cell denotes that the characteristic significantly influences the divestiture of state enterprises in the industry.

and transmission firms have better bargaining skills than the new
regulatory institutions, and small generation markets have made it
easier for firms to enjoy high price markups.
- Water and sanitation remains resistant to private participation. As
  mentioned earlier, only 11 percent of connections were private by
  2003. The risk that these services will be expropriated is high for
  private parties because they are perceived as an entitlement and an
  easy bargaining chip in local politics.
- The outcomes in transportation projects are ambiguous. Private participation was limited to segments of the primary road network and
  some ports and airports.

Instances of failure exist, but overwhelming evidence suggests this is no
argument to stop privatization. Privatization failures can be understood
within a political economy framework. The roots of failure can be traced
to substantial state participation in opaque processes; contract design
mismatched with specific institutional constraints; inadequate reregula-
tion; and insufficient deregulation and corporate governance reform that
increase the cost of capital and limit firm restructuring in a competitive
environment.

Using comprehensive data, a recent research effort by Chong and
López-de-Silanes (2005)[5] across Latin America expanded the detailed
privatization analysis for the region, helping to address the concerns raised
in this section. There were substantial gains in profitability after privatization, measured by net-income-to-sales and operating-income-to-sales
ratios (figure 8.6). For the countries in the sample, the median net-income-
to-sales ratio increased 14 percentage points and operating-income-to-
sales increased 12 percentage points. The largest gains were in Peru and
Argentina, where median changes reached about 20 percentage points
for each ratio. Brazil showed the smallest gains, between 2 and 5 percentage points depending on the ratio. Unlike their counterparts in other
countries, in Colombia, Costa Rica, and Uruguay some of the large state-
owned enterprises were profitable before privatization. For instance, the
Colombian levels of relative profitability are explained in part by the protective industrial policy implemented by the government during the 1980s,
which, in the case of telecommunications, resulted in a public monopoly
over long distance calls.

The main reason for the profitability gains was the improved operating
efficiency brought about by privatization. In fact, costs per unit plummeted,
with the median decline equivalent to 16 percent for the countries with
available data (figure 8.7). Sales-to-assets ratios show a similar trend in four
out of five countries. The median increase in that ratio is 26 percent. Peru
is the only country with a decrease, of about 20 percent, in sales-to-assets
because privatized state-owned enterprises engaged in large investments
that overtook output increases. Finally, the impact on sales-to-employment

Figure 8.6 Profitability Changes after Privatization

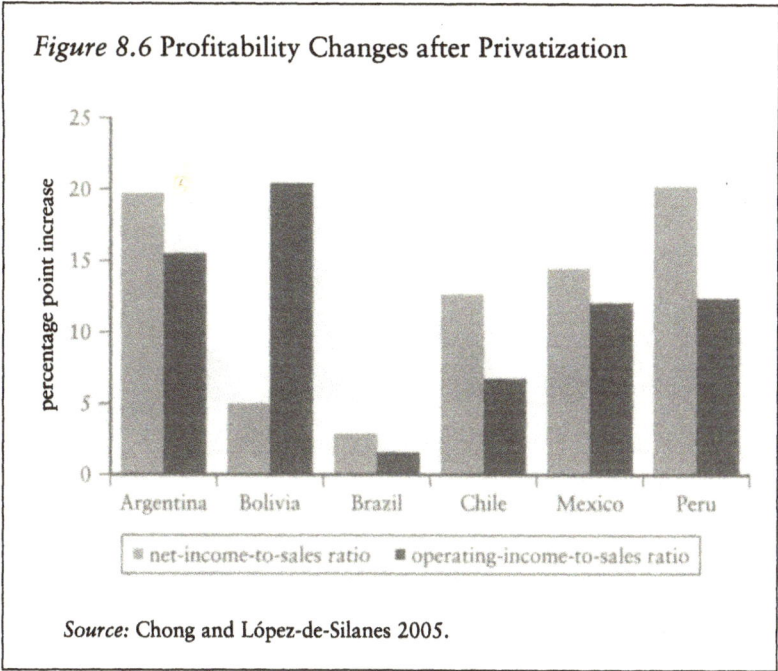

Source: Chong and López-de-Silanes 2005.

is dramatic with a median gain of almost 70 percent. Chile and Mexico show the most impressive results—the sales-per-employee ratio doubled. The analysis so far suggests that the profitability gains of privatized firms mostly result from efficiency gains and not from other related factors (lay-offs, for example). Most countries show drastic cuts in employment and fairly consistent capital stocks. Perhaps the most striking finding is that the output of privatized state-owned enterprises dramatically increased, despite dwindling employment and modest investment. The largest gains are in Mexico and Colombia, where median output increased 68 percent and 59 percent, respectively. The country with the lowest, albeit significant, increase in output is Brazil, where real sales went up 17 percent.

The Challenge for Governments: Regulation

Unquestionably, a key challenge for governments is the development of an appropriate regulatory framework after privatization, particularly for the majority of utilities, because they make basic services available to the poorest. Based on the evidence, a common element across many examples of failed privatization is inadequate regulation leading to suboptimal levels of competition or allowing producers to keep the gains from privatization

Figure 8.7 Operating Efficiency after Privatization

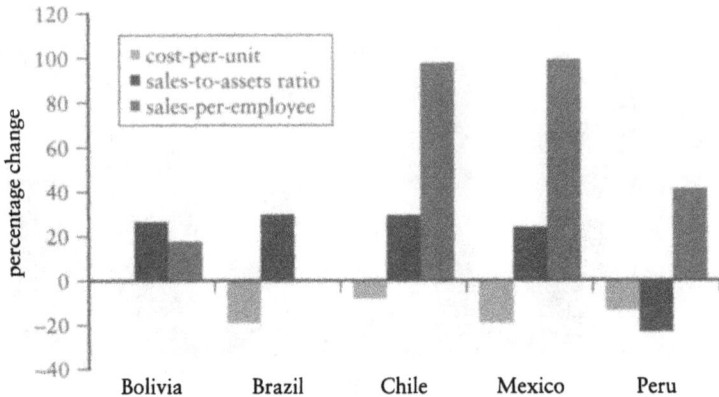

Source: Chong and López-de-Silanes 2005.

without sharing them with consumers. Although the classic position of critics is to argue against further privatization, ample empirical evidence shows that privatization can be done correctly, and can lead to social gains.

Two prominent instances call for the careful analysis of regulation in conjunction with privatization: industries that are natural monopolies or in which oligopolistic market structures exist; and industries in which the government owns most of the assets even if no individual firm has substantial market power. Sectors with heavy state presence tend to be protected by a web of regulations originally instituted to cut state-owned enterprises' losses and reduce fiscal deficits. In some of these cases, the necessary postprivatization regulatory effort can be better understood as deregulation to dismantle protective structures that shield companies from competition and could allow privatized firms to make extraordinary gains at the expense of consumers. As explained in both the early and more recent literature (Allen and Gale 1999; Yarrow 1986), competition and regulation should be carefully considered as part of the aftermath of the privatization process. Winston (1993) argues that adequate regulation has the power to produce efficiency improvements that can benefit consumers and producers; adequate regulation should work as well after privatization of overprotected industries. Regulation of oligopolistic sectors is complicated by weakness in regulatory governance. In oligopolistic sectors, the regulatory effort needs to be complemented with new rules and disclosure requirements to enhance supervision and reduce abuse of market power

Credible regulation complements privatization in two ways. First, at the most basic level, product market competition weeds out the least efficient firms. This process may take too long, or not work at all, if regulation inhibits new entry or makes exit costly. Wallsten (2002) undertook an econometric analysis of the effects of telecommunications privatization and regulation in a panel of 30 countries in Latin America and Africa. His results show that competition from mobile operators and privatization combined with the existence of a separate regulator are significantly associated with increases in labor efficiency, the number of main lines per capita, and connection capacity. A casual interpretation of his results suggests that privatization of oligopolistic industries without concurrent regulatory reform may not necessarily improve welfare. Chong and Galdo (forthcoming) also show that countries in which a regulatory agency existed before privatization were able to fetch higher privatization prices for their telecommunications industries.

Second, an adequate regulatory environment may also complement privatization by raising the cost of political intervention. Whereas an inefficient monopoly can squander its rents without endangering its existence, an inefficient firm in a competitive industry would have to receive a subsidy to stay afloat. The introduction of competition forces politicians to have to pay firms directly to engage in politically motivated actions whereas previously the costs of these measures were absorbed by a state-owned enterprise that did not have to worry about market performance. In fact, competition is often restricted precisely because it raises the costs of political influence. Colombia and Mexico provide good examples of adequate deregulatory policy actions that, when coupled with privatization, can be used as a lever to transform the economic landscape and reduce political interference in the economy. In the early 1990s, Colombia began an economic openness program through the promotion of market competition and deregulation. As Pombo and Ramírez (2005) explain, privatization was conceived as an instrument for economic deregulation and the promotion of market competition. A decade earlier, Mexico started to transform its previously closed economy characterized by capital controls, price regulation, restrictions on foreign direct investment, high tariffs, import quotas, and a large state-owned public sector. As in Colombia, privatization coupled with deregulation played a key role in the drive to restructure the economy and help privatized state-owned enterprises catch up to their private peers.

Adequate regulation can be imposed at three different moments: before privatization, at the time of privatization, or after the state-owned enterprise has been sold. The literature emphasizes the importance of having efficient regulation at an early stage. Regulation before privatization of the industry may increase the pace of divestiture and help companies to be sold at higher prices if it reduces regulatory risk as Bortolotti, Fantini, and Siniscalco (2001) argue for the electricity sector. Wallsten (2002) finds that countries that established a separate telecommunications regulatory authority before privatization not only benefited from increased investment and penetration, but also gained from investors' willingness to pay more for the firms. However, it is not easy to establish effective preprivatization regulation for at least three reasons: First, changes to the regulatory regime before privatization are likely to lower state-owned enterprise profits, translating into higher financial needs for the government at a very difficult time. Second, without the pressure of imminent privatization, the political will for true regulatory reform might not materialize. Finally, governments with little experience in privatization often find it difficult to carry out effective preprivatization regulatory reform.

Regulation at the time of privatization, clarifying the new set of rules, solves the first two problems and reduces regulatory risk discounts. Evidence shows that as long as a suitable regulatory framework is in place at or before the time of privatization, consumers and the government should benefit from the process. Lack of regulatory capabilities at the time of privatization coupled with a desire to maximize price at the time of the sale has led several governments to postpone full and clear regulation. Trying to establish an adequate regulatory scheme after privatization may be difficult from a political economy perspective. Because the agency charged with enforcing and regulating the contracts is often the same or a subordinate entity to the agency that carried out the privatization, there is an incentive for lax enforcement to avoid exposing past mistakes. Chong and Sánchez (2003) document that for a broad number of concessions in infrastructure projects, the private sector was able to bargain for and keep protective regulation after privatization because of the threat of bankruptcy, withdrawal, or desertion of future investment commitments. All of these affect the reputation and credibility of privatizing politicians. According to evidence in Guasch (2001), in the last 15 years, concession contracts in developing countries have often led to renegotiations. In Latin America and the Caribbean, 40 percent of all concession contracts were renegotiated just over 2.2 years after they were signed. Engel, Fischer, and Galetovic (forthcoming) argue that opportunistic renegotiations of concessions are common because of a "privatize now, regulate later" approach. Cost overruns in concessions and unclear rules governing contingencies provide private owners with the opportunity to extract economic rents from the government. Finally, attempting to substantially alter the regulatory framework after the sale may also prove difficult because new constituencies against regulation are created at the time of privatization. Shareholders and managers of privatized state-owned enterprises are joined by workers and even consumers who could benefit from the protective regulatory status of firms.

Using a recent survey from the World Bank (Wallsten and others 2004) on many aspects of governance in the telecommunications and electricity sectors, an overall index of regulatory reform for Latin America is constructed here as an attempt to measure the extent of after-privatization regulatory efforts in the region. In particular, it focuses on recent laws, regulatory bodies, and regulatory decisions in both sectors. Each question in each category is assigned a value of one when the answer is consistent with regulatory advancement. A value of zero is assigned otherwise. The questionnaire is shown in appendix 8A. For example, for the question, "Has parliament completely passed framework laws for the telecommunications sector?" a value of one was assigned if the respondent answered yes, because it reflects a characteristic typically associated with a higher level of regulation. The survey contains 22 questions for telecommunications firms and 24 for electricity providers, divided into three broad categories. They are summarized in an aggregate index, which is the simple sum of one-values assigned to each question. Figures 8.8 and 8.9 present comparative findings for telecommunications and electricity, respectively. The index shows the extent to which countries

Figure 8.8 Telecommunications Regulation Index

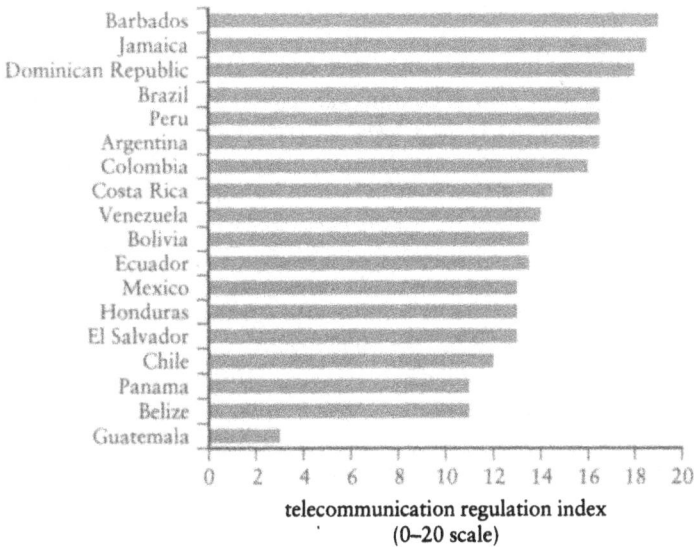

telecommunication regulation index
(0–20 scale)

Source: Wallsten and others 2004.
Note: The higher the index, the better the quality of the regulatory scheme of the country. See annex 8A.

Figure 8.9 Electricity Regulation Index

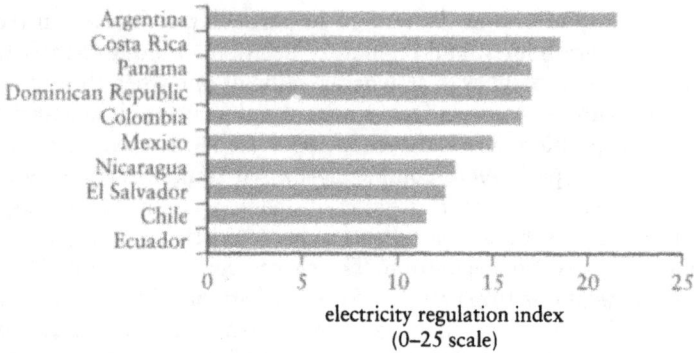

electricity regulation index
(0–25 scale)

Source: Wallsten and others 2004.
Note: The higher the index, the better the quality of the regulatory scheme of the country. See annex 8A.

---

were diligent in establishing formal sets of rules and procedures to implement regulation after privatization.

In telecommunications, the variance between the maximum value for the index (Barbados) and the minimum (Guatemala) is high. Overall, electricity reforms have not proceeded as quickly as telecommunications reforms, which is why fewer countries are covered in figure 8.9 than figure 8.8. Argentina has the highest level of rule-issuing activism when using this general index; Ecuador occupies last place. By construction, the index does not measure regulatory performance; its impact on outcome quality must be examined on a case-by-case basis. For example, Jamaica shows a high telecommunications regulation index, but it coexisted for a substantial time with a protected incumbent monopoly. In 2005, Argentina still had in place the formal rules for electricity regulation that were highly praised internationally before the 2002 macroeconomic crisis, but current policy measures and shortcuts in application (on prices, cost recovery, creation of public enterprises with discretion to intervene in the market, political appointment of regulators) make them ineffectual.

The effectiveness of regulation cannot be assessed in isolation. Regulation can be viewed as a component of the institutional possibility frontier of an industrial sector. Other components might include antitrust bodies, the courts, the executive power, both the national and the local levels of government, and the sector ministry, in the case of utilities. Countries with strong presidential regimes are often reluctant to grant actual independence to a regulator. Also, the regulatory body is subject to lower de

facto independence in countries in which politicians have room to interfere with decisions to limit the authority of the judiciary. Additionally, in
the smallest and poorest countries, privatization of an asset may become
the single most important business event of the country in several years,
providing fertile ground for development of a strong bilateral relationship
between the executive power and the firms. In those contexts, decisions of
the executive may override the competences of other sector institutions,
forcing regulation out of the role that it should perform. In sectors such
as water and sanitation, which can comprise hundreds of isolated and
heterogeneous firms at the subnational level and in countries where the
key problem is insufficient coverage, more than a centralized regulator is
needed to achieve adequate sector outcomes. The quality of regulation will
depend heavily on the decisions of sector and local authorities. Coordination of regulation will be important, particularly in light of the growth of
new independent and semi-independent regulatory agencies in all sectors
in the region, increasing from 43 in 1979 to 134 in 2002 (Jordana and
Levi-Faur 2005).

Conclusions

Privatization in Latin America started earlier and spread farther and more
rapidly than anywhere in the developing world. In the 1990s, the accumulated privatization revenues in 18 Latin American countries reached 6
percent of GDP. From 1990 to 2001, private investment in infrastructure
alone reached US$361 billion. More firms, and larger ones, were sold in
the region and more proceeds were raised than in almost any other part of
the world. However, privatization did not occur equally throughout the
region. Differences among countries are dramatic. Privatized sectors and
the potential for further privatization depend on the country and appear
not to be linked with purely economic variables, but with the institutional
endowment and the rule of law. Still, the overall privatization record is
remarkable, contrasting with the current idea that privatization is negative
for societies.

In fact, public opinion and policy makers in Latin America and other
regions have turned against privatization, and a large political backlash
to privatization has been brewing for some time. The findings reviewed in
this chapter do not mean that failures do not occur, but rather that they are
not the norm. Most instances of failure can be explained by two factors.
First, opaque processes with heavy state involvement open the door to
corruption and opportunistic behavior. Second, poor contract design and
regulatory capture are linked to a lack of adequate regulation. Overall, a
political economy approach explains why it is hard to bring about changes
in regulation after privatization and why privatized firms are frequently
able to renegotiate their contracts on more favorable terms. Despite the

regulatory advances in the region, changes in the regulatory framework need to be promoted, because the variance of outcomes in the region is high. However, perfection in developing new regulatory frameworks may take considerable time. Reasonable solutions may be required in the short term, to avoid a return to the mistakes of statism and the conceptual simplification that pushed the private alternative in circumstances where (with hindsight) it had little chance to flourish. Pro-growth policies linked with improvements in the business climate and the existing institutional endowment will make the private option increasingly feasible in the long run, once third-party enforcement of legal property rights becomes generally accepted.

Annex 8A: Regulation Index Questionnaire

1. Telecommunications

Telecommunications law

Has parliament completely passed framework laws for the telecommunications sector?	0 No; 1 Yes
Does the law explicitly forbid operators from being issued licenses that allow them to provide more than one telecommunications service?	0 No; 1 Yes
Is separate accounting for services compulsory?	0 No; 1 Yes

Regulatory bodies

Has a regulatory body that is separate from the utility and from the communications ministry started to work?	0 No; 1 Yes
Can the main regulator compel financial and performance information?	0 No; 1 Yes
Are financial and performance information publicly available?	0 No; 1 Yes
Is the regulatory body headed by a single person or by a group of people (for example, a regulatory board)?	0 Single; 1 Multiple
Is head appointed for a fixed term?	0 No; 1 Yes
Can regulator be fired at discretion of the executive?	0 No; 1 Yes
Can regulator be fired for conflict of interest?	0 No; 1 Yes
Can regulator be fired for incompetence?	0 No; 1 Yes
Can regulator be fired for corruption?	0 No; 1 Yes
Can consumers participate in regulatory proceedings?	0 No; 1 Yes
Can competitors participate in regulatory proceedings?	0 No; 1 Yes
Have regional regulatory bodies been created?	0 No; 1 Yes

Regulatory decisions

Are regulatory meetings open to the public in practice?	0 None; 1 All
Are regulatory meetings required to be open to the public by law?	0 No; 1 Yes
Are regulatory decisions publicly available?	0 No; 1 Yes
Does regulator publish decisions in practice?	0 No; 1 Yes
Does the law require the regulator to publish decisions?	0 No; 1 Yes
Does regulator publish explanations of decisions in practice?	0 No; 1 Yes
Does the law require the regulator to publish explanations of decisions?	0 No; 1 Yes

(continued)

Annex 8A: Regulation Index Questionnaire *(continued)*

2. Electricity

Electricity law

Has parliament passed any framework laws aiming at reforming the electricity sector?	0 No; 1 Yes
Does the law explicity forbid operators from joint ownership of electricity services (such as generation, transmission, distribution, and retail or supply)?	0 No; 1 Yes
Does the law allow the entry of new private power ownership?	0 No; 1 Yes

Regulatory bodies

Has a regulatory body that is separate from the utility and from the ministry started to work?	0 No; 1 Yes
Is the regulatory body headed by a single person or by a group of people (for example, a regulatory board)?	0 Single; 1 Board
Is head appointed for a fixed term? .	0 No; 1 Yes
Reasons to fire head or commissioners: conflict of interest	0 No; 1 Yes
Reasons to fire head or commissioners: incompetence	0 No; 1 Yes
Reasons to fire head or commissioners: corruption	0 No; 1 Yes
Are policy guidelines publicly available?	0 No; 1 Yes
Can the minister or president give verbal instructions to the regulator?	0 No; 1 Yes
Have regional regulatory bodies been created?	0 No; 1 Yes

Regulatory process/decisions

Can agency compel financial and performance information from utilities?	0 No; 1 Yes
Is the financial or performance information audited by a regulator?	0 No; 1 Yes
Does the regulator make financial and performance information publicly available?	0 No; 1 Yes
Is there a consultation process before regulator decisions?	0 No; 1 Yes
Have consumer groups the right to participate in regulatory proceedings?	0 No; 1 Yes
Are regulatory meetings open to the public in practice?	0 No; 1 All
Are regulatory meetings required to be open to the public by. law?	0 No; 1 Yes
Are regulatory decisions publicly available?	0 No; 1 Yes

(continued)

Annex 8A: Regulation Index Questionnaire *(continued)*

Regulatory process/decisions (continued)	
Does the law require the regulator to publish decisions?	0 No; 1 Yes
Does the regulator publish decisions in practice?	0 No; 1 Yes
Does the law require the regulator to publish explanations of decisions?	0 No; 1 Yes
Does the regulator publish explanations of decisions in practice?	0 No; 1 Yes

Source: Wallsten and others 2004.

Notes

1. Greenfield projects represented 29 percent and concessions represented 17 percent of the US$374 billion total value of infrastructure projects in the region that involved private participation between 1990 and 2003. The remaining 54 percent was generated by divestitures.

2. There has been a contraction in total public investment in infrastructure, sometimes larger than the improvements in the fiscal balance (3.08 percent and 2.8 percent of GDP, respectively, in Brazil; see Calderón, Easterly, and Servén [2003]).

3. Authors' calculations using Fay and Morrison (2005).

4. However, recent research shows that the privatization effort in Africa may have been highly underestimated. Bennell (1997) argues that most papers studying privatization in Africa have been based on low-quality or outdated samples. Using a comprehensive survey of privatization transactions that spans 16 years (1980–95) and includes over 2,000 privatizations, he concludes that African privatization programs are larger than previously thought and that they have increased substantially during the 1990s.

5. The countries included in the study are Argentina, Bolivia, Brazil, Chile, Colombia, Peru and Mexico.

References

Allen, Franklin, and Douglas Gale. 1999. "Corporate Governance and Competition." Center for Financial Institutions Working Paper 99-28, Wharton School Center for Financial Institutions, University of Pennsylvania, Philadelphia.

Benavides, Juan, and Antonio Vives. 2005. "Public–Private Partnerships: From Plain Vanilla to Local Flavors." *IFM Review* 11 (2): 1–5.

Bennell, Paul. 1997. "Privatization in Sub-Saharan Africa: Progress and Prospects during the 1990s." *World Development* 25: 1785–1803.

Birdsall, Nancy, and John Nellis. 2002. "Privatization's Bad Name Isn't Totally Deserved." *Christian Science Monitor*, September 26.

Bornstein, Morris. 1999. "Framework Issues in the Privatization Strategies of the Czech Republic, Hungary, and Poland." *Post-Communist Economies* 11(1): 47–77.

Bortolotti, Bernardo, Marcella Fantini, and Domenico Siniscalco. 2001. "Regulation and Privatisation: The Case of Electricity." In *The Anti-Competitive Impact of Regulation*, ed. G. Amato and I. Laudati. Northampton, United States: ELGAR Press.

Boycko, Maxim, Andrei Shleifer, and Robert Vishny. 1996. "A Theory of Privatization." *Economic Journal* 106: 309–19.

Calderón, C., W. Easterly, and L. Servén. 2003. "How Did Latin America's Infrastructure Fare in the Era of Macroeconomic Crises?" Working Paper 185, Central Bank of Chile, Santiago.

Chong, Alberto, and Virgilio Galdo. Forthcoming. "Streamlining and Privatization Prices in the Telecommunications Industry." *Economica*.

Chong, Alberto, and Florencio López-de-Silanes, eds. 2005. *Privatization in Latin America: Myths and Reality*. Palo Alto, CA: Stanford University Press.

Chong, Alberto, and José Miguel Sánchez, eds. 2003. *Medios privados para fines públicos: Arreglos contractuales y participación privada en infraestructura en América Latina*. Washington, DC: Inter-American Development Bank Press.

The Economist. 2001. "State-Owned Stockpiles." March 29.

Engel, Eduardo, Ronald Fischer, and Alexander Galetovic. Forthcoming. "Privatizing Highways in Latin America." *Economia, Journal of the Latin American and Caribbean Economic Association*.

Fay, M., and M. Morrison. 2005. *Infrastructure in Latin America and the Caribbean: Recent Developments and Key Challenges*. Washington, DC: World Bank.

Fischer, Ronald, and Pablo Serra. 2002. "Regulating the Electricity Sector in Latin America." *Economia* 1(1): 155–98.

Florio, Massimo. 2004. *The Great Divestiture: Evaluating the Welfare Impact of the British Privatizations, 1979–1997*. Cambridge, MA: MIT Press.

Florio, Massimo, Jorge Carrera, and Daniele Checchi. 2004. "Privatization Discontent and Its Determinants: Evidence from Latin America." IZA Discussion Paper No. 1587, Institute for the Study of Labor, Bonn, Germany.

Galiani, Sebastian, Paul Gertler, Ernesto Schargrodsky, and Federico Sturzenegger. 2005. "Costs and Benefits of Privatization in Argentina." In *Privatization in Latin America: Myths and Reality*, ed. Alberto Chong and Florencio López-de-Silanes. Palo Alto, CA: Stanford University Press.

Guasch, José Luis. 2001. "Contract Renegotiation in Latin America and the Caribbean." World Bank, Washington, DC.

———. 2004. *Granting and Renegotiating Infrastructure Concessions: Doing It Right*. Washington, DC: World Bank.

Jordana, Jacint, and David Levi-Faur. 2005. "Hacia un Estado Regulador Latinoamericano? La Difusión de Agencias Reguladoras Autónomas por Países y Sectores." Fundación CIDOB, No. 7. Barcelona, Spain.

Kikeri, Sunita. 1999. "Privatization and Labor: What Happens to Workers When Governments Divest?" World Bank Technical Paper 396, World Bank, Washington, DC.

Kikeri, Sunita, and John Nellis. 2004. "An Assessment of Privatization." *The World Bank Research Observer* 19 (1): 87–118.

La Porta, Rafael, and Florencio López-de-Silanes. 1999. "Benefits of Privatization: Evidence from Mexico." *Quarterly Journal of Economics* 114 (4): 1193–1242.

La Porta, Rafael, Florencio López-de-Silanes, and Andrei Shleifer. 2002. "Government Ownership of Banks." *Journal of Finance* 57: 265–302.

Latinobarometro. Various years. Available at: http://www.latinobarometro.org.

Lora, Eduardo. 2001. "Structural Reforms in Latin America: What Has Been Reformed and How to Measure It." Research Department Working Paper 466, Inter-American Development Bank, Washington, DC.

Megginson, William. 2005. *The Financial Economics of Privatization.* Oxford, UK: Oxford University Press.

Megginson, W., and Jeffry Netter. 2001. "From State to Market: A Survey of Empirical Studies on Privatization." *Journal of Economic Literature* 39 (2): 321–89.

OECD (Organisation for Economic Co-operation and Development). 2001. "Recent Privatization Trends in OECD Countries." Paris: OECD.

Pombo, Carlos, and Manuel Ramírez. 2005. "Privatization in Colombia: A Plant Performance Analysis." In *Privatization in Latin America: Myths and Reality,* ed. Alberto Chong and Florencio López-de-Silanes. Palo Alto, CA: Stanford University Press.

Sheshinski, E., and Luis Felipe López-Calva. 2003. "Privatization and Its Benefits: Theory and Evidence." *CESifo Economic Studies* 49 (3): 429–59.

Torero, Maximo. 2005. "Privatization in Peru." In *Privatization in Latin America: Myths and Reality,* ed. Alberto Chong and Florencio López-de-Silanes. Palo Alto, CA: Stanford University Press.

Vickers, John, and George Yarrow. 1988. *Privatization: An Economic Analysis.* Cambridge, MA: MIT Press.

Wallsten, Scott. 2002. "An Empirical Analysis of Competition, Privatization, and Regulation in Africa and Latin America." *Journal of Industrial Economics* 49 (1): 1–19.

Wallsten, Scott, George Clarke, Luke Haggarty, Rosario Kaneshiro, Roger Noll, Mary Shirley, and Lixin Colin Xu. 2004. "New Tools for Studying Network Industry Reforms in Developing Countries: The Telecommunications and Electricity Database." Policy Research Working Paper No. 3286, World Bank, Washington, DC.

Winston, Clifford. 1993. "Deregulation: Days of Reckoning for Microeconomists." *Journal of Economic Literature* 31: 1263–89.

Yarrow, George. 1986. "Privatization in Theory and Practice." *Economic Policy* 2: 324–64.

9

Two Decades of Financial Reforms

Arturo Galindo, Alejandro Micco,
and Ugo Panizza

A CRUCIAL INGREDIENT for long-term economic growth is a well-crafted financial system. The financial system must have the ability to respond to the financial needs of profitable activities to advance economic development. In fact, empirical research has shown that the major determinant of firms' growth is access to financial markets and that in countries where credit constraints are tighter, the productive sector is unable to grow. In Latin American countries, financial systems are very small. On average, the ratio of credit to the private sector to GDP is close to 30 percent—less than half the size of credit markets in East Asia and about one-third the size of those in Western Europe (IMF 2005). Recent data also show that the region is not catching up. Over the 2002–04 period, average credit growth in Latin America was virtually identical to that of East Asia; however, if the analysis does not consider Venezuela (which has an extremely small credit market and during the period was recovering from a deep political and economic crisis), credit growth in Latin America was well below that of East Asia.

The importance of the financial sector in economic growth has naturally raised the question of what role the government should play in promoting financial development and stability. Since the early works of Arthur Lewis, Alexander Gerschenkron, Gunnar Myrdal, and several other prominent development economists writing in the 1950s and 1960s, there has been some agreement that the state should play a key role in the financial sector. Greater disagreement among economists revolves around how intervention should take place, that is, if it should be directly through the state's ownership of first- or second-tier banks (or both) and by the imposition of interest rate caps and directed credit, or indirectly through the provision of basic infrastructure and regulation to promote the development of private markets.

Latin American countries sailed through conflicting waves of opinions in this matter. During the 1960s and early 1970s, direct intervention views predominated. During the mid-1970s, several Latin American countries engaged in rapid liberalization of their financial systems. In the Southern Cone, after an initial boost in credit, the laissez-faire financial policies that supported unrestricted private participation in financial markets led to a general financial crisis throughout the region (Díaz-Alejandro 1985). Countries then reversed their strategies, abandoned laissez-faire practices and introduced tighter regulations and restrictions on their financial systems. This came with a de facto nationalization of the banking sector and widespread application of interest rate caps and targeted credit.

The outlook on state intervention in the financial sector changed again in the 1990s. The new stance was that the government should not direct credit (either through regulation or direct ownership of banks) but that state intervention should be directed toward the enhancement of the regulatory and supervisory framework aimed at promoting stable financial systems. This led to the privatization of several public banks and the liberalization of credit markets (interest rate caps and directed credit were abolished or substantially diminished and reserve requirements were lowered). The main characteristics of this new liberalization were foreign participation and the implementation of regulatory and supervision mechanisms crafted to avoid the crises that affected the region in the 1980s. Despite these efforts, financial development during the 1990s was weak. By the end of the decade, and following a major international capital markets crisis, most financial systems were depressed, and many firms found their financing needs unattended.

Several lessons from failed attempts to develop adequate forms of state intervention in banking have been learned, and many novel approaches are currently being implemented. This chapter describes the major trends of state intervention in financial markets, and briefly describes the innovative outlook of many modern interventions. Before doing so, it must be emphasized that no financial sector reform can be successful in an environment characterized by macroeconomic instability. The Argentinean crisis of 2001–02 shows that even in the presence of an excellent regulatory framework, large macroeconomic shocks can have a devastating effect on the banking sector. In fact, the current characteristics of Latin American financial markets are deeply rooted in the macroeconomic history of the region. A history of high inflation, for instance, not only contributed to stunting the region's financial markets but is also at the root of its high degree of financial dollarization, which, in turn, is one of the region's main sources of macroeconomic vulnerability.

Banking Reforms

Standard arguments for state intervention in the banking sector can be classified into five broad groups: (a) mitigating market failures resulting from costly and asymmetric information, (b) financing socially valuable but financially unprofitable projects, (c) promoting financial development and providing residents of isolated areas access to competitive banking services, (d) maintaining the safety and soundness of the banking system, and (e) enabling the overall environment for private banks to function adequately.

First, financial markets in general and banking in particular are information intensive. The stock of information gathered by banks plays a role in increasing the pool of domestic savings channeled to available investment opportunities. However, because information has public-good characteristics (nonrival in consumption and high cost of exclusion) and often entails fixed acquisition costs, competitive markets will undersupply information and the presence of high fixed costs will lead to imperfect competition in the banking system. Moreover, information can be easily destroyed, increasing the cost of bank failures because customers of the failed bank may lose access to credit. Asymmetric information may also lead to credit rationing, that is, a situation in which good projects are underfinanced (or not financed at all) because of the lack of verifiable information.[1] A similar case can be made for the relationship between depositors and banks: lack of bank-specific information can dissuade savers from depositing their money in banks, particularly in incipient banking systems in which longstanding customer relationships are yet to be built.

Second, private lenders may have limited incentives to finance projects that produce externalities. Thus, direct state participation would be warranted to compensate for market imperfections that leave socially valuable (but financially unattractive) investments underfinanced. Alternatively, state intervention may be justified by big-push theories such as that originally formulated by Rosenstein-Rodan (1943). Another argument is that banks can frustrate expansionary monetary policy because they have limited incentives to lend during economic downturns and low interest rates and do not take the long view that, by increasing lending, they would push the economy out of recession (this is the macroeconomic view).[2] In such a case, state intervention could solve a coordination problem and make monetary policy more effective. A related theoretical argument for state intervention suggests that effective prudential regulation (and, in some cases, the banks' own incentives) tends to make private banks too risk averse to finance all potentially profitable investments.[3] Then, in the absence of developed capital markets that allow for alternative sources of financing, as in most developing countries, state intervention may be warranted.

The third argument often invoked by supporters of state intervention in the banking sector is that private banks may not find it profitable to open branches in rural and isolated areas so state intervention is necessary to provide banking services to residents there. Underlying the argument are beliefs that granting access to banking services may increase financial development, with positive externalities on growth or poverty reduction (see, for instance, Burgess and Pande [2004]), and that access to financial services is, at any rate, a right and the state should make an effort to guarantee its universal provision. Along similar lines, the presence of public banks has also been advocated as a means to guarantee competitive behavior in an otherwise collusive banking sector. This rationale, however, is relevant only if one accepts that while the regulatory and monitoring capacity of the state is limited or prone to capture, the ability to own public banks is not subject to similar problems.

These three sets of arguments have been used to justify two forms of interventions: through direct ownership of financial intermediaries (first or second tier) or through regulation of financial contracts by imposing interest rate ceilings or by establishing credit targets of private banks to certain sectors.

Fourth, banks are inherently fragile institutions because their liabilities consist of demand deposits and their assets consist of more illiquid loans. This situation can lead to self-fulfilling bank runs and widespread bank failures. However, banking fragility by itself does not justify government intervention aimed at guaranteeing the stability of the banking system unless bank failures generate large negative externalities. It is exactly in this sense that banks are special because, besides intermediating credit, they also provide two services that have a public-good nature: they are the backup source of liquidity for all other institutions and the transmission belt for monetary policy (Corrigan 1982). The need for state intervention also arises from the fact that, because of the large leverage ratios that characterize financial institutions in general, bank managers and owners may have strong incentives to pursue investment activities that are riskier than the ones that would be preferred by depositors.[4] This would not be a problem if depositors could effectively monitor bank managers. However, there is a problem in bank monitoring because bank liabilities are mostly held by small depositors who have very limited incentives and abilities to monitor bank activities.[5]

The final arguments are related to the overall contract environment in which banks work. The main tools with which banks relate to clients are deposit and loan contracts. If the overall contract environment does not work adequately, and the rules of the contract and obligations of every party involved are not clearly defined and enforced, the ability to engage in financial transactions may be dampened, and credit and deposit contracts may by worthless. The government's role then is to provide the necessary public goods (contract enforcement and adjudication) so that banks and clients can engage in contractual arrangements.

Recent Trends in State-Owned Banking

The share of bank assets controlled by the public sector varies widely across regions and countries. The industrial countries and Sub-Saharan

Africa have the lowest prevalence of state ownership of banks (about 30 percent in 1995, figure 9.1).[6] South Asia and the Middle East and North Africa have the largest share of state ownership of banks (close to 90 percent in South Asia and above 50 percent in the Middle East and North Africa). Transition economies of Eastern Europe and Central Asia, after the massive privatization programs of the 1990s, moved from almost full state ownership of banks (90 percent in 1985) to intermediate levels of state ownership in 1995 (data for 2001 indicate an even lower level of state ownership).[7]

The level of state ownership of banks in Latin America is similar to the developing country average, and shows a strongly declining trend. In 1995, government ownership of banks was 60 percent that of the 1970s. There are, however, large differences between countries in the region, with Costa Rica having the largest share of government ownership of

Figure 9.1 Share of State-Owned Banks in Total Bank Assets, by Region

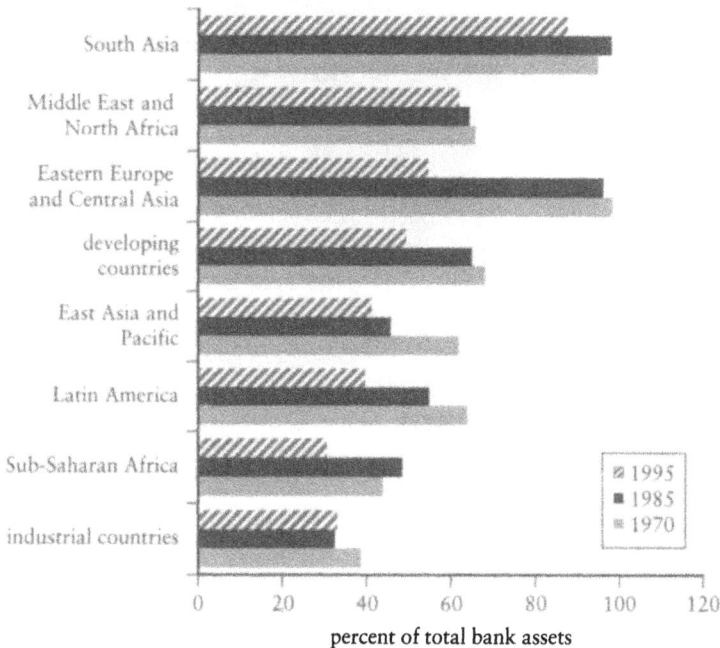

Source: La Porta, López-de-Silanes, and Shleifer 2002.

banks (90 percent in 1995, down from 100 percent in 1970, figure 9.2) and Trinidad and Tobago having the smallest share of state ownership of banks (1.5 percent). Most countries in the region privatized aggressively both in the 1970s (during the 1970–85 period, average state ownership of banks dropped from 64 to 55 percent) and 1990s (during the 1985–95 period, average state ownership of banks dropped from 55 to 40 percent).[8] Ecuador, Chile, and Peru privatized the most, moving from levels of state ownership hovering around 90 percent, to state ownership below 40 percent. Only Uruguay increased state ownership of banks, moving

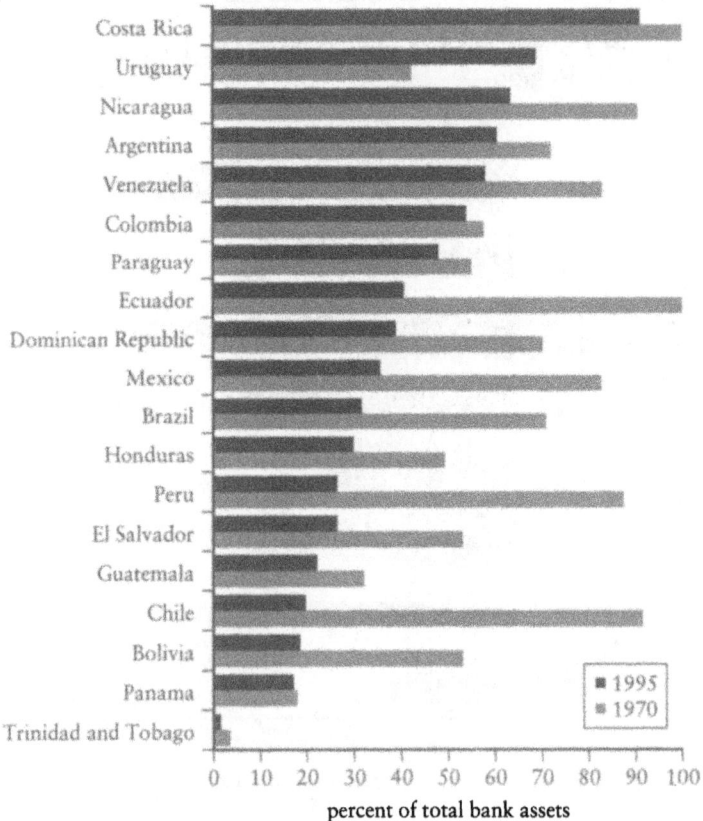

Figure 9.2 Share of State-Owned Banks in Total Bank Assets, Latin America

Source: La Porta, López-de-Silanes, and Shleifer 2002.

from 42 percent in 1970 to 69 percent in 1995. Other countries experienced large swings in the bank privatization and nationalization process. Mexico, for instance, moved from 82 percent state ownership in 1970 to 100 percent in 1985 and back to 35 percent in 1995. A similar pattern holds for Bolivia, Colombia, El Salvador, and Nicaragua.[9]

More recent data show that the pattern of bank privatization has continued in most countries. From 1995 to 2001, large bank privatizations raised US$5.5 billion in Brazil (with the privatization of BANESPA raising US$3.6 billion), US$800 million in Mexico, and more than US$500 million in both Colombia and Venezuela (Megginson 2003). Table 9.1 illustrates the recent evolution of state ownership of banks in 10 Latin American countries.[10] It shows that Argentina, Brazil, Costa Rica, and Nicaragua privatized the most. The share of assets controlled by state-owned banks also dropped in Chile, El Salvador, and Guatemala while it remained fairly constant in Colombia.

Two sets of factors drove privatization. The first set of factors was purely fiscal: during crises, the presence of public banks significantly increases the fiscal costs of dealing with distress and, when compared with private banks, the performance of public banks, measured by standard profitability indicators, is usually poor.[11] Thus, privatization was seen as an important source of both revenues and cost reduction for the public sector.

Figure 9.3 presents public bank performance indicators relative to those of private domestically owned banks.[12] It shows that public banks charge lower interest rates than their private counterparts and also pay lower interest rates on their deposits (0.9 percentage points less). Public banks also tend to lend more to the public sector (the difference between the

Table 9.1 Share of Public Bank Assets (percent)

Country	1995	1998	2000	2002
Argentina	42.5	29.2	25.7	—
Bolivia	0	0	0	0
Brazil	52.8	49.6	46.6	42.7
Chile	13.3	10.6	9.5	10.3
Colombia	19.6	16.3	21.1	19.4
Costa Rica	81.0	76.7	73.2	68.0
Guatemala	6.4	3.8	3.8	3.2
Honduras	n.a.	3.2	2.3	1.8
Nicaragua	53.0	13.3	0.5	n.a.
El Salvador	9.1	7.0	5.7	4.3

Source: IDB 2005.
Note: — = not available, n.a. = not applicable.

Figure 9.3 Relative Performance Indicators of State-Owned Banks vs. Private Banks

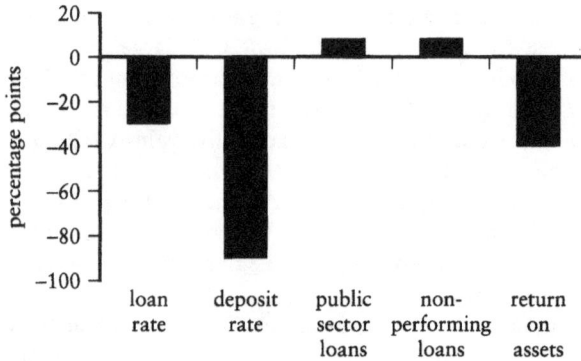

Source: IDB (2005) calculation based on balance sheet data for the 1993–2003 period. Includes banks from Argentina, Brazil, Chile, Colombia, Costa Rica, El Salvador, Mexico, and Peru.

Note: Loan rates, deposit rates, and return on assets are measured in basis points (100 basis points are 1 percent). Public sector loans and nonperforming loans are measured in percentage points.

share of public sector loans of private and public banks is 8 percentage points) and have a higher share of nonperforming loans (about 8 percentage points). Finally, public banks have lower profitability than their private counterparts (the difference in return on assets is 0.4 percentage points).

Although these results should be observed with caution because they are simple correlations that control only for bank size, they suggest that while public banks tend to be less efficient than their private counterparts (with higher nonperforming loans, more loans to the public sector, higher overhead, and lower returns) they are also perceived to be safer and hence able to pay lower rates on their deposits and extend credit at a lower rate.[13] An alternative explanation for these lower interest rates is that state-owned banks may benefit from indirect subsidies coming from government deposits paying no or low interest.[14]

The second driver of privatization was the empirical evidence that state-owned banks are often captured by politicians and that they do not achieve their social objectives (for instance, evidence indicates that public banks do not increase credit to the sectors that need it most, such as small and medium enterprises or economic sectors suffering from greater informational asymmetries).[15]

Toward New Forms of Public Banking

The fact that the pervasive reforms implemented in the 1990s did not yield the expected results in credit and GDP growth has led to skepticism about the reform process and to a renewed interest in public banking. However, policy makers aware of past experience with mismanaged public banks are trying to implement new, more focused and more sophisticated forms of intervention. This new wave of "smart" interventions is characterized by the design of specific interventions tailored to specific needs and institutional conditions. Examples of these forms of intervention include risk sharing through partial guarantees and risk pooling of otherwise atomized borrowers.

The recognized cases of successful public banks around the world share some common attributes that provide the following policy lessons:

- The social objective of the public bank needs to be clearly established and the institution should be subject to constant evaluation focusing on the achievement of the established objective.
- The subsidy received by the public bank should be clearly measured and used to conduct cost-benefit analyses of the activities of the institution.
- Public banks need to achieve their social objectives in the context of sound and competitive policies intended to maximize social return.
- The management of the public bank must be professional and its hiring policies transparent.
- Although the government should set the ultimate objectives for a state-owned bank, the management of the public bank should be operationally independent and fully autonomous from the government or any other form of political influence, especially with respect to the definition and implementation of its loan pricing and guarantee policies.
- The public bank must comply with all prudential requirements followed by private banks.

The main trend in state ownership of banks has been to reduce the state's participation in first-tier banks, and strengthen second-tier and development banks. Best practices have been identified, and novel forms of interventions in finance are currently being applied throughout the region.

Current Trends in the Involvement of the State in Financial Contracts

The government can intervene in credit markets directly through the own-ership of public financial intermediaries and indirectly through the regulation of the financial system. There are several types of regulations—those that directly shape and affect credit contracts, such as imposing limits on the interest rate, the maturity structure of loans, the allocation of credit, and the like, which are sometimes referred to as policies of financial repression; and those that indirectly affect the behavior of banking, such as prudential regulation and supervision, the enablement of the contract environment, and the like. This section discusses recent trends in the former, and the following section will discuss the latter.

In most regions, financial liberalization has been a gradual and continuous process; Latin America is the exception to this rule (figure 9.4). In fact, many Latin American countries engaged in rapid liberalization strategies in the mid-1970s and then, following a series of financial crises, reversed strategy in the early 1980s. At the beginning of the 1990s, Latin

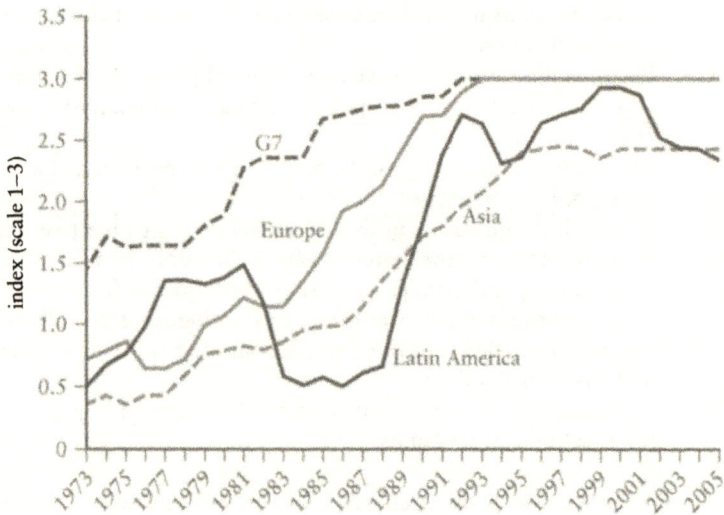

Figure 9.4 Financial Liberalization

Source: Financial liberalization is based on the indicators developed in Kaminsky and Schmuckler (2003) and authors' update of this index.

Note: The index plots the simple average of liberalization in the capital account, the domestic financial system, and the stock market. This measure ranges from 1 to 3, where 3 is full liberalization. The Average Liberalization Index in the graph is the simple average of the liberalization measure across countries in each year.

America engaged once again in a liberalization strategy that was again partly reversed in the last years of the 1990s. Figure 9.5 shows that the drop in the Latin American index of financial liberalization was completely due to the behavior of Argentina and Venezuela, both of which, in the last five years, went back to levels of financial repression similar to the early 1980s. This new swing was the result of politics, but also of the recent economic crises that were interpreted as failure of the neoliberal policies that characterized the 1990s (Panizza and Yáñez 2005).

It is worth mentioning that no theory provides a clear-cut answer on how liberalization should relate to economic performance. On the one hand, models of perfect markets in the tradition of Goldsmith (1969),

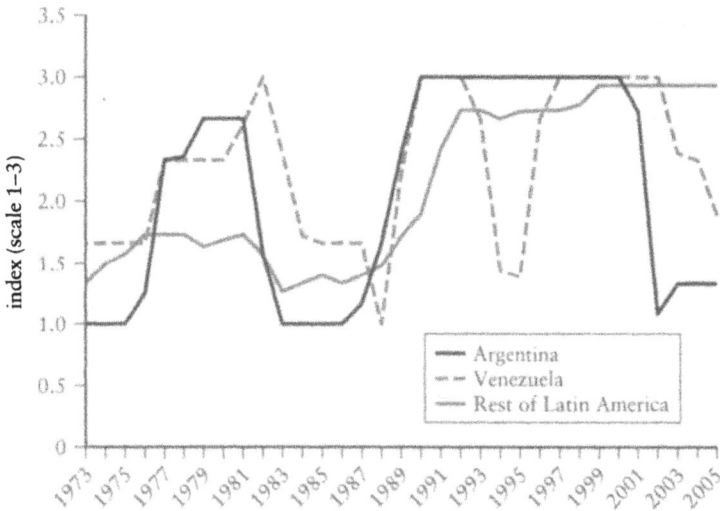

Figure 9.5 Financial Liberalization in Latin America

Source: Financial liberalization is based on the indicators developed in Kaminsky and Schmuckler (2003) and authors' update of this index.

Note: The index plots the simple average of liberalization in the capital account, the domestic financial system, and the stock market. This measure ranges from 1 to 3, where 3 is full liberalization. The Average Liberalization Index in the graph is the simple average of the liberalization measure across countries in each year. "Rest of Latin America" includes Brazil, Chile, Colombia, Mexico, and Peru.

McKinnon (1973), and Shaw (1973) suggest that removing restrictions on interest rates and credit controls should increase savings, expand the size of credit markets, and improve the efficiency with which funds are allocated. Through these mechanisms, liberalization should promote growth by effectively reducing the cost of funds for firms.[16] On the other hand, some authors claim that the efficient-markets paradigm is misleading when applied to the financial sector, which is plagued by serious problems of asymmetric information and moral hazard (Stiglitz 2000).

Interestingly, evidence now suggests that financial liberalization in Latin America did not deliver because of the lack of key complementary reforms. Galindo, Micco, and Ordóñez (2002) show that financial liberalization has little impact on growth in countries in which the institutions that support credit contracts and promote creditor rights are weak. Although financial liberalization increases the ability to manage and diversify risk, the advantages of liberalization cannot be exploited if the judicial system is not equally prepared and regulations inhibit the use of risk-mitigating instruments such as collateral.[17]

Toward the Promotion of Sound and Stable Banking

Strong reforms throughout the period since 1990 have occurred in the areas of prudential regulation and supervision. Prudential regulation and the supervision of banks are important tools for alleviating adverse selection and moral hazard in banking. The increased integration of financial markets requires standardized methods to promote financial stability.

There are two classic arguments for banking regulation. The first contends that regulation is necessary for the protection of small and unsophisticated depositors. Given their small size and their fragmentation, individual depositors do not have the ability to monitor whether bank managers are acting prudently and on their behalf. The regulator represents these depositors. Capital regulation, and the requirement to inject new capital when necessary or face closure, may be a way to create the incentives present in nonfinancial firms for managers to act on behalf of their shareholders (depositors in financial firms).[18]

The second rationale stems from the need to protect the payments system and the financial system more generally. For whatever reason, otherwise solvent banks may be subject to pure liquidity runs.[19] Moreover, if depositors run against a weak bank, contagion may cause them to run against other more healthy banks in the system fearing actual financial links between banks. Contagious bank runs can have significant negative effects on the rest of the economy and hence are generally thought to be costly, especially if they affect generally healthy banks or prevent the normal functioning of the payments system. In particular, if healthy banks fail client information can be lost (the private information those banks hold on their clients) and the economy may suffer a general "credit crunch."

Capital adequacy requirements have been among the most debated of the prudential regulations. Regardless of the theoretical debate, most countries around the world, and certainly Latin American countries, have adopted Basel Accord capital regulation (table 9.2). In fact, compared with international standards that suggest a minimum capital-to-assets-at-risk ratio of 8 percent, capital requirements in Latin America appear to be relatively stringent.

Although capital regulations are in place, many other areas of prudential regulation have yet to be adopted.[20] The 30 Basel principles for effective banking supervision are normally divided into seven chapters: (a) objectives, autonomy, powers, and resources; (b) licensing and structure; (c) prudential regulations and requirements; (d) methods of ongoing supervision; (e) information requirements; (f) formal powers of supervisors; and (g) cross-border banking. Figure 9.6 shows that Latin America does rather poorly in complying with these principles. In particular, the average Latin American country is compliant with only 6.8 of the 30 prin-

Table 9.2 Capital Requirements in Latin America

Country	Capital requirement percentage	Year of adoption of capital requirement
Chile	8.0	1989
Mexico	8.0	1994
Panama	8.0	1998
Trinidad and Tobago	8.0	1994
Belize	9.0	1996
Colombia	·9.0	1992
Ecuador	9.0	1995
Peru	9.0	1993
Bolivia	10.0	1995
Guatemala	10.0	1995
Honduras	10.0	1998
Nicaragua	10.0	1999
Paraguay	10.0	1991
Uruguay	10.0	1992
Brazil	11.0	1995
El Salvador	11.0	1993
Argentina	11.5	1991
Venezuela	12.0	1993

Source: Banking superintendencies.

Figure 9.6 Average Compliance with Basel Principles for Effective Banking Supervision

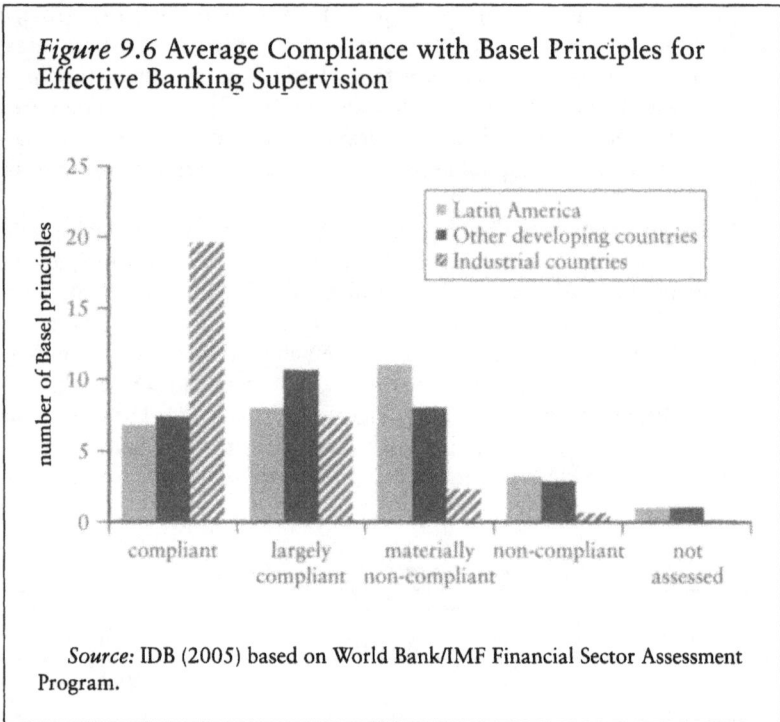

Legend:
- Latin America
- Other developing countries
- Industrial countries

Categories (x-axis): compliant, largely compliant, materially non-compliant, non-compliant, not assessed

y-axis: number of Basel principles (0 to 25)

Source: IDB (2005) based on World Bank/IMF Financial Sector Assessment Program.

ciples and largely compliant with only another 8. The figure shows that the region does slightly better than the average developing country but much worse than the average industrial country.

The region does particularly badly in three key areas. First, in the area of prudential regulation, less than 10 percent of countries are compliant with principles concerning loan evaluation and loan loss provisioning, interest rate risk, and liquidity risk. Second, countries in the region need to consolidate supervision on a national and global basis and properly supervise the links between banks and other financial companies including offshore entities. Third, quality and independence of the regulatory agencies are very deficient in most countries—less than 20 percent of countries are compliant with the principles related to operational independence and resources of the regulatory agency, suitable legal framework, and legal protection for supervisors and remedial measures.

Poor supervision is perhaps the biggest problem. Appropriate remedial measures are often not acted on because supervisors lack independence and they lack supervisory independence because they do not have effective legal protection. A lack of real supervisory independence can affect how all regulations function. Political or legal pressures may cause officials to overlook noncompliance with regulations and may produce loose monitoring of sensitive issues such as lending to companies or individuals related to the bank or with political connections. Moreover, poor supervision nullifies the positive effects of the high stated capital requirements. In particular, although all countries indicate that they follow a Basel methodology to calculate assets at risk there are different interpretations of what a Basel methodology implies. Furthermore, an assessment of whether capital is adequate must start with a determination of whether accounting practices value assets appropriately, whether nonperforming loans are treated appropriately, and whether banks are reasonably provisioned. Hence, while countries may have a headline Basel I capital requirement on the books, the reality is often quite different because exceptions are granted frequently and remedial action is weak. Inadequate risk analysis amplifies the problems.

Those who are critical of expanding the role of the state in bank supervision argue that, even in a system in which regulations are properly designed and supervisors have appropriate powers, supervisors may still lack the required information to effectively apply those regulations. According to this view, the only effective way to guarantee bank stability is to harness the market to discipline banks. While market and supervisory discipline may be thought of as substitutes, they are, in fact, strategic complements. Appropriate regulations can enhance the disciplining power of markets, and markets can enhance the disciplining power of supervisors; together they provide greater discipline than the simple sum of the two components.

Summing up, while in the recent past, the state has played an important role in adopting regulatory measures aimed at guaranteeing stable financial intermediation, these measures are often not enforced because of the institutional weakness of supervisory agencies. Policy makers in the region need to exert much greater effort toward improving the functioning of bank supervisory and regulatory agencies and taking advantage of the potential complementarities between regulation and market discipline.

Two key areas need more work. First, supervisory agencies must be guaranteed independence; second, agencies' ability to conduct consolidated supervision must be improved. Because the lack of consolidated supervision may prove to be a significant hurdle if the region wishes to adopt Basel II, banking supervisors must attempt to gain political support to increase their powers and ensure adequate resources. Moreover, as banking becomes ever more global this area will only increase in importance in the future.

Capital Market Reforms

During the 1990s, several Latin American countries focused on building the basis for capital market development by creating domestic securities and exchange commissions, developing regulatory and supervisory frameworks, and working toward easing market operations by designing centralized exchanges, securities clearance and settlement systems, custody arrangements, and by improving accounting and disclosure standards. Figure 9.7 summarizes the reforms undertaken by Latin American

countries. More recently, additional efforts have been made in passing
new laws and regulations intended to increase the protection of investors'
rights, particularly minority shareholders' rights, and deter insider trading
(World Bank 2004b).

So far, the outcome of these reforms has been far from satisfactory. The
size of the region's stock and bond markets remains very low by international standards. Figure 9.8 compares the domestic bond market of Latin
America with those of East Asia and the industrial countries and shows
that Latin America's bond market is not only small but heavily skewed
toward government bonds (as of 2004, corporate bonds were 2.5 percent
of GDP in Latin America and 9 percent of GDP in East Asia).[21]

The poor performance of the region's bond market is even more surprising because Latin America was a pioneer in the development of private
pension funds (table 9.3), which now manage approximately US$147
billion (approximately 12 percent of the region's GDP, figure 9.9).[22] The
creation of pension funds did not yield the expected impact on market
development because for prudential reasons pension fund portfolios were
limited to a few highly rated corporate bonds, government bonds, and
selected foreign claims. According to the *Asociación Internacional de*

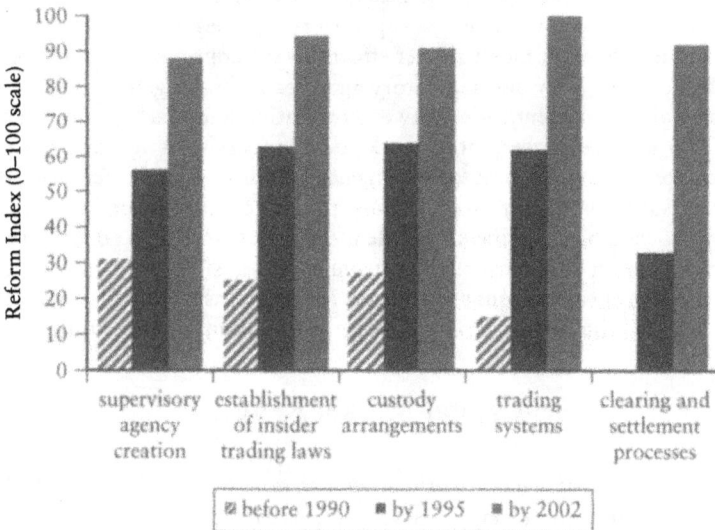

Figure 9.7 Capital Market Reforms in Latin America

Source: World Bank 2004b.

Figure 9.8 Domestic Bonds as a Share of GDP (weighted average)

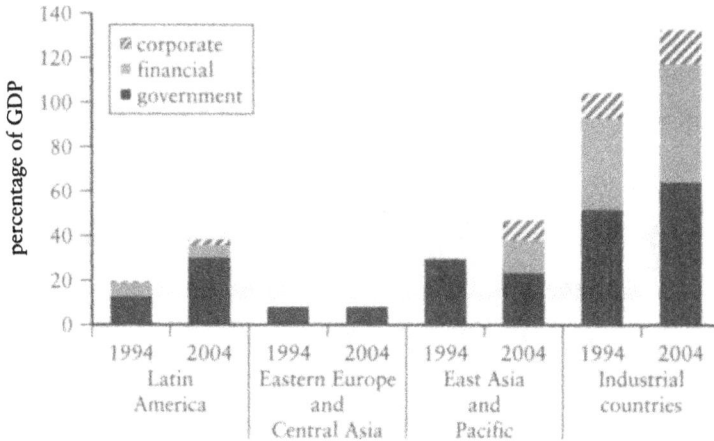

Source: Borensztein, Eichengreen, and Panizza 2006.

Table 9.3 Implementation of Private Pension Funds

Country	Year of implementation
Argentina	1993
Bolivia	1996
Chile	1980
Colombia	1993
Costa Rica	2000
Dominican Republic	2001
El Salvador	1997
Mexico	1996
Peru	1992
Uruguay	1995

Source: AIOS 2004.

Figure 9.9 Pension Fund Assets

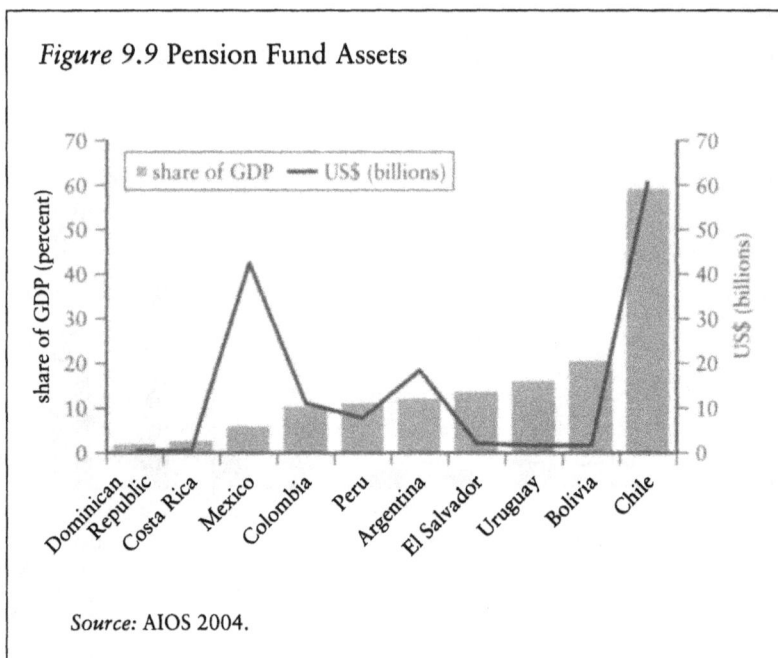

Source: AIOS 2004.

Organismos de Supervisión de Fondos de Pensiones (AIOS), by December 2004, on average, 48.1 percent of the assets of pension funds were government bonds, 16.8 percent were investments in financial institutions, 13.4 percent were investments abroad, and only 10.7 percent, 8.4 percent, and 2.1 percent were investments in local stocks, corporate bonds, and mutual funds, respectively.

Interestingly, while capital market reform had limited impact on the domestic capital market, it was a significant driver of internationalization and globalization. Notably, reforms led to a higher share of international activity relative to domestic activity (World Bank 2004b). Clearly, globalization had a positive impact on the firms that were able to access international markets, but it also had negative spillovers and reduced liquidity in domestic markets and hurt smaller firms that were unable to access the international markets.

As well as being small, the Latin American capital market is illiquid. The turnover ratio in the region is well below that observed in other emerging markets such as Hungary, India, and the Republic of Korea (table 9.4). The illiquidity of the equity market reflects both concentration of supply (concentrated firm ownership results in very low float ratios and concentration of demand (which in some countries is completely driven by institutional investors who mostly buy and hold). Chile is a clear example of concentration. The average free float in Chilean shares is less than 40 percent. The 10 largest shareholders in the 40 largest corporations

Table 9.4 Measures of Equity Market Development
for Selected Countries, 2003

	Listed companies	Market cap (% GDP)	Turnover ratio	Average free float (fraction of listed shares owned by minority shareholders)
Argentina	107	30	0.1	0.4
Brazil	367	46	0.3	0.7
Chile	240	105	0.1	0.4
Colombia	114	18	0.0	0.4
Hungary	49	20	0.5	0.6
India	5,644	48	1.0	0.4
Korea, Rep. of	1,563	64	2.1	0.7
Mexico	159	20	0.2	0.7

Source: Emerging Market Database of the International Finance Corporation available at http://fisher.osu.edu/fin/databases/emdb.htm.

own more than 80 percent of the company, and around 70 percent of the shares of the 60 most traded firms are held by controlling shareholders. In addition, most available free float shares are held by institutional investors with a buy-and-hold strategy.

Increasing liquidity is not an easy task. Liquidity is a positive function of market size, economies of scale, and network and agglomeration effects. As mentioned, in Latin America the adverse impact of small market size on liquidity has been amplified by a high concentration of trading in a few highly rated stocks. Thus, improvements to the market infrastructure can increase liquidity slightly but cannot lead to increases large enough to ensure stronger development.[23]

Protecting Creditor Rights: A Long Road Ahead

The provision of a suitable environment for contract enforcement is a key area for government intervention to guarantee deep and stable financial intermediation. For financial relationships to be entered into, the obligations of each party to a credit contract need to be made explicit, and an agent that enforces the obligations must be ready to act when required. Unfortunately, in Latin American countries, effective protection of property rights in financial contracts is weak, and except in few cases, including Brazil, Chile, and Mexico, very little reform has been seen.

The protection of creditor rights through rules and regulations that clearly dictate the ownership of assets involved in credit contracts, and the efficiency of their enforcement, have been identified as crucial areas to promote the development and stability of financial markets and increase access to credit for marginal sectors.[24] Recent research has shown that increasing the protection of creditor rights can have sizable impacts on the depth of credit markets, can contribute to increased credit market stability, and can promote access to credit for sectors that have usually faced greater credit constraints, such as small and medium enterprises.[25]

Several institutions limit the ability to secure creditor rights in Latin America. In most countries, laws are not designed to protect creditors, especially through ready access to different forms of collateral. Even when collateral can be pledge, the low levels of rule of law and of judiciary efficiency in the region fail to properly secure property rights.[26]

Latin American countries lag behind Organisation for Economic Co-operation and Development (OECD) and other emerging market countries in the protection of creditor rights (see figure 9.10). The measure

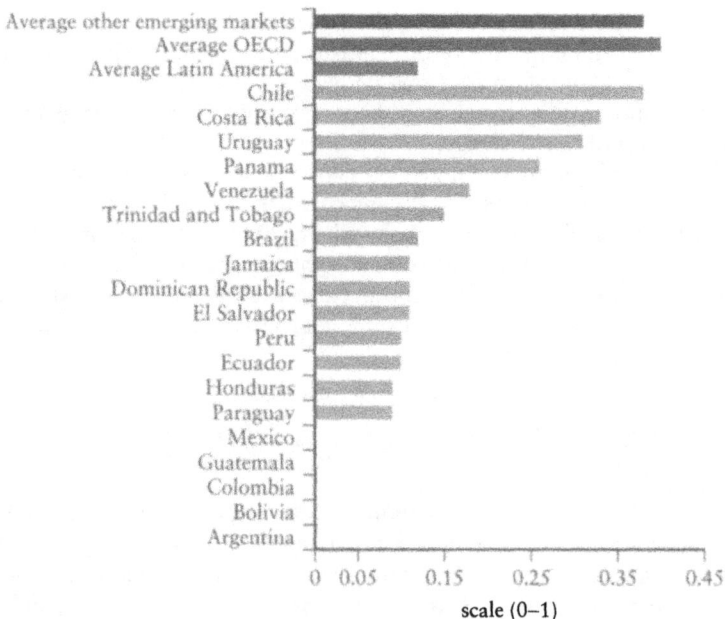

Figure 9.10 Effective Creditor Rights

Source: IDB 2005.

in the figure illustrates the extent to which regulations and law enforcement protect creditors.[27] The index suggests that the conditions for Latin America are precarious, because creditor rights in the region are not only weak, but barely enforced. Based on this methodology, creditor protection in Latin America is in extreme need of reform.

Latin American countries also fare badly in several other indicators commonly used as a proxy for the institutional environment and the ability to enter into contracts. The inefficiency of courts to handle contract disputes, and the prolonged duration of bankruptcy procedures (see figure 9.11), are notorious issues in the region.

The lack of reform in this crucial area prevented the first generation of market-oriented reforms from yielding stronger outcomes. The weakness of the contract environment indicates that it is an area in which the state needs to play a crucial role.

Conclusions

The role of the state in credit markets in Latin America has changed significantly since the mid-1980s. The region has moved from a realm of high

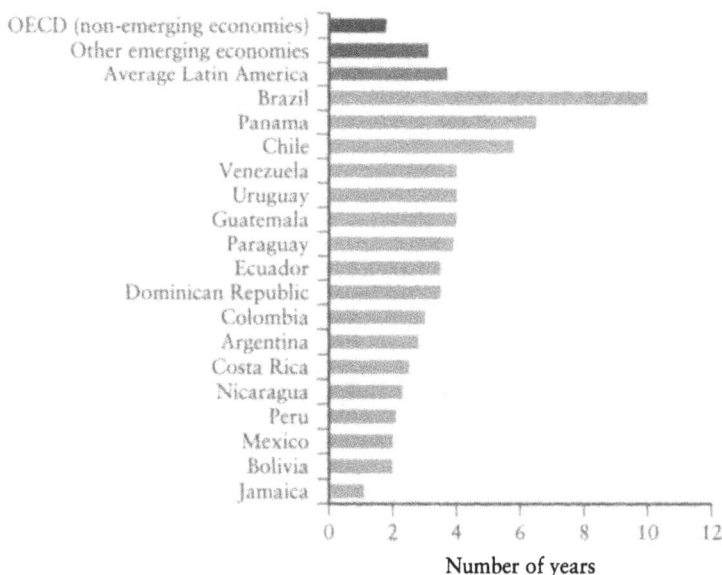

Figure 9.11 Duration of Bankruptcy Procedures

Source: World Bank 2004a.

intervention, both in the form of direct ownership and high repression, in the mid-1970s to the current environment of relatively less ownership and significantly less repression combined with stronger regulation and supervision.

Moreover, the focus of direct ownership is changing, as state interventions are becoming more oriented toward specific financing needs, and the charters of many public banks are being reformed to isolate them from possible political intervention in lending decisions.

Although many systems have been liberalized, evidence indicates a reversal in some countries. These reversals, as well as deficiencies in providing an adequate contracting environment, remain crucial challenges for Latin American states in the quest to achieve deeper and more stable financial systems.

Governments have played an important role in the past decade in the provision of proper prudential regulation and supervision. Compared to the 1980s, the region has made critical advances in this area. Nonetheless, many weaknesses need to be addressed, such as dealing with currency mismatches of borrowers, or assessing the risk of sovereign debt when the sovereign is poorly rated. Creative solutions must emerge from the region's regulators to address these and other issues. This is a crucial time for regional policy makers in their task of providing a framework for deep and stable financial intermediation, as the world moves toward the adoption of the new standards of regulation and supervision of Basel II.

Government efforts to promote deeper financial markets have gone beyond banking and credit markets. Significant efforts have been made to provide a suitable environment for the development of capital markets. The development of private pension funds, combined with reforms to the capital market's infrastructure, were notable areas of reform during the 1990s. The full benefits of these reforms have yet to be realized.

Notes

1. Indeed, rationing may occur as an adverse selection phenomenon in which, by pooling good and bad projects, the lender may increase financing costs to the point of driving good projects out of the market. For a detailed discussion of market failures arising from costly and asymmetric information, see Stiglitz (1994).

2. Prudential regulation may create an additional disincentive, because the quality of both banks' portfolios and prospective investments tend to deteriorate during a recession.

3. There are at least two reasons why this may be the case. First, because of the presence of externalities in the banking sector, the regulator may aim at a suboptimal risk level. Second, reputation costs and significant market power may induce large private banks to shy away from risky investments to protect their charter value.

4. See Jensen and Meckling (1976) and, for a textbook treatment, Freixas and Rochet (1997).

5. The same problem underpins the role of banks as delegated monitors of depositors' investments, as pointed out by Diamond (1984). These arguments have been invoked to reinforce the need for more stringent prudential regulation, as opposed to direct state participation in banking activities.

6. The data described here include both commercial and development banks.

7. For details of bank privatization in transition countries, see Bonin, Hasan, and Wachtel (2003).

8. Studies of bank privatization in Latin America include Beck, Crivelli, and Summerhill (2003); Clarke and Cull (2002); and Haber and Kantor (2003).

9. In Nicaragua, state ownership went from 90 percent (1970), to 100 percent (1985), to 63 percent. In Colombia, state ownership went from 57 percent (1970), to 75 percent (1985), then back to 53 percent (1995). In El Salvador, state ownership went from 53 percent (1970), to 100 percent (1985), to 26 percent (1995). In Bolivia, state ownership went from 53 percent, to 69 percent, then back to 18 percent (1995).

10. Table 9.1 is not directly comparable with figure 9.2 because the data in table 9.1 include only commercial banks and the data in figure 9.2 also include development banks. Furthermore, the data in figure 9.2 include only the assets of the 10 largest banks, while table 9.1 includes all the banks operating in the country. Finally, the data in table 9.1 were computed by assigning 100 percent government ownership to banks that have at least 50 percent of assets owned by the government and 0 percent government ownership to others.

11. See, for example, Córdoba (2005) for a discussion of the role of public banks in the Colombian financial crisis of the late 1990s. Despite the fact that public banks are designed with a social objective in mind, in most cases their performance is measured using standard private bank criteria, such as return on assets, net interest income, and so forth.

12. All the values were obtained by running a bank-level regression, controlling for size (expressed as log of total assets) and including a dummy taking value one for public banks and a dummy taking value one for foreign-owned banks. The values plotted in figure 9.3 are the coefficients of the public bank dummy.

13. Micco, Panizza, and Yáñez (2004) find similar results adding a complete set of bank level controls.

14. As in Chile, where the *Banco del Estado de Chile* manages the central government checking account.

15. See Galindo and Micco (2004) and IDB (2005) for discussions.

16. On the relationship between increasing the size and efficiency of financial markets and growth, see King and Levine (1993) and Beck, Levine, and Loayza (2000) for cross-country evidence, and Rajan and Zingales (1998) for cross-industry-country evidence. Galindo, Schiantarelli, and Weiss (2005) provide evidence on how financial liberalization has increased the efficiency of funds allocation.

17. Demirgüç-Kunt and Detragiache (1998) show that countries that liberalized their financial sectors were more likely to run into banking crises than those that did not, but depending strongly on the quality of the regulatory and supervisory institutions prevalent at the time of liberalization. Once again, many Latin American countries show important weakness in these areas.

18. For a discussion, see Dewatripont and Tirole (1994).

19. Such is the argument of Diamond and Dybvig (1983).

20. Because banks in the region are subject to much larger shocks than banks in industrial countries, it is reasonable to think that Basel's 8 percent may not be enough to guarantee bank stability and that capital requirements should be higher than the recommended minimum.

21. For a detailed analysis of the Latin American bond market, see Borensztein, Eichengreen, and Panizza (2006).

22. Private pension funds started to operate in Latin America during the 1990s. The exception is Chile, which started this system in 1980.

23. See World Bank (2004b) for a detailed discussion.

24. See IDB (2005) for a complete discussion.

25. See Galindo and Micco (2005) and IDB (2005) for detailed discussions.

26. Being unable to create collateral is also a major impediment to the development of credit markets in Latin America. In many Latin American countries, the types of assets that can be used as collateral are very limited and are mostly reduced to immovable assets, such as real estate. Using movable assets such as accounts receivable, inventories, agricultural production, or similar types of assets, is much more difficult, in part because rules and regulations do not accommodate adequate definitions of collateral that span into these assets, but also because immovable property registries are fairly underdeveloped. This last issue even diminishes the possibility of using real estate as collateral in many countries.

27. The index has two components. The first one, based on La Porta and others (1998), indicates the quality of the regulatory framework. It summarizes regulations determining creditors' rights to control collateral if firms file for reorganization or bankruptcy. The regulatory component of the index considers whether (a) regulations impose an automatic stay on assets in case of reorganization; (b) secured creditors have the right to be paid first in case of bankruptcy; (c) regulations require firms to consult with creditors before filing for reorganization; and (d) regulations mandate removal of the firm's management during reorganization. A positive response to each of the four elements of the index is interpreted as creditor rights protection. Regulations reflect what the law says, which is not necessarily what happens in practice. It is relevant to account for differences in law enforcement from country to country. The second component of the index is a measure of law enforcement. The index reported in the figure is the product of the legal quality measure and the law enforcement indicator. Higher values imply higher effective protection.

References

AIOS (Asociación Internacional de Organismos de Supervisión de Fondos de Pensiones). 2004. Boletín Estadístico No. 12. December.

Beck, Thorsten, Juan Miguel Crivelli, and William Summerhill. 2003. "State Bank Transformation in Brazil: Choices and Consequences." Paper presented at the World Bank Conference on Bank Privatization, Washington, DC, November 20–21.

Beck, Thorsten, Ross Levine, and Norman Loayza. 2000. "Finance and the Sources of Growth." *Journal of Financial Economics* 58(1–2): 261–300.

Bonin, John P., Iftekhar Hasan, and Paul Wachtel. 2003. "Privatization Matters: Bank Performance in Transition Countries." Paper presented at the World Bank Conference on Bank Privatization, Washington, DC, November 20–21.

Borensztein, Eduardo, Barry Eichengreen, and Ugo Panizza. 2006. "Building Bond Markets in Latin America." Inter-American Development Bank, Washington, DC.

Burgess, Robin, and Rohini Pande. 2004. "Do Rural Banks Matter? Evidence from the Indian Social Banking Experiment." CEPR Discussion Paper No. 4211, Centre for Economic Policy Research, London.

Clarke, George, and Robert Cull. 2002. "Political and Economic Determinants of the Likelihood of Privatizing Argentine Public Banks." *Journal of Law and Economics* 45(1): 165–97.

Córdoba, J. P. 2005. "Can Public Banks Work in Colombia?" Presentation at the Public Banks in Latin America: Myths and Realities Conference. Inter-American Development Bank, Research Department. Washington, DC, February. Available at http://www.iadb.org/res/pub_desc.cfm?pub_id=P-346.

Corrigan, E. Gerald. 1982. "Are Banks Special?" Annual Report Essay. Federal Reserve Board, Minneapolis, MN. Available at http://minneapolisfed.org/pubs/ar/ar1982a.cfm.

Demirgüç-Kunt, Asli, and Enrica Detragiache. 1998. "The Determinants of Banking Crises: Evidence from Developed and Developing Countries." *IMF Staff Papers* 45(1): 81–109.

Dewatripont, M., and J. Tirole. 1994. *The Prudential Regulation of Banks*. Cambridge and London: MIT Press.

Diamond, Douglas W. 1984. "Financial Intermediation and Delegated Monitoring." *Review of Economic Studies* 51(3): 393–414.

Diamond, Douglas W., and Philip H. Dybvig. 1983. "Bank Runs, Deposit Insurance, and Liquidity." *Journal of Political Economy* 91(3): 401–19.

Díaz-Alejandro, Carlos F. 1985. "Goodbye Financial Repression, Hello Financial Crash." *Journal of Development Economics* 19 (September–October): 1–24.

Emerging Market Database of the International Finance Corporation. Available at http://fisher.osu.edu/fin/databases/emdb.htm.

Freixas, Xavier, and Jean-Charles Rochet. 1997. *Microeconomics of Banking*. Cambridge, MA: MIT Press.

Galindo, Arturo, and Alejandro Micco. 2004. "Creditor Protection and Financial Markets: Empirical Evidence and Implications for Latin America." *Economic Review*, Federal Reserve Bank of Atlanta 89 (2): 29–37.

———. 2005. "Creditor Protection and Credit Volatility." Latin American Research Network Working Paper No. 528, Inter-American Development Bank, Washington, DC. Available at http://ssrn.com/abstract=669742.

Galindo, Arturo, Alejandro Micco, and Guillermo Ordóñez. 2002. "Financial Liberalization: Does It Pay to Join the Party?" *Economia* 3(1): 231–61.

Galindo, Arturo José, Fabio Schiantarelli, and Andrew M. Weiss. 2005. "Does Financial Liberalization Improve the Allocation of Investment? Micro Evidence from Developing Countries." Boston College Working Papers in Economics No. 625, Boston College, Boston, MA. Available at http://ssrn.com/abstract=698345.

Goldsmith, Raymond. 1969. *Financial Structure and Development*. New Haven, CT: Yale University Press.

Haber, Stephen, and Shawn Kantor. 2003. "Getting Privatization Wrong: The Mexican Banking System, 1991–2003." Paper presented at the World Bank Conference on Bank Privatization, Washington, DC, November 20–21.

IDB (Inter-American Development Bank). 2005. "Unlocking Credit: The Quest for Deep and Stable Bank Lending." In *Economic and Social Progress in Latin America*. Washington, DC: IDB.

IMF (International Monetary Fund). 2005. "Global Financial Stability Report: Market Developments and Issues." World Economic and Financial Surveys, International Monetary Fund, Washington, DC.

Jensen, Michael C., and William H. Meckling. 1976. "Theory of the Firm: Managerial Behavior, Agency Costs and Ownership Structure." *Journal of Financial Economics* 3(4): 305–60.

Kaminsky, Graciela, and Sergio Schmukler. 2003. "Short-Run Pain, Long-Run Gain: The Effects of Financial Liberalization." NBER Working Papers 9787, National Bureau of Economic Research, Cambridge, MA.

King, Robert, and Ross Levine. 1993. "Finance and Growth: Schumpeter Might Be Right." *Quarterly Journal of Economics* 108(3): 717–37.

La Porta, Rafael, Florencio López-de-Silanes, and Andrei Shleifer. 2002. "Government Ownership of Banks." *Journal of Finance* 57(1): 265–301.

La Porta, Rafael, Florencio López-de-Silanes, Andrei Shleifer, and Robert Vishny. 1998. "Law and Finance." *Journal of Political Economy* 106: 1113–1155.

McKinnon, Ronald I. 1973. *Money and Capital in Economic Development.* Washington, DC: Brookings Institution Press.

Megginson, William L. 2003. "The Economics of Bank Privatization." Paper presented at the World Bank Conference on Bank Privatization, Washington, DC, November 20–21.

Micco, Alejandro, Ugo Panizza, and Monica Yáñez. 2004. "Bank Ownership and Performance: Does Politics Matter?" Research Department Working Paper No. 518, Inter-American Development Bank, Washington, DC.

Panizza, Ugo, and Monica Yáñez. 2005. "Why Are Latin Americans So Unhappy About Reforms?" *Journal of Applied Economics* 8(1): 1–29.

Rajan, Raghuram G., and Luigi Zingales. 1998. "Financial Dependence and Growth." *American Economic Review* 88(3): 559–86.

Rosenstein-Rodan, Paul. 1943. "Problems of Industrialization in Eastern and Southeastern Europe." *Economic Journal* 53: 201–11.

Shaw, Edward S. 1973. *Financial Deepening in Economic Development.* New York: Oxford University Press.

Stiglitz, Joseph E. 1994. "The Role of the State in Financial Markets." In *Proceedings of the World Bank Annual Conference on Development Economics, 1993,* ed. Michael Bruno and Boris Pleskovic. Washington, DC: World Bank.

———. 2000. "Capital Market Liberalization, Economic Growth, and Instability." *World Development* 28(6): 1075–86.

World Bank. 2004a. *Doing Business in 2005: Removing Obstacles to Growth.* Washington, DC: World Bank.

———. 2004b. "Whither Latin American Capital Markets?" Office of the Chief Economist, Latin American and Caribbean Region, the World Bank, Washington, DC. Available at http://wbln1018.worldbank.org/LAC/LAC.nsf/ECADocbyUnid/01A51A58B764B8D585256EA9005BFE00?Opendocument.

10

Productive Development Policies and Supporting Institutions in Latin America and the Caribbean

Alberto Melo and Andrés Rodríguez-Clare

PRODUCTIVE DEVELOPMENT POLICIES CAN BE BROADLY defined as policies with the objective of strengthening the production structure of a particular national economy.[1] In this broad definition, they include any measure, policy, or program aimed at improving growth and competitiveness of large sectors of the economy (manufacturing industry, agriculture); specific sectors (textiles, the automobile industry, software production, and the like); or the growth of certain key activities (research and development, exports, fixed capital formation, human capital formation). The ultimate objective is to raise growth and improve competitiveness of the overall economy while increasing living standards. Productive development policy can target specific products, activities, or enterprises within a sector without targeting the sector as a whole. It can focus on horizontal issues directly related to production, such as technological innovation and investment, or focus on generic areas such as education, health, and work habits that have an indirect effect on production. Strictly speaking, productive development policies are not restricted to government policies (laws and regulations) and other policy measures that delineate the business environment and the institutional framework within which firms operate. They actually encompass any short-, medium-, or long-term program aimed at increasing growth and productivity whether formulated or executed by a public, private, or nongovernmental institution.

This chapter examines the evolution of productive development policies in Latin America in the last half century, with emphasis on the postreform period. The chapter begins with a review of the import-substitution era in the next section, followed by a section that describes productive development policies in the liberalization period. The last two sections provide a sample of current policies in the region and give a preliminary assessment of those policies.[2]

Productive Development Policies in the Import-Substitution Era

Post–World War II development policy in Latin America, as in most developing countries, was inspired by two ideas: first, that economic development is the process by which a poor country evolves into an economy with the broad characteristics of the more developed countries, with particular attention paid to their strong manufacturing sectors; and second, that the market by itself is unable to realize this transformation. There were several rationales for this second idea, including

- declining and volatile relative prices of the primary exports of developing countries (Prebisch 1950),
- dynamic (external) economies of scale favoring industry more than agriculture (arguing for protection of infant industries, see Bruton [1998]),
- abundance of imperfections in domestic markets that prevented resources from flowing toward sectors with the highest returns, and
- investment lumpiness and economies of scale that created "natural monopolies" and also led to the need for coordinated investments across multiple sectors for any individual project to be profitable (Rosenstein-Rodan 1943).

Development was a challenge whose solution required massive government intervention at multiple levels: trade protection in the form of high tariffs and quotas for certain industries; investment subsidies and subsidized loans; regulation to prevent competition in certain areas, so that economies of scale could be realized by one or a few companies; direct public investment in natural monopolies and industries that were either important for several downstream industries or that represented such large commitments as to make it unrealistic to expect the private sector to undertake them. Producing this "big push" implied an enormous transformation of the state, with new ministries and public institutes or agencies created to perform the many tasks associated with the new development policy. Governments thus created both public development and commercial banks, new utilities, and holding companies for the administration of public investments in manufacturing and agricultural operations. Ministries expanded to undertake their new regulatory and subsidy duties. Planning ministries were created to develop multiyear public investment plans.

Overall, the state grew significantly, and its new functions led to large accretions of power and discretionary action that were generally not matched by strong requirements for results and accountability. The goal of this section is to describe in more detail both the policies of this era and their implications for the state. The section focuses on the two most important areas—commercial policy and investment policy. After a brief review of the policies implemented, the discussion turns to the implications of these policies for the state.

Commercial Policy

Views regarding trade and development were very different during the late 1940s and the 1950s from the ones that are generally held today. There was nothing in the immediate postwar era like the miraculous growth rates of the export-oriented economies of East Asia during the 1970s and 1980s to convince economists and policy makers of the positive role that trade could play in the development process. On the contrary, as emphasized by Lindauer and Pritchett (2002), the "economic miracle" was the Soviet Union. It was simply difficult for most people to accept that opening up to trade could enable a poor agriculture-based economy to transform into a rich, industrial economy. As stated by Bruton (1998), the prevailing view was that the existence of already industrial economies in "the North" led to the belief that industrialization in the South required them to protect "their economies from imports from the North and concentrate on putting in place new activities that will produce an array of manufactured products currently imported. Thus would the structure of the economy be changed and, at some future time, make possible a foreign trade that contributes to the development objectives" (904).

The main instrument to protect the market was import duties, generally supplemented by quotas. As shown in table 10.1, average tariffs were very high in the Latin American region, with Central American countries exhibiting some of the highest average tariffs in the world. If the tariff equivalents of import quotas were included in these calculations, the rate of protection would look substantially higher.

The picture was further complicated by the large dispersion in tariffs across goods, which led both to high effective rates of protection for some industries, and to more cumbersome and complex customs procedures and administration. According to Balassa (1971) and Little, Scitovsky, and Scott (1971), Brazil, Chile, and Mexico had some of the most distorted trade regimes in the world, with very high variance in effective rates of protection across industries. Lin (1988) compared trade policies in the Republic of Korea, Taiwan (China), and Argentina during the 1970s and found that the effective rates of protection in the manufacturing sector were −1 percent in Korea, 19 percent in Taiwan, and almost 100 percent in Argentina.

Table 10.1 Import Protection in the Developing World in 1985 and in the 2000s (percentages)

	Total tariff protection in 1985[a]	Total tariff protection in the 2000s[b]	Nontariff barriers coverage in 1985[c]
South America	51.0	10.4	60.0
Central America	66.0	5.9	100.0
Caribbean	17.0	9.8	23.0
North Africa	39.0	20.7	85.0
Other Africa	36.0	14.7	86.0
West Asia	5.0	13.8	11.0
Other Asia	25.0	20.3	21.0

Sources: For the 1985 data the source is Edwards (1994), who took the data from Erzan and others (1989). For the 2000s, authors' own calculations.

Note:

a. Includes tariffs and paratariffs.

b. Year considered varies for each country, but all data are for years in the period 2000–04.

c. Measures as a percentage of import lines covered by nontariff barriers. The data on both tariffs and nontariff barriers reported here are weighted averages.

The grouping of countries in each region may differ slightly between 1985 and the 2000s.

Many countries entered into regional trading arrangements, with the idea that infant industry protection would be administered in larger markets so that economies of scale could be realized. This was the theory behind, in particular, the Central American Common Market and the Andean Pact, both created in the 1960s. These trading arrangement required tariffs to be negotiated at a very detailed level, and led to even more cumbersome customs procedures and requirements to validate origin and content.

One consequence of strong protection was the creation of an anti-export bias that resulted in low rates of export growth in many countries. A common reaction was the creation of fiscal incentives and subsidies to exports, which lessened somewhat the anti-export bias, but clearly imposed even stronger demands for bureaucracies to control and distribute such incentives.

The resulting commercial policy was complex and imposed heavy demands on the state apparatus for its design, implementation, and constant revision. However, as shown by Balassa (1971) and Little, Scitovsky, and Scott (1971), this does not appear to have produced the intended results.

Another result of strong protection under the import-substitution strategy was the triggering of directly unproductive profit-seeking activities, that is, activities that divert resources from productive use into directly unproductive but profitable lobbying aimed either at extracting a protective device (tariff seeking) or at having any revenues from protection awarded to the lobbyers (revenue seekers) (Bhagwati 1982; Rosendorff 2005). To the extent that these activities expend resources that might otherwise have gone to more productive activities, they are socially wasteful. Perhaps the most important subset of these directly unproductive but profitable activities under import substitution is rent seeking (Krueger 1974; Srinivasan and Bhagwati 1999) where protective tariffs are used to extract transfers of income and wealth from consumers by setting prices above those that would prevail under free trade. It is a well-documented fact that Latin America under import-substitution industrialization was a rent seekers' paradise. By the same token, it stands to reason that the demise of import substitution brought about a large-scale reduction in rent-seeking activities in the region.

Investment Policy

The view after World War II was that investment was crucial for economic development. To quote Arthur Lewis: "The central problem in the theory of economy growth is to understand the process by which a community is converted from being a 5 percent saver to a 12 percent saver" (Lewis 1955, 325–26). Aid to developing countries was viewed primarily as a way of alleviating this savings constraint on investment and growth. Moreover, governments used their ability to borrow to finance greater and greater shares of total investment, which was used not only for infrastructure, but also to invest in large-scale commercial ventures that were deemed too large or strategic to be left in private hands. Thus, the share of investment accounted for by public investment grew substantially, only to decrease again in the 1980s as a consequence of the financial crisis. For example, the share of the public sector in total investment increased from less than 20 percent in the early 1960s to more than 30 percent in the mid-1970s in Costa Rica, whereas the share of state-owned enterprises (SOEs) in the total capital stock increased from around 12 percent to close to 20 percent in the same period (Rodríguez-Clare, Sáenz, and Trejos, 2002). The creation of SOEs also led to a sizable increase in the share of GDP that was contributed by the state. This share declined subsequently during the 1990s as a direct result of the privatization efforts in many developing countries. Little and others (1993) calculate similar numbers for other Latin American countries and found that SOEs accounted for almost 30 percent of total investment in Mexico in the 1970–73 period, with Chile and Argentina exhibiting 20.0 percent and 17.5 percent, respectively. As shown in table 10.2, this phenomenon was widespread among developing countries (see also chapter 8).

One immediate consequence of the increase in the importance of public investment was the need for some kind of medium-term economic

Table 10.2 State-Owned Enterprises' Activity as a Percentage
of GDP (percentage points of GDP)

Countries (by income group)	1980	1997	Change
Low-income countries	15.0	3.0	−12.0
Lower-middle-income countries	11.0	5.0	−6.0
Upper-middle-income countries	10.5	5.0	−5.5
High-income countries	6.0	5.0	−1.0

Source: Sheshinski and López-Calva 1999.

planning. This led to the creation of planning ministries or agencies in most Latin American countries. In fact, multilateral financial institutions often imposed such plans as conditions for investment loans. In the words of Bruton (1998): "By the early 1960s virtually every development country had something that was called a plan. . . . Almost all plans announced a growth (of GDP and some sectors) target and then allocated the anticipated investment among the sectors of the economy believed necessary to achieve the target" (911).

Another area in which the state assumed a key role was banking. In many Latin American countries, banks were nationalized during the 1940s and 1950s, and in most of them the share of banking done by the state through public banks increased dramatically. By 1970, the share of banking assets held by public banks reached 70 percent in the region. This ratio fell significantly in the following decades, and the state's role shifted somewhat toward one of regulation and supervision rather than banker (see chapter 9).

The role of the state in promoting investment did not end there. Apart from undertaking direct investment, it also subsidized private investment in areas deemed consistent with the development strategy. This was accomplished through tariff exemptions on imported equipment and subsidized interest rates, although there were also direct subsidies granted for certain private projects.

Implications for the State

As mentioned, import substitution entailed a complex structure of tariffs, other import levies, and quotas that varied across fine categories of goods that were constantly being renegotiated between regional partners or unilaterally. This created the need for a technical bureaucracy responsible for this task, usually housed at the ministry of economics or ministry of industry. With unilateral liberalization and incorporation in the General Agreement on Tariffs and Trade (GATT), tariff structures became much simpler; overcharges and quotas were eliminated; thus, this bureaucracy lost much of its importance. Instead, with the new emphasis on outward-oriented free-trade agreements, a group of technocrats able to understand and negotiate such modern GATT-compatible agreements became essential. This group has generally been located in new ministries (for example, COMEX [*Ministerio de Comercio Exterior*] in Costa Rica) or in the ministry of foreign relations, as in Brazil and Chile. As a result, the balance of power shifted within government, from the ministries of economics or industry to the ministries of foreign relations or foreign trade.

Investment policy experienced a similar shift. The previous emphasis on investment and the high rates of public investment led to the creation of planning ministries or agencies. Such entities became very powerful during the 1960s. With the reforms of the 1980s and 1990s, however, public investment decreased, as did the role of SOEs. This led to a gradual weakening or even closure of such ministries. Investment planning is now mostly done at the Treasury, which exerts real power by controlling the budget.

The role of the state as producer almost disappeared except for utilities and certain services such as banking. The SOEs that remained acquired more restrictions and controls. The concept of state-owned companies that behaved like private companies almost disappeared. Agencies supervising such SOEs vanished.

The new incentives were supposed to avoid "picking winners," and instead strive to be sector-neutral. The tilt was toward transparency and eventual inclusion of any subsidies in the budget, except for fiscal incentives to foreign direct investment (FDI). The new incentives were also automatic, rather than discretionary. Thus, the offices and bureaucrats in charge of assigning incentives to particular firms disappeared, and in their place emerged offices or agencies responsible for checking that certain clear criteria were satisfied to merit certain subsidies or tax breaks.

In summary, the evolution of industrial policy had several major implications. It induced the state bureaucracy to become smaller, with fewer discretionary powers, acting under tougher and clearer restrictions, with more accountability and transparency. The presence of powerful ministries, such as ministries of planning and the ministry of the economy, which were supposed to plan and oversee large sums of investments, regulations, and incentives shriveled, giving way to a network of more decentralized agencies specialized in tasks such as export promotion, attraction of FDI, antitrust, and the like.

Productive Development Policies in the Liberalization Period

Radical policy changes tend to overshoot the mark. Thus, the rejection of the productive development policies characteristic of the import-substitution approach led, in many quarters, to the rejection of *any and every* industrial or sector policy. The possibility that there could exist a set of productive development policies both consistent with the process of structural reforms and necessary under the new conditions of more open economies was summarily disregarded by many. The underlying idea that market forces would spontaneously lead to an optimal reallocation of resources as the unquestionable result of the liberalizing reforms was a major factor in this intellectual and policy behavior.

Nonetheless, by the mid-1990s the policy atmosphere and policy makers' attitudes toward productive development policies changed noticeably. At that time, the perception was growing among economic agents and decision makers that the structural reforms were not delivering the promised results. Moreover, both the strains, imbalances, and difficulties of the industrial restructuring process and the unintended, undesirable outcomes of the reforms created conditions favorable to the emergence of a new type of industrial policy congruent with the new, market-oriented development strategy adopted by most countries in the region.

Melo (2001) examined the ensuing change in the direction of industrial policies in several key Latin American and Caribbean countries and found that it had three remarkable features. First, the turning point toward the adoption of the new industrial policies was almost simultaneous in a significant number of countries and can roughly be dated to the mid-1990s, with several critical policy pronouncements occurring in the 1994–96 period. Second, in most leading countries the change in direction took the form of the adoption and announcement of explicit, medium- to long-term plans, programs, and strategies for the industrial sector. Third, the policy turn was generally the outcome of (or, at the very least, was broadly related to) a public debate about the effects of the structural reforms and the need to improve the domestic industry's competitiveness in the new context of a more open national economy. To these features this chapter adds that the new industrial policies came to be juxtaposed in variable and complex ways with the remnants of the policies and institutions of the import-substitution era.

The new, productive development policies in Latin America are still an emerging phenomenon. Their defining feature can be encapsulated in the key idea that the new industrial polices aim at improving the competitiveness of domestic producers in the new, more integrated and open world economy. Instead of being designed to circumvent market outcomes, they seek to redress market failures through both the provision of public goods and government intervention to stimulate the supply of goods with positive externalities. The animating spirit behind the emerging policies is *not* to seek to return to the import-substitution model. *Nor* do they aim at interfering with the market mechanism through a systematic and generalized use of arbitrary subsidies. Moreover, in contrast to many policy makers of the import-substitution era, their proponents do *not* overlook the importance of macroeconomic stability and sound macroeconomic policies, either.

On the contrary, macroeconomic stability is not only explicitly but even forcefully prescribed as a condition for investment growth and industrial modernization.

A key generic feature of the new approaches to productive development policies is that they strive to address a core set of issues (such as productivity, efficiency, product quality, and so forth) revolving around the central question of how to raise the countries' competitiveness. The obvious background assumptions are that trade liberalization is necessary; that it is here to stay; that it is still not only desirable but also possible to change the prevailing world distribution of comparative advantage so as to increase the exports of manufactured goods (and even of high-technology goods and services) and decrease the dependence on primary sector–related exports; and that the government has a role to play in this pursuit.

The rest of this chapter places in context, describes, and assesses the current productive development policies in Latin America. It starts with a general discussion of emerging alternative approaches in the region, centering around the "two-paradigm hypothesis."

The Two-Paradigm Hypothesis

The two-paradigm hypothesis contends that two approaches to industrial policy making are emerging in the region. The first—the demand-driven approach—places the emphasis on responding to the needs of the existing sectors in the private economy with the principal aim of raising their international competitiveness. The second—the strategy-driven approach—is characterized by its emphasis on crisp definitions of the medium-term, and long-term, desired changes in the vector of goods and services produced by the economy and by the use of selective policies to promote a small number of industries.

To explore in greater detail the characteristics of the two paradigms, it helps to compare and contrast the ways productive development policies are conceived, designed, and implemented in the best empirical representatives of the two paradigms. The demand-driven approach is epitomized by Colombia's productive development policies; the best representative of the strategy-driven approach is Brazil.

The demand-driven approach. In Colombia, the discussion and definition of productive development policies and actions has, to a considerable extent, revolved around a public–private partnership and dialogue that has manifested itself through a set of organizational vehicles and instruments.[3] The first steps were taken in 1994 with the creation of the National Competitiveness Council, an organism directly ascribed to the Office of the President of the Republic and under the technical direction of the (now extinct) Ministry of Economic Development. The government adopted a strategy based on opening a dialogue with the private sector concerning the definition of competitiveness agreements by production chain. The competitiveness agreements aimed at improving the business environment and raising productivity. A quantum leap was made in 1999 with the inception of the National Conferences on Productivity and Competitiveness, conceived as forums for the public–private dialogue. The first of these conferences was held that year in Cartagena and was a trend-setting event. President Pastrana presented the National Policy for Productivity and Competitiveness, invited the private sector to work jointly to attain the objectives of the policy, and proposed the principles of (a) joint responsibility of the public and private sectors for its results, and (b) public sector officials' accountability for the commitments assumed by the government in the semiannual meetings of the National Conference. These meetings have since become a key institution for the public-private dialogue and for policy discussion. They are by far the most important public-private forum in Colombia.

The spirit of public-private dialogue was developed and deepened further through the establishment of the Colombia Competes Network and the Regional Advisory Committees for External Trade (CARCEs is the Spanish acronym). CARCEs is actually a set of 10 specialized networks. Each specialized network is thematically driven. Work and dialogue revolve around problem diagnosis and problem solving in connection with one key factor playing a determining role in shaping competitiveness. The factors in question were selected using as a guide the dimensions defined by the World Economic Forum as the main determinants of the competitiveness of any and every country, with suitable adaptations.[4] The specialized networks are an institutionalized meeting point and communication structure where representatives of the national government, the business sector, workers, regional and local governments, and academia carry out a joint diagnosis of the situation in connection with the factor and a policy and engage in a practical dialogue aimed at formulating solutions and programming actions.

The CARCEs are an instrument of a decentralization strategy. The underlying idea is that the attainment of competitiveness has an inescapable regional dimension. The CARCEs are organisms for public–private dialogue and policy discussion at the regional level.

A critical piece of the public–private partnership is the signing of export-oriented competitiveness agreements between the national government and the entrepreneurs and trade organizations of a particular production chain. The basic objectives are to raise productivity and improve the competitiveness of the particular chain. The agreements include commitments from both the public and the private sectors.

The Colombian experience has been very influential. Similar processes of public–private partnership and dialogue in Bolivia, Costa Rica, the Dominican Republic, Ecuador, and Peru have typically led to the establishment of national competitiveness councils with (varying) private-sector participation and to the definition of national competitiveness plans or strategies that summarize the joint vision of government and business classes in these countries.

The Colombian approach to industrial policy making is a bottom-up approach. The government addresses the entire organizational, policy, and activity efforts—the National Productivity and Competitiveness Policy, the National Conferences for Productivity and Competitiveness, the Export-Oriented Competitiveness Agreements, and the Regional Advisory Committees for External Trade—to existing export sectors. Since the replacement of the old Ministry of Economic Development with the new Ministry of Industry, Trade, and Tourism, there seems not to have been a single policy pronouncement or policy document from the Colombian authorities or governmental institutions with any statement about the need for the Colombian government to help create and develop new production chains or new industries to further a medium- to long-term development strategy.[5] The reference to this missing element in the Colombian approach sets the stage for the discussion of the alternative emerging approach—the strategy-driven approach.

The strategy-driven approach. On the face of it, industrial policy making in Brazil follows a more traditional style than in Colombia. The central government defines the policy and executes it through an array of agencies. A new industrial policy was launched in April 2004 and early in 2005 the Brazilian Agency for Industrial Development was created to coordinate the execution of industrial policies and monitor their progress in the different agencies.

The Brazilian industrial policy has a clear-cut strategic vision highlighting the need for choosing a small set of industrial sectors to be promoted through vertical, selective policies. That is, the Brazilian policy is the expression of a definite political will to change the vector of goods and services produced by the economy in a definite direction and is not simply a set of policy measures and actions aimed at promoting and assisting existing sectors. The industrial sectors selected for special attention fall into two categories. First, in the Brazilian policy's terminology, the "strategic-option" sectors are semiconductors, computer software, pharmaceutical products, and capital goods (Governo Federal do Brasil 2003). Second, there is a set of sectors deemed to be "bearers of future," presumably because of their potential to deeply affect productivity and competitiveness: biotechnology, nanotechnology, and biomass energy production (Jaguaribe 2004; Teixeira 2005).

Private-sector participation is also important in this approach. The foundational Brazilian policy document explicitly states that "both the multiplicity of situations and firm-level specificities reaffirm the need for the Industrial, Technological, and External Trade Policy to be discussed and negotiated with the private sector, as this is responsible for the productive investments and for industrial production" (Governo Federal do Brasil 2003, 10). Moreover, the newly constituted Brazilian Agency for Industrial Development is to be governed by a Deliberative Council made up of eight government representatives and seven representatives from the private sector and civil society. In addition, production chain–specific competitiveness forums have been organized as instruments of a public-private partnership to tackle issues that affect the competitiveness of selected production chains (to be discussed more later in this chapter).

A strategy-driven approach is practiced in relatively few countries—Argentina, Costa Rica, Mexico, and Venezuela in addition to Brazil. Costa Rica deserves careful consideration. As one of the authors of this chapter concluded, Costa Rica's development strategy is based on technology and human capital, with FDI from high-tech multinationals playing the leading role (Rodríguez-Clare 2001). However, two features differentiate Costa Rica's approach to attracting foreign investment from other approaches. First, in the context of a strong public-private partnership, the private sector, represented by the Costa Rican Coalition for Development Initiatives, plays a major role in FDI attraction. Second, since the early 1990s the strategy has focused on just a few sectors. For instance, the 1993 strategic plan focused on the electrical, electronic, and telecommunications industries (Rodríguez-Clare 2001).

Many features are common to both the strategy-driven and demand-driven approaches. All the general characteristics of emerging industrial policies in Latin America pointed out previously are shared by the two approaches, and they have many conceptions, themes, and policies in common.

What explains the simultaneous existence of the two approaches? This chapter suggests a preliminary hypothesis that combines political economy determinants with institutional elements. In this hypothesis, for a strategy-driven approach to become dominant in a country, the confluence of at least two of the three following elements is required: (a) the existence of a sufficiently strong technical and social-scientific intelligentsia, (b) the existence of government institutions where this technical intelligentsia can exercise its intellectual influence,[6] and (c) the existence of nuclei of private entrepreneurs who are able to go beyond a short-term corporatist stance and interact with the technical intelligentsia to generate a long-run, strategic perspective for productive development policies. In the Latin American experience, the technical and social-scientific intelligentsia sees itself as representing both the standpoint of the country's future and the interests of technical rationality. However, if this social segment is not sufficiently strong; if it is not sufficiently represented in the state bureaucracy; if the particular agencies through which it can express its views and rationality interests are weak or nonexistent; and if it does not have an ally in at least a segment of the entrepreneurial class, it cannot become a dominant influence in the shaping of public policy. The possibility of the particular country developing a strategy-driven approach comes to naught.

In the absence of a sufficiently strong technical intelligentsia expressing itself through strong, capable institutions (and possibly allied to a long-run-oriented segment of the business class), the political economy prevailing in Latin American countries spontaneously brings about productive development policies shaped by the political influence of existing production sectors, and long-term, strategic considerations take a backseat. A predominantly demand-driven approach results.

A Sample of Current Industrial
Policies in Latin America

Productive development policies include a diverse set of elements. Trade policies; investment policies; science and technology policies; policies aimed at promoting micro, small, and medium enterprises; human resources training and upgrading policies; and regional development policies belong to the set. Because this chapter aims only at providing a rough illustration of the types of productive development policies being used in the region, it confines itself to discussing four subsets of policies:

- those aimed at promoting innovation and technological development,
- those intended to foster the integration and strengthening of production networks,
- policies aimed at promoting output growth and investment, and
- export promotion policies.

More complete discussions of industrial policies in the region can be found in ECLAC (2004) and Melo and Rodríguez-Clare (2005).

Policies and Institutions to Promote Innovation
and Technological Development

The discussion starts with a review of the changes in the institutional dimension of science and technology policies in the last several decades, then examines the array of government interventions aimed at promoting technological innovation and development.

The institutional dimension. Major transformations in concepts and institutions have occurred in the last several decades in the policy field of technological development. As pointed out by ECLAC (2002), in the import-substitution era the public sector played a fundamental role in giving direct and indirect support to the development of technological capabilities. One way was by the creation of the institutional infrastructure for science and technology, consisting of two key pieces. The first was the establishment of autonomous, decentralized public agencies—the national science and technological councils—that were given the responsibility for formulating science and technology policies and promoting scientific research and technological development. The second piece, which to a considerable extent predated the establishment of the national councils, consisted of an array of public research institutes and laboratories, located both outside and within public universities.

The basic concept behind this institutional infrastructure was that it was sufficient for the state to organize and subsidize the supply of scientific knowledge and technological know-how as public goods. The belief was that solving the bottleneck on the supply side would lead almost automatically to technologies being adopted by enterprises on the demand side.[7]

The supply-based model resulted in crisis and came to be replaced in a number of countries in the 1990s by a new approach emphasizing demand-side incentives (ECLAC 2004).[8] In this approach, priority is on the design and use of instruments to promote the demand for technological innovation and support the transfer of technological know-how to firms in the production sectors. Demand subsidies play an important role in this model, but are allocated such that technology policies have turned more horizontal and neutral.

The new approach was accompanied by institutional reform. The main components of the reform were a greater legal formalization of the national science and technology system; the introduction of separate funding programs (or even agencies) for technological modernization, clearly differentiated from the traditional programs (or agencies) in charge of funding scientific research; implementation of a more participatory approach, which assigns a greater role to the business sector and allows for more dialogue with it; separation of the policy-making function from the programming, promotion, execution, and evaluation functions; and the assignment of responsibility for the two different sets of functions to different government agencies.

A conceptual and intellectual change that contributed to creating and shaping the atmosphere for reform was the increasing acceptance in the region of the idea of productive innovation as a social practice conducted by a wide variety of actors. Most science and technology policy elites adopted the conceptual tools of the national innovation systems approach and applied them to the analysis of strategic, institutional, and policy issues. A number of countries formally incorporated this systemic idea in their legal reforms of the 1990s, as will be presently seen.

The technology funds. The most important public policy instrument developed by countries in the region to support technological innovation is the technology fund. Technology funds provide loans, subsidies, or grants to firms engaging in technological innovation and modernization. Technology funds also represent the demarcation between the strategy-driven approach and the demand-driven approach. Thus, the Brazilian scheme of sector-oriented funds clearly epitomizes a long-term policy geared toward strengthening a particular set of productive sectors. The 14 Brazilian funds aim at promoting research and development (R&D) in the natural gas, information technology, water resources, energy, agribusiness, infrastructure, mining, land transportation, space, telecommunications, health, biotechnology, and aeronautical sectors, as well as supporting technological cooperation between university research centers and enterprises.[9] The Brazilian sector funds are typically financed with revenue from the sector enterprises. The laws setting up each individual sector fund define the share of company income that must be set aside for R&D activities (ECLAC 2004). Table 10.3 shows the characteristics of 7 of the 14 Brazilian sector funds.

On the other side of the divide, technology funds in most other countries are demand driven. In the typical demand-driven fund, resources come from the public budget, often as a counterpart to loans from the Inter-American Development Bank and the World Bank, which have been very active on this front. The funds are accessed through competition, which is consistent with a horizontal policy approach in that no particular sector is given any preference. (ECLAC 2004). The Chilean system of funds illustrates this demand subsidy–based approach (see Table 10.4).

Policies to Foster the Integration and Strengthening of Production Networks

Several alternative classifications can be used to organize information about the varied enterprise network policies being pursued in the region. For the purposes of this chapter, the classification proposed by Dini (2002) is used. Dini distinguishes between horizontal networks, vertical networks, and territorial networks. Horizontal networks are cooperation schemes among small and medium enterprises. Vertical networks result from links between large enterprises and their suppliers (which are frequently small and medium firms). Territorial networks are collaboration schemes between firms and other actors (local governments, universities, nongovernmental organizations, and so forth) in local communities (towns, regions, districts) aimed at developing competitive advantages appropriable by the participating firms. Table 10.5 provides a summary of the countries that have programs aimed at promoting horizontal, vertical, and territorial networks.

Fiscal and Financial Incentives for Production and Investment

Fiscal and financial incentives for production and investment are incentives that, at least in principle, are open to all producers that meet certain

Table 10.3 Technological Sector Funds in Brazil

Sector funds	Objectives	Origin of financial resources	Activities
CT-PETRO (1999) Sector fund for the oil and natural gas sector. Established by Law No. 9487 of 1997	Sector development through promotion of research and development and human resources training.	25 percent of value of royalties exceeding 5 percent of production of oil and natural gas	Collaboration in the definition of policies and the implementation of specific programs. In 2001, 144 projects worth 7 million *reais* were approved by the CNPq. Expenditure between January and November 2003: 16,431,002.70 *reais* (US$5,339,942)
CT-ENERG Sector fund for the energy sector. Established by Law No. 9991 of 2000	Sector development through promotion of research and development.	Between 0.75 percent and 1 percent of the net income of enterprises with concessions for the generation, transmission, and distribution of electricity	In 2001 the CNPq approved 132 research and development projects involving the investment of 8 million *reais* by the fund. In 2001 an association agreement was signed between the National Electric Power Agency and the CNPq to promote cooperation between research centers and enterprises. Total expenditures between January and November 2003: 8,397,983.70 *reais* (US$2,729,276)
CT-HYDRO Sector fund for water resources. Established by Law No. 9993 of 2000	Reduction of disparities between regions through investments in science and technology activities of importance for the sector. Strengthening of water resource sustainability.	Made up of 4 percent of the financial compensation of electricity generation enterprises	Financing of scientific and technological development projects and programs designed to improve water quality and use. In 2002, 28.6 million *reais* were invested, of which at least 4 million were for training of specialized personnel. Expenditure between January and November 2003: 3,735,635.85 *reais* (US$1,214,051)

(continued)

Table 10.3 Technological Sector Funds in Brazil (continued)

Sector funds	Objectives	Origin of financial resources	Activities
CT-INFO Sector fund for information technology. Established by Law No. 10176 of 2001	Promotion of the competitiveness of the sector through research and development programs and projects.	At least 5 percent of the gross annual turnover in the domestic information technology (IT) goods and services market of enterprises producing goods and services relating to IT that receive fiscal incentives under the law to promote the IT industry	It is estimated that over 50 million reais are spent each year on the promotion of research and development activities in this sector. Expenditure between January and November 2003 was 9,917,983.70 reais (US$3,223,264)
Sector fund for agribusiness. Established by Law No. 10332 of 2001	To consolidate the competitive position of products of this sector in international markets.	Law No. 10168 of 2000 lays down the sources of financing for this fund, which receives 17.5 percent of the resources covered by that law	Financing of research and development and science and technology activities. Expenditure between January and November 2003: 2,140,277.92 reais (US$695,573)

(continued)

Table 10.3 Technological Sector Funds in Brazil (continued)

Sector funds	Objectives	Origin of financial resources	Activities
FVA "Green and Yellow fund." Established by Law No. 10168 of 2000	Promotion of technological cooperation among universities, research centers, and enterprises.	Contributions in the form of royalties from enterprises holding user licenses or acquiring technological know-how abroad	A minimum of 30 percent of the resources is devoted to technological training and modernization in the northern, northwestern, and midwestern regions. Expenditure between January and November 2003: 58,071,768.19 reais (US$18,872,853)
CT-INFRA (2002) Infrastructure fund. Established by Law No. 10197 of 2001	Subsidies for maintenance and modernization of the technological infrastructure of public universities and research centers, to improve the competitiveness of the producing sectors.	The fund consists of 20 percent of the resources allocated to each sectoral fund from the National Technological Development Fund and from the other funds for financing science and technology activities	In 2002, 100 million reais were provided to create suitable conditions for the execution of science and technology activities in science and technology bodies. The northern, northwestern, and midwestern regions are to receive at least 30 percent of the resources. Expenditure between January and November 2003: 70,284,331.74 reais (US$22,841,837)

Source: ECLAC 2004.
Note: This table includes only the funds that spent more than 1,500,000 reais in 2003. CNPq = Conselho Nacional de Desenvolvimento Científico e Tecnologico (National Council for Scientific and Technological Development).

Table 10.4 Funds to Support Science and Technology Activities in Chile

Fund and administering body	Objectives	Beneficiaries	Origin and destination of financial resources
National Fund for Scientific and Technological Development (FONDECYT). Administered by CONICYT	To promote the development of fundamental scientific and technological research to create or improve methods and means of production of goods and services.	Natural persons or research institutes using various financing programs.	Contributions allocated under the National Budget law, legacies, and domestic and international donations that do not have any other specific purpose. The beneficiaries are selected by public competition.
Fund for the Promotion of Scientific and Technological Development (FONDET). Administered by CORFO	To strengthen the scientific and technological capacity of universities and research centers to increase the competitiveness of enterprises. The fund finances projects in priority areas (natural resources, promising areas for the creation of added value, and others of high social impact).	Nonprofit institutions, individually or in association, which carry on research and development (R&D) activities and have legally existed for at least five years. The fund requires the participation of enterprises, especially those working in the area of technology.	The fund finances up to 60 percent of the cost of projects, with a ceiling of 450 million *pesos* (US $640,000). Institutions and enterprises must contribute at least 20 percent themselves. The beneficiaries are selected by competition, by R&D projects, and on an open-window basis for technology transfer projects.

(continued)

Table 10.4 Funds to Support Science and Technology Activities in Chile *(continued)*

Fund and administering body	Objectives	Beneficiaries	Origin and destination of financial resources
Development and Innovation Fund (FDI). Administered by CORFO	To improve technological innovation in areas with strategic impacts on economic and social development.	Nonprofit institutions and technology centers engaged in R&D activities, technology transfer, and related services. Technological-entrepreneurial consortia made up of at least three enterprises not related in ownership before the date of application, associated with one or more technology centers.	Project completions; tenders for the execution of specific lines of work; and open-window arrangements (new form of allocation). The fund finances expenditure on operations, administration, human resources, subcontracts, and any other areas needed for the project.
Associate Development Projects (PROFOs). Administered by CORFO	To improve the competitiveness of a group of enterprises that seek to solve management and marketing problems on a joint basis.	Small and medium enterprises with annual sales of between 2,400 and 100,000 UF. Minimum sales are 1,200 UF for agricultural enterprises, while the maximum sales rise to 200,000 UF in the case of manufacturing enterprises that are associated in groups of at least five enterprises.	Open-window basis: the enterprises must contact intermediaries of CORFO who will provide application forms and designate professionals to diagnose the stage of preparation of the project.

(continued)

Table 10.4 Funds to Support Science and Technology Activities in Chile *(continued)*

Fund and administering body	Objectives	Beneficiaries	Origin and destination of financial resources
Technical Assistance Fund (FAT). Administered by CORFO	Through consultants, to incorporate management techniques into the operations of enterprises or new technologies into their production processes.	Chilean companies that require specialized outside support and have net annual sales of not more than 100,000 UF. The consultants are designated on an individual basis (at least three companies in the latter case).	Open-window basis (both cases): Individual FAT assistance: for the initial diagnosis, CORFO contributes 17 UF and the enterprise 3 UF, while CORFO subsequently finances up to 50 percent of the consultancy costs. In the case of collective arrangements, CORFO finances up to 50 percent of the consultancy costs, with a maximum of 100 UF per company.

(continued)

337

Table 10.4 Funds to Support Science and Technology Activities in Chile *(continued)*

Fund and administering body	Objectives	Beneficiaries	Origin and destination of financial resources
National Fund for Technological and Productive Development (FONTEC). Administered by CORFO	To promote, guide, and sponsor, through five lines of assistance, projects in the areas of technological innovation, associative technology transfer, and implementation of technological infrastructure.	Credit lines 1, 2, 3, and 5 finance private enterprises producing goods and services which can demonstrate the necessary technical, administrative, and financial capacity and are not in arrears with their debts. They can apply individually or in association, provided in the latter case that they are not linked with each other commercially. Credit line 4 finances enterprises producing goods and services that belong to a single sector of production and are applying for assistance in tackling technological problems of an associative nature.	Open-window basis: for credit lines 1, 2, 3, and 5, an application for the finance must be submitted to FONTEC or CORFO, which will consider the project in line with its rules for applications, together with information on the legal and financial status of the enterprises. Open-window basis: credit line 4 requires application for a diagnostic stage involving the preparation of a relevance analysis for FONTEC or CORFO.

Source: ECLAC 2004.
Note: UF = fiscal units.

Table 10.5 Programs to Promote Horizontal, Vertical, and Territorial Production Networks ·

Country	Horizontal	Vertical	Territorial
Argentina		x	
Brazil	x	x	x
Chile	x	x	x
Colombia	x	x	
Costa Rica		x	
Ecuador	x		
El Salvador	x		x
Honduras	x		
Mexico	x	x	x
Nicaragua	x	x	x
Peru	x		x
Uruguay	x		

Source: Dini 2002.

conditions (specific to the credit line or the fiscal incentive in question), regardless of whether they produce for domestic or external markets. They can be broken down into two wide categories, depending on whether a scheme of horizontal incentives or an emphasis on selective policies predominates. Horizontal policies are employed both by countries that practice a strategy-driven approach and by countries that implement a demand-driven approach. By contrast, selective policies are characteristic of the subset of countries practicing a strategy-driven approach. (A number of countries in the region belonging to both categories have traditionally enacted sector-specific tax incentives to attract FDI to their natural resource sectors, mainly hydrocarbons and mining.)

This discussion of incentives for investment and production is limited to a description of the practices through which selective policies are being implemented in those countries using the strategy-driven approach. Summary overviews of the horizontal forms of financial and fiscal support provided by governmental entities in the region can be found in ECLAC (2004) and Melo and Rodríguez-Clare (2005). ·

Since the mid-1990s, the way selective policies are practiced in the region has shifted significantly. To appreciate the contrast between the new and the old, it is illustrative to begin by recalling the situation as late as 2001. In that year, Melo (2001) found that, in those Latin American countries that employed selective financial or fiscal incentives to promote production and investment, natural resource–based sectors were the most frequent target of those incentives. The incentives in most cases were designed to attract FDI (see table 10.6).

Table 10.6 Financial and Fiscal Incentives for Specific Sectors in Latin America and the Caribbean, 2001

Country	Loans to specific sectors (other than agriculture)	Tax incentives to specific sectors
Argentina		Mining, forestry
Bahamas		Hotels, financial services, spirits and beer
Barbados		Financial services, insurance, information technology
Belize		Mining
Bolivia		Mining
Brazil	Oil, natural gas, shipping, power sector, telecom, software, motion picture industry	
Chile		Forestry, oil, nuclear materials
Colombia	Motion picture industry	
Costa Rica		Forestry, tourism
Dominican Republic		Tourism, agribusiness
Ecuador		Mining, tourism
El Salvador	Mining, services sector[a]	
Guyana		Agribusiness
Honduras	Transport sector, shrimp	
Jamaica		Motion picture industry, tourism, bauxite, aluminum, factory construction
Mexico	Motion picture industry	Forestry, motion picture industry, air and maritime transportation, publishing industry
Nicaragua		Tourism
Panama		Tourism, forestry
Peru		Tourism, mining, oil
Trinidad and Tobago		Hotels, construction

(continued)

Table 10.6 Financial and Fiscal Incentives for Specific Sectors in Latin America and the Caribbean, 2001 *(continued)*

Country	Loans to specific sectors (other than agriculture)	Tax incentives to specific sectors
Uruguay		Hydrocarbons, printing, shipping, forestry, military industry, airlines, newspapers, broadcasters, theaters, motion picture industry
Venezuela		Hydrocarbons and other primary sectors

Source: Melo 2001.
Note:
a. The services industries included with credit lines of their own are tourism, transportation, software, and other services.

Other than the bias toward natural resource sectors, the most salient feature of the information in table 10.6 is that tax incentives are used more intensively than credit lines as instruments to stimulate investment and production. The predominance of tax incentives reflects the circumstance that most of the incentives were intended to promote FDI in traditional primary sectors. As is well known, foreign investors are not usually credit constrained, thus credit lines are not much of an incentive for them.

Most of the incentives in table 10.6 still stand[10] and are an integral part of the set of productive development policies in those countries. However, new methods and policies have developed, representing the future direction.

To illustrate the thrust of the new policies, consider the way in which the idea of the competitiveness forums as the expression of a public–private partnership has been worked out in Argentina and Brazil in the last several years. Starting in 2000 in Brazil and in 2003 in Argentina, competitiveness forums for a number of selected production chains have been instituted by the authorities. Although the idea of organizing such forums for public–private dialogue and cooperation must have been inspired by the galvanizing Colombian experience of the National Competitiveness Conferences, the idea has undergone important transformations in the hands of Argentinian and Brazilian policy makers. As already pointed out, the competitiveness forums are now encompassed in the context of a strategy-driven approach. In addition, the Argentinian and Brazilian organizational format incorporates two major changes compared with the Colombian model. First, the forums are production-chain specific, so nothing like the National Competitiveness Conferences, which have played such a prominent role in the Colombian experience, exists. Second, Argentina and Brazil have refrained from replicating the thematic networks of the Colombian scheme.

Not unlike the Colombian model, the Argentinian and Brazilian forums aim at diagnosing the obstacles to competitiveness faced by the selected production chains and at agreeing on action plans and commitments to remove those obstacles. The Brazilian initiative also incorporates competitiveness contracts—to be signed by the government, the entrepreneurs, and the workers—defining the commitments assumed by all stakeholders represented in the particular forum. As of the time of writing (mid-2006), nine competitiveness forums had been established in Argentina and 16 in Brazil.

The idea and the practice of the competitiveness forums include a strong element of demand-side determination of policy measures. However, in Brazil and Argentina, the sectors given priority are not only the existing export sectors but also those production chains national industrial policies have prioritized. Moreover, some of the priority sectors have an economic-development status of infant industries and are treated as such. This is especially clear in Argentina, where these production chains have received differential treatment and are now the object of promotional legal regimes.[11] The special legal regimes include fiscal stability over a 10-year horizon; exemption from the income tax on profits; exemption from import duties for inputs, materials, and equipment destined to be used in R&D projects; and establishment of sector-specific funds to finance investment projects and contribute venture capital and seed capital to the creation of new firms in the selected sectors.[12] More consolidated sectors participating in the competitiveness forum framework, such as the civil construction materials sector and the wood-and-furniture chain, are supported in a variety of ways (such as labor training, quality improvement, external trade facilitation, market information, and strategic planning) but are not provided with a special promotional regime and thus are not given any substantial fiscal or financial incentives. In particular, unlike the cases of software and biotechnology, they are not given the benefit of a sector-specific financial fund for investment projects.

Fiscal and Financial Incentives for Exports

Fiscal incentives. Fiscal incentives to exports have a long tradition in the region. They were initiated in the 1960s under the import-substitution policy regime in countries such as Argentina, Brazil, Chile, and Colombia (ECLAC 2004); were subsequently adopted by most countries in the region; and have evolved in response to changes in multilateral trade rules, regional trade agreements, and the peculiarities and constraints of the fiscal situation in particular countries. More recently, following World Trade Organization rules, a number of countries in South America have reduced or eliminated tax and duty reimbursements for exporters. By contrast, tax exemptions (both on direct and indirect taxes) favoring export activities are common in Mexico, Central America, and the Caribbean. A mechanism for export promotion used in most countries is the special treatment accorded export processing zones. These zones are the favored instrument in the region to channel tax incentives to foreign investors willing to set up export-oriented production facilities in those enclaves. Table 10.7 summarizes fiscal incentives granted by countries in the region.

Financial support. Table 10.8 summarizes the various forms of financial support provided by public sector entities to exporters. Note the clear contrast between a group composed of the South American countries other than Bolivia and Peru, plus Mexico, Jamaica, Trinidad and Tobago, and Barbados, on the one hand, and the Central American countries, plus Bolivia and Peru, on the other hand. In the first group, availability of credit from government financial institutions is the dominant pattern. In the second group, the typical pattern is that no public resources are available for credit to exporters. They have to rely on private commercial banks for their financing needs. Of the 11 countries that provide public-sector financing to exporters, 4 of them do so through public financial agencies whose specific mission is to provide credit to domestic exporters,[13] and the remaining 7 do so through their main public development banks or other government financial institutions.[14]

A Preliminary Assessment of Current Productive Development Policies in the Region

A critical assessment of the productive development policies in the region is difficult because of the absence of systematic quantitative data, both on the scale of the interventions and on their outcomes and impacts. On the one hand, there appear to be no reliable data on the fiscal cost of industrial policies for the countries. Even data on the resources devoted by the public sector to providing credit and other forms of financial assistance to enterprises are incomplete. On the other hand, the demonstrable underdevelopment of results-oriented approaches to public sector management in the region means that public sector interventions to promote productive development typically lack the battery of baseline and outcome-and-impact indicators policy makers and third-party observers need to evaluate their effectiveness in attaining the stated objectives. At the design stage, productive development policies and programs in the region generally lack the information systems to allow outcome identification and measurement.

Table 10.7 Summary of Fiscal Incentives for Exports

	AR	BO	BR	CH	CO	EC	PE	UR	VE	ME	GU	ES	HO	NI	CR	JA	OC
Rebates	Yes	Yes	No	Yes	Yes	No	Yes	Yes	Yes	No	Yes	Yes	Yes	Yes	No	—	No
Tax credit certificates	No	Yes	No	No	Yes	Yes	Yes	Yes	Yes	No	No	No	No	No	No	—	No
Drawbacks	Yes	Yes	Yes	Yes	Yes	Yes	Yes	Yes	Yes	—	—	—	—	—	—	—	—
Exemption from value added tax	Yes	Yes	Yes	No	No	Yes	No	Yes	No	Yes	Yes	Yes	Yes	Yes	Yes	Yes	Yes
Exemption from other indirect taxes	Yes	No	No	No	Yes	No	No	Yes	No	Yes	Yes	Yes	Yes	Yes	Yes	Yes	Yes
Exemption from profit tax	No	No	No	No	Yes	No	Yes	No	Yes	Yes	Yes	Yes	Yes	Yes	No	—	Yes[a]
Performance-based incentives	Yes	No	Yes	Yes	No	No	No	No	No	Yes	No	No	No	No	No	—	Yes[b]
Incentives for trading companies	No	No	No	Yes	No	No	No	No	No	Yes	Yes	No	No	No	No	—	No
Maquila/free trade/ export processing zones	Yes	Yes	Yes	Yes	Yes	Yes	Yes	Yes	Yes	Yes	Yes	Yes	Yes	Yes	Yes	—	No
Deferred payment of customs duties	No	No	No	Yes	No	No	No	No	No	—	—	—	—	—	—	—	—

Source: ECLAC 2004.

Note: AR = Argentina; BO = Bolivia; BR = Brazil; CH = Chile; CO = Colombia; EC = Ecuador; PE = Peru; UR = Uruguay; VE = Venezuela; ME = Mexico; GU = Guatemala; ES = El Salvador; HO = Honduras; NI = Nicaragua; CR = Costa Rica; JA = Jamaica; OC = Other Caribbean countries; — = not available.

a. Grenada, Guyana, St. Lucia, and St. Vincent and the Grenadines are the countries that grant this exemption.
b. Guyana and the countries of the Organization of Eastern Caribbean States have this type of incentives.

Table 10.8 Financial Support for Exports from Government Financial Agencies

	AR	BO	BR	CH	CO	EC	PE	UR	VE	ME	GU	ES	HO	NI	CR	JA	OC
Pre- and postshipment credit	Yes	No	Yes	Yes	Yes	Yes	No	Yes	Yes	Yes	No	No	No	No	No	Yes	Yes[a]
Postshipment credit	Yes	No	Yes	Yes	Yes	No	No	Yes	Yes	Yes	No	No	No	No	No	Yes	Yes[a]
Trade promotion	Yes	No	Yes	Yes	No	Yes	Yes	Yes	Yes	Yes	No	No	No	No	No	Yes	Yes[b]
Fixed asset financing	No	No	Yes	Yes	Yes	Yes	No	Yes	Yes	Yes	No	No	No	No	No	—	—
Development of exportable products	No	No	Yes	Yes	Yes	No	No	No	Yes	Yes	No	No	Yes	No	No	—	—
Preshipment credit insurance	No	No	Yes	No	No	No	No	No	No	Yes	No	No	No	No	No	Yes	Yes[a]
Postshipment credit insurance	Yes	No	Yes	No	No	No	No	No	No	Yes	No	No	No	No	No	Yes	Yes[a]
Guarantee fund for exporters	No	No	Yes	Yes	No	No	No	No	No	Yes	No	No	No	No	No	Yes	Yes[a]
Coverage of bank loans to exporters	Yes	No	Yes	Yes	No	No	No	No	No	Yes	No	No	No	No	No	No	No
Financing for export-oriented SMEs	Yes	No	No	No	No	No	No	No	No	Yes	No	Yes	No	No	No	No	No

Source: ECLAC 2004.
Note: See table 10.7 for abbreviations; — = not available.
a. Trinidad and Tobago grant this support.
b. Barbados and Trinidad and Tobago grant this support.

345

The available literature on implementation and impact evaluation reflects these constraints. Because absence of monitoring and impact indicators results in uncertainty about the policies' effects, evaluation studies cannot go beyond conjecturing likely connections between certain trends developing after the policies have started and the policies themselves, but are not able to demonstrate close causal relationships between the policy interventions and the adduced phenomena.[15] An instance of this approach is Velasco's finding (2003) that nontraditional exports increased in those Colombian production chains that signed export-oriented competitiveness agreements with the national government. The hypothesized connection is plausible enough but how much of the increase in exports can be credited to government policies is still in question. In a similar vein, Alonso (2002) presents a good inventory of sector policies in Central America but is unable—because of sheer lack of data on policy outcomes—to gauge the effects of these policies.

Exceptions to the tentative character of existing impact evaluations occur when the scope of evaluation is narrowed to assessing the effects of particular achievements of sector policies or of specific programs. Larraín, López-Calva, and Rodríguez-Clare (2001) and Rodríguez-Clare (2001), for instance, evaluated Costa Rica's great policy success in attracting Intel to invest in the country. These authors point out the favorable effect that "having Intel inside" had on Costa Rica's efforts to attract high-tech FDI. They also mention the backward links generated by Intel's operations (particularly in logistics and transportation) and the significant externalities derived from Intel's training of its workforce and support of educational programs in public universities. A few programs to foster the integration and strengthening of enterprise networks have been evaluated. Thus, according to Dini (2002), Benavente and Crespi (1997a, 1997b) evaluated the Chilean PROFO and FAT programs for small and medium enterprises, ECLAC (2000) assessed Argentina's Centers for Entrepreneurial Development program, and Ventura (2001) evaluated Mexico's Entrepreneurial Reconversion for Exports program. Despite these efforts, the impact of productive development policies are not undergoing rigorous evaluation because of the data constraints.

Thus, the broad assessment here of these policies is merely qualitative and preliminary until a sufficient amount of hard data becomes available.

Latin America's incursions into activist development policies have been timid and inconsistent (Rodríguez-Clare 2004). To a great extent, this is because productive development policies have been hampered by their association with the old, import-substitution industrial policies. Although productive development policies are staging something of a comeback, no consensus on their potential and limits is yet widely shared. In addition, a number of analytical and institutional issues must be settled before the emerging productive development policies for open economies in this era of increasing globalization can be as reliable a part of the policy makers' toolbox as, say, fiscal and monetary policies are nowadays.

The clearest expression of the widespread timidity in implementing existing productive development policies are the minimal resources devoted to them. Although available information is limited, the resources mobilized by public development banks as a percentage of GDP (table 10.9) provides an indication of how limited they are. Taking the Republic of Korea as a benchmark, table 10.9 shows that even Mexico and Brazil, which make sizable efforts in absolute terms, fall quite short of the Korean effort of 6.7 percent of GDP. The only country in the same effort category is Costa Rica, where the loan portfolio of *Banco Nacional de Costa Rica* amounts to an impressive 6.5 percent of GDP. All along, a limiting factor for the funding of productive policies has been the chronic budgetary constraint characteristic of public sectors in countries with low tax-to-GDP ratios—an almost universal characteristic of Latin American tax structures—a constraint that worsens when fiscal adjustment efforts are undertaken.

In budgetary competition with needs that are perceived as more pressing (for instance, the need to increase social spending), industrial policies' funding requirements tend to get overlooked or simply discarded. In part, this outcome is also attributable to a more vigilant attitude toward rent seeking. The social costs of the pervasive rent seeking of the import-substitution era have not been forgotten and industrial policies are seen by many, albeit usually with no real justification, as suspicious. Quite frequently, a vicious circle sets in: agencies in charge of industrial policies that lack enough support and a strong enough constituency are allocated limited budgetary resources; the agencies perform below both needs and expectations; the agencies lose reputation and weight within the power structure of the state; their limited constituency tends to shrink further; new budgetary allocations are even scanter; and a new round of underperformance, loss of reputation, and new budgetary restrictions gets under way. As ECLAC (2004) concludes, implementation failures and the perception that "policies do not work" undermine their legitimacy among entrepreneurs and, somewhat paradoxically, lead to a situation where "entrepreneurs bemoan the lack of resources available for policies while at the same time failing to make full use of what is available"(ECLAC 2004, 258).

Budget constraints alone do not explain shortfalls in performance. Weak institutional capacity is widespread in the region's public sectors and is responsible for much of the ineffectiveness of many policies. However, a number of the government institutions responsible for productive development policies belong to the islands of competence and efficiency that can be found in almost every country in the region. These include some of the technology institutions, public development banks, and export promotion

Table 10.9 Credit Granted by Public Development Banks

	Brazil (BNDES)	Colombia (BANCOLDEX)	Costa Rica (BNCR)	Mexico (BANCOMEXT + NAFIN)	Peru (COFIDE)	Republic of Korea
Total credit (millions of US$)	12,542	1,152	1,090	23,723	573	45,844
As a percentage of GDP	2.8	1.4	6.5	3.7	1.0	6.7

Sources: ECLAC (2004), except for Korea, Costa Rica, and Peru. Credit figures for these three countries are from the Korean Development Bank (http://www.kdb.co.kr/), Costa Rica's General Superintendency of Financial Entities (http://www.sugef.fi.cr/), and Peru's Financial Corporation for Development (http://www.cofide.com.pe/).

Note: GDP figures for calculations are from World Bank, World Development Indicators, 2004 (http://www.worldbank.org/).

agencies where some of the best human capital of the region's public sectors is employed.

Quite apart from resource, implementation, and institutional capacity issues, some weaknesses stem from the fact that policy makers are finding their way even as they are immersed in the daily challenges of policy making and implementation. Much experimentation is going on in the region. Trial and error and a certain amount of learning by doing are unavoidable in an historical situation where unprecedented challenges are faced. These constraints include World Trade Organization agreements that impose constraints on industrial policies; regional and bilateral trade agreements that impose additional, sometimes even stronger, constraints of their own; international competition that is fiercer than ever; technological gaps that literally increase by the day; and so on. Much of the experimentation is relevant, fresh, and promising. But a good deal is reactive, or improvised, or inspired by passing fads.[16]

A particular weakness in the intellectual climate for industrial policy formulation in several countries in the region is that, if one is to base judgment on the actually existing policies, the only conclusion is that the lessons from other regions of the world have not been learned. For instance, two key policy principles from the East Asian experience—that subsidies must be contingent on performance and that they must be temporary—are absent in quite a few of the support policies practiced in the region. Current development policies are also vulnerable to special interest group pressures, and in that sense, continue to be dangerous. By allowing for the possibility of selective intervention or context-specific policies, they may end up, if applied in the wrong institutional contexts and under wrong rules of the game, opening the Pandora's box of rent-seeking behavior and related abuses.

However, on the positive side, some features of the emerging productive development policies constitute genuine contributions to the arsenal of economic development thinking and practice. First, the idea of a public-private partnership toward crucial development objectives (such as improving competitiveness and raising productivity) and the practice of systematic, organized, public-private dialogues to discuss problem diagnoses, policy measures, and action commitments are major contributions to shaping the industrial policies of the future. In these public-private dialogues, the joint effort to identify where the problems lie and where the possible solutions can be found is a harbinger of the new style of industrial policy making taking shape the world over, a new style where the process of discovery, or self-discovery as Hausmann and Rodrik (2002) have called it, of where the potential competitive advantages lie and what the obstacles to their development are, is as important as the content of the policies to address those obstacles.[17]

Second, the sheer amount of experimentation in the region bears the traits of all processes of innovation. New ways and means of policy making are tried and put to the hard tests of reality, conflicting domestic interests, and competition from abroad. The ongoing learning process is a necessary stage toward new, more consistent, and less timid policy frameworks where productive development policies can unfold effectively to contribute to the goals of economic growth and modernization. As the Spanish poet Antonio Machado wrote, "Wayfarer: there is not a single road. We find our way even as we walk."

Notes

1. Our definition follows quite closely the definition of industrial policy proposed by the Industrial Modernisation Centre (2003).
2. The chapter is a reduced version of a working paper written by the authors as a background document for this book. See Melo and Rodríguez-Clare (2005).
3. The description of the Colombian model of policy making and dialogue draws heavily upon Velasco (2003).
4. The 10 networks are Science and Technology, Finance, Internationalization-of-the-Economy, Institutions, Management, Education, Labor, Infrastructure, Transportation, and Telecommunications, Energy, and Gas.
5. The absence of any such policy pronouncement was not always the case in Colombia. As late as 2000, a policy document from the now defunct Colombian Ministry of Economic Development made a distinction between, on the one hand, existing production chains that required further strengthening and development and, on the other, new production chains that ought to be promoted to make the country a player in markets where, for the most part, it was and still is absent. On this, see Melo (2001).
6. The kinds of government agencies in mind are planning agencies, public development banks, industry and trade ministries, science and technology agencies, and external trade agencies.
7. This way of conceiving the relationship between science and technology and their productive applications by firms is known as the linear supply model. See the discussions in ECLAC (2002, 2004).
8. For a description of the process that led to this outcome, see Melo and Rodríguez-Clare (2005).
9. The fund devoted to this purpose is the *Verde e Amarelho Fund.*
10. A notable, well-known exception is the change in the taxation and royalty regime for private investment in the hydrocarbons sector in Venezuela under president Chávez's government.
11. For instance, the Promotional Regime for Software and the Promotional Regime for Biotechnology Industries.
12. Among the sector-specific funds, the biotechnology fund and the software industry fund have received special attention from the authorities.
13. The four countries and the respective export-promoting banks are Colombia with BANCOLDEX, Jamaica with the National Export-Import Bank of Jamaica, Mexico with BANCOMEXT, and Venezuela with BANCOEX.
14. The seven countries that provide credit to exporters through their main public development banks or other government financial institutions are Argentina (through the Investment and External Trade Bank, BICE), Barbados (through BIDC), Brazil (through BNDES), Chile (through the *Corporación de Fomento de*

la Producción, CORFO), Ecuador (through the National Finance Corporation, CFN), Trinidad and Tobago (through TIDGO), and Uruguay (through the *Banco de la República Oriental del Uruguay*).

15. This part of the discussion draws on ECLAC (2004).

16. For instance, in the authors' view, some of the things that are said and done in the matter of clusters have the trappings of a superficial, unreflective adherence to what is fashionable.

17. This issue is cleverly discussed in the penetrating article by Rodrik (2004).

References

Alonso, Eduardo. 2002. "Políticas para el fomento de los sectores productivos en Centroamérica." Productive and Entrepreneurial Development Division, Restructuring and Competitiveness Network, Economic Commission for Latin America and the Caribbean (ECLAC), Santiago, Chile.

Bhagwati, Jagdish. 1982. "Directly-Unproductive Profit-Seeking (DUP) Activities." *Journal of Political Economy* 90 (5): 988–1002.

Balassa, B. 1971. *The Structure of Protection in Developing Countries.* Baltimore: Johns Hopkins University Press for the World Bank and the Inter-American Development Bank.

Benavente, José Miguel, and Gustavo Crespi. 1997a. "Impacto del instrumento PROFO en la pequeña y mediana empresa." Departamento de Economía, Universidad de Chile, Santiago.

———. 1997b. "Impacto del instrumento FAT en la pequeña y mediana empresa." Departamento de Economía, Universidad de Chile, Santiago.

Bruton, H. 1998. "A Reconsideration of Import Substitution." *Journal of Economic Literature* 36 (2): 903–36.

Dini, Marco. 2002. "Programas de fomento de la articulación productiva: Experiencias en América Latina en los años noventa." In *Pequeñas y medianas empresas y eficiencia colectiva. Estudios de casos en América Latina,* ed. Marco Dini and Giovanni Stumpo. Economic Commission for Latin America and the Caribbean/Siglo XX, Mexico.

ECLAC (Economic Commission for Latin America and the Caribbean) 2000. "Buenas prácticas internacionales en apoyo a PYMES." ECLAC, Santiago, Chile.

———. 2002. "Globalization and Development." Economic Commission for Latin America and the Caribbean, Santiago, Chile.

———. 2004. "Productive Development in Open Economies." Thirtieth Session of the Economic Commission for Latin America and the Caribbean, United Nations, San Juan, Puerto Rico, June 28–July 2.

Edwards, Sebastian. 1994. "Trade and Industrial Policy Reform in Latin America." NBER Working Paper No. 4772, National Bureau of Economic Research, Cambridge, MA.

Erzan, Refik, K. Kuwahar, Sarafino Marchese, and Renée Vossenaar. 1989. "The Profile of Protection in Developing Countries." *UNCTAD Review* 1 (1): 29–49.

Governo Federal do Brasil. 2003. "Diretrizes de Política Industrial, Tecnológica e de Comércio Exterior." Brasilia.

Hausmann, Ricardo, and Dani Rodrik. 2002. "Economic Development as Self-Discovery." KSG Working Paper No. RWP02-023, Harvard University, Cambridge, MA.

Industrial Modernisation Centre. 2003. "Green Paper on Industrial Policy in Egypt." The Policy Support Unit, Industrial Modernisation Centre, Cairo, Egypt.

Jaguaribe, Roberto. 2004. "Política industrial de Brasil: Concepción general, la experiencia de MERCOSUR y la nueva PITCE." Presentation before the International Forum "Competitiveness Policies for the Industrial Sector vis-à-vis the Challenges Posed by Free Trade Agreements," Bogotá, Colombia, May 11.

Krueger, Anne O. 1974. "The Political Economy of the Rent Seeking Society." *The American Economic Review* 64 (3): 291–303.

Larraín, Felipe, Luis F. López-Calva, and Andrés Rodríguez-Clare. 2001. "Intel: A Case Study of Foreign Investment in Central America." In *Economic Development in Central America. Vol. I: Growth and Internationalization*, ed. Larraín, Felipe. Cambridge, MA: Harvard University Press.

Lewis, A. 1955. *The Theory of Economic Growth.* London: George Allen and Unwin.

Lin, Ching-Yuan. 1988. "East Asia and Latin America as Contrasting Models." *Economic Development and Cultural Change* Supplement: Why Does Overcrowded, Resource-Poor East Asia Succeed: Lessons for the LDCs? 36 (3): S153–197.

Lindauer, D., and L. Pritchett. 2002. "What's the Big Idea? The Third Generation of Policies for Economic Growth." *Economia* 3 (1): 1–39.

Little, Ian M. D., Tibor Scitovsky, and Maurice Scott. 1971. *Industry and Trade in Some Developing Countries.* Oxford, UK: Oxford University Press.

Little, I. M. D., R. N. Cooper, W. M. Corden, and S. Rajapatirana. 1993. *Booms, Crisis, and Adjustment.* New York: Oxford University Press for the World Bank.

Melo, Alberto. 2001. "Industrial Policy in Latin America and the Caribbean at the Turn of the Century." Working Paper No. 459, Research Department, Inter-American Development Bank, Washington, DC.

Melo, Alberto, and Andrés Rodríguez-Clare. 2005. "Productive Development Policies and Supporting Institutions in Latin America and the Caribbean." Working Paper C–106, Research Department, Inter-American Development Bank, Washington, DC.

Prebisch, R. 1950. *The Economic Development of Latin America and Its Principal Problems.* Lake Success, NY: United Nations Department of Social Affairs.

Rodríguez-Clare, Andrés. 2001. "Costa Rica's Development Strategy Based on Human Capital and Technology: How It Got There, the Impact of Technology, and Lessons for Other Countries." Paper written for the 2001 Human Development Report, United Nations Development Programme, New York.

———. 2004. "Microeconomic Interventions after the Washington Consensus." Working Paper No. 524, Research Department, Inter-American Development Bank, Washington, DC.

Rodríguez-Clare, A., M. Sáenz, and A. Trejos. 2002. "Economic Growth in Costa Rica: 1950–2000." Inter-American Development Bank, Washington, DC.

Rodrik, Dani. 2004. "Industrial Policies for the Twenty-First Century." John F. Kennedy School of Government, Harvard University, Cambridge, MA.

Rosendorff, B. Peter. 2005. "Ideas, Interests, Institutions, and Information: Jagdish Bhagwati and the Political Economy of Trade Policy." Paper presented at the Conference "International Trade and Factor Mobility: Theory and Policy," held in celebration of the 70th birthday of Jagdish Bhagwati, New York, August 5–6.

Rosenstein-Rodan, Paul. 1943. "Problems of Industrialisation of Eastern and South-Eastern Europe." *Economic Journal* 53 (210/211): 202–11.

Sheshinski, E., and L. F. López-Calva. 1999. "Privatization and its Benefits: Theory and Evidence." Harvard Institute for International Development, Harvard University, Cambridge, MA.

Srinivasan, T. N., and Jagdish Bhagwati. 1999. "Outward Orientation and Development: Are Revisionists Right?" Working Paper 806, Economic Growth Center, Yale University. Available at http://www.columbia.edu/%7Ejb38/Krueger.pdf.

Teixeira, Alessandro. 2005. "Industrial Development Policy." Presentation before a seminar at the Inter-American Development Bank, Washington, DC.

Velasco, María Piedad. 2003. "Políticas de productividad y competitividad en Colombia, 1998–2002." Report prepared for ECLAC and GTZ, Santiago, Chile. Available at http://www.eclac.cl/ddpe/noticias/paginas/8/15078/Ma PiedadVelasco.pdf.

Ventura, Juan Pablo. 2001. "Política de apoyo a las pequeñas y medianas empresas: análisis del Programa de Reconversión Empresarial para las Exportaciones." *Estudios y Perspectivas Series,* No. 1, March, ECLAC, Buenos Aires, Argentina.

11

Reform of Pension and Social Assistance Systems

Carmelo Mesa-Lago and Gustavo Márquez

SINCE THE MID-1980S, consolidation of democracy, macroeconomic instability, and changes in the way labor markets function in Latin America have contributed to strong demand for new instruments to protect incomes. Increases in unemployment and informal employment have led groups subsisting in extreme poverty or without access to formal labor markets to demand alternatives for protection from recurring macroeconomic shocks, particularly since the mid-1990s. In addition, efforts to reverse growing deficits in some public social security systems and the prospect of achieving greater efficiency and financial depth from the introduction of private pension systems have brought about reforms in traditional systems of insurance covering old age, disability, and survivors' benefits.

This chapter describes the changes in public policy management in social security and social assistance that have been taking place since the late 1980s, a time during which the view of the role of central government in this area has changed greatly. This introduction situates these reforms within the context of transformations in central government and the economy. The next section describes changes in pension systems, and the last section presents the evolution of social security and social assistance institutions and policies.

The 1990s were a time of concerted reform efforts in all aspects of social policy. Consolidation of democracy in most countries in the region allowed the expression of a series of social demands for greater coverage and better access to high-quality social services. The only way to meet these demands was to undertake institutional reform, given that increased spending did not seem possible or appropriate. National governments, financially precarious but committed to the new creed of macroeconomic stability, lacked the fiscal wherewithal to substantially increase social spending. At the same time, the urgency for institutional and operational reform was spurred by the perception that social service delivery systems were controlled by ineffective bureaucracies and groups that used resources as instruments of patronage to perpetuate their own power.[1]

In few other areas is this urgency as visible as in social security and social protection. The traditional view was reflected in import-substitution policies that assumed the creation of registered employment in modern, formal jobs for the entire labor force (Franco 1996). Against this backdrop, the public pension systems—which depended on employment-based contributions and were designed to cover the risks associated with old age, disability, and survivors' benefits—constituted the central axis of income-protection policy. Financing of these systems rested on the basic premise that ongoing expansion in registered employment would allow the benefits of retired workers to be funded by current workers paying into the system. Increases in informal employment and unemployment and greater employment in nonexport sectors[2] cut the number of contributors and the volume of contributions flowing into social security systems. Fiscal strains resulting from the need to cover running deficits in those systems were an important stimulus in the search for funding options and operational alternatives for these systems. Some countries opted for nonparametric reforms in an attempt to bring the levels of benefits from and contributions to the system into balance, without resorting to fundamental changes in their structure, and in particular, without creating private pension systems. Other countries, taking Chilean social security reform as a model, have made structural changes, such as creating private pension systems either to complement the public system or to replace it altogether. An important argument of the time was that private systems would create a series of long-term financial instruments that could deepen capital markets.

Against a panorama in which registered employment (with social security contributions and benefits) is losing its significance, social security reform will not be responsive to the demands of those who are excluded from the formal sector. For these groups, some of which are quite outspoken, reforms in social assistance programs become crucial. Where social assistance programs existed, they were very small and generally based on noncontributory pensions for elderly individuals not entitled to regular pensions. In this context, income policies in the 1980s consisted of instruments to manage aggregate demand; they were not designed with thought to social policy. Income policy depended on three basic instruments:

- price controls and subsidies for consumer goods
- management of aggregate demand through investment decisions and public sector employment
- wage policy, including wage indexing and general salary increases by decree

The prolonged crisis of the 1980s, with its recurrent fiscal adjustment processes, reduced the scope of action in which these policies could manage aggregate demand. Funding for these policies exacerbated high levels of indebtedness, and was a determining factor in the uncontrollable bouts of inflation that surfaced several times during the 1980s. The Washington Consensus represented a major new direction for public policy in most countries in the region, as the focus on management of aggregate demand gave way to maintaining equilibrium in key macroeconomic factors. This shift in the perspective and orientation of public policy naturally brought basic changes in the way social assistance systems operated.

Public and Private Pension Systems in Latin America: Characteristics, Performance, and Challenges

Pension system reform in the region was characteristic of the major changes in the actions of central governments in the 1990s. Using the Chilean reform as a model and under the imperative to curb growing current deficits in pension systems, a number of countries in the region undertook reforms. Despite a shared motivation, the systems that emerged were diverse and to varying degrees responded to the peculiarities of the local settings in which they were adopted. This section covers three topics: (a) concepts and characteristics of public and private pension systems, and a description of the two systems in 20 Latin American countries; (b) a comparison of private and public systems based on 10 performance indicators; and (c) upcoming challenges to both systems.[3]

Concepts and Characteristics of Public and Private Systems

Public and private social security pension systems can be distinguished from each other by four features: contributions, benefits, financial regime, and management. The public system has nondefined contributions (total contributions increase over time as the system matures and the population ages); defined benefits (determined and guaranteed by law); a distributive financial regime without reserves, and collective partial capitalization (the partial reserve for the insured pool of account holders); and public administration (whether by the social security administration or by the central government). The private system has defined individual contributions (which should not be increased over time); nondefined benefits (payouts will depend on the amount built up in the account of the individual holder based on his or her wage, contribution level, and investment yields); a financial regime of pooled and individual capitalization (an individual account belonging to the insured account holder whose funds are invested); and in most cases private management (undertaken by private, for-profit corporations, and handled exclusively, although the management can also be multiple—private, public, or a combination).

Table 11.1 Characteristics of Pension Systems in Latin America, 2005

Systems and countries	System	Contribution	Benefit	Financial regime	Administration
Systems with structural reform					
Substitution model	Private	Defined	Not defined	PIC	Private[a]
Chile: May 1981					
Bolivia: May 1997					
Mexico: Sept. 1997					
El Salvador: May 1998					
Dominican Republic: 2003–06					
Nicaragua[b]					
Parallel model	Public–Private	Not defined/ Defined	Defined/Not defined	Distributive with PIC	Public–Private
Peru: June 1993					
Colombia: April 1994					
Mixed model	Public–Private	Not defined/ Defined	Defined/Not defined	Distributive with PIC	Public–Multiple
Argentina: July 1994					
Uruguay: April 1996					
Costa Rica: May 2001					
Ecuador[b]					

(continued)

Table 11.1 Characteristics of Pension Systems in Latin America, 2005 *(continued)*

Systems and countries	System	Contribution	Benefit	Financial Regime	Administration
Public systems (without structural reforms)	Public	Not defined[c]	Defined	Distributive or CPC	Public
Brazil[d]					
Cuba[d]					
Guatemala					
Haiti					
Honduras					
Panama[d]					
Paraguay					
Venezuela[d]					

Source: Mesa-Lago 2004a, updated.

Note: CPC = collective partial capitalization; PIC = pooled and individual capitalization.

a. Multiple in Mexico, Dominican Republic, and Colombia.

b. In Nicaragua, indefinitely suspended due to high cost of transition; in Ecuador postponed due to constitutional appeal.

c. Defined contribution in part of private employee program in Brazil.

d. Parametric reforms recently approved or pending approval.

Parametric reforms strengthen the long-term financial condition of a public system, either by raising the retirement age or contributions, or by applying a more restrictive formula to calculate pensions. Structural reforms substitute, either entirely or partially, a private system for the public system. The 12 countries undergoing structural reform in Latin America have followed three distinct patterns: substitution, parallel, and mixed. In the upper portion of table 11.1, the countries are classified according to these three models; the date the private system began to function and its four features are also presented. The lower portion of the table lists eight countries with public systems, along with their four fundamental features. A footnote indicates whether they have undergone parametric reforms. Six countries followed the substitution model: Chile (the pioneering country, in 1981), Bolivia and Mexico (1997), El Salvador (1998), the Dominican Republic (gradually in 2003–06, although the process has ground to a halt), and Nicaragua (suspended indefinitely by a 2005 law reestablishing the public system because of the high fiscal costs the reform was incurring). The substitution model closes the public system to new affiliates and replaces it with a private system having the four features delineated above, except in Mexico, whose administrative system is multiple and offers both defined and nondefined benefits. The parallel model has been implemented in two countries: Peru in 1993 and Colombia in 1994. The public systems in those countries were reformed without being closed to new affiliates, and private systems, competing with the public systems, were created. The public systems are characterized by the four typical features (except in Colombia, where the financial regime is collective partial capitalization instead of distributive); while the private systems also fall within their typical features (except again in Colombia, which has multiple management types). The mixed model is followed in four countries: Argentina (1994), Uruguay (1996), Costa Rica (2001), and Ecuador (August 2005, although it is not yet in effect pending settlement of a Supreme Court appeal lodged on constitutional grounds). This model combines a public system, which provides a basic pension, with a private system offering a complementary pension, without closing the public system to new affiliates. Each of the systems is typified by its four features, except that the private systems have multiple management.

The other eight Latin American countries maintain public systems with the four typical features, and several of them recently approved parametric reforms: Brazil in its program for private sector employees in 1998–99, and for public employees in 2004; Costa Rica in the public portion of its mixed system in 2005; Cuba in 2005; Panama in 2005, although the president suspended its implementation in the face of public demonstrations; and Venezuela in 2002 and 2005. Structural and parametric reforms have been considered in Guatemala, Honduras, and Paraguay. No public discussion about reform had taken place in Haiti as of mid-2005.

Comparison of the Performance
of Private and Public Systems

This section compares public and private pension systems in Latin American on the basis of 10 performance indicators, four social and six financial:

- coverage of the economically active population
- retirement age and life expectancy
- pension amounts
- gender equity
- competition and administrative costs
- wage-based contribution rates
- reliability in making contributions
- impact on national savings, the stock market, and diversification of the investment portfolio
- investment performance
- fund accumulation and financial and actuarial equilibrium

Table 11.2 summarizes the statistics of the nine available performance indicators in 10 private systems (Ecuador and Nicaragua have been excluded because their systems are not yet in effect) and in seven public systems (Haiti is excluded for lack of data). The International Association of Latin American Pension Fund Supervisors (AIOS) publishes a semiannual report of standardized statistics for the 10 countries with private systems, but there is no similar association or statistical series for public systems.[4]

Coverage of economically active population. In 2004, 160 million people were covered by social security pension systems in the region, 67 percent by public systems (including the public component of mixed systems and the remaining account holders in closed public systems) and 33 percent in private systems and private components of mixed systems. The fraction covered in private systems varied as follows: 100 percent in Bolivia and Mexico; 87–98 percent in Argentina, Chile, the Dominican Republic, El Salvador, and Peru; and 50–54 percent in Colombia and Uruguay, where the public systems covered 46–50 percent. In Costa Rica, all pension account holders are covered by the mixed system.

In all countries, private system coverage declined between the year before the structural reform and 2004; the weighted average for the 10 countries fell from 38 percent to 26 percent; with the biggest drop in Argentina, from 50 percent to 20.7 percent (due to its economic crisis), and next in Peru, from 31 percent to 12 percent. No historical time series of statistical data exists that would allow coverage trends in public systems to be tracked. The comparison of static coverage between private systems (2004) and public systems (2001 to 2003) indicates that, regardless of

Table 11.2 Private and Public Systems: Performance Indicators, 2000–04

Systems and countries[a]	Coverage[b] (%)	Retirement age[c] (F/M)	Admin. cost[d] (%)	Contribution (percentage of salary)[e]			Paid current[f] (%)	Investment of funds		Funds accumulated		
				Total	Employee	Employer		Public debt[g] (%)	Yield[b] (%)	Millions (US$)	% GDP	Balance[j] (% GDP)
Private												
Argentina	20.7	60/65	17.4	7.0	7.0	0	35.4	62.0	9.9	18,306	12.0	-2.5
Bolivia	10.5	65	9.0	12.2	12.2	0	44.9	67.5	10.4	1,716	20.5	-3.5
Colombia	22.0	57/62	40.3	13.5	3.4	10.1	39.0	48.5	6.9	11,067	10.3	-1.6
Costa Rica	46.6	65	n.a.	4.5	2.5	1.8	68.1	73.1	6.7	476	2.7	–[j]
Chile	57.3	60/65	19.8	12.3	12.3	0	50.4	18.7	10.2	60,799	59.1	-7.2
Dominican Republic	14.5	60/65	7.0	7.0	2.0	5.0	49.8	32.5	-8.8	488	1.9	n.a.
El Salvador	20.1	55/60	33.5	13.0	6.0	7.0	41.9	83.5	9.9	2,148	13.7	-1.4
Mexico	28.0	65	18.7	11.0	2.6	6.2	38.8	85.5	7.7	42,524	5.8	-0.5
Peru	12.0	65	21.9	11.2	11.2	0	39.9	24.2	7.6	7,820	11.0	-0.7
Uruguay	58.8	60	11.9	5.0	5.0	0	52.2	57.9	12.9	1,678	16.1	-4.0
Average[k]	26.3	61/64	20.0	11.9	65.2[n]	24.5[n]	40.7	55.3	7.3	14,702	15.3	-2.7
Public												
Brazil	45.9	60/65	1.6	28.0	8.0	20.0	n.a.	0[l]	0[l]	80,000[m]	18.0[m]	-4.4
Cuba	n.a.	55/60	n.a.	12.0	–	12.0	n.a.	0[l]	0[l]	0	–	-2.2
Guatemala	21.8	60	8.7	5.5	1.8	3.7	n.a.	–	10.4	498	2.4	0.2
Honduras	15.7	60/65	0.5	3.5	1.0	2.0	n.a.	–	6.2	–	–	n.a.

Table 11.2 Private and Public Systems: Performance Indicators, 2000–04 (continued)

Systems and Countries[a]	Coverage[b] (%)	Retirement Age[c] (F/M)	Admin. Cost[d] (%)	Contribution (percentage of salary)[e]			Paid Current[f] (%)	Investment of Funds		Funds Accumulated		
				Total	Employee	Employer		Public Debt[g] (%)	Yield[h] (%)	Millions (US$)	% GDP	Balance[j] (% GDP)
Panama	58.9	57/63	4.8	9.5	6.8	2.7	n.a.	51.6	5.6	1,681	13.0	0.3
Paraguay	7.3	60	—	12.5	4.9	7.6	n.a.	—	—	—	—	0.4
Venezuela	26.3	55/60	—	6.8	0.8	5.9	n.a.	0[l]	0[l]	0	—	-2.4
Average[k]	41.4	59/61	3.9	11.1	3.3	7.7	n.a.	—	7.4	—	—	-1.4

Sources: Legislation on ages from countries; remainder from AIOS various years; Mesa-Lago 2004b, forthcoming.

Note:

n.a. = not applicable, — = not available.

a. Excludes Ecuador and Nicaragua, which have not yet introduced their private systems, and Haiti because of lack of data.

b. Percentage of economically active male and female population.

c. Early retirement is the norm in private systems.

d. Administrative costs as percentage of revenues; for private systems, only includes commission, not the fund reserves for disability and survivor benefits.

e. In private systems, includes deposit in individual account, commission, and account reserves. In Employee and Employer columns, percentages are for distribution of total contribution. Some systems also receive central government support, so Total column may be greater than sum of Employee and Employer columns.

f. Percentage of account holders contributing in previous month.

g. Percentage of portfolio invested in public debt.

h. Real annual yield; in private systems, from outset of operation until December 2004; in public systems, various periods.

i. Cost to public revenues from private systems in 2001; financial balance (revenues less expenses) in public systems, between 2000 and 2004.

j. The public system handles all pensions in process of payment, without transfer of fees, retirement funds, or the minimum pension, because the public system provides the basic pension.

k. The average for coverage is weighted by population. The average for administrative costs is based on total revenues and administrative expenses. Paid current is based on total account holders and contributors. The other figures are not weighted.

l. Distribution systems without reserves or investment.

m. These funds belong to a supplementary voluntary system and to the public system, which is distributive.

n. These values are shares of the total average contribution rate.

the type of system, the "pioneering" countries, with the oldest and most developed social security, had the highest coverage levels: 46–59 percent (Brazil, Chile, Costa Rica, Uruguay, with the exception of Argentina, at 21 percent; no figures are available for Cuba). These are followed by the "intermediate" countries: 22–59 percent (Colombia, Mexico, Panama, Venezuela, with the exception of Peru at 12 percent). Finally come the "late arrival" countries—the last to set up systems, and thus having the least developed systems: 7–22 percent (Bolivia, the Dominican Republic, El Salvador, Guatemala, Honduras, and Paraguay). The weighted average of private system coverage was 26.3 percent (lowered substantially by the scant coverage in Argentina) compared with 41.4 percent for public systems (strongly lifted by Brazil's high level of coverage).

The foregoing figures indicate that the expected increase in coverage has not taken place, despite the incentives of ownership of individual accounts and the close link between contributions and the pension amount, a point acknowledged in a recent World Bank study that assessed structural reforms over the past 10 years (Gill, Packard, and Yermo 2005). The two main causes for the decline in private system coverage, and in several public systems as well, are growth in the informal sector (especially self-employment) and the process of introducing greater labor flexibility, which promotes part-time employment, either through subcontracts or without contracts; workers in these sectors usually lack coverage. Non-contributory or "social assistance" pensions are provided to the poor only in the six pioneering countries, where coverage is highest and the informal sector and incidence of poverty the lowest.

Retirement age and life expectancy. Most structural reforms raised the age of retirement to increase amounts in individual accounts and ensure a minimum pension, although most systems allow early retirement when the amount deposited in the individual's retirement account is sufficient to fund a minimum pension. The average retirement age in the private systems is 61 for women and 64 for men, compared with 59 and 61, respectively, in the public systems. Given the higher age requirement in private systems, average life expectancy of a pensioned male upon retirement is 16.1 years and 21.0 years for a pensioned female, compared with 17.7 and 22.6 years, respectively, in the public systems. Increases in the retirement age in some countries, such as Chile, have been proportional to increases in the life expectancy of the population; however, in Uruguay, where life expectancy is third highest in the region, retirement at 60 is quite young. Conversely, in Bolivia, with the second lowest life expectancy in the region after Haiti, retirement at 65 is high and results in a shorter average life expectancy for pensioners (13.0 and 14.8 for men and women, respectively). As for public systems, retirement ages in Cuba (55 and 60, for men and women, respectively), with the second highest life expectancy in the region, are too low, resulting in longer life expectancy among pensioners upon retirement (20.5 and 27.2 years), considerably driving up system outlays, and contributing to the financial imbalances the system faces.

Pension amounts. Another implicit promise of structural reform has been that private pension systems will pay better than public ones, but this assumption cannot be readily confirmed in the absence of current time series data that would allow comparisons between the two systems; moreover, it would be hasty to predict relative payouts when the private systems have not been in place for long. In Chile, where the reformed systems have been in operation since 1981, only 20 percent of all pensions were under private systems as of 2002. Nevertheless, average private old-age pensions in Chile in 2001–02 (63 percent of total private pensions) were 24 percent lower than the average for public systems; the pension situation was reversed with disability and survivor benefits—the weighted average for all private pensions was 3 percent higher than the average for all public pensions. In Argentina, the crisis brought on a 65 percent drop in the private pension projected for the average holder. In Colombia, the average public pension was greater than the private pension; accordingly, most pension holders in Colombia are affiliated with the public system. A law passed in 2002, however, introduced changes to close this gap in a gradual fashion, and by 2004 most affiliates were in the private system. It is estimated that in Chile 30 percent of male and 50 percent of female affiliates fail to make the number of contributions required to obtain the minimum pension; in Peru, the proportions are 30 percent and 60 percent, respectively (Gill, Packard, and Yermo 2005).

Gender equity. For reasons both external and internal, coverage for women is usually lower than for men in both private and public social security systems, and pensions tend to be smaller. External factors are the lower rate of labor market participation and greater unemployment among women as compared to men, lower wages paid for the same job, and proportionally greater employment among women than men in unskilled positions and positions not covered by social security. For all these reasons, women build up lower contributions than do men during their working years. The system's internal causes of gender inequity include lower retirement ages than men (five years less in five private and five public systems), which, in combination with a life expectancy four or five years longer than men's, results in 9 or 10 years longer average life expectancy among female pensioners. Private systems exacerbate gender inequities in three ways: (a) they require a minimum number of contributions to qualify for pension payouts (most also have raised the number of years of contributions required to obtain a regular pension), heightening the difficulty women face in obtaining access; (b) they are based on contributions over the entire working life of the employee, and not just the last few years (as are most public systems), which is a disadvantage to women whose volume and pace of contributions are lower than an average man's;

and (c) they use actuarial tables that are differentiated by gender (whereas public systems use same-sex tables), and by dividing the amount built up in the individual account by the average years of life expectancy, they pay out less to women than men (further decreased if a woman retires five years earlier than a man). Some public systems use men's contributions to subsidize women's, partially offsetting the cost of childrearing, which mainly falls upon women. (In Chile before the reform, the public system for workers counted an additional year for a working mother for each living child.) Equalizing the normal retirement age of both sexes in five private systems facilitates the buildup of more contributions and greater funds in their individual accounts, to be distributed over a retirement period reduced by five years; however, it fails to completely compensate for longer life expectancy in women. This equalization of the retirement age reduces costs significantly in two public systems

The combined impact of these factors on gender was measured in Chile for 2001–02: the funds accrued in women's individual accounts varied between 32 percent and 46 percent of men's; the female wage replacement rate was 52–57 percent as opposed to 81–86 percent for men; the average pension of a female pensioner of 60 years of age was 60 percent that of a man's and 87 percent for retirement at 65. Mixed systems tend to offset gender inequity more than substitution systems, because the public portion lessens the inequity, whereas the private portion accentuates it; however, the effect depends on the share of the two portions. For instance, in Costa Rica the offsetting of gender inequities is greater than in other countries because the main pension payments are made under the public system, while the private is supplemental; in Argentina the reverse situation obtains.

Competition and administrative costs. It has been argued that private systems reduce administrative costs because they eliminate the monopoly situation of public systems and introduce competition and greater efficiency. In fact, greater efficiency is reflected in the handling of records and individual accounts and faster processing of pensions. However, with several different pension providers, the economies of scale from a single pension provider are lost; considerable resources are devoted to advertising and commissions for sales and marketing personnel, and to profits. Moreover, it has been shown that competition fails to function adequately in most private systems, because either there are only two providers (Bolivia, El Salvador) or the three largest providers are highly concentrated, for example, 71–86 percent market share in Chile, the Dominican Republic, Peru, and Uruguay (AIOS 2005). In addition, several countries fail to provide comparative information on commissions, fees, and yields that would enable pensioners to select the best provider. It is also alleged that the industry functions as an oligopoly with a captive clientele, that it restricts the number of times a customer can change pension companies (to reduce operating expenses), that competition among pension management companies for relatively narrow market shares leads to higher commission rates, and that only a fraction of the reduction in operating expenses is passed on to customers in the form of lower commissions (Gill, Packard, and Yermo 2005).

Administrative costs in private systems consist of a commission (usually in addition to a salary) paid to the manager for handling the individual account, the investments from the fund, and the old-age pension. The commission includes a fee that the manager pays a private insurance company to cover the risks of disability and death (done by the public system in Mexico and Colombia). Calculated as a percentage of revenues, administrative costs (not including the insurance fee component of the commission) in 2004 fluctuated between 7 percent in the Dominican Republic and 40 percent in Colombia, with a weighted average among the 10 countries of 20 percent (as calculated by Mesa-Lago [forthcoming]). Expenses for salaries, sales commissions, advertising, and other operations absorbed an average of 12 percent of revenues; the remaining 8 percent was profit (AIOS 2005). Information on public system administrative costs was only available in five countries (as a percentage of revenues) and ranged from 0.5 percent in Honduras to 8.7 percent in Guatemala; with a weighted average of 3.9 percent, that is, one-fifth the average level in private systems. The advantages of economies of scale, forgoing advertising and marketing, and the absence of profit in public systems offset the greater efficiency of private systems.

Contributions from wages. Contributions from salaries to private systems (which cover deposits to the individual account, commissions, and fees) range between 7.0 percent in Argentina (11 percent before the crisis) to 13 percent in El Salvador. In Costa Rica, the contribution of 4.5 percent accrues solely toward the deposit; other operating expenses are funded by a percentage of the investment yield. In the Dominican Republic, in addition to the 7.0 percent contribution, a percentage is also charged from the yield to cover some portion of administrative costs. Excluding these two countries, the weighted average contribution to private systems is 11.9 percent. The three mixed systems (Argentina, Costa Rica, and Uruguay) require an additional contribution that funds the public portion, so the total contribution significantly raises the average of private systems. Among public systems, contributions in Brazil are by far the greatest (28.0 percent), pulling the average among public systems up to 11.1 percent (slightly less than the average in private systems); if Brazil is excluded, the average falls to 8.3 percent.

Under the theory that employer contributions raise production costs, encourage capital input substitution for labor inputs, and undermine the competitiveness of exports, the structural reforms eliminated the employer contribution in Bolivia, Chile, and Peru, and pared it down in Argentina and Uruguay. Employee contributions were raised in six countries, but only three also raised employer contributions. In addition, commissions and fees are borne exclusively by employees in all but two countries, where they are shared with employers. There is neither an academic consensus nor an empirical justification for the theory about the negative effects of employer contributions. The counterargument is that the employer contribution may actually be paid by the employee or passed on to the consumer. Moreover, the elimination of the employer contribution has raised the burden on workers, increased the burden on the national treasury, or both, in addition to creating a disincentive to worker participation. (See next section.) Of total contributions, employees pay 65.2 percent, employers 24.5 percent, and the central government (in two countries) 10.3 percent. Public systems have maintained employer contributions, which account for 69.4 percent of the total, with employees paying only 30 percent, and the central government 0.6 percent (in one country).

Reliability in paying contributions. It is assumed that contributions to private systems are paid more punctually, given the ownership incentive of a private account and the close link between contributions and the pension level. However, increases in employees' levels of contribution can create a disincentive for meeting contribution requirements. In 1998–2004, the percentage of pension fund participants who had contributed in the previous month fell in all the private systems; the average dropped from 58 percent to about 41 percent (AIOS 2000 to 2005). In 2004, compliance with this requirement ranged from about 35 percent in Argentina (the lowest level, caused by the crisis) to over 68 percent in Costa Rica; the weighted average for the 10 systems was 40.7 percent, meaning that 59.3 percent failed to pay their contributions on time. Employer payments in Chile are significantly in arrears, where the outstanding debt in arrears expanded six times from 1990 to 2002, reaching US$526 million in the last year or the equivalent of 1 percent of the total value of pension funds, 43 percent of which will have to be written off because of bankruptcies. The dearth of time series statistics and up-to-date figures on fulfillment of obligations in public systems prevents meaningful comparison. Nevertheless, the little information that is available indicates that high levels of evasion and arrears are found in Panama, Paraguay, and Venezuela.

National savings, the stock market, and diversification of portfolios. Private systems are also supposed to raise savings at the national level, help stock markets develop, create new financial instruments, and diversify pension fund investments. Five studies have been carried out on the impact of this structural reform on national savings in Chile, the country with the longest period available for observation (see Mesa-Lago [forthcoming]). Three conclude that the effect was negative (approximately minus 3 percent of GDP), because the reduction in tax revenues has been greater than the capital accrued; one of the studies offers questionable results and another concludes that the impact has been positive. One of the studies also claims that empirical evidence is consistent with the notion that reform has contributed to the development of the national stock market, although the authors warn that other unrelated factors cannot be ruled out, so the evidence is inconclusive. By contrast, another study claims that pension fund resources have had a robust impact on the development of the national financial market.

In looking at portfolio diversification, the negative impact of the transition on tax revenues (see "Fund accumulation and financial and actuarial equilibrium" section) has led many governments to set ceilings on the amount that can be invested in certain instruments and to restrict investment in foreign securities to channel funds to finance the internal deficit. The domestic private sector attracts little investment from any investors through sales of stocks and bonds, and the high interest paid on public bonds provides public debt holders with high yields, which are unsustainable in the long run, particularly in countries where governments face large fiscal deficits and risk nonpayment (Gill, Packard, and Yermo 2005). By 2004, the portfolio was not close to the level of diversification that had been anticipated: the investment in public debt in seven countries was close to or over 50 percent, with two over 80 percent. Chile, the Dominican Republic, and Peru were the only countries in which less than a third of pension funds assets was in public debt. On average, public debt accounted for about 55 percent of the funds' investments. Stock investments averaged 8 percent, with significant levels in only three countries (13–38 percent). Several countries forbid investment in foreign securities, which averaged 5.6 percent, with only four countries showing significant investment (7–27 percent).

Half of the public systems operate as distributive regimens, without investment reserves (Brazil, Cuba, and Venezuela). The other four have reserves and do invest, but current information was available only from Panama, where about 52 percent of the fund investments were in public debt, and none were in foreign stocks or other securities. Less current information from Guatemala and Honduras indicates that most of their portfolios are also invested in national debt securities; the same is found in the public systems in Colombia and Costa Rica (82 percent and 89 percent, respectively) (AIOS various years). Thus, with few exceptions, both private and public systems have failed to diversify their portfolios and keep their holdings overly concentrated in public debt. The problem is aggravated in small countries where a local stock market either does not exist or is in an incipient stage.

Investment performance. For the 10 private systems, gross investment performance in real terms, beginning with the year each fund was set up until 2004, showed an annual average of 7.3 percent (ranging from minus 8.8 percent in the Dominican Republic to 12.9 percent in Uruguay). However, to calculate net return on investment, the costs of commissions for managing the retirement program have to be deducted from the gross yield, and neither the countries nor AIOS publish net performance figures. Using the figures on gross yields and commissions recorded by AIOS for

2000 to 2005, rough estimates are ventured for three countries: 7.6 percent gross yield and 4.3 percent net in Peru, 7.7 percent gross and 5.9 percent net in Mexico, and 9.9 percent gross and 8.1 percent net in El Salvador. In 1981–2000, the gross yield on the Chilean pension fund averaged 11.9 percentage points less than the Price Index of Select Stocks traded on the Santiago exchange; for 1993–2000, the performance of the Peruvian fund was lower than interest payments on bank savings accounts and Brady bonds. For the period 1993–95, gross performance was far better than for the period 1995–2000, as a result of several economic crises and plummeting stock markets. These fluctuations present significant risks to pension account holders, who will have good pensions if they retire when the stock market is peaking, but will see the value of their pensions diminish during recessionary periods, particularly prolonged ones, such as Argentina experienced. This risk is reduced in mixed models, which combine a guaranteed pension component with one that is sensitive to volatility in capital yields.

For public systems, annual average performance in real terms was available in only three countries for different periods between 1994 and 2002: 10.4 percent in Guatemala, 6.2 percent in Honduras, and 5.6 percent in Panama, for an average 7.4 percent for the three countries, quite close to the average for the 10 private systems. However, the four other public systems do not invest their funds, so the average would drop significantly if they were included. The guaranteed pensions in the public systems are less sensitive to market volatility than private pensions, but are not immune to the lack of portfolio diversification, as seen in several countries where pension fund balances have suffered from low or negative investment yields.

The concentration of investment in domestic public debt, seen in both public and private systems, leads to risky overdependence on the interest rates set by governments, which adversely affect investment performance and the long-term value of pensions. Until 2000, private systems in Argentina had the highest average yield in real terms (15 percent), thanks to the high interest rates paid by the national government. However, the government pressed pension fund managers to convert their dollar-based securities to bonds "guaranteed" in *pesos,* and the Superintendency of Pensions supported the shift by raising the ceiling on public debt holdings. The 2001–02 crisis provoked both the devaluation of the Argentine *peso* and a drop in interest rates, and the value and performance of the fund in real terms, previously projected in dollars, suffered a tailspin. By contrast, when the 1982–83 economic crisis threatened the existence of the new private Chilean system, the Superintendency played a crucial positive role in promoting the diversification of portfolios and reducing the overall share of public debt investments from 50 percent to 19 percent.

Fund accumulation and financial and actuarial equilibrium. Private systems are assumed to amass capital much more readily than public systems, and because they are based on set contributions and a financial regime of pooled, individually owned accounts, they can better handle the aging of the population, avoid having to raise contribution requirements, and in the long term eliminate the fiscal deficit. Nevertheless, increased life expectancy and longer retirement periods will make it necessary to raise contribution levels to avoid reductions in pension payouts. Private systems have managed significant capital accumulation, although with variations among countries depending on the size of their economies, salary levels, investment performance, and the length of time the private system has been in operation. The highest accumulation levels, as of late 2004, were in countries with the largest economies, highest number of account holders, and longest experience with reforms. Totals (in millions of U.S. dollars) were as follows: $60,799 in Chile, $42,524 in Mexico, $18,306 in Argentina, and $11,067 in Colombia. By contrast, the lowest totals were accumulated in the countries with the smallest economies, the least number of account holders, and where reforms were most recent: $488 million in the Dominican Republic and $476 million in Costa Rica. In proportion to GDP, accumulation ranged from 1.9 percent in the Dominican Republic to over 59 percent in Chile. The largest accumulation in the region ($80,000 million) was in Brazil, the country with the largest economy and the most pension account holders. Although Brazil does not have a private system, the monies were accumulated through voluntary supplementary funds paid for by employers and employees. In the two public systems for which data were available, reserves were $1,681 million in Panama and $498 million in Guatemala (13 percent and 2.4 percent of GDP, respectively), but two countries have no reserves, nor does the Brazilian public system. Thus, the data back up the claim that private systems achieve greater capital accumulation.

Nevertheless, capital accumulation needs to be balanced against three fiscal costs brought about by structural reform, all of which are financed by the central government: the operating deficit in the closed public system that remains responsible for current pension payments, with few or no contributing employees; the value of the contributions paid by account holders that is shifted from the closed public system to the private system (recognition bonds); and the minimum guaranteed pension, when the individual account is too small to finance the minimum pension. Pension funds face an operating deficit in all countries. Recognition bonds for past contributions are not paid out in the mixed models because account holders have not been moved into a different system. The minimum pension is not guaranteed in Bolivia, and only partially in Peru (the mixed models pay a pension under the private portion). The most generous benefits during the account holders' transition were those guaranteed in Chile, which also has the highest fiscal costs. Other countries restricted the pension reserves' being shifted to the new account and the minimum pension to curtail costs to public coffers. Estimates for 2001 of these fiscal costs as a percentage of GDP in private systems, ranged from –0.5 percent in Mexico to –7.2 percent in Chile (after 20 years of reform) and averaged –2.7 percent in eight countries, omitting Costa Rica and the Dominican Republic (Gill, Packard, and Yermo 2005).

Costa Rica's reform has not engendered losses to public revenues because the account holders belong to both the public and private systems.

The financial balance of the public systems, expressed as a percentage of GDP between 2000 and 2004, resulted in surpluses in three countries (Panama, Paraguay, and Guatemala; and deficits in three (Brazil, Cuba, Venezuela); the average deficit was –1.4 percent of GDP, whereas the average cost to public revenues from the private systems was –2.7 percent. The two figures are not technically comparable, however, because the former is a balance and the latter a fiscal cost to public coffers. In addition, the private systems have made the implicit debt for social assistance at least partially explicit (the present value of all pension obligations over the long term). Standardized long-term projections for the financial balance of public systems are not available, neither are the fiscal costs of the private systems. However, actuarial projections for six countries indicate that current contributions in two (Guatemala and Honduras) are sufficient or excessive (and thus would not need to be raised for a long time); Costa Rica, in 2005, decided to gradually increase the current level of contributions to maintain equilibrium; and in three other countries the contribution must increase substantially (Cuba, Panama, and Venezuela) (Mesa Lago 2004b).

Pending Challenges

Both public and private systems face challenges, some in common, others not. Challenges in common are

- reversal of the decreases in coverage resulting from growth of the informal sector and the introduction of flexible hiring arrangements; this will require special programs designed to incorporate self-employed workers and others in similar circumstances (through fiscal incentives for low-income earners, as in Costa Rica), and to support pensions tailored to the poor in the majority of countries;
- proportional adjustment of the retirement age to reflect longer life expectancy and introduction of a single retirement age for both sexes (which would require raising women's retirement age by five years in 10 countries);
- production of statistics that will allow comparisons between pension amounts in both systems;
- elimination of gender discrimination in the external job market, which reduces women's pensions;
- control of evasion and arrears in contributions (as is done in Costa Rica, where such behavior is defined as a criminal offense against social security and strong sanctions are imposed on offenders);
- adequate diversification of investment portfolios through the promotion of new financial instruments and allowing investment in foreign securities (as in Chile, Peru, and Colombia), particularly in small

countries that have no local stock market or where stock markets remain in an embryonic stage;

- examination of potential combinations of defined and nondefined benefits (guaranteed pension dependent on an individual account);
- formulation of robust long-term projections of the fiscal costs of transition in private systems and the financial and actuarial equilibrium in public systems; and
- unification of diverse systems into the general system in several countries (particularly those with public systems) to allow them to move with the employee; and
- standardization of access requirements and of the rules to calculate pensions, to promote equal treatment.

Challenges unique to private systems are

- reduction in the excessively high retirement age in some countries (such as Bolivia), which drastically shortens the length of retirement;
- reduction in the system's adverse impacts on gender equity, through single-sex life tables, individual accounts shared by spouses, and the like;
- improvement in competition in the system to facilitate entry of more pension management companies into the market, allowing them to make use of the infrastructure of existing financial entities;
- reduction in high administrative costs, including consideration of lower ceilings on commissions (as in Bolivia and the Dominican Republic) and changing part of the commission based on salary to base it on the balance or yield (as in Costa Rica);
- research on the causes of arrears in payments, including whether the requirements for higher workers' contributions outweigh system incentives;
- possible reintroduction of employer contributions in the three countries that eliminated them, and a more equitable distribution of the contribution burden on the worker and employer in the remaining countries;
- opportunity for the account holder to select an investment fund from among several options (as in Chile); and
- reinforcement of the autonomy of the supervision agency, which plays an active role in disseminating information and educating account holders, portfolio diversification, and passing on to account holders savings from reductions in fund managers' operating expenses.

Challenges unique to the public systems are

- formulation and regular publication of statistics on coverage, compliance with payment deadlines for contributions, administrative costs, portfolio diversification according to security type, investment yields, and amount of reserves;

- increases in very low retirement ages in several countries in relation to life expectancy (Cuba, Panama, Venezuela) to cut costs and improve financial sustainability;
- establishment of more sensitive links between contributions and pension amounts;
- increased efficiency in areas such as registration, holders' accounts, and processing pensions, as has been achieved in most private systems;
- promotion of supplementary pension programs to enhance the basic pension provided by the public system (as in Brazil);
- adjustment of contributions to maintain or reintroduce long-term financial and actuarial equilibrium; and
- creation of independent technical agencies to regulate and provide oversight for the system.

Characteristics and Performance of Social Assistance Programs

The expansion of off-the-books employment in the region has limited the scope of social security programs and left a growing portion of the population without protection. The reappearance of macroeconomic instability in the mid-1990s reinforced this trend and forced some national governments to seek alternatives to contain the social impact of unemployment and dependency on the informal economy. This section provides a structured description of these changes: first, the social and economic context in which demand for instruments to protect income originates; next, a synthesis of the new conditional modes of cash transfer; and finally, some reflections on the effectiveness of these new instruments.

Crisis Income Protection in the 1990s

The 1980s saw fundamental changes in labor markets in the region, along with changes to the conditions under which income policies and public policies in general operated. On the one hand, repeated retrenchment in public spending in the wake of the debt crisis (1981–3) reduced formal employment and pushed significant sectors of the population toward unregulated labor relationships that are less secure than those established under labor laws and that offer fewer protections against the loss of jobs. On the other hand, the labor market was dramatically unresponsive to the economic growth of the early 1990s. In contrast to the previous decade, the high growth rates in output that continued until the mid-1990s (tied to macroeconomic stability and structural reforms) failed to have an impact on unemployment. In fact, notwithstanding the relatively high growth from 1990 to 1994, the unemployment rate grew in several countries. Successive crises beginning in 1995 exacerbated the trend, and average unemployment rates in the region continued to rise until 2000. In some countries, the crisis at the end of the 20th century continued until 2003, and only in the past few years has unemployment begun to moderate.

The combination of unemployment and unregulated employment varied by country in the region (see Duryea, Jaramillo, and Pagés 2003), but serves to illustrate the new constraints on employment policies and the management of aggregate demand. Even during times of growth (such as 1991–94), the need to address the growing social demands of the groups affected by modernization and to assist the poorest groups, furthest removed from the public social services safety net, required changes in the composition of spending. In the 1990s, the countries increased public social spending in absolute terms and in proportion to overall public expenditure (ECLAC 2003).

Macroeconomic volatility associated with the various recessions, and the resulting abrupt increases in poverty and unemployment rates led to strong social demand for programs to protect the population against the risks of loss of jobs and incomes (Márquez 2000). This demand contributed to the creation of a series of programs intended to protect the most vulnerable groups from macroeconomic instability. These programs were inspired by the need to preserve political support for reform efforts, designed in a context of crisis, and frequently amid conditions in which unemployment soared as salaries plunged. Consequently, what resulted from the creation of these social safety nets was a collection of programs that generally lacked sufficient coherence and scope to meet the income-protection needs of the groups affected by modernization (Acosta and Ramírez 2004; Márquez 2000).

In lieu of a coherent system of social protection, diverse programs were created and activities undertaken that were geared toward revenue transfers to part of the population and could be expanded in the short term. The particular response of each country varied substantially, depending on its tradition and history in labor market interventions, and in terms of the political equation in which certain groups' income-protection needs figured to a greater or lesser degree. Countries that chose this route carried out a series of small-scale public works programs (organized either through Social Investment Funds[5] or through local or intermediate-level governments and nongovernmental organizations, as was the case in the *Programa Trabajar* [To Work Program] in Argentina).[6] Other program components (such as short-term training programs) were designed foremost to control the social impact of unemployment. These were temporary income-substitution programs with few, if any, conditions on the beneficiaries and thus did not result in human capital development or the attainment of useful skills. Additionally, these programs tend to create entitlements for beneficiaries, which makes it difficult for them to be canceled or modified.

In other countries, the prevailing view is that this type of income transfer cannot break through the vicious cycle that traverses from poverty to low investment in human capital to vulnerability and back to poverty. A cycle-breaking intervention would require income transfers to the poorest in society, conditioned on greater family investment in education, health, and child nutrition. To maximize these mutually reinforcing aspects, the various targeted programs are expected to operate within the parameters of a social safety net to safeguard the income of society's poorest, while providing incentives for them to make greater efforts to develop their human capital (Acosta and Ramírez 2004).

With these types of transfers, the distributional impact of public expenditure can be leveraged by using sophisticated means to select beneficiaries. As noted by Levy (2005), with the selection and strict application of target criteria, income transfers can be aimed at low-income groups.

Conditional Cash Transfer Programs

Under the institutional conditions in the region, the introduction of income transfer programs was not easy. Whereas in Organisation for Economic Co-operation and Development countries, income transfer programs are the main tools of social assistance, as measured in monetary terms and in the extent of population coverage (Tabor 2002), in Latin American countries spending on such programs is low and covers small proportions of the population (ILO 2000).

These programs have two features that stand out among the repertoire of social policies found in the region. First, by their own nature, these programs tend to be implemented alongside existing systems, which are normally controlled by the agencies and trade unions in the system that design and implement social policies. Social service delivery systems can be used to enroll beneficiaries, but normally cash transfer programs use separate human resources and systems from those of the front-line government agencies that design and deliver social services.

Second, cash transfer programs are grounded in the perception that the fundamental constraint on the target groups is the lack of access to the consumption levels required to maintain and develop human capital. Thus, the objective of these programs is to encourage demand for education, health, and nutritional services through conditioned access.

Conditional cash transfer programs carried out in the region in the late 1990s represented an attempt to address factors of human capital demand among the poorest social groups. Normally, these programs consist of cash transfers to poor households, conditioned on investments within the households in education, health, and nutrition. Six countries in the region at this point have adopted some type of conditional cash transfer programs: Brazil, Colombia, Honduras, Jamaica, Mexico (the first), and Nicaragua (see table 11.3).

Several other countries have debated the adoption of programs or the transformation of certain existing ones, and in the next few years more countries can be expected to adopt programs of this type.

Table 11.3 Characteristics of Conditional Cash Transfer Programs

Country program	Objectives	Components		Target population		
		Education	Health and nutrition	Education	Health and nutrition	
Bolsa Família—Brazil[a]	Increase families' investments in human capital	Income transfers	Income transfers	School-age children	Expectant mothers	
	To be part of the Social Protection Network				Children 0 to 15 years old	
PETI—Brazil	Eliminate worst forms of child labor, increase education achievement, reduce poverty	Income transfers Extension of school attendance	n.a.	Children 7 to 14 years old	n.a.	
Familias en Acción—Colombia	Increase human capital investment of families in extreme poverty Take part in social safety net	School subsidy	Nutritional grant Health education	Poor households with children 7 to 17 years attending school	Poor households with children 0 to 6 years not in any other program	
PRAF II—Honduras	Break cycle of intergenerational poverty by increasing human capital investment in children of poorest families	Education voucher as subsidy for demand Supply-side incentives in primary schools	Nutrition and health voucher, demand subsidy Incentives for health centers (supply) Nutritional training for mothers	Poor households with children 6 to 12 years who have not finished 4th grade in primary school	Poor households with expectant mothers or children under 3 years	

(continued)

Table 11.3 Characteristics of Conditional Cash Transfer Programs (*continued*)

Country program	Objectives	Components		Target population	
		Education	Health and nutrition	Education	Health and nutrition
PATH—Jamaica	Increase educational achievement, improve health outcomes, and thus reduce poverty	Grant for education	Health grant	Poor households with children 6 to 17 years	Poor households with children 0 to 6 years, expectant or nursing mothers, elderly over 65, disabled persons, and adults in extreme poverty under 65
	Reduce poverty		Health education		
	Reduce child labor				
	Take part in social safety net				
Oportunidades[b]—Mexico	Increase human capital stock of families in extreme poverty	Revenue transfer	Revenue transfer	Poor households with children in 3rd to 9th grade	Expectant or nursing mothers
		School supplies	Basic health care package		Infants 0 to 2 years and children 2 to 4 years with symptoms of malnutrition
		Incentives for educational centers (supply side)	Nutritional supplements		
			Instructions in health, nutrition, and disease prevention		
			Incentives for health centers (supply)		

(continued)

Table 11.3 Characteristics of Conditional Cash Transfer Programs *(continued)*

Country program	Objectives	Components			Target population	
		Education	Health and nutrition		Education	Health and nutrition
Red de Protección Social—Nicaragua	Promote buildup of human capital in households in extreme poverty	Grant for education	Cash grant for food		Children 6 to 13 years enrolled in primary school (1st to 4th grade)	Cash subsidy for poor homes, health services targeting children 0 to 5 years
		Support for school materials	Health and nutritional education			
		Supply incentives	Basic health care package for under-5 children			
			Supply incentives			

Source: Rawlings and Rubio (2004), adopted and updated by authors.

Note:
a. Under 2004 law, Bolsa Escola, Bolsa Alimentação, Carta Alimentação, and Auxilio-Gas all merged.
b. Poverty program continues, expanding to urban families in extreme poverty.

These programs target households in poverty for cash payments, conditioned on the beneficiaries' fulfillment of certain requirements for investment in human capital, such as educational assistance for their children, medical checkups for children and mothers, and nutritional instruction for adults. Within the range of existing programs, these three characteristics—cash transfers, targeting, and the condition or requirement of human capital investment—are inseparable and have important implications in the design and operation of the programs.

Direct cash transfer to families, instead of indirect funding of services or subsidizing certain consumer goods, offers the major advantage of allowing families to exercise their preferences in using the cash resources. At the same time, cash transfers involve lower transactions costs than equivalent programs of in-kind subsidies, and do not encourage secondary markets that could deplete the transfer of some of the resources (Rawlings 2004).

The targeting systems use identification instruments based on geographical location, income, and household assets. Centralized operations and the use of empirical verifiable information (social and topographical surveys) help to minimize erroneous inclusions and exclusions, although they generate significant program operating costs. Centralization also tends to reduce the scope of action of local government, which from a training perspective should be a major actor in the strategy to combat poverty (Rawlings 2004).

The conditioning of resources on health and education investment is one of the most promising features of this type of program. The requirements for school enrollment, academic assistance, medical checkups for children (and frequently, pregnant or nursing mothers), and nutritional education for mothers targeted by the program tend to leverage investment in family human capital and break the cycle of intergenerational poverty. Furthermore, these programs tend to raise public pressure to improve the availability and quality of educational and health services (Rawlings 2004).

Mexico was the pioneer when it introduced the *PROGRESA* (PROGRESS) program in August 1997. The program resulted from Mexican government concerns that high poverty levels persisted, particularly in rural areas, despite the quicker pace of growth in the 1990s. According to the diagnostic of the administration of then President Ernesto Zedillo, the existing transfer programs in Mexico failed to reach the poorest citizens (among other reasons, because they were subject to local political manipulation) and also had excessive administrative costs (the outcome of policy and program fragmentation, see Coady [2003]). With poverty correlated to extremely protracted and low-level human capital development, these programs failed to raise the ability of the poor to develop their human capital (Levy 1994).

PROGRESA was an innovative conditional cash transfer program that targeted families living in extreme poverty in rural areas for resource transfers. Few social policy programs in the region have been as successful. Evaluations of the program are unanimous in their identification of the important effects on the well-being and income-generating capabilities of the beneficiaries (Skoufias 2001). The program continues to be replicated in far-flung countries of the region, and in Mexico itself the program was extended to semi-urban and urban areas in 2001, under the name *Oportunidades* (Opportunities).

The program consists of cash transfers equivalent to approximately 20 percent of family consumption of targeted beneficiaries, who are among the poorest sectors of the population. The assistance is conditioned on the attendance of minor children at school, and family members attending health centers. The distinct feature of the program is the targeting mechanism that operates in three phases: first, the poorest rural communities are selected; next, the poorest families in the community are identified; in the third phase, the program meets with the local community to review the targeting and selection procedures.

The formal targeting procedure is intended to prevent local political interests from manipulating the selection process. The program is federal, the localities are selected by federal government employees, and the transfers go directly to the beneficiary families, bypassing the state and local governments.

From a decision-making perspective, one of the most outstanding features of the Oportunidades program was the emphasis on program evaluation conducted by independent outside evaluators. Facing the 2000 elections in which the official party's hold on government was seen to be slipping, an effective and credible assessment was essential to keep the program above reproach in the electoral contest and ensure its continued existence, notwithstanding a change in the party in power. The program evaluations, through objective, credible information, lent support to the perception that the program resources were reaching the poor (at least to a greater degree than in traditional programs) and reaching them and them alone (thus, program targeting was efficient).

Honduras began to implement the PRAF II program in late 2000, as the successor to the PRAF program, originally designed as nonconditioned income transfers that would boost aggregate demand. However, PRAF II became a program of conditional cash transfers, targeting families living in extreme poverty. The new program targeting was more attuned to identifying these families, and the program included a series of measures (demand subsidies) in the areas of education, health, and nutrition that were geared toward breaking the intergenerational cycle of poverty. It also included elaborate system monitoring and assessment.

The Nicaragua Social Safety Net (*la Red de Protección Social*) pilot program began in late 2000. It was geographically based to target groups in extreme poverty and had interventions in education, health, and nutrition designed to reinforce children's school attendance and to increase the use of health and nutritional services. Both sectors of the program include supply-side incentives in the form of additional budget support to respond to the greater use of services by the families incorporated into the program (Morley and Coady 2003).

In Jamaica, in 2001, the Programme of Advancement Through Health and Education (PATH) was launched as part of a comprehensive reform of the social safety net. Families living below the poverty line receive a cash transfer and assistance with free or subsidized access to selected health and education programs. The program consolidates a series of interventions that previously targeted children and senior citizens, who are incorporated into a sole beneficiary targeting and identification system.

Colombia began to implement the conditional cash transfer program, *Familias en Acción* (Families in Action), in 2002, in response to the most acute economic crisis in at least 70 years. The program was presented as a replacement for a series of benefits and services that were considered poorly focused and ineffective as a means to encourage family investment in human capital. Cash transfers are targeted to the poorest quintile of the urban and rural populations, and include monetary incentives for household investments in education, health, and nutrition (Attanasio and Mesnard 2005).

PETI was one of the first conditional cash transfer programs; it was designed to fight the most dangerous kinds of child labor in Brazil. The program attempts to induce families to register their children in the school system, and thus remove them from the labor market.

Bolsa Família (Family Basket) was launched in Brazil in 2003. The program consolidated within a single operation the subsidies provided under *Bolsa Escola* (School Bag), *Bolsa Alimentação* (Nutritional Basket), *Carta Alimentação* (Nutritional Record), and *Auxílio-Gas* (Fuel Assistance). The PETI program has been maintained separately, because its goal (to reduce child labor) is remedial and not preventive as is Bolsa Família. PETI awards a subsidy to families living below the poverty line, which is conditioned on school attendance and attendance at health centers by pregnant mothers and all children in the family. It is expected that the incorporation of all these programs into Bolsa Família will promote efficiency and improve targeting policies of social assistance in Brazil.[7]

Results and Pending Issues

The general view that emerges from the growing body of literature analyzing the effectiveness of direct cash transfer programs is that they are efficient in meeting their goal to reduce poverty. Levy (2005, 132) finds in reference to Mexico's PROGRESA program that "the evaluations of impact conducted in rural areas show that the program is cost effective, and has made a positive impact on education, health, and nutrition." The findings of the impact evaluations in rural areas show that the program is cost-effective, it selects its target population appropriately, and it has a positive impact on education, health, nutrition, and diet. The evaluators have indicated that these programs are effective in targeting groups that had never received support from the central government, that they are effective in inducing behavioral changes among the poor, and that the programs themselves have managed to avoid the pitfalls of patronage.

A key innovation of the conditional cash transfer programs has been the strategic use of evaluations as tools to improve the survival and growth of these programs. The evaluations are incorporated into the program design and show that the programs have been efficient and effective in protecting the incomes of the poor and promoting the buildup of human capital (Coady, Grosh, and Hoddinott 2004; Rawlings 2004; Rawlings and Rubio 2004). The evaluations have provided accurate measures of the impact on educational achievement and nutritional status of target populations; moreover, they have made information available on current and future program beneficiaries, which affords an additional element to protect them from political interventions and changes in priorities promoted by passing political majorities.

In recent years, an important body of literature has described and debated evaluations of conditional cash transfers.[8] All the cases reviewed found that these transfers increase primary school attendance and, where applicable, secondary school attendance. Another frequent effect observed is a reduction in child labor. Programs have had an impact on nutritional and health indicators, frequently associated with micronutrient distribution. Beneficiaries of these programs show fewer nutritional problems, low incidence of disease, and increased vaccination coverage. In all cases, the consumption level of beneficiary groups has improved as a result of their participation in the programs. The evaluations have found that more than 80 percent of the resources earmarked for these programs reach the poorest 40 percent of families.

Conditional cash transfer programs have become the cornerstone of social protection policies in several countries that have implemented them. None of these programs, however, are poised to create incentives for families to graduate from social assistance programs to regular social security programs that depend on employment. In the end, not even the most efficient social assistance program can eliminate poverty if the economy fails to produce the high-quality jobs necessary for program beneficiaries to enter into "normal" social security programs.

Moreover, many analysts argue that the design and implementation of these programs demand many scarce highly qualified human resources, diverting these resources from the key task of reforming the educational and health systems so that they can become more efficient. The poor quality of these systems is at the root of many of the problems that led these families to become vulnerable and trapped in poverty. Moreover, should the health and educational systems fail to improve the quality of services, the effect of the conditional cash transfer programs becomes that of turning low-income beneficiaries into consumers of low-quality services. Despite this, many defenders of these transfers argue that the pressure from the beneficiaries who now attend and use these services can become a catalyst for change. The available evidence does not confirm either of these two positions.

Finally, it is only reasonable to address the question of whether programs useful in attending to needs of families in extreme poverty in rural areas will be as helpful as an instrument for general social assistance. The preliminary evaluations of Oportunidades[9] suggest that the extension to urban areas of programs originally designed for rural areas has not led to a loss of effectiveness or efficiency. Even though these assessments give cause for optimism, it will be necessary to proceed with caution, in light of the small number of experiences available for observation.

Notes

1. For a detailed discussion of the "traditional model" in social policy and changes to it, see Franco (1996) and Molina (2002).
2. Traditional nonexport sectors record lower contribution rates than export sectors, possibly because of the smaller size of units in the former and their consequently lower revenue profile.
3. This section is based on Mesa-Lago (2004a, 2004b, forthcoming), unless a different source is specified.
4. AIOS groups managers of pension funds, and therefore does not include administrators of "traditional" prereform public pension systems.
5. See Tendler (2000).
6. See Ravallion (2000).
7. See PR-2912, Brazilian proposal for a loan to support the social protection system, Inter-American Development Bank, November 2004.
8. See Aedo (2005) and Rawlings (2004) for references to evaluations published on conditional cash transfer programs.
9. See PR-2919, Mexican proposal for a loan to support the Multiphase program for the consolidation and expansion of Oportunidades Human Development Program, Phase II, Inter-American Development Bank, February 2005.

References

Acosta, O., and J. C. Ramírez. 2004. "Las redes de protección social: modelo incompleto." Development Financing Series No. 41, Economic Commission for Latin America and the Caribbean, Santiago, Chile.

Aedo, Cristian. 2005. "Transferencias de ingreso: Una nueva forma para asignar el gasto social." Inter-American Development Bank, Washington, DC.

AIOS (International Association of Latin American Pension Fund Supervisors). 2000 to 2005. *Boletín Estadístico AIOS,* Vol. 1–12.

Attanasio, O., and A. Mesnard. 2005. "The Impact of a Conditional Cash Transfer Programme on Consumption in Colombia." Institute for Fiscal Studies, London.

Coady, D. 2003. "Alleviating Structural Poverty in Developing Countries: The Approach of PROGRESA in Mexico." Background paper for the 2004 *World Development Report*, World Bank, Washington, DC.

Coady, D., M. Grosh, and J. Hoddinott. 2004. *Targeting of Transfers in Developing Countries: Review of Lessons and Experience.* Washington, DC: The World Bank and the International Food Policy Research Institute.

Duryea, Suzanne, Olga Lucía Jaramillo, and Carmen Pagés. 2003. "Latin American Labor Markets in the 1990s: Deciphering the Decade." Research Department Working Paper WP-486, Inter-American Development Bank, Washington, DC.

ECLAC (Economic Commission for Latin America and the Caribbean). 2003. *Social Panorama of Latin America and the Caribbean, 2002–2003.* Santiago, Chile: Economic Commission for Latin America and the Caribbean.

Franco, Rolando. 1996. "Los paradigmas de la política social en América Latina." Division of Social Development, Economic Commission for Latin America and the Caribbean, Santiago, Chile.

Gill, Indermit, Truman Packard, and Juan Yermo. 2005. *Keeping the Promise of Social Security in Latin America.* Palo Alto, CA: Stanford University Press and World Bank.

ILO (International Labor Organization). 2000. *World Labor Report 2000: Income Security and Social Protection in a Changing World.* Geneva: ILO.

Levy, S. 1994. "La pobreza en Mexico." In *La pobreza en Mexico: Causas y políticas para combatirla,* ed. F. Velez. Mexico City, Mexico: ITAM/FCE.

———. 2005. "Economic Crisis, Political Transition and Safety Nets Reform: Mexico's *Oportunidades.*" Inter-American Development Bank, Washington, DC.

Márquez, Gustavo. 2000. "Labor Markets and Income Support: What Did We Learn from the Crises?" Research Department Working Paper WP-425, Inter-American Development Bank, Washington, DC.

Mesa-Lago, Carmelo. 2004a. "Evaluación de un Cuarto de Siglo de Reformas Estructurales de Pensiones en América Latina." *Revista de la CEPAL* 84 (December): 59–82.

———. 2004b. "Las Reformas de Pensiones en América Latina y su Impacto en los Principios de la Seguridad Social." Serie Financiamiento del Desarrollo 144, CEPAL, Santiago, Chile.

———. Forthcoming. "Private and Pension Systems Compared: An Evaluation of the Latin American Experience." *Review of Political Economy.*

Molina, Carlos G. 2002. "La entrega de los servicios sociales: modalidades y cambios recientes en América Latina." Working Paper No. I-50, IDB/Inter-American Institute for Social Development (INDES), Washington, DC.

Morley, S. A., and D. Coady. 2003. "From Social Assistance to Social Development: Targeted Education Subsidies in Developing Countries." International Food Policy Research Institute, Washington, DC.

Ravallion, Martin. 2000. "Monitoring Targeting Performance When Decentralized Allocation to the Poor Are Unobserved." *World Bank Economic Review* 14 (2): 331–45.

Rawlings, Laura. 2004. "A New Approach to Social Assistance: Latin American Experience with Conditional Cash Transfer Programs." Social Protection Discussion Paper No. 0416, World Bank, Washington, DC.

Rawlings, Laura, and G. Rubio. 2004. "Evaluating the Impact of Conditional Cash Transfer Programs: Lessons from Latin America." Policy Research Working Paper No. 3119, World Bank, Washington, DC.

Skoufias, E. 2001. "PROGRESA and Its Impacts on the Human Capital and Welfare of Households in Rural Mexico: A Synthesis of the Results of an Evaluation by IFPRI." International Food Policy Research Institute, Washington, DC.

Tabor, Steven. 2002. "Assisting the Poor with Cash: Design and Implementation of Social Transfer Programs." Social Protection Discussion Paper No. 0223, World Bank, Washington, DC.

Tendler, Judith. 2000. "Safety Nets and Service Delivery: What Are the Social Funds Really Telling Us?" In Social Development in America Latina: The Politics of Reform, ed. J. Tulchin and A. Garland. Washington, DC and Boulder, CO: Woodrow Wilson Center and Lynne Rienner Publishers, Inc.

12

Education Reform as Reform of the State: Latin America Since 1980

Juan Carlos Navarro

BETWEEN 1980 AND THE START of the 21st century, Latin American education systems underwent a constant wave of reforms. The backdrop for this reformist activism was a broad social agreement to bring all children and young people into the education system, and make their stay in the education system longer and more significant.

Education reform took place in practically all countries of the region, although with a wide range of intensity and consistency. In Brazil, the reform process affected most aspects of education policy during the eight years of the Cardoso administration (1995–2002) and had a visible and positive impact on education indicators. In the Brazilian interior, various state governments implemented noteworthy reforms in areas such as school autonomy (Minas Gerais) and accountability (Curitiba). Chile, under the *Concertación* governments since 1990 has maintained a constant rate of reform thanks to a national consensus establishing education reform as a priority. Chile implemented more education reforms than any other country in the region (see box 12.1), and now has outstanding education indicators, although it faced severe problems improving the quality of learning. Since 1990, Colombia made successive attempts to introduce legal reforms by decentralizing the provision of education services and introduced impressive innovations in school districts and specific regions in areas such as education vouchers, teacher evaluation, and public-private partnerships for school administration. Uruguay adopted original reforms in the 1990s that produced well-documented results. Argentina decentralized the education system and changed the curriculum dramatically, but the execution of reform has been uneven and some of the initial designs have been altered and even reversed due partly to economic volatility.

Since 1993, Mexico has been ambitiously decentralizing education and implementing numerous special programs designed to improve its equity and quality, with visible results. The Dominican Republic, after the adoption of a 10-year plan in the early 1990s, followed a straight and continuous path in which successive administrations prioritized education development, producing a significant jump in coverage and the quantity and quality of resources devoted to education. El Salvador came out of its civil war of the 1980s amid a national dialogue on the importance of education in national development, which has generated consistent and effective education policy for over a decade. Nicaragua has been a pioneer in experimentation with school autonomy, giving parent-teacher associations unusual powers to organize the school process. Since the early 1990s Bolivia has maintained vigorous education reform, which has had some successes and failures, but has not come to a halt.

These broad strokes do not do justice to the dimension and richness of the reforms in each country, and leave out important reforms in countries not included in this short list. The countries of the region have diverse educational conditions, which make any significant attempt at synthesis difficult (Urquiola and Calderón 2005). The development of an exhaustive and detailed overview of education reform in Latin America, a more ambitious task for which there are excellent sources,[1] is outside the scope and intent of this chapter.

The starting point for this chapter is the evidence that most of the important education reforms since the mid-1980s in Latin America were institutional. The prevailing consensus among experts and education authorities in the region was that it was not sufficient to improve the strictly pedagogical aspects of the education process—changes were also needed in decision making, the relation of government to citizens, and the responsibilities of the various levels of government and their structure and capacities. So, curriculum reform; investments in infrastructure, textbooks, and teacher training; and provision of computers for schools had, as always, a good space in the activity of the ministries of education. At the same time, however, issues such as decentralization, evaluation, accountability, community participation, and school autonomy became part of the shared language of education reformers throughout the continent.

This chapter reviews the main trends in education reform insofar as they relate to state reform. One of the most radical ways in which a state can reform is through redistribution of the responsibilities of each level of government—three in most countries: national or federal, state or provincial, and municipal or local. Another important reform mechanism is to strengthen the capacity of a government to perform an essential function for which it previously lacked adequate power or structure. Finally, the third major current of state reform involves the redistribution of tasks that

Box 12.1 A Catalog of Education Reforms:
Broad and Sustained Education Reform in Chile

Although the experience of any one country in particular should not be taken as a model or paradigm for reforms in others with different conditions, histories, and resources, the Chilean education reform is remarkable for its continuity and its features, present in most Latin American reforms in different combinations. After the stimulus of municipalization and introduction of the voucher system in the 1980s under the military government, neither of which was reversed, the governments of the democratic *Concertación* directed their reform efforts into (according to the synthesis by Arellano 2005) the following:

- Expansion of coverage, particularly in secondary education, and increased time on task through the introduction of full-time schooling
- New teaching materials, complete curriculum modernization, and intensive teacher training, all aimed at improving classroom work
- Stimulus for programs focused on assisting students in difficulty or at risk of dropping out, in the poorest urban schools, and in rural and remote areas
- Improvement of the working conditions for teachers, contributing to a recovery in the prestige of the teaching profession
- Gradual introduction of new information and communication technologies in the schools
- Improvement of performance evaluation instruments in the school system (modernization of the national evaluation system and participation in international comparative testing)

Although no other country in the region has launched a general voucher program (Colombia made some local experiments that were not continued) most have tried some variant of decentralization, as will be seen later in this chapter. The 1990s was the decade of expansion of secondary education in almost the entire region, and also the era of recovery of education funding (after the penury of the 1980s), as well as curriculum change. In most countries, these initiatives were implemented using targeting mechanisms in combination with numerous compensatory programs. Teacher pay levels recovered, although no country succeeded in introducing incentive and evaluation measures as well defined as Chile's. Attempts, often ambitious although not always successful, to introduce information technology into the learning process have been widespread, and the development of assessment systems has also been common.

Source: Author's compilation.

public policy assigns to the public sector rather than the private sector in a defined area of activity. Based on the broad spectrum of education reforms implemented in Latin America in recent years, the key aspects of the three main lines of reform are described below:

- Decentralization—the transfer of responsibility for managing significant aspects of the education system from the national government to other levels.[2] This point also includes extreme cases of decentralization, such as the reforms centered around the notion of school autonomy.
- Development of evaluation systems—the institutionalization of systems for measuring the quality of learning in schools and universities, together with their use in improving education policy and debate.
- Public-private partnerships—associations in which private provision of education gains special prominence through some process, sometimes spontaneous but preferably planned, complementary to public action on education.

These three lines encompass many of the aspects of reform that have led to fundamental changes in the public organization of the provision of education. Decentralization introduced subnational governments as actors with responsibility for education. Evaluation systems involved the acquisition of a capacity, generally at a national or central level, that was previously nonexistent in the public education sector—state reform resulted from the creation and institutionalization of this capacity. Finally, public-private partnerships led to a change, although in limited areas, of the basic organization of the education sector, modifying the traditional model consisting of a public monopoly accompanied by a group of private schools restricted to an elite clientele. As will be seen, these three lines of reform represent sweeping changes experienced throughout the length and breadth of Latin America, on which there is sufficient experience, although not always conclusive evaluations, to attempt a preliminary assessment from which some lessons can be extracted.

Decentralization

The most common institutional reform in education in the 1990s was the transfer of administration and, to a lesser extent, financing of public school systems to subnational levels of government, especially in the geographically largest countries (table 12.1).

The Argument for Decentralization

In the 1980s, decentralization had already made good headway in Brazil and Chile.[3] The main justification for decentralization was the complexity

Table 12.1 Level of Government with Responsibility for Education

Country	1980	2005 [a]	When decentralization began [b]
Argentina	National	Provincial	1976, 1991
Bolivia	National	Municipal	1994
Brazil	National/state	State/municipal	1988, 1995
Chile	National	Municipal	1981
Colombia	National	Dep./municipal	1991, 2000
Costa Rica	National	National	–
Dominican Rep.	National	National	–
Ecuador	National	National	–
El Salvador	National	National/school	1991
Guatemala	National	National/school	1994
Honduras	National	National	1995
Mexico	National	State	1993
Nicaragua	National	National/school	1993
Panama	National	National	1998
Paraguay	National	National	1998
Peru	National	National	–
Uruguay	National	National	–
Venezuela	National	National	1989

Source: Author's compilation.
Note:
a. Cases in which a country had education decentralization initiatives but the level of government is still national in 2005 means an unconsolidated or completely reversed process of decentralization.
b. Multiple years indicate various important decentralization initiatives.

and diversity of the education system, which made management difficult for a bureaucratic center devoted to controlling the last administrative detail of schools that were often thousands of kilometers away in systems counting students in millions and teachers in the hundreds of thousands.

This is a well-founded diagnosis. Latin American education systems have been strongly controlled during most of their histories by central ministries. Decisions on who teaches, how and how much teachers are paid, and what is taught have been remote from the local and regional communities and the authorities that represent them. The central ministry has rarely had the capacity to supervise school operations, even in areas as simple as checking whether classes actually take place, if teachers and students attend, and if the content stipulated in national study programs is covered, much less to know if any significant learning is taking place. The central education ministries came to be in many cases more effective at suppressing innovation than at guaranteeing the functioning and the quality of education processes and results. Decentralizing reforms were intended to correct this incompetent centralism.

Bringing decisions closer to users also offers the expectation of improving accountability and democratic control of public decisions. Taking for granted the heterogeneity of preferences among citizens of different jurisdictions on the level and characteristics of a semipublic good such as education, subnational governments have some advantages in producing it more efficiently. From the start, this argument provided a strong foundation for decentralizing initiatives in education, and counteracted the reservations of those who saw in decentralization a serious risk to the coherence of the systems and even to the maintenance of a unified national culture.[4]

Experiences of School Autonomy

The principles of efficiency, participation, and convergence between the information and decisions that underpin the education decentralization processes, just described, had their boldest realization in a series of experiences of school autonomy implemented by several countries in the 1990s. Following Espínola (2000), school autonomy experiences can be classified into two groups according to whether the autonomy transferred to the school is mainly concerned with managing the school process or with the teaching strategies to be practiced in each school. The best documented and disseminated experiences of the first type are those of Nicaragua and Minas Gerais state in Brazil, while Argentina, Chile, Colombia, and Uruguay introduced important initiatives of the second type.

For management autonomy, three areas of decision making have been generally transferred to the school level: election of directors, evaluation and supervision of teaching staff, and administration of modest financial resources, generally for maintenance of the structure or for special programs supplemental to the basic curriculum. Of these three areas, election of directors seems to have had the least consequence; in contrast, teacher evaluation has had a stronger impact. A series of evaluations of these experiences of management autonomy shows that they were effective in increasing student enrollment and attendance, reducing teacher absenteeism, improving the contribution and involvement of parents in the education of their children, and improving use of the resources under management (Arcia and Belli 2001; Espínola 2000; King, Rawlings, and Ozler 1996; Paes de Barros and Mendonca 1998; PREAL 2000; Winkler and

Gershberg 2000). The evidence does not support, however, the existence of a causal link between autonomy and better learning results; Nicaragua, for example, provides indications that the inequality of results between schools may have increased. The few clear results for teacher autonomy are mainly restricted to a positive impact on the motivation of teachers and directors.

An important fact documented by the latest research in the area (Gunnarsson and others 2004) is that adoption of a school autonomy policy tends to benefit schools that previously had greater management capacity and better leadership from the director or the education community, but may not have appreciable effects on schools that lack these characteristics. Experience shows that effective adoption of school autonomy schemes is a gradual process requiring a competent and prolonged commitment by the central authorities to guide and educate the actors in the school context (families, teachers, students, directors).

Decentralization in Context

Education decentralization must also be examined in the broader context of the political and administrative decentralization in the region during this period (see chapter 7). The state organization devoted to education services was affected by the general trend toward greater political and social participation, and development of directly elected subnational governments with growing autonomy and management capacity. This helps explain why education decentralization made progress even with opposition from the teachers' unions, which in general have viewed such reform as a serious threat to their negotiating power at a national level.

In fact, despite strong arguments in favor of education decentralization reforms whereby education policy itself dictates the decisions and the timing of the process, it has been usual for changes or circumstances that are beyond the strict education policy sphere to lead to education decentralization.

In Argentina, decentralization suffered from an early association with the military government, which promoted the decentralization of primary education. When the democratic government embarked on decentralization of secondary education in the 1990s, the initiative was led by the Ministry of Finance and, to a large extent, imposed on the provinces, which resisted taking on the new responsibilities without corresponding financial support. So what could have been a carefully implemented core education policy, appeared from the start to be part of a fiscal austerity program of a central government keen to strip itself of expenditure responsibilities.

Venezuela provides another example of the impact of comprehensive state reform on education. In the late 1980s, the direct election of governors and mayors led to legislation that explicitly transferred education responsibilities, among others, to states and municipalities. The result was a wave of education innovations sponsored by state and local governments, as well as considerable expansion of public expenditure on education resulting in an explosion of social demands directed at the new subnational authorities (Navarro 2000). In this case, the appearance of a new relationship between voters and elected authorities in the framework of the state reform process created incentives that intensified collective action in education and spurred the introduction of new approaches and experiments at the local level, some of which later became influential at the national level.

Even in Mexico, in which it can be argued that decentralization was part of a policy of improving the efficiency and quality of education, the elected governors—particularly governors elected from political parties other than the party that had historically controlled the national government—were decisive players in the adoption and implementation of ANMEB (*Acuerdo Nacional para la Modernización de la Educación Básica,* or National Agreement for the Modernization of Basic Education), the political agreement that initiated education decentralization in Mexico.

It should not be inferred from cases such as this, however, that subnational governments have always welcomed education decentralization. In Colombia in the early 1990s, municipalities resisted taking on responsibilities for which they were not physically or organizationally prepared, which led to the stagnation of the education decentralization process in that country (Lowden 2004). In Venezuela, education decentralization moved toward giving subnational governments more to do in education, but not in the usual sense of accepting transfers of responsibilities and schools that had been in the hands of the national government. The main reason was that the practical fiscal aspects of these transfers could never be defined to the satisfaction of the subnational authorities.

Impact of Decentralization

To understand the dynamic of decentralization, its impact and results must be analyzed. These can be discussed on at least two levels:

- Educational outcomes—has education decentralization led to better-quality learning, to more equitable opportunities and better education results, or to more efficient education systems?
- Education policy making—after the decentralizing reforms, to what extent have education policies become more stable, presided over by better technical and managerial capacities, in tune with the public interest, capable of resisting drastic changes in the economic and political environment, and less conflictive?

Relatively little is known about the impact of decentralization on learning results. In the most rigorous study available, Galiani and Shargrodsky

(2002) found that, on average, a positive effect can be detected in the scores on standardized examinations taken by Argentinian children as a result of the decentralization process. However, in what seems to clearly parallel the results of studies on the impact of school autonomy, the same researchers detected that the favorable effects of decentralization were concentrated in schools and provinces that started off with better capacity to manage resources, but was not discernible in schools or provinces with precarious institutional or socioeconomic conditions.

Nonetheless, overwhelming evidence suggests that attempts to decentralize education have produced a legacy of institutional capacity for formulating and implementing education policy in subnational governments, where before it was practically nonexistent. No doubt, the growth of institutional capacity has been irregular. Local politics has been shown to be equally powerful but not necessarily more constructive than national politics when it directly influences the functioning of education systems.[5] In some countries, years of decentralization have failed to produce growth in capacity commensurate with the importance of the responsibilities assigned in education, and as expected, in all countries, institutional strengthening has progressed much more rapidly in some jurisdictions than in others.[6] Finally, education decentralization has not been without pure and simple failures and reversals.

However, because the development of subnational public administrations is a benefit, decentralization comes out favorably in the balance. The reforms began a dynamic of change that has taken on its own momentum. In a decision-making process in which the teachers' unions and national authorities were normally the exclusive participants, there is now a third actor—the subnational governments—with the strength to make their points of view heard.[7]

Especially in large countries, improvement in capacity of subnational governments has facilitated management of education systems. Certain institutional developments in Argentina, Brazil, and Mexico reveal that the maturing of the education decentralization processes is leading to coordination between levels of government that goes beyond the original design of the decentralizing reforms. The Federal Council in Argentina or the regular policy dialogue meetings between the Secretariats of Education of the states and the federal authorities in Mexico are examples of coordination that are improving the coherence of education policies, 10 years or more after the initial decentralization measures.

Additionally, on several occasions state or municipal governments have produced education innovations of great value for the design of national reforms. Much of the knowledge about the effects of a radical program of school autonomy is due to the extraordinary experience gained since the mid-1980s in Minas Gerais state in Brazil. The introduction of full-time schools by the Mérida state government in Venezuela created, over the years, a national consensus on the need to move the entire education system in the direction of full-time schools, a consensus that is still being implemented despite a succession of administrations with diverse political orientations and persistent and deep disagreements on decentralization of education policy. In Colombia, the Bogotá School District has justifiably gained a reputation as a source of innovations in education policy, and has attracted international attention and become a source of inspiration for other reformers. The examples could be expanded.

These positive changes have to be contrasted with other facets of decentralization that were not always equally constructive. Although decentralization was frequently understood as a policy that required changes in the structure and functions of the traditional central ministry, in practice the consequences of this principle were not always correctly interpreted. In some cases, this led to a weakening or deterioration of the capacities of the Ministry of Education at a time when the subnational levels were still institutionally underdeveloped, leaving a negative balance in capacity for design and implementation of education policies.[8]

Education Decentralization and Fiscal Federalism

The most serious weakness of education decentralization processes in Latin America has been in another area: the difficulty of adjusting the fiscal system to the decentralization of administrative policy of the sector. Although important decisions have been made on transfers of powers to states and municipalities, and in some cases the autonomy enjoyed by these levels of government in education policy has increased, these transformations have rarely been accompanied by fiscal transfers or tax schemes capable of creating well-financed systems with incentives that maximize the welfare of citizens.

This is a basic problem of public choice: if a certain level of government is given a responsibility—especially a significant and visible one such as the school system—maximization of citizen welfare requires that the transfer be financed, either through local taxes or through transfers from the central government that are credible and stable and that do not undermine the incentives for subnational governments to maintain fiscal discipline and efficiently provide services. Both alternatives are technically and politically complex. In practice, the complexity of this situation has prevented the development of reasonably stable fiscal arrangements that support education decentralization.

In Argentina, Brazil, Mexico, and Venezuela, education decentralization took place and existed for years without efficient arrangements in fiscal federalism. In Argentina, the collapse of education financing by the states when fiscal revenue fell because of the recession in the late 1990s led to the temporary closure of various provincial systems, to an increase in labor conflicts in the education sector, and, ironically, to a de facto return to federal government financing of education, in the form of "teacher incentive" payments.

In Mexico, with the exception of some elements of rationality introduced in the last few years through intense coordination between the Secretariat of Public Education and the Secretaries of Education of the states, fiscal transfers to the states for financing decentralized schools has followed largely ad hoc procedures that are in continuous negotiation year after year and state by state. In Venezuela the process of transferring schools from the central government to subnational governments came to a standstill following the refusal of state governments to assume the commitments with teachers on social benefits and pensions previously contracted by the central government.

In this context, Brazil is the exception because of the financing reforms for the decentralized education system introduced in the mid-1990s. With the creation of FUNDEF (*Fundo para Manutenção e Desenvolvimento do Ensino Fundamental e Valorização do Magisterio*, or Fund for Maintenance and Development of the Fundamental Education and Valorization of Teaching), the education responsibilities of states and municipalities were established by law, and an adequate financing structure was created to meet the system's need for funds. Additionally, the central government's role was to guarantee equity in expenditure, defining a spending floor per student and committing the ministry to supplementing the funds for states that could not achieve the minimum on their own. These reforms produced substantial improvements in student flows, equitable access, and educational achievement in Brazil, proving that an efficient financing scheme can make the difference between decentralization that creates problems and decentralization that creates excellent education results (Draibe 2004).

The Future of Decentralization

Decentralization reforms in Latin America have failed to solve several of the fundamental deficiencies of education in the region. These include the low quality of learning, which, according to all available evidence, is not improving and is still well below the achievements of the countries of East Asia and Organisation for Economic Co-operation and Development (OECD) countries. Although this issue will be returned to in more detail, a provisional conclusion is that the abundant and intense education decentralization initiatives did not correct these deficient results. It is now clear that the change in the level of government responsible for management of certain schools does not necessarily lead to an improvement in the quality of learning. The schools may be better managed, or have better capacity to respond to the communities in which they operate, without necessarily producing a change in teaching practices, the capacities of teachers, the support they receive on the job, or the leadership that each school director can offer. The probability that conditions conducive to making such changes exist in the schools can be higher when the education administration resides in the local or provincial administration instead of in a remote bureaucratized central ministry, but even so, decentralization is not a sufficient condition in itself.

Consequently, although the most advanced and vigorous decentralization processes will continue their courses, especially in geographically larger countries, in the next few years, decentralization will probably move to a secondary place on the menu of reforms favored by the education authorities in the region.

The Development of Assessment Systems

In the mid-1980s, immediately preceding the wave of education reforms covered by this chapter, it was not possible to determine how much students were learning in the schools. With the exception of some pioneering efforts in a few countries, the capacity to collect standardized and representative information about learning results simply did not exist. This issue is extremely important because one of the recurring objections to the management of school systems is that they are usually guided by measures of input—enrollment, expenditure per student, and the like—rather than by results. Learning is the final result of the school system; without information on this aspect, it is impossible to speak of a results-oriented education policy. The education results of a society are the product of innumerable decisions made by students and their families based on the information they acquire about the value of education and the quality and effectiveness with which providers are capable of delivering education. Lack of information on the results of learning considerably impoverishes these private decisions as well as public policy.

The 1990s, in contrast, saw an exceptional chapter in the history of capacity building in evaluation of education systems in Latin America. Table 12.2 summarizes the progress of several countries.[9]

What Has Been Gained

Each of the countries in table 12.2 has now, to differing degrees, attained the main components of solid institutional development in the evaluation area:

- a group (although not always sufficient to form a critical mass) of highly qualified specialists in the technical aspects of education evaluation
- sufficient funds to maintain the minimum effort needed to regularly collect information on learning achievement in primary and secondary education
- social and political legitimacy to develop their activities[10]

Table 12.2 Evaluation Systems in Latin America

Country	Starting year	Institutionalization	International Tests				
			LLECE	PISA	TIMSS	PIRLS	Others
Argentina	1993	Intermediate	X	X			X
Bolivia	1996	Intermediate	X				
Brazil	1988	Advanced	X	X			X
Chile	1988	Advanced	X	X	X	X	X
Colombia	1991	Intermediate	X		X		X
Costa Rica	1988	Intermediate	X				
Dominican Republic	1991	Intermediate	X				
Ecuador	1996	Initial					
El Salvador	1993	Advanced					X
Guatemala	1997	Intermediate					
Honduras	1990	Intermediate	X				
Mexico	1992	Advanced	X	X	X		
Nicaragua	1997	Initial					
Panama	1997	Intermediate					
Paraguay	1995	Intermediate	X				X
Peru	1997	Intermediate	X	X			X
Uruguay	1996	Advanced		X			X
Venezuela	1995	Initial	X			X	X

Sources: Author's compilation based on Ferrer (2005), Wolff and Gurría (2005), and Tiana (2000).
Note: LLECE = Laboratorio Latinoamericano de Evaluación de la Calidad de la Educación; PISA = Program for International Student Assessment; TIMSS = Third International Math and Science Study; and PIRLS = Program in International Reading Literacy Study.

- networks and international relations that nurture and support evaluation activities in each country, and frequently lead countries to participate in comparative international tests[11]
- a degree of institutionalization in the form of well-established ministerial departments or semi-independent institutes devoted to the organization, implementation, and analysis of learning assessment tests.

The countries of the region exhibit great disparities in consolidating these elements. Where they have matured most, they can be seen as an "evaluation-based education reform," as occurred during the Cardoso administration in Brazil, thanks to the development of INEP (*Instituto Nacional de Estudos e Pesquisas Educacionais*, or National Institute for Education Studies and Research), a sophisticated and powerful institute of education assessment in the Ministry of Education. Overall, these elements exemplify the acquisition of critical institutional capacities by the education ministries of Latin America without parallel in any other aspect of education policy. The education authorities now have extremely valuable information to steer their policies and establish priorities. A good part of the education debate and public pressure to produce improvements in the education systems—which comes from the media, the business community, the political opposition, and families—are based directly on results of national and international standardized assessment tests. The inclusion of education as a distinctively important component of concern for the competitiveness of Latin American economies is largely driven by information on test scores in mathematics, science, or language.

Evaluation and Higher Education

The growth of public capacities for education evaluation is not limited to primary and secondary levels. The tertiary level has also been a fertile area for the introduction of various evaluation initiatives. Many countries now have—unlike before 1990—university evaluation and accreditation programs. These mechanisms flourish because they are designed to improve the quality and accountability of higher education institutions and are characteristically accepted and even welcomed by those institutions, in contrast to reforms dealing with financing or governance mechanisms. The implementation of evaluation and accreditation systems in tertiary institutions and programs is a fundamental change in the function of the state in education because it incorporates the principle of accountability and the notion that production and dissemination of information that helps society and individuals make better choices, in this case in tertiary education, is an important public function.

It is impossible to do justice here to the progress made in many countries in this area. Some examples, however, can illustrate the changes involved.[12] In El Salvador, the introduction of evaluation instruments in the late 1990s brought guiding principles and quality standards, which had been absent because of the armed conflict in previous years, into private higher education. In various countries specialized institutions have been created to promote and supervise accreditation processes, and in some cases, such as in Central America, international networks are being created to work in this direction. Brazil, in what is one of the most original cases, created *Provão* ("big test" in Portuguese) in 1997, an instrument that subjects all students in the final academic year of certain professional areas to a knowledge test considered the minimum necessary for later professional practice. The results, which rate the study programs of each institution with a letter grade that qualifies the students, are widely disseminated, stimulating the programs and institutions that did not come out well in the first rounds to invest in improving their performance (Guimaraes 2002).

The Next Frontier: Using the Evaluations

The performance evaluations in primary and secondary education are not used as effectively as at the tertiary level, which is the Achilles heel of all this effort (Iaies 2003). Abundant information on how much children and young people are learning in Latin American schools is now available, but this information suffers from (a) underutilization—although the databases are often available they are not adequately exploited in education research; (b) lack of dissemination—sometimes the supposed beneficiaries do not receive the information or receive it late and in an inadequate format; (c) poor adaptation of the design to the original purpose, such as when feedback is offered to schools based on sampling information that is inadequately disaggregated; and (d) negative political reaction that prevents the efficient use of the information collected, which usually happens either because the results are distributed to the public inadequately or because the government decides not to disclose the information because it appears to be unfavorable (Ravela 2002).

Nonetheless, on certain occasions results of education evaluations have become a constructive part of public policy (Cueto 2005). The experiences of Chile with SNED (*Sistema Nacional de Evaluación de Desempeño de los Establecimientos Educacionales*, or National System of Evaluation of Performance of the Educational Establishment) and Mexico with *Carrera Magisterial* deserve special mention. In both cases, in the context of complex methodologies for granting monetary incentives to teachers, test results provide irreplaceable information for determining which teachers made better contributions to student learning (Vegas and Unmansky 2005).

How to Build Institutional Capacity in Education

Why exceptional achievements in this area of state capacities have been made and not in others has yet to be examined in depth. The following reasons can be suggested:

- The creation of these capacities is related, to a point, to general improvement in the professionalism and institutional capacity of the education ministries, but has gone much further, much more rapidly, than improvements in other areas. Even areas seemingly directly related to evaluative capacities, such as education statistics, have failed to achieve similar institutional development. In countries in which stagnation, or even reversal, of the capacities of the education ministries can be detected, the evaluation area has remained solid. This progress has been sufficiently rapid, general, and substantial as to be the exclusive result of better public education management. Consistency and continuity in the development of education evaluation capacities are even more worthy of recognition seeing as the test results tend to be very disappointing, showing that learning in schools leaves a lot to be desired across the region.[13]
- From a political point of view, the growing priority given to education by the political, social, and business leadership of Latin American societies may have been a contributing factor. The trigger for many of the most important education reforms in many countries has been the conviction of the elites that the competitiveness of the national economy has to be improved and that investment in human capital is critical in the contemporary global economy. Hand in hand with political priority has been priority in the assignment of resources,[14] which affected accountability and the demand for information by finance ministries, lawmakers, and taxpayers in general.
- At least part of the achievements in evaluation capacity can be credited to the consistency of international efforts in this area. The regional summits of heads of state have recognized the importance of evaluation. In particular, the Summit of the Americas in Santiago, Chile, in 1999 created a regional program for exchange of experiences and consensus building on initiatives on learning evaluation. Both the Inter-American Development Bank and the World Bank have been prioritizing evaluation capacity in their education operations for over a decade, thus strengthening the priorities of the governments. They have also played an important role in regional cooperation efforts, particularly the Latin American Laboratory of Education Quality (LLECE, a UNESCO initiative), which not only conducted a regional comparative test, but accompanied the test with programs deliber-

ately designed to strengthen countries' technical evaluation capacity. Additionally, the operation of networks, originating in OECD countries through initiatives such as Program for International Student Assessment (PISA) and Third International Math and Science Study (TIMSS), have had a beneficial effect, acting as sources of technological transfer and contributing legitimate international standards to education evaluation programs in Latin America (Tiana 2000). Finally, professional and specialized networks such as the one promoted by Partnership for Educational Revitalization in the Americas/Group for the Analysis of Development (PREAL/GRADE) continue to play a vital role in disseminating experiences and refining technical advances in education evaluation.

Public–Private Partnerships for the Provision of Education Services

Formal education services are organized with surprising similarity around the world. A large public education system administers schools and hires teachers, who teach in schools that are free for families and students because they are financed from taxes. The Ministry of Education supervises the activities of the schools, regulates the duties and rights of teachers and directors, and provides them with tools for their work.

This form of organization has been questioned by a series of initiatives in different countries, but all alternative forms of organization have been exceptional or short-lived in their application.

Latin America is no different. With only the partial exception of Chile, public organization of education systems in the region is uniform, and entirely adapted to the general model. As in most countries of the world, Latin America also has a private education sector. The universal explanation for the presence of this sector, especially at primary and secondary levels, is so-called idiosyncratic demand from families that wish to impress a particular tone on their children's education—certain religious values, for example—that, by definition, is difficult to find in public schools.

Recent history in Latin America, however, suggests that something more than social groups with special preferences is at stake. It could be called "government failure" in contrast to the usual expression of "market failure"—that is, a situation in which the supply of public education no longer provides the minimum quantity or quality to satisfy the demand of a large number of the families that would normally send their children to schools administered directly by the state. In these circumstances, the private sector comes in to fill a void that, under standard economic and social conditions, would have been filled by the public school.

The most extreme cases of this phenomenon can be found in the well-known models of independent schools in various countries of Central America, of which the EDUCO (*Educación con participación de la comunidad* or Community-Managed Schools Program) system is probably the best known. The origin of this network of schools is a quasi-Hobbesian situation, in which the state no longer has control—even in the capacity to govern and maintain a monopoly on violence—over certain areas of its territory. This makes it incapable of meeting the demand for education, but this demand creates its own supply in the form of schools that did not originally belong to the formal education system, with teachers directly hired by the communities in which they work, creating a completely different employment relationship from the usual one in conventional education systems.[15]

Other forms of private education provision have also emerged, closely related to some degree of government failure. Revealingly, the institutional slogan of the *Fe y Alegría* school network is "the school where the asphalt ends," transmitting in a phrase the idea that it is devoted to serving poor children, specializing in localities that regular education services cannot always reach, or where they have problems in establishing and consolidating themselves.

The most important institutional development in the case of private schools is the gradual process through which the public systems have begun to channel the activity of private providers of education so that they become aligned with the quality, efficiency, and equity objectives of society.

An Opportunity for Mutual Gains

The experience of countries with schools administered by nongovernmental bodies, but that receive public financing, is especially relevant in this context. The quality and capacity of private schools vary as much or more than those in the public sector, which makes any conclusion about the superiority of one type of school over another inappropriate. Several studies show that, for a given level of quality, private schools tend to operate with lower costs. The management and incentives scheme with which they operate is usually different from that of the public schools, resulting in more proactive directors with a more significant margin for action, greater involvement of parents in running the school, better teaching support, and better enforcement of rules. Also, the size of private schools is generally restricted because of the low ability to pay of many families that, although they appreciate the quality that some private schools have to offer, are unable to afford private education.

In such situations, there is much space for cooperation between the public sector and private education providers. With public financing, private schools could expand a low-cost supply of education, and provide their services to low-income populations, while the public system could benefit from the savings that these schools produce, as well as from the administrative and teaching expertise of the private sector with a view to delivering better education to children living in poverty, especially in areas that are remote or unreachable by the public system. This space for mutual gains is being deliberately exploited by various Latin American countries with a variety of approaches, depending on their institutional history and regulatory capacities.

Three Approaches to Public–Private Partnerships

Leaving aside EDUCO, which emerged from extreme needs in extraordinary circumstances, three types of public–private partnerships can be illustrated from cases that have been studied in depth:

- The expansion of private supply through public subsidies granted to students, in essence the education voucher originally proposed by Milton Friedman (1955), was initiated by Chile in the mid-1980s, generating rapid growth of private supply, eventually representing about 40 percent of enrollment in primary and secondary education. In this scheme, the financing "follows the child," so a family can send their children to public or private schools wherever they are (except for a small group of schools with very high-income clientele) (Peirano and Vargas 2004).
- The "bidding" model, which turns public schools over to private providers is exemplified in its purest state by the concession schools of the Bogotá District in Colombia. In this case, the public sector builds the schools needed to expand enrollment but invites private bidders to propose school administration schemes in exchange for a subsidy per student. After selecting the winning bid, an agreement is signed with the private entity—generally a school or private school network of recognized quality—to achieve certain results in enrollment and learning in a defined time frame (Villa and Duarte 2004).
- The "negotiated agreement" model is characterized by a global multiyear agreement negotiated between the government and a group of private education networks. Under the agreement, the government finances a number of privately administered schools in exchange for meeting certain targets, emphasizing children from low-income families or isolated rural or marginal urban areas. This model has achieved a formal and well-institutionalized expression in Venezuela in the agreement between the Ministry of Education and AVEC (Venezuelan Catholic Schools Association), to finance the activities of *Fe y Alegría* and other networks of Catholic schools. These arrangements have some predictability

and flexibility so that the networks can apply for expansions every year when unmet needs are demonstrated and they have the installed capacity to respond to the growing demand for education from certain communities (González and Arévalo 2004).

Controversy over Impact

Although cost-effectiveness is an advantage shared by all three approaches to public–private partnerships in education, normally additional benefits are expected to come from other sources specific to each approach.

In the vouchers model, a quasi-market for education is stimulated by the introduction of competitive pressures between schools. In this case, a mechanism is created in which the consolidation of a good reputation is essential for privately administered schools—this good reputation supposedly must come from results. The public schools in Chile depend on the municipality, which should also respond to incentives to make continuous improvements created by the pressures caused by private competition and other municipalities.

Measuring these potential benefits is a recurring theme in recent education research. Given that Chile is still one of very few countries, if not the only one, that have adopted a school system based on vouchers, and given the excellent database provided by SIMCE (*Sistema Nacional de Medición de Calidad de la Educación*, or National System for the Measurement of the Quality of Education), abundant quantitative analyses have produced observable benefits in the quality of education and offer a comparison between private subsidized schools and public schools. The controversy centers on calibrating the consequences of the effect of adverse selection, where the best students tend to be attracted to the few subsidized private schools, leaving the municipal system with an overwhelming concentration of less advantaged students. In contrast, the results could be better because the mix of inputs in the private subsidized schools tends to be more efficient, and because of the positive externalities of competition.[16] Given that the Chilean experience constitutes by far the largest experiment with the voucher model, the debates and efforts to obtain more refined results through the application of increasingly sophisticated analytical methods are unlikely to end soon.

In the Bogotá concession schools, the advantages of a public–private alliance should come from the competition to win the bidding process, and from better-defined, results-oriented agreements, with transparent rules for renewal, and sanctions and rewards, instead of the traditional systems based on measurement of inputs better suited to the conventional organization of public school systems. The Bogotá case has shown that it is possible in practice to write performance contracts that seem compatible with creating the correct incentives so that administrators and teachers maximize the welfare and learning of children. Although the concessions schools are in full operation and abundant qualitative observations indicate that they seem to deliver good results, the fact that the experience is very recent prevents any conclusive evaluations.

In the model based on an AVEC-style convention, the advantages of competition do not exist because from the start the public subsidies are restricted to schools previously declared eligible. Likewise, this model does not produce the efficiency expected of a bidding model or, in the present form of the convention, from the presence of performance agreements. The benefits come from the fact that the public subsidy expands the radius of action of schools that have contractual relations aimed at obtaining good results, such as proactive directors and teachers who are better motivated or receive better teaching support; in short, a more efficient school management model. The available research, concentrated on the *Fe y Alegría* network schools, shows some positive intermediate indicators—reduction of repetition, over-age and dropout rates—particularly in comparison with the public schools, although this superiority does not apply consistently to learning results (Bruni-Celli 2005; Navarro and de la Cruz 1998). Some *Fe y Alegría* schools report better results than comparable public schools, but not all or always, which suggests the model does not give uniformly superior learning results.

It is also clear that the first model is designed to improve efficiency, while the second and third are related more directly to the objectives of equity and access for the most disadvantaged children and young people. For all three, improvement of the quality of learning is a primary goal.

Selecting the Model Best for Each Circumstance

In addition to the illustrative cases that have been developed in detail, similar models have been attempted in other contexts in the region. Las Condes municipality in Santiago, Chile, has experimented with a concession model. Various Latin American countries have extensive networks of private schools that have reached agreements with the public sector with varying degrees of definition and stability, such as Bolivia and, at least partly, Peru. The *Fe y Alegría* schools operate in a dozen countries in the region, in all cases under some arrangement that gives them access to public subsidies, although in no case have these arrangements reached the formal level of the Venezuelan agreement. Some governments have not revised their practices of public subsidies for private education, and continue to misuse the space available for obtaining public benefits through public-private partnerships, even producing effects that are openly contrary to public policy, such as the maintenance of large public subsidies for elite private schools, as in Argentina. In cases of "no regulation" like these, the transaction costs of the relation between private education providers and the government tend to be very high. The nongovernmental schools have difficulty predicting what will happen the next year in relation to growth and stability because the subsidy has to be renegotiated annually.

Neither can it be maintained that one of the three models is superior in all circumstances. Experience has conclusively shown that the voucher model requires high levels of information and supervision, which are not available in any ministry of education. Although the experience with the bidding model is limited, at first sight the information costs are also considerable. In contrast, the "negotiated agreement" model seems to be more easily adapted to situations in which the capacity to supervise the conduct and quality of private supply is much more limited. The introduction of this model, however, is valuable only to the extent that, by making the conduct of the public sector predictable, it opens the way for the orderly development of private provision in line with public priorities.

If this conclusion is accepted, each country faces a trade-off between, on the one hand, the institutional and informational complexity required to operate a system based on incentives and highly efficient contracts, and, on the other hand, information simplicity accompanied by higher transaction costs and lower incentives for efficiency in relations between government and private providers of education. Each country has to choose an optimal point between these extremes based on their particular characteristics and institutional capacities (Navarro 2004).

Latin American education systems are overwhelmingly public and no doubt will continue to be so. The size of the challenges and the weakness of the state show, however, that no effort should be spared in improving education in the region. Education policy must assimilate as its own the principle that responsibility for education is not only a matter for the state but also for society in the broadest sense. Policy makers should welcome all the nongovernmental energy that is available for channeling into the education sector, exploiting it to the maximum and, from the public policy point of view, integrating it the best possible way into the objectives of education policy.

Education Results and Reforms

The 1990s saw significant progress in the performance of education systems in Latin America. Table 12.3 compares the enrollment rates for 1990 and 2000 in 12 countries in the region for various age groups, and reveals the breadth of the progress—extraordinary in Brazil and Nicaragua. The only countries that exhibit reversals in all three age groups are Colombia and Ecuador, possibly due to the effects of their deep economic recessions toward the end the of the 1990s.

The results shown in table 12.4 present a very similar conclusion, this time based on a comparison of average years of enrollment. Again, in most countries, children and young people improved their educational achievements in the 1990s.

These advances, however, left a number of critical problems in Latin American education in relation to equity and the quality of learning

Table 12.3 Enrollment Rates, 1990 and 2000 (percent)

Country	Ages 6–11			Ages 12–14			Ages 15–19		
	2000	1990	Change	2000	1990	Change	2000	1990	Change
Brazil	96.76	86.73	10.03	94.04	80.04	14.00	68.14	50.63	17.51
Colombia	92.11	93.46	-1.35	84.96	91.85	-6.90	55.18	65.45	-10.27
Dominican Republic	95.65	93.58	2.08	97.28	96.34	0.93	74.53	73.16	1.37
Ecuador	93.35	96.87	-3.52	80.26	92.34	-12.08	55.93	70.64	-14.71
Honduras	83.77	78.15	5.62	68.48	67.55	0.92	35.01	29.46	5.56
Mexico	96.54	96.68	-0.14	88.41	83.80	4.60	88.41	83.80	4.60
Nicaragua	83.85	64.15	19.70	82.39	63.04	19.35	49.58	35.49	14.09
Panama	97.79	95.20	2.60	92.78	86.52	6.27	65.09	58.22	6.87
Paraguay	94.12	92.55	1.57	87.56	89.24	-1.68	55.13	56.33	-1.21
Peru	96.92	95.08	1.85	91.97	93.82	-1.85	57.89	67.51	-9.62
Uruguay	98.35	97.80	0.55	93.85	91.67	2.18	63.92	61.61	2.31
Venezuela	96.37	95.94	0.44	92.02	91.67	0.35	57.52	58.83	-1.31

Source: Marshall 2005.

Table 12.4 Years of Enrollment, 1990 and 2000

Country	Ages 6–11			Ages 12–14			Ages 15–19		
	2000	1990	Change	2000	1990	Change	2000	1990	Change
Brazil	2.48	2.03	0.44	5.24	4.41	0.83	7.08	6.04	1.04
Colombia	1.84	2.05	–0.21	5.29	5.54	–0.25	7.86	7.89	–0.03
Dominican Republic	2.12	2.30	–0.19	5.28	5.78	–0.49	7.88	8.16	–0.28
Ecuador	2.86	2.27	0.59	6.29	6.10	0.19	8.41	8.70	–0.29
Honduras	1.39	1.22	0.17	4.50	3.96	0.54	6.01	5.17	0.84
Mexico	2.31	1.43	0.88	6.22	4.96	1.26	8.45	6.80	1.65
Nicaragua	1.48	1.38	0.11	4.42	3.58	0.84	6.13	5.00	1.13
Panama	2.15	2.18	–0.03	6.11	5.91	0.19	8.92	8.50	0.43
Paraguay	1.89	1.56	0.34	5.03	5.26	–0.23	7.50	7.84	–0.34
Peru	2.03	1.97	0.06	5.56	5.65	–0.09	7.92	8.57	–0.66
Uruguay	2.45	2.16	0.29	6.28	6.14	0.14	8.57	8.30	0.27
Venezuela	2.38	2.35	0.03	6.07	5.90	0.17	8.07	7.77	0.30

Source: Marshall 2005.

unresolved. Table 12.5 compares the enrollment ratio for children and young people from households in the first quintile of income distribution with those from households in the fifth quintile. In all countries, the participation of children and young people in the school system is very unequal, particularly at postprimary ages. In the countries with lower incomes, and Brazil, this difference extends even to children of primary school age. Although the new Latin American generations generally have higher education achievement, and the goal of universal primary education is no longer remote, considerable inequalities persist in access to education.

However, it is important to ask how much headway education in Latin America has made compared with other regions of the world, because in a knowledge-intensive globalized economy with high mobility of factors of production, countries need to be able to attract investments and generate well-paying jobs, specifically in export sectors. The latest international comparative measurements reveal that the region's performance in quality of education leaves a lot to be desired. Not only are the learning results of Latin American countries that have participated in the TIMMS or PISA tests well below OECD countries, expected spending on education per student is also lower (Bruneforth, Motivans, and Zhang 2004).[17]

Unfortunately, sufficient research has not been done to establish whether reforms such as those described in this chapter explain the mixed results of the education systems during the last decade. Several of the reforms—Brazil's FUNDEF, for example—have been associated with extraordinary advances in education. It cannot be concluded, however, that a specific type of reform produces significant impacts because in each country the reforms are part of complex packages of education policies, which range from institutional reforms such as those described here to pure and simple school construction.

In the framework of these "packages," two regularities can be noted:

- The most frequent reforms are those aligned with the preferences of the teachers' unions, while those that never go through, or only go through under extremely exceptional conditions, are the ones that are frontally opposed by the teachers' unions (Navarro 2005). So, despite the reformist zeal of recent years, little has been done to introduce evaluation or incentives into the teaching career. Decentralization, often opposed by teachers' unions, has generally made headway when it is stipulated that decentralization will not affect the national-level functioning and influence of the union.
- Those areas in which some solid achievements have been made in the way the state functions are those in which it has been feasible to create general agreements on medium- and long-term objectives, and to maintain cooperation between the main actors in education policy. The clearest case is the acquisition of capacities to evaluate the performance of education systems, and also to evaluate education decentralization where it has been successful.

Table 12.5 Comparison of Enrollment Rates in Income Distribution, Quintiles 1 and 5

Country	Ages 6–11 Quintile 1	Ages 6–11 Quintile 5	Ages 6–11 Gap	Ages 12–14 Quintile 1	Ages 12–14 Quintile 5	Ages 12–14 Gap	Ages 15–19 Quintile 1	Ages 15–19 Quintile 5	Ages 15–19 Gap
Argentina	98.0	99.7	1.7	96.4	99.0	2.6	67.7	87.5	19.8
Brazil	90.7	98.7	8.0	90.9	98.8	7.9	61.3	82.5	21.2
Bolivia	90.5	97.4	6.9	71.2	97.1	25.9	38.9	81.7	42.8
Chile	97.0	97.7	0.7	96.5	98.6	2.1	62.9	63.7	0.8
Colombia	89.6	96.7	7.1	80.1	92.8	12.7	53.5	66.1	12.6
Costa Rica	93.7	98.5	4.8	76.9	96.3	19.4	92.2	98.5	6.3
Dominican Republic	94.0	99.2	5.2	96.1	99.6	3.5	74.8	79.5	4.7
Ecuador	92.3	96.1	3.8	77.3	90.8	13.5	47.4	78.2	30.8
El Salvador	76.9	97.1	20.2	79.6	93.9	14.3	43.8	65.4	21.6
Guatemala	75.5	94.7	19.2	67.7	86.7	19.0	26.1	54.8	28.7
Honduras	76.1	92.8	16.7	59.8	84.1	24.3	24.2	50.4	26.2
Mexico	93.6	99.0	5.4	82.0	98.0	16.0	30.7	70.1	39.4
Nicaragua	81.0	89.5	8.5	81.0	83.5	2.5	43.5	47.5	4.0
Panama	96.3	99.6	3.3	83.8	97.1	13.3	46.4	76.8	30.4
Paraguay	91.1	98.8	7.7	77.4	94.8	17.4	42.6	74.6	32.0
Peru	94.3	97.6	3.3	86.4	94.4	8.0	49.2	60.1	10.9
Uruguay	97.9	100.0	2.1	84.1	97.6	13.5	43.1	83.9	40.8
Venezuela	93.9	98.1	4.2	88.1	96.4	8.3	50.0	66.6	16.6

Source: Marshall 2005.

This does not necessarily mean that the reforms discussed in this chapter lack importance and do not affect the underlying problems of education. Many recent education policies have had beneficial effects. But a definite bias can be detected in the reforms as described above; on the reasonable assumption that progress in education quality depends mainly on a substantial improvement in teaching and therefore on teacher performance—by definition, objectives only realizable over rather long periods—the corollary has to be that reform has had less effect on quality than on other areas, such as access and equity.

On balance, the opinion that the recent reforms have failed cannot be endorsed: in many respects, the education results of the period have been favorable. But it can be stated that, whatever the achievements have been, they did not produce clear progress on important problems in Latin American education, particularly its low quality. Some specific and valuable lessons have been learned, and perhaps can now lead to a better understanding of the problems facing education reform. The next section presents conclusions in an effort to synthesize these lessons.

Conclusion: Limits and Possibilities of State Reform in Education

The preceding review shows the state has transformed the education sector in three important respects:

- The level of government responsible for providing or regulating education has been diversified, as illustrated by decentralization reforms.
- Public capacities have been built as a result of the strengthening of central government institutions in critical areas, such as education assessment.
- The role of the state as a direct provider of education has changed in some cases—including a few countries and, for the most part, within the boundaries of programs that do not directly challenge the mainstream public education system—to financier and regulator of private supply, as illustrated by public-private partnerships.

Every Latin American country followed at least one of these paths during the last two decades. Several tried two or three at the same time. From this rich experience of successes and failures, achievements, and lessons learned, some general messages emerge:

- These reforms are feasible, despite enormous difficulties. Education decentralization failed or was distorted in various cases, but also produced clear, observable benefits in others. Institutional strengthening of the education ministries is often considered a lost cause by external observers, but the creation and strengthening of national assessment systems shows that it is possible, with an adequate combination of consistency, political will, and international and regional cooperation. The move to models that exploit the potential of private education providers in conjunction with the goals of public policy is probably the most difficult of all the reforms because of the basic changes in the function of the state that are involved; even so, it has been making progress in the region.

- There is no unique model for implementing these reforms. Each country must consider its own historical, cultural, and geographical conditions, particularly the strengths and weaknesses of the public administration, and choose the model that best fits with these conditions.

- From the point of view of the stability of education policies, and their coherence and capacity to serve the public interest, on balance, the institutionally oriented education reforms—which have directly affected the structure, functions, or capacities of the state—are positive. However, what cannot be ignored are the numerous, and sometimes costly, errors that have been committed by the incomplete adoption of some of these reforms, with unrealistic expectations or with lack of sensitivity to local conditions.

- The reforms have not led to a significant improvement in the quality of learning. Although it could be argued that decentralization has improved equity because of the expanded enrollment achieved by many subnational governments and subsidized private networks, quality remains elusive. This suggests that the institutional reforms in education have to be linked with policies that aim to affect what takes place in the classroom.

An "intelligent state," in terms of education, is capable of distributing the responsibility for the provision of education services at the optimal level of government, succeeds in extracting the greatest social benefit from alliances with private education providers, and is capable of obtaining information on education results and using it effectively (Wolf and de Moura Castro 2003). Latin America has made good progress toward a state of this type, but there is still a long way to go, and not all countries are positioned equally. Deepening the institutional education reforms, which involves changes in the way the state functions, continues to be a challenge for education policy makers.

Notes

1. Gajardo (2003) recently produced an extensive and well-organized review of the reforms of the 1990s; the volume edited by Gajardo and Puryear (2003) is an excellent general introduction to the subject of education reform in Latin America. The International Commission on Education, Equity and Economic Competitive-

ness in Latin America and the Caribbean produced in 2001 a report full of information and reviews on reform in the region (PREAL 2001). Navarro, Carnoy, and de Moura Castro (2000) discuss the main lines of the reforms in the period. Each country or subregion has considerable sources for study: for Chile see Cox (2004), OECD (2004), and Delannoy (2000). Carnoy and others (2004) edited a comprehensive comparative analysis of the reforms in Argentina, Chile, and Uruguay. Recent reviews of the reforms in Argentina and the results can be found in Rivas (2004) and Tedesco (2005). The most important source for the Bolivian case is Contreras and Talavera Simoni (2004). Pardo (1999) contains analysis of the reforms in Mexico during the period the chapter is concerned with, and the most recent volume published by CENEVAL (2004) offers ample information on the impacts of the reforms in that country. An excellent description of the reforms in Uruguay can be found in ANEP (2000). The report of the Central American Commission for Education Reform (2003) presents an excellence synthesis of the achievements and challenges of education policy in that region (PREAL 2003); a volume edited by Navarro and others (2000) collects cases of education reform throughout the region, especially Central America and the Dominican Republic; the reforms in the latter country can be reviewed in more depth in Alvarez (2004). The building of national agreements on education as the basis for reforms in El Salvador has been well described and contextualized in Reimers and McGinn (1997). De Moura Castro (2003) presents a compact review of education reforms in Brazil in the 1990s, and many other sources cover particular aspects of education in Brazil in recent years. For Colombia, see Aldana and Caballero (1997). At least three important works have appeared in recent years that review Latin American education reforms emphasizing aspects of political economy and the mechanism of adoption and implementation of the reforms rather than their impact on education as such. They deal with Argentina, Bolivia, Brazil, Chile, Colombia, Ecuador, Mexico, Nicaragua, and Venezuela. These works are Angell, Lowden, and Thorp (2001), Grindle (2004), and Kauffman and Nelson (2004).

2. Although there are wide variations in the specific details as to which education activities or responsibilities have been transferred in the numerous decentralization processes, they typically include maintenance of school infrastructure, teacher pay, and management of teaching staff. In general, control of curriculum has remained in the hands of national authorities, although opening a space to accommodate regional and local issues. The responsibility for evaluating the system has generally remained under central control.

3. The analysis of these cases has produced an abundant literature: McGinn and Street (1986); Winkler (1989); Espínola (1997); Hanson (1997); Winkler and Gershberg (2000); Raczynski and Serrano (2001); Kaufman and Nelson (2004), among others.

4. In its curious history, the argument in favor of decentralization shifted in 10 years—roughly from 1990 to 2000—from being on the defensive as a technocratic imposition that ignored national education traditions, to becoming a cultural imperative, dictated by the ethnic, regional, and racial diversity of the countries.

5. It is interesting to note, however, that sometimes—for example, the reform in Minas Gerais state in Brazil—policies, such as promoting school autonomy, have been deliberately proposed with the objective of rescuing schools from the corruption and political cronyism that, at certain times and places, has marked the state and municipal administration of education (dos Mares Guia 1999).

6. This general description of the institutional effects of education decentralization has been documented for various countries, but probably the most detailed and in-depth study was done by the Centro de Implementación de Políticas Públicas para la Equidad y el Crecimiento (CIPPEC) in Argentina (Rivas 2004). Adding to factors such as those mentioned above, this study finds a positive association between growth of enrollment and the implementation of reforms in the Argentinian provinces, although in some of them the central government ended up "taking

over" decentralization and its main initiatives by putting them in the hands of teams resident in the provinces but financed by the central ministry. The study concludes with a positive balance of the decentralization process of the 1990s but identifies a high level of conflict and fragmentation—heterogeneous implementation and results of the reform—as features of the Argentinian experience.

7. A more extensive treatment of the implications of the entry of a third important actor into the basic game of education policy making can be found in Navarro (2005). A deeper analysis of the issue of the economics of education reform is beyond the scope of this chapter.

8. A·weighty argument used in all cases to stop or delay education decentralization was the low level of management capacity in subnational governments. Although this factor is worth taking into account in the design of decentralization policies, the experience of the last two decades indicates that, paradoxically, the best way to develop the capacity of subnational governments is to give them responsibilities. It is not easy to find cases of institutional strengthening of municipalities or provinces without a real transfer of power to these levels.

9. A very complete review of the recent trend in learning evaluation systems in Latin America can be found in Ferrer (2005).

10. In contrast, for example, to the strong criticism in the United States of the use of standardized learning tests as a basic part of education policy.

11. Many Latin American countries have regularly participated in the most recognized international comparative tests of student performance, including TIMSS (Third International Math and Science Study), PISA (Program for International Student Assessment), and PIRLS (Program in International Reading Literacy Study). Most have participated in an initiative of this type that originated in the region: the Latin American Laboratory of Education Quality, *Laboratorio Latinamericano de Evaluación de la Calidad de la Educación* (LLECE), organized by UNESCO-OREALC.

12. Tyler and Bernasconi (2002) discuss the principles on which this change in the action of the state in higher education was founded, and describe the progress made in the region, mainly in Central America. The cases of Argentina, Brazil, and Chile can be found in Mora and Fernández-Lamarra (2005).

13. In comparing various national learning tests for third and fourth grade of primary education in Paraguay, El Salvador, Ecuador, Honduras, Brazil, and Chile, a recent report states that in three of the six countries only between 1 percent and 33 percent of the students in the socioeconomically lower half of the student body could correctly answer comprehension questions on a written test. In the other three countries the correct proportion of answers was indistinguishable from random answers. These results are for 2001 (Schiefelbein 2004).

14. Although there is considerable variability from country to country, the fraction of GDP devoted to education expenditure by the public sector grew from 4.1 percent to 4.9 percent between 1990 and 2000 (Bruneforth, Motivans, and Zhang 2004). Unfortunately for the discussion in this chapter, there is no systematic account of how much education expenditure relates to each level of regional government.

15. After the armed conflict, El Salvador put through a cautious process of integrating EDUCO schools into the formal system, in an effort not to lose the main advantages of the original spontaneous and autonomous model.

16. A recent account of the scientific debate on the effects of the Chilean voucher system can be found in Contreras and others (2005). Important background on the debate can be found in the works of Aedo and Larrañaga (1994); Aedo and Sapelli (2001); Hsieh and Urquiola (2002); McEwan and Carnoy (1999); and Mizala and Romaguera (2000).

17. A benchmarking exercise of Latin American education for an extensive range of aspects and indicators can be found in IDB (2006).

References

Aedo, Christian, and Oswaldo Larrañaga. 1994. "Sistema de entrega de los servicios sociales: La experiencia Chilena." In *Sistemas de Entrega de los Servicios Sociales: Una Agenda para la Reforma*, ed. C. Aedo and O. Larrañaga. Washington, DC: Inter-American Development Bank.

Aedo, Christian, and C. Sapelli. 2001. "El sistema de vouchers en educación: Una revisión de la teoría y evidencia empírica para Chile." ILADES Georgetown University Working Paper No. 133, Georgetown University, Washington, DC.

Aldana, Eduardo, and Piedad Caballero, eds. 1997. "La reforma educativa en Colombia: Desafíos y perspectivas." PREAL-Instituto SER, Bogotá, DC, Colombia.

Alvarez, Carola. 2004. "La Educación en la República Dominicana: Logros y Desafíos Pendientes." Inter-American Development Bank, Washington, DC.

ANEP (Administración Nacional de Educación Pública). 2000. "Una visión integral del proceso de reforma educativa en Uruguay: 1995–1999." Administración Nacional de Educación Pública, Montevideo, Uruguay.

Angell, Alan, Pamela Lowden, and Rosemary Thorp. 2001. *Decentralizing Development: The Political Economy of Institutional Change in Colombia and Chile.* Great Britain: Oxford University Press.

Arcia, Gustavo, and Humberto Belli. 2001. "La autonomía escolar en Nicaragua: Reestableciendo el contrato social." Working Paper No. 21, PREAL, Santiago, Chile.

Arellano, José Pablo. 2005. "Prioridades estratégicas para mejorar la calidad de la educación en Chile." Fundación Chile, Santiago, Chile.

Bruneforth, Michael, Albert Motivans, and Yanhong Zhang. 2004. "Investing in the Future: Financing the Expansion of Educational Opportunity in Latin America and the Caribbean." Working paper, UNESCO Institute for Statistics, Montreal, Quebec, Canada. http://www.uis.unesco.org/ev.php?ID=5743_201 &ID2=DO_TOPIC.

Bruni-Celli, Josefina. 2005. "Evaluación de la calidad de la educación de Fe y Alegría." Instituto de Estudios Superiores de Administración, Caracas, Venezuela.

Carnoy, Martin, G. Cosse, and C. Cox. 2004. *Las Reformas Educativas en la Década de 1990: Un estudio comparado de Argentina, Chile y Uruguay.* Buenos Aires, Argentina: Banco Interamericano de Desarrollo and Ministerios de Educación de Argentina, Chile y Uruguay.

CENEVAL (Centro Nacional de Evaluación para la Educación Superior). 2004. "Evaluación de la Educación en México." Centro Nacional de Evaluación para la Educación Superior, Mexico City.

Contreras, Dante, Oswaldo Larrañaga, Lorena Flores, Félix Lobato, and Víctor Macías. 2005. "Políticas educacionales en Chile: Vouchers, concentración, incentivos y rendimiento." In *Uso e impacto de la información educativa en América Latina*, ed. Santiago Cueto. Santiago, Chile: PREAL.

Contreras, Manuel, and María Luisa Talavera Simoni. 2004. *Examen Parcial: La Reforma Educativa Boliviana 1992–2002.* La Paz, Bolivia: PIEB-ASDI.

Cox, Christian. 2004. "Las políticas educacionales de Chile en las últimas dos décadas del siglo XX: Compromiso público e instrumentos de Estado y mercado." In *Las Reformas Educativas en la Década de 1990: Un estudio comparado de Argentina, Chile y Uruguay*, ed. Martin Carnoy, G. Cosse, and C. Cox. Buenos

Aires, Argentina: Banco Interamericano de Desarrollo and Ministerios de Educación de Argentina, Chile y Uruguay.

Cueto, Santiago, ed. 2005. *Uso e impacto de la información educativa en América Latina.* PREAL.

Delannoy, Francoise. 2000. *Education Reforms in Chile, 1980–98: A Lesson in Pragmatism.* Washington, DC: World Bank.

De Moura Castro, Claudio. 2003. *Despertar do Gigante: Com menos ufanismo e mais directo, a educaçâo Brasileira acorda.* Belo Horizonte: Pitágoras.

Dos Mares Guia, Walfrido. 1999. "As reformas educationais no estado de Minas Gerais." In *Reformas Educacionais e Autonomia das Escolas.* Washington, DC: World Bank.

Draibe, Sonia M. 2004."Federal Leverage in a Decentralized System: Education Reform in Brazil." In *Crucial Needs, Weak Incentives: Social Sector Reform, Democratization, and Globalization in Latin America.* Washington, DC: Woodrow Wilson Center Press.

Espínola, Viola. 1997. "Descentralización del sistema educativo en Chile: Impacto en la gestión de las escuelas." Report No. 10, Human Development Group, World Bank, Washington, DC.

——. 2000. "Autonomía escolar: Factores que contribuyen a una escuela más efectiva." Inter-American Development Bank, Washington, DC.

Ferrer, Guillermo. 2005. "Estado de situación de los sistemas nacionales de medición de los logros de aprendizaje en América Latina." PREAL, Washington, DC.

Friedman, Milton. 1955. "The Role of Government in Education." In *Economics and the Public Interest*, ed. Robert A. Solo. Livingston, NJ: Rutgers University Press.

Gajardo, Marcela. 2003. "Reformas Educativas en América Latina: Balance de una década." In *Formas y Reformas de la Educación en América Latina*, ed. Marcela Gajardo and Jeffrey M. Puryear. Santiago, Chile: PREAL.

Gajardo, Marcela, and Jeffrey M. Puryear, eds. 2003. *Formas y Reformas de la Educación en América Latina.* Santiago, Chile: PREAL.

Galiani, Sebastián, and E. Shargrodsky. 2002. "Evaluating the Impact of School Decentralization on Educational Quality." *Economía* 2 (2): 275–302.

González, Rosa Amelia, and Gregorio Arévalo. 2004. "El caso de las escuelas católicas subvencionadas en Venezuela." In *Alianzas público-privadas en educación: innovaciones en América Latina*, ed. Juan Carlos Navarro, Jaime Vargas, Jesús Duarte, and Gregorio Arévalo. Washington, DC: Inter-American Development Bank.

Grindle, Merilee. 2004. *Despite the Odds: The Contentious Politics of Education Reform.* Trenton, NJ: Princeton University Press.

Guimaraes Castro, Maria Helena. 2002. "Sistemas emergentes de evaluación y evaluación: El caso de Brasil. Seminario Internacional sobre Educación Superior Ciencia y Tecnología en América Latina y el Caribe: Respuestas frente a la expansión y la diversificación." Banco Interamericano de Desarrollo, Fortaleza, Brazil.

Gunnarsson, Victoria, Meter F. Orazem, Mario Sánchez, and Aimee Verdisco. 2004. "Decentralization and Student Achievement: International Evidence on the Roles of School Autonomy and Community Participation." Inter-American Development Bank, Washington, DC.

Iaies, Gustavo, ed. 2003. *Evaluar las evaluaciones. Una mirada política acerca de las evaluaciones de la calidad educativa.* Buenos Aires, Argentina: IIPE-UNESCO.

IDB (Inter-American Development Bank). 2006. "Education in Latin America: A Statistical Profile." IDB-Education Unit, Washington, DC.

Hanson, Mark E. 1997. "La descentralización educacional: Problemas y retos." Working Paper No. 9, PREAL, Santiago, Chile.

Hsieh, C., and M. Urquiola. 2002. "When Schools Compete, How Do They Compete? An Assessment of Chile's Nationwide School Voucher Program." Occasional Paper No 43, National Center for the Study of Privatization in Education. January.

Kauffman, Robert R., and Joan M. Nelson. 2004. *Crucial Needs, Weak Incentives: Social Sector Reform, Democratization, and Globalization in Latin America.* Washington, DC: Woodrow Wilson Center Press. Copublished by the Johns Hopkins University Press.

King, Elizabeth M., Laura Rawlings, and Berk Ozler. 1996. "Nicaragua's School Autonomy Reform: A First Look." World Bank, Washington, DC.

Lowden, P. 2004. "Education Reform in Colombia: Elusive Quest for Effectiveness." In *Crucial Needs, Weak Incentives. Social Sector Reform, Democratization and Globalization in Latin America,* ed. Robert K. Kauffman and Joan Nelson. Washington, DC: Woodrow Wilson Center Press. Copublished by the Johns Hopkins University Press.

Marshall, Jeffrey. 2005. "Social Exclusion in Education in Latin America and the Caribbean." Inter-American Development Bank, Washington, DC.

McEwan, Patrick, and Martin Carnoy. 1999. "The Effectiveness and Efficiency of Private Schools in Chile's Voucher System." *Education Evaluation and Policy Analysis* 22: 213–40.

McGinn, Noel, and Susan Street. 1986. "La descentralización educacional en América Latina: ¿Política nacional o lucha de facciones?" *La Educación.* 99: 20–45.

Mizala, Alejandra, and Pilar Romaguera. 2000. "School Performance and Choice: The Chilean Experience." *Journal of Human Resources* 35 (2): 392–417.

Mora, José-Ginés, and Norberto Fernández-Lamarra. 2005. "Educación superior: convergencia entre América Latina y Europa. Proceso de evaluación y acreditación de la calidad." Proyecto Alfa-Acre, Comisión Europea, Universidad Nacional Tres de Febrero, Buenos Aires, Argentina.

Navarro, Juan Carlos. 2000. "The Social Consequences of Political Reforms: Decentralization and Social Policy in Venezuela." In *Social Development in Latin America: The Politics of Reform,* ed. Joseph S. Tulchin and Allison M. Garland. Boulder, CO: Woodrow Wilson Center and Lynne Rienner Publishers.

———. 2004. "Conclusiones." In *Alianzas público-privadas en educación: innovaciones en América Latina,* ed. Juan Carlos Navarro, Jaime Vargas, Jesús Duarte, and Gregorio Arévalo. Washington, DC: Inter-American Development Bank.

———. 2005. "One Core Conflict, Diverse Arenas: The Interplay Between Sector-Specific and Nationwide Political Dynamics in the Education Reforms of Latin America." Inter-American Development Bank, Washington, DC.

Navarro, Juan Carlos, Martin Carnoy, and Claudio de Moura Castro. 2000. "La reforma educativa en América Latina: Temas, componentes e instrumentos." In *Perspectivas sobre la Reforma Educativa: América Central en el contexto de políticas de educación de las Américas,* ed. Juan Carlos Navarro, Katherine Taylor, Andrés Bernasconi, and Lewis Tyler. Washington, DC: Inter-American Development Bank, Harvard Institute for International Development, and US Agency for International Development (USAID).

Navarro, Juan Carlos, and Rafael de la Cruz. 1998. "Escuelas federales,estatales y sin fines de lucro en Venezuela." In *La organización marca la diferencia. Educación y Salud en América Latina*, ed. William Savedoff. Washington DC: Inter-American Development Bank.

Navarro, Juan Carlos, Jaime Vargas, Jesús Duarte, and Gregorio Arévalo, eds. 2004. *Alianzas público-privadas en educación: innovaciones en América Latina.* Washington, DC: Inter-American Development Bank.

OECD (Organisation for Economic Co-operation and Development). 2004. *Reviews of National Policies for Education: Chile.* Paris, France.

Paes de Barros, Ricardo, and Rosane Mendonca. 1998. "El impacto de tres innovaciones institucionales en la educación brasileña." In *La organización marca la diferencia. Educación y Salud en América Latina*, ed. William Savedoff. Washington, DC: Inter-American Development Bank.

Pardo, María del Carmen, ed. 1999. *Federalización e innovación educativa en México.* Mexico City: El Colegio de México.

Peirano, Claudia, and Jaime Vargas. 2004. "Escuelas privadas con financiamiento público en Chile." In *Alianzas público-privadas en educación: innovaciones en América Latina*, ed. Juan Carlos Navarro, Jaime Vargas, Jesús Duarte, and Gregorio Arévalo. Washington, DC: Inter-American Development Bank.

PREAL. 2000. "Creando Autonomía en las Escuelas." PREAL, Santiago, Chile.

———. 2001. *Quedándonos Atrás: Un informe del progreso educativo en América Latina.* Informe de la Comisión Internacional sobre Educación, Equidad y Competitividad Económica en América Latina y el Caribe. Santiago, Chile.

———. 2003. Comisión Centroamericana para la Reforma Educativa. 2003. "Es Hora de Actuar: Informe de progreso educativo en Centroamérica y la República Dominicana." PREAL, Santiago, Chile.

Raczynski, Dagmar, and Claudia Serrano, eds. 2001. *Descentralización: Nudos críticos.* Santiago, Chile: CIEPLAN.

Ravela, Pedro. 2002. "¿Cómo Presentan sus Resultados los sistemas nacionales de evaluación educativa en América Latina?" Working Paper No. 22, PREAL, Santiago, Chile.

Reimers, Fernando, and Noel McGinn. 1997. *Informed Dialogue: Using Research to Shape Education Policy around the World.* Westport, CT: Praeger Publishers.

Rivas, Axel. 2004. *Gobernar la educación: Estudio comparado sobre el poder y la educación en las provincias argentinas.* Buenos Aires, Argentina: Granica-Universidad de San Andrés.

Schiefelbein, Ernesto. 2004. "Paraguay: Education Sector Analysis." World Bank, Washington, DC.

Tedesco, Juan Carlos, ed. 2005. *¿Cómo superar la desigualdad y la fragmentación del sistema educativo Argentino?* Buenos Aires, Argentina: IIPE-UNESCO.

Tiana, Alejandro. 2000. "Cooperación internacional en evaluación de la educación en América Latina y el Caribe: Análisis de la situación y propuestas de actuación." Technical Report Series of Sustainable Development Department, Inter-American Development Bank, Washington, DC.

Tyler, Lewis, and Andrés Bernasconi. 2002. "Factores de promoción de la calidad en sistemas de evaluación de la educación superior en América Latina." In *Perspectivas sobre la Reforma Educativa: América Central en el contexto de políticas de educación de las Américas*, ed. Juan Carlos Navarro, Katherine Taylor, Andrés Bernasconi, and Lewis Tyler. Washington, DC: Inter-American Development Bank, Harvard Institute for International Development, and U.S. Agency for International Development (USAID).

Urquiola, Miguel, and Valentina Calderón. 2005. "Apples and Oranges: Educational Enrollment and Attainment across Countries in Latin America and the Caribbean." Inter-American Development Bank, Washington, DC.

Vegas, Emiliana, and Ilana Unmansky. 2005. "Mejorar la enseñanza y el aprendizaje por medio de incentivos: ¿Qué lecciones nos entregan las reformas educativas de América Latina?" World Bank, Washington, DC.

Villa, Leonardo, and Jesús Duarte. 2004. "Colegios en Concesión de Bogotá: Una experiencia innovadora de gestión escolar en Colombia." In *Alianzas público-privadas en educación: Innovaciones en América Latina*, ed. Juan Carlos Navarro, Jaime Vargas, Jesús Duarte, and Gregorio Arévalo. Washington, DC: Inter-American Development Bank.

Winkler, Donald R. 1989. "Decentralization in Education: An Economic Perspective." Working Paper No. 143, World Bank, Washington, DC.

Winkler, Donald R., and Alec Ian Gershberg. 2000. "Los efectos de la descentralización del sistema educacional sobre la calidad de la educación en América Latina." Working Paper No. 17, PREAL, Santiago, Chile.

Wolf, Lawrence, and Claudio de Moura Castro. 2003. "Education and Training: The Task Ahead." In *After the Washington Consensus: Restarting Growth and Reform in Latin America*, ed. Pedro-Pablo Kucynski and John Williamson. Washington, DC: Institute for International Economics.

Wolff, Laurence, and Martin Gurría. 2005. "Money Counts: Projecting Education Expenditures in Latin America and the Caribbean to the Year 2015." Working paper, UNESCO Institute for Statistics, Montreal, Quebec, Canada. http://www.uis.unesco.org/ev.php?ID=6088_201&ID2=DO_TOPIC.

Index

Page numbers for boxes, figures, and tables are italicized. Notes are indicated by *n*.

A

accountability
  in judicial reform, 90, 99, *110,*
    112, 116
  in public administration, 135,
    138, 138–39
activity decentralization index
    (ADI), *236,* 236–37
administration
  pension systems, costs of public
    vs. private, 366–67
  public, reform of. *See* public
    administration and public
    employment reform
  tax systems, administrative
    reform of, 194–95
Africa, Sub-Saharan
  privatization in, 267, 270
  share of bank assets controlled
    by public sector, 294–95
AIOS (International Association of
    Latin American Pension
    Fund Supervisors), 361
Alesina, Alberto, 19, 22, 172
Alonso, Eduardo, 346
Andean countries. *See also* specific
    countries
  sectoral policy reform in, 36
  tax reform in, 207
Andean Pact, 320
Andrews, Josephine T., 113

Argentina
  budgetary institutions, reform
    of, 19, 161, 164, 166,
    168–72, 177, 182*n*19
  crisis and silent revolution in
    state reform, 2, 3
  decentralization, fiscal and
    political, 25–27, 213, 216,
    219–25, 226, 237, 239,
    242, 245–47, 252, 254,
    255, 258*n*4–5, 260*n*24
  democratic government, Latin
    American support for, 6
  education reform, 48, 387, 392,
    393, 395, 396, 407, 415*n*6
  financial crisis (2001-02), 292
  financial sector reform, 33, 292,
    297, 301
  judicial reform, 13, 91, 95, 96,
    99, 104
  pension system reform, 40, 44,
    360, 361, 364, 365–68,
    370, 371
  political reform, 7, 12, 57, 59,
    61, 62, 63, 66, 68, 69, 72,
    76, 77
  privatization, 31, 270, 272, 273,
    276, 282
  productive development policy
    reform, 36, 319, 321, 328,
    341, 342, 346, 350*n*14

Argentina (*continued*)
  public administration, 16, 133,
    138, 139, 141, 143, 149,
    151, *152*
  social assistance reform, 375
  social assistance system reform,
    44
  tax reform, 23, 185, 195, 199,
    201, 207, 208
Asia
  capital market reform in India,
    308
  Central Asia. *See* Eastern Europe
    and Central Asia
  East Asia
    capital markets compared to
      those of Latin America,
      306
    credit markets compared to
      those of Latin America,
      291
    educational performance in
      Latin America compared,
      397
    subsidies and productive
      development policy reform
      in, 349
  financial crisis of 1997, 267
  share of bank assets controlled
    by public sector, *295*
  South Korea. *See* Korea,
    Republic of
  Southeast Asia, examples of
    state reform in, 3
assessment systems. *See* evaluation
  systems
Australian public administration
  system, 127
authoritarian government, Latin
  American support for, 6

B
Bahamas, productive development
  policy reform in, 36
Balaguer, Joaquín, 67, 69
Balassa, Bela, 319, 320

bankruptcy procedures, duration
  of, *311*
banks and banking, 292–305
  arguments for state intervention
    in, 292–94
  capital adequacy requirements,
    303
  central banks
    independence granted to, 18
    limitation of government
      access to financing from, 18
  national savings, effects of
    public *vs.* private pension
    systems on, 368–69
  new forms of public banking, 299
  privatization, 296–98, *298*
  prudential regulation, 302–04
  regulatory controls, 299–300,
    302–04
  share of bank assets controlled
    by public sector, 294–97,
    295–97
  supervisory controls, 302,
    303–05, *304*
Barbados, productive development
  policy reform in, 350*n*14
Barzeleay, Michael, 154*n*1
Basel Accord, 34, 54*n*29, 303, *304*,
  305, 312
Belize, fiscal and political
  decentralization in, 219
Benavente, José Miguel, 346
Benavides, Juan, 269
bidding model of public–private
  education partnerships, 405
Bird, Richard, 23
Blair, Harry, 90
Bolivia
  budgetary institutions, reform of,
    19, 168, 176, 181*n*16–17,
    182*n*19, 182*n*27
  decentralization, fiscal and
    political, 25, 27, 220, 225,
    228, 246, 248, 254, 255
  education reform, 48, 388, 407
  financial sector reform, 33, 297

judicial reform, 13, 91, *96*
pension system reform, 40, 360, 361, 364, 366, 367, 371, 373
political reform, 12, 57, 66, 69, 71, 76, 77, 78
privatization, 31, 270, 273
productive development policy reform, 326, 343
public administration, 16, 133, 139, 141, 144, 146, 149, *152*
social public expenditure in, 37
tax reform, 23, 185, 192, 195
bond market. *See* capital markets
Bornstein, Morris, 273
borrowing autonomy of subnational governments, 216, 248–51, *249*
Bortolotti, Bernardo, 280
Brady Plan, 3, 50, 157
Brazil
   budgetary institutions, reform of, 161, 166, *167*, 168–70, 172, 178, 182*n*19
   crisis and silent revolution in state reform, 2, 4
   decentralization, fiscal and political, 25–27, 51, 213, 216, 220–25, 226–27, 237–39, 241, 245–50, 252, 254, 255, 258*n*4
   education reform, 48, 49, 387, 390, 392, 395, 396, 397, 400, 401, 408, 411, 415*n*5
   financial sector reform, 33, 34, 297, 309
   judicial reform, 13, 14, 91, *96*, 100, 104
   pension system reform, 40, 44, 360, 364, 367, 369, 371, 372, 374
   political reform, 7, 12, 59, 66, 67, 68, 69, 72
   privatization, 31, 270, 272, 273, 274, 276, 277

productive development policy reform, 36
   current policies, 331, *332–34,* 341–42, 347, 350*n*14
   in import-substitution era, 319, 320
   liberalization era, 325, 327–28
   technology funds, *332–34*
public administration, 16–18, 126–33, *130–31*, 138, 139, 141–43, *145, 146*, 151, 153
social assistance reform, 376, 382
social assistance system reform, 44
tax reform, 23, 185, 195, 196, 200
Bresser Pereira, Luiz Carlos, 4
Bruton, Henry J., 319, 322
budgetary institutions, reform of, 157–84
   analytical framework, 19, *20–21,* 159–60
   collegiate rules, 181*n*6
   common resources, problem of, 159, 172, 180*n*3
   crisis and silent revolution in, 18–22
   democratization and, 157, 179
   executive branch and. *See under* executive branch
   fiscal results, index of, 172–74, *173, 175*
   fiscal rules, 159–60, 161–67, *162–63*
      multiyear frameworks, 165–66
      numerical restrictions, 164, *165*
      in practice, 177–78
      results, 172–74, *175*
      stabilization funds, 166
      subnational government restrictions, 166–67, *167*, 178
   hierarchy. *See* subhead "procedural rules"

budgetary institutions, reform of, (*continued*)
  importance of budgetary institutions, 158–59
  international conditions contributing to, 180*n*2
  judicial budget, 104, *109, 111,* 115
  legislature
    interbranch relations, procedural rules for, 168, *169*
    "parliamentary assistance," 177, 183*n*30
    policy recommendations for, 180
    political reform intertwined with, 158, 176–78, 182*n*25
    in practice, 174–78
  procedural rules, 160, 167–70
    cash management, 170, *171*
    interbranch relations, 168, *169*
    intrabranch relations, 168–70, *170*
    results, 172–74, *175*
  progress of, 160–61, *164*
  transparency rules
    function of, 160, 171–72
    results, 172–74, *175*
bureaucracies. *See* public administration and public employment reform
Burgess, Robin, 294
business taxes, 190–92, *191–92*

C
capital gains taxes for businesses, 190–92, *191–92*
capital markets
  public *vs.* private pension systems and, 368–69
  reform of, 305–9, *306–9*
Cardoso, Fernando Henrique, 4, 127, 270, 387, 400

Caribbean countries. *See also* specific countries
  productive development policy reform, 36, 343
Carrera, Jorge, 272
Central America. *See also* specific countries
  crisis and silent revolution in, 2, 3
  education reform, 48, 49, 401, 404, 416*n*12
  political reform, 12, 57
  productive development policy reform, 36, 319, 320, 323, 343, 346
  public administration and public employment reform, 16, 17, 139, 149, *150–51*
  tax reform, 192, 194, 206
Central American Market, 320
Central Asia. *See* Eastern Europe and Central Asia
central banks
  independence granted to, 18
  limitation of government access to financing from, 18
centralization in conditional cash transfer programs, 380
Chávez, Hugo, xviii, 54*n*37
Checchi, Daniele, 272
Chile
  budgetary institutions, reform of, 19, 164, 166, 168, 170, 171
  crisis and silent revolution in state reform, 2, 3
  decentralization, fiscal and political, 26, 27, 220, 225, 232, 240, 241, 246, 254, 259*n*17
  democratic government, Latin American support for, 6
  education reform, 48, 49, 387, *389,* 390, 392, 401, 402, 403, 405, 406, 407
  financial sector reform, 296, 297, 308, 309

judicial reform, 13, 14, 91, 95, 96, 104, 108
pension system reform, 40, 44
pension system reform in, 356, 357, 360, 361, 364, 365–73
political reform, 12, 57, 66, 69, 72, 77, 85n9
privatization, 31, 269, 270, 272, 273, 274, 277
productive development policy reform, 36
    current policies, 331, 335–38, 342, 346, 350n14
    in import-substitution era, 319, 321, 323
    technology funds, 335–38
public administration, 16, 17, 126, 128, 129–32, 130–31, 138–42, 140, 146, 151–54, 152
social assistance system reform, 44
social public expenditure in, 39
tax reform, 23, 196, 199, 205
China, privatization in, 267
Chong, Alberto, 264, 272, 276, 279, 280
Churchill, Winston, 6
clientelist bureaucracies, 148–49, 150–51
collateral and financial sector reform, 314n26
Colombia
    budgetary institutions, reform of, 19, 161, 166–67, 168, 171–72, 177, 182n28–29
    crisis and silent revolution in state reform, 2
    decentralization, fiscal and political, 25–27, 51, 216, 220, 224–25, 227, 237, 239, 242, 245–50, 252, 254, 258n5
    education reform, 48, 49, 387, 389, 392, 394, 396, 405, 408

financial sector reform, 33, 297, 313n11
judicial reform, 13, 91, 96, 104
pension system reform, 40, 360, 361, 364, 365, 367, 369, 371, 372
political reform, 7, 12, 57, 63, 68, 69, 71, 72, 76
privatization, 31, 272, 273, 274, 276, 277, 279
productive development policy reform, 35, 325–27, 341–42, 346, 350n5, 350n13
public administration, 16, 138, 139, 141, 143, 144, 148, 149, 152
social assistance reform, 44, 45, 376, 382
social public expenditure in, 37
tax reform, 23, 185, 195, 200, 203, 206, 208, 209n10
common resources
    budgetary institutions, reform of, 159, 172, 180n3
    poor division of functions and responsibilities between central and subnational governments, 216
competitiveness forums and productive development policy reform, 341–42
competitiveness of public $vs.$ private pension systems, 366–67
concentration of business ownership, 308–9
Concertación governments, Chile, 387
concession schools, Bogotá District, Colombia, 405, 406, 407
conditional cash transfer programs, 44–45, 376–84, 377–79
contract environment generally and financial sector reform, 294, 300, 309, 310, 311
corporate taxes, 190–92, 191–92

corruption
  decentralization, fiscal and
      political, 216, *238*
  judicial reform and, 94, 95, 100,
      108, 117*n*12
  as major weakness in Latin
      American institutions,
      xviii, 2, 7, *9*
  political party and electoral
      financing, 78
  privatization and, 32, 267, 283,
      285, 286
  regulation and regulatory
      reform, *285, 286*
  social policy reform and, 356
  transfers to local government
      instead of local of tax
      collection reducing, 28–29
  Uribe on budgetary institutions
      and, 183*n*30
Costa Rica
  budgetary institutions, reform
      of, 164, 167, 168, 170,
      172, 180*n*4
  crisis and silent revolution in
      state reform, 2
  decentralization, fiscal and
      political, 26, 219, 220,
      225, 233, 238, 248, *255*
  democratic government, Latin
      American support for, 6
  financial sector reform, 295, 297
  judicial reform, 13, 14, 91, *96,*
      99, 100, 108
  pension system reform, 40, 360,
      361, 364, 366–69, 371–73
  political reform, 7, 12, 61, 62,
      66, 68, 72, 85*n*7
  privatization, 31, 272, 276
  productive development policy
      reform, 321, 323, 326,
      328, 346, 347
  public administration, 16, 17,
      138, 139, 141, *143, 144,*
      148, 149, *150*
  tax reform, 192, 200
councils, judicial, 100, *101–3*

credit markets, 291, 309–11, *310,*
      311
Crespi, Gustavo, 346
Cuba, pension system reform in,
      360, 364, 369, 372, 374

D
Dakolias, María, 90
de Moura Castro, Claudio, 414
debt crisis of 1980s, 157
decentralization, educational. *See*
      under education reform
decentralization, fiscal and political,
      213–61
  ADI (activity decentralization
      index), *236,* 236–37
· borrowing autonomy of
      subnational governments,
      216, 248–51, *249*
  citizen autonomy and political
      participation, reforms
      affecting, *221–23*
  corruption, 216, *238*
  crisis and silent revolution in,
      25–28
  critical risk areas, 215–16
  democratization and, 213–14,
      224
  division of functions and
      responsibilities between
      central and subnational
      governments, 216
  educational decentralization
      broader political and
          administrative
          decentralization, in
          context of, 393–94
      fiscal federalism and, 396–97
  effectiveness, measuring, 251–55
  electoral reforms, 213–14, 217–
      20, *218, 219*
  low fiscal decentralization
      reforms, countries with,
      225, 232–35
  major fiscal decentralization
      reforms, countries with,
      220–25, *226–27*

maturity matrix or index (DMI), 28, 29, 217, 251–55, 253
moderate fiscal decentralization reforms, countries with, 225, 228–31
obstacles to, 238
policy considerations, 256–57
priorities, trends in, 217
public expenditures, 214, 220, 223, 231–40
recentralization, oscillation with, 224
sectoral decentralization, 236, 236–40, 238
tax responsibilities, 240–46, 243, 244
transfers, intergovernmental, 28–29, 215–16, 246–48, 259n16
demand-driven approach to productive development policy reform, 325–27
democratization, 3
budgetary institutions, reform of, 157, 179
decentralization, fiscal and political, 213–14, 224
judicial reform and, 88
political parties, internal democratization of, 77
popular support for democratic government across Latin America, 6
social policy reforms and, 355
stability, political, 81
developing economies, extent of privatization in, 267–68, 268
development, productive. See productive development policy reform
D'Hondt system, 71, 85n8
Di Palma, Giuseppe, 59
differences between countries
judicial reform, differential results of, 100–04
privatization, 272, 283

Dini, Marco, 331, 346
DMI, See decentralization maturity index or matrix
Dominican Republic
budgetary institutions, reform of, 167, 168, 170-71
decentralization, fiscal and political, 26, 219, 220
democratic government, Latin American support for, 6
education reform, 388
judicial reform, 13, 91, 96
pension system reform, 40, 360, 361, 364, 366, 367, 369, 371, 373
political reform, 7, 63, 66, 67, 68, 69, 76, 77, 78
productive development policy reform, 326
public administration, 141, 144, 146, 149
social public expenditure in, 37
tax reform, 23, 185, 195, 200

E
East Asia. See under Asia
Eastern Europe and Central Asia
capital market reform in Hungary, 308
communist systems, collapse of, 3
privatization, 267, 270
share of bank assets controlled by public sector, 295
Economic Commission for Latin America and the Caribbean (ECLAC), 329, 339, 347
Ecuador
budgetary institutions, reform of, 19, 161, 164, 166–68, 171–72, 176, 181n12, 181n18, 182n26
decentralization, fiscal and political, 26, 27, 220, 225, 228–29, 239, 240, 246, 248, 250, 254, 255, 258n9

Ecuador (*continued*)
   education reform, 408
   financial sector reform, 33, 296
   judicial reform, 13, 14, 91, 97,
     99, 100, 104, 114
   pension system reform, 40, 360,
     361
   political reform, 7, 57, 62, 63,
     66, 68, 71, 72, 76, 77
   privatization, 31, 270, 273, 274,
     282
   productive development policy
     reform, 326, 351*n*14
   public administration, 16, 139,
     141, 144, *152*
   social assistance system reform,
     44
   social public expenditure in, 37
   tax reform, 199, 205, 209*n*10
Educación con participación de
   la comunidad (EDUCO)
   or Community-Managed
   Schools Program, 404,
   405, 416*n*15
education reform, 387–421
   bidding model, 405
   comparisons with East Asia and
     OECD countries, 397, 411
   concession schools, Bogotá
     District, Colombia, 405-07
   conditional cash transfer
     programs, 380, 383
   crisis and silent revolution in,
     45–49
   decentralization, 48, 390–98, *391*
     broader political and
       administrative
       decentralization, in
       context of, 393–94
     fiscal federalism and, 396–97
     future challenges, 397–98
     impact of, 394–96
     school autonomy experiences,
       392–93
   enrollment rates, 408–11,
     409–10, 412

evaluation systems, 48–49, 390,
    398–403, *399*
Fe y Alegría school network, 49,
    404, 405, 407
higher education, assessment
    systems in, 400–401
income and enrollment rates,
    411, *412*
institutional nature of, 388, 395,
    402–03
judiciary, educational
    requirements for, *109,*
    111, 114
negotiated agreement model,
    405–06
networks supporting evaluation
    capacity, 403
public–private partnerships, 49,
    390, 403–08
quality of learning, effect on,
    411–13, 414
results of, 408–13, *409–10, 412*
stability and, 414
subsidies model, 405, 407
teachers' buy-in and, 411–13
types of, 45, *46–47*
vouchers, 387, *389,* 405, 406,
    408, 416*n*16
EDUCO. *See Educación con*
    participación de
    la comunidad or
    Community-Managed
    Schools Program)
El Salvador
   budgetary institutions, reform
    of, 168, 170
   decentralization, fiscal and
    political, 27, 219, 225,
    233–34, 246, 248, 255
   democratic government, Latin
    American support for, 6
   education reform, 48, 388, 401,
    416*n*15
   financial sector reform, 297
   judicial reform, 13, 14, 91,
    97, 108

pension system reform, 40, 360,
361, 364, 366-67, 370
political reform, 7, 12, 60, 72,
77-78
public administration, 141, 144,
150, 151
tax reform, 188, 192
electoral reforms
financing of parties and election
campaigns, 78–80, *79,*
81–83
legislature
presidential elections timing
relative to, 63–67
reform efforts, 69–76, *73–75*
presidential. *See* presidential
election reform
primary elections, 77, *78*
subnational governments,
213–14, 217–20, *218-19*
electricity
privatization, 272-74
regulations, 280–82, *281, 286–87*
employment
import-substitution era,
assumptions about
employment in, 355
pensions. *See* pension system
reform
public. *See* public administration
and public employment
reform
unemployment assistance. *See*
social assistance system
reform
Engel, Eduardo, 203, *204,* 280
equity market development, 308–9,
309
European Union, Treaty of
Maastricht, 180*n*2
evaluation systems
education reform, 48–49, 390,
398–403, *399*
social assistance system reform,
383
excise taxes, 194

executive branch
budgetary institution reform and
cash management, 170, *171*
interbranch relations, 168,
169
intrabranch relations, 168–70,
170
political reform, practical
dependence on, 176–77
sustainability of public
accounts, vested interest
in, 180*n*4
elections. *See* presidential
election reform
exports, fiscal and financial
incentives for, 342–43,
344, 345

F
Fantini, Marcella, 280
FDI. *See* foreign direct investment
Fe y Alegría school network, 49,
404, 405, 407
Fernández Reyna, Leonel, 67
financial sector reform, 291–316
banking. *See* banks and banking
bankruptcy procedures, duration
of, *311*
capital markets
effects of reform on, 305–9,
306–9, 368–69
public *vs.* private pension
systems and, 368–69
collateral, 314n26
complementary reforms required
for, 302
contract environment generally
and, 294, 300, 309, 310-11
credit markets, 291, 309–11,
310, 311
crisis and silent revolution in,
32–34
equity market development,
308–09, *309*
exports, financial support for,
343, *345*

financial sector reform (*continued*)
  long-term economic growth, as
    key to, 291
  patterns of financial liberalization
    in Latin America, *300,*
    300–02, 301
  pension systems, public *vs.*
    private, 368–69
  productive development. *See*
    investment policy and
    productive development
    policy reform
  regulation of banking, 299–300,
    302–04
  stability, importance of, 292
  state intervention in, 291–92
financial transactions taxes, 201, *202*
fiscal reforms, 18–28
  budgetary institutions, 18–22,
    157–84. *See also* budgetary
    institutions, reform of
  debt crisis of 1980s, 157
  decentralization, 25–28, 215–61.
    See also decentralization,
    fiscal and political
  export incentives, 342–43, *344*
  financial sector, 32–34, 291–316.
    See also financial sector
    reform
  judicial budgets, 104, *109, 111,*
    115
  political parties and election
    campaigns, financing of,
    78–80, *79, 81–83*
  tax reform, 22–26, 185–212. *See*
    also tax reform
Fiscal Responsibility Act (New
    Zealand), 180n2
Fischer, Ronald, 280
flexibility in public administration,
    143–44
Florio, Massimo, 272
foreign direct investment (FDI),
    323, 328, 339, 341, 346

free trade agreements, tax revenue
    loss from, *207*
Friedman, Milton, 405
Fujimori administration, Peru, 58,
    128

G
Galdo, Virgilio, 279
Galetovic, Alexander, 203, *204,*
    280
Galiani, Sebastián, 394
Galindo, Arturo, 302
GATT. *See* General Agreement on
    Tariffs and Trade
gender equity in pension systems,
    365–66
General Agreement on Tariffs and
    Trade (GATT), 322–23
Gerschenkron, Alexander, 291
globalization
  capital market reform and, 308
  tax reform and, 185–86, 187,
    206–7, *207,* 208
Gramm-Rudman-Hollings Act
    (United States), 180n2
Griner, Steven, 80
Grisanti, Alejandro, 172
Guasch, José Luis, 280
Guatemala
  budgetary institutions, reform
    of, 19, 164, 166, 168, 170
  decentralization, fiscal and
    political, 219, 225, *234,*
    238, 240, 246, *255*
  education reform, 48
  financial sector reform, 297
  judicial reform, 13, 14, 91, *95,*
    97, 108
  pension system reform, 360, 364,
    367, 369, 370, 371, 372
  political reform, 66, 69, 76, 78
  privatization, 274, 282
  public administration, 16, 133,
    141, 144, *150–52*

social public expenditure in, 37
tax reform, 192, 196, 203, 206
Guyana, privatization in, 270

H
Haiti
  pension system reform, 360,
    361, 364
  productive development policy
    reform, 36
Hammergren, Linn, 90
Hansen, Gary, 90
Harden, Ian, 182n20
Hare and greatest remainder
    system, 71, 85n8
Hausmann, Ricardo, 349
health care incentives and
    conditional cash transfer
    programs, 380, 383
Hobbes, Thomas, 404
Honduras
  budgetary institutions, reform
    of, 19, 166, 167, 168, 170
  decentralization, fiscal and
    political, 219, 220, 225,
    238, 254
  democratic government, Latin
    American support for, 6
  education reform, 48
  judicial reform, 13, 14, 91, 95,
    97, 108
  pension system reform, 360,
    364, 367, 369, 370, 372
  political reform, 7, 60, 62, 66,
    76, 77
  public administration, 141, *150–52*
  social assistance reform, 376, 381
  social assistance system reform,
    44
  tax reform, 188, 192, 200
horizontal equity as goal of tax
    reform, 187
Hungary, capital market reform in,
    308

I
import-substitution era
  assumptions about employment
    in, 355
  productive development policy.
    See under productive
    development policy reform
incentives
  conditional cash transfer
    programs, health care and
    educational incentives
    attached to, 380, 383
  exports, fiscal and financial
    incentives for, 342–43,
    344, 345
  productive development policy
    reform, 331–42
  public administration, effective-
    ness in, *142,* 142–43, *145*
  tax reform
    costs of exemptions and
      incentives, *206*
    export incentives, 343, *344*
income tax
  business taxes, 190–92, *191–92*
  personal taxes, 192–93, *193,*
    207–8
independence
  of bank supervisors, 304–5
  of central banks, 18
  judicial reform
    independent actor in policy-
      making process, judiciary
      as (Type III reforms), 91, 94
    quality in, independence of
      judiciary as sign of, 104,
      106, 107, 117n11
  public administration and public
    employment reform, 136,
    139, 140, 149
India, capital market reform in, 308
industrial development. *See*
    productive development
    policy reform

inflation, 18, 180n1, 197, 292
informal employment and social
        policy reform, 356, 374–75
infrastructure privatization, 264–65,
        269, 270
institutional frameworks and state
        reform
    budgetary institutions,
        importance of, 158–59
    confusion over mechanisms of,
        xv–xvi
    consensus on importance of, xv
    continuing weaknesses in Latin
        America, xviii
    crisis and silent revolution in, 1–6
    education reform, institutional
        nature of, 388, 395,
        402–03
    fiscal issues. See fiscal reform
    major areas of, 5
    political issues. See political
        institutions and
        organizations of state
    productive development policy
        reform, institutional
        dimension of, 329–30, 347
    progress of reform in Latin
        America, xvi–xviii
    sectoral policy. See sectoral
        policy institutions
    social policy. See social policy
        reforms
    unbundling of, 50–51
International Association of Latin
        American Pension Fund
        Supervisors (AIOS), 361
investments
    capital markets
        public vs. private pension
            systems and, 368–69
        reform of, 305–9, 306–9
    pension systems, public vs. private
        capital markets, effect on,
            368–69
        comparison of investment
            performance, 369–70
        national savings, 368–69

productive development policy
        reform and
    current fiscal and financial
        incentives for production
        and investment, 331–42
    FDI, 323, 328, 339, 341, 346
    import-substitution era, 321–
        22, 322, 323

J
Jamaica
    decentralization, fiscal and
        political, 220
    productive development policy
        reform, 343, 350n13
    social assistance system reform,
        44, 376, 382
    tax reform, 196, 209, 209n13
JRI (judicial reform index). See
        under judicial reform
judicial reform, 87–121
    accountability, 90, 99, 110, 112,
        116
    bankruptcy procedures, duration
        of, 311
    broader reform agendas,
        coordination with, 100
    budget, judicial, 104, 109, 111,
        115
    challenges and obstacles to,
        95–99, 96–98
    common determinants of
        successful reform, 99–100
    corruption, problem of, 94, 95,
        100, 108, 117n12
    councils, judicial, 100, 101–3
    crisis and silent revolution in,
        13–14
    democratization and, 88
    differential results, 100–04
    education of judiciary, 109, 111,
        114
    efficiency, 110, 112, 116–17
    factors of, 114–17
    financial sector reform
        dependent on, 302
    goals of, 88–90, 89

independence of judiciary as sign
of quality in, 104, *106,*
107, 117*n*11
independent actor in policy-
making process, judiciary
as (Type III reforms), 91, 94
JRI (judicial reform index), 104–8,
109–12, 114–17
factors of judicial reform,
114–17
table of results, *109–12*
law itself, changes in (Type I
reforms), 90, 91, 94
law-related institutions, changes
in (Type II reforms), 91–94
means, methods, and strategies,
88–90, *89,* 99–100
policy-making process
implications of judicial
reform for, 108–14
judiciary as independent
actor in (Type III reforms),
91, 94
role of judiciary in, 113–14
powers of judiciary, *109, 111,* 115
professional qualifications, *109,*
111, 114
promoters of, 88–90, *89*
public confidence in judiciary, 99
quality indicators, 14, *15*
education and professional
qualifications, *109, 111,* 114
independence of judiciary,
104, *106, 107,* 117*n*11
salaries, judicial, 100–104, *105,*
109, 111, 115
structural safeguards, *109, 112,*
115–16
Supreme Courts, 87, 95, 104
transparency, 99, *110, 112,* 116
typology of, 90–95, *92–93*

K
Kakwani measure of tax
progressivity, 203, *204*
Kaufmann, Daniel, 6–7, 30
Kirchner, Néstor, 54*n*37

Korea, Republic of
capital market reform, 308
infrastructure assets, *265*
productive development policy
reform, 36, 319, 347
Kraay, Aart, 6–7, 30

L
La Porta, Rafael, 270
Larraín, Felipe, 346
Latin American Laboratory of
Education Quality
(LLECE), 402
Latinobarometer survey, 6, 99
legislature
budgetary institution reform and
interbranch relations,
procedural rules for, 168,
169
"parliamentary assistance,"
177, 183*n*30
elections
presidential elections timing
relative to, 63–67
reform efforts, 69–76, *73–75*
Levy, Santiago, 376
Lewis, Arthur, 291, 321
liberalization
financial. *See* financial sector
reform
political. *See* political reform
productive development policy
reform and, 323–29
trade liberalization, 3, 4
productive development
policy reform and, 323–29
taxation capacity affected
by globalization, 185–86,
187, 206–07, *207*
Lindauer, David L., 319
Linz, Juan J., *59*
Little, Ian M. D., 319, 320
LLECE. *See* Latin American
Laboratory of Education
Quality
local governments. *See* subnational
governments

López-Calva, Luis Felipe, 267, 346
López-de-Silanes, Florencio, 264,
    270, 272, 276

M
Maastricht, Treaty of (European
    Union), 180n2
Machado, Antonio, 350
macroeconomic stability. See
    stability
Mastruzzi, Massimo, 6–7, 30
McKinnon, Ronald I., 302
Megginson, William, 273
Melo, Alberto, 324
Menem, Carlos, 95
meritocratic bureaucracies, 139,
    140, 150–53, 152, 154
Mexico
    budgetary institutions, reform
        of, 19, 166, 168, 170,
        171, 180n4, 181n13
    crisis and silent revolution in
        state reform, 1-4
    decentralization, fiscal and
        political, 25–37, 220, 225,
        229–30, 237, 239, 246,
        247, 251, 255, 259n15
    democratic government, Latin
        American support for, 6
    education reform, 48, 388, 394,
        395, 396, 397, 401
    financial sector reform, 33, 34,
        297, 309
    judicial reform, 13, 91, 97, 99
    Oportunidades program, 4, 51,
        381
    pension system reform, 40, 44,
        360, 361, 364, 367, 370,
        371
    political reform, 7, 12, 57, 59,
        60, 62, 71, 72, 76, 77
    privatization, 269–70, 273, 277,
        279
    productive development policy
        reform, 36, 319, 321, 343,
        346, 347, 350n13

public administration, 16, 138,
    139, 141, 143, 149, 151,
    152, 153
social assistance reform, 370,
    376, 381, 382
social assistance system reform,
    44-45
tax reform, 23, 196, 206,
    209n10
Micco, Alejandro, 302
Montinola, Gabriella R., 113
multiyear frameworks and reform
    of budgetary institutions,
    165–66
Myrdal, Gunnar, 291

N
Naím, Moisés, 5
national savings, effects of public
    vs. private pension systems
    on, 368–69
negotiated agreement model of
    public-private education
    partnerships, 405–06
networks
    educational evaluation capacity,
        networks supporting, 403
    Fe y Alegría school network, 49,
        404-05, 407
    production networks, integration
        and strengthening of, 331,
        339
neutrality and tax reform
    corporate taxes, sector neutrality
        in, 192
    goal of tax reform, neutrality
        as, 187
    results of tax reform regarding,
        199–201, 201, 202
New Zealand
    Fiscal Responsibility Act as part
        of international conditions
        contributing to budgetary
        institution reform, 180n2
    public administration and public
        employment systems, 127

Nicaragua
  budgetary institutions, reform
      of, 164, 166–72
  decentralization, fiscal and
      political, 26, 220, 225,
      238, 240, 246, 255
  democratic government, Latin
      American support for, 6
  education reform, 48, 388, 392,
      393, 408
  financial sector reform, 297
  judicial reform, 13, 14, 91, *98,*
      104
  pension system reform, 40, 360,
      361
  political reform, 12, 62, 63, 66,
      68, 69, 77
  privatization, 31, 270, 273, 274
  public administration and public
      employment reform, 133,
      141, 144, *150, 151*
  social assistance reform, 376, 381
  social assistance system reform,
      44, 45
  tax reform, 192
numerical restrictions and reform
    of budgetary institutions,
    164, *165*

O
OECD countries. *See* Organisation
    for Economic Co-operation
    and Development (OECD)
    countries
oil stabilization funds, 166
Oportunidades program, Mexico,
    4, 51, 381
Ordóñez, Guillermo, 302
Organisation for Economic
    Co-operation and
    Development (OECD)
    countries. *See also* specific
    countries
  budgetary institution reform,
      international conditions
      contributing to, 180*n*2

  credit markets, 310
  educational performance in
      Latin America compared,
      397, 411
  income transfer programs, 378
  public administration and public
      employment systems in,
      127
  public expenditure
      decentralization trends, 214
Ortega, Daniel, 69

P
Panama
  budgetary institutions, reform
      of, 19, 161, 164, 167,
      168, 171
  decentralization, fiscal and
      political, 225, 240, 246,
      255
  democratic government, Latin
      American support for, 6
  education reform, 48
  judicial reform, 13, 91, 95, *98*
  pension system reform, 360, 364,
      368, 369, 370–72, 374
  political reform, 7, 60, 62, 66,
      76, 77, 78
  privatization, 270
  public administration, 16, 141,
      144, *150*
  tax reform, 23, 196, 209*n*10
Pande, Rohini, 294
Paraguay
  budgetary institutions, reform
      of, 19, 166, 168, 170,
      178, 182*n*19, 183*n*37
  decentralization, fiscal and
      political, 26, 220, 225, 254
  education reform, 48
  judicial reform, 13, 14, 91, *98,*
      99, 104
  pension system reform, 360,
      364, 368, 372
  political reform, 12, 57, 62, 66,
      68, 69, 71, 76, 77

Paraguay (*continued*)
  productive development policy
    reform, 36
  public administration, 139, 141,
    144, 149
  social public expenditure in, 37
  tax reform, 192, 196
  "parliamentary assistance" and
    budgetary institution
    reform, 177, 183*n*30
  party political reform, 77–80,
    78–79, 81
Pastrana, Andrés, 326
Payne, J. Mark, 80
pension system reform, 357–74
  capital market and, 306–8, 307,
    308
  challenges faced in, 372–74
  characteristics of public and
    private systems, 357,
    358–59, 360
  comparison of performance
    of public and private
    systems, 361–72, 362–63
    administrative costs, 366–67
    amount paid, 365
    competitiveness, 366–67
    coverage, 361–64
    employer and employee
      contributions, 367–68
    financial sector effects,
      368–69
    fund accumulation and
      equilibrium, 370–72
    gender equity, 365–66
    investment performance,
      369–70
    life expectancy, 364–65
    reliability of payment of
      contributions, 368
    retirement age, 364
  crisis and silent revolution in,
    39–45, 355–57
  investments
    capital markets, effect on,
      368–69

comparison of investment
    performance, 369–70
  national savings, 368–69
  mixed model, 360
  models and characteristics, 41–43
  parallel model, 360
  parametric reforms, 360
  privatization, 306–8, 307, 308,
    355, 360
  structural reforms, 360
  substitution model, 360
performance evaluation systems.
    See evaluation systems
personal taxes
  income tax, 192–93, 193, 207–8
  property and net worth taxes,
    207–08, 245
Peru
  budgetary institutions, reform
    of, 19, 161, 164, 166,
    168–72
  decentralization, fiscal and
    political, 26, 27, 220, 225,
    230–31, 237, 240, 248,
    250, 254, 255
  education reform, 407
  financial sector reform, 33, 296
  judicial reform, 13, 91, 95, 98
  pension system reform, 40, 360,
    361, 364, 365–67, 369–72
  political reform, 7, 12, 58, 60,
    66, 69, 71, 72, 76–77
  privatization, 31, 270, 272, 273–
    74, 276
  productive development policy
    reform, 326, 343
  public administration, 16–17,
    128–33, 130–31, 137, 139,
    141, 144, 146–51, 152
  social public expenditure in, 37
  tax reform, 192, 195, 199
policy and policy making
  budgetary institutions, reform
    of, 180
  decentralization, fiscal and
    political, 256–57

judicial reform
implications of judicial
reform for, 108–14
judiciary as independent
actor in (Type III reforms),
91, 94
role of judiciary in, 113–14
sectoral policy. *See* sectoral
policy institutions
social policy. *See* social policy
reforms
political institutions and
organizations of state, 6–18
decentralization, 25–28, 215–61.
See also decentralization,
fiscal and political
judicial reform, 13–14, 87–121.
See also judicial reform
political reform, 7–13, 57–86.
See also political reform
privatization, political economy
of, 265–66, 284
productive development policy
reform, political economy
hypothesis of, 328–29
public administration, 14–18,
123–55. *See also* public
administration and public
employment reform
political reform, 57–86
budgetary institution reform
intertwined with, 158,
176–78, 182n25
crisis and silent revolution in,
7–13
federalist and unitary regimes in
Latin America, 59
financing of parties and election
campaigns, 78–80, 79, 81–83
legislative elections
presidential elections timing
relative to, 63–67
reform efforts, 69–76, 73–75
parties, 77–80, 78–79, 81
presidential elections. *See*
presidential election reform

primary elections, 77, 78
stability, political, 6–7, 8,
59–60, 81
tax reform's relationship to, 206
Pombo, Carlos, 279
presidential election reform
changes in rules across Latin
America, 7, 10–11, 61,
64–65
legislative elections, timing
relative to, 63–67
reelection rules and term limits,
67–69, 68, 70
system of election used, 60–63,
63–65
price stabilization, 3–4, 196
primary elections, 77, 78
Pritchett, Lant, 319
privatization, 263–89
banks and banking, 296–98, 298
corruption and, 267, 283, 285,
286
corruption associated with, 32
crisis and silent revolution in,
31–32
differences between countries,
272, 283
electricity, 272, 273, 274
expropriation risks, 269
extent of
in Latin America, 269–74,
271, 283
by sector, 269, 270, 271, 272
in transition economies,
267–68, 268
worldwide, 266, 266–69,
271, 272
failures of, 276, 277, 283
infrastructure, 264–65, 269, 270
pension system reform, 306–8,
307, 308, 355, 360
political economy of, 265–66, 284
profitability and, 274–77, 277,
288
public companies, general
ineffectiveness of, 263–65

privatization (*continued*)
    regulatory challenges, 31,
        277–83, *281, 282*, 284,
        285–87
    sequencing of, 273–74, *275*
    tax reform and, 185–86
    telecommunications, 264, 267,
        269, 271, 272–74, 276
procedural rules for budgetary
    institutions. *See under*
    budgetary institutions,
    reform of
productive development policy
    reform, 317–53
    competitiveness forums, 341–42
    crisis and silent revolution in,
        34–37
    current policies, 329–50
        assessment of, 343–50, *348*
        exports, fiscal and financial
            incentives for, 342–43,
            344, 345
        innovation and technical
            development, promotion
            of, 329–31
        institutional dimensions,
            329–30, 347
        production and investment,
            fiscal and financial
            incentives for, 331–42,
            340–41
        production networks,
            integration and
            strengthening of, 331, *339*
        technology funds, 330–31,
            332–38
    definition of productive
        development, 317
    demand-driven approach, 325–27
    exports, fiscal and financial
        incentives for, 342–43,
        344, 345
    import-substitution era, 318–23
        implications for state, 322–23
        investment policy, 321–22,
        322, 323
        trade policy, 319–21, *320*

innovation and technical
    development, promotion
    of, 329–31
institutional dimensions, 329–30,
    347
intellectual climate for, 349
investment policy
    current fiscal and financial
        incentives for production
        and investment, 331–42
    FDI, 323, 328, 339, 341, 346
    in import-substitution era,
        321–22, *322*, 323
    liberalization period, 323–29
    political economy hypothesis,
        328–29
    public-private partnerships, 326,
        327–28, 341
    strategy-driven approach, 327–28
    technology funds, 330–31,
        332–38
    two-paradigm hypothesis,
        325–29
professional qualifications
    judicial reform, *109, 111*, 114
    public administration and public
        employment reform, *142*,
        144
progressivity of taxes, 203–5, *204*
public administration and public
    employment reform,
    123–55
    accountability, 135, *138*, 138–39
    breadth and depth factors, *127*
    classic or administrative
        bureaucracies, 147–48
    clientelist bureaucracies, 148–
        49, *150–51*
    crisis and silent revolution in,
        14–18
    decisionmaking process, 129,
        130–31
    flexibility, 143, *143–44*
    as goal of reform policy, 124–26
    heterogeneity of systems in Latin
        America, 146
    implementation of, 129, *130–31*

incentive effectiveness, *142,*
    142–43, 145
independence, 136, *139, 140, 149*
merit index, *139*
meritocratic bureaucracies, 139,
    140, 150–53, *152,* 154
parallelist bureaucracies, 149–50
predecision processes, 129,
    130–31
professional qualifications, *142*
quality indicators, 16, *17,*
    135–46, *147*
salaries, 141–46
size of administration, impact
    of reform on, 133–34,
    134–37, 147
strategic consistency index, *138,*
    138–39
strategies for, 126–33, *130–31*
technical and functional
    capacity, 136, *141–45,*
    141–46, 149
types of bureaucratic forms,
    146–53, *149*
public banking reforms. *See* banks
    and banking
public companies
    continuing investment in, 267,
        268
    general ineffectiveness of, 263–65
    privatization of. *See*
        privatization
Public Policy Management and
    Transparency Dialogue
    of the Inter-American
    Development Bank, 16
public–private partnerships
    circumstances indicating need
        for, 269
    education reform, 49, 390, 403–8
    productive development policy
        reform, 326, 327–28, 341
public subsidies
    productive development policy
        reform in East Asia, 349
    public-private education
        partnerships, 405, 407

Q
quality indicators
    education reform's effect on
        quality of learning, 411–14
    judicial reform, 14, *15*
        education and professional
            qualifications, *109, 111,* 114
        independence of judiciary,
            104, *106, 107,* 117n11
    public administration and public
        employment reform, 16,
        17, 135–46, *147*
    regulation and regulatory
        reform, *30*
quality inspectors, judiciary as, 113

R
Raddatz, Claudio, 203, *204*
Ramírez, Manuel, 279
Rawlings, Laura, 380
recentralization and decentralization,
    oscillation between, 224
redistribution of income and tax
    reform
    abandonment as goal, 187–88
    enhancement of redistributive
        capacity as result of
        reforms, 195
reform generally. *See* institutional
    frameworks and state
    reform
regressivity *vs.* progressivity of
    taxes, 203–05, *204*
regulation and regulatory reform
    banking, 299–300, 302–4
    corruption, *285, 286*
    crisis and silent revolution in,
        30–31
    electricity sector, 280–82, *281,*
        286–87
    privatization and, 31, 277–83,
        281, 282, 284, 285–87
    quality indicators, *30*
    telecommunications sector,
        279–82, *281, 285*
Republic of Korea. *See* Korea,
    Republic of

retirement systems. *See* pension
system reform
Reynolds-Smolensky measure of
tax progressivity, 203, *204*
Rodríguez-Clare, Andrés, 329, 339,
346
Rodrik, Dani, 349
Rosenn, Keith S., 117*n*11
Rosenstein-Rodan, Paul, 293
rule of law, 7, *9*
Russian crisis of 1998, 177

S
salaries
judicial, 100–104, *105, 109,
111,* 115
public administration, 141–46
public and private pension
systems, employer and
employee contributions to,
367–68
Sánchez, José Miguel, 280
Scitovsky, Tibor, 319, 320
Scott, Maurice, 319, 320
sectoral policy institutions, 28–37
decentralization of sectoral
expenditures, *236,* 236–40,
238
financial sector, 32–34. *See also*
financial sector reform
privatization, 31–32, 263–89.
See also privatization
productive development,
34–37, 317–53. *See also*
productive development
policy reform
regulation, 30–31. *See also*
regulation and regulatory
reform
sequencing of privatization, 273–74,
275
Shargrodsky, Ernesto, 394
Shaw, Edward S., 302
Sheshinski, Eytan, 267
SIMCE. *See Sistema Nacional de
Medición de Calidad*

de la Educación or
National System for the
Measurement of the
Quality of Education
Siniscalco, Domenico, 280
*Sistema Nacional de Medición
de Calidad de la
Educación* (SIMCE),
or National System for
the Measurement of the
Quality of Education, 406
social assistance system reform,
374–84
conditional cash transfer
programs, 44–45, 376–84,
377–79
crisis and silent revolution in,
44–45
crisis income protection programs,
inadequacy of, 374–76
evaluation tools, 383
informal employment and, 356,
374–75
successes and challenges, 382–84
unemployment rates, 374–75
social policy reforms
corruption and, 356
crisis and silent revolution in,
37–49, 355–57
decentralization of sectoral
expenditures, *236,* 236–40,
238
democratization and, 355
distribution of expenditure,
37–39, *39*
education, 44–49, 387–421. *See
also* education reform
expenditure per capita, 37, *38*
informal employment and, 356,
374–75
pensions, 39–45, 357–74. *See
also* pension system reform
social assistance systems, 44–45,
374–84. *See also* social
assistance system reform
stability, macroeconomic, 355

society representative, judiciary as,
  113–14
Somoza, Anastasio, 69
South Korea. *See* Korea,
  Republic of
Southeast Asia. *See also* Asia
  examples of state reform in, 3
Southern Cone. *See also* specific
  countries
  financial sector reform in, 292
  political reform in, 57
Soviet Union, regarded as economic
  miracle in post-War
  period, 319
stability
  budgetary institution reform and
    stabilization funds, 166
  education reform and, 414
  financial sector reform's need
    for, 292
  political stability, 6–7, *8, 59*–60,
    81
  price stabilization, 3–4, 196
  social policy reforms and, 355,
    375
state-owned banks. *See* banks and
  banking
state-owned enterprises. *See* public
  companies
state reform generally. *See*
  institutional frameworks
  and state reform
Stein, Ernesto, 2, 5, 45, 172
Stepan, Alfred, 59
stock market. *See* capital markets
strategic consistency index of public
  administration, *138,*
  138–39
strategy-driven approach to
  productive development
  policy reform, 327–28
Stroessner, Alfredo, 69
Sub-Saharan Africa
  privatization in, 267, 270
  share of bank assets controlled
    by public sector, 294–95

subnational governments. *See also*
  decentralization, fiscal and
  political
  borrowing autonomy and fiscal
    responsibility, 216, 248–51,
    249
  budgetary institutions, reform
    of, 166–67, *167,* 178
  division of functions and
    responsibilities with
    central government, 216
  educational decentralization,
    impact of, 395
  electoral reforms, 213–14,
    217–20, *218, 219*
  tax reform
    decentralization of tax
      responsibilities to, 240–46,
      243, 244
    personal property and net
      worth taxes, 208, 245
    transfers replacing local tax
      collection, 28–29, 215–16,
      246–48, 259*n*16
  transfers rather than revenues,
    dependence on, 28–29,
    215–16, 246–48, 259*n*16
  weak institutional capacity of,
    216
subsidies
  productive development policy
    reform in East Asia, 349
  public-private education
    partnerships, 405, 407
Supreme Courts, 87, *95,* 104
Suriname
  political decentralization in, 218
  productive development policy
    reform, 36

T
Taiwan (China), productive
  development policy reform
  in import-substitution era
  in, 319
Talvi, Ernesto, 172

Tanzi effect, 197
tariffs
    productive development
        policy reform in import-
        substitution era, 319, *320*,
        322–23
    tax reform, 188, *189*
tax reform, 185–212
    administration, 194–95
    collection of taxes, 28–29,
        195–99, *199*
    consumption taxes, 194
    corporate taxes, 190–92, *191–92*
    costs of exemptions and
        incentives, *206*
    crisis and silent revolution in,
        22–26
    decentralization, fiscal and
        political, 240–46, *243, 244*
    excise taxes, 194
    export incentives, 343, *344*
    financial transactions taxes, 201,
        202
    future challenges in, 205–8
    globalization and, 185–86, 187,
        206–7, *207*, 208
    goals of, 186–88
    horizontal equity as goal of
        reform, 187
    incentives
        costs of exemptions and
            incentives, *206*
        export incentives, 343, *344*
    income tax
        business taxes, 190–92,
            191–92
        personal taxes, 192–93, *193*,
            207–8
    meritocratic bureaucracies and,
        151, *152*
    neutrality
        corporate taxes, sector
            neutrality in, 192
        as goal of reform, 187
        results of tax reform regarding,
            199–201, *201, 202*

    personal taxes
        income tax, 192–93, *193,*
            207–8
        property and net worth taxes,
            207–8, 245
    political reform, relationship to,
        206
    privatization and, 185–86
    productivity calculations, 54*n*21,
        200
    progressivity/regressivity, 203–5,
        204
    redistribution of income
        abandonment of goal of,
            187–88
        enhancement of redistributive
            capacity as result of
            reforms, 195
    results of, 195
    revenue trends, 23, *24–25*, 185,
        195–98, *196–98*
    subnational governments
        decentralization of tax
            responsibilities to, 240–46,
            243, 244
        personal property and net
            worth taxes, 208, 245
        transfers replacing local tax
            collection, 28–29, 215–16,
            246–48, 259*n*16
    tariffs, 188, *189*
    transparency in, 206
    VAT. *See* valued-added tax
technology funds, 330–31
telecommunications
    privatization, 264, 267, 269,
        271, 272–74, 276
    regulations, 279–82, *281, 285*
trade liberalization, 3, 4
    productive development policy
        reform and, 323–29
    taxation capacity affected by
        globalization, 185–86,
        187, 206–7, *207*
    trade policy in import-substitution
        era, 319–21, *320*

transition economies, extent of
  privatization in, 267–68,
  268
transparency
  budgetary institutions, reform of
    function of transparency
    rules, 160, 171–72
    results of transparency rules,
    172–74, 175
  in budgetary reform. See
    budgetary institutions,
    reform of
  in judicial reform, 99, 110, 112,
    116
  in tax reform, 206
Treaty of Maastricht (European
  Union), 180n2
Trinidad and Tobago
  decentralization, fiscal and
    political, 220
  financial sector reform, 296
  productive development policy
    reform, 343, 351n14
  tax reform, 23, 196, 209n10,
    209n13
Tsebelis, George, 113
two-paradigm hypothesis,
    productive development
    policy reform, 325–29

U
unemployment assistance. See social
    assistance system reform
United Kingdom, public
    administration in, 127
United States, Gramm-Rudman-
    Hollings Act, 180n2
Uribe, Álvaro, 177, 183n30
Uruguay
  budgetary institutions, reform
    of, 166, 167, 168, 170,
    181n9
  crisis and silent revolution in
    state reform, 2
  decentralization, fiscal and
    political, 220, 225, 235

democratic government, Latin
    American support for, 6
education reform, 387, 392
financial sector reform, 296
judicial reform, 13, 14, 91, 98,
    104
pension system reform, 40, 360,
    361, 364, 367, 369
political reform, 57, 63, 77, 78
privatization, 31, 270, 272, 273,
    276
productive development policy
    reform, 351n14
public administration, 16, 133,
    135, 138, 139, 141, 143,
    144, 147–49, 153
tax reform, 207

V
Valenzuela, Arturo, 59
valued-added tax (VAT), 194
  administrative tax reform, 195
  collection of tax, 26, 198
  globalization and, 207, 208
  limits on raising, 208
  as major tax on reform agendas,
    23, 186, 205
  neutrality and, 200, 209n18
  productivity calculations, 54n21,
    200
  progressivity measures, 203–5,
    204
Velasco, María Piedad, 346
Venezuela
  budgetary institutions, reform
    of, 19, 161, 166–68, 170,
    172, 181n10
  crisis and silent revolution in
    state reform, 1, 2
  decentralization, fiscal and
    political, 25, 26, 220, 225,
    231, 246, 247, 255
  democratic government, Latin
    American support for, 6
  education reform, 48, 49, 393, 394,
    395, 396, 397, 405, 407

Venezuela (*continued*)
  financial sector reform, 33, 291,
    297, 301
  judicial reform, 13, 14, 91, *98*, 114
  pension system reform, 40, 360,
    364, 368, 369, 372, 374
  political reform, 7, 12, 57, 59,
    60, 62, 66, 67, 68, 69, 71,
    72, 76, 77, 78
  productive development policy
    reform, 328, 350*n*10,
    350*n*13
  public administration, 16, 138,
    139, 141, 143-44, 148, *152*
  tax reform, 23, 196, 200,
    209*n*10
Ventura, Juan Pablo, 346
veto players, judiciary as, 113
Vives, Antonio, 269

voice and accountability, 6–7, *8*
Von Hagen, Jürgen., 182*n*20
vouchers in education reform,
    387, *389*, 405, 406, 408,
    416*n*16

W
Wallsten, Scott, 279, 280
Washington Consensus, 5, 125, 357
welfare systems. *See* social
    assistance system reform
Winston, Clifford, 278
Wolf, Lawrence, 414
World Trade Organization (WTO),
    36, 343, 349

Z
Zedillo, Ernesto, 380
Zovatto, Daniel, 80

The authorized representative in the EU for product safety and compliance is:
Mare Nostrum Group
B.V Doelen 72
4831 GR Breda
The Netherlands

www.ingramcontent.com/pod-product-compliance
Lightning Source LLC
Chambersburg PA
CBHW021842020426
42334CB00013B/157